Yearbook 136

2020 New In Chess – The Netherlands

Yearbook

NEW IN CHESS 136

Contributing Authors

Adams • Bosch • Flear • Giri • Gupta • Ikonnikov • Ilczuk • Jankovic • Jones
Karolyi • Külaots • Lalic • l'Ami • Mchedlishvili • Moll • P.H.Nielsen • Ninov
Ntirlis • Olthof • Panczyk • Petrov • Ponomariov • Ris • Saric • Sasikiran • Schut
I.Sokolov • Stella • Suleymanli • K.Szabo • Tekeyev • Timman • Yu Yangyi

CHESS OPENING NEWS

Edited by Jan Timman

Colophon

Editor-in-chief: Jan Timman
Managing editor: Peter Boel
Editors: René Olthof, Frank Erwich
Production: Anton Schermer, Joop de Groot, Sandra Keetman

New In Chess Yearbook
ed. by Jan Timman
ISSN 0168-7697
4 times a year
Yearbook 136 (2020)
ISBN: 978-90-5691-907-8 hardcover
ISBN: 978-90-5691-906-1 softcover

Photos: New In Chess Archives, unless indicated otherwise.

E-mail: editors@newinchess.com
Subscriptions: www.newinchess.com

New In Chess Code System

White stands slightly better	⩲	excellent move	!!	see	−
Black stands slightly better	⩱	bad move	?	editorial comment	RR
White stands better	±	blunder	??	Yearbook	YB
Black stands better	∓	interesting move	!?	championship	ch
White has a decisive advantage	+−	dubious move	?!	zonal tournament	zt
Black has a decisive advantage	−+	only move	□	interzonal tournament	izt
balanced position	=	with the idea	△	candidates tournament	ct
unclear position	∞	attack	→	team tournament	tt
compensation for the material	⯗	initiative	↑	olympiad	ol
strong (sufficient)	>	counterplay	⇄	match	m
weak (insufficient)	<	mate	#	correspondence	cr
better is	≥	novelty	N	junior	jr
weaker is	≤	zugzwang	Z		
good move	!	time	T		

From the editor

Classical

It is a strange experience: for months I have only seen rapid games, played on the Internet, with all their peculiar mistakes. I really miss the classical games. As a consequence, I have also included rapid games in my Survey, which normally I don't do.

So I was glad to see that Ivan Sokolov had decided to base his Survey on a classical game between two promising youngsters from the period just before the lockdown. It reminded me of the Karpov-Kasparov matches. This also goes for Krishnan Sasikiran's contribution to Erwin l'Ami's correspondence column. Just one small correction on his analysis: the move 9...e3 is generally attributed to Igor Zaitsev. However, as I have pointed out in my book *The Longest Game*, it was first mentioned by John Watson, back in 1979.

We welcome Yu Yangyi as a contributor. He has been a top player for years, but we hardly ever saw any of his commentaries. His views are obviously very interesting.

Another welcome to Zaur Tekeyev from Russia. He tackles an interesting option in the main line of the Caro-Kann.

Of course there were some rapid games from the last months that were worthwhile. The best example is Magnus Carlsen's victory over Anish Giri in the Semi-Tarrasch. Ivan Saric examines this line.

While Giri and Ian Nepomniachtchi frequently play the Semi-Tarrasch as Black, Hikaru Nakamura sticks to his own line in the Blackburne Variation of the Classical Queen's Gambit. Michael Adams writes the Survey; while working on it, he himself played the Black side of the system to beat Noël Studer in a game in Biel – the first big tournament in which classical chess was played again.

Jan Timman

Opening Highlights

Anish Giri

The Dutch super-GM boosted his speed chess in the past Covid-19 months. He won the strong Mr Dodgy Invitational and reached the final of the Chessable Masters event. Anish brilliantly defeated another specialist, Ian Nepomniachtchi, with **a fresh treatment of a distinguished Tarrasch line**, only to succumb to Magnus Carlsen in the final in an even more brilliant game with the same line! We have Peter Heine Nielsen's analysis in a Survey where Ivan Saric tells the whole story on page 131.

Aydin Suleymanli

The latest sensation before lockdown was this 14-year-old boy outstripping dozens of high-class GMs at the Aeroflot Open. In the crucial game, the young Azeri tempted Parham Maghsoodloo into **grabbing a pawn on b7 in the Exchange QGD** and then outplayed the former Junior World Champ. Aydin analyses this game in Ivan Sokolov's Survey on page 121. Also, newcomer Zaur Tekeyev (see facing page) looked at Suleymanli's exploits as Black in the Classical Caro-Kann.

Sergey Karjakin

Leaving all the jokes about Ministers and Defence aside, we see that Sergey Karjakin has also rejuvenated himself online. He's been experimenting with **yet another 6th move against the Najdorf: bishop to d3**. It's just online chess, you may say, but if you try such things against the likes of Giri, Duda, Nepomniachtchi, and even Najdorf guru Vachier-Lagrave, you better know what you're doing. Kaido Külaots has collected and deeply analysed all the relevant games in his Survey on page 38.

Krishnan Sasikiran

The strong Indian GM already featured several times as a correspondence player – you know, that slower and deeper version of the current online hype – in Erwin l'Ami's column. In this issue, Sasikiran contributes analysis to our 'correspondence corner' of **a novelty on the 11th move which breathes new life into the famous 9...e3 idea in the Reversed Sicilian** which Karpov used in his 1987 match with Kasparov. See page 29 for Sasikiran's assemblage of new, fantastic variations!

Yu Yangyi

We are proud to present a Survey by absolute top player Yu Yangyi! At the Nations Cup, one of the first big online events after the lockdown, Yangyi was the big man of the Chinese team with a 7½ out of 10 score. Moreover, he bounced back from a loss against Wesley So in the preliminaries to beat the American with **a crushing 8th move novelty in the Nimzo-Indian Ragozin**, winning the Cup for his country! Yangyi's analysis of this gorgeous game and others in this line can be found on page 165.

Hikaru Nakamura

Starting in the Magnus Invitational, speed chess wizard Nakamura took on all comers in the same QGD line. Michael Adams aptly calls it 'Rest of the World v Nakamura' in his Survey on the subject (page 112). Nakamura kept showing that the set-up with **6...♘bd7 and 7...c6 is super-solid against the Blackburne Variation**, but can also lead to great complications and highly varied ramifications. Anish Giri got fascinated too and added a lot of comments on this line.

Zaur Tekeyev

We welcome our new contributor, Russian FM Zaur Tekeyev, current champion of the North-Caucasian Federal District and former student champion in Russia. Tekeyev is an active chess coach and opening expert who makes his debut with a Survey on **the Classical Caro-Kann where White squeezes in 7.♗d3 even before committing to h4-h5 and a move with his king's knight**. This gambit move may look a little brusque but it hides many subtleties, as Tekeyev nicely demonstrates on page 70.

Arne Moll

Some openings are considered just blatantly incorrect. But with computer analysis running to move 25 or further, what can we still call 'correct' in chess? Anyway, Arne Moll doesn't make any unrealistic claims for **the audacious 3...f5 in the Philidor Defence**. He just proves in his Survey on page 85 that it leads to wild tactics, fun games, and yes, the occasional loss against a White player who knows all the ins and outs of this obscure line. You think you're going to face many of those?

Your Variations

Trends & Opinions

Forum

Surveys

1.e4 openings

1.d4 openings

Others

Views

Reviews by Glenn Flear

HOT! = a trendy line or an important discovery

SOS = an early deviation

GAMBIT = a pawn sacrifice in the opening

TRENDS & OPINIONS

Featuring

Forum

From Our Own Correspondent

Forum

Cloud-busting

The FORUM is a platform for discussion of developments in chess opening theory in general and particularly in variations discussed in previous Yearbook issues.

Contributions to these pages should be sent to: editors@newinchess.com

No toilet move

by Han Schut

RL 7.1 (C65)   YB 97

During the semifinals of the Lindores Abbey chess24.com Rapid Challenge, Magnus Carlsen played an interesting piece sacrifice and novelty against Hikaru Nakamura. As early as move 8, Black sacrifices a piece for two pawns and an attack on the white king.

position after 10.♗e3

White's king is vulnerable, and it takes White time to unpin himself. Black has the bishop pair, and his attacking plan is simple: steamroll with the f-, g-, and h-pawns, castle queenside, bring on attackers and checkmate. And if White is able to organize a defence, then there is a plan B: create two passed pawns that keep White's major pieces occupied with defensive tasks. It is difficult for White to untangle himself and create counterplay. Nakamura's defensive play

in this rapid game was impressive.

Peter Leko was one of the commentators on Chess24. Coincidentally, he'd had the position after 10.♗e3 against David Navara with white in Linares 2018. After the game, Navara had told him that his preparation was 10...♗e7 but that he was in a rush to go to the bathroom and made a mistake. So, this time not the 'toilet' move 10...♗d6 but the new 10...♗e7!.

It looks like White's best defence is to unpin himself immediately by protecting the pinned knight with his king (♔g2) and subsequently moving his queen out of the pin (♕e1).

Hikaru Nakamura
Magnus Carlsen
Lindores Abbey Online 2020 (2)
1.e4 e5 2.♘f3 ♘c6 3.♗b5 ♘f6 4.d3 ♗c5 5.♗xc6 dxc6 6.0-0 ♗g4 7.h3 ♗h5 8.g4 ♘xg4 9.hxg4 ♗xg4 10.♗e3 ♗e7N
Up till now only the move 10...♗d6 had been played. The essential difference between 10...♗d6 and 10...♗e7 is that in the variation 11.♔h1 h5 12.♖g1 f5, White can take on f5 if the bishop is on d6. This is impossible in the line with 10...♗e7 as 13.exf5 e4 14.dxe4 ♕xd1 15.♖xd1 ♗xf3 loses the knight on f3.
Moreover,
– 10...♗d6 protects pawn e5 and allows the black queen to go to f6 or h4 but the bishop

is also under the threat of being traded after ♘bd2-c4. – 10...♗e7 does not protect the pawn on e5 and blocks the black queen from going to f6 or h4, but maintains the flexibility of going to f6 if pawn e5 is under attack. Notice that in both predecessors with 10...♗d6 White reduced the pressure by taking exf5:

A) 11.♘bd2 f5 12.exf5 0-0 13.♕e1 ♗xf3 14.♘xf3 ♖xf5 15.♕e2 ♕f6 16.♘h2 e4 17.♕g4 exd3 18.cxd3 ♖e8 19.♖ae1 ♖e6 20.f4= ½-½ (50) Wei Yi-Xiu Deshun, China tt 2015;

B) 11.♔h1 f5 12.♖g1 h5 13.exf5 ♕f6 14.♘bd2 ♕xf5 15.♖g3 h4 16.♖xg4 ♕xg4+− ½-½ (44) Leko-Navara, Linares 2018.

11.♔h1?!
Can White unpin himself? The engines prefer the immediate ♔g2/♕e1. It looks dangerous to give the king this defensive task, but concrete analysis shows it is possible: 11.♔g2 f5 12.♕e1 (White has unpinned the knight on f3, making both 13.♘xe5 and 13.♘h2 possible) 12...♗xf3+ (12...h5 13.♘xe5; 12...♗f6 13.♘h2) 13.♔xf3 f4 14.♗d2

14...g5. Lc0 believes Black has full compensation, while Stockfish prefers White. A plausible continuation is 15.♗c3 ♗f6 16.♖h1 h5 17.♔e2 g4 18.f3 g3 19.♕f1 ♕e7 20.♕h3 ♔f7 21.♘d2 ♖ag8 and

Black's two passed pawns give Black ample compensation for the piece.
11...f5
White gets steamrolled with ...f7-f5/...g7-g5/...h7-h5 etc.
12.♖g1 h5 13.♘c3
13.exf5 e4 loses because of 14.dxe4 ♕xd1 15.♖xd1 ♗xf3+.
13...f4 14.♗d2 g5 15.♘b1
White wants to create counterplay with ♗c3 and ♘b1-d2.
15...♗c5
Simpler was 15...♗xf3+ 16.♕xf3 g4 17.♕g2 ♕d7−+ followed by ...0-0-0 and ...♖g8 and the advance of the g- and h-pawn. White is not able to generate any counterplay. The king on h1 prevents White from setting up a blockade with ♖h1 and ♕h3.
16.♗c3 ♗xf2 17.♘bd2 ♕e7 18.♕f1 ♗xg1 19.♕xg1 ♗xf3+ 20.♘xf3 g4 21.♘xe5
Threatening 22.♘g6 with a double attack on the ♖h8 and the ♕e7.
21...♖g8 22.♖f1 ♕g5 23.♕d4
Threatening ♕d4-d7-f7 mate.
23...♕h4+ 24.♔g1
Carlsen was facing a tough choice with less than one minute on the clock: take the draw by perpetual check or continue to play for a win with ...g4-g3. This choice is even harder considering he had a clearly winning position earlier in the game.
24...♕g3+ 25.♔h1 ♕h3+ 26.♔g1

26...g3?
Now White is better!

CARLSEN WINS 1st SET

26...♖d8! 27.♕c4 is winning for Black. Three key elements for the evaluation of a position are the material balance, time (development) and space. Black can win by giving a full rook (material) for 1 move (time) with 27...♖d5!! 28.exd5 f3 29.♖f2 (29.♔f2 g3+ 30.♔e3 f2 31.♕e4 (31.dxc6 g2+ 32.♔d2 gxf1♘+−+) 31...g2+ 32.♘f3+ ♔d8−+) 29...g3 30.♘xf3 gxf2+ 31.♔xf2 ♖g4 32.d4 ♕g2+ 33.♔e3 ♕xc2. Very complicated lines that are impossible to find with so little time.
27.♘f3
Covering 27...♕h2 mate.
27...g2 28.♖e1 ♕xf3
White has a forced mate.
29.♕e5+ ♔d8 30.♕f6+ ♔e8 31.♗b4 c5
Threatening mate on e7.
32.♗xc5 ♔d7 33.♕f7+ 1-0
A fantastic defensive performance by Nakamura.

Covid creativity
a letter by Wayne Gradl

NI 30.1 (E20)   YB 134

Covid-19 confinement did not lead to any 'cabin fever' for this chess fan. Instead, home isolation freed up more time for the study of our beloved game. The

Internet and email allowed this extra chess study time to be put into practice against other homebound chess fans. The following email game I believe is important to Nimzo-Indian Defense theory.

GB
Wayne Gradl
email April 24 – May 4, 2020

1.d4 ♘f6 2.c4 e6 3.♘c3 ♗b4 4.f3!? c5

Turns out Yearbook 134 and Ikonnikov's article 'No real threat to the Kmoch' arrived just in time for this game, although 4...c5 is also the move recommended in GM Michael Roiz's book on the Nimzo-Indian (Quality Chess 2017). Even without these book recommendations though, the other main line 4...d5 5.a3 ♗xc3+ 6.bxc3 c5 7.cxd5 ♘xd5 8.dxc5 leads to one of those positions where I personally dislike both sides. White has the coveted bishop pair, but shattered queenside pawns and weak squares on b3, c4 and d3. Black has weak dark squares, is a pawn down, and seems to be playing mainly to win back the pawn and gain a draw. My view of the White side improved when I found Palliser-Sundararajan, Port Erin 2005, which continued 8...♘d7 9.e4 ♘e7 10.♗e3 0-0 11.♗b5 ♕a5 12.♕b3 ♕c7 13.♗xd7 ♗xd7 14.♖b1 ♖ab8 15.♘e2 e5 16.c4! ♘c6 17.♘c3 ♘d4 18.♗xd4 exd4 19.♘d5 ♕xc5 20.♕b4 b6 21.♕xc5 bxc5 22.♔d2 and Black suffers in this ending with Palliser bringing home the full point on move 42. The plan of 16.c4! and hopping with the knight from e2 to d5 looked like a very good one to me. Hence 4...c5 was my move.

5.d5 b5 6.e4 d6 7.♗d2

Here I had a choice to make, as was laid out in Yearbook 134. I could follow in the footsteps of the World Champion and play 7...♗xc3 8.♗xc3 b4, but I really did not want to close the queenside. Very tempting was 7...exd5 of Mamedyarov-Rapport, St Louis rapid 2019, given that Black won convincingly in only 23 moves, but it looked to me like White had opportunities to improve. Ultimately, I decided to keep my position flexible and follow GM Roiz's recommended repertoire.

7...a6 8.a3?!

Flicking in 8.a3?! to kick the bishop is an easy move to play, especially on move 8. It gets you one move closer to the time control and defers the need for serious thought. It is the kind of move that but for this game, I might play myself. In fact, in the above-mentioned game, super-GM Mamedyarov played 9.a3?! after 7...exd5 8.cxd5 a6. Despite the ease of this seemingly innocuous move, the future course of this game shows that with the weakening of b3 and the clearing of the bishop from the b-file White's troubles start here.

The most commonly played move is 8.a4. On the white side I would have not wasted time with either 7.♗d2 or 8.a3?!, but would have immediately played 7.dxe6

♗xe6 8.♗f4 0-0 9.♗xd6 ♖e8 10.♗f4. GM Roiz considers 10.♗f4 in a note which continues 10...♕a5 11.♕c1 bxc5 12.a3 ♗xc3+ 13.♕xc3 ♕a4 (13...♕b6!?) 14.♖c1 ♘c6 15.♘e2 ♘d7 16.♗g3 f5 17.♘f4 ♗f7 18.♗xc4 ♗xc4 19.♕xc4+ ♕xc4 20.♖xc4 fxe4 21.fxe4 ♘d4=. However, as White I would prefer further simplification with 21.♖xe4 and after 21...♖xe4+ 22.fxe4 ♘f6, I would be nervous about this ending if I were Black, given the weak pawn on c5 and White's current bishop over knight advantage and centralized king, although with precise play Black can hold.

8...♗a5 9.dxe6 ♗xe6 10.♗f4 0-0 11.♗xd6 ♘c6

Offering the exchange was my engine's first choice.

12.♗xc5 bxc4 13.♘ge2

13...♕c7!

Your computer will tell you that there is no longer any need for Black to offer the exchange to get a comfortable game. I was not interested in a comfortable game though. I wanted to play for a win. So I ignored my engine's recommendations and left the forbidden fruit dangling for one more move.

14.♗xf8

Eating the dangling exchange cannot really be criticized. Alternatives give Black a sizable edge due to White's lack of development and poor piece coordination. Taking

the exchange also gets an engine endorsement which at this point indicates that Black has compensation, but nothing close to a significant advantage.

14...♖xf8 15.♕c2 ♖d8!
A key move. The logical 16...♖b8?! would allow White to castle queenside and ultimately complete development in a reasonable manner.
16.♖d1 ♖b8

Mission accomplished! White's king will now stay stuck in the center for the rest of the game and the rook on h1 will never see action. In subsequent play my computer offered a number of first and second choices that would lead to positions where Black had significant edges, but nonetheless did not look winning to me. Via a series of 'inferior' moves I was able to convert Black's advantage in development and piece coordination to a full point.
17.♕c1 ♖b3 18.♘f4 ♕b6 19.♗e2 ♖xb2 20.♔f1 ♕b3 21.♘cd5 c3 22.♕e3 c2 23.♕xb3 ♖xb3 24.♖c1 ♗xd5 25.exd5 ♘d4 26.♗c4 ♖xa3 27.♔f2 ♗b6 28.♔e1 ♖c3 29.♗xa6 ♘b3 30.♘e2 ♖c5 31.♗d3 ♘xc1 32.♘xc1 ♘xd5 33.g3 ♖c7 34.♔e2 ♘c3+ 0-1
White loses a piece after 35.♔d2 ♘d1 36.♗xc2 ♘f2 due to the threat of 37...♗a5+.
My colleague could not believe that a computer-

Michael Roiz

assisted email game could be so one-sided. My thoughts dwelled on 8.a3?! and that poor opening choices can indeed lead to a lost game before the fighting even starts; hence my ongoing subscription to the New In Chess Yearbook.

Wayne R. Gradl
U.S. National Master
Getzville NY, USA

Duda's novelty
by René Olthof

SI 8.8 (B97)   YB 53, 132

The nature of theoretical experiments in the rapid and blitz events during these pandemic times may be slightly different compared to over-the-board tournaments, but there is definitely no shortage of new opening developments, both on and off the well-trodden paths.

Sergey Karjakin
Jan-Krzysztof Duda
Lindores Abbey blitz 2020 (4)
1.e4 c5 2.♘f3 d6 3.d4 cxd4 4.♘xd4 ♘f6 5.♘c3 a6 6.♗g5 e6 7.f4 ♕b6 8.♕d2 ♕xb2 9.♖b1 ♕a3 10.f5 ♘c6
Only one more game has been played in the new *tabiya* position after 10...♗e7 11.fxe6

♗xe6!? 12.♘xe6 fxe6 13.♗c4 ♘bd7 14.♗xe6 ♘c5 since my FORUM contribution in Yearbook 132: 15.♗f5 g6 16.♗h3 ♘cxe4 17.♘xe4 ♘xe4 18.♕d4 ♘c3+ 19.♕xc3 ♕xc3 20.♗xe7 ♔xe7 21.♖xb7+ (diverging from 21.♖b3 ♘e4 22.♖xb7+ ♔f6 23.0-0+ ♔g5 24.g3 ♖ab8 in Wei Yi-Nepomniachtchi, Moscow rapid 2019) 21...♔f6 22.0-0+ ♔g5 23.g3 ♖ab8 24.♖c7! ♘d5 (½-½ (46) Wei Yi-Vachier-Lagrave, Internet blitz, September 2019) 25.♖c6!? ♖b6 26.♖xb6 ♘xb6 27.♖f7 and White still has a slight pull.
11.fxe6 fxe6 12.♘xc6 bxc6
The former main line – long time no see!
13.♗e2
Thousands of games with 13.e5. But the success rate is below 50 percent!
13...♗e7

14.e5!?
Anish Giri has wiped the dust off this ancient continuation. There are literally hundreds of draws with either 14.0-0 0-0 15.♖b3 ♕c5+ 16.♗e3 ♕e5 17.♗d4 ♕a5 18.♗b6 ♕e5 19.♗d4 or 17.♗f4 ♕c5+ 18.♗e3. 18.♔h1 is the only way to play for more, as explained in Yearbook 53, over 20 years ago!
Likewise, the scoring percentage of 14.♖b3, played twice by our editor-in-chief in the mid-1980s, is below 50 after 14...♕a5!.
14...dxe5 15.♗xf6 ♗xf6 16.♗h5+

16.♘e4 0-0 17.0-0 is easy for Black, who comfortably sits on his material advantage.

Now Black has to decide how to stop the check.

16...g6

16...♔e7 17.♖d1 ♕c5! (17...e4? 18.♘xe4 ♖a7 19.0-0 ♖d7 20.♕f2 ♖f8 fails to 21.♖xd7+! (even stronger than 21.♔h1?!, Giri-Korobov, Moscow blitz 2019, in view of 21...♕a5!) 21...♗xd7 22.♕d2! and the poor placement of his king is a permanent problem for Black. If 22...♖b8 23.♘xf6 gxf6 24.♕h6 with decisive penetration) 18.♘e4 ♕d4 19.♕e2 ♕b6 (inserting 19...♕b4+ 20.c3 is not necessarily helpful for Black, viz. 20...♕b6 21.♕f3 and now:
  A) 21...♖f8?! 22.♕g3! ♖d8 23.♘xf6 ♖xd1+ (Gunnas-A. Roze, cr 1986) 24.♔xd1! gxf6 25.♔c2 ♗f8 26.♖f1 ♖b8 27.♖xf6+ ♔e7 28.♖f7+ ♔d6 29.♕d3+ ♔c5 30.♕e3+ ♔d6 31.♕xb6 ♖xb6 32.♖xh7±;
  B) 21...♖b8?? is a blunder with the white pawn on c3: 22.♘xf6 gxf6 23.♖f1 ♖f8 and here 'everything' wins for White;
  C) 21...♖d8 22.♖xd8 ♔xd8 23.♘xf6 ♕b1+ 24.♔f2 ♕xh1 25.♕xc6 gxf6 26.♕d6+ ♗d7 27.♕b6+ with a perpetual) 20.♕f3 ♖b8!? (a combative idea of 12-year-old Duda; 20...♖d8 21.♖xd8 ♔xd8 22.♘xf6 ♕b4+! 23.c3 ♕b1+ transposes to the 'insertion' 19...♕b4+ 20.c3 above)

21.♘xf6?! (an inaccurate move order; 21.♖f1 ♖d8 22.♖xd8 ♔xd8 23.♘xf6 ♕b4+ 24.♔d1 ♕d4+ 25.♔e2 ♕c4+ 26.♕d3+ ♕xd3+ 27.♔xd3 gxf6 28.♖xf6=) 21...gxf6 22.♖f1?! (22.c3 ♗b7 23.♖f1 ♖bf8±; 22.♕g3 ♕b4+! 23.c3 ♕e4+ 24.♗e2 ♔f7 and White's compensation is not quite sufficient, e.g. 25.♕f2 ♕f5 26.♕h4 ♕f4 27.♕h5+ ♔e7 28.♖f1 ♕g5 29.♕xg5 fxg5∓ 30.♗h5 ♖f8 31.♖xf8 ♔xf8 32.♖d8+ ♔e7 33.♖h8 ♖b1+ 34.♔d2 ♗d7 35.♖xh7+ ♔d6∓) 22...f5! (this would not have been possible otherwise) 23.♖f2 (23.♕g3? ♕b4+–+ Warakomska-Duda, Wroclaw 2010) 23...♖d8! 24.♕g3 ♖d5! (creating a nice shelter on the d-file) 25.c4 ♕b4+ 26.♖fd2 ♕xc4 27.♗f3 ♗d7 28.♗xd5 cxd5 29.♕xe5 ♕e4+ 30.♗e2 ♕xe5 31.♖xe5 ♔d6∓.
The choice between 16...♔e7 and 16...g6 is hard.

17.♘e4 0-0 18.0-0 ♗g7
19.♖xf8+ ♕xf8 20.♗f3
20.♗g4 ♕e7 21.c4 c5= Azarov-A.Zhigalko, Minsk ch-BLR 2017.

20...♖a7
Duda's novelty is a frequent guest in various lines of the Najdorf Poisoned Pawn. 20...♕e7 21.♕a5 (21.c4 a5 22.c5 ♗a6 23.♕xa5 ♕f8 24.♕b6 (24.♕c3) 24...♗c4 25.♕xc6 ♗d5 26.♕d6? (26.♕d7 ♕f4 27.♖e1=) 26...♕f4! 27.♖e1 (the real refutation of 27.♖b8+? from

the stem game Hennings-Bobotsov, Leipzig 1965, would have been 27...♗f8!–+) 27...♗f8 (an important gain of time!) 28.♕b6 ♖xa2∓) 21...♖d7 (21...♕a7+ 22.♔h1 ♗d7 Carbonnel-Fröhlich, Germany Bundesliga B 2000/01, stops the invasion of the rook on b7, but 23.c4 (△ 24.c5) tightens the screws on Black's position, which is difficult to play) 22.♖b7 ♕d8 23.♕c7 ♕xc7 24.♖xc7 ♖d8! (24...♗e8?! (De La Fuente Gonzalez-I.Herrera, Madrid 2000) 25.♗g4!± △ 26.♗xe6+ is really awkward for Black) 25.♗e2 and despite the two-pawn plus Black still needs to actively seek equality.
21.♖b8 ♖d7 22.♕a5

22...♕d8?
A hideous oversight. There were several alternatives to hold the balance:
  A) 22...♖h6 23.♔f2 ♕d8 24.♕xe5 ♖f7 25.♕d6 ♖f8 26.♕xd8 ♖xd8 27.♗g4 ♔g7 – a handy spot;
  B) 22...h5 23.♕b6 ♕d8 24.♕xc6 ♖c7 25.♕d6 ♖d7 26.♕xe6+ ♔h7 27.♕b3;
  C) 22...h6 23.♕b6 ♕d8 24.♕xd8+ ♖xd8 25.♗g4 ♔h7 (another handy spot) 26.♔f2 ♖f8+ 27.♔e2.
23.♕xd8+! ♖xd8 24.♗g4+–
It's not about what goes off the board but what is left behind! Suddenly there is no defence to the back-rank pin.
24...♔f7 25.♖xc8 ♖xc8
26.♘d6+ ♔f6 27.♘xc8 ♗f8

Jan-Krzysztof Duda

Black pretends he has some compensation for the lost piece. There is always time to resign later.
28.♗f3 ♔f5 29.♗xc6 e4 30.♔f2 ♗c5+ 31.♔e2 ♔f4 32.a4 a5 33.♔d2 ♗b4+ 34.c3 ♗c5 35.♔e2 ♔f5 36.g3 ♔e5 37.♔d2 ♗g1 38.h3 ♗f2 39.♗b7 ♗c5 40.♔c2 h5 41.♔b3 g5 42.♔c4 ♗f2 43.g4 h4 44.♘e7 ♔f4 45.♘c6 ♔g3 46.♘xa5 ♔xh3

47.♘b3?
Especially in blitz chess there are always decisions to make. 47.♘c6! would have been the proper approach: 47...♔xg4 48.a5 ♔f4 49.♘d4 g4 50.♘xe6+ ♔f3 51.♘d4+ ♔xd4 52.♔xd4 g3 53.♗xe4+ ♔f2 54.a6 h3 55.a7 g2 56.a8♕ g1♕ and the c3-pawn decides.
47...♔xg4 48.a5
48.♗xe4 ♔f4 49.♔d3 g4 50.♘d4 h3 51.a5 g3 52.♘xe6+ ♔e5 53.♘g5 g2 54.♘xh3 g1♕ 55.♘xg1 ♗xg1 is a drawn opposite-coloured bishops ending.

48...♗a7!
This is the difference with 47.♘c6!. 48...♔f4? 49.♘d4! transposes to the line given at move 47.
49.♘d4 h3?
So close, and yet so far away! 49...e5! secures the draw:
  A) 50.♘e6 e3! (50...♔f5? 51.♘xg5!+−) 51.♔d3 ♔f5=;
  B) 50.♗xe4 ♔f4 51.♗h1 exd4 52.cxd4 g4 53.d5 ♔e5=;
  C) 50.♘c8+ ♔g3 51.♘f5+ ♔f3 52.♗b7 ♔f4 53.♘e7 ♔f3=.
50.♗xe4 e5
Too late!
51.♘e2 ♔h4 52.♔d5 g4 53.c4 g3 54.♘xg3 ♔xg3 55.c5 1-0

New points to Anikaev's idea

by Rafal Ogiewka

CA 2.4 (E04)

Here is a nice novelty in the Open Catalan.
1.d4 ♘f6 2.c4 e6 3.g3 d5 4.♗g2 dxc4 5.♘f3 a6! 6.0-0 ♘c6 7.e3 ♖b8 8.♘fd2 e5!!
An excellent move and a great idea, introduced in 1982 by Yury Anikaev!
9.♗xc6+ bxc6 10.dxe5 ♘g4 11.♘f3!?
11.♘xc4 ♗e6 12.♘bd2 ♗b4! (Jan Smeets, 2012)

with massive complications, for instance: 13.b3 h5 14.♕e2 h4! 15.♘f3 hxg3 16.fxg3 ♕d5!!N – instead of 16...♗c3 Barp-Gilevich, Padova 2019 – 17.h4 ♗c3! (right now!) – and, in my opinion, Black is OK

in all variations, e.g. 18.♖b1 ♗xe5 19.♘cxe5 ♘xe5 20.♘xe5 ♕xe5 21.♕f3 d5 22.♗b2 ♕e6 23.♕f4 0-0 24.♖be1 ♗e4! and a draw was agreed in the friendly game Czak-Ogiewka, Poland 2020.

After the knight move to f3 Black can choose between:
  A) 11...♕e7 12.♕d4 c5 13.♕c3!N (instead of 13.♕e4, Zanan-Timofeev, Jerusalem 2015) and it is not easy for Black to finish development, for instance: 13...♕e6 14.e4 ♗e7 15.h3 ♘h6 16.♗g5! f6 17.exf6 ♗xf6 18.♗xf6 ♕xf6 19.♕xf6 gxf6 20.♖c1 ♖xb2 21.♘fd2!;
  B) 11...♕xd1!!N 12.♖xd1 ♖b5 13.♖d4! (13.♘c3 ♘xe5!) 13...♘xe5 14.♘xe5 ♖xe5 15.♖xc4

15...h5!! (the point!), and now:
  B1) 16.♖xc6 h4! 17.♖xc7 ♗e6 18.♖c2 hxg3 19.fxg3 ♗d6! 20.♘c3 ♖eh5 21.♖g2 ♗d7! 22.h4 (22.♗d2 ♗h3! 23.♖e2 ♗g4=) 22...♗g4! 23.e4 ♗c5+ 24.♔h2 ♗d6 25.♔g1=;
  B2) 16.e4 ♖c5! 17.♖xc5 ♗xc5 18.♗f4 ♗d4 19.♘d2

♗xb2 20.♖b1 ♗c3 21.♘b3
♗b4 22.♖c1 ♗d7 23.♖xc7 h4!
24.♗b6 ♖h5! 25.♗c5 a5! 26.f3
hxg3 27.hxg3 a4! 28.♗xb4
axb3 29.axb3 ♖b5 30.♗c3
♖xb3 and Black is OK!;

B3) 16.h4! g5! 17.b3 ♖g8
18.♗b2 ♖c5 19.♖xc5 ♗xc5
20.hxg5 ♖xg5 21.♘d2 ♗e7!
– with enough chances for
Black, for instance: 22.♔f1
a5! 23.♘e4 ♖f5 24.♖c1 a4
25.bxa4 ♖a5 26.♖xc6 ♗b7
27.♘f6+ ♔d8 28.♖c2 ♖xa4
29.♖d2+ (29.♘xh5 ♖xa2=)
29...♔c8 30.♘d5 ♗d8 31.♘c3
♖c4 32.♔e2 h4 33.gxh4 ♖xh4
34.♖d4 ♗a6+ 35.♔d2 ♖xd4
36.exd4 ♗c4 – the ending is
a draw.

With best wishes,
Rafal Ogiewka
Nisa, Poland

Don't play the bishop to e6!

by René Olthof

GI 3.3 (D85)   YB 31, 51, 108

There seems to be no end to
Carlsen's incredible string of
tournament victories, be it in
real time or online. Does this
mean that he is infallible?
No, it doesn't. Like any other
mere mortal, Magnus trips up
big-time from time to time –
just not quite as often as his
adversaries.
On page 48 of my Survey
in Yearbook 135 I presented
the blatant blunder 7.♘xe6??
coming out of Carlsen's
hands in the obscure anti-
Sicilian gambit 1.e4 c5 2.♘f3
d6 3.d4 cxd4 4.♘xd4 ♘f6
5.♗c4 ♘xe6 6.♕h5 e6 against
Ian Nepomniachtchi during
the Carlsen Invitational on
April 28, 2020.

One week later the following
happened to his opponent in
the Online Nations Cup.

Viswanathan Anand
Ian Nepomniachtchi
Nations Cup Online 2020 (5)
**1.d4 ♘f6 2.c4 g6 3.♘c3 d5
4.cxd5 ♘xd5 5.♗d2 ♗g7 6.e4
♘xc3**
6...♘b6 7.♗e3 0-0 is the main
line.
7.♗xc3

This is one of the tabiya
positions during these
Covid-19 times with dozens
of games being played all
over the world.
7...c5
The major alternative
is 7...0-0 8.♕d2 ♘c6
(8...c5!? is the main reply)
9.♘f3 ♗g4 10.d5 ♗xf3
11.♗xg7 (11.gxf3 ♘e5 12.♗e2)
11...♔xg7 12.gxf3 ♘e5
13.0-0-0 c6 14.♕c3 f6 15.f4
(15.♗h3 cxd5 16.exd5 ♘f7
17.f4 was seen in the first
World Championship match
Anand-Carlsen, Sochi 2014)
15...♘f7 16.d6!? exd6 17.h4
♕b6N 18.♕g3 d5 19.exd5
and Giri had reached a very
promising position against
Nepomniachtchi, Legends
of Chess Online 23.7.2020.
In the first match game he
stumbled and later even lost
after 19...♖ad8 20.h5 ♕c5+
21.♔b1 ♖xd5 22.♖c1, while he
again failed to convert his
advantage in the third match
game after 19...cxd5 20.h5
♖ac8+ 21.♔b1 ♖fe8 22.hxg6
hxg6 23.♗d3.
8.d5 ♗xc3+ 9.bxc3 ♕d6
A relatively recent addition
to Black's armoury. 9...0-0

and 9...♕a5 are the oldest and
most common moves.
10.♕d2 0-0 11.f4
11.♘f3 is the main
alternative and Ivanchuk
has even ventured upon the
adventurous 11.h4 f5 12.h5
fxe4 13.hxg6 ♕xg6 14.♘e2
♘d7 15.♖h6 ♕f7 16.♗g5+
(16.♘g3 ♘f6 17.♖h4 ♕xd5
18.♕xd5+ ♘xd5 19.♗c4 ♗e6
20.♘xe4=) 16...♔h8 17.0-0-0
♕xf2 (17...♖g8!?) 18.♗e6!?

Viswanathan Anand

♘f6 19.♖xe7 ♖g8 20.♕h6
♖g6 (20...♗g4=) 21.♖xh7+
♘xh7 22.♕xg6 ♗f5 (22...♗d7
23.♕xe4 ♖e8 24.♕f3 ♕xf3
25.gxf3 ♖e3=) 23.♕h6
(23.♕g3 ♕xg3 24.♘xg3 ♗g6
25.♔d2 △ 26.♔e3+=) 23...♗g4
24.d6= Ivanchuk-Dominguez
Perez, Beijing rapid 2014.
White won in 71 moves.
11...e6 12.♘f3!?N
A nice novelty.
12.♗c4 b5 13.♗xb5 exd5
14.♗c4 (14.exd5 ♘d7=)
14...♗b7 15.♘f3 ♘d7 (15...♖d8
may be a simpler route
towards equality: 16.♗xd5
♗xd5 17.♕xd5 ♕xd5
18.exd5 ♖xd5 19.♖d1 ♖xd1+
20.♔xd1= Tomashevsky-
Nepomniachtchi, Satka
ch-RUS 2018) 16.0-0 ♘b6
17.♗e2 d4 18.e5 ♕d7 19.cxd4
♖ad8 20.♖ad1 ♗xf3 21.♖xf3
♕xd4+ 22.♕xd4 ♖xd4
23.♖xd4 cxd4. White has
two small advantages here:
bishop v knight and fewer

pawn islands, but in the game Giri-Vachier-Lagrave, Yekaterinburg 19.3.2020, White didn't really try: 24.♖d3 (24.♖a3) 24...♖d8 25.♗d1 (25.♔f2) 25...♘c4 26.♔f2 ♘b2 27.♖d2 ♘c4 28.♖d3 ♘b2 29.♖d2 ♘c4 30.♖d3 ½-½.

12...exd5 13.♗c4

13...♗e6?
This is already the decisive mistake. And Anand knew it! 13...♘c6 14.♗xd5 ♗e6 is the right way. If Black wanted to play ...d5-d4, this was the right moment.

14.0-0! d4?
Black's situation is already quite desperate, but this doesn't help.
14...♖d8 also fails to 15.f5 dxc4 16.♕h6 ♕f8 17.♕h4 gxf5 (17...f6 18.fxe6 ♖e8 19.♘g5 ♖e7 20.e5 f5 21.♖ad1 ♘c6 22.♖d7 △ 23.♖fd1) 18.♘g5 h6 19.exf5 ♗d5 20.♘e6+−.
Black should acquiesce to an inferior position after 14...♘d7 15.f5 ♘e5 16.♘xe5 (16.♗b5!? ♗c8 17.♖ad1±) 16...♕xe5 17.♗b3 c4 18.♗c2 dxe4 19.fxe6 ♕xe6 20.♕e3 f5 21.♖ab1± or 14...♕d8 15.exd5 ♗f5 16.d6 ♘d7 17.♘e5±.

15.f5!+−
Did MVL really miss this in his preparation?

15...♗xc4 16.e5! ♕d7 17.f6!
1-0
It's mate in 4!

The message from this game is loud and clear: don't play

---

the bishop to e6. But two months later this message was wasted on our World Champion.

Anish Giri
Magnus Carlsen
Chessable Online 2020 (3)
1.d4 ♘f6 2.c4 g6 3.♘c3 d5 4.cxd5 ♘xd5 5.♗d2 ♗g7 6.e4 ♘xc3 7.♗xc3 0-0 8.♕d2
The line with 7.♗xc3 is not particulary new and has been around since the mid-80s. By transposition, 8.♘f3 was already seen in Nürnberg-Teschner, German Championship, Essen 1948!

8...c5 9.d5 e6
Inserting 9...♗xc3 10.bxc3 doesn't make much difference: 10...e6 (10...♕d6 – Anand-Nepomniachtchi above) 11.d6 (Anand-Hammer, Stavanger 2013) was examined in depth by Tibor Karolyi in Yearbook 108, while 11.♗c4 is a direct transposition to the game.

10.♗c4
10.♗xg7 ♔xg7 has also been seen.

10...♗xc3
10...exd5 11.♗xd5 ♘d7 (11...♘c6 – Mikhalevski) 12.♗xg7 ♔xg7 13.♘e2 or 13.h4.

11.bxc3 exd5
The most popular move here but by no means the only option: there are also 11...b5 12.♗xb5 exd5 13.exd5, 11...♕h4, and 11...♕f6.

12.♗xd5 ♘d7
In the stem game, Gelfand-Grischuk, London ct 2013, 12...♘c6 13.♘f3 ♕f6 14.0-0 ♗g4 was played.

13.♘f3 ♘b6
The odd choice.
There are a dozen games with 13...♘f6 14.0-0 ♘xd5 15.exd5 or 14...♖e8 15.♖fe1 ♗g4 16.♘g5 ♗e6 17.c4 ♗xd5 18.exd5 b5= Kasimdzhanov-Radjabov, Tbilisi 2015.

14.0-0

14...♗e6??N
Again this basic blunder! 14...♗g4; 14...♘xd5 (Martinez Martin-Duda, Banter blitz 2019) transposes to 13...♘f6 14.0-0 ♘xd5 15.exd5.

15.♗xe6?
You don't expect the World Champion to make such a monumental mistake. Otherwise Giri would have had no problem finding 15.♕h6!, going for the king. Black is busted! 15...♖e8 (15...♘f6 16.♘g5 ♕g7 17.♕xg7+ ♔xg7 18.♗xe6 h6 19.♘xf7 ♖ae8 20.♗b3+−; 15...♗xd5 16.♘g5 ♕xg5 17.♕xg5 ♗xe4 18.♖fe1+−) 16.♘g5 ♗xd5 17.exd5 ♕f6 18.♕xh7+ ♔f8 19.d6+−.
If you're not looking for mate, there were two alternatives to retain a small edge:
  A) 15.c4 ♗xd5 16.cxd5 f5 17.♖ad1 fxe4 18.♘g5 ♖f5 19.♘xe4 ♖xd5 20.♕c2 ♖xd1 21.♖xd1 ♕e7 22.♘xc5±;
  B) 15.♗xb7 ♕xd2 16.♘xd2 ♖ab8 17.♗a6 ♖fd8 18.♘b3 ♘a4 19.♖fc1 c4 20.♘d4 ♖d6 21.♘xe6 ♖xa6 22.♘c7 ♖ab6 23.♘d5±.

15...♕xd2
A more practical solution than 15...fxe6 16.♕e2±. The fractured pawn structure makes Black feel slightly uncomfortable.

16.♗xf7+ ♖xf7 17.♘xd2 ♖d8⇆
18.♘b3?!
18.♖fd1?? ♖fd7−+; 18.♘f3=.

18...c4! 19.♘c5
19.♘d4?! ♘a4! 20.♖fc1 ♘xc3 21.♖xc3 ♖xd4∓.

19...♖e8

20.a4!
The only way to leave the scene unscathed.
20...♖c7 21.a5 ♞c8 22.♞a4 ♖xe4
The material balance has been restored.
23.♖fe1 ♖xe1+ 24.♖xe1 b5 25.axb6 axb6 26.g4 b5 27.♞b2 ♔f7
27...♞b6!?.
28.♖e5 ♞d6 29.♔g2 ♖e7 30.♖xe7+ ♔xe7 31.f4 h5 32.h3 hxg4 33.hxg4 g5 34.♔f3 ♔f6 35.♞d1 gxf4 36.♔xf4 ♞c8 37.♞e3 ♞b6 38.g5+ ♔g6 39.♔g4 ♞d7 40.♔f4 ♞c5 41.♔e5 ♞xg5 42.♞xc4 bxc4 43.♔d5 ♞a4 44.♔xc4 ♞xc3
½-½

Ambitious move

by Rafal Ogiewka

NI 27.16 (D39)   YB 74, 111, 121

1.d4 e6
I like the French Defence...
2.c4 ♞f6 3.♞f3 d5 4.♞c3 dxc4 5.e4 ♝b4 6.♝g5 c5 7.♝xc4 cxd4 8.♞xd4 ♝xc3+ 9.bxc3 ♛a5 10.♝b5+!?

And now my recommendation:
10...♞bd7!
I like this ambitious move! Let's look at the most important lines:
11.♝xf6 ♛xc3+ 12.♔f1 gxf6 13.h4 ♛b4!
A move order with a trap!
14.♖b1 ♛d6 15.♖h3 a6 15.♝e2 ♞c5! and White is in trouble (e4 is hit). The most common move is 13...a6.
14.♖h3! a6 15.♝e2 ♞e5

And now:
A) 16.h5 ♛d6 17.♛d2 ♞c6 18.♖d3 ♛h2 19.♞f3!? (19. f4 ♖g8 20.♝f3 ♞d7 21.♞e2 Anand-Kramnik, Khanty-Mansiysk 2014, was examined in Yearbook 111) 19...♛h1+ 20.♞g1 ♖g8 21.♖g3 ♖xg3 22.fxg3 ♝d7!N (instead of 22...e5, Fröwis-Hölzl, Austria Bundesliga 2011/12) 23.♖c1 ♞e5 24.♖c7 ♖d8 25.♛f4 (25.♔f2 ♝c6 26.♛b4 ♖d7 27.♖c8+ ♖d8=)

25...♝b5! 26.♝xb5+ axb5 27.♛xf6 ♖d1+ 28.♔e2 ♖e1+! 29.♔xe1 ♛xg1+ 30.♛f1 ♞f3+! 31.gxf3 ♛xg3+ 32.♔d2

♛xc7 33.♛xb5+ ♔f8 and the ending is a draw;
B) 16.♖b1 ♛d6 17.♖c3 (17.♛d2 ♝d7! 18.♖xb7 ♝b5 – and Black is OK! So-Aronian, Wijk aan Zee 2017, as mentioned by Adorjan in Yearbook 121) 17...0-0!! 18.h5 ♖d8 19.♛g3+ (19.♛b3 h6!N – instead of 19...♝d7 Giri-Harikrishna, Shenzhen 2017 – 20.♖d1 ♛e7 with the idea 21.f4 ♞c6! and Black is OK!) 19...♔f8 20.♛b3 ♛c5! 21.♞f3

21...♔e7!! This is the point! Square e7 is a safe haven for the king and ♖g7 is not dangerous for Black. 22.♞xe5 ♛xe5 23.♛b4+ (23.♛a3+ ♛d6 24.♛e3 ♛d4 25.♛c1 ♛d2 26.♛c7+ ♖d7! 27.♛c5+ ♛d6 28.♛e3 ♛d4 29.♛h6 b6! 30.♛xh7 ♝b7 31.♖d1 ♛a4= Heilala-Doppelhammer, cr 2018) 23...♛d6 24.♛b2 ♛e5 25.♖c3!? (25.♛c1 b5! 26.f4 ♛xe4 27.♛c5+ ♖d6 28.♖d3 ♛c6 29.♛xc6 ♖xc6 30.♝f3 ♝b7 31.♝xc6 ♝xc6= Williamson-Cousins, cr 2019) 25...♖d4! 26.♛a3+ ♛d6 27.♖c7+ ♔e8 28.♛c3 ♝d7! 29.♖bxb7 ♖d1+! 30.♝xd1 ♛xd1+ 31.♛e1 ♝b5+ 32.♖xb5 ♛xe1+ 33.♔xe1 axb5 and this ending is also drawn.

With best wishes,
**Rafal Ogiewka
Nisa, Poland**

Please be healthy y'all!

Sheer enthusiasm

by Erwin l'Ami

In this column, Dutch grandmaster and top chess coach Erwin l'Ami scours the thousands of new correspondence games that are played every month for important novelties that may start new waves in OTB chess also. Every three months it's your chance to check out the best discoveries from this rich chess source that tends to be underexposed.

Even though Corona-times have stopped more or less all OTB-events, for obvious reasons it has not affected Correspondence Chess. There was once again plenty of material!

The King's Gambit always speaks to the imagination of chess lovers. When I saw the following game passing by, I decided to grab my chance and do a full overview on this fantastic opening. I may have gotten a bit carried away, but it's sheer enthusiasm, dear reader!

A fantastic opening
KG 1.6 (C37)

John Claridge
Michael Höppenstein
GER-WLS ICCF 2019
1.e4 e5 2.f4
This ancient opening wasn't featured before in this column. This game gives me the opportunity to right that wrong. We are in for a fun journey!
2...exf4
Hein Donner claimed that an attempt to refute the King's Gambit has to start with 2...d5, which is the Falkbeer Countergambit. Donner made this statement back in 1965, and a lot has happened since. The Falkbeer remains a viable option, but 3.exd5 e4, which was Falbeer's idea, has fallen from grace recently, due to 4.d3! ♘f6 5.dxe4 (5.♘c3 ♗b4 6.♗d2 e3! 7.♗xe3

0-0 is known to give Black dangerous compensation) 5...♘xe4 6.♘f3 ♗c5 7.♕e2 ♗f5 (if 7...♕xd5 8.♘fd2! just wins a pawn after 8...f5 9.♘c3 followed by taking on e4)

8.♘c3 ♕e7 9.♗e3 ♗xe3 10.♕xe3 ♘xc3 11.♕xe7+ ♔xe7 12.bxc3 ♗xc2, an endgame that arises more or less by force. Now after 13.♔d2 Black has three bishop moves, but none are overly satisfactory:
A) 13...♗g6 14.♖e1+ ♔d8 15.♘d4 looks fantastic for White, despite Black actually winning this game in Wheatcroft-Keres, Margate 1939;
B) 13...♗a4 14.♖e1+ ♔f8 (on both king moves to the 6th rank, 15.♘g5! is a strong reply) 15.♖e4 followed by ♗c4 and ♖he1, is bad for Black;
C) 13...♗f5 14.♖e1+ ♔f6 15.♘e5 (threatening 16.g4!) 15...h5 16.h3 is very dangerous. A sample line is 16...c6 17.d6! ♖d8 18.g4! ♖xd6+ 19.♔c1 ♗e6 20.f5 ♘d7 21.fxe6 ♘xe5 22.exf7 and Black is in big trouble as ♗c4! is a huge threat. For instance, 22...♖f8 23.♗c4!

♘xc4 24.♖hf1+ ♔g6 25.gxh5+ ♔xh5 26.♖e8 and the f-pawn decides.

3...exf4 is likely better, and even Nimzowitsch' move 3...c6 deserves serious attention. Back in the 'Romantic Era' of our game (generally considered to have lasted from the 15th century until the 1880s, though Willy Hendriks's excellent recent book *On the Origin of Good Moves* may change the perception of what that era was about – but I digress!) the King's Gambit was the main opening and so it has an incredibly rich past. On move three a lot of options have been tried. We will look at them briefly:

3.♘f3

The most conventional way of continuing.

A) 3.♘c3 invites the check 3...♕h4+ after which White calmly plays 4.♔e2 and claims to have good central control and the ability to kick away the queen with ♘f3 next. Reality is quite different though. 4...♕d8!?, which is how Karjakin played in a 2017 blitz game against Garry Kasparov, is perfectly reasonable, but...

A1) An attempt to refute this way of playing is the energetic 4...d5!? 5.♘xd5 ♗g4+ 6.♘f3 ♘c6! which was already recommended by Keres many decades ago.

I believe White is in huge trouble here as 7.♘xc7+ ♔d8 8.♘xa8 ♘e5 (not 8...♘d4+ 9.♔d3!) 9.♕e1 (9.h3 ♗h5! 10.d4 ♘xf3 11.gxf3 ♗xf3+ 12.♔xf3 ♕h5+ 13.♔g2 ♕xd1 14.♗d3 ♕h5 15.♗xf4 was assessed by Keres as 'surely not worse for White', but actually it is. Best is 15...♘e7 with the idea to open up the kingside with ...f7-f5 and ...g7-g5; Black is – close to – winning) 9...♘xf3 10.♕xh4+ ♘xh4+ 11.♔e1 as in Rapport-Bromberger, Austria Bundesliga 2014, should be better for Black after 11...g5. Black will proceed to pick up the a8-knight with a great endgame ahead;

A2) Of course, 4...g5 is highly critical as well. Here, 5.d4 d6 (5...♘e7 6.g3! fxg3 7.♘f3 ♕h5 8.♗xg5 g2 9.♗xg2 ♖g8 is what Stockfish initially comes up with, but 10.h4 f6 11.♕d3! is very messy) 6.♘f3 ♕h5 begs the question if White can really be happy, with a pawn down and his king on e2.

B) The Bishop Gambit, 3.♗c4, has a better reputation but is also not too worrisome for Black. Now White has the f1-square for the king, after the check on h4, and I think better is 3...♘c6 4.d4 (or 4.♘f3 g5!) 4...♘f6 when 5.e5 d5! is an important point, and 5.♘c3 ♗b4! is fine too;

C) The above moves are stronger than 3.d4 when 3...♕h4+ 4.♔e2 d5! is the big difference with 3.♘c3 and 3.♗c4: Black has this freeing pawn break;

D) A ChessBase article from 2012 claimed 3.♗e2 to be the only move to make a draw, but I am not sure what White should do after 3...f5! which looks really strong;

E) Last but not least, there is the move 3.♕f3 which

was played by two World Champions! True, Euwe was not yet the Champion when he played the move and Capablanca used it only in simultaneous exhibitions. Needless to say, the rule that you should not move your queen too early applies here as well. White's idea is that 3...g5 4.h4! wins back the pawn under favourable circumstances. Much stronger is 3...♘c6! and now:

E1) After 4.♕xf4 White falls too far behind in development. There are multiple ways to punish this but the simplest is 4...d5 (4...♗d6 5.♕e3 ♘f6 is very strong too, with the idea to quickly castle kingside and start attacking) because 5.exd5 ♘b4 is quite unpleasant for White;

E2) 4.c3 ♕h4+ (famous is the following game: 4...♘f6 5.d4 d5 6.e5 ♘e4 7.♗xf4 g5 8.♗e3 h5 (8...g4! 9.♕e2 ♕h4+ 10.♔d1 f6! 11.exf6 ♗f5 is how modern engines treat this position) 9.♘d2 ♗g4 10.♘xe4! ♗xf3 11.♘f6+ ♔e7 12.♘xf3 and White won in great style in Capablanca-Chase, New York simul 1922) when White has no good response. Likely, best is 5.g3 (5.♔d1 d5! threatens 6...♗g4) 5...fxg3 6.hxg3 and now the simple 6...♕e7 7.d4 d5 gives a huge advantage.

3...g5

The sharpest reply!

A) Fischer's recommendation was 3...d6, which became a popular move as a direct result. It plans to protect the f4-pawn on the next move, thereby avoiding the sharp lines after 3...g5 4.h4.

A1) After 4.♗c4 h6 (4...g5 5.h4! has a bad reputation, though the mega-ugly 5...f6! is not easy to refute at all!) 5.d4 g5 6.0-0 ♗g7 Black has been doing well;

A2) The main line runs 4.d4 g5 5.h4 g4 6.♘g1 (6.♘g5 can be met by both 6...f6 and 6...h6) 6...♕f6 with a very unclear position. Practice has seen 7.♘c3 ♘e7 8.♘ge2 ♗h6 9.♕d2 ♘bc6 10.♘b5 ♔d8 where Black is not doing badly.

B) Perhaps the main line these days is 3...♘f6! which I give an exclam because it is an easy-to-learn variation where White is unlikely to equalize. Jan Gustafsson recommends it in his 1.e4 e5 Chessable course and it does seem like the most straightforward solution.

The idea is 4.e5 (4.♘c3 d5! is easy for Black) 4...♘h5 where Black simply protects the f4-pawn with the knight and prepares to play ...d7-d5 next. We recommend this line to the practical player when faced with the King's Gambit.

4.♘c3
The so-called Quaade Gambit.

A) The old reply is 4.h4.

A1) Here modern engines spit out the move 4...d5, which is extremely rare, played in just a handful of games. Two of them are high-level correspondence outings though, forcing us to take this move seriously!

A11) 5.exd5 g4 6.♘e5 ♕e7 7.♕e2 ♘f6 8.d4 ♘h5! 9.♘d3 ♗f5 is pleasant for Black;

A12) 5.d4 is critical, and now 5...dxe4 6.♘xg5 ♘f6 7.♘c3 (both 7.♗c4 ♗g4! and 7.♗xf4 h6 8.♘h3 ♘c6 are great for Black) 7...♗b4 looks okay for Black. One game continued 8.♗b5+ (8.♗xf4 h6 9.♗c4 hxg5 10.♗xg5 could be an interesting direction as well) 8...♗d7 9.♗e2 h6 10.♘xf7 ♔xf7 11.♗xf4 ♘c6 12.0-0 ♔g7 13.d5 ♕e7 14.dxc6 ♗c5+ 15.♔h1 ♗xc6 16.♗h2 e3 17.♖f5 ♖hd8 18.♕f1 ♖d4 19.♗e5 ♖xh4+ 20.♔g1 ♗d4 21.♕e1 ♖h1+ 22.♔xh1 ♗xe5 23.♕h4 ♖d8 24.♖af1 ♖d4 25.♖1f4 ♖xf4 26.♖xf4 ♗xf4 27.♕xf4 a6 28.♔g1 and White barely

managed to hold in Kögler-Pessoa, ICCF 2019.

A2) The classical main line is 4...g4 5.♘e5 (the Allgaier Variation, 5.♘g5 h6 6.♘xf7, has a particularly bad reputation for White. The compensation is of a very speculative nature) 5...♘f6 and is very comfortable for Black too.

B) 4.♗c4 is the introduction to the Muzio Gambit. I would decline the offer with 4...♘c6 (transposing to the note given after 3.♗c4) as the following mess is hard to remember over the board: 4...g4 5.0-0 gxf3 6.♕xf3 (a sacrifice that actually looks half-decent. One of my first trainers, Rob Brunia, implemented me with a set of rules on sacrifices in the opening. For 1 tempo you can sacrifice a pawn, for 2 tempi two pawns and for 3 tempi a piece can be sacrificed. White is certainly up in development here and Black's next move can't be considered a developing move either. I'm afraid it's one of those examples of chess being very hard to bring down to clear rules) 6...♕f6 and now:

B1) 7.d3 is too slow;

B2) An interesting thing to observe is the difference in evaluation that Stockfish and Leela show after 7.♘c3!?? ♕d4+ 8.♔h1 ♕xc4 9.b3

where Stockfish initially goes as high as -5, while Leela thinks it's just around -1. With ♘d5 and ♗b2 coming next it isn't that clear, but objectively Black should be doing well here;

B3) 7.e5 is the only way to keep the fire burning: 7...♕xe5 8.♗xf7+ ♔xf7 9.d4.

This position first appeared in 1889 and the best move was played: 9...♕f5! (9...♕xd4+ 10.♗e3 ♕f6 11.♗xf4 ♘e8 12.♘c3 ♘c6 13.♘d5 ♕g6 14.♖ae1+ ♗e7 15.♗d6!! was a nice miniature by the young Alexei Shirov against Lapinsky, Daugavpils 1990) 10.♗xf4 (after 10.g4 ♕g6 11.♘c3 ♘f6 12.♗xf4 d6 13.♗g3 ♔g7 Black soon won in Showalter-Taubenhaus, New York 1889, which, remarkably, is still a relevant game today!) 10...♘f6 11.♘c3 d6 and Black is doing well as the two extra pieces will have their say.

C) The final move that deserves attention is 4.d4, which is the Rosentreter Gambit.

It is not particularly good, and 4...g4 5.♗xf4 (5.♘e5 ♕h4+ 6.g3 fxg3 7.♕xg4 ♕xg4 8.♘xg4 ♘c6 9.c3 d5 is a comfortable endgame, but the complications after 7...g2+ 8.♔xh4 gxh1♕ 9.♘c3 are best avoided, I think) 5...gxf3 6.♕xf3 ♘c6! is generally considered to be the reason why 7.♗c4 ♕f6 8.e5 ♕g7 just doesn't give White enough attacking prospects.

4...d6
Black has a wealth of possibilities here.

A) 4...♗g7 is decent...;
B) And so is 4...g4 5.♘e5 d5! (5...♕h4+ 6.g3 fxg3 7.♕xg4 is less clear, as White has compensation after the exchange of queens while 7...g2+ 8.♔xh4 gxh1♕ 9.♕h5! is just lost) 6.♘xd5 (instead, 6.♘xg4 d4 (6...dxe4 7.♘f2 ♗e7 8.♗c4 ♘f6 9.0-0 gave White good play in Spielmann-Leonhardt, Opatija 1912) 7.♘b1 ♕h4+ 8.♘f2 ♗d6 is excellent for Black) 6...♕h4+ 7.♔e2 f3+ 8.gxf3 gxf3+ 9.♔d3 f5! is very dangerous for White. The main idea is 10.♘xc7+ ♔d8 11.♘xa8 fxe4+ 12.♔c3 ♕e7 13.a3 ♕xe5+ with a winning position. 10.♕xf3 is tougher, but following 10...♗g7 Black keeps the initiative;
C) Last but not least, 4...♘c6 5.g3!? is a modern interpretation of this line. Now 5...g4 6.♘h4 ♘d4! is

a very strong response, physically stopping d2-d4: 7.♘d5 ♗d6! 8.♕xg4 ♗e5! (Black prepares to take on c2 while preventing ♕g7. The immediate 8...♘xc2+? 9.♔d1 ♘xa1 10.♕g7 is curtains) 9.gxf4 d6 10.♕g3.

It looks like White is for choice here, but after 10...♗f6! 11.♘xf6+ ♕xf6 Black threatens both 12...♘xc2+ and 12...♕xh4. The only way to avert both threats is 12.♔d1 but then 12...♘e7 13.f5 ♕h6! is very convincing. The idea is to give a check on h5 and lure the king to e1, in order to either take on c2 or h4(!) next. White has other options on move 5 but they aren't overly convincing either.

5.d4 g4
Forcing White to invest a piece. Also fine for Black is 5...♗g7 6.g3 ♘c6, but I would refrain from 6...g4 7.♘h4 f3 8.♗e3 ♘c6 9.♕d2 which gave White good compensation in Ponomariov-Dominguez Perez, Huai'an (blitz) 2016.
6.♗xf4 gxf3 7.♕xf3

7...♕h4+

This line also caught my attention because of two recent games between Leela and Stockfish. Both these games continued 7...♘c6 8.♗b5 ♗d7 and here the play diverged. Stockfish chose 9.0-0-0 ♕h4 10.♔b1 0-0-0 (10...♗g4 11.♕e3 ♗xd1 12.d5! is something White is of course happy to invite) 11.d5 ♘b8 12.♖d4 and found just enough counterplay to eventually make a draw in Stockfish-Leela, TCEC 2020. With the white pieces, Leela chose 9.♗xc6 instead. After 9...bxc6 10.0-0 the calm 10...♗g7! followed and it turned out White's threats on the f-file aren't that serious. 11.♗e5 f6!, for instance, leads nowhere. Stockfish eventually held on to the material and turned it into a full point.

I am not sure what to think of Höppenstein's check as it seems to lose a lot of time.

8.g3 ♕g4 9.♕e3 ♘e7 10.♗e2 ♕g6

A fascinating position!

11.0-0

White has two serious alternatives:

A) 11.0-0-0 looks the most natural to me. White intends to go ♖he1 and ♘d5. Black has a wide area of options here but optically, and considering White's 2nd move, this looks to me like an excellent King's Gambit;

Michael Höppenstein

B) 11.g4!? is Leela's suggestion, preventing any future ...♗g4 and playing against the queen on g6. A sample line is 11...♗d7 12.0-0-0 ♘bc6 13.h4, planning h4-h5 to kick the queen further back.

11...♖g8 12.♘b5

More direct is 12.e5 d5 13.♘b5 ♘a6 (13...♘f5 14.♘xc7+ ♔d8 15.♕c3 ♘c6 is certainly possible too!?) 14.♘d6+ cxd6 15.exd6 when 15...♕e4 is likely the easiest reply.

12...♘a6

12...♔d8 is also a typical move in the King's Gambit, but here 13.c4 gives White excellent compensation.

13.♖ae1 ♗e6 14.♗d3

I am sure both players spent a lot of time on 14.c4!? h5 15.♗d3 (15.d5 ♗h3 16.♗d3 ♗xf1 17.♖xf1 is also not out of the question, with e4-e5 coming next) 15...h4 16.e5 ♗f5 17.exd6 ♗xd3 18.dxe7 ♗h6! 19.♗xh6 hxg3 20.h4 ♗xc4 and Black seems to survive. Obviously these lines are so complex that I wouldn't be surprised if there is a huge improvement somewhere along the way.

14...♕h5 15.d5 ♗h3 16.♖f2 ♔d7

Fearless!

Unless I am missing something, Black could have bailed out with 16...♘g6

17.e5 (or 17.♗e2 ♗g4 18.♗xg4 ♕xg4 19.e5 dxe5, transposing) 17...dxe5 18.♗e2 ♗g4 19.♗xg4 ♕xg4 20.♗xe5 0-0-0 when White is forced to play 21.♗xa7+ ♔b8 22.♘c6+ ♔c8 with a repetition. Note that 22...bxc6 23.♕b6+! is not possible.

17.♗e2 ♕g6 18.♘d4 ♔c8 19.♗xa6 bxa6

Certainly a risky winning attempt! Apart from the game continuation, also 20.c4 ♗g7 21.e5!? is a serious question here.

20.♕e2 ♔b7

20...♗g7 21.e5! ♔b7 22.♘c6! is a line Leela initially missed – the reason why a good engine analysis is always a joint venture between Leela and Stockfish. White wins after 22...♖ae8 23.e6! ♗xe6 24.♘a5+ ♔a8 25.dxe6 ♕xe6 26.♕f3+ ♕d5 27.♖xe7! and Black can resign because after 27...♕xf3 there is the intermediate move 28.♖xe8+, winning a piece.

21.♕c4 ♖b8!

The only move, but a strong one!

The king's journey that started with 16...♔d7 is about to end on a8!

22.♘f5

The only try. Instead, 22.♘c6 ♘xc6 23.♕xc6+ ♔c8 24.♕e8+ ♔b7 25.♕c6+ is a draw by perpetual check on which neither side can improve.

22...♔a8 23.♕xc7 ♖b7 24.♕d8+ ♖b8 25.♕d7 ♖b7

26.♕e8+ ♖b8 27.♕a4 ♖b6 28.♕c4!?

A tricky move, as it is hard for Black to do anything constructive. White just intends to play a4-a5 next. Instead, 28.c4 would have allowed Black to regroup with 28...♘c8 29.b4 ♖b7 with an unclear game that can go either way.

28...h5!?

In order, after 29.a4, to get counterplay with 29...h4 30.♘xh4 ♕h5, when 31.a5 ♖b7 seems to be fine for Black.

29.c3 h4 30.♘xh4 ♕h5 31.♘f5

After 31.♔h1 ♗g7! Black is fully mobilized and can count on a big advantage. White's king is considerably weaker compared to his colleague on a8.

31...♘xf5 32.♕c8+ ♖b8 33.♕c6+ ♖b7 34.exf5!?

A final attempt, instead of immediately agreeing to perpetual check.

34...♗e7 35.♗xd6 ♗xd6 36.♕xd6 ♗xf5 37.♕e5 ♗g4

Draw agreed.

Indeed, in the endgame after 38.♕xh5 ♗xh5 White has three pawns for the bishop, which is enough to keep the balance, but nothing more. A sample line is 39.b3 a5 40.c4 a4! 41.bxa4 ♘c7 42.♖f4 ♔b7 and here White's pawns aren't too dangerous as Black's pawn sacrifice on move 40 has weakened the c4-pawn.

And now for a game with much more restraint. The Slow Slav with 4.e3 is a popular way of avoiding the heavy theoretical 4.♘c3 and aims for a small but workable advantage. The most popular replies are 4...♗f5 and 4...♗g4, but Black can also continue in Meran style with 4...e6. The following game gives a good idea how White can treat such a set-up.

Marauding the Meran

SL 1.5 (D11)

Andreas Brugger
Sergejs Klimakovs
MT-Strautins ICCF 2018

1.d4 d5 2.c4 c6 3.♘f3 ♘f6 4.e3 e6

Instead of taking the opportunity to bring the bishop out, to f5 or g4. Of course White can now transpose to main lines with 5.♘c3, but it is more interesting to try and make use of the fact that the knight is still on b1. This gives White some extra options.

5.b3

This pawn move makes a lot of sense now that Black has already committed to ...c7-c6 and ...e7-e6. Other options include 5.♗d3 and 5.♘bd2.

5...♘bd7

Black has plenty of valid alternatives at this point. One is 5...c5 which looks like a loss of time but Black is challenging the centre and given that White's previous moves were 4.e3 and 5.b3, it is not at all clear that the tempo Black loses with this move has any meaningful significance.

In his latest Chessable course on the Semi-Slav, Sam Shankland recommends 5...♘e4!? with the intention

of setting up a Stonewall structure with ...f7-f5. He certainly makes a compelling argument, and I expect to see more of this move in the future.

6.♘bd2 ♗d6 7.♗b2 0-0 8.♗d3

A standard type of position, but one which usually arises with the knight on c3, rather than on d2, and this certainly favours White.

8...b6 9.0-0

An automatic move, but perhaps the new idea 9.e4!? also deserves consideration. The idea is that after 9...dxe4 10.♘xe4 ♘xe4 11.♗xe4 ♗b7 (if 11...♗b4+ 12.♔f1 ♗b7 13.h4! starts a serious attack on the kingside) 12.♗c2 White will follow-up with ♕d3 and 0-0-0. Definitely worth a look!

9...♗b7 10.♕e2

Kramnik played 10.♘e5 back in 2008, beating Van Wely

Sergejs Klimakovs

in a model game: 10...♕e7 11.♕f3 ♖fd8 12.♕h3 h6 13.f4 ♗b4 14.♘df3 ♘e4 15.♘xd7

♖xd7 16.♘e5 ♖c7 17.♗xe4 dxe4 18.c5 bxc5 19.a3 ♗a5 20.dxc5 ♕xc5 21.b4 and White won after a few more moves in Kramnik-Van Wely, Dortmund 2008. Ding Liren later showed that 10...c5 11.cxd5 ♗xd5!? is a good way to go. He easily made a draw in this way against Wesley So in Wijk aan Zee 2016.

10...♕e7
Once again, I refer to Ding Liren for the move 10...c5 which the Chinese played in no less than three games. White, as usual in this line, keeps some pressure with 11.♖ad1. Instead 11.cxd5 stops 11...♗xd5, which loses a piece now after 12.e4 followed by 13.e5. But after 11...exd5 12.♗a6 ♗xa6 13.♕xa6 ♕e7 14.♖fd1 ♖fd8 15.♖ac1 ♕e6 16.♘f1 ♘e4 the position was comfortable for Black in Giri-Ding Liren, Wijk aan Zee 2016.

11.♖ad1 ♖fe8
The 'freeing' move 11...e5 just backfires after 12.dxe5 ♘xe5 13.cxd5 ♘xd3 14.♕xd3 (14.♗xf6 ♕xf6 15.♘e4 ♕g6! is messy, because after 16.♘xd6 Black has the surprising resource 16...♗a6!) 14...♘xd5 (14...cxd5 15.♘d4 is pleasant for White) 15.♘e4 (threatening to take on d6, followed by e3-e4) 15...♗a3 16.♘eg5! g6 17.♗a1! and Black experiences discomfort along the long diagonal.

12.♘e5
Black intended to meet 12.e4 with 12...e5.

12...a5
I am not very fond of this plan, though I'm uncertain whether it is here where Black's problems start. More natural is 12...c5 when 13.f4 cxd4 14.exd4 ♖ac8 15.♖f2 ♘f8 16.h3 ♘g6 was eventually drawn in Sommerbauer-Mrkvicka, ICCF 2020. White

can play more aggressively with 15.g4, but that could also backfire after, for instance, 15...♘f8 16.g5 ♘6d7 when it is not clear how White breaks through while pushing the pawns forward does create certain weaknesses.

13.g4!?
Stockfish's top choice, while Lc0 prefers 13.f4 a4 14.♘df3. Both plans give White good chances for an advantage, but the game continuation is obviously more critical.

13...g6
13...♘f8 14.g5 ♘6d7 is an interesting way to regroup, like in the Sommerbauer-Mrkvicka game; however, it may be a bit too late. Following 15.f4 ♘xe5 16.dxe5 ♗b4 17.♘f3 a4 18.cxd5 cxd5 19.♘d4 axb3 20.axb3 the position was great for White in Tleptsok-Aleksandrov, ICCF 2015; a long torture that finally ended in a 1-0 result after 82 moves.
13...c5 seems to make little sense, as Black has already committed to the plan of ...a7-a5-a4 earlier, but the g2-g4 push does ask for a break in the centre: 14.g5:
A) Not 14...♘e4 15.♗xe4 dxe4 16.♘xd7 ♕xd7 17.♕g4! cxd4 18.♘xe4 ♕c6 (18...♗e4 19.♕xe4 ♕e7 20.h4 dxe3 21.♕xe3 also looks more pleasant for White) 19.f3 ♗f8 20.exd4 and White is doing great. Note that after 20...b5 21.♖f2! bxc4 22.♘f6+

gxf6 23.gxf6+ ♔h8 24.♗c1!! threatens 25.♖g2, which is now unstoppable. The immediate 24.♖g2 would be met with 24...♗h6! and ...♖e8-g8 next;
B) 14...♗xe5! 15.dxe5 ♘e4 16.f4. Stockfish initially shows a near winning advantage here, but eventually has to admit that 16...♘xd2 17.♖xd2 ♘f8 18.cxd5 (18.h4 ♖ed8 19.♖fd1 a4 is similar) 18...♗xd5 19.♗b5 ♖ec8 followed by ...♗d5-c6 is actually pretty solid, which is exactly what Leela was claiming from the very start.

14.f4 a4

This is one of those positions that are heavily discussed in Correspondence Chess (59 high-level games), but not at all OTB.

15.♗b1
A rare move, featured in only two of the 59 games, and one of those two is the current one. However, it actually does make sense to prevent the black rook from entering on a2.
15.♖f2 axb3 16.axb3 ♖a2 17.♘f1 c5 18.g5 dxc4 19.bxc4 (19.♗b1 looks strong, but so is the reply 19...♖xb2! 20.♕xb2 ♗xe5 21.dxe5 ♘g4! with ideas of playing ...♘dxe5 and ...♕xg5 next, with a raging attack) 19...♗xe5 20.dxe5 ♘e4 21.♗xe4 ♗xe4 has been seen in a number of correspondence games and seems to be fine for Black.

I also find the position after 15.♘df3 ♗xe5 16.♘xe5 axb3 17.axb3 ♕b4 looking somewhat dubious, without the dark-squared bishop, but this line has done fine for Black in correspondence games as well.

15...axb3 16.axb3 ♗a3

16...c5!? comes into consideration too, with the idea that 17.g5 ♗xe5 18.dxe5 ♘h5 is very unclear. Once again, Leela and Stock have widely different opinions.

17.♗c3 ♘xe5

A big question is whether Black can try to force a repetition with 17...♗b4, but, rather than dropping back to b2, White can play 18.♗xb4 ♕xb4 19.♕f2!? with ideas of going g4-g5 as well as bringing the queen over to h4. This looks dangerous though I'm not 100% sure how to proceed after 19...♕e7.

18.dxe5 ♘d7 19.♘f3 ♗b4

Novelty on move 20

20.♗b2

The first new move in the game! 20.♗xb4 ♕xb4 21.♘d4 ♗a6 isn't clear at all, and 20.♗d4 dxc4 21.bxc4 b5 22.cxb5 cxb5 23.f5 exf5 24.gxf5 ♗xf3 25.♕xf3 ♘xe5 26.♕d5 was agreed drawn in Konstantinov-Korabliov, ICCF 2017. The position after, say, 26...♖ad8 27.♕xb5 ♗d6 indeed does look very balanced.

20...dxc4

And perhaps this is already the decisive mistake! Once again, the question of how to answer 20...♗a3 is an important one. The position is fascinating and very dangerous for Black: 21.h4!? ♕b4 (the most straightforward answer, starting counterplay on the queenside) 22.♗a1!? and now:

A) 22...♕xb3 23.♗c2 ♕b4 24.h5 is very dangerous. A sample line is 24...♗b2 25.hxg6 hxg6 26.♗xb2 ♕xb2 27.♕h2 (threatening 28.♘g5!) 27...♔g7 28.f5! ♖h8 29.♕f4 ♕xc2 30.fxe6 fxe6 31.♘d4 and Black's best is probably to give back material with 31...♕h2+ 32.♕xh2 ♖xh2 33.♘xe6+! ♔g8 34.♔xh2 and White should win;

B) 22...♗a6 23.♘d2 (first securing the queenside, though even 23.h5 ♕xb3 24.♘d4 ♗xc4 25.♕f3 ♕b4 26.hxg6 hxg6 27.♗d3 is not completely out of the question, when White intends to go all in on the kingside) 23...♘c5 24.♗c2 ♖ed8 25.f5 and now the position after 25...♘xb3! 26.fxe6 (26.♗xb3 dxc4 27.♗xc4 ♖xd2! is the point, when 28.♕xd2 ♕xd2 29.♖xd2 ♗xc4 is an OK endgame for Black) 26...♘xa1 27.exf7+ ♔g7 28.♖xa1 ♗xc4 29.♘xc4 ♕xc4 30.♗d3 ♕c3 31.♖xa3 ♕xa3 32.♕f3 ♕e7 33.♕f4 is an exercise in itself. Black saves the game with 33...b5!! intending ...♖a8-a4.

21.bxc4 b5

Very slow, but at this point there is already no stopping what is coming next.

22.f5 ♖ed8

Another instructive line is 22...♘b6 23.f6 ♕f8 24.h4! with the idea 24...♘xc4 25.♖d7 ♗c8 26.♖xf7! ♕xf7 27.♘g5 followed by f6-f7 and Black is collapsing.

23.f6 ♕f8

If 23...c5, 24.♕f2! sets up deadly threats, for instance: 24...bxc4 25.♗xg6! c3 (25...hxg6 26.♗d4 ♕d5 27.♘g5 and ♕h4 next, is mating) 26.♗xf7+! ♔h8 27.♗c1 is just winning, as 27...♘xe5 28.♖xd8+ ♖xd8 29.♘g5, again with ♕h4 coming, leaves Black defenceless.

24.h4 ♕h6 25.h5

Rolling forward!

25...bxc4

Pretty is the variation 25...c5 26.hxg6 hxg6 27.♔f2!, preparing ♖f1-h1. Forced is 27...♗xf3 but after 28.♔xf3 ♕h3+ White calmly plays 29.♔e4! and it turns out that the threat of ♖h1 ♕g3 ♖dg1, trapping the queen, can only be prevented by shedding a serious amount of material.

26.hxg6 c3

If 26...hxg6, 27.♔f2! wins on the spot, with ♖h1 coming.

27.gxf7+ ♔xf7 28.♗c1 ♗a6 29.♗d3 ♗xd3 30.♖xd3 ♕g6 31.♔h2 ♘c5

If 31...♕xg4 32.♖d4! wins the bishop on b4.

32.♖xd8 ♖xd8 33.e4!

This pawn cannot be taken because White always has a check on g5. The pawn push has the added advantage that it indirectly protects g4, because of that same knight check on g5. In an OTB game this may still be a fight, but this is not an OTB game.

33...h6 34.♖d1 ♗a5 35.♖xd8 ♗xd8 36.g5 ♔e8

It is interesting that Lc0 is unable to find the win after 36...♗c7 even after it is shown the first couple of moves! Stockfish does immediately show 37.♘h4! ♗xe5+ 38.♔h3 ♕xe4 39.♕h5+ ♔f8 40.♘g6+ ♔g8 41.♘e7+ ♔f8 42.♕xh6+ ♔e8 43.♕h8+ ♔d7 44.♕c8+ ♔d6 45.♕d8+ ♘d7 46.♗a3+ c5 47.♘c8+ ♔c6 48.♘a7+ ♔d6 49.♘b5+ ♔c6 50.♕a8+! and wins. A very beautiful variation!

37.♔g2 ♕xe4 38.♕xe4 ♘xe4 39.gxh6

Black resigned; after 39...♘xf6 40.exf6 ♗xf6 41.♘g5 the h-pawn will decide.

It's a great pleasure to have a guest contribution by Krishnan Sasikiran. The Indian top grandmaster is an active correspondence player and has featured on these pages a number of times before. He takes an in-depth look at his game against Iotov which featured a line of the English Four Knights Variation I wrote a Survey on in Yearbook 119. The move 9...e3 is an innovation of Zaitsev which gained popularity in 1987, when Karpov used it against Kasparov in their World Championship match. Since then it has been under constant discussion with evaluations changing back and forth. In the game at hand, Sasikiran introduces

a new idea on move 11 that is very relevant for the evaluation of the entire variation. We end the column with his analysis.

A completely new direction
by Krishnan Sasikiran

EO 1.10 (A29)

Valentin Dimitrov Iotov
Krishnan Sasikiran
CC022/S4 ICCF 2020

1.c4 e5 2.♘c3 ♘f6 3.♘f3 ♘c6 4.g3 ♗b4 5.♗g2 0-0 6.0-0 e4 7.♘g5 ♗xc3 8.bxc3 ♖e8 9.f3 e3 10.d3 d5 11.♕a4

Nothing new so far. The line is considered quite good for White and I had won a nice game with it some years ago.

> A natural novelty?!

11...♗d7!?N

Opening a completely new direction for investigation. I am surprised that this natural move has not been tried before.

11...d4 and now:

A) 12.♕c2 dxc3 (12...h6 13.♘e4 ♘xe4 14.fxe4 ♗g4 15.h3 ♗h5 16.g4 ♗g6 17.cxd4 ♕xd4 18.♕b2± and with the queens off, I can simply surround the e3-pawn. White won later in Sasikiran-Gerzina, ICCF 2016) 13.♕xc3 ♘d4 14.♖e1 c5 15.♘e4 ♘xe4 16.dxe4 ♕f6 17.♗b2 ♕a6 18.♕xe3 ♕xc4 (Petkov-

Tropf, ICCF 2017) 19.♖ed1!? ♘xe2+ 20.♔f2 ♘d4 21.♗f1 ♕b4 22.♗c3 ♕b6 23.♗xd4 cxd4 24.♕xd4 ♕a5=;

B) 12.♗b2 h6 13.♘e4 ♘xe4 14.fxe4 dxc3 15.♗xc3 ♗g4 16.♗f3 ♗h3 17.♗g2 ♗g4 18.♕c2 ♘d4 19.♗xd4 ♕xd4 20.♖ab1 ♖ab8 21.♕b2 c5 22.h3 ♗d7 23.♕xd4 cxd4 24.e5! ♖xe5 25.♗f4 ♗e6 26.♖xd4 b6 27.♖b3 Czudek-Weber, ICCF 2018. Although Black held this position in the end, it did not appeal to me. White has active pieces and the e3-pawn might come under attack in the future after an eventual g3-g4 by White. Naturally, when I was looking for alternatives in various directions, 11...♗d7 looked plausible and I decided to go for it.

12.cxd5

A) 12.f4 is one of the critical directions, opening the way for the g2-bishop: 12...h6 13.cxd5 ♘e7 14.♕c4 b5 15.♕b3 hxg5 16.fxg5 ♘g4 17.d6 ♘f5 18.g6 ♘e5 19.gxf7+ ♘xf7 20.♗d5 ♖f8 21.dxc7 ♕xc7 22.♖f4 (22.♗a3 ♘xg3 23.♗xf8 ♘xe2+ 24.♔h1 ♗c6 25.♖xf7 ♕xf7 26.♗xc6 ♕xb3 27.axb3 ♖xf8=) 22...g5! (making space for the king; now Black is alright) 23.♖f3 (23.♖g4 ♔g7!=) 23...♔g7!?=;

B) 12.♕b3!? hits b7 and d5, which is a common theme in this line. Now:

B1) 12...b6 13.cxd5 ♘a5 14.♕b2 ♘xd5 15.f4 ♘f6 16.♘f3! (16.♗xa8 ♕xa8 gives excellent compensation as the light squares are crea-king) 16...c5 17.♘e5 ♖c8 18.♖f3 c4 19.♖xe3 ♗e6 20.d4!?±;

B2) 12...♘a5 13.♕a3 c6 (13...b6 14.cxd5 ♘xd5 15.f4 ♘f6 16.c4!? ♗c6 17.♗b2 ♗xg2 18.♔xg2±) 14.cxd5 cxd5 15.f4 leads to complex play and future tests will tell us about the viability of 11...♗d7.

12...♘xd5 13.♘e4

The endgame after 13.♕c4 ♕xg5 14.f4 ♘b6 15.fxg5 ♘xc4 16.dxc4 ♘a5 17.♖b1 c6!? should be defensible despite White having two bishops, as White's pawn structure is broken.

13...f5

Rather forced as the e3-pawn is in danger if White manages to get in c3-c4.

14.♘g5

I think this is the only way to continue the game, as ♘c5 leads to a draw when Black gets in ...♖e6-g6/h6 in most lines, e.g. 14.♘c5 f4. White had to be stopped from playing f3-f4 as otherwise his pieces start to control a lot of squares from the flank. Now: 15.♕b3 (15.♘xb7 ♕f6 16.♕c4 ♕f7 gives Black excellent compensation in view of the activity and the bind – the pawns on e3 and f4 restricting both bishops) 15...♗c8 16.a4 (clearing a2 for the queen in case of ...♘a5; 16.♘e4 ♖e6!? is similar to the main line and mostly ends in a draw after the rook manoeuvre to h6) 16...b6 17.♘e4 ♖e6! 18.gxf4 ♖g6 19.♘g3 ♖h6 20.f5 (20.♗xe3 ♘a5 21.♕a2 ♗e6 22.f5 ♘xe3 23.fxe6 ♕h4 24.♔f2 ♕f4=) 20...♘a5! (avoiding ♕c4 just in case; 20...♗e6 21.♕c4 ♗f7 22.♕e4 ♕f6 23.♗xe3 ♖h4 24.f4 ♖e8 25.♕xe8+! ♗xe8 26.♗xd5+ ♗f7 27.♗g2 ♕h6!? 28.♖f2!?) 21.♕a2

21...♗e6! (a neat trick, securing the draw) 22.fxe6 ♕h4 23.h3 ♘f4 24.♗xe3 ♘xh3+ 25.♗xh3 ♕xg3+ 26.♗g2 ♕h2+ 27.♔f2 ♕h4+=.

14...f4!?

After 14...♕xg5 15.f4 ♘xf4 16.♕xf4 ♕xf4 17.gxf4!? ♘a5 18.♖f3 ♗c6 19.♖xe3 ♖xe3 20.♗xe3 ♖e8 21.♗xc6 ♘xc6 22.♔f2 the bishop is stronger than the knight on the open board and White has good scope to improve on the queenside with ♖b1, c3-c4 etc.

15.gxf4

15.♘e4 ♖e6! 16.♕c4 ♗c8! 17.gxf4 ♖h6 18.f5 ♗xf5 19.♗xe3 ♘a5 20.♕d4 ♘c6 21.♕c4 ♘a5=.

15...h6!?

Here there was a wide choice, and it was not easy. It became clear to me that in all these lines, Black had to aim for activity before White can manage ♔h1/♖g1 and ♗f1, achieving coordination.

A) 15...♖f8!? 16.♕b3 ♗f5 17.♘e4 ♘a5!? 18.♕d1 b5!? (everything hinges on the e3-pawn and Black is making every effort to stop c3-c4; 18...♕h4 19.♕e1!±) 19.a4 (19.♔h1 c5 20.a4 b4 21.c4 ♘xf4 22.♗xe3 ♘xg2 23.♔xg2 ♗xe4 24.fxe4 ♕d6 is equal as the open position of the white king and the passed pawn on the b-file compensate for the lost material) 19...b4 20.cxb4 ♘c6! 21.♔h1 ♘d4! 22.♖g1 ♖b8! (naturally aiming for activity, and the rook can go to h6 as

now the f6-square is covered) 23.♗f1 ♖b6 24.♗b2 ♖h6.

Now, White has a rather simple plan to activate the c1-bishop along the a1-h8 diagonal and the rook can be activated via c1. So I was not sure when I started investigating this line. It seems alright, although there are many directions still unexplored: 25.♕e1!? (stopping ...♕h4; 25.♘g5 ♕d6 26.♖g3 ♘xf4 27.♗xd4 ♕xd4 28.♖c1!? ♕b2=) 25...♘xf4 26.♖c1 ♗xe4! (26...♘de6 27.♗e5 ♗xe4 28.dxe4 ♖h5 29.♗a1) 27.dxe4 ♖ff6 28.♖g4 ♘d3! 29.♕c3 ♘f2+ 30.♔g1 ♘h3+ 31.♔g2 ♘f4+ 32.♖xf4 ♖xf4 33.♕xd4 ♕g5+ 34.♔h1 ♕g3 35.♕xg7+ ♕xg7 36.♗xg7 ♔xg7 37.♖xc7+ ♔f7 38.♖c3 ♖a6=;
   B) 15...♗f5!? 16.♔h1 ♖b8 17.♖g1 b5 18.♕c2 ♘xf4 19.♘e4 ♘d5 20.♘g3 ♗g6 21.f4 ♕d7 22.♖f1 ♗f7 23.♗b2 ♘f6!?.

16.♕c4

   A) 16.♘e4 ♘xf4 17.♔h1 (17.♕d1?! ♕c8! 18.♗xe3 ♘xg2 19.♔xg2 ♗h3+) 17...♕h4 18.♗xe3 ♘xg2 19.♔xg2 ♗h3+ 20.♔h1 ♗xf1 21.♖xf1 (White's knight on e4 is an octopus controlling many squares, compensating for the lost exchange) 21...♖h8!∞ – prophylaxis before White can latch on to g7;
   B) 16.♕b3!? ♘ce7 17.♘e4 ♗e6! and now:
   B1) 18.♗xe3 ♘g6! (18...♘xe3!? 19.♕xe6+ ♔h7

30

20.♘f6+ gxf6 21.♕xe3 ♘d5
22.♕d2 ♘e3 23.♔h1! ♘xf1
24.♖xf1 ♕d7 25.e4) 19.♗d2
♘dxf4 20.♕d1 ♕d7! with
excellent compensation for
the pawn as white's king is
comparatively weaker with
the knight well placed on
f4, e.g. 21.♘c5 (21.♘f2 ♗f7!=)
21...♕b5 22.♘e4 (22.♘xe6
♖xe6 23.♖f2 ♖ae8 24.♗f1
♕g5+ 25.♔h1 ♕h4 26.♗e1
♖e3 27.♖b1 a5!?) 22...♕h5=;
  B2) 18.♕c2 ♘f5 19.♗h3
♘h4 20.♗g4 ♕d7! (stepping
into the fork. But the light-
squared bishop is easily
worth the exchange as the
knights become stable)
21.♘c5 ♕f7 22.♘xe6 ♖xe6
23.♗xe6 ♕xe6 24.♔h1 ♘xf4
25.♖g1 ♖e8! 26.♖g4 g5=.
16...♘ce7 17.♘e4

17...♖f8!?
17...♔h8!? 18.♔h1 c6 19.♖g1
(this is a familiar plan for
White, clearing f1 for the
bishop and trying to hit g7)
19...♗e6 20.♕a4 ♘xf4 21.♘g3
(21.♘f6 ♘xe2 22.♘xe8 ♕xe8
23.♖e1 ♘xc3 24.♕c2 ♘cd5
25.♗xe3 ♘f5 – this position
is extremely appealing for
human players with nice
outposts and play on the
light squares, but the comp
says Black has enough
compensation – that is
all!) 21...♘ed5!? 22.c4 ♘c3
(22...♘f6!?) 23.♕c2 ♘cxe2!
24.♘xe2 ♕xd3 25.♕xd3
♘xd3 26.♗f1 ♘f2+ 27.♔g2
♘h3 28.♘g3 ♖ad8 29.♗xe3
♘xg1 30.♗xg1 ♖d2+ 31.♔h1

Krishnan Sasikiran

♖c2 and probably there is
enough counterplay to make
a draw.
18.♔h1
18.f5!? ♖xf5 19.♗xe3 ♗b5 and
now:
  A) 20.♕d4 c5! 21.♕xc5
b6 22.♕xb5 ♘xe3 23.♕b3+
♔h8 24.f4 ♘g6! (eschewing
material in favour of
the initiative. The line
follows the same principle:
maximum activity for all
pieces!) 25.♘g3 ♖xf4 26.♗xa8
♕xa8 27.♖f2 ♘h4! 28.♕e6
♘g4 29.♖af1 ♘xf2 30.♖xf2
♖xf2 31.♔xf2 ♕g2+ 32.♔e1
♕xh2=;
  B) 20.♕b3 ♗a4 21.♕xa4
♘xe3 22.♗h3 ♖h5 23.♗e6+
♔h8 24.♖f2 ♖h4! 25.♕d4
(25.♕b5 b6 26.f4 c6!?=)
25...♕xd4 26.cxd4 ♘g6!?=.
18...♔h7!
It was quite difficult to spot
the difference between the
text move and 18...♔h8.
In some lines Black needs
...g7-g5 to create counterplay
with ...g5-g4. With the king
on h8 this may expose it to
unnecessary checks, e.g.
18...♔h8 19.♖g1! (19.♕b3 ♘xf4
20.♗xe3 ♘xe2 21.♖ae1 ♘f4
22.♗xf4 ♖xf4 23.♕xb7 a5!?)
19...♗c6 (19...♘xf4 20.♗f1
♘f5 21.♘g3 ♘xg3+ 22.♖xg3
♘h5 23.♖g1 ♖f4 24.♕c5
♖h4 25.♕e5 ♕f8 (25...♗c6
26.♗xe3 – here is another
difference between ...♔h7
and ...♔h8. The threat to h6

stops Black from activating
his queen normally) 26.♗xe3
♖e8 27.♕c5) 20.♗a3 ♘xf4
21.♗f1 ♘f5 22.♖g4 g5 23.♗xf8
♕xf8 24.♘g3 ♕f6 25.♖xf4
♘xg3+ 26.hxg3 gxf4 27.♕xf4
♕xf4 28.gxf4 ♔g7 29.♗h3
♔f6 30.c4.
19.♖g1
19.♕d4!? c6 20.♗a3 ♘f5
21.♕c4 ♖f7 22.♗h3 ♗e6
23.♗xf5+ ♖xf5 24.♕d4 ♖h5
25.f5 ♗xf5 26.♘d6!? ♗xe4
27.♕xe4+ ♔h8 28.♗e5 ♕g5
29.f4 ♕h4 30.f5 ♕xe4+
31.dxe4 ♖e8 32.exd5 ♖xe5=;
19.♗a3 ♘xf4 20.♕c5 ♘f5!
21.♕xf8 ♕xf8 22.♗xf8
♖xf8 23.♖fe1 g5! with good
compensation as e2 has to
be defended all the time and
there is not enough room for
the white rooks to operate.
19...♘xf4 20.♗f1 ♘f5 21.♘g3!
Of course White needs to
eliminate e3. 21.♗a3!? ♖g8
22.♗b2 b6!?=.
21...♘xg3+ 22.♖xg3 ♘h5!
It is imperative that Black
keeps the queens on the
board in order to compensate
for the weak e3-pawn and the
pair of bishops, as White's
king is considerably weaker:
22...♕e8?! 23.♕e4+! and the
e3-pawn goes.
23.♖g1 ♖f4 24.♕c5
24.♕d5 ♖h4 25.♕e5 merely
transposes to the game.
24...♖h4 25.♕e5 ♗c6!

Black's counterplay lies in
creating threats to the white
king. The h1-a8 diagonal
serves this purpose best.

26.♖b1
26.♗xe3!? ♕d7! (making way for the a8-rook) 27.♗d2 ♕f7!? (27...♖e8 28.♗c5 g5 29.e4 b6 30.♕d4! (30.♕f2 ♖f8 31.♗e2 ♕h3 32.♖g2 ♗e8 33.♕g1 c5☒) 30...♕f7 31.♗e2 ♗d7 32.♖af1 ♕h3 33.♖f2±) 28.♖g2 (28.♕c5 ♖f8 29.♖g2 g5☒) 28...b6! (stopping the ♕c5 manoeuvre) 29.c4 (29.e4 ♖e8 30.♕d4 ♕xf3 31.♔g1 ♕f8=; 29.♕e3 ♘f4 (that is the difference as ♗f4 is not available; 30.♖g3 ♘h5=) 29...g5!). Time and again this theme occurs in this game. The main point is to clear the h1-a8 diagonal.

26...a5!
The rook on h4 is very well placed and Black has to keep it on the board. The text prevents ♖b4 in some lines.

27.c4!?
White is unable to chop off e3 immediately without allowing a draw. The variation is quite amusing and I am sure this would make it into an chess exercise book: 27.♗xe3 ♕d7 28.♗f2 ♖e8!, activating the last piece. What follows is an example of perfect coordination: 29.♕xa5 b6 30.♕a3 ♖h3!! (clearing the a8-h1 diagonal with a sacrifice) 31.♕b4 (31.♕b2 ♕f7! 32.♗xh3 ♖xe2 33.♕xe2 ♗xf3+ 34.♕xf3 ♕xf3+ 35.♗g2 ♕xf2 36.♗e4+ ♔g8!=) 31...♖xe2! 32.♗xe2 ♖xf3 33.♗xf3 ♗xf3+ 34.♖g2 c5! (the queen has to move

away from the 4th rank to allow the knight to land on f4) 35.♕b2 (35.♕h4 g5 36.♕c4 ♘f4) 35...♗xg2+! (the easiest. The typical queen and knight combination works very well here) 36.♔xg2 ♘f4+ 37.♔g1 (37.♔f3 g5! and despite being a rook ahead White is unable to prevent the draw) 37...♘h3+ 38.♔f1 ♕xd3+ 39.♔e1 ♘f4 40.♗g3 ♕e4+ 41.♔d1 ♕d3+ 42.♔e1 ♕e4+=.

27...♕f8
27...♕d7! 28.♕xe3 ♕d6 29.♕f2 g5 was a better way to reach the game continuation, avoiding the extra possibility of ♗b2. Cutting down your opponent's options is an important aspect while studying openings, which is why I mention this move-order trick.

28.♕xe3
28.♗b2 ♖e8 29.♕xc7 ♗xf3+ 30.exf3 ♖e7 31.♕d6 e2 32.♗e5 (32.♗xe2 ♖xe2! 33.♖xg7+ ♘xg7 34.♕xf8 ♖hxh2+ 35.♔g1 ♖hg2+=) 32...exf1♕ 33.♖bxf1 ♕f7 34.d4 ♘f4 35.♕a3 ♕f5=.

28...♕d6 29.♕f2 g5 30.e4
White has managed to shut down the h1-a8 diagonal but now Black latches onto the weakness on f3:

30...♖f8! 31.♗e2
31.c5 ♕e7 32.♗e2 g4.

31...b6!? 32.c5!?
A) 32.♗e3 ♕e7 (getting away from the c4-c5 break) 33.♖bf1 ♘f4 34.♗xf4 ♖hxf4 and Black has nice positional compensation and ...♗c6-e8-h5 is coming. I shall give a sample line although there are many alternatives for both sides: 35.♕e3 ♕a3 36.♕d2 ♗e8!? 37.♖g4 ♖xg4 38.fxg4 ♖xf1+ 39.♗xf1 ♔g7!? 40.e5 b5!=;
B) 32.♗d2 ♖xe4! 33.♗xg5 hxg5 34.dxe4 ♔h6! with ♘f4 coming this is excellent compensation for the pawn;

C) 32.♗xg5 hxg5 33.♖xg5 ♕f4 34.♖bg1 ♖f7!=.

32...♕xc5 33.♕xc5 bxc5 34.♔g2
34.♖b2 c4! breaks up the centre at the cost of a pawn:
A) 35.♖c2 cxd3 36.♗xd3 ♖xf3 37.♖xc6 ♖xd3 38.♖xh6+ ♔xh6 39.♗xg5+ ♔h7 40.♗xh4 (although the computer indicated some small edge for White, I was sure this was a draw as too much material has left the board already) 40...♖d4 41.♖c1 ♖xe4 42.♗d8 c5 43.♖xc5 ♖e1+ 44.♔g2 ♘f4+ 45.♔g3 ♘e6 46.♗xa5 ♖e3+ 47.♔f2 ♖h3 48.♔g2 ♖xh2+ 49.♔xh2 ♘xc5=;
B) 35.dxc4 ♔g6! (simply aiming for positional compensation as the white rooks do not have any entry points) 36.c5 ♘f4 37.♗xf4 ♖hxf4 38.h3 h5!?=.

34...c4

Draw agreed on Black's proposal.
If 35.d4, 35...g4!, finally breaking the impressive centre from the flank. The following variation is fairly linear: 36.d5 gxf3+ 37.♗xf3 ♗d7 38.♖b7 ♖g8+ 39.♔f1 ♖f8 40.♔e2 ♖xh2+ 41.♖g2 ♘g3+ 42.♔f2 ♘xe4+ 43.♔e3 ♖xg2 44.♗xe4+ ♖g6 45.♖xc7 ♖f7!=

Analysing this game was a lot of fun, with amazing ideas sprinkled all over the place. I hope Yearbook readers will like it too.

SURVEYS

Featuring
25 Opening Variations

Sicilian Defence Hungarian Variation SI 2.4 (B53)

Time for some old guns to come out of Quarantine!

by Abhijeet Gupta

1.	e4	c5
2.	♘f3	d6
3.	d4	cxd4
4.	♕xd4	♘c6
5.	♕e3	♘f6
6.	♗e2	

Pentala Harikrishna

The Hungarian Variation is finding more takers than the last time I was checking this line introduced by 4.♕xd4. The reason was clearly some new ideas that had surfaced wherein White first of all dumped what used to be the main line once upon a time.

After 4...♘c6 the move 5.♕e3 is the new world order. Well – not new exactly, but it has gained in popularity hugely over 5.♗b5 which used to be the favoured move by many!

White's idea is quite simple here: going either for a Hedgehog kind of structure or the Maroczy Bind coming out of a move-order akin to the Accelerated Dragon. Modern-day theory has a huge package with loads of new analysis coming out in the Najdorf, Rauzer etc. This seems worth a try as the opponents

also have to be well-versed with the intricacies of these structures.

The high point is that White seems to be doing well after 5...♘f6 6.♗e2.

6...e6 (Game 1)
In Demchenko-Gajewski, for example, White had a small advantage till the former went berserk with a highly dubious g2-g4. Funnily enough he still had a decent position a few moves later but the rapid-chess took its toll, I guess.

6...♗g4 (Games 2-3)
Quite impressive was the way Harikrishna handled his position against Navara in 2018, holding on to a slight advantage till the Czech grandmaster crumbled, while in Vaibhav Suri-Deepan Chakkravarthy you can only admire the very matured handling of the middle-game and later the ending.

While Navara went for 6...♗g4, capturing the knight on f3 and surrendering

the bishop pair and then developing the other bishop on g7, Korobov was outplayed gradually as he tried the same thing against Andreikin while developing the bishop on e7.

6...g6 (Games 4-6)

That finally brings us to a proper Accelerated Dragon structure, and here, in a correspondence game, the key idea was explained. After 6...g6 7.h3 ♗g7 8.0-0 0-0 9.♖d1 ♗e6 White should just drive the bishop away with 10.♘g5 and then build on the queenside and in the centre.

Conclusion

This is already my second attempt at work during the Quarantine and I have just been thinking about training my sights on taking out old guns, oiling them up and making them ready for battle. So far, a clear path to equality for Black is still not known to me in this variation and the freshness it presents is simply tempting. Surely, this line is going to see many games in the months to come. And hopefully Black will be able to complicate matters.

Till then, let's just wait for some OTB tournaments to begin and then unleash this!

6...e6

Anton Demchenko   1
Grzegorz Gajewski
Moscow Wch rapid 2019 (3)
1.e4 c5 2.♘f3 d6 3.d4 cxd4 4.♕xd4 ♘c6 5.♗e3 ♘f6 6.♗e2 e6 7.0-0 ♗e7 7...d5 8.exd5 ♘xd5 9.♕d2 (with the idea c2-c4) 9...♗e7 10.c4 ♘f6 11.♕xd8+ ♗xd8 12.♘c3 0-0 13.♗e3 with a more pleasant endgame for White. **8.♖d1 ♕c7 9.c4**

9...♗g4 9...0-0 10.♘c3 a6 11.b3 b6 (Black enters an inferior version of the Hedgehog as Black's knight belongs on d7 and not on c6, in order to defend the b6-pawn. The main drawback of having the knight on c6 is that White can play ♖ac1 threatening ♘d5 since ...exd5 is met by cxd5.

11...♘g4 12.♕f4 ♘ge5 (12...♗f6 13.♗b2 ♘ge5 14.♘e1!± – we have learned all our lives not to exchange pieces when we have more space ☺) 13.♖b1 ♗f6 14.♗b2 ♖d8 15.♘e1!; 11...♗d7 12.h3 ♖fd8 13.♗b2 ♖ac8 14.♖ac1 (threatening 15.♘d5) 14...♘a5 15.♘a4 ♖b8 16.♗c3 ♕c7 17.♘e1±) 12.♘a3 ♗b7 13.♖ac1. Again ♘d5 is coming, which would be very hard to stop for Black. **10.♕f4 ♘ce5 11.♘c3** 11.h3 clarifies the situation a lot: 11...♘xf3+ 12.♕xf3 ♘e5 13.♕g3 ♘xc4? 14.♗xg7+−. **11...h5 12.♘xe5 dxe5 13.♕g3 ♗d7 14.h3 ♘f6 15.♗e3 h4 16.♕h2?!** 16.♕f3 with the idea of bringing back the queen with ♗d3/♕e2 and White is still a bit better. **16...♗c5** 16...0-0 feels normal for Black here. **17.♗xc5 ♕xc5 18.a3 0-0-0 19.b4** Now again White is better. **19...♕c7 20.g4?** I don't know what to say about this move: it feels ugly, looks ugly, and is bad. **20...hxg3 21.♕xg3 ♖h6 22.♕e3 ♖dh8 23.♗f1 ♖g6+ 24.♔h1 ♔b8 25.♘b5??** After 25.♖a2 the position is really scary but the computer gives a slight edge for White. **25...♗xb5 26.cxb5 ♘g4! 27.♕f3 ♕c2 0-1**

6...♗g4

Pentala Harikrishna   2
David Navara
Prague m rapid 2018 (10)
1.e4 c5 2.♘f3 d6 3.d4 cxd4 4.♕xd4 ♘f6 5.♗e2 ♘c6 6.♕e3 ♗g4

7.0-0 g6 8.♖d1 ♗xf3 8...♗g7 9.e5±; 8...♕c7 9.c4 ♗g7 10.♘c3 0-0 (10...♗xf3 transposes to the game) 11.♖b1 – Black is forced to take on f3 at some point. **9.♗xf3 ♗g7 10.c4 ♕c7 11.♘c3 ♘e5** 11...0-0 12.b3±; White has two bishops and a strong centre, thus depriving Black of any active play. **12.b3 ♘xf3+ 13.♕xf3 0-0 14.♗e3** White changes the plan by changing the bishop's diagonal so that he now intends to play ♖ac1, thus reducing the power of the g7-bishop. **14.♗b2 is**

also possible. The idea is to go ♘d5 at the correct time, capture back with the e-pawn, and put pressure on the e7-pawn. **14...♕a5 15.♖ac1 a6** Black threatens to play 16...b5, thus creating some counterplay. **16.♗d2 ♖fc8** 16...b5 17.♘xb5 ♕xa2 18.♘d4!+–. **17.h3** A slow move, asking Black: How do you improve your position? **17...b5?!** Black decides to act first as he does not have any useful waiting moves: 17...♕c7 18.♗g5 followed by ♗xf6 and ♘d5; 17...♕b6 18.♗g5. **18.♘d5?!** 18.e5! would have done the job for Hari, e.g. 18...dxe5 19.♘a4 b4 20.a3±. **18...♕d8 19.♗e3 ♘xd5 20.cxd5 ♖c3** After 20...♖xc1 21.♖xc1 ♖c8 White is still better but winning this is a whole different ball game. **21.♖xc3 ♗xc3 22.♖c1 ♖c8** 22...b4 23.a4!±. White eliminates his weakness on the a-file and can now shift his attention to the kingside. **23.♕e2** Although the pawn structure is symmetrical, White retains pressure due to his space advantage and the weak c6-square. **23...♕a5 24.♖c2 ♖c7 25.♕d1 ♗e5?** 25...b4 26.♕d3±. **26.♖c6! ♖xc6 27.dxc6 b4 28.f4 ♗f6 29.♕e2 e6 30.♕d3 d5 31.exd5 exd5 32.♗d4 ♗xd4+ 33.♕xd4 ♕c7 1-0**

Dmitry Andreikin   **3**
Anton Korobov
Minsk rapid 2018 (6)
1.e4 c5 2.♘f3 d6 3.d4 cxd4 4.♕xd4 ♘f6 5.♗e2 ♘c6 6.♕e3 ♗g4 7.0-0 e6 8.♖d1 ♗e7 9.c4 ♕c7 10.♘c3 a6 11.b3 0-0 12.♗b2 So here Black's bishop is out, but it doesn't really change anything. White has a solid grip. **12...♘e5 13.♖ac1 ♗xf3 14.♗xf3 ♕c5**

15.♕e2 Personally I would have taken the queens off – 15.♕xc5 dxc5 16.♗e2 ♘c6 17.f4 ♘d4 18.♗f1± but keeping them on also gives White a slight edge. **15...♖ac8 16.g3 ♘xf3+ 17.♕xf3 ♕c6 18.♕e2 ♖fe8 19.♖d2 h5 20.♖cd1 h4 21.gxh4 b5 22.cxb5 axb5 23.♘xb5 ♘xe4 24.♘a7 ♕a8 25.♘xc8 ♖xc8 26.♕g4** Although it's a rapid game, still a very high-class game by Dmitry. **26...e5 27.♖e2 ♘f6 28.♕g2 ♕a6 29.f4 ♘h5 30.♖f1 ♕a7+ 31.♔h1 exf4 32.♕g4 ♘c5 33.♗d4 ♕b7+ 34.♕g2 ♖b5 35.♕xb7 ♖xb7 36.a4 ♗f6 37.♗xf6 ♘xf6 38.a5 ♖b3 39.♖a1 2-1 1-0** Just a perfect game of chess by Andreikin.

6...g6

Suri Vaibhav   **4**
J. Deepan Chakkravarthy
Jammu ch-IND 2018 (12)
1.e4 c5 2.♘f3 d6 3.d4 cxd4 4.♕xd4 ♘c6 5.♕e3 g6 6.♗e2 ♗g7 7.0-0 ♘f6 8.h3 0-0 9.♖d1

9...♗d7 10.♘c3 10.c4 ♕b6! 11.♘c3 (11.♕d2 ♘c5 – Black is doing really well here) 11...♘xe3 12.♗xe3 ♗xc3!∓. **10...♘b4** 10...♕b6 11.♕f4± with the idea ♕h4 and ♗h6. **11.♘e1 b6 12.a3** After 12.♕g3 ♗a6 13.a3 ♗xe2 14.♘xe2 ♘a6 15.♖b1 ♘ac5 16.f3 White still holds some bind. **12...♘a6 13.b4** I prefer 13.b3, e.g. 13...♘ac5 14.♗b2 ♗b7 15.♖ab1. **13...♗b7 14.♖b1 ♕c7 15.♗b2 ♖c8 16.♘d5 ♘e5** 16...♘xb2 17.♖xb2 e5! (not an easy move to foresee; 17...♘xd5 18.exd5 ♖e8) 18.♘xc7 (18.c4 ♘xd5 19.cxd5 f5 with loads of counterplay on the kingside)

18...♕xc7 19.c4 ♘f6 20.f3 ♘h5 21.♖bd2 ♖cd8 22.♗f1 ♘g3 23.♗d3 ♘h5 24.♗f1 with a very weird repetition. **17.c4 ♘xd5 18.cxd5** Now White is simply better. **18...♕d7 19.♕b3!** Taking control of the c4- and c2-squares. **19...b5 20.♖bc1** 20.♘c2! with the idea ♘e3 was more to the point. **20...♖xc1 21.♖xc1 ♗h6 22.♖c2 a6 23.♗xe5! dxe5 24.♘d3 ♕d6 25.♘c5** Now the game is really over. **25...♗c8 26.a4 ♗d7 27.♘xd7 ♕xd7 28.♖c6 ♕a7 29.axb5 axb5 30.♗xb5 ♕d4 31.♗f1 ♕d2 32.♖c4 ♕a7 33.♕b2 ♗f4 34.b5 ♖b8 35.♕c3 ♔g7 36.h4 ♖b6 37.g3 ♗h6 38.♖c7 ♕a2 39.♕xe5+ ♖f6 40.f4 ♕b3 41.♕c3 ♕d1 42.e5 1-0**

Mateusz Paszewski   **5**
Bharathakoti Harsha
Warsaw 2019 (7)
1.e4 c5 2.♘f3 d6 3.d4 cxd4 4.♕xd4 ♘c6 5.♕e3 ♘f6 6.♗e2 g6 7.h3 ♗g7 8.0-0 0-0 9.♖d1 ♗e6 10.♘c3 ♖c8! This is the reason I don't like ♘c3 and hence I prefer 10.♘g5!. **11.a3 ♕c7**

Black's whole idea is not to let White move his knight from c3. **12.♖b1 a6 13.♗d2** 13.♘d5 ♗xd5 14.exd5 ♘a5 15.c3 b5 (thematic) 16.♕d3 ♕c4 17.♗g5 ♕xd3 18.♗xd3 ♘c4 19.♗xf6 ♗xf6 20.♘e1 a5 21.♗e2 Demchenko-Volokitin, Germany Bundesliga 2018/19. **13...♖fd8 14.♘g5 d5! 15.♘xe6 fxe6 16.exd5 exd5 17.♕f4 e5 18.♕h4 ♘d4 19.♗g5 ♕f7 20.♖d3** 20.♗d3∓. **20...h6–+ 21.♗xf6 ♗xf6 22.♕g4 h5 23.♕g3 ♘f5 24.♕h2 ♗g5 25.♖dd1 ♗f4 26.g3 ♗h6 27.♕g2 ♘d4 28.♗d3 e4 29.♗f1 ♘f3+ 30.♔h1 ♗g7 31.♗e2 ♗xc3 32.bxc3 ♖xc3 0-1**

Hueseyin Ozalp   **6**
Osman Levent Mollamustafaoglu
cr email 2013

**1.e4 c5 2.♘f3 d6 3.d4 cxd4
4.♕xd4 ♘c6 5.♕e3 g6 6.♗e2
♗g7 7.0-0 ♘f6 8.♖d1 0-0 9.h3
♗e6 10.♘g5**

This is the line I would play
as White, as shown by the
correspondence guys. **10...♗d7**
10...♗c8. The point is if White

goes for the Maroczy Bind with
c2-c4, Black has ...♕b6 with the
idea ...♘f6-d7-c5 later on, but
of course White can simply go
11.♘c3± here. 11.c4 ♕b6 12.♘c3
♕xe3 13.♗xe3 ♘d7!=. **11.c4
♘b4** 11...♖c8 12.♘c3 ♘a5 13.b3
h6 14.♘f3 ♘xe4. If it works,
it will solve Black's position
instantly – but unfortunately it
doesn't: 15.♘xe4 ♗xa1 16.♕xh6
♗g7 17.♕h4 f6 18.c5±; 11...♕b6
12.♘c3 ♕xe3 13.♗xe3 – although
Black is fairly solid here, still
White has more space and easier
play. **12.♕b3 ♘a6** 12...a5 has to
be played, e.g. 13.a3 (13.♘c3 h6
14.♘f3 ♗c6 15.♘d4 ♗xe4 16.♗e3
♕b8 17.♖e1) 13...♘a6 14.♘c3 h6
15.♘f3 ♘c5 16.♕c2 ♗c6 17.♗d3
(17.e5 ♘fe4 18.♗e3 ♘xc3 19.♕xc3

♕c8=; 17.♘d4 ♗xe4 18.♘xe4
♘fxe4 19.♗e3 a4) 17...a4 18.♗e3.
The comp says it's equal but
I still prefer White. **13.♘c3
♗c6 14.e5!± ♘e8 15.♘f3 ♕a5
16.♗g5 f6 17.c5+ ♔h8 18.♗xa6
♗xf3 19.gxf3 ♕xa6 20.exd6
exd6 21.♗e3 dxc5 22.♗xc5
♖g8 23.♖d7 ♖c8 24.♗e3 ♘d6
25.♖d1 ♘f5 26.♕xb7 ♕c4
27.♗xa7 ♕h4 28.♕e4 ♕xh3
29.♕g4 ♕h6 30.♘e4 ♖c2 31.b4
♖xa2 32.♗c5 ♖ga8 33.b5 ♗f8
34.b6 ♖b2 35.b7 ♖b8 36.♖f7
♗xc5 37.♘xc5 ♖e8 38.♖fd7
♖xf2 39.♔xf2 ♕h2+ 40.♕g2
♕h4+ 41.♔f1 ♘e3+ 42.♔g1
♘xd1 43.♘e4 ♘c3 44.♕h2
♕xh2+ 45.♔xh2 ♘xe4 46.fxe4
♖b8 47.♖c7 ♖xb7 48.♖xb7 ♔g8
49.♔g3 1-0**

Exercise 1

position after 25.♘c3-b5

How can Black finish White
off? Remember, it's about the
third move!

(solutions on page 246)

Exercise 2

position after 17...♕a5xa2

White to play and win.

Exercise 3

position after 17.♖b1xb2

What strategic decision would
you take here as Black?

Looking for material from previous Yearbooks?

Visit our website www.newinchess.com and see under 'Games and Downloads' in the page footer.
Here you can find games, Surveys and contributors from all our Yearbooks.
Surveys are indexed by opening, by author and by Yearbook.

The Young Masters Variation – Part I

by Kaido Külaots

1.	e4	c5
2.	♘f3	d6
3.	d4	cxd4
4.	♘xd4	♘f6
5.	♘c3	a6
6.	♗d3	e5

The Najdorf keeps its place as one of the most popular opening systems in (sub-)elite tournaments. Black normally chooses it not necessarily because he badly wants to win the game, but rather because he simply feels comfortable in the resulting positions. Additionally, by playing a system that is being perceived as aggressive and also somewhat risky to some, he provokes White to prove all that.

David Paravyan

The fact is that the Najdorf is irrefutable, and White will be scratching his head in his efforts to find a line that could possibly be the most unpleasant against a certain opponent on a certain day. There's a lot to choose from. And when the white player sacrifices a morning walk for the sake of digging ever deeper into the labyrinths, this is already a small victory for the black player.

The subject of our Survey is the move 6.♗d3.

To a starting player this looks like a very sound developing move. To the trained eye, however, it immediately looks unusual. But maybe it is just because the move has never yet made it to the top of White's choices.

So where are the roots of this weird, but healthy move? Curiously, it occurred no less than four times at the Young Masters tournament in Vilnius in 1988. This was an annual tournament, where the most promising young Soviet players 26 years and down (this was considered to be young then) fought it out. The youngest of the participants that year, Vladimir Akopian, employed the move three times! Unfortunately I cannot ask

details from my countryman Lembit
Oll, who defended the black side in two
games, because he left us tragically early
11 years after the event as a young elite
grandmaster.

Later, it was English super-GM Michael
Adams who occasionally employed the
move, then the Russian GM Alexander
Motylev showed some ideas, and very
recently Sergey Karjakin and David
Paravyan have amassed a huge number of
games here – though in the online chess
arena mostly.

Black certainly has a number of options
in reply to 6.♗d3, but I will put the
emphasis on the replies that aim to bring
the (possible) drawbacks of the move
into daylight.

The Najdorf reply

In the first instalment, we will be
looking at the move that most Najdorf
aficionados will be itching to make:
6...e5.

Now 7.♘de2 is surely the main path.
7.♘f5 has been tried occasionally too, but
Nepo's direct answer in his game with
Grischuk is quite sufficient (Game 1).
7...♗e7 8.0-0 (8.♘g3 might limit White's
own options) and now:

A) 8...♗e6!? has been chosen on high
level by the likes of Giri, Dominguez
and Cheparinov. Black has a specific
idea in mind: 9.♘g3 (9.f4 is the direct

try to take advantage of Black playing
...♗e6 before castling. Some good players
don't much mind, however – see Games
2-3. But I do think White can hope for
some pull here; there is one new idea
I am proposing after 9...0-0 10.f5 ♗d7)
9...♘c6!?, avoiding the structure White
would obtain after 9...0-0 10.♘d5 ♗xd5
11.exd5, see Game 4;

B) 8...0-0 9.♘g3 ♗e6 (9...♗g4 turns out
to help rather than disturb White, see
Game 5, and I do not fully trust 9...g6.
Still, it has been employed twice by
Russian GM Kokarev and no less a player
than Wei Yi – in online blitz, truth be
told. A very young Duda played it too,
but then he was probably even more
adventurous than now. See Game 6. For
9...♘c6 I refer to Game 7, an online blitz
game) 10.♘d5 (there is no good way to
wait with this) 10...♗xd5 (apparently this
exchange should be executed right away,
as MVL learnt at his expense: 10...♘bd7
11.c4 g6?! 12.♘xe7+ ♕xe7 and White
was almost winning already, Karjakin-
Vachier-Lagrave, St Louis blitz 2019)
11.exd5 g6.

Here White has two approaches. He can
either put the pawn on c4 right away
and take it from there (Games 8-9), or
he can first try to advance his a-pawn all
the way to a5 and only then proceed with
c2-c4 (Game 10). The latter is a fresh
approach, but White should not forget

about the possibility of a capture on d5 along the way.

Conclusion

The move 6.♗d3 is far from a refutation of the Big Najdorf. But as I said above, such a variation does not exist. I would say it still comes with some surprise value, although people are catching up as even some elite players are employing

it in large quantities in online chess (where else?). How to answer with black is largely a matter of taste.

6...e5 is very playable for Black!

> In the **next instalment** I will examine various alternatives to the main line 6...e5, ranging from **6...e6** and **6...g6** to **6...♘c6**.

An occasional try
7.♘f5

Alexander Grischuk   1
Ian Nepomniachtchi

Riga rapid 2013 (4)

1.e4 c5 2.♘f3 d6 3.d4 cxd4 4.♘xd4 ♘f6 5.♘c3 a6 6.♗d3 e5 7.♘f5 7.♘b3; 7.♘f3. **7...♗xf5** 7...g6 8.♘e3 ♘bd7 (8...♗e6 9.0-0 ♗g7 10.♗c4 0-0 11.♘ed5±) 9.a4 ♘c5 10.♗c4 ♗e6 11.♗xe6 fxe6 12.f3± Xiong-Indjic, chess.com blitz 2020. **8.exf5 d5**

9.♗g5 9.0-0 also scores badly. **9...♗b4 10.0-0 ♘c6 11.♗xf6 gxf6 12.♕g4 ♕a5⇄ 13.♘d1** 13.♕h4 ♗e7=. **13...♗d2 14.c3 h5 15.♕e2 ♗g5 16.b4** 16.f4?! ♗h6. **16...♕c7 17.b5 axb5 18.♗xb5 ♔f8 19.♘e3 ♘e7∓ 20.c4 ♗xe3 21.fxe3 ♕c5** 21...♖a3!∓. **22.a4 ♖d8 23.♖ad1 ♔g7 24.♔h1 dxc4 25.♖xd8 ♖xd8 26.♗xc4 ♕b4 27.♗d3?** 27.♗b5. **27...♕xa4 28.h3 ♘d5 29.♕f3 ♘c3-+ 30.e4 b5 31.♔h2 ♔f8 32.♖e1 h4 33.♗f1 b4 34.♗c4 ♖d4 35.♗xf7 ♔xf7 36.♕h5+ ♔e7 37.♕h7+ ♔d6 38.♕xh4 ♕c5 39.♕xf6 ♕e8! 40.♕g7 ♖d7 41.♕g3 ♕e7? 41...♔c4-+. **42.♕f2+! ♔c4 43.f6!**

♕e6 **44.♕f1+ ♔c5 45.♕f2+ ♔c4 46.♕f1+** 46.g4!=. **46...♔b3 47.♖e3?** ≥ 47.g4 ♕d6 48.♔h1 (48.f7? ♕f8-+) 48...♖f7 49.g5 ♕d2 50.♕g1 (50.g6? ♖xf6! 51.g7 ♖xf1+ 52.♖xf1 ♕d8 53.f8♕ ♕d1+ 54.♔g2 ♕c2+ 55.♔h1 ♕xe4+ 56.♔h2 ♕e2+ 57.♔h1 ♕d1+ 58.♔h2 ♕d2+ 59.♔h1 ♔b2 60.g8♕ e4-+) 50...♕c2 51.g6 ♖xf6 52.g7 ♖g6 53.♕xg6 ♕xe1+ 54.♔h2 ♕e2+ 55.♔g2 ♕xg2+ 56.♔xg2 b3 57.g8♕ b2 58.♕g7 b1♕ 59.♕xe5 should be a draw. **47...♖f7 48.♖f3 ♕c4?** 48...♔a4! 49.g4 ♕xe4∓. **49.♕d1+! ♔a3 50.♕a1+ ♔b3 51.♕d1+ ♔a3 52.♕a1+ ♔b3 ½-½**

Variation A
7.♘de2 ♗e7 8.0-0 ♗e6

David Paravyan   2
Mustafa Yilmaz

Gibraltar 2020 (10)

1.e4 c5 2.♘f3 d6 3.d4 cxd4 4.♘xd4 ♘f6 5.♘c3 a6 6.♗d3 e5 7.♘de2 ♗e7 8.0-0 ♗e6 9.f4 The principled continuation. **9...exf4 10.♘xf4** It seems that Black has played right into White's hands, but in fact, Black is quite solid.

10...♘c6 11.♘xe6 11.♗e3 ♘e5 12.a4 0-0 13.♗d4 (13.a5 – Game 3) 13...♖c8 14.♔h1 (14.♕d2 ♖e8 15.♘cd5 ♗xd5 16.exd5 ♘fd7 17.♗f5 ♗g5=) Abdusattarov-Dominguez Perez, chess 24 Banter blitz 2020) 14...♘fd7 Paravyan-Sarana, Lichess 2020. **11...fxe6 12.♕f3** I would consider 12.♗c4 to be the main test: 12...♕d7 13.a4N (13.♗f4 b5 14.♗b3 ♘a5= Stany-Gopal, Biel 2019) 13...0-0 14.♗f4 ♔h8 15.♔h1±. **12...♘e5** Now Black is rock-solid and should be fine. **13.♕h3 ♕d7** 13...♘fg4 is a very ambitious move with the king in the centre, e.g. 14.♗e2 (14.♔h1 h5⇄) 14...♕b6+ 15.♔h1 ♘f2+ (15...h5) 16.♖xf2 ♕xf2 17.♗e3 ♕f7 18.♖f1 ♗f6 19.g4 ♕d7! 20.g5 ♗e7 21.♗d4 0-0-0 22.♖d1 and White has compensation, but not more. **14.♗e3 0-0** 14...♘fg4!? 15.♗d4 ♗f6∞. **15.♗d4 ♖ae8= 16.♖ad1 ♕c8 17.♔h1 ♗d8 18.♘d5** This leads to simplification, but White was short of other active ideas. **18...♘c6 19.♗xe5 dxe5 20.♘xf6+ ♖xf6 21.b3 b5 22.♕h5 ♖xf1+ 23.♖xf1 ♗f6 24.♕e2 ♖f8 25.c4 b4 26.c5 ♗g5 27.♗xa6 ♖xf1+ 28.♕xf1 ♕xc5 29.♗c4 ♕d6 30.g3 ♗f6 31.♕e2 g6 32.♔g2 ♔f7 33.h4 ½-½**

Krishnan Sasikiran   3
Ivan Cheparinov

Spain tt 2019 (4)

1.e4 c5 2.♘f3 d6 3.d4 cxd4 4.♘xd4 ♘f6 5.♘c3 a6 6.♗d3 e5 7.♘de2 ♗e7 8.0-0 ♗e6 9.f4 0-0 One provocative move after another.

10.a4 After 10.f5 ♗d7 the problem for White is that the knight on e2 is interfering with the g2-g4 push. So he needs to find other plans to mount the pressure. Or maybe not?!

A) 11.♘d5 ♘xd5 12.exd5 ♗b5!? 13.c4 (13.♘c3 ♘d7 14.♖f3 ♗xd3 15.cxd3 ♘f6 16.♖g3 ♔h8 17.♗e3 b5⇄) 13...e4 14.cxb5 exd3 15.♕xd3 ♘f6 16.♔h1 ♘d7 and Black has nice piece play for the pawn;

B) 11.g4!? (this novelty is a very interesting proposition) 11...♘xg4 12.♘d5 (12.♘g3 ♘f6) 12...♘f6 (12...♗g5 13.♘ef4!? and it remains tense) 13.♘ec3 ♗c6 14.♘xf6+ ♗xf6 15.♕g4 ♘d7 16.♖f3 – this will need to be investigated further, but the play White has for the pawn is evident. **10...exf4 11.♘xf4 ♘c6 12.♗e3 ♘e5** Now, generally speaking, Black should be fine. There are still many pieces on the board, however. **13.a5 ♖c8 14.♗d4 ♘fd7** 14...♖e8 15.♔h1 ♘fd7 16.♘cd5 ♗g5 Nguyen-O. Bronstein, Bratislava jr 2019. **15.♘cd5** The point of not taking on e6 earlier. **15...♗g5 16.b4 ♖e8 17.♖b1** 17.c3 ♘xd3!. **17...♘c6 18.♖a1 ♘ce5 19.♔h1 ♘f6?!** White's keeping of the tension starts to bear fruit. Now Black will be suffering. 19...♘g6!? 20.♘h5 ♘de5∞. **20.♗xe5 dxe5 21.♘xe6 fxe6** 21...♖xe6 22.c4 and with the pawns fixed on light squares, this is surprisingly hopeless. **22.♘xf6+** An understandable choice in a team game, but 22.♘b6 had its virtues too. **22...♗xf6 23.♕e1** 23.c4!?, aiming to fix the queenside for good. **23...♗h4 24.g3 ♗f6 25.b5 axb5 26.♖xb5 ♖c7 27.♕b4 h5 28.♔g2 ♕e7 29.♖b1 ♕xb4 30.♖1xb4 ♖ee7** The lateral defence is the solid one. **31.h4 ♔f8**

32.♖c4 ♔e8 33.♖b6 ♔d8 34.♖xc7 ♔xc7 35.♔h3 ♖d7! 36.♖xe6 ♖d6 37.♖e8 ♖d8= 38.♖e6 ♖d6 39.♖xd6 ♔xd6 40.♗b5 ♗d8 41.♗e8 ♗xa5 42.♗xh5 ♗e6 43.♗e8 ♔f6 44.g4 g5 45.h5 ♔g7 46.♔g2 b6 47.♔f3 ♗e1 48.♔e3 ♔h6 49.♔d3 ♗f2 50.♔c4 ♗g1 51.c3 ♗f2 52.♔d5 ♗g3 53.♔e6 ♗h2 54.♔f7 ♗g3 55.♔g8 ♗h2 56.♔h8 ♗g3 ½-½

Michael Adams 4
Anish Giri
Batumi Ech tt 2019 (4)
1.e4 c5 2.♘f3 d6 3.d4 cxd4 4.♘xd4 ♘f6 5.♘c3 a6 6.♗d3 e5 7.♘de2 ♗e7 8.0-0 ♗e6 9.♘g3 ♘c6!? 9...0-0 – Variation B below; 9...♘bd7 10.♕f3 ♗g4 11.♕e3 0-0 (11...♖c8 12.♗e2 (12.h3 ♗e6) 12...♗e6 13.♖d1 0-0 14.a4 ♘b6 15.a5 ♘c4 16.♗xc4 ♖xc4 17.b3 ♖c6 18.♗b2 ♕c7∓ Fedoseev-Sarana, Lichess blitz 2020) 12.h3 ♗e6 13.♕f3 ♘e8 14.♘f5 ♗g5 15.♖d1 ♗xc1 16.♖axc1 g6 17.♗f1 ♘b6 18.♘e3 0-1 (40) Akopian-Oll, Vilnius 1988. **10.♘h5** 10.a3 ♖c8 11.♖e1 h6 12.♗f1 d5 13.exd5 ♘xd5 14.♘xd5 ♕xd5 15.♘e3 ♕d7= Nepomniachtchi-Ding Liren, chess.com blitz 2019.

10...♘xh5 11.♕xh5 ♘b4 Without having to do anything excessive, Black now gains the bishop pair. He should be content with the outcome of the opening. **12.♖d1** White chooses to aim for Black's traditional soft spots on the d-file. Black, in turn, has considerable play along the c-file. **12...♕d7 13.♕e2 ♖c8 14.a3 ♘xd3 15.♕xd3 0-0 16.♗e3 ♖c7 17.a4 ♖fc8 18.a5 ♖c4 19.f3 h6 20.♗f2 ♔h8 21.♕e3 ♗d8!?** Instead of preparing the play with ...f7-f5, Giri looks in another direction; a fine approach.

22.♖d3 ♖4c6! 22...♖4c5? 23.♕xc5 dxc5 24.♖xd7 ♗xd7 25.♘d5 is the structural transformation Sicilian players will always try to avoid. **23.♕e1 b5** Giving up the bishop pair, but freeing himself from the queenside bind. **24.axb6 ♗xb6 25.♗xb6 ♖xb6 26.♘a4 ♖bc6 27.♘c3 ♕b7** A reasonable try. **28.♖b1** Alas, there is no ♖a2. **28...a5 29.h3 a4 30.♔h2 ♕b4 31.♕d2 a3** This releases the tension a bit too soon. 31...♖c4!? would have kept the pull, and would maybe have helped the Netherlands to keep the balance in the match. This, of course, is hindsight wisdom. The idea on the chessboard is to put the rook on d4 and try and eventually take White's defensive formation apart. **32.bxa3 ♕xa3 33.♘d1!** Heading to e3, where the knight keeps everything in check. **33...♕a7=** ½-½

Variation B
8...0-0 9.♘g3

Sergey Karjakin 5
Anish Giri
Riga rapid 2019 (1)
1.e4 c5 2.♘f3 d6 3.d4 cxd4 4.♘xd4 ♘f6 5.♘c3 a6 6.♗d3 e5 7.♘de2 ♗e7 8.0-0 0-0 9.♘g3 The most popular continuation. 9.f4 and 9.♔h1 are common alternatives, but in the very early days of the Najdorf, 9.♗g5 was a move sometimes seen, as in the stem game K.Grossner-M.Kahn, Großröhrdorf 1949: 9...♘bd7 (9...♘xe4 10.♗xe7 ♘xc3 11.♗xd8 ♘xd1 12.♗e7 ♖e8 13.♖fxd1 ♖xe7 14.♗e4 ♗e6 15.♖xd6±) 10.♕d2 (10.♘g3) 10...b5 11.♘g3 ♘b6 and now 12.a4 would have been indicated. **9... ♗g4** Aiming to provoke f2-f3. **10.♗e2 ♗e6 11.♗e3** A very normal Najdorf now, with the 'small' nuance that the knight is on g3 instead of b3. On g3 it is asking for ...g7-g6, and then we will have a position with its own little details. 11.♘d5 is less

effective with the bishop having retreated to e2: 11...♘xd5! 12.exd5 ♗c8 with no-nonsense play starting with a quick ...f7-f5.

11...g6 12.a4 ♘bd7 13.♕d2 ♗c8 14.a5 Before jumping to d5, White will need to fix this, in order to prevent Black fixing it himself by ...a6-a5. **14...♖e8 15.♘d5 ♗xd5 16.exd5 ♘c5?** As there is a white pawn on a5 and not a black one, this knight is by no means solidly placed here. It will only invite White to roll on with his pawns. The invitation is politely accepted, following a little preparation. After 16...h5 17.f3 Black is two tempi up compared to the game and this should yield him some chances, e.g. 17...h4 18.♘e4 ♘h5. **17.f3!** Keeping all the pieces on. **17...h5 18.b4 ♘cd7 19.c4± h4 20.♘e4 h3 21.g3 ♘xe4 22.fxe4 ♘f6 23.♕d3 ♕d7 24.♖ac1 ♘g4 25.♗b6** 25.♗d2 would have kept Black's counterplay at a minimum. **25...♗g5 26.♖c3 ♖f8 27.c5** 27.♕d1 f5 28.♗xg4? fxg4⇄. **27...dxc5 27...♗e3+! 28.♔h1 ♘f2+ 29.♖xf2 ♗xf2 30.c6 bxc6 31.dxc6 ♖xc6 32.♖xc6 ♗xc6 33.♗xf2 and if not for that little pawn on h3, Black's resignation would be fully justified. As it is, it is hard to tell what the situation is exactly – especially in rapid. **28.♗xc5 ♖xc5 29.bxc5 ♗e3+ 30.♔h1 ♘f2+ 31.♖xf2 ♗xf2 32.c6 bxc6 33.dxc6 ♕c7** 33...♕xd3! 34.♖xd3 ♗e1 35.♖d5 ♗c8 36.♖c5±. **34.♖c1 ♗d4 35.♕xa6 ♖b8 36.♗g4 ♗c3 37.♗xh3 ♖xa5 38.♗d7 ♔g7 39.♖f1 ♖f8 40.♖b1 ♕d8 41.♔g2 ♗c7 42.♖b7 ♗d6 43.♕d3 ♗b8 44.♕d5 ♗c7 45.h4 ♖h8 46.♗e6 1-0**

Maxim Chigaev   **6**
Dmitry Kokarev
Khanty-Mansiysk 2019 (2)
1.e4 c5 2.♘f3 d6 3.d4 cxd4 4.♘xd4 ♘f6 5.♘c3 a6 6.♗d3 e5 7.♘de2 ♗e7 8.0-0 0-0 9.♘g3 g6 10.♗c4 ♗e6 11.♘d5 ♘bd7 11...♘xd5 12.♗xd5 ♗xd5 13.♕xd5 ♘c6 14.♗h6 ♖e8 15.c3±. **12.♘xe7+ ♕xe7 13.♗d3** Compared to Karjakin-Vachier-Lagrave, St Louis blitz 2019, Black is two tempi up here. This being said, I still have some issues trusting his position. **13...d5 14.♗g5 ♕b4 15.exd5 ♘xd5 16.b3 ♘c5 17.c4 ♘f4 18.♗c2 f6 19.♗xf4 exf4 20.♘e4 ♖ad8 21.♕e1 ♕xe1 22.♖fxe1 ♘xe4 23.♗xe4 b5 24.♗c6! ♗d7 25.♗d5+ ♔g7 26.c5 ♗c8 27.♖ad1 b4 28.c6 f5 29.♗e7+?! 29.h4!±. **29...♘f6 30.♖xh7 ♗e6 31.♗f3 ♖xd1+ 32.♗xd1 ♖d8 33.♗f3 ♖d2 34.h4 ♖xa2 35.♖a7** 35.h5!! (echoes of Botvinnik-Fischer, Varna ol 1962!) 35...gxh5 36.c7 ♗c2 37.♗b7+– with ♖h6+ coming up. **35...♗xb3 36.c7 ♗e6= 37.♗d5 ♖a1+ 38.♔h2 ♗d7 39.♗c6 ♗e6 40.♗d5 ♗d7 ½-½**

Sergey Karjakin   **7**
Vitaliy Bernadskiy
chess.com blitz 2020 (3)
1.e4 c5 2.♘f3 d6 3.d4 cxd4 4.♘xd4 ♘f6 5.♘c3 a6 6.♗d3 e5 7.♘de2 ♗e7 8.0-0 0-0 9.♘g3 ♘c6 9...b5. **10.♗c4** 10.a3 ♗e6 11.♘h5 ♘xh5 12.♕xh5 g6 13.♕d1 f5 14.♗h6 ♖f7 15.♘d5 ♗g5 16.♗xg5 ♕xg5= Louma-Brat, Jablonec 1954(!); 10.♘d5 ♘xd5 11.exd5. **10...♗e6**

11.♘d5 11.♗b3 ♖c8 12.f4 b5 13.♘d5 ♘d4 14.♗e3 ♘xb3

15.axb3 exf4 16.♘xf4 ♕c7 17.c3 ♕b7 18.♗d4± 1-0 (41) Rowson-Tihonov, Zagan jr 1997. **11...♖c8 12.c3 ♘a5 13.♘xf6+ ♗xf6 14.♗xe6 fxe6 15.♕g4** 15.♕h5!?. **15...♕e7 16.♖d1 b5 17.♕e2 ♖fd8 18.♕g4 ♕f7 19.♘f1?! ♘c4** 19...d5!∞. **20.b3 ♘a5 21.♗a3 ♘b7 22.♖d3 ♘c5 23.♗xc5 ♖xc5 24.♖ad1 ♗e7** 24...d5!?. **25.♘d2 ♕g6 26.♕xg6 hxg6 27.c4 ♖dc8 28.g3 ♔f7 29.♔g2 g5 30.♔f3 ♗g6 31.h3 ♖f8+ 32.♔g2 ♖fc8 33.♖a1 ♖5c6?!** 33...♖b8 34.a4 bxa4 35.♖xa4 a5⇄. **34.a4! b4 35.a5!± ♖c5 36.♖a4 ♖b8 37.♘f3 ♔f7 38.♖d2 ♗e8 39.♘e1 ♖c7 40.♔f3 ♔f7 41.♘d3 ♖cb7 42.c5 ♖b5** 42...dxc5 43.♘xe5+ ♔e8±. **43.cxd6 ♗xd6 44.♘b2** 44.♖c2!+–. **44...♗c5 45.♘c4 ♔f6 46.♖d7 ♖f8?!** 47.♖a2 ♗d4 48.♔g4 ♖c5 49.♖b7 ♗c3?** 49...♖fc8 50.♖xb4 ♖5c7+ **50.♖b6?** 50.♘b6!+–. **50...♖fc8** 50...♗d4±. **51.♖xa6 ♖xc4 52.bxc4 b3 53.♖a3 b2 54.♖b6 ♖xc4 55.a6 ♗d4 56.♖b7 ♖c1 57.♔h5 b1♕ 58.♖f3# 1-0**

Variation B
9...♗e6

Hikaru Nakamura   **8**
Maxime Vachier-Lagrave
Stavanger 2017 (4)
1.e4 c5 2.♘f3 d6 3.d4 cxd4 4.♘xd4 ♘f6 5.♘c3 a6 6.♗d3 e5 7.♘de2 ♗e7 8.0-0 0-0 9.♘g3 ♗e6 10.♘d5 ♗xd5 10...♘bd7 11.c4 g6 12.♘xe7+ ♕xe7 13.b3± is not to be recommended, Karjakin-Vachier-Lagrave, St Louis blitz 2019. **11.exd5**

11...g6 11...♘xd5 has not yet appealed to anybody – probably with reason. 12.♗xh7+ ♔xh7 13.♕xd5 ♘c6 14.♘f5 (going for play with the superior minor piece) 14...g6 15.♘xe7 ♕xe7 16.♗e3±. **12.c4 ♗e8?!** As Alex Yermolinsky put it in his comments, this narrows down Black's options of a kingside attack. **13.♗h6 ♗g7 14.b4 ♘d7 15.♖c1 a5 16.a3 axb4 17.axb4 ♖a3** 17...b6 18.♕d2!, preventing the exchange and connecting the rooks; 17...f5 18.c5!±. **18.♘e4** Nakamura assessed that here the exchange of bishops would not solve all Black's problems. **18...f5 19.♘c3 e4 20.♗e2 ♗g5 21.♗xg5 ♕xg5 22.c5!** Exploiting the tactical vulnerability of the ♖a3. **22...♘e5** 22...dxc5 23.bxc5 ♘xc5 24.♘b5! ♖d3 25.♗xd3 ♘xd3 26.♗c7 f4 27.♖xg7+! ♔xg7 28.♘c7± – Yermolinsky. **23.c6+– ♘h5 24.♗xh5 gxh5 25.♔h1 ♕h4 26.♕d4 ♗g4 27.h3 f4 28.♔g1 e3 29.hxg4 hxg4 30.cxb7 exf2+ 31.♖xf2 g3 32.♖xf4 ♕h2+ 33.♔f1 1-0**

Ian Nepomniachtchi   **9**
Radoslaw Wojtaszek
Moscow 2019 (3)

1.e4 c5 2.♘f3 d6 3.d4 cxd4 4.♘xd4 ♘f6 5.♘c3 a6 6.♗d3 e5 7.♘de2 ♗e7 8.0-0 0-0 9.♘g3 ♗e6 10.♘d5 ♗xd5 11.exd5 g6 12.c4 ♘bd7 13.♗h6 ♖e8 For Radoslaw this is not the first experience with this position.

14.♖c1 A generally useful move. 14.b4 ♗f8 15.♗g5 h6 16.♗d2 e4 17.♗e2 ♗g7∞ Najer-Wojtaszek, Batumi Ech 2018; 17...h5!? 18.♗g5

♗e7⇄. **14...♘c5** Wojtaszek is not in a hurry with the seemingly automatic ...♗f8; he seeks immediate counterplay.

A) 14...♗f8 15.♗g5 h6 16.♗d2 a5 17.b3 and Vishy eventually managed to outplay the young newcomer in the super-tournament, Anand-Keymer, Baden-Baden 2019;

B) 14...a5 15.b3 ♘c5 16.♗c2 (16.♗b1 – game) 16...♘fd7 17.f4 exf4 18.♗xf4 ♗g5 19.♕f3 ♗xf4 20.♕xf4 ♘e5∞ 1-0 (27) Wang Yu A-Zhao Shengxin, China tt 2018. **15.♗b1 a5 16.b3 ♖b8** With the white bishop settled on the b1-h7 diagonal for good, ...b7-b5 becomes a desirable push. **17.f4 exf4 18.♗xf4** 18.♖xf4, intending to put everything on the f-file. This idea is too naive, though: 18...b5! and Black appears to be in time to distract White from his evil intentions: 19.♕f3 bxc4 20.bxc4 (the weakness on b1 and that of the back rank are much more relevant than anything that might happen on the f-file) 20...♘cd7∓. **18...b5 19.♕f3** 19.♗e2 (c6 just got vacated) 19...bxc4 20.♘d4 cxb3 21.♘c6 ♕b6 22.♗e3 looks like a mess, but Black is in control, e.g. 22...b2 23.♖c2 ♖b7 24.♕f3 ♗f8! 25.♗d4 ♘fe4 26.♖xb2 ♕c7 27.♖e2 f5∞ – a rather entertaining sample line. **19...bxc4 20.♖xc4** Ian is no fan of opening the whole file for the ♖b8; 20.bxc4 ♘fd7⇄. **20...♘b4 21.♗d2** 21.♖xc5?! dxc5 22.d6 ♗xd6 23.♗xd6 ♕xd6 24.♕xf6 ♕xf6 25.♖xf6 and White is not really risking to win here. **21...♖xc4 22.bxc4 ♘cd7!** The knight has completed its mission on c5. **23.♗c3! ♕b6+ 24.♔h1 ♖f8!= 25.♕f4 ♗d8 26.h3 ½-½**

Jorden van Foreest   **10**
Andrei Volokitin
Germany Bundesliga 2019/20 (2)

1.e4 c5 2.♘f3 d6 3.d4 cxd4 4.♘xd4 ♘f6 5.♘c3 a6 6.♗d3 e5 7.♘de2 ♗e7 8.0-0 0-0 9.♘g3 ♗e6 10.♘d5 ♗xd5 11.exd5 g6 12.a4!?N

An interesting concept. Before playing c2-c4 White wants to make sure that Black won't have any ideas with ...♘c5 and ...a6-a5. **12...♘bd7** Here, however, 12...♘xd5 would have been a slightly different story: 13.♗xg6 (13.♗e4 feels like looking in the wrong direction, e.g. 13...♘f6 14.♗xb7 ♖a7 15.♗f3 d5 16.♗h6 ♖e8 17.c3 ♕d6⇄) 13...hxg6 14.♕xd5 ♘c6 (now there is no jump to f5, but White's active pieces still give him some interesting possibilities) 15.♗h6 ♖e8 16.f4 (Black needs to know what he is doing here) 16...♕a5! 17.♕f3 exf4 18.♗xf4 ♘c5+ 19.♗e3 ♘c4 and Black probably holds, but the scare is not over yet. **13.a5 b5** A big decision. **14.c4 b4** To secure the outpost on c5 after all. If only Black could keep his b4-pawn intact. **15.b3 ♘c5 16.♗c2 ♘fd7 17.♗d2 ♖b8 18.♕e1 ♖b7! 19.♘e2** 19.♗xb4 ♕b8 also gives Black counterplay. **19...♗g5∓ 20.♗xb4 ♕b8 21.♗a3 ♘xb3 22.♗xb3 ♖xb3 23.♘c3 f5↑ 24.♘a4 ♕c7** 24...e4!. **25.♕e2 ♖c8 26.c5! ♕xa5 27.c6 ♕xa4 28.♗xd6 ♕b5 29.cxd7 ♕xd7 30.♗xe5 ♕xd5 31.♕xa6 ♖e8 32.f4 ♕e6 33.♕xe6+ ♖xe6 34.♖a8+ ♔f7 35.♖h8 ♗f6** 35...h5 36.♖h7+ ♔g8 37.♖g7+ ♔f8 38.fxg5 ♖xe5 39.♖xg6 ♖b2 40.♖f6+ ♔g7 41.♖6xf5 ♖xf5 42.♖xf5 ♔g6 is just about sufficient. But so is in fact also the text. **36.♖xh7+ ♔g8 37.♖d7 ♗xe5 38.fxe5 ♖e3 39.♖a1 ♖3xe5 40.♖aa7 ♖e1+ 41.♔f2 ♖1e2+ 42.♔f3 ♖2e3+ 43.♔f2 ♖e2+ 44.♔f3 ♖2e3+ 45.♔f4 ♖3e4+ 46.♔g3 ♖e3+ 47.♔h4 ♖3e4+ 48.♔h3 ♔f8 49.♖h7**

49...♖e7?? The problem is that White will achieve a general exchange on e8, after which the pawn ending will be lost for Black. Could it be that Volokitin, who is known to be an excellent calculator, trusted his capabilities and decided to end the game right away, unfortunately missing the strength of White's 56th move?

49...♔g8=. **50.♖a8+ ♖e8 51.♖h8+ ♔f7 52.♖hxe8 ♖xe8 53.♖xe8 ♔xe8 54.♔h4 ♔f8 55.♔g5 ♔f7 56.h3!!** 56.g3? ♔g7 57.h4 ♔f7 58.h5 gxh5 59.♔xf5 h4 and the white pawn moves to the h-file. **56...♔g7 57.h4 ♔h7** 57...♔f7 58.h5 gxh5 59.♔xf5 h4 60.♔g4+−. **58.h5 gxh5 59.♔xh5 f4 60.♔g5 ♔g7 61.♔xf4 ♔f6 62.♔g4 ♔g6 63.g3 1-0**

Exercise 1

position after 32...♕b4xa3

White has an inferior pawn structure. How can he save himself?

(solutions on page 246)

Exercise 2

position after 24...♘f6-g4

White is clearly better. What is the best way for him to contain Black's counterplay?

Exercise 3

position after 24.♔g1-h1

There is imminent danger along the f-file. How should Black deal with this?

French Defence   Tarrasch Variation   FR 14.1 (C03)

The 3...h6 Tarrasch

by Gawain Jones

1.	e4	e6
2.	d4	d5
3.	♘d2	h6
4.	♘gf3	♘f6
5.	e5	♘fd7
6.	c3	c5
7.	♗d3	♘c6

The top English players have taken some interest in this little pawn push, with Nigel Short, Matthew Sadler, and even David Howell giving it a whirl from time to time.

I'm not a French player, but, as the Tarrasch is my main weapon, I've faced it quite often. Black waits to see how White develops his minor pieces; his principal point being to bypass the mainline of 3...♘f6 4.e5 ♘fd7 5.♗d3 c5 6.c3 ♘c6 7.♘e2. Black is not trying to equalize. Instead, he aims for unusual double-edged positions where Black has his fair share of winning chances and White might not feel so comfortable. As I've been playing the Universal System (7.♘gf3) there anyway, 3...h6 hasn't move-ordered me out of my type of positions, and it will be the subject of this Survey.

In the main-line Universal System Black's main approach preparing ...g7-g5 is 7...♗e7. After 8.0-0, 8...g5 9.dxc5 is the sharp main line. Via the Universal System move order, 7...h6 makes a strange impression but does have some logic. Black is preparing to fight on the kingside with ...g7-g5 once White has castled. If we compare the positions with bishop on e7 versus pawn on h6 we see some advantages for Black. The g5-square is firmly defended, while e7 isn't the most natural square for the black bishop once White takes on c5. It can now either capture on c5 in one go or fianchetto itself on g7.

Instead, the immediate 7...g5 doesn't make any sense before White has castled, as after 8.h3 Black can't get any further with his kingside push. 8...h5 doesn't threaten ...g5-g4 due to the pin along the h-file, and White is doing well after 9.dxc5. Therefore 7...h6 is a good waiting move.

White castles

With the pawn on h6 rather than the bishop on e7 White has a broad range of options following 8.0-0 g5 (the only logical continuation).

These can be condensed into two different strategies:

Plan A: He can elect to open up the centre immediately, trying to exploit Black's delayed development and potentially vulnerable king.

Plan B: The other strategy is to try and hold onto the centre. If White successfully manages to keep his d4/e5 wedge intact without too many concessions he'll be doing well. Both strategies often require a pawn sacrifice.

The main line

The main line remains 9.dxc5, but I think this is a move Black is happy to see. White opens up the centre but Black has a few routes to a sharp double-edged battle.

Hikaru Nakamura has defended the black side a few times here, and opts for 9...♘xc5, see Ding-Nakamura and O'Gorman-McPhillips. 9...♝xc5 is the more popular recapture, see the game

Mamedov-Nevednichy. There Black dropped the bishop back to b6, but it seems more accurate to retreat all the way with 10...♝f8, see the game Krebs-Relyea.

The c3-c4 lever

The most direct route to 'Plan A' is with the c3-c4 lever, either on move nine or on move ten (after 9.h3 h5). It seems better for White to delay it one move, when Black's structure is looser. Black will have to defend extremely accurately, but if he does he has his fair share of the chances. See Akopian-Christiansen. White can prevent the threat of ...g5-g4 for one move with 9.h3. After 9...h5 White has to be careful not to get overrun on the kingside.

10.g4?! prevents the g-pawn from getting any further, and is an attempt at 'Plan B', but leaves White's king rather too airy for my liking, see Kuybokarov-Antipov. Likewise, 10.♖e1 was considered inaccurate, but new analysis by Andrew Liu rehabilitates the line. Still I would advise to steer clear of these positions. I cover this in Grimberg-Meister.

A tricky hybrid

While in the process of writing this article I managed to have another game in the line, this time at a semi-classical (45 15) time control. This time I opted

for 9.b3!? which is pretty tricky for Black.

Gawain Jones

This is really a hybrid of plans. White simply continues developing and allows ...g5-g4. Black can grab the central pawns but then White has a good version of the 'Plan A' positions. If Black declines the pawn White will be able to hold onto his centre without having made any major kingside concessions. See Jones-Harvey and Predojevic-Bukal.

A strategic alternative

Instead of going into the complications that Black is aiming for with this variation, White has the alternative option of 8.♗c2!?, a move I've tried a few times myself.

This is definitely playing in the secondary strategic spirit. As White delays castling, the ...g7-g5 break loses its impact, while White can now safely defend the d4-pawn with ♘d2-b3 without allowing a fork with ...c5-c4. The game becomes quite strategic, as both sides attempt to develop their pieces actively. See Jones-Camus de Solliers and Jones-Harvey (same opponent, different game – this was my first attempt against Marcus).

Conclusion

With 3...h6 Black is declaring his intentions early, and he's not content with a draw. The main lines with 8.0-0 g5 9.dxc5 are double-edged but seem fully playable for Black. Lines where White opens up the position with a quick c3-c4 are very dangerous, but Black is fine with accurate play. I'd advise against trying to block up the kingside with g2-g4 from White, as his position can quickly become very dangerous. Instead White has quite a few interesting sidelines, most involving a pawn sacrifice. The most serious to me looks to be 9.b3!?, as I tried last time I had this line.

If you wish to have a more strategic battle then I think my pet line 8.♗c2!? is a good option. White is willing to invest some time to keep control of his centre. The game will be much slower to develop than after 8.0-0, but strategically I believe White to be doing well.

Main line
8.0-0 g5 9.dxc5

Ding Liren 1
Hikaru Nakamura

PRO League Stage 2019 (7)

1.♘f3 h6 Hikaru opts for this trolling move order, but soon we get back to the critical tabiya. **2.e4 e6 3.d4 d5 4.♘bd2 ♘f6 5.e5 ♘fd7 6.♗d3 c5 7.c3 ♘c6 8.0-0 g5** Nothing else makes sense, as then Black's ...h7-h6 would have very limited value. Black has to force a concession out of White, or he'll just be suffering with his lack of space and White's big centre. 8...♕b6?! 9.dxc5! – this is strong in the theoretical position with a pawn on g6 rather than h6, see Kasparov-Bareev (2001). Here Black is simply in trouble, e.g. 9...♗xc5 (9...♕c7 10.♘b3 ♘xc5 11.♘xc5 ♗xc5 (Semenova-Grebnev, Ekaterinburg 2019) 12.b4±) 10.b4 ♗e7 11.♖e1± Ripperger-Meyer, Neustadt an der Weinstrasse 2012; 8...♗e7 9.♖e1± – again, what is the point of ...h7-h6 here?; 8...a5 9.♗c2. A typical idea in these structures. The bishop gets out of the way so it's now easier for White to defend his d4-pawn: 9...cxd4 (9...g5 10.♘b1!± as given by Watson; White keeps control of his centre and Black is just left with his weaknesses) 10.cxd4 b5 11.♖e1 ♗a6 12.♘f1 ♖c8 (Drozdowski-Piorun, Poland tt 2013). Eingorn gave this as level but really Black is in some trouble. Here 13.♘g3± would be very pleasant for White. **9.dxc5 ♘xc5** Nakamura's preference. White already has a question where to park the bishop.

10.♗b5 10.♗c2!? see O'Gorman-McPhillips. **10...♘d7** Hikaru's novelty, but I don't think this improves on his previous game. 10...a6 was how he'd played against Vishy Anand a few years previously: 11.♗xc6+ bxc6 12.b4 ♘d7 13.♖e1 (perhaps White should try 13.♘b3N g4 (13...♗g7 14.♗e3 0-0 15.♗c5 ♘xc5 16.♘xc5∞) 14.♘fd4 ♘xe5 15.♗f4 ♘g6 16.♗e3⩲) 13...a5= Anand-Nakamura, Zurich 2014; 10...♗g7 11.♘b3 (11.♖e1 ♘d7 transposes) 11...♘d7 (11...♘xb3 makes no sense as here Black isn't winning the e5-pawn, e.g. 12.axb3 0-0 (M.Rudolf-De Francesco, Zadar 2017) 13.♗xc6+) 12.♘bd4 ♕c7 13.♖e1 a6 14.♗a4 ♘b6?! (Gabuzyan-Legky, Milan 2014; 14...b5 15.♗c2 ♘cxe5 16.♘xe5 ♗xe5∞) 15.♘xc6 bxc6 16.♗e3±. **11.♖e1 ♗g7 12.c4** 12.♘f1! (eyeing up the h5-square, a major downside of Black's early kingside expansion) 12...g4 (12...0-0 13.♗xc6 bxc6 14.♘g3±; 12...♕c7 13.♘g3 ♘dxe5 14.♘h5 0-0 15.♘xe5 ♘xe5 (15...♗xe5 16.f4±) 16.♘xg7 ♔xg7 17.f4±) 13.♘d4 ♘cxe5 (13...dxe5 14.♖xe5! ♗xe5 15.♘xc6±) 14.♗f4 (14.♘g3!±) 14...0-0 15.♗xd7 ♘xd7 16.♕xg4± Ghaem Maghami-Short, Teheran 2013. **12...a6** 12...0-0!∓; White will be forced to capture on c6 now, to retain his e5-pawn, as he has no initiative – see the game. **13.♗a4** 13.♗xc6! bxc6 14.cxd5 cxd5 (in principle Black would like to be able to put more pressure on the e5-pawn with 14...exd5?! but here it's obviously too weakening: 15.♘d4±) 15.♕a4±. **13...0-0 14.cxd5 exd5 15.♗xc6 bxc6 16.♘b3 ♖e8∓** The e5-pawn is dropping for insufficient compensation. **17.♘bd4?!** 17.♗e3 ♘xe5 18.♘xe5 ♖xe5 19.♖c1∓ would grant White some compensation for the pawn. **17...♘c5?** Black won't get another opportunity to win the pawn. 17...c5! would leave White in trouble: 18.♘c6 ♕c7 19.♕xd5 ♗b7 20.e6 fxe6 21.♖xe6 ♔h8! 22.♕d6 ♕xd6 23.♖xd6

g4∓. **18.♗e3± ♘e4 19.♘xc6 ♕d7 20.♖c1 ♗b7 21.♘a5 ♕b5 22.♘xb7 ♕xb7 23.♗d4** Now it's White who is a clear pawn up. **23...♖ac8 24.h3 ♗f8 25.♖xc8 ♖xc8 26.h4 g4 27.♘h2 h5 28.♘f1 ♗e7 29.g3 ♘c5 30.♘e3 ♘e6 31.♘f5 ♕d7 32.♕d3 ♗f8 33.♖d1 ♖c6 34.♗c3 ♕c7 35.♘e3 ♖c5 36.♗b4 ♖b5 37.♗xf8 ♔xf8 38.♕h7 ♕e6 39.♕xh5 ♖xh2 40.♖c1 d4 1-0**

Tom O'Gorman 2
Joseph McPhillips

Dundalk 2019 (3)

1.e4 e6 2.d4 d5 3.♘d2 h6 4.♘gf3 ♘f6 5.e5 ♘fd7 6.♗d3 c5 7.c3 ♘c6 8.0-0 g5 9.dxc5 ♘xc5 10.♗c2!?

Here White accepts he'll lose the e5-pawn but hopes his initiative will be strong enough. **10...♘d7** 10...♗g7 11.♖e1 (I think 11.♘b3N is more thematic. White would rather have the rook on f1 to support the f2-f4 break once Black grabs the e5-pawn, e.g. 11...♘d7 (11...♘xb3 12.axb3 ♘xe5 13.♘xe5 ♗xe5 14.f4⩱) 12.♘bd4 ♘dxe5 13.♘xe5 ♗xe5 (13...♘xe5 14.f4⩱) 14.f4 ♘c6 15.♗e3⩱) 11...♘d7 12.♘b3 ♕c7 (12...♘dxe5 was already playable: 13.♘xe5 ♗xe5 14.♗e3 ♗d7 15.♘c5⩱) 13.♘bd4 ♘dxe5 14.♘xe5 ♗xe5 15.♘b5 (15.♘f3 ♗d6 16.♕xd5 ♗d7=) 15...♕b8 16.f4 (16.♗e3!=) 16...gxf4 17.♕h5 ♗d7 18.♖xe5 ♕xe5 19.♕xe5 ♘xe5 20.♘c7+ ♔e7 21.♘xa8 ♖xa8 22.♗xf4 f6 23.♗xh6 ♖g8∓. The smoke cleared and Black had the better chances in the ending in Naroditsky-Nakamura, chess. com INT 2019. **11.c4!?** 11.♘b3 ♗g7 transposes to 10...♗g7. **11...♗g7 12.cxd5 exd5 13.♘b3** 13.e6!? is a

complete mess: 13...fxe6 14.♗g6+ ♔f8 15.♖e1 g4 (15...e5 16.b4!∞) 16.♖xe6∞. **13...♘dxe5 14.♘xe5 ♗xe5 15.f4 gxf4 16.♗xf4 ♗xf4 17.♖xf4 ♗e6** Perhaps Black should start with 17...♕d6!? 18.♕d2 ♗e6 19.♘d4 0-0-0∞. **18.♘d4± ♕b6** 18...♕d6 19.♘xe6 fxe6 20.♕h5+ ♔d8 21.♖f7 ♖c8 22.♗a4♗. **19.♔h1** 19.♗a4! 0-0-0 20.♖c1 ♗d7 21.♗xc6 ♗xc6 22.♖f3±. **19...0-0-0 20.♖c1 ♔b8∓** Black has managed to get his king to safety, and is better with his extra pawn. **21.♘xc6+ ♕xc6 22.♗b3 ♕b6 23.♕d4 ♕xd4 24.♖xd4 ♖hg8 25.h3 ♖g5 26.♔h2 ♖e5 27.♖cd1 ♔c7 28.♖1d2 ♔d6 29.♔h1 a6 30.♔h2 ♖g8 31.♗d1 ♖c8 32.♗f3 ♖g5 33.a3 b5 34.♖h4 ♖g6 35.♖h5 f5 36.♗xd5 ♗xd5 37.♖xf5 ♖xg2+ 38.♖xg2 ♗xg2 39.♔xg2 ♖c2+ 40.♔g3 ♖xb2 41.♖f6+ ♔d5 42.♖xa6 ♖a2 43.♔g4 ♔c4 44.♖c6+ ♔b3 45.♖b6 ♔c4 46.♖c6+ ♔b3 47.♖b6 ♔c4 48.♖c6+ ½-½**

Rauf Mamedov — 3
Vladislav Nevednichy

Turkey tt 2013 (7)

1.e4 e6 2.d4 d5 3.♘d2 h6 4.♘gf3 ♘f6 5.e5 ♘fd7 6.♗d3 c5 7.c3 ♘c6 8.0-0 g5 9.dxc5 ♗xc5 9...♘dxe5 is the rarer capture, but this also looks fully playable: 10.♘xe5 ♘xe5 11.♘b3 (11.♗b5+ ♗d7 12.♗xd7+ ♕xd7 13.♘b3 ♘g6 (13...♘c4∓) 14.♗e3 (14.f4!∞) 14...♗g7 15.♕e2 0-0∓ Guid-Skoberne, Slovenia tt 2019; perhaps 11.♘f3!?N is White's best try here, for example: 11...♘xd3 (11...♘xf3+ 12.♕xf3 ♗xc5 13.c4!♗) 12.♕xd3 ♗g7 (12...♗xc5? 13.♕b5+) 13.♖e1 0-0 14.h4 g4 15.♘e5 ♕xh4 16.♗f4♗) 11...♘xd3 12.♕xd3 ♗g7 13.f4 ♗d7?! (13...0-0 14.♕g3 ♕c7 15.h4 f6 with a weird, extremely complicated position. Exactly what Black is going for in this variation) 14.♘d4± Van den Doel-Meessen, Germany Bundesliga B 2009/10. The move 9...g4 doesn't combine well with ...h7-h6: 10.♘d4 ♘dxe5 11.♗b5!? (11.♘2b3∓ H. Hunt-Wilks, London 2018) 11...♗xc5 12.f4 was

very dangerous for Black in C. Balogh-Hoang, Hungary tt 2011/12. **10.♘b3** This time it's Black's turn to decide where he should put the bishop. **10...♗b6** The more common, but I don't think this is best. 10...♗f8 has been the choice of Matthew Sadler, amongst others, and he can normally be relied upon. See the next game. **11.♕e2!** It's more flexible to leave the rook on f1 to support the f2-f4 lever, as explained earlier.

11...a6 Not the most useful tempo.

A) 11...g4 12.♘fd4 ♘cxe5 was given as unclear by Eingorn. I'd prefer White after 13.♗c2♗ with the idea of ♔h1 and f2-f3 or f2-f4. 13.♗b5 was Botta-Borgo, Switzerland tt 2015;

B) Eingorn also offered 11...♗c7 with the idea of immediately snaffling the pawn. This is probably critical: 12.♗c2 (12.♗b5 is possible here, although I don't really like ceding the bishop pair: 12...a6 13.♗xc6 bxc6∓) 12...♘dxe5 13.♘xe5 ♗xe5 14.f4 ♗d6∞ — **12.♗c2!** A useful retreat. Now Black won't gain a tempo when he captures on e5. **12...♕c7** 12...♗c7 13.♘fd4 ♘dxe5 14.f4!±; 12...g4 13.♘fd4 ♘cxe5 14.♔h1± — Watson. White is ready for the thematic f2-f4 next move. **13.♖e1 ♗a7** 13...g4 14.♘fd4 ♕xe5 15.♗e3♗. **14.g3!?** 14.h3! ♗b8 (14...♖g8 15.♘bd4±) 15.♗e3 ♘dxe5 16.♖ad1± — the pressure down the long diagonal looks scary but it doesn't seem like Black can make use of it. **14...b5** 14...♖g8!=, preparing ...g5-g4. 15.h3 can now be met with 15...f6!, exploiting the hanging g3-pawn. **15.a4 b4 16.♗d2± bxc3** 16...g4 17.♘h4 bxc3 18.bxc3! (18.♗xc3 ♖g8=) 18...♘cxe5

19.♗f4 ♕xc3 20.♖ac1↑ looks far too dangerous. **17.bxc3** 17.♗xc3 here was a decent option as 17...g4 18.♘fd4± is now possible. **17...♘c5** 17...g4 18.♘h4 (see 16...g4. White has to be careful, as 18.♘fd4? drops material: 18...♘xd4 19.♖xd4 ♗xd4 20.cxd4 ♕xc2). **18.♘xc5 ♗xc5 19.♗e3!± ♗a5 20.♗d3 ♗xe3 21.♕xe3** Black's counterplay has dissipated and he's just left with his weaknesses and exposed king. **21...♗d7 22.♘d4 ♘c6 23.♘b3! ♘e7 24.♘c5 ♗c8 25.a5 h5 26.♖ab1+− g4 27.♖b6 ♘c6 28.♕g5 ♗xa5 29.♖d6 ♕e7 30.♕g7 ♖f8 31.♖a1 ♕c7 32.♘xe6 ♗xe6 33.♖xe6+ ♔d7 34.♖d6+ ♔e8 35.♗f5 ♘c4 36.♖e6+ fxe6 37.♕xc7 exf5 38.e6 1-0**

Jürgen Krebs — 4
Alexander Relyea

cr 2019

1.e4 e6 2.d4 d5 3.♘d2 h6 4.♘gf3 ♘f6 5.e5 ♘fd7 6.♗d3 c5 7.c3 ♘c6 8.0-0 g5 9.dxc5 ♗xc5 10.♘b3 ♗f8

Rerouting the bishop to g7 looks like Black's most reliable plan. Black isn't actually losing time; via b6 the bishop would normally drop back to c7 to target the e5-pawn anyway.

11.♗c2!? A rare move-order.

A) 11.♘bd4 ♘dxe5 (11...g4?! just loosens Black's position: 12.♘xc6 bxc6 13.♘d4 ♘xe5 (13...c5 14.♘b5 (14.♘xe6!? fxe6 15.♗g6+ ♔e7 16.f4↑) 14...♘xe5 15.♗f4 ♗g7 16.♖e1 f6 17.♗g6+! ♔f8 (17...♖xg6 18.♕xg4±) 18.♗h5♗) 14.♗f4↑; as given by Eingorn, 14.♗c2 0-1 was the abrupt end to Lagerman-Arizmendi Martinez, Belgrade 2009; 11...♗g7 12.♗b5 (12.♘xc6 bxc6 13.♖e1 c5∞) 12...♕c7 13.♕a4?!

(13.♖e1=) 13...♘cxe5 14.♘xe5 ♗xe5 15.f4 gxf4 16.♗d2 ♔d8!?∓; Boix Moreno-Torrecillas Martinez, Barcelona 2018; 16...0-0∓) 12.♘xe5 ♘xe5 13.♘c2 ♗g7 14.f4 ♘c6 and we'd be back in the game;

B) 11.♖e1 is the most common but again I would be reluctant to move the rook off the f-file: 11...♗g7 12.♗b5 (sacrificing the pawn with 12.♘bd4 is, as usual, the alternative plan: 12...♘dxe5 (12...a6?! 13.♘xc6 bxc6 14.h4↑ Eingorn) 13.♘xe5 ♘xe5 14.♗b5+ (14.f4 should be preferred, but then it's unclear why White plays ♖e1, e.g. 14...♘xd3 15.♕xd3 ♗d7=) 14...♗d7 15.f4 ♗xb5 16.fxe5 (Kerigan-Fiebig, Belgium tt 2013/14) 16...♗d7∓) 12...0-0 13.♗xc6 bxc6 14.h4 gxh4?! (14...g4 15.♘fd4 ♕xh4 16.♘xc6 ♗b7 17.♘ca5 ♖ab8 with extremely complicated equality) 15.♘bd4 ♗b7 (Carnic-R. Perez Garcia, Obrenovac 2010) 16.b4!±;

C) 11.♘fd4!? is the most direct path. White immediately gives the e5-pawn and prepares to push f2-f4, e.g. 11...♘dxe5 12.f4 (12.♗c2!?♔) 12...♘xd3 13.♕xd3 ♗d7 (perhaps Black should start with 13...♘xd4!? before White can recapture with the bishop: 14.♘xd4 ♗d7 15.♗e3♔) 14.♗e3!?± Eingorn; 14.♗d2 ♘xd4 15.♘xd4 ♕c7∓ Rendle-Sadler, London 2014;

D) 11.♗b5, holding onto the e5-pawn for now, but as usual I don't really trust this approach: 11...a6 12.♗xc6 bxc6 13.♘fd4 ♘xe5 (13...♕b6! is more circumspect, e.g. 14.f4 c5 15.♘f3 g4 16.♘h4 ♖g8⇄) 14.f4 gxf4?! 15.♗xf4 ♘g6 16.♘xc6 ♕b6+ 17.♘bd4 ♗g7 18.♕h5± Solak-Haria, Batumi 2018. **11...♗g7** 11...♘dxe5 12.♘xe5 ♘xe5 13.f4 ♘c4 14.♕h5↑. **12.♘bd4 ♘dxe5** 12...g4 13.♘e1!? (13.♘xc6 bxc6 14.♘d4 ♘xe5 15.♗f4♔) 13...♘dxe5 14.f4 ♘xd4 15.fxe5 ♘xc2 16.♕xg4 ♗xe5 17.♘xc2♔. **13.♘xe5 ♗xe5** 13...♘xe5 14.f4 ♘c6 comes to the same thing. **14.f4 ♗g7 15.♗e3** A typical position for the variation. Black has grabbed a pawn but White has decent compensation

with his lead in development and Black's somewhat vulnerable king. **15...♘xd4 16.cxd4 ♗d7 17.♕h5 ♕e7 18.♗d3♔**

A complicated and well played game ensued, with the assessment never really deviating from equality: **18...♔f8 19.♖ac1 ♖c8 20.♖xc8+ ♗xc8 21.♖c1 ♗d7 22.♖c7 ♕b4 23.♔f1 ♔e8 24.fxg5 hxg5 25.♕xg5 ♗xd4 26.♕g4 ♗c3 27.♕xb4 ♗xb4 28.♖xb7 ♗d6 29.h3 a5 30.♖a7 ♗c6 31.♖xa5 e5 32.♗f5 d4 33.♗d2 ♖h5 34.♗g4 ♖h7 35.♗e2 ♔d7 36.♖a7+ ♔c8 37.♗d3 ♖h5 38.a4 ♗b7 39.♖a5 ♔c7 40.♔f2 f5 41.♔g1 ♗b8 42.♖b5 ♔c7 43.♖a5 ½-½**

The c3-c4 lever
8.0-0 g5 9.h3

Vladimir Akopian   **5**
Johan-Sebastian Christiansen
Dubai 2018 (7)

1.e4 e6 2.d4 d5 3.♘d2 h6 The actual move-order was 3...♗e7 4.♘gf3 ♘f6 5.e5 ♘fd7 6.♗d3 c5 7.0-0 ♘c6 8.♖e1 g5 9.h3 h5 10.c4 and with one move less each we're back to the game position after 11.♖e1. **4.♘gf3 ♘f6 5.e5 ♘fd7 6.♗d3 c5 7.c3 ♘c6 8.0-0 g5 9.h3** If you want to break in the centre then it seems to be better to first include the h-pawn moves. 9.c4 ♗g7?! (9...g4?! 10.cxd5 exd5 11.e6!, as seen in Bocharov-Antipov, Sochi 2018, is incredibly complicated) as given by Watson seems to work out well for Black: 10.cxd5 exd5 11.♗f5 (11.e6 would of course be the critical test, but here it doesn't look too challenging for Black. The crucial

difference is that Black can now use the f8-square for his king: 11...fxe6 12.♗g6+ ♔f8 13.dxc5 (13.♖e1!?♔) 13...♔g8!∓) 11...0-0 12.e6 (Semenov-L.H.Bech Hansen, cr 2005) 12...fxe6 13.♗xe6+ ♔h8 looks more comfortable for Black to me. **9...h5**

10.c4!? ♗e7 Much choice here:

A) 10...g4 11.cxd5 exd5 12.e6!. This pawn sacrifice is generally more dangerous when Black's bishop remains on f8. Watson provides some good analysis here: 12...fxe6 13.♗g6+ ♔e7 14.♖e1!? gxf3 15.♘xf3 ♗h6 16.dxc5 ♗xc1 17.♖xc1 ♘f6 (– Watson. He doesn't think White has quite enough compensation, although my engine is quite happy with White after 17...♖g8!?) 18.b4!♔;

B) 10...♖g8!? defends the g5-pawn but, more importantly, prevents the check on g6: 11.cxd5 exd5 12.♘h2?! (White's position becomes very dangerous here. Therefore 12.♖e1!? should be investigated: 12...g4 (12...♘db8= looks more circumspect) 13.e6 fxe6 14.♖xe6+ ♔f7 15.♕e2 ♗g7! with complete chaos! 16.♖h6!? (16.h4!?) 16...♕e7 17.♕d1∞) 12...g4 13.hxg4 (13.♖e1 ♘xd4∓) 13...hxg4 14.♘xg4 ♕h4! (this is much more challenging with the knights still on the board; 14...♘xd4 15.♘b3 ♘xb3 16.axb3 ♕h4 17.♗f5 ♗e7? (17...♖h8 18.f3±) 18.g3 ♕h8 19.♕xd5+– Bernadskiy-Skawinski, Karlsruhe 2018) 15.♗f5 (15.♘h2 ♘xd4+!) 15...♖h8 16.f4 ♗e7!→;

C) 10...♗g7?! is now no longer so good after the immediate 11.cxd5 (11.♘b3 is also enough for a big advantage) 11...exd5 12.♘xg5! looks crushing, e.g. 12...♕xg5 13.♘e4

♕e7 14.♗g5+–. **11.♖e1!?** This looks to be the most challenging. 11.cxd5 exd5 12.e6 fxe6 13.♗g6+ (again this check isn't as strong with the black bishop having vacated f8) 13...♔f8 14.♖e1 ♔g7! 15.♗c2 g4!? (15...♗f6!? Watson) 16.hxg4 hxg4 17.♘e5?! (17.♘h2 was required: 17...♘f6 18.♘xg4 ♘xd4∞) 17...♘dxe5 18.dxe5 ♖g8! 19.♕xg4+ ♔f7∓ Antipov-Bauer, Linares 2013. **11...g4** 11...dxc4?! 12.♘xc4 cxd4 (12...g4 13.d5! exd5 14.♘d6+ ♗xd6 (14...♔f8 15.♘xf7! ♔xf7 16.e6+ ♔g7 17.exd7 ♗xd7 18.♘e5±) 15.exd6+ ♔f8 16.♗g5! f6 17.♗f4+– Thilakarathne-Sankalp, New Delhi 2018) 13.♗e4 g4 14.♗xc6 bxc6 15.♘xd4± Czebe-Toth, Gyula 2013; 11...♘b4 12.♗b1 g4 (12...dxc4 13.♘xc4 g4 14.♘fd2 cxd4 15.♘e4 (15.hxg4±) 15...♘c6 16.♗f4± Asrian-Prasca Sosa, Turin ol 2006) 13.a3!? (13.hxg4 hxg4 14.♘h2 g3 15.fxg3 cxd4 16.a3 ♘c6 17.cxd5 exd5 18.♘g4±) 13...gxf3? (13...♘c6! was necessary, e.g. 14.cxd5 exd5 15.e6 fxe6 16.♗g6+ ♔f8 17.hxg4 hxg4 18.♘e5 ♘dxe5 19.dxe5 ♔g7 (19...♗f6!? 20.exf6 ♕xf6 21.♕xg4 ♖g8 22.♕e4!±) 20.♕xg4 ♖h4 (20...♕g8 here isn't so strong as the black king is unable to run back to the queenside) 21.♕g3 ♘d4 22.♘f3 ♘xf3+ 23.gxf3 ♕h8 24.♔g2±) 14.axb4+– Dragnev-Lahav, Skopje 2019. **12.cxd5**

12...♘b4? 12...exd5 is necessary, albeit dangerous, for example: 13.e6 fxe6 14.♗g6+ ♔f8 15.hxg4 hxg4 16.♘e5 ♘dxe5 (16...♗d6 17.♕xg4 ♗xe5 18.dxe5 ♕h4 19.♕xh4 ♖xh4 20.♘f3±) 17.dxe5 ♗f6!? 18.exf6 ♕xf6 19.♕xg4 ♖g8 20.♘e4! ♕xg6. This is all given by Watson. Here I think a slight

refinement is 21.♕f3+ (21.♕f4+ ♕f7 22.♕h6+ ♕g7 23.♕f4+ ♕f7= Watson) 21...♕f7 22.♗h6+ ♔e7 23.♗g5+ ♔f8 (or 23...♖xg5 24.♕xf7+ ♔xf7 25.♘xg5+ which comes to the same thing) 24.♘f6 ♖xg5 25.♘h7+ ♔e7 26.♕xf7+ ♔xf7 27.♘xg5+ ♔f6 28.f4 e5 with a very complicated endgame. **13.♘e4** 13.d6!? is also very promising, e.g. 13...♗h4? (13...♗xd6 14.♘e4 ♗e7 15.♗g5→) 14.♘e4 gxf3 15.♘xf3+– Nisipeanu-Czebe, Tusnad 2004. **13...♕xd3** 13...♘xd5 14.♘fg5+–; 14.hxg4 Tesik-Berchtenreiter, Pardubice 2012. **14.♕xd3 gxf3 15.d6! ♗f8** 15...♗h4 16.g3+–. **16.♗g5 ♕a5 17.d5** With an absolutely crushing position. **17...c4 18.♕xf3 ♗g7 19.♖ad1 ♖h7 20.♗f6 ♗xf6 21.exf6 ♘f8 22.d7+ ♘xd7 23.♘d6+ ♔d8 24.dxe6 fxe6 25.♖xe6 ♕b4 26.f7 ♔c7 27.♘e8+ 1-0**

Temur Kuybokarov   6
Mikhail Antipov
Moscow 2017 (2)

1.e4 e6 2.d4 d5 3.♘d2 h6 4.♘gf3 ♘f6 5.♗d3 c5 6.e5 ♘fd7 7.c3 ♘c6 8.0-0 g5 9.h3 h5 10.g4 White prevents Black from expanding further, but now White's king is very draughty. **10...hxg4 11.hxg4 ♕b6**

12.dxc5?! 12.♕a4 ♗e7 (12...a6 was given by Eingorn in Yearbook 115 but I think it's unnecessary) 13.♖e1 cxd4 14.cxd4 (Kilian-Göcke, Germany tt 2015/16) 14...f5!∓, a beautiful move, blowing open White's kingside; 12.a4!? is Lc0's offering to keep the game balanced. Its idea is to sacrifice a pawn: 12...cxd4 (12...a5 13.♖e1 cxd4 14.♘b3!≙) 13.a5 ♘xa5

14.cxd4≙. **12...♕c7!∓** White is going to lose his e5-pawn anyway, and now he has none of that long-term compensation. **13.♔g2** 13.♖e1 is better, although after 13...♘dxe5 14.♘xe5 ♘xe5 15.♘f3 (15.♗b5+ ♗d7 16.♕e2 (Pourramezanali-Rastbod, Rasht 2017) 16...f6!–+) 15...♘xd3 16.♕xd3 (J. Houska-Wiley, Olomouc 2018) 16...f6 Black still has a clear advantage. **13...♘dxe5 14.♘xe5 ♘xe5 15.♗b5+ ♗d7 16.♗xd7+ ♔xd7–+ 17.♘e4 ♗e7 18.♗xg5 ♗xg5 19.♘xg5 ♖h4 20.f3 ♖h2+ 21.♔g3 ♖ah8 22.f4 f6 23.♖f2 fxg5 24.♕a4+ ♘c6 0-1**

Boris Grimberg   7
Peter Meister
Immenstadt 2009 (8)

1.e4 e6 2.d4 d5 3.♘d2 h6 4.♘gf3 ♘f6 5.♗d3 c5 6.e5 ♘fd7 7.c3 ♘c6 8.0-0 g5 9.h3 h5

10.♖e1 This move has been criticized but it appears playable. There are a couple of novelties here that could be considered:

A) 10.h4!? with the idea 10...g4 (10...gxh4 11.♖e1≙) 11.♘g5 cxd4 12.f4!∞;

B) And one that I find quite attractive: 10.b4!?N cxb4 (10...g4 11.b5!±) 11.cxb4 ♘xb4 (11...g4 12.b5 ♘b4 13.♘e1±) 12.♘b3±;

C) 10.♘b3!? meanwhile isn't a novelty, but an interesting piece offer:

C1) 10...c4 11.♗xg5! (11.♘xg5 cxd3∓ didn't grant White sufficient compensation in Paszewski-Zaleski, Warsaw 2018) 11...♗e7 12.♗xe7 ♕xe7 13.♗xc4 (I'd be inclined to keep the bishop with 13.♗c2 cxb3 14.axb3∞) 13...dxc4 14.♘bd2∞ Eingorn;

C2) 10...♖g8 11.h4! (11.♗e2 c4 12.♘bd2 g4 13.♔h2 f5⇄ – a complete mess, but I'd be quite scared as White) 11...gxh4 12.♗h7 (12.♗e2!?) 12...♗g7 13.♗c2 c4?! 14.♘bd2 h3 15.g3 h4 16.♔h2 hxg3+ 17.fxg3± f6?! 18.♘h4!+– O'Gorman-Wiley, Dundalk 2019;

C3) 10...♗e7 11.♘xc5 ♘xc5 12.dxc5 g4 (Levi-Suarez Gomez, Gijon 2018) 13.♘d4 gxh3 14.♘xc6 bxc6 15.g3±;

C4) 10...g4 11.♘g5 was given as unclear by Eingorn. Since his Survey there was an email game: 11...♗e7 (11...♗h6 12.f4!? c4 13.♗b1 cxb3 14.hxg4 looks like fun compensation, while 12.♘xe6 is a forcing line: 12...fxe6 13.♗xh6 ♖xh6 14.♕d2! ♖h8 15.♗g6+ ♔f8 16.♕f4+ ♗g7 17.♕f7+ ♔h6 18.♗xh5 ♕g8 19.♕xg8 ♖xg8 20.♗xg4 ♖e8 21.f4 with an unclear but probably fairly balanced ending) 12.♘xe6 fxe6 13.♗g6+ ♔f8 14.hxg4 (14.f4! appeals to me: 14...gxh3 15.g4!→) 14...hxg4 15.♕xg4 ♖h4 16.♕f3+ ♔g7 17.♕f7+ ♔h8 18.f4∞ Angermann-Kern, email 2017. **10...g4**

11.hxg4? But here 11.♘h2! is necessary. Elliot Liu and John Watson went into a lot of detail in this position on ChessPublishing. I don't want to simply repeat their analysis, I'll merely mention they indicate 11...cxd4 as Black's best option here, with a very complicated position. **11...hxg4 12.♘h2 cxd4 13.cxd4 ♖xh2!** Eingorn correctly gave this as winning last time this opening appeared in the Yearbook. **14.♔xh2** 14.g3 was tried in a strange correspondence game: 14...♖h8 15.♕xg4 ♕e7 16.♘f3 f5–+.

16...♗h6 17.♔g2 ♗xc1 18.♖axc1 1-0, Sherwood-Yeo, cr 2019, is a strange find in the database. **14...♕h4+ 15.♔g1 g3** Black immediately regains the sacrificed material, with an ongoing attack. **16.fxg3 ♕xd4+ 17.♔h2 ♕xd3 18.♕h5 ♘dxe5 19.♘b3 ♗g7 20.♗g5 ♕g6 21.♕h4 f6 22.♗d2 ♘g4+ 23.♔g1 ♗d7 0-1**

A tricky hybrid
8.0-0 g5 9.b3

Gawain Jones   8
Marcus Harvey
England 4NCL Online pff 2020 (12)
1.e4 e6 2.d4 d5 3.♘d2 h6 4.♘gf3 ♘f6 5.e5 ♘fd7 6.♗d3 c5 7.c3 ♘c6 8.0-0 g5 9.b3!? I noticed White has a very good score with this move. **9...cxd4** Black logically goes after the pawn. For alternatives please check out the next game. **10.cxd4 g4** If Black doesn't immediately grab the pawn, play will be much slower. Generally I believe White should have some advantage there with his extra space, e.g. 10...♕b6 11.♗b2 ♗e7 12.♖c1 (12.♘b1!?) 12...a5 13.a4 ♘db8 (13...h5 14.♗b5 ♘a7 15.♗e2 g4 16.♘e1 ♘b8 17.♔h1 ♘bc6 18.f3± Abolins Abols-Bishop, cr 2018) 14.♘b1 ♘a6 15.♘a3 ♘c7 16.♘e1 ♗d7 17.♘b5 ♘xb5 18.♗xb5± Santos Latasa-Ider, Porto 2015; 10...h5 11.♗b2 ♗e7 12.♘e1 ♕b6 13.♘c2± Tarjan-Ragnarsson, Sault Ste Marie 2017. **11.♘e1 ♘xd4 12.♕xg4 ♘c6 13.♘df3!?** I'd spent some time studying this position and decided this was the most practical approach. It's useful to keep the knight on e1 so it can recapture on d3 on the way to jumping into e5. 13.f4 was played in the correspondence game that inspired me: 13...♘c5 14.♘df3 ♘xd3 15.♘xd3 h5 16.♕h3 ♕b6+ 17.♔h1 ♗d7 18.♖e1 ♘b4 19.♗e3 ♕a6 20.♘xb4 ♗xb4 21.♗d2 ♗xd2 22.♘xd2 0-0-0 23.♘f3± and White has managed to end up with the

dream good knight v. bad bishop position, Wharrier-Lundberg, cr 2018. **13...♘dxe5 14.♗xe5 ♘xe5 15.♕g3** I thought all queen moves were promising here, but this one has the advantage of keeping an eye on the g7-square. **15...♘xd3** My line before the game ran 15...♗d6 16.f4 ♘xd3 17.♘xd3 ♗d7 18.♗b2 ♖f8 19.♗d4⩲; 19.♖fc1!?. **16.♘xd3± ♖h7** Now I was on my own. I spent a fair chunk of my time, I think something like a third of my 45 minutes, and found the most accurate continuation: **17.♖e1! ♖g7 18.♕f3 ♗e7**

19.♗b2 Already White has a choice of winning lines. The engine is perplexed why I didn't simply grab 19.♗xh6. I didn't want to allow Black potential counterplay along the h-file and control of the long diagonal, but 19...♖h7 20.♘e5! is a strong intermezzo, e.g. 20...♗d6 21.♘g4!+–. **19...♖g5** 19...f6 20.♖ad1+–. **20.h4! ♖f5 21.♕g4 h5 22.♕g7** And here I couldn't figure out whether I wanted to force things. The most precise would have been 22.♕g8+! ♔d7 23.♕h7 ♗f6 24.♕xf7+ (the engine informs me that 24.♘e5+! ♗xe5 25.♖xe5 is even stronger. Black is completely powerless without his queenside pieces) 24...♕e7 25.♕g8!+–. **22...♗xh4 23.♖ac1 ♕d6 24.♕h8+** 24.♕h7!+– was better. I wasn't sure if I wanted to force the queen back to f8 or not. 24...♗e7 was the reason I threw in the check, but 25.♗e5 ♕b6 26.♖c7! is completely winning. **24...♕f8 25.♕h7 ♗e7??** Short on time Marcus cracks. 25...♖g5! was strictly the only move according to the engine, although

it's hard to believe Black will really survive after 26.♘f4; 25...♔d8 (I thought this was forced) 26.♗g7 ♕e8 (26...♕e7 27.g3! ♗g5 28.f4 and the bishop runs out of squares: 28...♗f6 29.♕h8+ ♔d7 30.♗xf6 ♕xf6 31.♘e5+ ♔d6 32.♕e8+−) 27.g4!+− ♖f3 28.♘e5! ♗xf2+ (28...♖xf2 29.♕xh5+−; 28...♖f4 29.♕h6!) 29.♔g2 ♗xe1 30.♔xf3!+−. **26.♗g7 1-0**

Borki Predojevic   **9**
Vladimir Bukal jr
Zadar 2019 (4)
1.e4 e6 2.d4 d5 3.♘d2 h6 4.♘gf3 ♘f6 5.e5 ♘fd7 6.♗d3 c5 7.c3 ♘c6 8.0-0 g5 9.b3 ♗g7 9...a5 10.a4 g4 is quite similar to the previous game: 11.♘e1 cxd4 12.cxd4 ♘xd4 13.♕xg4 ♘c6 14.♘df3 ♘c5 (how does White respond to 14...h5 ? See Exercise 2) 15.♗e3 b6 16.♕h5 ♗a6 17.♗xa6 ♘xa6 18.♖c1 ♗c5 19.♗g5 ♕d7 20.♘f6+− Metsemakers-Baumann, cr 2018; 9...♗e7 10.♗b2 ♕b6 11.c4! (switching from Plan B to Plan A) 11...cxd4 12.cxd5 exd5 13.e6 ♘f6 (13...fxe6 14.♘xd4 ♘xd4 15.♘c4 ♕c7 16.♗xd4±) 14.exf7+ ♔xf7 15.♖c1↑ Höxter-Kern, cr 2017. **10.♗b2** 10.h3 h5 11.b4!? is an amusing pawn sacrifice offered by my engine, e.g. 11...cxd4 (11...g4 12.b5±) 12.cxd4 ♘xb4 13.♘b3♕. **10...0-0** Black should probably try and open the kingside either this move or next. After 10...f5!? 11.exf6 ♕xf6 12.dxc5 0-0 13.♖b1!? ♘xc5 14.♗c2 g4 15.♘e1 h5 16.b4 ♘d7 17.♘d3 I prefer White but the position is extremely double-edged. **11.h3**

11...a6 Black's last chance was 11...f6! 12.exf6 ♕xf6 13.♖c1!? (13.b4!?) 13...e5 14.c4 exd4 15.cxd5 ♘b4

16.♘e4 ♕f4∞. **12.♖e1 b5 13.♖c1±** Now White has total control of the position. **13...♕b6?! 14.♗b1+− f5 15.exf6 ♘xf6 16.dxc5 ♕xc5 17.c4! bxc4 18.bxc4 ♕b6 19.cxd5 exd5 20.♘b3 d4 21.♘bxd4 ♗d7 22.♗a3 ♖fd8 23.♗c5 ♕b7 24.♕c2 ♖ac8 25.♕g6 ♘xd4 26.♗xd4 ♖xc1 27.♗xf6 ♖xe1+ 28.♘xe1 ♗f5 29.♗xf5 1-0**

A strategic alternative 8.♗c2

Gawain Jones   **10**
Guillaume Camus de Solliers
England 4NCL 2012/13 (4)
1.e4 e6 2.d4 d5 3.♘d2 h6 4.♘gf3 ♘f6 5.e5 ♘fd7 6.c3 c5 7.♗d3 ♘c6 8.♗c2!? This was my first game facing 3...h6. I hadn't checked the main lines for a while and so went for this quieter Plan B approach. The ensuing positions are much more strategic than those we've seen after 8.0-0.

8...♕b6 Targeting the d4-pawn is how all my opponents have reacted. 8...g5?! no longer makes much sense: 9.h3 ♗e7 (Garcia Pardo-Largo Barbero, Madrid 2019; 9...h5 would be an empty move without a threat of ...g5-g4; 10.♘b3±) 10.a3 b6 11.b4± . **9.♘b3 cxd4** 9...a5 was played against me in another recent online game. Here I think White's most accurate reaction is to ignore it with 10.0-0!? (I continued on autopilot with 10.a4 when after 10...g5?! (Jones-Saravana, chess.com 2020) John Watson points out I could have ignored the threat with 11.0-0! as Black isn't collecting on d4 here: 11...cxd4

12.cxd4 g4 13.♘e1 h5 14.♗e3± Watson) 10...cxd4 (10...a4?! 11.♘xc5 ♘xc5 12.dxc5± and White collects the a4-pawn) 11.♖e1!? (not 11.cxd4?! a4) 11...dxc3 12.bxc3♕. **10.cxd4 a5 11.a4 ♘b4** 11...♕b4+ was another recent competitive online game. At blitz the right move isn't so straightforward, but Watson points out I should have gone for 12.♗e2! (12.♔f1 ♘b6 (12...b5!?) 13.♘e1!? (13.♗d2! ♕c4+ 14.♔g1 ♗d7 15.h4± Watson) 13...♘c4= Jones-S.Chow, chess.com 2020) 12...♕b6 (12...b6 13.♗d3! ♗a6 14.♗xa6 ♖xa6 15.♕d3 ♖a7 16.♗d2± − Black has succeeded in exchanging his bad bishop but still stands passively; the key point appears to be that 12...♘b6 13.♗d2 ♕c4+? now loses to 14.♗d3 as the bishop is defended) 13.♔f1! (now that Black's queen is in the way on b6) 13...♕c7 14.h4 ♘b6 15.♗d2 ♗d7 16.♔g1± Watson. **12.♗b1 ♕c7** 12...♕a6, preventing castling, is what I was expecting: 13.♗e3 (13.♘g1!? was an idea I was toying with but is unnecessary) 13...b6 (13...b5!?) (Watson) 14.0-0 bxa4 15.♖xa4 ♕b5 16.♖a1 a4 17.♘c1 ♘b6±; 13...♗e7 14.h4) 14.♘g1!?±. This seems slow but Black is hardly attacking. White follows up with 15.♘e2 and 0-0. **13.0-0 ♘b6** As Watson observed in similar positions, Black should really be going long with his king here: 13...b6 14.h4 ♗a6 15.♖e1 0-0-0!?∞. I'd still prefer White but it'll be much harder to generate attacking chances against Black's king. **14.♖e1 ♗d7**

15.♘c5! A thematic pawn sacrifice. In return White gets a beautiful outpost on d4 and uncontested dark squares. **15...♗xc5?!** It

was better for Black again to ignore with 15...0-0-0!?±. **16.dxc5 ♕xc5 17.♗e3 ♕c7 18.b3 ♖c8** The engine wants to defend with 18...♕c3! 19.♗d4 ♕c7±. Apparently it's vital to deflect the bishop. How does White exploit 18...0-0 ? See Exercise 3. **19.♕d4!** It's always pleasant to force Black to retreat his knight into the corner. **19...♘a8 20.♕g4±** **♔f8 21.♗d2 ♕b6 22.♘d4 ♘c7 23.♖e3 ♘e8 24.♖f3 f5** This loses immediately but it doesn't look like Black can escape: 24...♔g8 25.♕h5 ♘f6 26.♖xf6! gxf6 27.♕g4+ ♔f8 28.exf6 ♔e8 29.♕g7 ♖f8 30.♘f3 e5 31.♗xh6+−. **25.♘xf5! h5 26.♘xg7+ ♔g8 1-0**

Gawain Jones   11
Marcus Harvey
London blitz KO 2019 (4)
This was actually an Armageddon game. **1.e4 e6 2.d4 d5 3.♘d2 h6 4.♘gf3 ♘f6 5.e5 ♘fd7 6.♗d3 c5 7.c3 ♘c6 8.♗c2 cxd4** Going after the d4-pawn is logical, but we've seen White successfully holding on to it. Instead, 8...b6 is an alternative plan: 9.0-0 and now:

A) 9...cxd4 (Aydogdu-Sahin, Antalya 2017) 10.♗a4! (an accurate intermezzo) 10...dxc3 (10...♗b7 11.♘xd4!? (11.cxd4±) 11...♘cxe5 12.f4 ♘g6 13.f5 exf5 14.♘2b3±) 11.♗xc6 cxd2 12.♗xa8 (12.♗xd2 ♖b8 13.♖c1⩱) 12...dxc1♕ 13.♖xc1±;
B) 9...g5!? (Mösl-Sattler, Germany tt 2012/13) is suggested by Watson at this point. Here I'd go 10.h3 h5 11.♗a4! (a strange circuit for the bishop but we indirectly protect our centre) 11...♗b7 12.c4! ♘xd4 (12...g4 13.cxd5 exd5 14.♖e1! ♗e7 15.e6 fxe6 16.♖xe6 ♕c7 17.♘b3! gxf3 18.♗xc6 ♗xc6 19.♗g5+−) 13.♘xd4 cxd4 14.♖e1⩱;
C) 9...♗a6 10.♖e1 g5 (Tölly-Schieder, Leitersdorf 2014) 11.h3± h5? 12.c4!+−; again Black is far too loose. **9.cxd4 ♕b6 10.♘b3 ♗b4+ 11.♔f1 a5 12.♗e3!?** 12.a4 would be very similar to the previous game. **12...a4 13.♘c1** White's pieces have been pushed back but if Black can't make any progress on the queenside White will have great long-term chances. I was quite pleased with how I had coordinated my pieces.

13...a3 14.bxa3 ♖xa3 15.♖b1! **♕a6+ 16.♔g1 ♗e7 17.h4 ♘b4 18.♗b3± ♘b8** 18...♘b6!? 19.♗d2 ♘c4 20.♗xb4 ♗xb4 21.♖h3±. **19.♖h3 ♘8c6 20.♖g3± ♔f8 21.♗d2 ♘d3?!** Black was running out of a plan but objectively this loses. **22.♘xd3 ♕xd3 23.♖c1** Normally I'd have hoped to spot 23.♖xg7+− even with only a minute or so on the clock. Still I succeed in winning without needing to resort to any tactics: **23...♕a6 24.♗c3 ♗d7 25.♕e1 ♕b6 26.♖b1 ♕a7 27.♗b2 ♖a6 28.h5 ♖b6 29.♖c1 ♕a5 30.♕e3 ♗a3 31.♗xa3+ ♕xa3 32.♕f4 ♕a8 33.♘h4 ♘e7 34.♘g6+ ♘xg6 35.hxg6 ♕e8 36.♖f3 ♖c6 37.♖xc6 ♗xc6 38.♕h4 f5 39.exf6 ♕xg6 40.fxg7+ ♔xg7 41.♕e7+ 1-0**

Exercise 1

position after 15.h2-h3

How could Black create counterplay here?

(*solutions on page 246*)

Exercise 2

position after 14...h6-h5

How should White respond?

Exercise 3

position after 18...0-0

How can White crash through?

Caro-Kann Defence   Exchange Variation   CK 2.8 (B13)

An early surprise

by Mikheil Mchedlishvili

1.	e4	c6
2.	d4	d5
3.	exd5	cxd5
4.	♗d3	♘f6
5.	c3	♗g4

I would like to share my thoughts about the line I introduced first in grandmaster practice. As a long-time Caro-Kann player I never really considered the 3.exd5 line as a serious try for White, I thought I would always find an adequate answer against it. Then, after the London System become popular, it made me look at the 3.exd5 Caro-Kann with a new eye, as there are many similar positions, and positions which were thought to be comfortable for Black are now no longer considered so – especially if Black is not fast enough to make ...b7-b5-b4 work and White can slowly build up a kingside attack.
It is clear that Black has to do something with his light-squared bishop. Normally, when it is exchanged then Black solves his problems. I thought that saving a tempo on ...♘c6 by playing 4...♘f6 and 5...♗g4 immediately was an interesting try, and though this is connected with a pawn sacrifice I analysed it a bit with the engine and gave it a try in a game against

Adam Tukhaev, who was unaware of this possibility. He spent a lot of time in the opening and blundered in time pressure. I was happy with how things had gone, and with scoring a win in an interesting game with a new line.
Let us look at the options for both sides step by step.

Caruana's choice
Blackburne's 6.♘e2 from 1907(!) was played by Caruana in the ProChess League 2019 (Game 1).

After 6...♘c6 7.0-0 e6 8.♕b3 ♕d7 9.♘f4 I think that instead of 9...♗d6, which was played in that game and which led to a typical advantage for White, 9...g6 is an interesting idea leading to a double-edged position. I didn't find any special problems for Black here.

The main move
6.♕b3 is of course the main move. After 6...♕c7, 7.♘e2 is also possible. While considering the lines with 7.♘e2, I wanted at some point to exchange on e2, which forces White to retake with the bishop, which stands worse on e2 than on d3. I thought this was enough to

Mikheil Mchedlishvili

get a nice position (Game 2). I thought somewhere I could even consider playing ...♘f6-e4 and ...f7-f5, especially if White's pawn is on h3. Instead of taking on e2, ...♘c6 is also OK.

7.♗g5, as played by Praggnanandhaa, is not a problem for Black (Game 3).

Eljanov's unusual retreat

7.h3 is our main line.

Now, 7...♗d7 looks very unusual, Black suddenly changes plans and wants to put the bishop on c6 and the knight on d7. Then he can threaten to play ...♘e4. The very interesting new game Ganguly-Eljanov was played at Tata Steel this year (Game 4), where a complicated fight ended in Black's favour. It is still early to say if 7...♗d7 is enough for equality.

The pawn sacrifice

After 7...♗h5 8.♘e2, Aryan Gholami took on 8...♗xe2 against Idani, and his opponent missed the interesting novelty 9.♗f4! which is critical in this line. After 9.♗xe2 Black had absolutely no problems (Game 5).

Maybe 8...♘c6 is also interesting, with the idea to exchange the bishop via h5-g6. This looks solid for Black.

Of course, when preparing this line I focused my attention mainly on 8.g4, when White is winning a pawn.

I thought Black was getting nice compensation after 8...♗g6 9.♗xg6 hxg6 10.g5 ♘fd7 11.♕xd5 with his lead in development and mainly because of the weaknesses which White has created in his camp to win the pawn. In the comments to my game against Tukhaev (Game 6) I mention possibilities for White on the 14th move; he can choose from three different queen moves and it is really not an easy choice – after my analysis, it is still hard to say which move is the best. Personally, I believe in Black's position, and also I think that in a practical game this is easier to play as Black.

Conclusion

Overall, the line with the immediate 4...♘f6 and 5...♗g4 is still new and fresh. I believe it is an interesting choice, and together with Eljanov's move 7...♗d7, sacrificing a pawn with 7...♗h5 also deserves serious attention. I don't think that the lines with ♘e2 can worry Black much; probably taking the pawn is critical. I hope we will soon have more games with this line.

Fabiano Caruana   **1**
Shiyam Thavandiran
PRO League rapid 2019 (3)
**1.e4 c6 2.d4 d5 3.exd5 cxd5
4.♗d3 ♘f6 5.c3 ♗g4 6.♘e2 ♘c6**

7.0-0 7.♕b3 e5!? (a very interesting sacrifice. 7...♗xe2 is of course possible and leading to a typical positions for this line) 8.♕xb7 (8.dxe5 doesn't pose Black problems: 8...♘xe5 9.♗b5+ ♘d7=) 8...♗d7 9.♗f5 (the only move; 9.♕a6 ♖b8 10.♗c2 ♗d6 and Black has very strong compensation) 9...♗xf5 10.♕xc6+ ♗d7 11.♕a6 and Black has good compensation after for example 11...e4. **7...e6** 7...♕c7 is not a very accurate move in view of the recent 8.♕e1; 7...♕d7!? (Black is trying to exchange bishops) 8.♕b3 (8.♕c2 ♖c8; 8.h3 ♗f5) 8...♗h5 9.♘f4 ♗g6 10.♘xg6 hxg6 11.♘d2 e6 12.♘f3 ♗d6 13.♖e1 and as usual White is a bit better in this type of position. **8.♕b3 ♕d7** 8...♗xe2 9.♗xe2 ♖b8 10.♘d2; 8...♖b8, connected with the idea to play ...♘h5 after White's ♘g3, is not working well: 9.♘g3 ♗d6 (9...♘h5 10.♖e1 ♘xg3 11.hxg3 ♗h5 12.♗f4 (with tempo) 12...♗d6 13.♕xd5+–) 10.♖e1 0-0 11.h3 ♗h5 12.♘xh5±) **9.♘f4** 9.♘g3!? (a typical way to exchange the knight for the bishop) 9...♘h5!? (Black is trying to exchange the g3-knight for his f6-knight instead of allowing White to get the two-bishops advantage by allowing White to exchange his light-squared bishop; 9...h5 10.f3 h4 11.fxg4 hxg3 12.h3 and White is better in this unusual position; 9...♗d6 10.♖e1 0-0 11.♗g5! (11.h3? ♘xg3 12.fxg3 ♗f5 and Black gets

the important e4-square) 11...♘h5 12.h3 ♗f5 13.♘xf5 exf5 14.♘d2 (after 14.♕d1 ♖fe8 15.♖xe8+ ♖xe8 16.♘d2 ♘f4 Black has good chances to equalize, as doubled pawns are not such an important weakness in this position) 14...♘f4 15.♗xf4 ♘xf4 16.♗f1 – Black doesn't equalize fully here) 10.h3 (10.♖e1 ♘xg3 11.hxg3 ♗e7 and after this Black will play ... ♗g4-h5-g6 and have a good position) 10...♘xg3 11.fxg3 ♗h5∞ – Black looks fine. **9...♗d6** 9...g6!?; I like this very unusual idea. Black has counterchances based on the idea of ...h7-h5, ...♗d6 and ...♗f5. White cannot really attack the bishop when it will be on f5: 10.f3 ♗f5 11.♕c2 (11.♗e2?! ♗d6; the bishop on f5 is in fact strong now) 11...♗d6 with an unclear position in which I like Black's chances. **10.h3** 10.f3 ♗h5 11.♘xh5 ♘xh5 12.f4 f5 and then Black will transfer his knight to e4 via f6. **10...♗h5** This is a lazy move. Much more interesting was 10...g5. Black has this very surprising move here which is giving him good counterplay, e.g. 11.hxg4 gxf4 12.g5 ♘g4 13.♕d1 f5 with a messy position. **11.♘xh5 ♘xh5 12.♖e1±** White tends to be slightly better after exchanging knight for bishop. **12...0-0 13.♕d1** Another typical idea which we will see many times in this line. On b3 the queen is no longer doing anything. **13...♘f4** 13...g6 14.♘d2 ♗f4 15.♗e2±. **14.♗c2 ♖ae8 15.h4** An interesting move, preparing g2-g3. 15.♘d2 e5 (without this move Black is worse; 15...♕c7 16.♘f3) 16.dxe5 ♘xe5 17.♗f1 ♘eg6 18.♗xg6 hxg6 19.♗xf4 ♗xf4 20.♕d3 and White is slightly better. 15.♗e3 was another solid move. **15...e5** I don't like the structure arising from this move for Black. 15...g6 16.g3 (16.♕f3 ♕c7) 16...♘h5 17.♗h6±; 15...f5 16.♗xf4 (16.♘d2?! e5 17.dxe5 ♘xe5↑) 16...♗xf4 17.♘d2±; 15...♕d8!? is an interesting move with the idea to meet 16.g3 with the unexpected 16...e5! 17.gxf4 exd4≅. **16.♗xf4 exf4 17.♖xe8 ♖xe8 18.♘d2 ♕e7?** Just blundering a pawn; 18...g6±. **19.♕h5 g6 20.♕xd5 ♕xh4 21.♗b3**

21.♕xd6 ♖e2 22.♘e4 ♖xc2 23.♖e1+–. **21...♖e7** 21...♖e6 22.♘f3; 21...♕e7±. **22.♕xd6 ♖e2 23.g3 fxg3 24.♘f3 gxf2+ 25.♔f1+– ♕e4 26.♕f6 ♘d8 27.♕xd8+ ♔g7 28.♕d5 ♕d3 29.♕xf7+ ♔h6 30.♗c4 ♖e1+ 31.♔xf2 ♕e3+ 32.♔g2 ♖xa1 33.♕f8+ ♔h5 34.♕g7 h6 35.♕xb7 ♖b1 36.♕d5+ ♔g4 37.♕d7+ ♔f4 38.♕f7+ 1-0**

Arghyadip Das   **2**
Teja Sanka Ravi
Yogyakarta 2019 (5)
**1.e4 c6 2.d4 d5 3.exd5 cxd5
4.♗d3 ♘f6 5.c3 ♗g4 6.♕b3 ♕c7
7.♘e2**

7...♗xe2 Black takes the knight immediately, not allowing 8.♗f4. 7...♘c6 8.♗f4 ♕d7 9.♘g3 (9.♘d2 e6 10.0-0 ♗h5) 9...♗h5! (Black must remember this typical idea to meet ♘g3 with ...♗h5) 10.♗e3 e6 11.f3 ♘xg3 12.hxg3 ♗f5 looks okay for Black. **8.♗xe2** 8.♗f4, without the insertion of h3 ♗h5 (see the notes to Game 5), is not working due to 8...♗xf4 9.♕xb7 ♗g4!. **8...♘c6** 8...e6 is more in the spirit of the line, fighting against ♗f4: 9.0-0 (9.♘a3 a6 10.♗f4!? (still) 10...♕xf4 11.♕xb7 ♗xa3 12.bxa3 ♘e4 13.0-0 0-0 14.♕xa8 ♘xc3 15.♗xa6 with a really messy position) 9...♗d6 10.g3 ♘c6 11.♘d2 h5!? (going for active play; 11...0-0 12.♘f3 (12.♗d3?! e5) 12...♘e4⇄) 12.♘f3 h4 is very much possible, e.g. 13.♘xh4 0-0-0-0∞ and Black will use the h-file for an attack. **9.♘a3!? e6** I like 9...♖c8!?, forcing White to play g2-g3 in case he wants to put his bishop on f4

10.g3 e6 11.♗f4 ♕d7. **10.♗f4 ♕d7 11.0-0 ♗e7** 11...a6 and then ...b7-b5 is also possible. **12.♘b1** White decides that on a3 the knight has no future, which is indeed the case. **12...0-0 13.♕d2 ♗d6 14.♗xd6** 14.♗g5 ♕c7 (14...♖e8) 15.g3 ♘d7 16.♗e3 f5!?∞ is a typical idea for Black to get counterchances in such positions. **14...♕xd6=** This is a very typical position. I believe that when the dark-squared bishops are exchanged the position is equal. **15.♖fe1 ♖ab8 16.a4 ♕c7 17.♕d1 a6** 17...e5 18.dxe5 ♘xe5 19.♘f3 ♖fe8 20.♗b5 ♘xf3+ 21.♕xf3 ♖e5 – this is very close to equal, but I understand that Black didn't want to play with the isolated d5-pawn. **18.♗f1 ♖fc8 19.♖c1 ♘a5** It's not easy to suggest an active plan for Black. ...e6-e5 is possible of course, but this knight move, provoking b2-b4, looks fine too. 19...b5 20.b4 is not very good for Black; 19...♕b6!? 20.♖b1 (20. b4 a5). **20.b4 ♘c6** Black lost time but at least now the c3-pawn is weak; 20...♘c4 21.♗xc4 dxc4 22.a5±. **21.♘b3** I think 21.a5 is White's only chance for an advantage. He doesn't have to allow ...a7-a5: 21... e5 22.dxe5 ♘xe5 23.♘f3±. **21...♖e8** It's hard to understand this useless move. After 21...a5!? 22.b5 ♘e7 Black is very solid. A plan can be to play ...b7-b6 and then transfer the knight from e7 to d6, slowly improving the position. Black is not worse at all. **22.g3** 22.♘c5 a5 23.♕d2 ♖ec8; 22.a5!?. **22...♖a8** This was also not necessary at all; 22...a5. **23.f4** I think 23.a5!? was better, when White has some pressure. **23...b6** Finally Black stops a4-a5. **24.♘d2 ♖ed8 25.♗d3 ♘e7 26.♕e2 a5 27.b5 ♖ac8 28.♘f3 ♘d6 29.♕b2 ♖c7 30.♘e5 ♖dc8 31.♖c2 ♕d8** and the players decided that it was hard for both sides to improve their position, so... **½-½**

Rameshbabu Praggnanandhaa 3
Le Quang Liem
Xingtai 2019 (3)

1.e4 c6 2.d4 d5 3.exd5 cxd5 4.♗d3 ♘f6 5.c3 ♗g4 6.♕b3 ♕c7 7.♗g5 Just a move to have a game.

7...e6 8.♘d2 ♘c6 9.♘gf3 ♗h5 9...♗d6 is also fine. **10.♗h4** 10.♗f4, intending 10...♕xf4? 11.♗xb7, doesn't give anything after 10...♗d6. **10...♗g6 11.♗g3 ♗d6=** Black has equalized comfortably. **12.♕c2 ♖c8 13.0-0 ♗xg3** 13...0-0 was of course possible, but Black wants to keep the possibility to push his h-pawn in case of an exchange on g3. **14.hxg3** Now the manoeuvring phase of the game starts, when it's hard for both opponents to create activity.

14...♔f8 14...0-0 is of course also fine. Black is trying to create some imbalance. **15.a3 ♗xd3 16.♕xd3 g6 17.♕e3 ♗g7 18.a4 ♘d7** This move looks strange, the knight has no business on d7; 18...♘g4 19.♕f4 ♕xf4 20.gxf4 h6 and Black can hope to play ...f7-f6 and ... g6-g5 and open the h-file; 18...♘e7 19.♘e5 h5 20.♕f4 ♘f5 with the idea of ...♗g4. **19.♖fe1 h6 20.♘b3 ♗e7 21.a5 ♘f5** It's risky to prevent a queen swap with 21...g5 in view of 22.♘e5. **22.♕f4** 22.♕e2 h5. **22...♗xf4 23.gxf4 ♖c7 24.♘c1** Good regrouping. **24...♘f6 25.♘d2 g5 26.fxg5** 26.♘d3 g4. **26...hxg5** Now it's Black who is pressing but there is nothing real. **27.♘d3 ♖cc8** 27...♘g4 can be met by 28.g3 and 29.f3. **28.g3** Black is not in time to exploit the open h-file. **28...♘g4** 28...♖h6 29.♔g2 ♖ch8 30.♖h1 ♖xh1 31.♖xh1 ♖xh1 32.♔xh1=. **29.♘f3 ♖h5 30.♔g2 ♖ch8 31.♖h1 ♖xh1** 31...♘ge3+ 32.fxe3 ♘xe3+ 33.♔f2 ♘g4+= (33...♖xh1 34.♖xh1 ♖xh1 35.♔xe3 is also approximately equal, but it can be risky for Black). **32.♖xh1 ♖xh1 33.♔xh1** The resulting knight ending is very drawish. **33...f6 34.♔g2 ♘d6** Black is still trying to push a bit. **35.♘d2 ♔f7 36.♘c5 ♘h6**

37.♔f3 ♗e7 38.♔e2 ♘hf7 39.♔d3 ♘d8 40.c4 White tries to exchange some pawns. This was not necessary: 40.b4 ♘c6 41.♗f1=; 40.f3. **40...♘c6 41.cxd5 ♘b4+ 42.♔e2** 42.♔c3 ♘xd5+ 43.♔d3=. **42...♘xd5** 42... exd5!?∓ – Black's knights are slighly more active but it's hard to imagine any result other than a draw. **43.♘de4 b6 44.axb6 axb6 45.♘xd6 ♔xd6 46.♘c4+ ♔c6 47.♔d3 ♔b5 48.b3 ♘b4 49.♘c2 g4 50.♘d6 ♘e7 51.♘e8 ♘c6?!** 51...♘d5=. It was better to agree the draw here as there is nothing real. **52.d5** Now it is again White who is slightly pressing. **52...♘d4+ 53.♔d3 ♘xb3 54.dxe6 ♘c5+ 55.♔c2** 55.♔d2 ♘xe6 56.♔xf6 ♔c4 57.♘xg4 ♔d4** and White is a pawn up but still this position is drawish. **55...♘xe6 56.♘xf6 ♔c4 57.♘xg4 ♔d4 58.♔b3 ♔e4 59.♘h2 ♔d3 60.♔b4 ♔e2 61.f4 ♔f2 62.♔b5 ♔xg3 63.♔xb6 ♔xf4 ½-½**

Surya Shekhar Ganguly 4
Pavel Eljanov
Wijk aan Zee B 2020 (12)

1.e4 c6 2.d4 d5 3.exd5 cxd5 4.♗d3 ♘f6 5.c3 ♗g4 6.♕b3 ♕c7 7.h3 ♗d7

8.♘f3 This set-up looks more logical to me than the one involving 8.♘e2 ♘c6 9.♗f4 e5 (perfectly fine) 10.dxe5 ♘xe5 11.♗b5 ♗d6 (11...0-0-0 (Santos Ruiz-Rozum, Moscow rapid 2019) 12.♗xd7+ ♘fxd7 13.♕c2 (trying to be smart; 13.0-0 allows 13...g5!?↑ 14.♗xg5? ♘f3+) 13...♗d6 14.♘d2 ♖he8 15.0-0. Black still has to justify his decision to castle

queenside) 12.♗xd7+ ♕xd7 13.0-0 0-0 14.♘d2 ♖fe8 – Black has no real problems here. **8...e6 9.0-0 ♗d6 10.♖e1 ♗c6!?** It is possible of course to play 10...0-0 11.♕d1 ♘c6 but the bishop is passive on d7. From c6 it can support the move ...♘f6-e4. **11.♕d1** An interesting regrouping. The queen has nothing to do on b3 any longer. 11.♗g5 ♘bd7 12.♘bd2 ♘h5; 11.♘e5 ♘bd7 12.♗f4 ♘h5 (12...♘e4 13.♘a3±) 13.♗h2 f6 14.♘f3 ♗xh2+ 15.♘xh2 ♘f4 16.♗f1 e5 17.♘a3 0-0∞ and Black has active play. **11...♘bd7 12.♕e2 0-0** 12...♘e4?! 13.c4 seems premature. **13.♘bd2** 13.♘e5 ♗xe5 (of course Black cannot allow White's knight to stay on e5. He must create play before White is fully developed) 14.dxe5 ♘e4 15.f3 ♘xe5!? (a very enterprising piece sacrifice) 16.fxe4 (16.♗f4 ♕b6+ 17.♗e3 ♕c7 can lead to a draw, e.g. 18.fxe4 dxe4 19.♗c2 ♘f3+! 20.gxf3 ♕g3+ 21.♔h1 exf3 22.♕f2 ♕xh3+ 23.♔g1 ♕g4+ is also an interesting draw) 16...♘xd3 17.♕xd3 dxe4♙ and Black will push the f-pawn next. **13...♘h5** This move is quite risky but it's the only real try for Black to create some play. **14.♗xh7+** Very interesting and tempting. Other moves offer no advantage: 14.♘b3 ♘f4=; 14.♘g5 ♘hf6. **14...♔xh7 15.♘g5+ ♔g6** 15...♔h6?! was probably worse in view of 16.♘df3 ♘f4 (16...♗f4 17.♗xf4 ♕xf4 18.g3 ♕f5 (18...♕xg3 19.fxg3 ♕xg3+ 20.♔h1+−) 19.♕e3) 17.♕e3 (17.♕d2 g6 18.g3 ♔g7 19.gxf4 ♖h8; 17.♕c2 g6 18.g3 ♔g7 19.♗xf4 ♗xf4 20.gxf4 ♕xf4 21.♖xe6 ♖ae8♙) 17...g6 18.g3 ♔g7 19.gxf4↑ ♖ae8 (19...♖h8? 20.♘xf7 – hence 17.♕e3) 20.f5 gxf5 21.♘e5 ♗xe5 22.dxe5 f6 23.exf6+ ♖xf6 24.♕d4. **16.♘df3 ♘f4** Black must be very careful; 16...♗f4 17.g3 (17.♗xf4 ♘xf4 18.♕d2 ♔f6∞ 19.♕e3 ♔e7; 17.h4!? ♖xc1 18.♖axc1 ♕f4 19.g3 ♕g4 20.♕d2!→; 20.♕d3+ ♕f5 21.♕d1 ♕g4=; 17.g4 ♘hf6 18.♕c2+ ♘e4 19.♘xe4 dxe4 20.♖xe4 ♗xe4 21.♕xe4+ f5 22.♘h4+ ♔f6!? (22...♔h7 23.♗xf4

fxe4 24.♗xc7) 23.gxf5 (23.♗xf4 fxe4 24.♗xc7 (24.g5+ ♔f7 25.♗xc7 ♖h8 26.♗g3 ♖h5∓) 24...♖h8 (that's why Black played 22...♔f6) 25.♗g3 g5 26.♘g2 ♖xh3 27.♘e3∓) 23...♖h2+ 24.♔h1 ♖ae8 25.fxe6 ♖xe6 26.♕g6+ ♔e7 27.♗g5+ f6 with a messy position; 17.♗d2!? ♖ae8 18.♖ac1) 17...♗xc1 18.♖axc1 ♘hf6 19.♕e3 (19.c4 ♕a5) 19...♘e4 20.c4→. **17.♕c2+** Strangely enough it seems like White doesn't have a decisive blow. 17.♕d2 ♘f6 18.g3 ♘g6 19.♕d3 (19.♕e3 ♖ae8∞) 19...♖ae8 with a very messy position; 17.♗xf4? ♗xf4 18.h4 ♖ae8; 17.♕e3 ♖ae8 offers nothing for White. **17...♘f6 18.g3 ♘g6 19.♘xf7** 19.a4; 19.b4 – moves like this are too deep for a practical game; 19.♕e2 ♖ae8. **19...♔xf7 20.♘g5+ ♔g8 21.♕xg6 ♘f6 22.♘xe6 ♕d7** Black has a choice: 22...♖ae8 was also possible, e.g. 23.♗h6 ♖xe6 (23...♔f7 24.♕g7+ ♕xg7 25.♗xg7 ♖f7 26.♗xf6 ♖xf6 27.♘g5∞. White has 4 pawns for a piece but Black's bishops are strong. Probably the position is dynamically balanced) 24.♖xe6 ♘e4 and both sides have their chances. **23.♗h6** 23.♗g5 ♘e4. **23...♘e4! 24.♖xe4!** 24.♗xg7?! ♕f7 25.♕xf7+ ♖xf7 and Black is better. **24...dxe4 25.♘g5 ♖f7!** The only move. **26.♕h7+** 26.♘xf7 ♕xf7 27.♕xd6 gxh6 28.♕xh6∞ and probably the game will end in perpetual check. **26...♔f8 27.♘xf7 ♕xf7** Now, after a well-played game, mistakes from both sides start to happen.

28.d5? 28.♕h8+ ♕g8 29.♗xg7+ ♔e7 (29...♔f7 30.♕h6 ♖d8 with a balanced position) 30.♕xg8 ♖xg8 31.♗h6 ♗b5∓ – I slightly prefer

Black here but White should hold the draw. **28...♕xd5** 28...♗xd5 was simple and good: 29.♕h8+ ♕g8 30.♗xg7+ ♔e7∓. **29.♕xg7+ ♔e8 30.♕g6+?** 30.c4! is really not an easy move to make, its idea is to disturb Black's piece coordination and to allow the rook to enter the game from the d1-square, e.g. 30...♕xc4 (30...♕f5 31.♖d1 e3 (31...♗f8 32.♕g8! ♔f7 33.♕g5 with a messy and dynamically balanced position) 32.♗xe3 ♕e4 33.♕h8+=) 31.♕h8+ ♔d7 32.♕g7+ ♔c8 (32...♔e8=) 33.♖c1 ♕e6 34.♗e3♙ (White has two pawns and Black's king is weak) 34...♔e7 35.♕h8+ ♔f8 36.♕h7 ♗e7 37.♗f4=; 30.♕h8+ ♔d7 31.♕xa8 e3−+. **30...♔d7 31.♕g7+ ♔e8 32.♕g6+ ♔d7 33.♕g7+ ♗e7** Black correctly decides to play on. 33...♔c8 was also good, e.g. 34.c4 ♕f5. **34.c4 ♕f5 35.b4?** 35.♖d1+ ♔e6 36.♗f4 would have given more practical chances. **35...♔e6?!** 35...e3−+. **36.♖d1** 36.g4 ♕f6∓. **36...♗f6 37.♖d6+** 37.g4 has to be played, but after 37...♕xg4 38.hxg4 ♗a4 White doesn't really have any hope of survival. **37...♔xd6** Now it's over. **38.♕f7 ♗d7 39.♗f4+ ♔c6 40.b5+ ♔c5 0-1**

The pawn sacrifice 7.h3 ♗h5

Pouya Idani 5
Aryan Gholami
Bushehr ch-IRI 2019 (1)
1.e4 c6 2.d4 d5 3.exd5 cxd5 4.♗d3 ♘f6 5.c3 ♗g4 6.♕b3 ♕c7 7.h3 ♗h5 8.♘e2

8...♗xe2 8...♘c6 is another, probably more accurate move:

9.♗f4 ♕d7 10.0-0 e6 11.♖e1 ♗e7 (11...♗g6!?= 12.♖c1 ♗d6, exchanging both bishops with equality; 12...♘e4 is also interesting; Black will either exchange the knight or transfer it to the better square d6) 12.♘d2 0-0 13.♗g3 ♗d6 14.♘f4 ♖ab8 (14...♗g6 15.♘xg6 hxg6=) 15.a4 (a draw was agreed in Santos Ruiz-Eljanov, France tt 2019. 15.♘xh5 was more logical, e.g. 15...♘xh5 16.♗xd6 ♕xd6 17.♘f3 ♘f6 (such positions are typical for this line) 18.♕d1 ♕c7 19.♕e2 and White is very slightly better.

9.♗xe2 The surprising 9.♗f4! improves White's position if Black doesn't take the bishop: 9...♕d7 (9...♕xf4 leads to complications which are favourable for White after accurate play: 10.♕xb7 e6 11.♗xe2 ♘fd7 (11...♘e4 12.♗f1) 12.♗b5 (12.g3 ♕d6 13.♕xa8 ♕c7 14.♗a6 ♕b6 15.♗c8 ♗d8 16.♕b7 ♕xb7 17.♗xb7 ♗c7 18.♗xd5 exd5 19.♘d2 and I prefer White's position) 12...♕e4+ (12...♗e7 13.a4) 13.♔d1 ♕xg2 14.♖f1 ♕f3+ 15.♔c2 ♕f5+ 16.♔b3±) 10.♗xe2 ♘c6 11.♘d2±. **9...e6 10.♘a3** 10.♗e3 is another possibility, e.g. 10...♗d6 11.♘d2 ♘c6 12.g3 0-0 and Black is fine. **10...a6** Black has a nice position. **11.0-0 ♗d6 12.c4!?** White is trying to be creative but this doesn't bother Black at all. White can continue in a normal way, let's say 12.♗e3, but the knight on a3 is misplaced then. **12...♘c6 13.c5 ♗e7 14.♗e3 0-0 15.♘c2 ♘e4 16.♗d3 ♖ad8** 16...f5 and Black has the easier game. **17.♖ad1 ♗h4** An interesting move; Black is becoming active. Of course 17...f7-f5 was also possible. **18.♗xe4?!** 18.♘e1 f5 19.♘f3 ♗f6 – I prefer Black's position; his next plan can be ...♔h8, ...♖g8 and ...g7-g5. **18...dxe4 19.♖fe1 ♗f6** 19...♖d5∓ 20.♖c1 ♗e7 – Black is preparing to take on c5 if White takes on e4. **20.♕c4 ♖d5 21.♗c1 b5?!** Black is playing for compensation but it was possible for him to press without taking any risk: 21...♘xd4!? 22.♘xd4 ♖fd8 23.♗e3 ♕d7 24.♕e2 e5 (24...♖xd4

25.♖xd4 ♖xd4 26.♗xd4 ♕xd4 27.♕xe4 ♕xb2 28.♖b1=) 25.c6! (this strong intermediate move equalizes for White) 25...bxc6 26.♗xc6 ♕xc6 27.♖xd5 ♕xd5 28.b3 ♕d3 29.♗c5 ♖d5 30.b4=; 21...♖fd8!? (this was probably the most accurate move) 22.♖xe4 ♕d7. **22.cxb6 ♕xb6 23.♖xe4 ♖fd8 24.♗e3 h6** 24...♖c8 25.b3 ♗e7 26.♕d3 ♗f5⩲. **25.♖d3 ♕b5?!** 25...♘a5 26.♕c3 ♕b7⩲; 25...♘e7 was the logical move, and then depending on circumstances Black can play ...♘f5 or move the rook from d5 and play ...♘d5. **26.♖c3 ♗e7 27.♕xb5 ♖xb5 28.b3 ♘f5 29.♗c6** Now White is pressing, Black must be very precise to prove compensation for the pawn. **29...a5 30.g4 ♘d6** 30...♘xe3 31.fxe3 a4 32.b4 ♖bb8 33.♔f2 ♖dc8 34.♖c5! (preparing for a strong exchange sacrifice and the only way to fight for an advantage) 34...♗e7 35.a3 ♗xc5 36.dxc5♕ and White has the much better endgame. **31.♖f4 ♖d5 32.♔g2 ♕b5 33.♖c5 ♗e7 34.♖c4** 34.♖xd5 ♖xd5 35.a4 was another good possibility. **34...♘d6 35.♖a4** The rook has nothing to do on a4. 35.♖c7! and Black doesn't have enough for the pawn. **35...♖c8** It seems both players missed the strong knight move 35...♘c8 36.♖c4 ♘b6 and the knight is on its way to occupy the nice d5-square. **36.♘a3** Now again White is clearly better. **36...g5 37.♖f3 ♘e4 38.♖c4 ♗d8 39.♘e5 ♘d6**

40.♗d2?! It was not necessary to allow Black's rook to come to c2. 40.♘c4!±. **40...♖c2?!** 40...f6! 41.♘c4 (41.♘d3 ♖c2∞ – only now, after pushing White's knight back) 41...♘xc4 42.bxc4 ♖xd4 43.♗xa5 ♖a8=. **41.♗e1 ♗b6** Again,

41...f6 was clearly the best move. **42.♖c3** Now White is much better. **42...♖e2 43.♘c6 ♔f8 44.♔f1 ♖b2 45.♖d3** Black's rook can be trapped: 45.♖c1 ♘e4 46.♘e5+−. **45...♖b1 46.♔e2** 46.b4 axb4 47.♖xb4 ♖xb4 48.♗xb4+. **46...♖c1 47.♘e5 ♔e8 48.♘c4 ♘xc4 49.♖xc4 ♖a1 50.♖a4 ♔d7 51.♗c3** 51.♖d1, exchanging the active rook on a1, seems best. Black cannot really take the pawn on d4 with a piece as the important a5-pawn is weak: 51...♖xd1 52.♔xd1 e5 53.♔c2 exd4 54.♔d3±. **51...♖c1 52.♗d2 ♖a1 53.♖f3 f5 54.gxf5 exf5 55.♖e3** 55.h4±. **55...♔d6 56.♖e8 ♖xd4 57.♖d8+ ♗xd8 58.♗xd4+ ♔e7= 59.♖a4 ♖h1 60.♗xa5 ♖xh3** Suddenly it becomes sharp, but within the realms of equality. **61.♗b4+ ♔d7 62.♖a7+ ♔c6 63.♗d2** 63.♗a5=. **63...f4 64.♖f7 h5 65.♗b4 h4 66.♗e7 f3+ 67.♔e3 ♗b6+ 68.♔e4 g4** Now it looks very dangerous for White. **69.♖f6+!** The only move. **69...♔b7 70.♖f7 ♔c6** 70...♔c8 71.♗d5! ♖h1 72.♗g5! – Black's king cannot escape so White is able to make a draw. **71.♖f6+ ♔b7 72.♖f7 ♔c6 ½-½**

Adam Tukhaev   **6**
Mikheil Mchedlishvili
Turkey tt 2018 (3)
1.e4 c6 2.d4 d5 3.exd5 cxd5 4.♗d3 ♘f6 5.c3 ♗g4 6.♕b3 ♕c7 7.h3 ♗h5 8.g4 ♗g6 9.♗xg6 hxg6 10.g5 ♘fd7 11.♕xd5

11...e5 11...♘c6 is also possible: 12.♘f3 e5 13.dxe5? 0-0-0! (this is surprisingly already very bad for White; Black will take on e5 next. 13...♘dxe5 Safarli-Postny, Moscow Wch rapid 2019)

14.♕xf7 ♘cxe5 15.♘xe5 ♕xe5+ 16.♗e3 ♕e4. **12.♘e2** 12.♗e3 ♘c6 (12...exd4) 13.♕d2 0-0-0!? (I like this move, sacrificing a second pawn for rapid development; 13...exd4 14.♕e4+ ♗e7 15.cxd4 ♘b6♕ (this is a common position in this line. It becomes clear that Black has sacrificed a pawn for positional compensation, and for the d5-square, where the knight will be very strong) 15...♔f8 16.♘gf3± ; 16.♘e2 ♖e8) 16.♖c1 ♕d7; 13...♘b6 14.♕e4 0-0-0 15.♘gf3 f5 16.gxf6 gxf6 17.dxe5 f5 18.♗xb6 ♕xb6 19.♕c4 ♔b8 20.0-0-0 ♕xf2 21.♖h2±) 14.♕xf7 exd4 15.cxd4 ♗b4 (with the idea to play ...♖hf8 and then ...♘b6-d5; on d5 the knight will be very strong) 16.♘e2 (16.♖c1 ♖hf8 17.♕xg6 ♕a5∞) 16...♖hf8 17.♕b3 ♘b6 18.♖c1 ♔b8 and Black has positional compensation for two pawns; 12.♘f3 ♘c6 13.♗e3 0-0-0 14.♕xf7 exd4 15.♘xd4 ♘ce5 16.♕e6 ♗c5♕ – I like Black's chances here despite the fact that he is two pawns down. **12...♘c6 13.♗e3**

13...♘b6 This is probably the main move, but 13...exd4 deserves serious attention as well. 13...0-0-0? 14.♕xf7 exd4 15.cxd4; with 13...exd4!? Black is playing for rapid development: 14.cxd4 (14.♕e4+ ♗e5 15.♕xe5+ ♘dxe5 16.cxd4 ♘c4 and Black has enough compensation; 14.♘xd4 0-0-0 15.♘b5 ♕e5 16.♕xe5 ♘dxe5∞) 14...♗b4+ (14...♘b6 15.♕e4+ ♗e7 16.♘bc3 ♕xe4 17.♘xe4 ♘b4 18.♔f1 ♘6d5 and Black has positional compensation, but probably not quite enough for a pawn) 15.♘bc3 ♘b6 (with 15...0-0!? Black can play for activity: 16.0-0-0 ♘b6 17.♕b3

♗xc3 18.♘xc3 ♘a5 19.♕b4 ♘d5 20.♕c5 ♕xc5 21.dxc5 ♘xc3 22.bxc3 ♘c4 and Black has good chances for a draw) 16.♕b3 (16.♕e4+ ♘e7) 16...0-0-0 17.0-0-0 ♗xc3 18.♘xc3 ♘a5♕ – probably this will transpose to some bishop against knight endgame with a pawn up for White but without any realistic winning chances. **14.♕e4** The most natural move, and the one I was expecting.

A) Probably 14.♕f3!? (with the idea, just like ♕g2, to avoid ...f7-f5 for now) is the best chance for an advantage:

A1) With 14...0-0-0!? Black is trying to hide the king on the queenside and then open the position: 15.♘d2 ♔b8 (15...exd4 16.♘xd4 ♘xd4 17.♗xd4 ♖h4 (17...♘c5 18.♗xc5 ♕xc5 19.0-0-0± and Black didn't have enough compensation in Chigaev-Rozum, Moscow Wch rapid 2019) 18.♕g3 ♖e8+ 19.♔d1 ♖f4 20.♔c2 ♗d6 21.♗e3±) 16.♘e4 f5 (a typical move for this line, creating counterplay; 16...♖h4 17.0-0-0 ♘d5 18.♔b1 ♗e7 19.♖hg1± and White consolidates) 17.gxf6 gxf6 18.0-0-0 f5 19.♘g5 ♘c4 20.♘e6 ♕b6 (20...♕a5 is a very interesting move, e.g. 21.♔b1 ♖d6 22.♘xf8 ♖xf8. This position is very unclear. White is a pawn up but with his strong knight on c4 Black has counterchances) 21.b3 ♗a3+ (21...♘a6!? 22.♔b1 ♘a3+ with a very messy position) 22.♔b1 ♖de8 23.♘c5±; 23.d5 ♘xe3 24.♕xe3 ♕xe3 25.fxe3 ♖d8±;

A2) Probably 14...exd4 is not enough for equality: 15.♘xd4 ♘c4 16.♘d2 ♘xb2 (16...♘xd2 17.♔xd2 ♖d8 18.♖ad1) 17.♕e4+ ♘e5 18.♖b1 ♕xe4 19.♘xe4 ♘c4 20.♖xb7 ♘6a5 21.♖b5±;

A3) 14...♖d8 15.♘d2 ♗e7 and now:

A31) 16.♘e4 ♖h4 (the rook can be useful on the 4th rank) 17.0-0-0 exd4 (17...♘c4 deserves serious attention: 18.♔b1 ♕b6 19.b3 ♘a3+ 20.♔b2 (20.♔c1 ♕b5∞) 20...♕b5 21.d5 ♘a5. The position is really messy. Black's king is stuck in the centre but Black has very active

pieces trying to attack White's king. Play could continue 22.♗c1 ♔f8 23.d6 ♘3c4+ 24.♔c2 ♘xd6 25.♘xd6 ♖xd6 26.♖xd6 ♗xd6 27.♖d1 ♗c7 28.c4 ♕c6 – the smoke has cleared and the position is approximately equal) 18.♗f4 (18.♗xd4 ♔f8 19.♗xb6 (19.♔b1 ♘c4 20.b3 ♘a3+ 21.♔b2 ♕a5∞) 19...♕xb6 and I think Black has full compensation here; 18.♘xd4 ♘e5 19.♕g2 ♘ec4∞ – the knight is very strong on c4) 18...♘c8 19.♕g3 ♕e6! 20.♕xh4 (20.♘d6+ ♖xd6 21.♗xd6 ♖e4 22.♗xe7 ♖xe2♕) 20...♕xa2 (Black has sacrificed a rook to get close to White's king) 21.♔d2 ♘c4+ 22.♔e1 ♘xb2∞ and Black has a strong attack;

A32) 16.h4 ♘d5 17.♘e4 (maybe 17.0-0-0!? was the best chance for an advantage, e.g. 17...♘xe3 18.fxe3 exd4 19.exd4 ♘xd4 20.♘xd4 ♖xd4 21.♖df1 0-0 22.♕b3 ♖d6± – material is equal but Black's king's position may be endangered; 17.a3 is not critical, e.g. 17...0-0 18.♕h3 exd4 and Black has full compensation: 19.cxd4 ♘de8=) 17...♘a5 18.♔f1 (18.a3 exd4 19.♗xd4 0-0 20.0-0-0 ♗xa3 with a mess) 18...♘b5 19.b3 exd4 20.♗xd4 ♘xd4 21.cxd4 f6∞.

B) 14.♕g2!? is probably too deep: 14...♖d8 (here 14...♘c4!? is better than after ♕f3: 15.♘d2 (15.b3 exd4 16.♗xd4 ♘d6∞ and Black will transfer his knight to the nice f5-square; 16...♘4e5) 15...♘xb2 (15...♘xd2 16.♗xd2 exd4 looks okay; Black will always have positional compensation for the pawn) 16.♖b1 ♗a3 17.♕d5 exd4 18.cxd4 ♘b4∞; 14...0-0-0 is the usual move, e.g. 15.♘d2 ♔b8∞) 15.♘d2 ♗e7 (15...exd4 is premature, e.g. 16.♘xd4 ♘xd4 17.♗xd4 ♖xd4 18.cxd4 ♗b4 19.a3 ♗xd2+ 20.♔xd2 0-0 21.♖he1±) 16.h4 (16.♘e4 ♖h4 (16...♘c4 17.d5 ♘xe3 18.fxe3 ♖xd5 19.♘f6+ ♗xf6 20.♕xd5 ♗xg5 21.0-0-0 and with an exchange up White's position looks preferable) 17.f3 exd4 18.♗xd4 (18.♗f2 ♖xe4 19.fxe4 d3 20.♘d4 d2+ is good for Black) 18...♘xd4 19.♘xd4 ♘c4 (19...♕f4 is a solid positional

move, the queen is strong on f4: 20.♔f2 ♖d5 21.♖ae1 ♘f8∞) 20.♕e2 ♖xe4 (Black has very good compensation for the exchange) 21.fxe4 ♗xg5; 21...♗a3) 16...♘d5 17.♕e4 exd4 18.♘xd4 (18.cxd4 0-0) 18...0-0 and Black has good compensation. **14...0-0-0** Probably this is the best move. **15.♘d2 f5!** This is the idea I wanted to try. 15...exd4 16.♘xd4 ♘xd4 17.♗xd4 ♗c5 18.♕g4+ (0-1 (29) Predojevic-Postny, Internet blitz 2020) 18...♖d7 19.0-0 ♗xd4 20.cxd4 ♔b8 21.♖ac1 ♖d8 22.♘f3±. **16.gxf6 gxf6 17.♕xg6** Very principled, but also a risky move. 17.dxe5 was the safer choice, e.g. 17...f5 18.♕g2 ♘xe5 19.0-0-0 (before the game I was unsure about this position) 19...♗c5!? 20.♔f4 (20.♔b1 ♗xe3 21.fxe3 ♘d3♕) 20...♗xe3 21.fxe3 ♕c5 (21...♕a4 immediately targets the weak b2-pawn: 22.♘b3 ♘c4 with compensation) 22.♖he1 ♘a4 23.♘b3 (23.♔c2 ♕b5 24.♘b3 ♖d1 25.♖xd1 ♘c4⇄; 23.♔b1 ♔b8 24.e4 ♕b6 25.♘b3 ♖xd1+ 26.♖xd1 ♕e3 and his active queen gives Black enough compensation) 23...♖xd1+ 24.♔xd1 ♕d6+ 25.♔c2 ♘c4 26.♘d4 ♘axb2 27.♕xg6 ♕xg6 28.♘xg6 ♖xh3 and most probably the game

will peter out to a draw. **17...exd4 18.cxd4** 18.♘xd4 ♘xd4 19.♗xd4 ♗h6∞ and it's not easy for White to hide his king; 18.♗xd4 ♘xd4 19.♘xd4 ♔b8∞; 19...♗a3. **18...♘d5♕**

The position is very unclear, but in a practical game I think it is easier to play with Black. This is where my pre-game preparation ended. **19.♖c1** 19.♘c3 ♘xe3 20.fxe3 ♗h6 with fine compensation. **19...♔b8** 19...♕d7 is also possible, but Black will have to play ...♔b8 at some point anyway. At this point I was satisfied with the opening outcome. **20.♕g3 ♗d6 21.♕f3 ♕f7** 21...♘db4!? was possible, but I didn't want to move the knight from its strong square. There could follow: 22.♔f1 ♘xa2 23.♖c4 ♘ab4; 21...♖he8, with the nice idea 22.♕xd5? ♖xe3!, was also

possible. **22.♘e4 ♗c7 23.a3?!** 23.♔f1 ♖he8♕. **23...♖he8?!** This looks logical, but superior was 23...f5 with a strong attack, despite being two pawns down. **24.♘4c3 ♘xe3 24...f5!?. 25.fxe3 ♕b3** Again, the immediate pawn push 25...f5 deserved serious attention. **26.♔f2 f5 27.♖hd1 ♖d7 28.♖d2?** Quite a weak move, probably my opponent missed my next move. 28.♘f4 was probably the best option, giving pawns back but activating pieces: 28...♕xb2+ 29.♘ce2 ♕xa3. I still prefer Black slightly after 30.♖d3. **28...♘e5! 29.♕h5 ♖ed8** 29...♕e6→. **30.♘f4?** My opponent had spent a lot of time in the opening, and he was in time pressure now, so he blundered. 30.♕h6 was necessary, though White's position is very dangerous already. **30...♘c4 31.♖e2 ♘xe3−+** After this capture, White's position collapses. **32.♘g2** Here Black has many ways to win. **32...♘c4 33.♕f3 ♖xd4 34.♔g1 ♕b6 35.♕f2 ♕d6 36.♘e1 ♖g8+ 37.♔h1 ♖f4 38.♘f3 ♕h6 39.♖g1 ♕xh3+ 40.♘h2 ♖h8 41.♕e1 ♕xh2+ 42.♖xh2 ♖xh2+ 43.♔xh2 ♖f2+ 44.♔h3 ♖h2# 0-1**

Exercise 1

position after 9.♘e2-g3

White is threatening h2-h3 or f2-f3 to gain the bishop pair. What is an interesting way for Black to counter this plan?'

Exercise 2

position after 13.♘b1-d2

Black is well developed, now it's time to think what to do.

Exercise 3

position after 13.d4xe5

White carelessly took on e5 in a rapid game. How can Black punish this mistake?

(*solutions on page 247*)

Caro-Kann Defence   Advance Variation   CK 4.7 (B12)

Radulski's straight approach

by Marian Petrov

1.	e4	c6
2.	d4	d5
3.	e5	♗f5
4.	c4	

A long time ago, I used to play the Caro-Kann with 3.♘c3. Then, with time, I wanted to try something else. A friend of mine, the late GM Julian Radulski, showed me a very rare line, which he claimed was good for White.

The idea is to push c2-c4 and then develop the knights, make some pawn moves until Black takes on c4, so White can put the bishop on c4 in one move. If not, White plays b2-b3 and keeps control over the potentially good outpost d5 for his knights.

Ever since then I took this idea on board and played it – very successfully. I have around 15 games with it, and won almost all of them. Even in the games I drew, I had an advantage or even a winning position.

The idea of the line is to get more space, even if White will have a potentially backward pawn on d4. Black has a solid but slightly passive position and White can try to set up an attack.

Black has a few options:

Black takes the pawn

If Black exchanges on b1 and then takes the pawn on a2, he is behind in development. See Game 1 in the Game Section. This line is much better for White.

Black puts his bishop on b4

With 4...e6 and 5...♗b4 Black pins the knight, but he is giving the pair of bishops to White. See Game 2. White has more space here, and the bishop pair – he has a slight advantage.

Black takes on c4 early

In this line, Black has a good outpost on d5 for his knights. But White has the option to play ♘ge2 and then to push the f-pawn, which gives him an advantage. Now he has an outpost on e4 and from there his knight has many good options. See the comments to Petrov-Eldengawy in Game 3. If Black doesn't put a knight on d5 right away, White can play ♘f4 and trade on d5 after ...♘d5. White is better.

Black postpones taking on c4

If Black takes after White has played ♘f3, he has better chances to equalize as now it is not so easy for White to organize an attack on the kingside. See Games 4, 5, 6. Black has a solid, but slightly passive position. White has more space and a good chance to keep the initiative.

Plans for White

After 4...e6 5.♘c3 Black's main moves are 5...♘d7 and 5...♘e7. Here White has several options. If Black does not take on

Julian Radulski

c4, White can play b2-b3 and keep the pressure in the centre (see Games 7 and 8). Black has to find a good plan here, as now he doesn't have the outpost on d5. If Black fails, he may get problems. White can play on both sides of the board and is more flexible.

Another idea for White is to play 6.♘ge2 and sacrifice the c-pawn – see Games 9 and 10. The idea of bringing the knight to f4 and trading on d5 is interesting (see

Game 10), and for Black it is not so easy to find the right answer.

White can also close the centre by playing c4-c5 and then try to advance his pawns on the queenside – see Game 11. Here White is trying to get more space by blocking the queenside. This plan is a bit slow and Black gets good counterplay. Another option for White is to take on d5 (see Game 12). This plan is not dangerous for Black as the pawn structure is symmetrical and White doesn't have any attack.

Conclusion

I think that in most of the lines White has a more pleasant position. The move 4.c4 also avoids the usual long theoretical lines and Black has to think how to set up his pieces in the best way and get an equal position. But even then it's still a long game and plenty of pieces remain on the board.

Black takes the pawn
4...♗xb1

Tim Krabbé   **1**
Comp Mirage
The Hague 1995 (2)
1.e4 c6 2.d4 d5 3.e5 ♗f5 4.c4 ♗xb1?! There is no need to give up the pair of bishops without a fight. **5.♖xb1 ♕a5+? 6.♗d2 ♕xa2**

A typical case of poisoned pawn. Black has lost a lot of time already. Now his queen is in trouble, and she will be lucky to

get away with eating that pawn. **7.c5** 7.b3 e6 8.c5 also gives a big advantage to White. **7...b5** The only way to defend Her Majesty. 7...e6 8.♕c1 ♕b3 9.♖a1 b6 10.♖a3 loses the queen. **8.♖a1 ♕xb2 9.♘e2 b4** 9...e6 10.♘c3+−. **10.♕a4 b3** 10...a5 11.♗c1+−. **11.♘c1** Also winning was 11.♘c3 ♕c2 12.♖a3 ♕f5 13.♕xb3+−. **11...e6 12.♗d3** 12.♘xb3 ♕c2 13.♗a6+−. **12...♗xc5** 12...♘e7 13.♖b1+−. **13.♘xb3 ♗xd4 14.♘xd4 ♕b6** Black has managed to escape with only a piece less, but hit is far behind in development as well, and White has full control of the position. **15.♗a5 ♕b7 16.♖b1 ♕c8 17.0-0 ♘e7 18.♗b4 g6 19.♗d6** Now Black can hardly move and the end is near. **19...♖g8 20.♖fc1 ♘d7 21.♖xc6 ♘xc6 22.♖xc6 ♕d8 23.♖c7 ♖c8 24.♖xc8 ♕xc8**
1-0

Black puts his bishop on b4
4...♗b4

Marian Petrov   **2**
Athanasios Serntedakis
Crete tt 2018 (4)
1.e4 c6 2.d4 d5 3.e5 ♗f5 4.c4 e6 5.♘c3 ♗b4

When all your pawns are on light squares, usually it's not such a great idea to trade your dark-squared bishop. But here this idea is not so bad. **6.♕b3** 6.a3 ♗xc3+ 7.bxc3. **6...a5 7.c5** This seems like a novelty. The alternatives are:

A) 7.♘f3 ♘e7 8.♗g5 dxc4 9.♗xc4 h6 10.♗h4 ♗e4 11.0-0? ♗xf3 12.gxf3 b5∓ Fedoseev-Riazantsev, Kaliningrad 2015;

B) 7.a3 dxc4 8.♗xc4 ♗xc3+ 9.bxc3 b5 10.♗e2 a4 11.♕d1 ♘e7 12.♘f3 h6 13.0-0= Todorovic-Musovic, Montenegro tt 2013.

7...♘d7 8.a3 ♗xc3+ 9.♕xc3 My plan was to wait until Black tries to open some files or diagonals and then use my pair of bishops and try to explore the dark squares. **9...b6 10.b4 bxc5** 10...axb4 11.axb4 ♘e7 12.♗e2 0-0 13.g4 ♗g6 14.h4±. **11.bxc5 a4 12.♕g3 ♗g6 13.h4** Insisting on the same strategy, pushing the pawns to dark squares. **13...h5 14.♗e2 ♖b8** 14...♘e7 15.♘f3 0-0 16.♗d2±. **15.♗d1 ♕a5+ 16.♗d2 ♕b5 17.♗b4 ♕c4 18.♘e2 ♘e7 19.♖c1 ♕a6 20.♘f4** While Black was trying to create counterplay with his queen, White has managed to get a big advantage by developing with simple moves. **20...♗f5 21.♕c3 ♘f8 22.♗e2 ♗a7 23.g3 ♕e7 24.♗d1 ♖a8 25.0-0+−** It's never too late to castle. White has done it now, while Black is still hoping to do it soon. **25...♗h7 26.♕d2 ♘d7 27.♘h3** 27.♗xh5 ♘xh4 28.gxh4 ♕xh4 allows Black counterplay, which I wanted to avoid. **27...♗g6 28.♖e1 ♖a7 29.♗c3 0-0 30.♘f4 ♖b8 31.♗b4 ♗h7 32.♘xh5** Now already I can take the pawn without complications. **32...f6 33.exf6 ♘xf6 34.♘xf6+ ♕xf6 35.♖e5+− ♘h6 36.♕e1 ♗e4 37.♗d2 ♗f7 38.♗f4 ♖b2 39.♖xe4 dxe4 40.♕xe4 ♘h6 41.♕xc6 ♘f5 42.♕e8+ ♔h7 43.♕h5+ ♔g8 44.♗e5 ♕f8 45.♗c2 ♕f7 46.♕xf7+ ♔xf7 47.♗xf5 exf5 48.c6 ... 1-0 (51)**

Black takes on c4 early 4...dxc4

Alexander Morozevich   **3**
Krishnan Sasikiran
Moscow FIDE Wch KO 2001 (2.2)
1.e4 c6 2.d4 d5 3.e5 ♗f5 4.c4 dxc4?! 5.♗xc4 e6 6.♘c3 ♘d7 7.♘ge2!

This set-up is possible if Black takes on c4 early. Now White can prepare to advance his pawns on the kingside. **7...♘b6 8.♗b3 ♘e7 9.0-0 ♕d7** 9...♘ed5 10.♘g3 ♗g6 11.f4 (White has to prepare f4-f5 as soon as possible) 11...♕d7 12.♘ce4 h5 13.♘f3 h4? 14.f5! hxg3 15.fxg6 0-0-0 16.♕xg3+− Petrov-Eldengawy, Cairo 2016. **10.♘f4** Preparing to take on d5, when the black knight moves there. **10...h6 11.♗e3 ♗h7 12.♖c1** White could force the black king to castle queenside with 12.♘h5 ♘ed5 13.♕g4 0-0-0± but it's not so easy to attack it there. **12...♘ed5 13.♘cxd5 ♘xd5 14.♘xd5 exd5** 14...cxd5 15.♗c2 ♕xc2 16.♖xc2 and if 16...♖c8 17.♖xc8+ ♕xc8 18.♕a4+ ♕d7 19.♕xa7±. **15.♗d2** White wants to bring on his rook, but I think here it's better to just push his pawns forward: 15.h3 ♗e7 16.f4 0-0 17.g4 ♗e4 18.f5±. **15...♗e7 16.♖c3 ♗f5?!** 16...0-0±. **17.♗c2 h5 18.♗xf5 ♕xf5 19.♕b3 ♕d7 20.f4** 20.♕g3 g6 21.e6 fxe6 22.♕xg6±. **20...f5 21.♖g3 ♔f7 22.♗b4 ♗xb4 23.♕xb4 ♖ae8 24.♖ff3 ♖e6 25.♖g5 g6** Black is trying to build a fortress and White has to be creative to find a way to improve his position. **26.♖a3 b6 27.h3 h4 28.♔h2 ♕e7 29.♕a4 a5 30.♖b3 ♕c7 31.♖c3 ♖c8?!** 31...c5±. **32.♕c2 ♕e7??** Black loses his sense of danger, and will soon regret this. 32...♖h8±. **33.g4!** Now is the time to open up the kingside. **33...hxg3+ 34.♖cxg3+− ♖h8 35.♖xg6!** Simple, but elegant. **35...♖xg6 36.♕xf5+ ♖f6 37.exf6 ♕xf6 38.♕d7+ ♔f8 39.♕c8+ ♔f7 40.♕c7+ ♔f8 41.♖g5 ♖h4 42.♕c8+ ♔e7 43.♖f5 ♕xd4 44.♕c7+ ♔e6 45.♖e5+ 1-0**

Black postpones taking on c4

Marian Petrov   **4**
Spyridon Skembris
Greece tt 2014 (5)
1.e4 c6 2.d4 d5 3.e5 ♗f5 4.c4 e6 5.♘c3 ♘e7 6.h3

This move was suggested to me by my friend the late Julian Radulski once, and since then I've been playing it almost every time, even for nostalgic reasons. Actually the move is not bad. White is waiting for Black to take on c4 and is delaying the development of his king's bishop. **6...♘d7 7.♘f3 dxc4 8.♗xc4 ♘b6 9.♗b3 ♘ed5 10.0-0 ♗e7** This is the set-up which I have faced many times in my games. It looks like Black has a comfortable position, but he does not have any threats. Meanwhile White enjoys more space and could try to attack on the kingside. **11.♕e2** I think the knight has to go to e4, so it needs protection there. I prefer to move the queen to the e-file and the rook to the d-file. It is possible to reverse this in case you need to trade the bishops on c2 later, because then the queen moves again from e2 and maybe White could lose a move. **11...0-0 12.♘e4 h6 13.♗d2 a5 14.a3 ♘d7** I faced this idea a few times in my games. It is interesting that usually my opponents play this move fast, so I guess this is what the engine thinks is best for Black. **15.♖fc1 ♕b6 16.♗c2 ♖fd8** Playing it safe. White is not winning after 16...♕xb2 17.♖ab1 ♕xa3 18.♕d1 a4 19.♖a1 because of 19...♗xe4! 20.♗xe4 (20.♖xa3

♗xc2 21.♕xc2 ♗xa3 22.♖a1 ♗e7 23.♖xa4=) 20...♕b3 21.♗c2 ♕b5=. **17.g4 ♗xe4?!** I was surprised by this move, since now White gets the initiative. 17...♗g6 18.♖ab1=. **18.♕xe4 ♘f8 19.♗d3 c5 20.♖c2 ♕a7?!** 20...♖ac8 21.♖ac1 ♖c6=. **21.♖ac1 b6 22.h4!** White has a dominant position, and he should try to open some files on the kingside now. **22...♕d7 23.h5 ♖a7 24.♔h2** Preparing ♖g1. **24...f6 25.♕e2 ♕e8 26.♖g1 ♕f7 27.♖g3 ♖ad7 28.exf6 gxf6 29.♔h1** White should have been braver and given the exchange with 29.♗xh6!, as he has great compensation after 29...♗d6 30.♗b5 ♗c7 31.dxc5 ♗xc5 32.♖xc5 bxc5 33.♗d2± . **29...♗d6 30.♖g1±** ♘f4 31. ♗xf4 In time trouble I could not find what to do and decided to offer a draw: ½-½

Marian Petrov 5
Ufuk Sezen Arat

Izmir Urla 2017 (5)

1.e4 c6 2.d4 d5 3.e5 ♗f5 4.c4 e6 5.♘c3 ♘e7 6.♘f3 ♘d7 7.h3 dxc4 8.♗xc4 ♘d5 9.0-0

9...♘xc3 This is another possible plan for Black. I think it's not the best as now White gets better control in the centre. The same idea but in a worse version was played in Radulski-Bjorneboe, Helsingor 2011: 9...♗e7 and White was much better after 10.♕e2 ♘7b6 11.♗b3 ♘xc3 12.bxc3 0-0 13.c4 h6 14.♖d1± . **10.bxc3 b5 11.♗b3** 11.♗d3!? – probably White has to exchange the bishops and bring the knight to e4: 11...♗xd3 12.♕xd3 ♘b6 13.♘g5 h6 (13...♗e7 14.♗xh7) 14.♘e4 ♘d5 15.♕e2± . **11...♘b6 12.a4 ♗e7 13.axb5 cxb5 14.♕e2** 14.d5!? ♘xd5 15.♘d4

♗g6 16.♘xb5 0-0 17.♗xd5 ♕xd5 (17...exd5 18.♘d6±) 18.♕xd5 exd5 19.♘c7 ♖ac8 20.♘xd5 ♗c5± . **14...♕d7 15.♖a5?** White should have opened the position with 15.d5!?. I saw this idea, but I thought it was nothing special for White: 15...♘xd5 (15...exd5 16.e6 ♗xe6 17.♘e5 ♕c7 18.♕xb5+→) 16.♘d4 ♗g6 17.♘xb5 0-0 18.c4± . **15...a6 16.♗a3 ♗xa3 17.♖xa3 0-0 18.♖fa1** The whole plan is wrong and not only has White lost his advantage but soon he will be worse. **18...♕b7 19.♕a2 ♗e4 20.♘e1 a5 21.f3** 21.♖xa5?? ♖xa5 22.♕xa5 ♖a8–+. **21...a4 22.fxe4 axb3 23.♕xb3 ♖xa3 24.♖xa3 ♕xe4∓ 25.♘f3 ♕e3+ 26.♔h2 ♘d5 27.♕b2 ♕f4+ 28.♔h1 g6?** 28...g5!∓. **29.♕d2 ♕e4 30.♕h6 ♕e3 31.♕xe3 ♘xe3 32.♘g5 ♖c8 33.♘e4 ♘d5 34.♖b3 ♗g7 35.♔h2=** ... ½-½ (50)

Julian Radulski 6
Robert Hafner

Lienz 2011 (2)

1.e4 c6 2.d4 d5 3.e5 ♗f5 4.c4 e6 5.♘c3 ♗e7 6.♘f3 ♘d7 7.h3 ♗g6 8.♗e2 dxc4 9.♗xc4 ♘d5 10.0-0 ♗e7

11.♖e1 White can also use the rook to bring his knight to e4 and the queen can later help to trade the bishops on c2 without moving. **11...0-0 12.♘e4 h6 13.♗d2 ♘5b6 14.♗a5 ♕b8 15.♗d3** 15.♗b3 ♘d5=. **15...♘d5 16.♖c1** A common position for this set-up. Both players can be happy. White has more space, while Black has a solid position. **16...b6 17.♗d2 ♕b7** 17...c5 18.♕a4 ♖d8 19.♗b5 ♕c7=. **18.♕e2** White could provoke ...b6-b5 and then

try to exploit the dark squares with 18.♕a4!? b5 19.♕b3. **18...a6** 18...c5 19.♗a6 ♕b8=. **19.♘g3** Interesting was 19.♗c2 with the idea 19...♖fd8 20.♘d6 ♗xd6 21.♗xg6 fxg6 22.exd6 ♘f8 23.♕e5 ♕d7 24.♗f4 ♘xf4 25.♕xf4 ♕xd6 26.♘e5± . **19...♗xd3 20.♕xd3 c5 21.♘h5 cxd4** 21...♖fd8 22.♖e4! ♗f8 23.♖g4 ♔h8 24.♗xh6! gxh6 25.♘h4 ♘e7 26.♕g3 ♕d5 27.♖g7+–. **22.♘xd4 ♕h8 23.♘xe6** 23.♕f3 ♖ac8 24.♘xg7 ♕xg7 25.♕g4+ ♔h8 26.♕h5+–. **23...fxe6 24.♕g6 ♖g8 25.♗xh6 ♗f8 26.♗g5 ♗e7?** Closing the 7th-rank corridor for the queen. Now she can't help the king. 26...♗c5= 27.♕xe6 ♘f8 28.♖c4 (28.♕g4 ♕f7 29.♖xc5 bxc5 30.e6 ♕g6 31.♕h4 ♕h7 32.♕g4 ♕g6=) 28...♖xe6 29.♖h4 g6 30.♘f6+ ♔g7 31.♖h7+ ♔f8 32.♖xb7 ♘xg5 33.♘xd5 ♖g7 34.♖xg7 ♔xg7 35.b4♗. **27.♘f6! ♘7xf6 28.exf6 1-0**

Marian Petrov 7
Nikolaus Stanec

Vienna 2011 (5)

1.e4 c6 2.d4 d5 3.e5 ♗f5 4.c4 e6 5.♘c3 ♘d7 6.♘f3 h6 7.h3 ♗e7

8.b3 An important part of my plan. Now Black doesn't have the d5 outpost. **8...a6 9.♗e2 ♘h7 10.0-0 ♘f8 11.c5** I decided to close the centre and advance the b-pawn. The other option is 11.♗d3 ♗b4 12.♘e2± . **11...♗e7 12.b4 ♘h4** I'm not sure if the trading of the knight is worth wasting two moves with the bishop. 12...0-0 13.♗d3± . **13.♘xh4 ♗xh4 14.a4 0-0 15.♗e3 ♗e7 16.f4** 16.b5 (16.a5 f6 17.f4±)

After the game we both thought that White is better here, but Black has 16...b6 (16...axb5 17.axb5 ♖xa1 18.♕xa1 f6 19.♗g4±) 17.bxc6 ♘b8 18.♕b3 ♘xc6 (18...bxc5 19.♕b7 ♘xc6 20.♕xc6 ♖c8 21.♕xa6 ♖a8 22.♕b5 ♖b8 23.dxc5±) 19.♕xb6. White wins a pawn but Black is fine after 19...♕xb6 20.cxb6 ♘a5=. **16...b6 17.a5 b5 18.♗g4 f5 19.exf6** After 19.♗h5 g6 20.♗f3 ♔h8 21.g3 ♖g8 22.♔h2 g5 the engine claims that White is almost winning, but to me it's not so clear how exactly. Sure, White has an advantage because he has more space, but Black's position is hard to break. **19...♖xf6 20.♕e2 ♘f8 21.♗d2 ♗f5 22.♖ae1** White has a big advantage but I could not find what to do until the end of the game ... ½-½ **(47)**

Marian Petrov 8
Ketevan Tsatsalashvili
Cesme 2015 (8)

1.e4 c6 2.d4 d5 3.e5 ♗f5 4.c4 e6 5.♘c3 ♘d7 6.♘f3 h6 7.h3 ♘e7 8.b3 This move was also an idea of GM Radulski, which we analysed back then. The idea is to not allow Black to get the outpost on d5, so now he has to search for another plan. **8...a6**

With the idea ...b7-b5. **9.c5** A common idea, to close the centre. I think here, after Black has played ...a7-a6, this is even better, because now if Black goes for ...b7-b6, White can take and Black has to retake with a piece, leaving a potential weakness on c5. RR: 9.♗e2 – Petrov-Stanec. **9...♗h7 10.♗d3** I think 10.♗e2 is slightly better here. I thought I had to trade the bishops to get b1 for

the rook. But now in the future the black queen could get to b5. Even so, if Black finds 10...g5 he has good counterplay. **10...♗xd3 11.♕xd3 b6** If Black doesn't play this, he has a passive position, e.g. 11...♘f5 12.0-0 ♗e7 13.♗d2 0-0 14.♘a4+. **12.cxb6** 12.b4?? a5∓. **12...♕xb6** Black loses the control over c5 after 12...♘xb6 13.♗a3 ♘f5 14.♗xf8 ♔xf8 15.♘e2±.

13.0-0 13.♘a4. When I analysed this position in the past, I thought I would always be better after this. But now I realized that my bishop is not there, and after 13...♕b5 Black is fine. **13...c5** More cautious was 13...♘g6 14.h4 h5±. **14.♘a4** I played this, hoping for: **14...♕a7?** After 14...♕b5!? 15.♕xb5 axb5 16.♘xc5 ♘xc5 17.dxc5 ♘c6 18.♗d2 Black has good compensation for the pawn. This was a better option than the move in the game. **15.♘xc5 ♘xc5 16.dxc5 ♕xc5** I was expecting 16...♘c6 17.♗d2 ♗xc5 18.♖ac1 and White has the initiative after 18...♘e7 19.b4 ♗b6 20.a4 0-0 21.a5 ♗c7 22.♖c2 ♕b7 23.♖fc1±. **17.♗e3 ♕a5?!** 17...♕b5 18.♕xb5+ axb5 19.a4 bxa4 20.♖xa4±; I was wondering how to use the fact that the black king is still in the centre, and how to keep it there. The first step is to prevent the development of the knight. **18.♘d4! g6** Black needs two moves to castle, so I thought what can I do during these two moves to prevent it? 18...♘g6 19.♘xe6+−. **19.b4!** White needs to very quickly open some files, and this is the only way to do this. **19...♕xb4 20.♖fc1** 20.♖ab1 ♕c4 21.♕d2!+− also works. **20...♘f5 21.♖ab1 ♕a5** 21...♕a4 22.♘xf5 gxf5 23.♖c7 ♗g7

24.♗c5+−. **22.♘xf5 gxf5 23.♕c2** Using the open files in the best possible way. **1-0**

Dimitrios Mastrovasilis 9
Vilka Sipila
Tromsø ol 2014 (3)

1.e4 c6 2.d4 d5 3.e5 ♗f5 4.c4 e6 5.♘c3 ♘e7 6.♘ge2 This is an attempt to bring the knight to g3 and then White could try to push the h-pawn, or, in case Black takes on c4, both knights will have the outpost e4. **6...dxc4 7.♘g3**

7...b5 The most critical line: Black is trying to keep his pawn. If Black develops normally with 7...♘d7 then White has the better chances after 8.♗xc4 ♘b6 9.♗b3 ♕d7 10.0-0 ♗g6 11.h4 h6 12.h5 ♗h7 13.a4 a5 14.♕g4 (it is not clear which side Black will castle) 14...♘f5 15.♖d1 ♘xg3 16.♕xg3 ♖g8 17.♗f4 (17.♗e3±) ½-½ (36) Efimenko-Bareev, Russia tt 2009. **8.a4 b4** As yet, nobody has tried to defend the pawn with 8...♕b6, but I think in this case White has the initiative after 9.axb5 cxb5 10.♗e3 ♕b7 11.♗e2 ♘bc6 12.0-0±. **9.♘ce4** Of course White has to play actively. 9.♘a2? b3 10.♘c3 c2 11.♕d2 and now Black has the edge after 11...c5 (11...♘d5 0-1 (48) Nevednichy-Jobava, Heraklion 2007) 12.dxc5 ♕xd2+ 13.♔xd2 ♘ec6∓. **9...♗xe4 10.♘xe4 ♘f5!** Black is almost lost after all the other moves, say 10...♘d5 11.♗xc4+−. **11.♗e3 ♘d7** 11...♕d5 12.♘g3 ♘h4 13.f3 c3?! (13...c5 14.♖c1=) 14.bxc3 bxc3 15.♕c2 ♕d7 16.♖b1 (White should have entered the complications without fear: 16.♕xc3! ♖b8 17.♔f2

♖b3 18.♕c2 ♘xe5 19.♖d1 (19.dxe5 leads only to a draw after 19...♖xe3 20.♔xe3 ♕xe5+ 21.♔e4 ♕xa1 22.♕xc6+ ♔d8 23.♗b5) 19...♖xe3 20.♔xe3± 16...♘b6 ½-½ (46) D. Mastrovasilis-Svetushkin, Serbia tt 2008. **12.♗xc4 ♗e7?!** Missing the chance to take the pawn and get an equal game with 12...♘xe3! 13.fxe3 ♘xe5=. **13.0-0 0-0 14.♗a2** 14.♘g3 ♘xe3 15.fxe3 ♘h6 16.♗h3±. **14...♕a5?!** A very bad square for the queen, and this move gives an important tempo to White. 14...♖c8 15.♖c1 ♕b6=. **15.♗g5!** **♕d8 16.g4** This is the key. Now White takes control of the d6 outpost. **16...♗xg5 17.gxf5 exf5 18.♘d6 ♘b6?** 18...g6±. **19.♕c2?!** 19.f4! and White has full control in the centre after 19...♗xf4 20.♕f3 ♗h6 21.♘xf5+−. **19...♗e7 20.♘xf5 ♖c8** 20...g6±. **21.♖ad1** Better was 21.a5! ♘d5 (21...♘d7 22.♕c4+−) 22.♗xd5+−. **21...g6 22.♘e3 ♘h8 23.f4 ♕e8 24.a5** Finally White pushes the pawn, pushing back the knight to a very bad square. **24...♘a8 25.f5+−** f6 **26.♖f3 fxe5 27.dxe5 ♗g5 28.e6 ♘c7 29.♘c4 ♖d8 30.♘d6 ♖xd6 31.♖xd6 gxf5 32.♕xc6 ♘h5 33.♖dd3 ♖g8 34.♔h1 ♘e8 35.e7 ♖g7 36.♖xf5 h6 37.♖f8+ ♔h7 38.♕e4+ ♖g6 39.♗f7 ♕h3 40.♕xg6# 1-0**

Zahar Efimenko 10
Zoltan Gyimesi
Germany Bundesliga 2008/09 (12)
1.e4 c6 2.d4 d5 3.e5 ♗f5 4.c4 e6 5.♘c3 ♘e7 6.♘ge2 ♘d7

7.♘f4 A rare move, with an interesting idea. **7...dxc4** 7...h6 8.cxd5 cxd5 9.♗d3 ♗xd3 10.♕xd3± Manik-Villegas, Pardubice 2017. **8.♗xc4 ♘b6** Black is following his

---

usual plan to jump to d5. **9.♗b3 ♘ed5**

10.♘cxd5 This is the key. White uses the position of his knight on f4 to change the pawn structure; 10.♘h5 looks tempting, but does not promise much after 10...♗g6 11.0-0 a5 12.a3=. **10...cxd5?** 10...♘xd5 11.♘xd5 exd5 (11...cxd5 12.♗a4++−) 12.0-0 ♕d7 13.h3 ♗e7 14.♗e3 g5⇄; 14...0-0 15.g4 ♗g6 16.f4 f5 17.♔h2±. **11.g4!** Of course. When the centre is closed, White can make such moves. **11...♗e4 12.f3 ♕h4+** 12...♗g6 13.h4+−. **13.♔e2 ♗g6 14.♗e3 0-0-0?** 14...♗e7 15.♕d2 0-0 (15...♖d8 16.♗f2 ♕e7 17.h4±) 16.♗f2 ♕h6 17.h4+−. **15.♕c1+** White wins material. **15...♗d7 16.♘xg6 hxg6 17.♗g5 ♕h3 18.♗xd8 ♕g2+ 19.♔e3 ♗xd8 20.♕d2 ♕h3 21.♖ag1 ♗e7 22.♕g2** 22.♔e2 ♗d7 23.♕e1 ♗g5 24.♕g3+− ... **1-0 (50)**

Ruslan Ponomariov 11
Jan Timman
Pamplona 2005 (5)
1.e4 c6 2.d4 d5 3.e5 ♗f5 4.c4 e6 5.♘c3 ♘d7 6.a3 A waiting move, which can also be a preparation for c4-c5, if Black doesn't take on c4. **6...♘e7**

7.c5 One of the main plans in this set-up. White wants to expand on the queenside by pushing all the

---

pawns there, if given the chance. **7...b6** The most obvious reply. Black doesn't want to sit and wait until the pawns come knocking on his door. **8.b4** Of course White should support his pawn. **8...a5 9.♗e3 axb4** The other plan is 9...g6 10.♘f3 ♕c7 11.♗e2 (a better try is 11.♘h4 ♘f5 12.♘xf5 ♗xf5 and now 13.b5!? bxc5 14.bxc6 ♕xc6 15.♗b5 ♕c7 16.g4 ♗g6 17.f4→) 11...♘f5 12.0-0 ♘xe3 13.fxe3 ♗e7 14.♗d3= Najer-Dreev, playchess. com blitz 2004. **10.axb4 bxc5 11.bxc5 ♖xa1 12.♕xa1**

Black has managed to trade a few pawns and a pair of rooks, but now White can try to explore the open files. That is why Black has to do something on the other side. **12...f6 13.f4 g5** Black has to go all out in his attempt to destroy White's pawn chain. If he plays passively and gives White time to develop, he will have problems; 13...♘xc5 14.dxc5 d4 15.♘b5 cxb5 16.♗xb5+ ♔f7 17.♖xd4 ♗d5 18.♘f3 ♕c7 19.♕a3 ♗xc5?! 20.♕xc5 ♕xc5 21.♗xc5 ♖c8 22.♗a3? (22.♗g1!±) 22...♖xc3 23.0-0 ♖xa3= Bukhteeva-Gromova, Russia tt W 2010. **14.exf6 ♘xf6 15.fxg5** White has to take the pawn if he wants to get an advantage. **15...♘g4** Winning a tempo, but putting the knight in slight danger. It is strange that the move 15...♘e4 hasn't been played yet. This is a far better outpost for the knight, and now Black has good compensation, e.g. 16.♘f3 ♗g7=. **16.♗d2 ♕b8 17.♘ge2** 17.♘f3 looks more natural, but still White needs to bring the other knight to e2 after this: 17...♗g7 18.♘e2 ♕b3? (it's hard to see where this queen is going;

18...h6=) 19.♘c1! (19.♕c3? 1-0 (56) Zhang Zhong-Li Wenliang, Beijing 1996) 19...♕c2 20.♗e2+−. **17...h6** 17...♖xh2? 18.♗f4+−. **18.h3 hxg5 19.♗xg5 ♗g6?** 19...♗g7!. It's not easy to calculate and evaluate all the complications after this, but actually Black is fine, for example: 20.hxg4 ♖xh1 21.♗xe7 ♕h2! 22.gxf5 ♕xg2 23.♔d2 ♕xf1=. **20.♖g1** 20.g3 gives White an edge after 20...e5 21.♗g2 exd4 22.0-0 dxc3 23.hxg4 ♗d3 24.♗f4+−. **20...♗h6 21.♕c1!** Allowing the activation of his queen and slowing down Black's initiative. **21...♗xg5 22.♕xg5 ♘h6 23.♕f4** 23.g4 is tempting, but not clear, as after 23...♘f7 24.♕e3 e5 Black has compensation. **23...♕b4?!** Black should have tried 23...e5! 24.♕xe5 ♕xe5 25.dxe5 when he has good compensation because of his active pieces: 25...♘f7 26.e6 ♘e5 27.♘d4 ♘f5 28.♘ce2 ♔e7. **24.g4!** Now the black knights don't have any good outposts. **24...♘f7 25.♕e3** 25.♖g3!. **25...♗e4 26.♗g2?** 26.♖g3±. **26...e5?** Missing a great chance: 26...♗xg2 27.♖xg2 e5! 28.dxe5 d4! 29.♕xd4 ♕xd4 30.♘xd4 ♖xh3 31.♘e4 ♘xe5=. **27.♗xe4 dxe4 28.♖g3** Finally White has made this move and he has a big edge now. **28...exd4 29.♕xd4?** White should have played for an attack

with 29.♘xd4 ♕xc5 30.♘xe4 ♕e5 31.♖f3 0-0 32.♘f6++−. **29...♕xd4 30.♘xd4 ♘g5 31.♔e2 ♔d7 32.♘f5?** ♘g6 33.♔e3 Suddenly White has lost his advantage. **33...♖xh3** 33...♘xh3 34.♘xe4 ♖a8=. **34.♘xe4 ♖xg3+ 35.♘fxg3 ♘f7 36.♘h5 ♔e6 37.♔d4 ♘fe5 38.♘f2 ♘f3+ 39.♔e3 ♘fe5 40.♔e4 ♘d7 41.♘d3 ♘gf8** 41...♘f6+=. **42.g5 ♔f7?? 42...♔e7!** 43.♘hf4 ♘e6= **43.♘hf4 ♔g8** Black has lost the plot, and now loses the game. **44.♔f5 ♔g7 45.♘e6+ ♘xe6 46.♔xe6 ♘f8+ 47.♔e7 ♘h7 48.♘f4 1-0**

Andrey Zhigalko   **12**
Maxim Rodshtein
Jerusalem Ech 2015 (3)
1.e4 c6 2.d4 d5 3.e5 ♗f5 4.c4 e6 5.a3 ♘e7 6.♘c3 ♘d7 7.♘f3 ♗g4 This is the reason why I usually play h2-h3. I think that after ...♘f5 there could be some danger for the d4-pawn. **8.♗e3 ♘f5**

9.cxd5 And then White has to trade the pawns to reduce the pressure. **9...cxd5 10.h3 ♗h5** 10...♘xe3 11.fxe3 ♗f5=. **11.♗d3 ♗g6** Black does not want to trade off his knight, so now White can keep his bishop. **12.♗f4 a6 13.h4 ♘e7 14.h5 ♗xd3 15.♕xd3** Somehow Black has lost a lot of time in the past few moves and now White has the edge. **15...h6 16.0-0?** 16.♔f1 ♖c8 17.♔h3 ♘c6 18.♖g3±. **16...♖c8** 16...♘c6 allows some complications after 17.♘xd5 exd5 18.e6 ♘f6♔. **17.♖fc1 ♘b6 18.b3** 18.♘e2 ♘c6 19.♘d2 ♗e7 20.♕g3±. **18...♘c6 19.♗d2 ♗e7 20.♘e2 ♔d7** It's not clear what the safest place for the king is: 20...0-0 21.g4↑. **21.♘e1** 21.a4 ♘b4 22.♗xb4 ♗xb4 23.♘e1±. **21...♕g8 22.♕f3** 22.a4 g6 23.a5 ♘a8 24.b4 ♗c7 25.♘c3 ♘xb4 26.♕e3↑. **22...g6 23.♘d3 gxh5 24.♕xh5 ♕g6 25.♘df4 ♕h7 26.♖c3 ♖cg8 27.♕h3 h5 28.a4 a5 29.♖ac1** 29.♖xc6! bxc6 30.♗xa5 ♖b8 31.♕c3±. **29...♖g4?? 30.f3** 30.♖xc6! was the last chance to win the game, e.g. 30...bxc6 31.♕c3 ♖c8 32.♕xa5 ♘a8 33.♕a7++−. **30...♖g7 31.♔f2 h4 32.♔e1?! ♗b4 33.♖c5?** 33.♖d3. **33...♗xc5 34.dxc5 ♘c8 34...**♘a8 35.♘xd5 ♔c8−+. **35.♘xd5 ♕d3 36.♘f6+?** 36.♗c3♔. **36...♔c7 37.f4 ♕xh3−+ ... 0-1 (56)**

Exercise 1

position after 19...♘g6-e7

White to move.

Exercise 2

position after 22...0-0-0

White to move.

Exercise 3

position after 35...h6-h5

White to move.

(solutions on page 247)

A fresh idea in the Classical Caro-Kann

by Zaur Tekeyev

1.	e4	c6
2.	d4	d5
3.	♘c3	dxe4
4.	♘xe4	♗f5
5.	♘g3	♗g6
6.	h4	h6
7.	♗d3	

Zaur Tekeyev

7.♗d3 is a very rare option in this line; usually White trades the light-squared bishops only with 7.♘f3 ♘d7 8.h5 ♗h7 included, winning some time to advance the h-pawn a bit further. It used to be debatable whether White should push the pawn till h5 or leave it to stay on h4, until in 1966 the former option took the upper hand when Boris Spassky used it to defeat Tigran Petrosian in the 13th game of their World Championship match. The idea was to tie up Black's kingside with the h5-pawn to restrict any activities there and possibly achieve a better endgame.

However, then Black found a possibility to castle kingside and get more dynamic play. Even though the h-pawn is advanced and there is a hook on h6, it is still difficult for White to create an attack on the kingside. The g2-g4 push is usually a pawn sacrifice, but the centre is not closed and Black often use the d5-square to activate his queen and either force some more exchanges or create active counterplay. Often the h5-pawn even becomes a weakness.

The white king's knight

Sometimes White develops the knight to f3 and transposes to the main lines with the pawn on h4. But one of the ideas of 7.♗d3 is also to keep the possibility of developing the king's knight to e2. Then it can go to f4, controlling the d5-square, and sometimes to h5, trading the black king's defender and creating more pressure on the kingside. Now it is also easier for White to launch a pawn storm with f2-f3 and g2-g4-g5. In this Survey, we will focus on the approach with ♘g1-e2.

There are not many games played yet with this move, but I found the idea very fresh and interesting (even though the

first time it was played was back in 1948 in a correspondence game). And recently some grandmasters started using this rare weapon with good results.

So what can Black do? There are three main directions. After 7...♗xd3 8.♕xd3 Black can try to castle either kingside or queenside. The latter option is more popular in practice.

The third option is to take the d4-pawn on the 7th move. It looks risky, but it needs to be well analysed.

Black castles kingside

The winner of the Aeroflot Open 2020, Aydin Suleymanli, met this system twice in World Rapid and Blitz Championships. In a rapid game against Evgeny Najer, he went for queenside castling, got a solid but slightly worse position, and eventually lost in the endgame (see notes to Game 3). The next day he met the same variation in a blitz game against another strong Russian grandmaster, Sergey Grigoriants. Now Aydin decided to castle kingside and start an attack on the queenside (Game 1). This time he was objectively worse after the opening, but managed to outplay his opponent in time trouble. Nevertheless, this is a good game to start the analysis, because it shows that Black's attack is slower. In Game 2, Philipp Wenninger against Evgeny Vorobiev decided to stop White's attack by exchanging the queens, but the endgame turned out to be worse for Black.

Black castles queenside

Castling queenside is by no means a safer option, but it usually leaves Black with a rather passive position. We will start covering it with a very exciting game played by Alexander Predke and

Ivan Rozum, where Black placed his queen on c7 (Game 3). It looks like White can obtain some advantage, but Black's position is solid. In Van Foreest-Dziuba (Game 4), the queen went to b6. In the notes to this game, you will find that Black has an interesting equalizing manoeuvre, but it seems like Jorden van Foreest knew about it, and he prevented it in time. In general in such positions White has a wider choice of plans.

Black accepts the gambit

But what if Black just takes the central pawn with 7...♕xd4 ? After 8.♘f3 ♕d6 9.♗xg6 ♕xg6

White can choose between the sharp 10.♕e2 (Game 5) and the calmer 10.♗e3 (Game 6). The latter option forces Black to enter a somewhat worse endgame, but it seems like Black can hold with precise play. 10.♕e2 leads to very sharp positions with full compensation for the sacrificed pawn. So taking the pawn on d4 doesn't seem to be a good option for a practical game.

Conclusion

There is not much theory in this line yet, but it leads to very interesting and fresh positions. The set-up with ♘g1-e2 looks quite promising for White, so I assume (and hope!) we will see more games with this in future practice.

**Black castles kingside
7...♗xd3 8.♕xd3**

Sergey Grigoriants   **1**
Aydin Suleymanli

Moscow Wch blitz 2019 (7)

**1.e4 c6 2.d4 d5 3.♘c3 dxe4
4.♘xe4 ♗f5 5.♘g3 ♗g6 6.h4 h6
7.♗d3 ♗xd3 8.♕xd3 ♘f6 9.♘1e2**

This variation was already used
against Aydin Suleymanli just
one day before this game. In that
game, against Evgeny Najer, Black
preferred castling queenside, but
lost, so now Aydin decides to
change the strategy and goes for
a position with opposite-castled
kings: **9...e6 10.♗d2 ♗e7** In case
of 10...c5 White should play 11.♘e4
♘c6 12.♘xc5 ♗xc5 13.dxc5 ♕xd3
14.cxd3. White is a pawn up, but
Black has good compensation, so
some precision is required from
White, for example: 14...0-0-0
15.♖h3 ♖d5 16.b4 ♖hd8 17.b5 ♘d4
18.♘xd4 ♖xd4 19.♔e2±. **11.0-0-0
0-0** If Black tries to play ...c6-c5
before castling kingside, White has
a very interesting pawn sacrifice:
11...♘bd7 12.♔b1 c5 (12...0-0 is
covered in Vorobiev-Wenninger)
13.d5!. Not an obvious decision!
Now:

A) 13...♘e5 14.♕b5+ ♕d7
15.♕xd7+ ♘exd7 16.dxe6 fxe6
17.♘f4 ♔f7 18.♖he1↑ with a better
endgame for White;

B) 13...exd5 14.♘f5 g6 (14...0-0?
falls immediately to 15.♗xh6+−)
15.♘xe7 ♕xe7 16.♘c3 0-0-0 (if
16...♕d6 White takes a pawn
and retains the initiative after
17.♗xh6↑) 17.♗f4! (17.♘xd5 is also
possible, but not so great: 17...♘xd5
18.♕xd5 ♘e5 19.♕b3 ♘c6 20.a3
♖d7 21.♗e3±) 17...♖he8 18.♘b5 ♘e5

19.♘xa7+ ♔b8 20.♘b5 g5 21.hxg5
hxg5 22.♗xe5+ ♕xe5 23.♕a3→;

C) 13...♘xd5 14.♘h5 and now:

C1) 14...g6? 15.♘g7+ ♔f8
16.♘xe6+ fxe6 17.c4! ♘e5 (17...♘5f6
18.♕xg6+− ; ♗xh6+ is coming
and Black is lost) 18.♕c2 ♘xc4
19.♕xc4±;

C2) 14...♘f6 15.♗c3 (15.♕g3
is also possible, e.g. 15...♕b6
16.♘xf6+ gxf6 17.♘c3! 0-0-0
18.♘xd5 exd5 19.♖he1 and White's
chances are a bit better) 15...0-0
16.♕g3 g6 17.♘xf6+ ♘7xf6
18.♗e5±. White will exchange one
pair of knights to reduce Black's
defensive potential;

C3) 14...♘f8 15.♕g3 g6 (15...♖h7
16.c4 ♘5f6 17.♘xf6 ♗xf6 18.♗c3
♗xc3 19.♘xc3 ♕e7 20.♖he1 and
White is better) 16.c4 (16.♘hf4
♕c7 17.♘c3!? ♘7f6 18.♘cxd5 ♘xd5
19.♗c1 (threatening 20.♖xd5 and
then 21.♘e6+) 19...♗e8 20.♕f3
with some compensation for
the sacrificed pawn) 16...gxh5
(16...♘5f6 17.♘xf6 ♗xf6 18.h5 g5
19.♗c3 ♗xc3 20.♘xc3 ♕e7 21.f4↑)
17.cxd5 exd5 18.♕d3 d4 19.♘g3
with some advantage for White;

C4) 14...♘g8! is the best defence,
e.g. 15.♕g3 ♕b6 16.♗xh6 0-0-0
(16...♘f6?! 17.♘xf6+ ♘7xf6 18.♗xg7
0-0-0 19.♗xf6 (19.h5 is also
possible) 19...♖xg3 20.♗xd8 ♔xd8
21.fxg3±) 17.♗c1. White can create
a passed pawn on the h-file at
some point: 17...♘d6 18.♘hf4 ♘5f6
(18...♘7f6 19.♘xd5 exd5 20.♕f3
♖ge8 21.♘f4 ♗xf4 22.♕xf4∓) 19.f3,
preparing ♕f2, g2-g4, h4-h5. For
example, 19...♘e5 20.♕f2 ♗c7
21.h5 ♔b8 22.g4 ♘d5 23.♕d3 ♘d3
24.♖xd3 f6 25.f4±.
The immediate 11...c5 can be met
by 12.♗c3 0-0 13.dxc5, aiming for a

preferable endgame, e.g. 13...♕xd3
14.♖xd3 ♘xc5 (14...♘bd7 15.b4 a5
16.a3 axb4 17.axb4 ♘d5 18.♘f4!
♘xc3 19.♖xd7 ♘f6 20.♘d3±)
15.♗xf6 gxf6 16.♘e4 ♗e7 17.g4±.
Or 12.♘e4 (preparing g2-g4!)
12...cxd4 13.♘xd4 ♘bd7 14.g4!? ♖c8
15.♗e3 ♘d5 16.g5 hxg5 17.hxg5
♖xh1 18.♖xh1±. **12.♔b1 b5?!**
13.♘e4 This is White's main idea
in this variation. Now the g-pawn
is ready to march towards Black's
king. **13...♘bd7** 13...♘xe4 was
probably better, e.g. 14.♕xe4 ♕d5
15.♕e3 ♘d7 16.g4 ♘b6 17.♘f4 ♕d8
18.♕f3 ♖fd8 19.♗c1 g6 20.♘d3±.
14.♘xf6+ 14.g4! ♘xe4 (14...♘xg4
15.♕g3 f5 16.♘f4 ♕b8 17.f3 ♘gf6
18.♖dg1 ♘e8 19.g5!+−) 15.♕xe4
♘f6 16.♕xc6±. **14...♘xf6**

15.f3 This looks a bit slow. 15.g4
could be strong here, because Black
shouldn't take the pawn anyway,
for example: 15...♘xg4 16.♖dg1
f5 17.♕g3 ♗d6 18.♕g2 ♕e7 19.f3
♘f6 20.♗xh6± and White's attack
is too strong. **15...c5** 15...♘d5!?
16.g4 a5 17.♖dg1 (17.g5 h5 18.g6 a4
19.gxf7+ ♖xf7 20.♕g6 b4 21.♕xh5
♕b6 22.♕g6 b3∓) 17...a4 18.♘g3
a3 19.b3 c5 20.g5 c4∞. **16.♕xb5**
Now Black's compensation for
the pawn doesn't seem to be
enough. **16...cxd4** 16...♖b8 17.♕a5
cxd4 18.♕xd4 ♖bxd8 19.♗f4 ♗c5
20.♗e5 ♖d5 21.♗xf6 gxf6 22.♖d2±.
**17.♗a5 ♕d5 18.♕xd5 ♘xd5
19.♘xd4** 19.♖xd4+− would have
been more precise. **19...♗f6 20.g3
♖ab8 21.♘b3** 21.♖d3 ♖fc8 22.b3
♖c5 23.♗d2+−. **21...♖fc8 22.♖he1
g5 23.hxg5 hxg5** White was
objectively much better, but it was
a blitz game and Black managed to
win. The rest is not important for
us ... **0-1 (64)**

Evgeny Vorobiov   **2**
Philipp Wenninger
Schwäbisch Gmünd 2020 (8)
**1.e4 c6 2.d4 d5 3.♘c3 dxe4
4.♘xe4 ♗f5 5.♘g3 ♗g6 6.h4 h6
7.♗d3 ♗xd3 8.♕xd3 e6 9.♗d2
♘f6 10.♘1e2 ♘bd7 11.0-0-0 ♗e7
12.♔b1 0-0 13.♘e4 ♘xe4** 13...c5
14.♘xf6+ ♘xf6 (14...♗xf6 15.g4
♗xd4 16.♘xd4 cxd4 17.♕xd4 ♘b6
18.♕e4 ♕d5 19.♕xd5 ♘xd5 20.c4
♘f6 21.f3 ♖fd8 22.♗b4±; White
will try to take control over the
d-file by ♗b4-e7 at some point)
15.g4 ♘d5 16.g5 h5 17.c4 ♘b6
18.♖he1 cxd4 19.♘g3±; 13...♕b6
14.♘xf6+ ♘xf6 15.g4!→. **14.♕xe4
♘f6 15.♕d3!** White's main plan is
to start attacking on the kingside,
so Black would like to exchange
the queens. That is why d3 seems
to be a better square for White's
queen than f3. **15...♕d5** After
15...b5 16.g4 Black should forget
about the attack on the queenside
and start defending anyway. **16.f3**
Not only preparing the g2-g4 push,
but also preventing 16...♕e4!. Here
16.g4 is no longer strong, because
Black is ready to exchange the
queens: 16...♕e4 17.♕xe4 ♘xe4
18.♗e3 ♘f6 19.f3 ♘d5 20.♗d2
b5=. **16...h5** Trying to slow down
White's play on the kingside and
also preparing ...♕f5, while the
pawn will not be hanging on h6.
After 16...♕f5 17.♕xf5 exf5 18.♘g3
g6 19.♗xh6 ♖fe8± Black loses
a pawn, but can hope for some
counterplay.

17.♗g5 A clever way to prevent
17...♕f5. The more straightforward
17.♘f4N leads to an endgame with
some advantage for White, but
Black is solid: 17...♕f5 18.♕xf5
exf5 19.♖he1 ♖fe8 20.c4 ♖ad8

21.♗c3 ♗d6 22.♖xe8+ ♘xe8 23.♗d2
♗e7 24.♗a5 b6 25.♗e1 g6 26.♔c2±.
17...♕f5?! 17...♖ad8 18.c3 ♖fe8
19.♘f4 ♗d6 20.♕e2 c5 21.♗xf6
♕xf4 22.♗xe7 ♖xe7 23.dxc5 ♖ed7.
After this sequence of precise
moves Black could hope for
equality, but 24.b4!± looks strong
for White. **18.♕xf5 exf5 19.♘f4**
19.♖he1! was more precise. **19...g6**
19...♗d6! 20.c4 ♖fe8±. **20.♖he1
♗d8** Now if 20...♗d6 21.♗xf6 ♗xf4
22.c4!+− and d4-d5 is coming; or
22.♖e7±. **21.c4 ♔g7 22.♔c2** Black
is passive and White can improve
slowly. **22...♖e8 23.♖xe8 ♘xe8
24.♗xd8** The immediate 24.d5 was
also promising. **24...♖xd8 25.♔c3
♔f6 26.b4 ♘c7** Here 26...g5
27.hxg5+ ♔xg5 28.♘d3 ♘g7± could
have given Black some hopes for
counterplay. **27.d5 cxd5 28.♘xd5+
♔g7 29.a4 ♘e6 30.a5 a6 31.♖d2
♔f8 32.f4 ♖d7 33.g3 ♖d8? 34.♘c7
1-0** A nice game!

Black castles queenside
7...♗xd3 8.♕xd3

Alexander Predke   **3**
Ivan Rozum
Khanty-Mansiysk 2018 (6)
**1.e4 c6 2.d4 d5 3.♘c3 dxe4
4.♘xe4 ♗f5 5.♘g3 ♗g6 6.h4
h6 7.♗d3 ♗xd3 8.♕xd3 e6**
8...♘f6 9.♗d2 ♘bd7 10.0-0-0 e6
11.♔b1 ♕c7 12.c4!? 0-0-0 13.♗c3.
White delays the development
of the g1-knight and keeps Black
guessing. This interesting plan was
seen in a game between two chess
legends back in 1966! 13...c5 14.d5
♘b6 15.♘e4? (surprisingly enough,
this move should lose immediately.
After 15.♕c2!? exd5 16.♗xf6
gxf6 17.cxd5 ♖xd5 18.♖xd5 ♘xd5
19.♘1e2 ♘b4 20.♕f5+ ♔b8 21.♖d1
White has some edge) 15...♗e7?
(15...bxd5!−+) 16.♘xf6 ♗xf6
17.♘f3 ♕f4 18.♗xf6 gxf6 19.♕c3
♕xc4 20.♕xc4 ♘xc4 21.dxe6 fxe6
22.♖c1 ♘d2+ (22...b5!?∓) 23.♘xd2
♖xd2 24.♖xc5+ ♔b8 25.♖c2 ♖hd8
26.♔c1 ♖xc2+ 27.♔xc2 ♖d4 28.♖e1
½-½ Matanovic-Pomar, Palma

de Mallorca 1966. **9.♗d2 ♘f6
10.♘1e2 ♘bd7 11.0-0-0 ♕c7**
11...♕b6!? is more active and will be
covered in Game 4.

12.♘e4 Even if Black's king
goes to the queenside, one of
White's main plans here is to
push g2-g4-g5 anyway, so the
knight doesn't block the g-pawn.
The next step is probably to go
♕f3 to support the pawn. That
is why Black's next move seems
to be inaccurate. Waiting with
12.♔b1 doesn't change much, but
if White's plan is to exchange the
knights with ♘e4 to open the
road for the g-pawn it should be
done immediately. Because now
after 12...0-0-0 (in case of 12...♗e7
here is a sample line where White
can get some advantage: 13.♘e4
0-0-0 14.♗f4 ♕a5 15.♘d6+ ♗xd6
16.♗xd6 ♘b6 17.♔h2! (threatening
18.♕g3) 17...♘g4 (if Black plays
something like 17...♕b4?!, White
can start a strong attack with
pieces: 18.♕g3 ♘bd5 19.a3 ♕b5
20.♖d3 ♘e4 21.♕b8+ ♗d7 22.♕e5
♘df6 23.♕f4↑) 18.♗g3 ♘f6 19.f3
♕b5 20.b3 ♕xd3 21.♖xd3 ♘bd5
22.h5 ♖d7 23.♗e5 and White has
some advantage, but Black is
solid) 13.♘e4?? loses on the spot
due to 13...♘e5! 14.♕e3 ♘eg4
15.♕f3 ♘xe4 16.♕xe4 ♘xf2−+,
so be careful! Instead, 13.♖he1!?
was played in two games by two
famous Russian players: 13...♗d6
14.♘e4 (14.c4 ♖he8 15.♕f3 ♗f8
16.♘c3 ♘b4 17.♗f4?! (17.a3!? ♗f8
(17...♖xc3 18.♗xc3 ♗b8 19.♘f1
♘b6 20.b3 ♗c8 21.g4±) 18.♗f4
♗d6 19.♗xd6 ♕xd6 20.♘ge4
♕c7 21.c5±) 17...♕a5 18.♗d2 ♘b6
19.♕d3 ♘g4 20.a3? ♗xf2 21.♕c2?
♘xc4! 22.♖c1 ♖xd4 23.♗e3 ♘xa3+?

(23...♘xe3 24.♖xe3 ♘g4–+)
24.bxa3 ♗c4 25.♕b3 ♗xc3 26.♖e2
♕d5 27.♖xc3 ♖xc3 28.♕xc3 ♘d1
29.♕c2 ♖d8? 30.♗xa7? (30.♗d2=)
30...♕a5 31.♗e3 ♘c3+ 32.♔b2
♘xe2 33.♘xe2 ♕e5+ 34.♕c3
♕b5+ 0-1 Gunina-Sargsyan,
Batumi 2019) 14...♘xe4 15.♕xe4
♖he8 16.♕g4 ♖g8 17.♘c1+ ♔b8
18.♕d3 (18.♕f3!? ♕b6 19.♘d3±)
18...e5 19.dxe5 ♘xe5 20.♘xe5 ♗xe5
21.♗e3 ♖xd1+ 22.♖xd1 ♖d8 23.h5
♖xd1+ 24.♕xd1 ♕d6? (it seems it
would have been easier to defend
this position with the queens
on the board) 25.♕xd6+ ♗xd6
26.c3 ♗c7 27.♔c2 a6 28.♔d3 ♗d7
29.♔e4 ♗e6 30.g4± f6 31.♗b6 ♗e7
32.b4 ♗d6 33.f4 ♗e7 34.♗c5 ♗xc5
35.bxc5 f5+?? (35...♗e7 36.♔f5
♔f7 and Black holds) 36.gxf5+
♔f6 37.a3 a5 38.a4 ♔f7 39.♔e5
♗e7 40.f6+ 1-0 Najer-Suleymanli,
Moscow rapid 2019. **12...♘xe4**
12...0-0-0 could save some time
for Black, e.g. 13.♕f3 and only
now 13...♘xe4 14.♕xe4 ♘f6 15.♕f3
♕b6!?=. **13.♕xe4 ♘f6 14.♕f3
h5** After 14...0-0-0 15.♔b1 c5!?
16.dxc5 ♗xc5 17.♗c3 (or 17.♘c1±)
17...♖xd1+ 18.♖xd1 ♖d8 19.♖xd8+
♕xd8 20.♘c1 White has some
advantage. **15.♔b1 0-0-0**

16.♘c1 Here, 16.♗g5 was also
interesting. After 16...♗e7 17.♖d3
♕a5 (aiming to go to d5) 18.c4 ♖d7
19.♖hd1 it is difficult for either
side to make progress, but White's
position is slightly preferable. For
example, the natural 19...♖hd8
is already a slight inaccuracy,
because the h-pawn is vulnerable
now: 20.c5 (threatening 21.♖a3)
20...♔b8 21.♗f4 ♖h8 22.♗xf6 ♗xf6
23.♘xh5 ♗xd4. White has a nice
tactical trick: 24.♘f6 gxf6 25.♖xd4

♖xd4 26.♖xd4 and White is better,
but 24.♖xd4 could also give some
advantage, e.g. 24...♖xd4 25.♖xd4
♕xc5 26.♕d3 ♖xh5 27.♖d8+
♔c7 28.♕d7+ ♔b6 29.♖b8 ♕f5+
30.♔a1±. The computer suggests
a long sequence of manoeuvres,
for example: 19...♕a6 20.♖c1
♕a5 21.♘c3 ♕b8 22.♖cd1 ♖hd8
23.g3 ♕a6 24.b3 ♕a5 25.♔b2
♘g4 26.♗xe7 ♖xe7 27.♕e2 ♕c7
28.♘e4 but White's position is
still slightly preferable. **16.♗e7**
16...♕g4!? 17.♕b3 g6 18.♗g5 ♗e7
19.♗c1 ♗f8 20.♖d3 ♔b8 21.♕e2±;
16...♗e7 17.♘b3 ♗d7 18.g3 ♖hd8
19.♖he1 ♖d5 20.c4 ♖5d7 21.♖c1±;
16...♖xd4?! 17.♗a5 ♖xd1 18.♗xc7
♖xh1 19.♗g3±. **17.♘b3 ♖d7 18.c4
♕d8 19.♔a1 ♕g8 20.♗f4** 20.♗g5
♕h7 21.♖he1 ♖hd8 22.a3 ♔b8
23.♖e2 ♖a8 24.♘a2±. **20...♕h7
21.g3 ♕f5 22.♕e3 ♖hd8 23.d5!?**
Sharpening the game. **23...e5
24.♕xa7 exf4 25.♖he1** 25.♕d4!?
♕e5 26.dxc6 bxc6 27.♕a8+ ♔c7
28.♕xc6+ ♔b8 29.♖xd7 ♘xd7
30.♘c6+ ♔c7 31.♘xe5 ♘xe5
32.♖d8 ♖xd8 33.♖d1±. **25...c5?**
25...♕e4! 26.f3 ♕c5 27.♖xe7 ♘xb3+
28.axb3 ♖xe7 29.♕a8+ ♔c7
30.♕a5+ ♔c8 31.♕a8+=. **26.♖xe7**
26.♘a5!? ♕e4 27.♕a8+ ♔c7
28.♕xb7+ ♔d6 29.♘c6+ ♔e5
30.f3+–. **26...♖xe7 27.♘xc5+–
♕c2 28.♕a8+?** 28.♖b1!+–.
**28...♔c7 29.♕xb7+ ♔d6
30.♕b6+ ♔e5 31.♖g1!** The only
move that doesn't lose! **31...♖a8
32.gxf4+ ♔xf4?** 32...♔f5! 33.♖g5+
♔xf4 34.♕d6+ ♔f3 35.♖g3+ ♔e2
36.♕xe7+ ♔f1= and Black's king
is safe! **33.♘e6+! ♖xe6 34.dxe6
♕e4 35.exf7 ♕e5 36.♕b4 ♕b8
37.♕c5 ♘g4 38.♕d4+ ♔f5 39.f3
♘f6 40.♕e3 ♘d7 41.♕d3+ ♔e6
42.♖e1+ ♔xf7 43.♕xd7+ ♔g8
44.♕e6+ ♔h8 45.♖e5 1-0**

Jorden van Foreest 4
Marcin Dziuba
Germany Bundesliga 2019/20 (7)
**1.e4 c6 2.d4 d5 3.♘d2 dxe4
4.♘xe4 ♗f5 5.♘g3 ♗g6 6.h4 h6
7.♗d3 ♗xd3 8.♕xd3 e6 9.♘1e2
♘f6 10.♗d2 ♘bd7 11.0-0-0 ♕b6**

A more active square for the
queen. In this game Black tried
to attack on the queenside, but
sometimes there is also an option
of ...♕b5, trying to exchange the
queens. I think in general it works
well when White has a bishop on
f4 and has played ♘e4, so if White
meets ...♕b5 with c2-c4, Black's
queen will jump to f5. It was seen
in one correspondence game:
11...♗e7 12.♔b1 ♕b6:
A) Here 13.♘f4!?N could be
interesting. 13...0-0-0 (if Black
now castles kingside, White has
a little trick: 13...0-0 14.♘gh5
♘xh5 15.♘xh5 ♘f6 16.♗g5! ♘xh5
17.♗xe7 ♖fe8 18.♕a3 ♕b5 19.g4
♘f4 20.♗d6 ♕d5 21.g5 h5 22.g6↑)
14.♖he1 ♖he8 15.♗c1 ♗f8 16.a3!?±
– White is slowly improving
his position. If Black keeps
manoeuvring, White's plan can
be something like ♕f3, ♘gh5 and
g2-g4-g5;
B) 13.♘e4 0-0-0 (now it's
dangerous to castle kingside:
13...0-0 14.♘xf6+ ♘xf6 15.g4±)
14.♗f4 ♕b5 15.♕xb5 (15.c4 ♕f5
16.♘xf6 ♘xf6 17.f3 ♕xd3+ 18.♖xd3
h5=; or even 18...g5!?=) 15...cxb5.
The endgame is more or less equal:
16.♘xf6 ♘xf6 17.♖d3 ♖d5 18.♗g3
b4 19.♖f3 ♗f6 20.a3 bxa3 21.♖xa3
a6 22.c4 ♘e7 23.♖d3 ♘f5 24.d5
exd5 25.cxd5 ♗d7 26.♘f4 ♘xg3
27.♖xg3 ♗e5 28.♖f3 ♔d6 29.♖e1
♖d7 30.♘h5 ♖e7 31.♘g3 g6 32.♘e4+
♔xd5 33.h5 ♖g8 34.g3 ♗c6 35.♘f6
♗xf6 36.♖xf6+ ♔d7 37.♖xe7+
♔xe7 38.♖b6 gxh5 39.♖xb7+ ½-½
Leupold-Ruggieri, cr 2014. **12.♔b1
0-0-0**

13.♘c3!? Now Black no longer
has ...♕b5 and also White at
some point can meet ...c6-c5 with

d4-d5. Here again 13.♘e4?? runs into 13...♘e5−+. Something like 13.♗f4N is also interesting. In case of 13...♗e7 14.c4 (note that 14.♘e4 allows 14...♗b5! 15.♕xb5 cxb5 16.♘xf6 ♘xf6 17.a3 ♘g4 18.♖df1 ♗d6 19.♗xd6 ♖xd6 20.c3 ♖e8=) 14...♖he8 15.♕c2±. White can push c4-c5 or d4-d5 in the future. **13...♗e7 14.♗f4** In case of 14.♖he1, 14...♖e8!? could be interesting, e.g. 15.♕f3 ♘d6 16.b3 ♖he8 17.♗f4 ♘f6 18.♗c1 ♕a5 19.♗b2 ♗d7 20.♖e5 ♕c7 21.♘a4±. **14...♖he8 15.♕f3** 15.♖he1 ♕a5 16.♘ce4 ♘xe4 17.♘xe4 ♘f6 18.♗e5 ♘xe4 19.♖xe4±, White retains some pressure. **15...♕a5 16.♖he1 ♘b6** Black tries to be active on the queenside, but White has enough defensive resources. **17.♘ce4** More precise could be 17.♗c1!? or 17.♖e5 ♕a6 18.♘h5!?. **17...♘c4** 17...♖xd4!? 18.♖xd4 ♕xe1+ 19.♖d1 ♕a5 20.♘xf6 ♗xf6 21.♘e4 ♗e7 22.♘d6 ♕f5 23.♕e2 ♕b5 – it seems like Black could equalize here. Also good was 17...♘fd5 18.♗c1 f5 19.♘d2 ♗xh4 20.♘h5∞. **18.♗c1 ♖d5?!** This move allows White to damage Black's kingside pawn structure. After 18...♘xe4 19.♘xe4 ♕f5 20.♕g3 ♖g8 21.f3 ♕b5 White would be a bit better. **19.♘xf6 gxf6** If 19...♗xf6 White could try the direct 20.♘e4 (or 20.c3!? ♖e7 21.♘e4 ♗xh4 22.♕d3 b5 23.♖h1 ♗g5 24.f4 ♗f6 25.g4 ♖ed7 26.♖xh6!±) 20...♖xd4 21.c3 f5 22.cxd4 fxe4 23.♕xe4 ♕b4 24.♕g6 with good chances. **20.♕d3 ♕a6 21.b3 ♘a3+ 22.♔b2 b5?** Black had to enter a worse endgame: 22...♕xd3 23.♖xd3 ♗d7 24.c3 ♘b5 25.♘h5 f5 26.g3 ♖h8 27.♔c2 ♗c7 28.a4 ♘d5 29.♗d2±. **23.♕h7!+− ♖f8 24.♖xe6! b4** The last chance, but White calculated everything well. Of course, after 24...fxe6 25.♕xe7 ♖fd8 26.♕xa3 White is simply winning. **25.♖xe7 ♖a5 26.♗f4 ♔d8 27.♖xf7 ♘c4+ 28.♔c1 ♖xf7 29.♕xf7 ♖d5 30.♕c7+ ♔e8 31.bxc4 ♕a3+ 32.♔b1 1-0**

Dragoljub Minic   5
Milan Vukic

Vrnjacka Banja ch-YUG sf 1966

1.e4 c6 2.d4 d5 3.♘c3 dxe4 4.♘xe4 ♗f5 5.♘g3 ♗g6 6.h4 h6 7.♗d3 ♕xd4 This leaves Black behind in development, but it is not obvious how White can exploit this. **8.♘f3 ♕d6 9.♗xg6 ♕xg6** 9...♕xd1+ 10.♔xd1 fxg6 11.♘e5±.

10.♕e2 The sharpest plan. White wants to attack with the queens on the board. After 10.♗e3!? Black can choose from two worse endgames. This is covered in Game 6 in the notes to move 9. **10...♕d6?!** 10...♕d7 was played in the same year in the same country! Now White has a choice, but in any case it seems like Black should hold with precise play. But is it possible in a practical game?

A) 11.♗f4 ♕g4! (if 11...e6 12.0-0-0 ♘gf6 13.h5 ♕h7 14.♘d4 ♗e7 15.♘df5 exf5 16.♖he1↑ Black's queen is out of play) 12.♗c7! ♖c8 (12...♘gf6 13.0-0-0 ♘d5 14.♖d4 ♕e6 15.♕xe6 fxe6 16.♗a5±) 13.♘e4 e6 14.♘d6+ ♗xd6 15.♗xd6 ♘gf6 16.0-0-0∞;

B) 11.h5 ♕d6 12.♖h4?! (here, 12.0-0 ♕c7 13.♖d1 e6 14.♘d4 ♘gf6 15.♗f4∞ would lead to more or less the same, but with the king being in a safer place) 12...e6 13.♖d4 ♕c7 14.♗f4 ♕a5+ 15.♗d2 ♕b5∓ 16.c4 ♕xb2 17.♖d1 ♘gf6 18.♘e4 0-0-0 (18...♗e7!? 19.♘xf6+ ♘xf6 20.♖d3 0-0 21.♖b3 ♕xa2 22.♖xb7 ♗c5−+; White's doesn't have enough compensation) 19.♘xf6 gxf6 20.♕d3 ♕a3 21.♗c3 ♗b4 22.♗xb4

♕xb4+ 23.♔f1 ♕e7 24.♕e3 ♕b4 25.♔g1 ♕a5 26.♖d6 a6 27.a7 ♕c7?? (27...♕b6! 28.♖a8+ ♘b8 29.c5 ♖xd6 30.cxb6 ♖xd1+ 31.♔h2 ♖hd8−+) 28.♖xd7 ♖xd7 29.♕a8+ ♕b8 30.♕xb8+ ♔xb8 31.♖xd7 1-0 Maric-Susic, Yugoslavia 1966. **11.0-0 e6 12.♖d1 ♕c7 13.♖d4** 13.♘e5! ♘f6 14.♗f4+− g5 (14...♕b6 15.♘g6 ♖h7 16.♘xf8 ♔xf8 17.♖d6 ♘bd7 18.♖ad1±; 14...♘c8 15.♘c4 ♘bd7 16.♘f5+−) 15.♘e4! (also good for White would be the simplest option: 15.hxg5 hxg5 16.♗xg5+−) 15...♘xe4 16.♗h2 ♘d6 17.♘c4 ♖g8 18.♖xd6+ ♗xd6 19.♖xd6 ♕e7 20.♖ad1+−. **13...♘f6 14.♗f4 ♕a5 15.♘e5 c5 16.b4** The most beautiful, but not the best. 16.♖d3 ♘bd7 17.♘g6 ♖h7 18.♘xf8 ♔xf8 19.♕f3+−. **16...♕a4?** Black should have taken the pawn, but, of course, the position was too complicated: 16...cxb4! 17.♘h5 ♕a6 18.♖d3 ♘bd7 19.♘xd7 ♘xd7 20.♖ad1 ♘c5 21.♕e5 ♘xd3 22.♕xg7+ ♔xg7 23.♕xg7 ♔e7 24.♖xd3↑.

17.♖d8+! ♔xd8 18.♘xf7+ ♔c8 19.♕xe6+ ♘bd7 20.♖e1! b6 21.♘f5 21.♘e4!+−. **21...♖g8** 21...♔b7 22.b5 ♕xf4 23.♕c6+ ♔b8 24.♘5d6 ♗xd6 25.♘xd6 ♕xd6 26.♕xd6+ ♔b7 27.♕c6+ ♔b8 28.♗e7 a6 29.♖xd7 ♘xd7 30.♕xd7 axb5 31.♕xg7. **22.♘5d6+** 22.♖d1! cxb4 23.♘7d6+ ♔c7 24.♘b5+ ♔b7 25.♖xd7+ ♗a6 26.♘c7+ ♔b7 27.♖f7+−. **22...♗xd6 23.♘xd6+?** This hands Black an escape route. 23.♕xd6! ♗b7 24.♕c7+ ♔a6 25.♘d6 cxb4 26.♕b7+ ♔a5 27.a3!!+−. The only winning move! **23...♔c7! 24.♘c4+ ♔b7! 25.♘d6+** 25.b5! ♖ac8 26.♖d1 ♘b8! (26...♔a8?! 27.♖xd7! ♕xb5 28.♖xg7

♕c6 29.♕xc6+ ♖xc6 30.♗xh6±)
27.♘d6+ ♚a8 28.♕e3 (Black is a
rook up but finds it surprisingly
difficult to take care of the
precarious placement of his king)
28...♖ce8! 29.♕f3+ ♘e4 30.♖e1 g5!
31.♖xe4 ♖xe4 32.♘xe4 g4 33.♕d3
♕d4 34.♗xh6 and Black has
not equalized yet, viz. 34...♕xd3
35.cxd3 ♗d7 36.♚h2 ♘e5 37.♚g3
♘xd3 38.♗g5. **25...♚c7 26.♘b5+
♚b7 27.♘d6+ ♚c7 ½-½**

**Jose Maria Gutierrez Dopino
Pedro Canizares Cuadra   6**
cr 2011
**1.e4 c6 2.d4 d5 3.♘c3 dxe4
4.♘xe4 ♗f5 5.♘g3 ♗g6 6.h4 h6
7.♗d3 ♕xd4 8.♘f3 ♕g4**

9.♗e3!? White could also develop
this bishop after the exchange of

the light-squared bishops, but now
with this move-order Black can't
switch to 10...♕d6 (see 9.♗xg6). Of
course, it gives Black some other
possibilities, but it seems they
are not so good. 9.♗xg6 ♕xg6
10.♗e3 ♕d6 (10...♘f6? 11.♘e5 ♕h7
12.♕d2 ♘d5 13.0-0-0± – c2-c4 is
coming, White is already winning;
10...♘d7 transposes to the game)
11.♕xd6 exd6 12.0-0-0 ♘d7 13.♗f4
(also interesting may be 13.♘f5
d5 (13...0-0-0 14.♘xd6+ ♗xd6
15.♖xd6 ♘gf6 16.♖d2 c5 17.♖hd1
♖he8 18.♗f4±) 14.♗d4 ♖h7 15.c4 c5
16.♖he1+ ♚d8 17.♗e5 d4 18.♗d6 g6
19.♗xf8 gxf5 20.♗d6∞) 13...0-0-0
(13...d5 14.♖he1+ ♚d8 15.c4 ♘gf6
16.♘e5 ♘xe5 17.♗xe5 ♗g4 18.♗d4
♚c7 19.f3 ♘f6 20.♘f5±) 14.♗xd6
♗xd6 15.♖xd6 ♘gf6 16.♖d4 and
White is a bit better. **9...♘d7** After
9...♕xd3 10.♕xd3 Black is too late
with his development: 10...♕b4+
(10...♘d7 11.0-0-0 ♘gf6 12.♕b3 b5
13.♘d4 ♖c8 (13...a6 14.♘xc6 ♕c4
15.♕xc4 bxc4 16.♖d4±) 14.♘gf5↑)
11.♗d2 ♕d6 12.♕e2 ♕c7 13.♘e5
♘d7 14.♘xd7 ♕xd7 15.0-0-0↑.
10.♗xg6 ♕xg6 11.c4 Probably
better was 11.♕xd7+ ♚xd7 12.♘e5+

♚e8 13.♘xg6 fxg6 14.0-0-0 ♘f6
15.♖he1 e6 16.♗d4 ♗e7 (16...♚f7?!
17.♗xf6! gxf6 18.♖d7+ ♗e7 19.h5!
♖he8 (19...g5? 20.♘f5+–) 20.hxg6+
♚xg6 21.♖xb7 ♗d6 22.♘e4±)
17.♖xe6 ♚f7=; Black's doubled
pawns are not weak. **11...♕d6!
12.♕xd6 exd6 13.0-0-0 0-0-0
14.♘e4 c5 15.♘xd6+ ♗xd6
16.♖xd6 ♘gf6 17.♖hd1 ♘g4** Now
it's probably White who should be
precise. **18.♖1d3 ♖he8**

19.♚c2?! 19.♚d2!?=. **19...♖e4
20.♚c3** 20.b3!? ♘xe3+ 21.fxe3 b6∓.
**20...♘xe3 21.fxe3 ♖e7∓ 22.♖6d5
♖de8 23.g4 ♘f6?!** 23...b6 24.g5
hxg5 25.hxg5 ♘b8 26.♖f5 ♘c6∓.
**24.♖xc5+ ♚b8 25.♘d2 b6 26.♖f5
♘xg4 27.e4 ♗b7 28.b4 f6 29.h5
♘e5 30.♖d4 ♖c7 31.♖f1 ♖e6
32.a3 ♖e8 ½-½**

Exercise 1

position after 15.♘g3-e4

This position was reached in a
game of two famous GMs back
in 1966. It seems like they both
missed something important.
Can you find it?

(solutions on page 247)

Exercise 2

position after 14.♗d2-f4

Can you find the equalizing
manoeuvre?

Exercise 3

position after 22...b7-b5

Find the best continuation.

The pressure is on Black – Part II

by Robert Ris (special contribution by Anish Giri)

1.	e4	e5
2.	♘f3	♘f6
3.	d4	♘xe4
4.	♗d3	d5
5.	♘xe5	♘d7
6.	0-0	

In Yearbook 134 I wrote a Survey on the double-edged continuation 6.♘c3!?, as World Champion Magnus Carlsen and Wesley So both won impressive games in that line. This time, I will have a look at 6.0-0, which proves to be another critical test for Black as Caruana won a very nice game against Yu Yangyi in Wijk aan Zee this year. At first glance, the position after 6...♘xe5 7.dxe5 ♘c5 doesn't seem to offer White much, but apparently things are much trickier for Black, as there are a lot of hidden subtleties with move-orders.

The board has been divided into two parts with the white pawn on e5 vs the black pawn on d5. White will often try to generate a quick attack on the kingside with f2-f4-f5, whereas Black aims to set up a blockade on the light squares with ...g7-g6 and/or challenge the head of White's pawn chain (pawn on e5) with a quick ...f7-f6. White on the other hand has a choice whether to break on the queenside with c2-c4 or not. As you see, it's hard to make general statements, as it simply depends on the exact placement of every single piece whether these plans will work out well for either side.

A critical position

One critical position arises after 8.♗e3 c6 9.f4 ♘xd3 10.♕xd3 g6 11.♘c3.

In Caruana-Yu Yangyi, Black played 11...b6!?, while after 11...♗e7 12.♘e2 play would have transposed to the main line of the variation with 6.0-0. In the analyses of the games Areschenko-Rustemov (12...♗f5, Game 2) and Adams-Sandipan (12...0-0, Game 3) we will have a closer look at the current status of this line.

Fabiano Caruana

The ♘c3-e2 manoeuvre

In Caruana-Villanueva (Game 4), 8.♘c3 c6 9.f4 g6 10.♘e2 was tested.

The ♘c3-e2 manoeuvre is quite common in these structures (either going to d4 or to g3 to prepare f4-f5), though in certain lines White prefers to postpone the development of the knight to c3 and rather bring it to d2 or play c2-c4 first. In this particular case, as White hasn't developed his bishop to e3 yet, Black decided to play 10...♗g7, though in the ensuing structure with ...♘xd3, cxd3 the bishop isn't particularly well placed on the long diagonal in my opinion.

Various options

On move 8, White has tried various options. To remain as flexible as possible is usually good advice, but as you will understand, all the alternatives have their pros and cons. For instance, the move 8.♗e2, not allowing Black to grab the pair of bishops, has mainly been played, but I doubt if giving up a tempo by making another move with the bishop is really worth it. Recently this old move has disappeared from the highest level. However, in the analysis of the game Tkachiev-Giri (Game 5) you'll be shown in several lines how things can go wrong for Black. It's worth remembering that in the structures after ...f7-f6, exf6 ♖xf6 White often will launch his 3 vs 2 kingside with the aggressive idea g2-g4!.

Finally, it is also possible to start with 8.f4, not revealing the exact developing plans of the pieces on the queenside. In Kamsky-Gelfand (Game 6), Black opted for 8...g6, though in my annotations you will see that I prefer to start by taking the bishop on d3. A transposition to one of the positions reached in Games 1-3 seems inevitable.

Conclusion

As you have seen, this particular variation against the Petroff leads to strategically complex middlegames. White has so many tricky move-order ideas that Black has to be very careful. Objectively speaking, this line shouldn't pose Black too many problems from a theoretical viewpoint, but in general I tend to believe that White's position is easier to play (i.e. he is certainly risking less than his opponent!). All in all, I believe that both this line with 6.0-0 as well as 6.♘c3 are dangerous practical attempts, unbalancing the ultra-solid Petroff.

A critical position
8.♗e3

Fabiano Caruana 1
Yu Yangyi

Wijk aan Zee 2020 (3)

1.e4 e5 2.♘f3 ♘f6 Yu Yangyi likes his Petroff, but so does Fabiano Caruana. He is a well-known expert in this opening, so it was to be expected that he would bring something to the table here. **3.d4 ♘xe4 4.♗d3 d5 5.♘xe5 ♘d7 6.0-0 ♘xe5 7.dxe5 ♘c5 8.♗e3 c6** Yu Yangyi was most likely prepared, because postponing the move ...♗e7 seems to make sense. 8...♘xd3 9.♕xd3 ♗e7 10.f4 g6 11.♘c3 c6 is a major tabiya that White wanted to get in this game and that Yu Yangyi avoided. **9.f4 ♘xd3 10.♕xd3 g6 11.♘c3 b6!?** An idea of Ju Wenjun, and again, I don't know if it was preparation of improvisation, but developing the bishop to g7 makes a lot of sense here. 11...♗e7 12.♘e2 is the main line, if we can call the most played continuation a main line.

12.♖ad1 Fabi improves on a game between the Women's World Champion and her recent challenger. That game saw 12.♘e2 ♗g7 13.♘g3 0-0 14.c3 c5 15.♖ad1 ♗b7 and White was just getting outplayed (0-1, 54) in Goryachkina-Ju Wenjun, St Petersburg rapid 2018. **12...♗g7** 12...♗f5 is an alternative. **13.b4** Using the fact that the bishop has left the diagonal. But Yu Yangyi responds very well. **13...♗f5 14.♕e2 ♖c8 15.h3 0-0** Now 16.b5 can be met with 16...f6, with lots of simplifications incoming. Black is about to survive the opening test.

16.g4 ♗e6 17.b5 f5! Essentially the same as 17...f6. **18.exf6 ♗xf6 19.♗d4 ♗xd4+ 20.♖xd4 cxb5 21.♘xb5** Black has an ugly bishop, but White's knight hasn't yet reached the d4-square. Yu Yangyi uses the opportunity to simplify further. **21...♗d7!?** A very human way to try to solve things. Black gives up a pawn, but has obvious counterplay against both the queenside weaknesses and the f4-pawn. In fact, all he now needs is to trade queens and then any rook endgame would be too drawish not to hold. **22.♖xd5 ♗xb5 23.♖xb5** 23.♕xb5 ♕xc2 24.♖d7 ♕c5+ is going to peter out quickly, clearly. **23...♕c3 24.♖b3**

24...♕c5+? This is the main mistake in the game. In fact, I happened to walk right past their board at this point and from Fabiano's whole demeanour I could see that he didn't believe in his position, and rightly so, as the endgame would be totally holdable for Black. Therefore Black should have played 24...♕d4+! 25.♕e3 (25.♔g2 just invites 25...♕xf4) 25...♕xe3+ 26.♖xe3 ♖ac8 27.c3 ♖c4 and it's more or less a forced draw, besides just being drawish in general. Very strange that a defender of Yu's calibre didn't go for this! **25.♔g2** In fact, it is not so easy for Black, as with queens on it turns out that Black's king can be a target too, after a well timed f4-f5 push. 25.♔h2!? was also interesting, giving the queen space on g2. **25...♖ae8?** 25...♖fe8! was better, as after 26.♕d2 ♖ad8 Black causes White more trouble than in the game. **26.♕d2 ♖e4 27.♖f2 ♕c6?** And here 27...♖c4 was better, as White may want to go ♔g3 anyway. **28.♔g3 ♖c4 29.♖d3** Now White has sort of consolidated

and is still a pawn up. It's getting very unpleasant for Black. **29...♖f7 30.♖d6 ♕c5 31.f5** 31.♖d8+ ♔g7 32.f5 was possible too. **31...♕e5+?** 31...♖f8! would still have kept things together. But this would have required very clear calculation, and for that a lot of time is needed and preferably no pressure. **32.♔g2 ♖c3** This all doesn't work out as ...gxf5 is never possible. **33.♖f3! ♖xf3 34.♔xf3 ♖e7 35.♖d5?** This allows Black to get back onto the defensive track, but in time trouble Yu Yangyi doesn't manage. Both 35.♕d3 or 35.f6 were cleaner, apparently. **35...♕e4+ 36.♔g3**

36...♔g7? Missing 36...gxf5!. A rook or queen endgame would be a blessing for Black at this point: 37.♖xf5 (or 37.♕g5+ ♔h8 38.♕f6+ ♔g8 39.♖d8+ ♖e8) 37...♕e1+ with clearly better chances to hold. **37.♖d6?** A gross miscalculation. Here 37.♔h4! was an elegant prophylactic move, when Black, unable to trade queens in a favourable version, is losing, for instance after 37...♖f7 38.♕c3+ ♔h6 39.fxg6 ♖xd5 40.gxf7 ♕xf7. Another brilliant idea of the engine is 37.c4!, anticipating the rook endgame: 37...♕e3+ 38.♕xe3 ♖xe3+ 39.♔f4 ♖xh3 40.♖d7+ ♔f8 41.fxg6 h6 42.♖xa7 and White wins. **37...♕e5+?** This is losing by force. There were two ways to try and hold the game. To begin with, 37...gxf5!, when after 38.♕g5+ ♔h8 39.♖d8+ ♖e8 40.♖xe8+ ♕xe8 41.♕xf5 ♕e1+ 42.♔f4 ♕c1+ 43.♔e5 ♕a1+ 44.♔d6 ♕xa2! it's a draw as the queen is just in time to come back to g8 after picking up a vital pawn. And most likely Black should be able

to hold the rook ending after 37...♕e3+ 38.♕xe3 ♖xe3+ 39.♔f4 ♖xh3 40.♖d7+ ♔f8! and the battle continues. **38.♔h4! gxf5** 38...♔f7! would have prolonged the game, but it is already very lost at this point. **39.♕h6+ ♔g8 40.♖d8+ ♖e8 41.♖d7!** And now it's not hard to see that White gets a won pawn endgame by force: **41...♖e7 42.♕g5+ ♔f7 43.♖xe7+ ♕xe7 44.♕xe7+ ♔xe7 45.gxf5 ♔f6 46.♔g4** The rest is elementary. **46...♔e5 47.♔g5 b5 48.c3 1-0**

M/20-2-13 Giri

Alexander Areschenko 2
Alexander Rustemov
Germany Bundesliga 2012/13 (12)
1.e4 e5 2.♘f3 ♘f6 3.d4 ♘xe4 4.♗d3 d5 5.♘xe5 ♘d7 6.0-0 ♘xe5 7.dxe5 ♘c5 8.♘c3 c6 9.♘e2 g6 10.♗e3 ♗e7 11.f4 ♘xd3 12.♕xd3

12...♗f5 12...h5?! 13.♖ad1 0-0 14.f5! with a crushing attack for White. Compared with Polgar-Gelfand (in the notes to Game 3), the pawn on h5 has further weakened Black's kingside: 14...♗xf5 15.♕xf5 gxf5 16.♕xf5 ♗g7 17.♘g3 ♖h8 18.♖f1 ♕g8 19.♘xh5+ ♔f8 20.e6 ♖h7 21.♘f6 ♗xf6 22.♕xf6 ♔e8 23.♗c5 fxe6 24.♕f8+ ♕xf8 25.♖xf8+ ♔d7 26.♖xa8 1-0 Perunovic-Fridman, Skopje blitz 2018. **13.♕b3** The critical move. White keeps an eye on the b7-pawn and intends to increase the pressure on the f5-square as well. 13.♕c3 0-0 14.♘g3 (14.♗c5? ♗xc5+ 15.♕xc5 ♕b6! actually favours Black) 14...♕d7 15.♗c5 ♗xc5+ 16.♕xc5 b6 is fine for Black, Predke-Sychev, Moscow 2017. 13.♕d2 ♕d7 14.♘g3 0-0 15.♘xf5 ♕xf5 16.♖ae1 f6 and Black was in control in Sidenko-

Häusler, cr 2012. **13...♕d7** There is no reason to opt for the more passive 13...♕c8?! 14.♘g3 b6 15.c4 dxc4 16.♕xc4 ♗e6 (16...♕e6!? is tougher) 17.♕c2 with a powerful initiative for White in Firouzja-Niese, Tegernsee 2018. **14.♘g3** 14.h3?! was seen in Jones-A. Smirnov, PRO League blitz 2018, and now Black could just take control of the centre by means of 14...c5!. 14.♖ad1 was seen in Pali-Gunnarsson, San Agustin 1998, but it looks pretty harmless as Black can at least consider to swap his light-squared bishop for the knight with 14...♗g4=. **14...c5?!** I would rather not allow White to capture on f5. 14...b6 and now in Grandelius-A.Smith, Ronneby 2018, White could have played more energetically with 15.♘xf5 gxf5 (15...♕xf5 16.♕a4! is inconvenient for Black) 16.a4! with pressure on both sides of the board. I had a look at the new move 14...♗e6!? 15.♕d3 (15.♕c3 c5! 16.f5 (16.♗xc5? ♖c8 drops a piece) 16...gxf5 17.♘xf5 d4 (17...♗xf5? 18.e6! and White wins) 18.♘g7+ ♔f8 19.♘xe6+ ♕xe6 20.♕b3 ♕xb3 21.♗h6+ ♔e8 22.axb3 which is about equal; 15.f5 gxf5 16.♕d3 c5 17.♘xf5 0-0-0 doesn't seem to be too bad for Black, as the pawn on e5 becomes a possible target) 15...c5 16.c3 0-0-0. White will eventually decide whether to break on the queenside (b2-b4) or the kingside (f4-f5), but Black is very solid and ready when the position will be opened. **15.♘xf5 gxf5 16.♖ad1 0-0-0 17.♖d2 ♕e6 18.c3 ♖d7 19.♖fd1 ♖hd8**

After a logical sequence it seems that both sides have optimalized their pieces. However, Black's

position is pretty passive and he needs to wait for White to start any action on the queenside with b2-b4. Besides that, the isolated pawns on the kingside, and in particular the pawn on f5, are pretty vulnerable and require permanent protection from the black queen. **20.♕a4 b6 21.b4 d4 22.cxd4 cxb4** In case of 22...cxd4 23.♗xd4 Black seems to be just a pawn down. **23.a3 a5** 23...bxa3? 24.d5! was White's idea, as 24...♖xd5 fails to 25.♕c4+, winning the rook. **24.♕b5**

24...♖d5? More stubborn was 24...♕d5! 25.♕a6+ (25.♕xb6? ♖b7 26.♕a6 bxa3 could easily go wrong for White) 25...♔b8 26.axb4 ♗xb4 and Black is still fighting. In that sense we may draw the conclusion that White's queenside operation between move 20-24 could have been prepared more carefully. **25.♕a6+ ♔b8 26.axb4 ♖c8 27.♕d3?** After this move Black gets back into the game. Quite an instructive idea is 27.g4! ♖g8 (27...fxg4 28.f5 and White breaks through the centre) 28.♖c1 ♖xg4+ 29.♔f1 ♖g8 30.♖dc2 and White is just winning. **27...♗xb4 28.♖c2 ♖xc2 29.♕xc2 ♔b7 30.g4 fxg4 31.f5 ♕c6 32.♕e4 a4** 32...h5!?. **33.e6 fxe6 34.fxe6 ♗e7 35.♗f2 ♕a6 36.♕xh7 ♕d6 37.♗g3 ♕a3 38.♕g8 ♖d8 39.♕xg4 ♖d5** 39...♕a2=. **40.♕e2+ ♔b7** ≥ 40...b5!. **41.♕c2 ♕e3+?!** ≥ 41...b3. **42.♔g2 ♕b3** 42...♕xe6!? 43.♕c7+ ♔a6 44.♖e1 ♕d7 45.♖xe7 ♕xc7 46.♖xc7 with 47.h4+− to come; 42...♕g5 43.d5! ♗c5 44.♕h7+! ♔a6 45.♕d3+ ♕xd3 46.♖xd3 a3 47.♖d1 a2 48.♖a1 ♖xd5 49.♖xa2+ ♔b5 50.♖e2 ♗e7 51.♔f3+−.

43.♕c7+ 43.♕xb3! axb3 44.♔f3 △ 45.♔e4+−. **43...♔a6 44.♕c8+**

44...♔b5 Far more tenacious would have been 44...♔a5! but in the end it won't save Black in view of 45.♖f1!, providing shelter for the monarch: 45...♕b2+ (45...♖g5 46.♕a8+ ♔b4 47.♕e4! ♕d5 48.♕xd5 ♖xd5 49.♖f7 ♔d8 50.♗e5 a3 51.♖a7 ♔b3 52.♔f3 ♖xe5 53.dxe5 a2 54.♔g4 ♗e7 55.h4 b5 56.h5 ♗a3 57.♖xa3+ ♔xa3 58.e7 a1♕ 59.e8♕+−) 46.♖f2 ♕xd4 47.♕a8+ ♔b5 48.♕e8+ ♔a6 49.♖f4! ♗d8 50.♕xe7 ♕d5+ 51.♖f3 ♕a2+ 52.♔h3 ♖h8+ 53.♗h4 ♖h6 54.♕e8 ♕xe6+ 55.♕xe6 ♖xe6 56.♔g4. **45.♕e8+ ♔a6 46.♖d2** 46.♕a8+! ♔b5 47.♖b1 ♕xb1 48.♕xd5+ ♔a6 49.♕a8+ ♔b5 50.♕e8+ ♔c4 51.♕xe7+−. **46...♖f5 47.♕a8+! ♔b5 48.♕e4 ♕d5 49.♕xd5+ ♖xd5 50.♔f3 a3 51.♔e4 ♔c4 52.♗e5 ♖a5 53.d5 a2 54.♖d1 b5 55.d6 ♗xd6 56.♖xd6 a1♕ 57.♗xa1 ♖xa1 58.♖c6+ ♔b3 59.♔d5 ♖d1+ 60.♔c5 b4 61.e7 ♖e1 62.♔d6 1-0**

Michael Adams   3
Chanda Sandipan
Gibraltar 2018 (8)
1.e4 e5 2.♘f3 ♘f6 3.d4 ♘xe4
4.♗d3 d5 5.♘xe5 ♘d7 6.0-0 ♘xe5
7.dxe5 ♘c5 8.♗e3 ♗e7 9.f4 ♘xd3
10.♕xd3 g6 11.♘c3 c6

So here we are at the main tabiya that Giri was referring to in his notes to Caruana-Yu Yangyi. Black has established nice control over the light squares, so White's main idea is to improve the knight from c3 to get in the move f4-f5. **12.♘e2 0-0** 12...♗f5 – Game 2. **13.♘g3** Since Black has castled, the move 13.f5?! looks very tempting, but after 13...♗xf5 14.♖xf5 gxf5 15.♗h6 (15.♕xf5 ♕c8! is unproblematic for Black) 15...♔h8 16.♗xf8 ♗xf8 Black is better, Polgar-Gelfand, Khanty-Mansiysk 2009. At first, the black kingside may seem too weakened, but Black will be quickly coordinated with moves like ...♔g7, ...♔b6, ...♖e8, after which the pawn on e5 will drop. **13...♗h4** Premature is 13...f5?! 14.exf6 ♗xf6 15.f5 ♗xf5 16.♘xf5 gxf5 which was seen in Sengupta-Fridman, Warsaw 2017, and now a small refinement upon the immediate recapture on f5 is 17.♗c5!? and Black's position feels shaky. **14.♗c5 ♖e8** The only move, as the exchange of dark-squared bishops with 14...♗e7? is positionally not desirable for Black.

15.♖ad1 As Black is often intending to block the centre with ...f7-f5, the rook is likely to be best placed on d1.

A) Another game went 15.♖ae1 b6 16.♗d6 f5 and White decided to play 17.♖d1 anyway, as was seen in Kosteniuk-Ju Wenjun, Khanty-Mansiysk 2016. Black decided to exchange the dark-squared bishops with ...♗e7, but personally I would prefer to start with 17...a5!?, not allowing the knight to be improved with ♘g3-e2-d4;

B) 15.♔h1 ♗xg3 (the following game shows how dangerous Black's position could become in case the kingside gets opened: 15...b6 16.♗d6 a5 17.♖f3 f6?! (this move doesn't appeal to me at all) 18.c4! fxe5 19.fxe5 ♗e6 20.♖af1 dxc4 21.♕d2 ♗xg3 22.♖xg3 ♖a7 23.♕h6 ♗f5 24.h4 (24.♖xf5 ♕xd6 was Black's defensive resource) 24...♖f7 25.♔g1 (25.h5? ♕h4+!) 25...♗e6 26.♖xf7 ♗xf7 27.♖f3 ♕c8 28.♖f6 ♗e6 29.♕g5 ♔g7 30.h5 ♕d7 31.hxg6 h6 32.♕d2 a4 33.♖f7+! ♗xf7 34.♖f8+ ♔xf8 35.♕xd7 ♗xg6 36.♕xc6 ♔g7 37.♕xa4 ♖xe5 38.♕xc4 and White went on to win in Shablinsky-Biedermann, cr 2013) 16.♕xg3 ♗f5 17.c3 h5 18.h3 ♔h7 19.♔h2 b6 20.♗f2 (20.♗d6 is possible, but Black is very solid and frankly I don't see a constructive plan for White to improve his position) 20...♗e4 21.♕h4 ♕xh4 22.♗xh4 f5! (this excellent move must have been overlooked by Adams. Black is just in time before White starts pressing on the kingside by installing a bishop on f6 and playing g2-g4) 23.exf6 ♘g8 and soon a draw was agreed in Adams-Gelfand, Plovdiv 2010;

C) 15.♕c3 f6 (in conjunction with the Adams-Gelfand game I would recommend 15...♗xg3 16.♕xg3 ♗f5 17.c3 b6 18.♗d6 ♕d7 19.♖ad1 ♖ad8 20.♖d2 ♕e6 21.a4 and a draw was agreed in Lockwood-Larsen, cr 2008. Black is indeed very solid, though in a practical game anything could still happen here) 16.♖ad1 ♗d7 (16...b6 17.♗d6 ♕d7 18.f5! gives White exactly what he is looking for in this variation, e.g. 18...♗a6 19.♖f4 ♗g5 20.♖f3 fxe5 21.♖xe5 ♕e7 22.♗f4 ♗xf4 23.♖xf4 ♕d6 (23...♕e3+ 24.♕xe3 ♖xe3 25.fxg6 hxg6 26.♖f6 wins a pawn) 24.♕d4 ♖e7 25.fxg6 hxg6 26.c4 (26.♘e4?! ♕e5!) 26...♖ae8 27.♘e4 ♕xf4 (27...♕e5 28.♘f6+ now wins the exchange) 28.♘f6+ ♔xf6 29.♕xf6 and White converted his material plus in Kilichenko-Balshaw,

cr 2012) 17.♖d2 b6 18.♗d6 ♖c8
19.♖df2 f5 20.♖d2 ♗e6 21.♖fd1 c5
22.♕f3 ♗e7 23.♗xe7 ♖xe7 24.♘e2
♕e8. This position was reached
in Sidenko-Canibal, cr 2013. Two
moves later a draw was agreed,
but Black's position seems very
suspicious to me:

1) White always has ideas to
include the h-pawn in the attack,
which is something he could start
with;

2) Another important idea
could be to provoke Black playing
...d5-d4 with ♘c3-e2 and follow it
up with c2-c3, opening the centre.
However, this also activates the
bishop, so White shouldn't take
this too lightly either. **15...b6
16.♗d6 f5 17.♘e2 a5!** Black is
just in time, not allowing White
to install a knight on d4. **18.♖d2
♗a6 19.♕f3 ♗e7 20.♗xe7
♕xe7 21.♖fd1 ♗xe2 22.♕xe2**
The protected passed pawn on e5
ensures White an edge, though,
as the present game shows, once
the files are opened Black simply
becomes too active. **22...a4 23.c4
♕c5+ 24.♖d4 dxc4 25.♔f1** Also
after 25.♕xc4+ ♕xc4 26.♖xc4
a3! Black shouldn't have any
difficulties holding the rook
ending. **25...b5 26.a3 c3 27.♕c2
♖ab8 28.♕xc3 ♕xc3 29.bxc3 c5
30.♖d7 b4 31.cxb4 cxb4 32.♖a7
bxa3 33.♖dd7 ½-½**

9.f4 9.♕f3?! has been played by
various strong players, but after
9...♕h4! Black obtains excellent
play. The spectacular idea 10.♘xd5?
(10.h3 ♗e7 11.♖e1 ♘xd3 12.cxd3 0-0
is unproblematic for Black, Geller-
Smejkal, Moscow 1981) is easily
refuted: 10...cxd5 11.♗b5+ ♗d7
(11...♘d7, as played in Smirin-A.
Smith, Helsingor 2015, may also
work for Black, but is certainly
less convincing) 12.♗xd7+ ♘xd7
13.♕xd5 0-0-0 (13...♘c5 was seen
in A.David-Isonzo, Bratto 2007,
and is also good for Black) 14.♗e3
♕e7 15.f4 ♘b6 16.♕b3 ♕e6 and
White doesn't have sufficient
compensation for the piece,
Grabowski-Kraujunas, cr 2013.
9.♘e2 ♗e7 (9...g6 10.♗e3 ♗e7
11.f4 ♘xd3 12.♕xd3 transposes
to Games 2-3) 10.f4 f6 doesn't
offer White anything, e.g. 11.♗e3
♘xd3 12.♕xd3 0-0 13.c4 fxe5
14.fxe5 ♗e6 15.♘f4 ♗f5 16.♕d4
♗g5 17.cxd5 ♗xf4 18.♖xf4 ♕xd5
and soon a draw was agreed in
Mamedyarov-Kramnik, Wijk aan
Zee 2008. **9...g6** Black shouldn't
commit his structure too early
by means of 9...f5?!, as White
obtains an easy game after 10.♘e2!,
though he definitely has to refrain
from playing 10.exf6?! ♕xf6
11.f5 ♘xd3 12.♕xd3 ♗e7 which
was positionally quite disastrous
already for White in Rozentalis-
Turov, Quebec 2001. **10.♘e2 ♗g7**
Given the choice, as Black is very
likely to take on d3 anyway, I
think Black shouldn't place his
bishop on g7: 10...♘xd3 11.cxd3
(11.♕xd3 ♗f5 is unproblematic)
11...♕b6+ 12.d4 ♗g4 13.♖f2 h5 14.h3
♗e6 15.♖f3 and now in Minasian-
Petrosian, Yerevan 2005, Black

---

went 15...h4?! but it seems to me
this pawn can only become a
weakness, as White has plenty of
time regrouping his pieces with
♗e3-f2, ♔h2, ♘g1-f3 etc. Instead,
after something like 15...♗e7
Black seems to be doing alright.
11.♗e3 ♘xd3 11...♕e7 12.b4!?
(12.c4 is probably more testing)
12...♘xd3 13.cxd3 ♕xb4 14.♕c2
♗f8? (14...♕a5 is more sensible,
though White's compensation
is beyond doubt) 15.♖ab1 ♕a5
16.f5 gxf5 17.♘g3 ♗a6 18.♘xf5
with a dangerous initiative for
White in Minasian-Dutreeuw,
Batumi 1999. **12.cxd3** 12.♕xd3
b6!? actually transposes to the
game Goryachkina-Ju Wenjun,
St Petersburg rapid 2018, as
mentioned in the notes to Game 1.
12...0-0 13.d4 ♗g4 Rather than
trading off the light-squared
bishop, I would prefer 13...f6 which
seems to be perfectly playable for
Black. **14.h3 ♗xe2 15.♕xe2**

The bishop on g7 has been boxed
in by a massive pawn chain and
hence White can count on a clear,
risk-free edge, though Black is
very solid. **15...♕d7 16.♕d3 f6
17.b4 a5 18.a3 axb4 19.axb4 ♖xa1
20.♖xa1 fxe5 21.fxe5 ♕f7 22.♖a3
h5 23.♔h2 ♔h7 24.♗g5 ♕c7
25.♖a3 ♖f5 26.h4 ♗h6 27.♗xh6
♔xh6 28.♕g3 ♕e7 29.♖b3 g5
30.hxg5+ ♕xg5 31.♕xg5+ ♖xg5
32.♖g3 b6 33.♖xg5 ♔xg5 34.♔g3
♔f5 35.b5 h4+ 36.♔f3 cxb5
37.♔e3 ♔e6 38.♔d3 ♔d7 39.♔c3
♔c7 40.♔b4 ♔c6 41.♔a3 ♔c7
42.♔b3 ♔d7 43.♔c2 ♔c7 44.♔d3
♔d7 45.♔e3 ♔e7 46.♔f4 ♔e6
47.♔e3 ♔e7 48.♔d2 ♔d7 49.♔c3
♔c7 50.♔b4 ♔c6 51.♔a3 ♔c7
52.♔b3 ♔d7 53.♔b4 ♔c6 ½-½**

**The ♘c3-e2 manoeuvre
8.♘c3**

**Fabiano Caruana   4
Mario Nicolas Villanueva**
PRO League rapid 2020 (6)
**1.e4 e5 2.♘f3 ♘f6 3.d4 ♘xe4
4.♗d3 d5 5.♘xe5 ♘d7 6.0-0 ♘xe5
7.dxe5 ♘c5 8.♘c3 c6** 8...♘xd3
has been played in quite a number
of games as well, but I don't see
the need for Black releasing the
tension so early, as it actually
helps White to complete his
development. 8...♗e7? is simply
bad, in view of 9.♘xd5!.

Various options
8.♗e2/8.f4

Vladislav Tkachiev   **5**
Anish Giri

France tt 2010 (3)

**1.e4 e5 2.♘f3 ♘f6 3.d4 ♘xe4
4.♗d3 d5 5.♘xe5 ♘d7 6.0-0 ♘xe5
7.dxe5 ♘c5 8.♗e2**

Not allowing the exchange of
White's light-squared bishop
has been White's top choice,
but it shouldn't pose Black any
serious problems. **8...♗e7** The
most natural response, although
8...c6 and 8...♗f5 are reasonable
alternatives. **9.♗e3** 9.c4 d4! 10.b4
d3 11.bxc5 dxe2 12.♕xe2 and now,
rather than taking the pawn on
c5 which was played in Fedoseev-
Nyzhnyk, PRO League rapid 2020,
Black should play 12...♕d4 13.♗b2
♗g4 and Black's position already
has to be preferred. **9...0-0 10.f4**
Nothing can be gained from 10.c4
dxc4 11.♗xc4 ♗e6 12.♗xe6 ♘xe6
13.♘c3 ♗c5 and Black manages
to equalize comfortably. **10...f6**
The alternative 10...c6 has been
seen here as well, but the text is
more in accordance with Black's
plan to undermine White's centre.
However, as we will see, in the
ensuing lines Black still needs
to play precisely as otherwise
the rook on f6 could easily be
misplaced. **11.exf6 ♖xf6 12.c4
♗e6 13.cxd5**

13...♗xd5?! To my mind,
exchanging the queens with
13...♕xd5 is a better attempt
to equalize, e.g. 14.♘c3 (more
challenging than 14.♕xd5 ♗xd5
15.♘c3 ♗f7 16.♖ad1 ♖e6 17.♗d4
♘a4! and Black was OK in
Efimenko-Nabaty, Plovdiv 2012)

14...♕xd1 15.♖axd1 c6 16.g4!?
(16.♖d2 a5! as played in Wedberg-
Rozentalis, Upplands Vasby 2000,
enables Black to stabilize the
position) 16...♖ff8 (16...g6? 17.♗d4
♖ff8 18.b4?! (more accurate is 18.f5!
gxf5 (18...♗f7? runs into 19.f6 ♗d6
20.♗f2! and Black can't parry the
threat of ♖xd6) 19.b4 ♘e4 (19...♘d7
20.gxf5 with a transposition to the
line 18.b4) 20.gxf5 ♘xc3 21.♗xc3
♗xa2 22.♖d2 and Black's position
looks very dangerous, e.g. 22...♗d5
23.f6 ♗d6 24.♗h5! and White
threatens ♖xd5 followed by f6-f7+)
18...♘d7 19.f5 gxf5? (Black should
have played 19...♗f7! when the
knight on d7 prevents White from
advancing the f-pawn) 20.gxf5 ♗d5
(after both 20...♖xf5 21.♖xf5 ♗xf5
22.♗c4+ ♔f8 23.♖f1 and 20...♗xf5
21.♗c4+ White wins material,
while 20...♗f7 21.♘e4 gives White a
dangerous initiative) 21.♘xd5 cxd5
and White had a huge advantage
in A.Muzychuk-Tan Zhongyi,
Shenzhen 2011) 17.f5 ♗f7 18.b4
♘a6 19.♗xa6 bxa6 20.♗c5 ♗xc5+
21.bxc5 ♖ab8 22.♖b1 was seen in
Arslanov-Mikheev, St Petersburg
2011, and now Black should
consider 22...a5! preparing ...♖b4
with excellent play to compensate
his weakened pawn structure.
14.♘c3 ♗c6 14...♗f7 15.♕c2 just
looks very unpleasant for Black.
15.♕c2 ♖g6 An illustrative
miniature: 15...♕f8? 16.b4! ♘e6
17.f5 ♘d8 18.b5 ♗c5 19.♕b3+ ♔h8
20.♗xc5 ♕xc5+ 21.♔h1 and Black
resigned in Wedberg-Ingbrandt,
Örebro 2000, in view of 21...♗e8
22.♘e4 and White wins material.

16.♗c4+ At first sight, the
move 16.g3! may seem to be too
weakening, but due to White's

central control, Black isn't able
to take advantage. White's main
idea is b2-b4, though also the
centralizing ♖ad1 in combination
with ♘d5 offers White a clear
advantage. **16...♔h8 17.♖ad1 ♗d6
18.♘d5 ♕e8 19.♖f3 ♖e6 20.♖h3
♖h6 21.♗xc6 bxc6 22.♖f3 ♖e6
23.♘d4 ♖d8 24.♖df1 ♗f8 25.♖h3
h6 26.♗e5 ♘d7 27.♗d4 c5 28.f5
♖b6 29.♗f2 ♘f6 30.♗e3 ♕h5
31.♗e2 ♖b4 32.♗g3 ♗d6 33.♕d3
♕g4 34.♗e5 ♔h7 35.h3 ♗xe5
36.♕xd8 ♕g3 37.♖xe5 ♕xe5
38.♕d2 ½-½**

Gata Kamsky   **6**
Boris Gelfand

Moscow 2008 (3)

**1.e4 e5 2.♘f3 ♘f6 3.d4 ♘xe4
4.♗d3 d5 5.♘xe5 ♘d7 6.0-0 ♘xe5
7.dxe5 ♘c5 8.f4**

8...g6 Black's main response
has been 8...♘xd3 9.♕xd3 g6
(9...♗c5+? is badly timed: 10.♔h1!
c6 (there is no time to play 10...g6?
in view of 11.♕b5+) 11.f5 0-0
12.♕g3 ♕c7 13.f6 with a crushing
attack for White in Funke-
Braziulis, cr 2009) 10.♗e3 (in case
White starts with 10.♘c3?! Black
has the additional option to play
10...♗c5+ (10...c6 likely transposes
after 11.♗e3) 11.♔h1 (11.♗e3? loses,
because of 11...♗xe3+ 12.♕xe3
d4-+) 11...c6 12.♘e2 ♗f5 13.♕c3
♕b6 was first seen in G.Papp-G.
Pap, Szombathely 2010: Black is
very comfortable) 10...c6 (10...♗e7
leads to Game 3) 11.♘d2 (11.♘c3
see Game 1) 11...♗e7 12.♘f3 c5!?
(12...0-0 13.c3 ♗f5 14.♕d2 f6
15.♖ae1 ♗e4 16.exf6 ♗xf6 17.♘g5
may give White a little pressure
(Grandelius-Low, Reykjavik 2019),
though objectively it shouldn't be

much either) 13.♖ad1 d4 14.♗f2 ♗f5 15.♕d2 0-0 with a good game for Black in Jones-Smirin, Batumi 2018. **9.♗e3** 9.♗e2 ♗f5 10.♗e3 c6 11.♘d2 ♗e7 12.♘f3 ♘e6 13.♗d3 ♗xd3 14.cxd3 d4 15.♗d2 ♕d5 16.b4 and now in Karjakin-Topalov, Nice rapid 2009, Black went astray by playing 16...a5? as Black doesn't have to open up the queenside at all. A better option is 16...0-0 with approximate equality. **9...♗e7** Again, 9...♘xd3 10.♕xd3 likely transposes to one of the earlier games from this article. **10.♗e2** 10.♘d2?! ♘xd3 11.cxd3 c5 12.d4 c4 and in Maze-Blohberger, Germany Bundesliga 2019/20, White had to be careful not to get steamrolled by Black's queenside majority. **10...0-0 11.♔h1** 11.♘d2 c6 (11...d4!? is worth examining) 12.c3 f6 (12...a5!? makes sense as well) 13.exf6 ♖xf6 14.b4 ♘e6 15.♘b3 was seen in T.Kosintseva-Illner, Gibraltar 2011, and now I quite like 15...♘g7!? with a roughly even game. **11...f6?!** I like better the following set-up:

11...c6 12.♘d2 a5!? 13.♘f3 ♕c7 14.c4 (what else? Otherwise Black will likely follow-up with ...b7-b5 anyway) 14...dxc4 15.♗xc4 ♗f5 16.♘d4 ♗e4 17.♕e1 ♖ad8 18.♖d1 b5 19.♗e2 ♘a4 with mutual chances in Simmelink-Ghyssens, cr 2009. **12.exf6 ♖xf6 13.c4** Another promising continuation is 13.♘c3 ♗e6 (13...c6? allows 14.♗xc5 ♗xc5 15.♘e4 which wins the exchange) 14.g4!? and, having a simple plan to expand on the kingside, White's position seems to be very easy to play. **13...♗e6 14.cxd5 ♕xd5 15.♘c3 ♕xd1 16.♖axd1 ♖f7**

The position looks very similar to the line 13...♕xd5 which was covered in Game 5. White has a

pleasant advantage, but it's not clear whether it's enough to play for a win. In any case, Kamsky shows that Black likely has to suffer the rest of the game. **17.b4 ♗f6 18.♗d4 ♗xd4 19.♖xd4 ♘d7 20.♖e4 ♗f5 21.♖e3 ♘b6 22.♖d1 ♔f8 23.♔g1 ♖e7 24.♔f2 ♖xe3 25.♔xe3 ♖e8+ 26.♔f2 c6 27.♖d4 ♗e6 28.♗f3 ♘d5 29.♘e4 ♖e7 30.♘c5 ♘c3 31.♖d8+ ♔f7 32.♖h8 ♔g7 33.♖b8 ♗d5 34.♘xb7 ♘e4+ 35.♔g1 ♗xa2 36.♘c5 ♗d5 37.♖xe4 ♗xe4 38.♔f2 ♗d5 39.g4 ♔f6 40.♖d8 ♖c7 41.♔e3 ♔e7 42.♖b8 ♔d6 43.♘b7+ ♔e6 44.♔d4 h5 45.♘c5+ ♔f6 46.h3 hxg4 47.hxg4 ♖h7 48.♖d8 ♖h1 49.♖d6+ ♔g7 50.g5 ♖c1 51.♖d7+ ♔h8 52.♘e5 ♖c4 53.♔f6** 53.f5! gxf5 54.g6 and with the f-pawn serving as a shield against the checks, White could have converted his advantage in style. **53...♖xf4+ 54.♔xg6 ♖xb4 55.♖xa7 ♗g8 56.♘e7 ♖h4 57.♖e8 ♖d4 58.♖e7 ♖d6+ 59.♔h5 ♗h7 60.♘d7 ♖d1 61.♖e8+ ½-½**

Exercise 1

position after 13...0-0

Does Black have a stable blockade on the light squares?

(solutions on page 248)

Exercise 2

position after 17.♘g3-e2

White's protected passed pawn on e5 is a serious asset. How should Black deal with it?

Exercise 3

position after 15...c7-c6

Do you see White's thematic plan?

Living on the edge

by Arne Moll

1. e4 e5
2. ♘f3 d6
3. d4 f5

François-André Danican Philidor

Some people like to play chess, others prefer bungee jumping. But even in chess, there's safe play and there's living on the edge – or jumping off a cliff. An extreme case is the Philidor Countergambit, which is characterized by the move 3...f5. This was declared refuted as early as the year 1763, when the Italian Ercole del Rio found a massive improvement in the opening promoted by (and later named after) the great François-André Danican Philidor (1726-1795). Philidor, famously declaring pawns 'the very life of this game' in his influential book *Analyse du Jeu des Échecs* (1749), argued that the f-pawn should always be pushed before developing a knight to f6 (or f3), but history would prove him wrong. After more than 250 years, Del Rio's move still stands, while Philidor's original variation has been considered busted ever since.

Despite its bad reputation, the Philidor Countergambit has been rearing its head a few times per century since its invention, always relying on a few loyal supporters who just loved its colourful history. And what a history it is! After Philidor, the American prodigy Paul Morphy picked up the variation when he arrived in England in the summer of 1858. He employed it successfully in his only recorded (consultation) game with black against Howard Staunton, his greatest rival.

Morphy's successor, Wilhelm Steinitz, analysed the gambit extensively in his *Modern Chess Instructor* (1889) and concluded it was 'absolutely unsound'. Lasker, Euwe and others were equally dismissive. Still, the opening bounced back in the 1970s and the British grandmaster Tony Kosten opined, in 1992, that the Philidor Countergambit was 'completely viable'. Around that same time, the chess world saw its first strong chess computers, and the cat was out of the bag. Now, everyone could analyse the gambit deeply and make some sense of its wild tactics.

I was no exception. As a youngster, captivated by its rich past, I played

and analysed it, with the help of my computer. Each time I thought I'd found a definitive refutation, the machine showed there were still hidden possibilities for Black. Others, too, kept believing in the resilience of Black's position – despite its obvious weaknesses – and some even played it against very strong opposition. The American James West, a life-long believer in the system who wrote a book on it in the mid-90s, played hundreds of games with it and has found innumerable new ideas in positions long considered dead. Twenty-five years later, the latest generation of chess engines (Stockfish and Leela Chess Zero in particular) are now boldly going where no man (or machine) has gone before. For the first time in perhaps the history of chess, we're beginning to see glimpses of what lies beyond ordinary human opening comprehension. Del Rio, Staunton, Steinitz, Euwe: they couldn't refute the Philidor Countergambit conclusively, even though they thought they had. But today's chess engines are well on their way. A similar fate may await the King's Gambit, or even more topical lines. Is this the ultimate fate of all chess openings? Will we reach a point where we'll just have to trust our engines and accept that we have no clue what's going on? Is that a beautiful idea, or a frightening one? We may have to accept that there is a point beyond which there is no understanding, no explanation, no logic. Just concrete moves, calculation, and the awful buzzing of the engines.
For this Survey, I have looked at the existing literature dating back more than 300 years with the newest engines (the most recent Stockfish 2020 Dev builds running on 20 CPU Core, and LCZero

0.24/0.25 running on RTX 2080 GPU), and am presenting some of their most interesting findings. The move ♗f1-c4! is a recurring theme among these improvements. There are also some recent games since the last Survey on this subject in Yearbook 63. Traditionally, there have been four 'refutations' of Black's third move.

White's most popular choice
The oldest attempt is 4.dxe5, forcing Black's hand immediately. This is White's most popular choice in practice. It was also played once by Bobby Fischer in a simul game, incidentally on the day after he visited Morphy's old house in New Orleans. Philidor liked Black's massive pawn centre after 4...fxe4 5.♘g5 d5

but he gave only 6.f4?. Del Rio was quick to point out the obvious 6.e6!, highlighting the weak spot f7. The move 6...♘h6 was the only reply considered in the 18th and early 19th centuries, and is best met by the obscure but logical 7.g3! (Game 1).
It was Morphy who first came up with the dynamic 6...♗c5!?, sacrificing the rook on h8 for active piece play. Still, things looked rosy for White after 7.♘xe4! (Game 2), so Black needed to look further. In Van Keulen-Moll (Game 3), I tried to improve on 6...♘f6 (Bird's idea) by temporarily keeping the square

f6 available for the queen and simply developing a piece (6...♞c6!?). It worked out decently, but 7.♗b5! is the critical test. The line 6.c4 remains popular as well (Game 4), but Black seems to somehow hold on.

Zukertort's 'refutation'

Another 'known' refutation (recommended by Zukertort) is 4.♞c3. Since the 1990s, it's been known that 4...fxe4 5.♞xe4 d5 6.♞eg5! is good for White (though some still believe in Black's chances even there). For this reason, most contemporary authors now recommend Zukertort's move as the easiest way to gain the upper hand with white. However, 5...♞f6! is much more tenacious (Game 5).

Black's position seems playable after the natural 6.♞xf6+, so 6.♗g5!? deserves attention.

A tough nut to crack

Then there is the innocuous-looking capture 4.exf5.
Philidor didn't think much of this move, but Steinitz later said it was White's best. Modern-day engines confirm it's a tough nut to crack. Even here, though, there are possibilities still. After 4...e4 5.♞g5 Black can either go 5...♞f6 (Game 6) or the usual 5...♗xf5, which happened in Charbonneau-Nakamura (2010).

The American, however, immediately committed hara-kiri after 6.f3! by 6...exf3?, while the surprising positional pawn sacrifice 6...♗e7! – Leela's remarkable choice – may yet prove viable, as in the training game Stockfish-Leela Chess Zero (Game 7). Perhaps White should return to the simple 6.♞c3 (Game 8). It won't be easy to come up with improvements for Black here.

Euwe's preference
Finally, there is 4.♗c4.

This position (although from a different move order) was analysed already before Philidor, in the Traitté de Lausanne (1698). It was also Euwe's preferred refutation, and it is certainly the most natural move of all. Now 4...fxe4? has been considered unplayable for over 200 years and the engines confirm this is also true of 4...exd4?. With simple piece development White builds up a winning position. And so again we return to Morphy, who favoured 4...♞c6!?. White can then choose to enter an endgame where he has an advantage, which nevertheless isn't entirely straightforward (Game 9); or close the centre in King's Indian style and play for a space advantage and domination on the light squares. The game Owens-Aymard (Game 10) is a template for how play might develop. So far, things look rather grim for Black.

Conclusion

Black is definitely jumping from cliffs in the Philidor Countergambit – and the ropes may not be secured. Kasparov called the line 'objectively more than dubious, perhaps even losing', but Bronstein (who also played the gambit once as Black) wrote of 3...f5 that 'the inquisitive reader may wish independently to study the variations (...). My most sincere advice is not to believe the leading figures of chess but to try and bring this opening into your own personal tournament practice.' Indeed, one has to be a bit of a contrarian to analyse and play this variation at all (perhaps this is also reflected in some of my evaluations

above), but the engines confirm that White is still doing very well in most lines. Nevertheless, as the West games show, even titled players can easily stumble against well-prepared opposition. This echoes my own recent experience in online blitz games against IMs and GMs: hardly anyone opts for the critical lines discussed below. 4.exf5! and 4.♗c4! are White's most promising ways to obtain a clear (if not winning) advantage, but even here, a good understanding of tactical nuances and positional themes is essential. With an engine running in the background it's easy to criticize this risky opening, but in a real game the pieces tend to move differently.

The most popular choice
4.dxe5

George Atwood　　　　　　**1**
Jonathan Bruhl
London 1796
1.e4 e5 2.♘f3 d6 3.d4 f5 4.dxe5 fxe4 5.♘g5 d5 6.e6 ♘h6

7.g3!± This modest move, aiming to protect the outpost on e6 by means of ♗f1-h3, has been neglected by theory for over 200 years. The old main line started with 7.♘c3 c6 and now Atwood's spectacular piece sacrifice 8.♘gxe4!? (8.g3!) was the subject of endless debate in the late 18th and early 19th centuries: 8...dxe4? (8...♘f5! is much better, after which Black seems to be

OK) 9.♕h5+ g6 10.♕e5 ♖g8 was analysed by all the great names of the Romantic era. However, so far nobody seems to have discovered the powerful 11.♗c4!!+− as indicated by Stockfish (11.♗xh6 ♗xh6 12.♖d1 ♕g5! led to a spectacular victory for Black in Staunton & Owen-Morphy & Barnes, London 1858 – YB/63-142; 11.♗g5 ♗g7 12.e7 was initially regarded as winning for White, but Black can still play on after 12...♕d2+!? 13.♔xd2 (superior to 13.♗xd2 ♗xe5 14.♗xh6 as analysed in Yearbook 76) 13...♗xe5 14.♗xh6 g5 15.h4 gxh4 16.♖xh4 ♖g6 and now 17.♗e3! should be winning): 11...♗g7 (11...♘f5 12.♗f4! (12.♘xe4±) 12...♗g7 13.♕xe4 ♕d4 14.♖d1 ♕xe4+ 15.♘xe4 ♘d4 16.0-0. Despite being a piece down, albeit for two pawns, White has a terrific grip on the position: 16...b5 17.♗g5! ♗xe6 (17...bxc4 18.♘d6+ ♔f8 19.e7#; 17...♘xe6 18.♗xe6 ♗xe6 19.♖d8+ ♔f7 20.♘d6#) 18.♖xd4 ♗xd4 19.♗xe6 ♖h8 20.c3+−) 12.♕xe4 ♖f8 (12...♗xc3+ 13.bxc3 ♘f5 14.♗a3!+−)

13.h4! ♘f5 14.♗g5 ♗f6 (14...♕b6 15.0-0-0) 15.♖d1 ♕e7 16.0-0+−. White just quietly completes his development before striking. It's remarkable how natural it all looks in hindsight. Still, it took more than two centuries before this was found! **7...c6** 7...♘c6!? is the more active try, but 8.♗h3 ♗b4+ 9.c3 ♗e5 10.0-0!± seems to be good for White. **8.♗h3 ♘a6** 8...♕f6 9.e7+−. **9.0-0** 9.c4!. **9...♘c7?!** 9...g6 10.♘xe4!? dxe4 11.♕xd8+ ♔xd8 12.♖d1+ ♔e8 (12...♔c7 13.♗f4+ ♔b6 14.a4+−) 13.♗g5 ♗xe6 14.♗xe6±.

10.f4? A very static move, typical of those days. 10.c4! was the correct move, when White's position is close to winning

already. **10...♗c5+ 11.♔g2** ≥
11.♔h1. **11...0-0 12.f5?!** 12.c4 ♕e7
13.♘c3 b6∓. **12...♕f6?!** 12...e3!−+.
13.c3?! ♔h8? Now the play
deteriorates. It's clear that the
principles of dynamic chess hadn't
been formulated yet. 13...e3−+.
14.g4? ♘g8?? 14...e3−+. **15.♗f4?**
15.♘xh7! ♖xh7 16.g5 ♕e7 17.g6+
♔h8 18.♕h5+ ♘h6 19.♗xh6 gxh6
20.f6+−; the pawn front is quite
spectacular. **15...♘e8? 16.♗f7+?**
16.♘xh7 ♔xh7 17.g5+−. **16...♖xf7**
17.exf7 ♕xf7∞ 18.♗e5 ♗d7
19.g5 ♕e7 20.♗f4 ♘d6 21.♖c1?
♖f8 22.f6 ♗xh3+ 23.♔xh3 gxf6
24.gxf6 ♕e6+ 25.♔g2 ♖xf6
26.♗f4 ♖g6+ 27.♗g3 ♘f5 28.♕e1
♘xg3 29.hxg3 ♗d6 0-1

Samuel Rosenthal   2
Karl Pitschel

Paris 1878

1.e4 e5 2.♘f3 d6 3.d4 f5 4.dxe5
fxe5 5.♘g5 d5 6.e6 ♗c5 6...♗b4+
7.c3 ♗c5 8.♘xe4 ♗e7 9.♕g4±.

7.♘xe4! This move spoils the
fun for Black. 7.♘f7?! ♕f6 8.♗e3
♗xe3!? (8...d4 9.♘g5 ♕f5 was
Barnes-Morphy, London 1858
(− YB/63-142), but now 10.♗c4!!
(10.♘xh8 ♕xg5♔) seems to be
simply winning for White, e.g.
10...h6 (10...♗xe6 11.♗xe6 ♕xe6
12.♘xh8 △ 12...h6 13.♕h5++−;
10...♘c6 11.g4+− Sinding-West,
Parsippany tt 2000 − YB/63-
143) 11.g4! ♕h7 12.♗h4+−;
8...♗xe6!? 9.♗xc5? ♕xf7∓) 9.fxe3
♗xe6 10.♘xh8 ♕xb2 11.♘d2
♕c3♔; 7.♘c3?! c6 (or 7...♘f6
8.♘f7 ♕e7 9.♘xh8 ♗xe6) 8.♗f7
♕f6 (8...♕b6? (Sveshnikov-
Skvortsov, Riga rapid 2018)
9.♕g4!+−) 9.e3 ♗xe6 10.♘xh8
♗xe6 11.fxe3 ♘h6 12.♕h5+ ♔e7

13.♗e2 ♘d7±. **7...♗e7** 7...dxe4?
8.♕h5+ g6 9.♕xc5+− Salmon-D.
Szabo, Birmingham 1858. This
game was observed by Morphy,
who was a spectator during the
tournament and suggested 7...♗e7
as an improvement; 7...♗b4+ 8.c3
dxe4 9.♕xd8+ ♔xd8 10.cxb4
♗xe6 11.♘c3±. **8.♕g4!?** The
most principled move, going for
the attack. 8.♘g5 ♗xg5 (8...♕d6
9.♗b5+! c6 10.0-0-0!±) 9.♕h5+
g6 10.♕xg5 ♕xg5 11.♗xg5 c6
(11...♗xe6 12.♗f4!±) 12.♘d2 ♗xe6
13.0-0-0 is somewhat better for
White but certainly a good deal for
Black, all things considered. **8...g6**
9.♘g5 ♘h6 Better than 9...♕f6
Geenen-Henris, Genk ch-BEL
1995 − YB/63-143, which should
be met by 10.♕h3!±. **10.♕h4 ♘f5**
10...♗f8 (West) fails to the simple
11.♕d4+−. **11.♕a4+ c6 12.♘f7**
♕b6?! Slightly better was 12...♕c7
13.♘xh8 ♕e5+ 14.♗e2 ♗xe6
15.♘xg6 hxg6 16.♗f4 ♕g7± when
Black has at least some active
pieces for the material deficit.
13.♘xh8 ♗c5 13...♗xe6 14.♗d3+−.
14.♕f4 ♗xe6 15.♘c3 15.♗d3!+−.
15...♗d6 16.♕g5 ... 1-0 (31)

Onno van Keulen   3
Arne Moll

Barcelona rapid 2019

1.e4 e5 2.♘f3 d6 3.d4 f5 4.dxe5
fxe4 5.♘g5 d5 6.e6 ♘c6!?

Trying to keep f6 free for the
queen whilst not allowing the
neutralizing ♘xe4 after ...♗c5.
Also, it keeps the option of ...♘g8-
e7 open, defending the other
knight in case of ♗b5xc6. 6...♘f6
was already tried by Henry Bird
in the 19th century, but White
seems to be doing well after

7.♘f7 ♕e7 8.♘xh8 ♗xe6 and now
the accurate 9.♘c3! △ 9...♘c6
10.♗b5±. **7.♘f7** 7.♘c3!? ♗b4! (the
typical response after White's
knight move) 8.♘f7 (8.♗b5!? ♕f6
9.0-0 ♗xc3 10.bxc3 ♘ge7 11.f3 e3
12.♘h3±) 8...♕f6 9.♗b5? (9.♗g5∞)
9...♗xe6∓ B.Thomas-J.Turner,
Cardiff 2014. Critical is 7.♗b5!,
trying to ruin Black's pawn
structure immediately: 7...♗c5
(7...♘f6?! 8.♘f7 ♕e7 9.♘xh8 ♗xe6
10.♗xc6+ bxc6 11.0-0±; 7...♕f6?
8.♕xd5; 7...♘h6 8.♘c3) 8.♗xe4!
(this annoying move spoils Black's
attacking hopes; 8.♘f7 ♕f6 9.0-0
♗xe6 10.♗xc6+ bxc6 11.♘xh8
♘h6♔) 8...♗e7 (8...♗b4+ 9.c3 dxe4
10.♗xc6+ bxc6 11.♕xd8+ ♔xd8
12.cxb4 ♗xe6 13.♘c3±) 9.♘g5
(9.♕h5+!?; 9.♕g4!?) 9...♗xg5
10.♕h5+ g6 11.♕xg5 ♘ge7!?.
Black will regain the e-pawn but
White has the two bishops. Then
again, compared to some other
positions we'll see in the next
games, this looks like a reasonably
good deal for Black. **7...♕f6**
8.♘xh8 ♗c5 9.♗e3 9.♕h5+?! g6
10.♕xh7 ♕xf2+ 11.♔d1 ♗xe6 is
very dangerous for White, and
after 12.♕xg6+? ♔d7 Black was
already winning in Hrabinska-
Moll, Titled Tuesday blitz 2020.
9...♗xe3 9...d4? 10.♕h5+. **10.fxe3**
♗xe6 11.♘c3 11.♗b5 ♕xb2;
11.♕h5+ g6 12.♕xh7 ♕xb2 with
the idea of 13.♕xg6+? ♔d7−+.
11...0-0-0♔ A prototypical
situation for many lines in the
Philidor Countergambit. Black
will at some point regain the
knight on h8 and has the mighty
'Philidor' pawn centre. White's
weak pawn on e3 gives Black just
enough counterplay. **12.♕d2!**
The best move. 12.♗b5?! (Fahad
Rahman-Moll, Titled Tuesday
blitz 2020) fails to 12...d4! 13.♘xe4
♕h4+ 14.♘g3 dxe3−+. **12...♕h4+**
Here, 12...d4 doesn't work: after
13.♘xe4 ♕h4+ 14.♘g3 dxe3
15.♕xe3 ♕b4+ White has 16.♕c3.
13.g3 13.♗f2 ♕xf2+ 14.♔xf2 ♘ge7.
13...♕e7 14.0-0-0 ♘f6 15.♗b5
♗g4 Now White liquidates into a

slightly better endgame, but Black can hold it without too much effort. **16.♗xc6 ♗xd1 17.♗xb7+ ♔xb7 18.♖xd1± c6 19.♘a4 ♖xh8 20.♕a5 ♔a8 21.♘b6+ ♔b7 22.♘a4 ♔a8 23.♘b6+ ♔b7 24.♘a4 ½-½**

Alexandre Dgebuadze   **4**
Pieter Claesen
Aalst ch BEL 2006 (0)

1.e4 e5 2.♘f3 d6 3.d4 f5 4.dxe5 fxe4 5.♘g5 5.♘d4!? is completely obscure but might be a decent alternative, e.g. 5...d5 6.c4 c5 7.cxd5 cxd4

8.♕xd4≌ with interesting play for the piece. **5...d5 6.c4!?** This logical move, attacking Black's pawn centre immediately, is frequently seen in club and blitz games. 6.♘c3?! should be met by 6...♗b4!∞, not 6...♘e7?? 7.e6+− Fischer-Chaney, Houston (simul) 1964. **6...♗b4+ 7.♘c3** 7.♗d2?! ♕xg5 8.♗xb4 d4! 9.♕xd4 ♘c6 10.♕d2 e3!∓ Martemianov-Moll, Titled Tuesday blitz 2020. **7...d4** 7...c6 8.cxd5 ♕xd5 (8...cxd5 9.♗b5+ ♘c6 10.e6±) 9.♗d2 ♕xe5 10.♕b3 ♕e7 11.♘cxe4 ♗xd2+ 12.♔xd2± Van der Tak – YB/76-21. **8.a3 ♗xc3+ 9.bxc3 ♘c6!?** 9...e3 is the move Philidor players would love to play in principle (ideally followed by ...c7-c5), but it just doesn't seem to work concretely: 10.f4 (Van der Tak examined 10.♗xe3 dxe3 11.♕xd8+ ♔xd8 12.♘f7+ ♔e8 13.♘xh8 in Yearbook 76) 10...♘c6 (10...c5 (Van der Sterren-Mestel, Tjentiste Wch-jr 1975) 11.♘e4!+−) 11.♗d3 ♘xe5 12.fxe5!N (12.cxd4? ♗g4? (Kaunas-Arkhipkin, Haapsalu tt 1978 – YB/63-143) 13.♗e2!+−) 12...♕xg5

13.0-0 c5 14.cxd4 cxd4 15.♕f3 ♘h6 16.♕d5! and White must be winning. **10.♘xe4 ♕h4?** This pseudo-active move was proposed by Mestel in 1975 but leads to a lost position. 10...♗f5! (Black must develop pieces as quickly as possible) 11.♘g3 ♗g6 12.♗d3 ♘ge7≌ and Black has some fun for a meagre pawn. **11.♗d3! ♘xe5 12.0xd4** Also good was 12.0-0. **12...♘xd3+ 13.♕xd3 ♗f5** 13...♘f6 14.♘xf6+ ♕xf6 15.♕e2+. **14.♘d6+ cxd6 15.♕xf5+−** ... **1-0 (29)**

Zukertort's refutation 4.♘c3

Peter Green   **5**
Vilnis Strautins
cr 2017

1.e4 e5 2.♘f3 f5 3.♘c3 d6 4.d4 fxe4 4...exd4? seems to be just losing after 5.♘xd4 fxe4 6.♗c4! ♘f6 7.0-0 c6 8.♘xe4! d5 (8...♘xe4 9.♖e1 d5 10.♕h5+ g6 11.♕e5++−) 9.♘xf6+ ♕xf6 10.♕h5+ ♕f7 11.♖e1+ ♗e7 12.♖xe7+!? (12.♕h4+−) 12...♔xe7 13.♕h4+ ♔f8 14.♗d2 1-0 Feetham-Akrill, Great Britain 2017. **5.♘xe4** 5.♘g5 d5 6.dxe5 ♗b4 transposes to Fischer-Chaney, as quoted in the previous game.

5...♘f6! Development is now a priority for Black. 5...d5? was long regarded as Black's principled reply.
A) 6.♘g3?! e4 leads to the famous game Bird-Morphy, London 1858 – YB/63-144. Black has his ideal Philidor pawn centre;
B) 6.♘xe5!? dxe4 7.♕h5+ g6 8.♘xg6 is highly complex. While it may ultimately prove to be good for White, it plays into Black's

hands, who gets active piece play for the relatively minor material sacrifice (the rook on h8). This is a recurring theme in the entire gambit;
C) 6.♘eg5! throws a spanner in the works: 6...exd4 (6...e4 7.♘e5 ♘h6 8.♘xe4! ruins Black's position. If 8...dxe4 9.♗xh6+−; 6...h6 is refuted by the elegant 7.♘f7! ♔xf7 8.♘xe5+ +− Pavlovic-Van Dooren, Cappelle-la-Grande 2006 – YB/84-15) 7.♗b5+! (7.♘xd4 ♘f6 (Ehlvest-West, New York 1999) is less accurate) 7...c6 and now the Morphy-style 8.0-0!! (Shirov) leaves Black defenceless in all lines, as the engines confirm, albeit with sometimes rather hard-to-find moves: 8...cxb5 9.♖e1+ ♗e7 10.♘e5+−. **6.♘xf6+** 6.♗d3?! ♘xe4 7.♗xe4 d5 8.♘xe5 dxe4 9.♕h5+ g6 10.♘xg6 hxg6 11.♕xh8 ♗f5 is what Black wants (Kairbekova-Moll, Titled Tuesday blitz 2020), but 6.♗g5!? deserves serious attention: 6...♗e7 7.♗xf6 gxf6 This is unclear according to Bauer. Having the bishop pair should give Black some relief, but it's not easy after the engine's suggestion 8.♘g3! (8.dxe5 dxe5 9.♕e2 ♕d5 or 9.♗c4 ♕xd1+ 10.♖xd1 ♘c6= Golubev-Moll, Titled Tuesday blitz 2020) 8...♗e6 (8...c5!? is more in the style of Philidor, intending 9.dxc5 d5) 9.♘h4!? d5 10.♘hf5 and now Black must resort to the cool-headed 10...♗f8! in order not to be overrun quickly, e.g. 11.♕h5+ ♔d7 with a typical, crazy Philidor Countergambit position that looks completely lost for Black at first sight, but might just be holdable with accurate (engine) play. Not for the faint-hearted. **6...gxf6** A critical position for the evaluation of 4.♘c3. Black's kingside is clearly weakened, but he still has his strong centre. In practice, White usually takes on e5 at this point, but fast development may be better. A typical manoeuvre for Black would then be ...♕d7-g7 (or f7) followed by slow development

of the queenside. The engines consider it better for White but not dramatically so.

7.dxe5 This may not be White's best. After 7.♗d3 White has an 'obvious plus' according to Bauer but the engines like 7...♕d7!? 8.0-0 ♘c6 9.c3 ♕f7 and Black is somehow still hanging on; 7.♗c4!?; 7.♘h4!?; 7.♗e2!? (Haring-Moll, Titled Tuesday blitz 2020) 7...♗g7!±. **7...dxe5 8.♘d2** This somewhat odd-looking move, usually followed by ♕d1-f3, is seen surprisingly often. White may have a symbolic plus but not more. 8.♕xd8+ ♔xd8 9.♗e3 ♗e6= Werksma-Moll, blitz 2020; or 8.♗e3 ♕xd1+ 9.♖xd1 ♗e6= Yoo-Moll, Titled Tuesday blitz 2020. **8...♕e7!?** Parrying ♕h5+ by ...♕f7 is a recurring theme in this opening. 8...♗e6 9.♕f3 ♘c6 10.c3 occurred in H.Visser-Moll, blitz 2020, and now 10...f5∞ would not have been bad for Black, e.g. 11.♕h5+ ♔d7∞ followed by ...♕e8 and artificial castling. **9.♕h5+ ♕f7 10.♘e4 ♗e7 11.♗e2 ♗e6 12.♗e3** 12.f4!?± **12...♘d7 13.♕xf7+ ♗xf7** The position is roughly equal. **14.0-0-0 ♖g8 15.g4 ♘b6 16.♘c5 ♖b8** 16...♘d5=. **17.♘e4 ♘d5 18.♗d2 ♖d8 19.♗f3 ♗e6 20.♖hg1 c6 21.h4 ♖d7 22.b3 ♔d8 23.♔b2 ♔c7 24.♖df1 b6 25.a4 a5 26.♖e1 ♗b4 27.c3 ♗e7 28.h5 ♖dd8 29.♗h6 ♗c8 30.♗e2 ♘f4 31.♗xf4 exf4 32.♔c2 ♖g7 33.♘d2 ♗f8 34.♘e4 ♗e7 35.♗d3 ♖de8 36.♔d2 ♗g7 37.f3 h6 38.♘f2 ♗e3 39.♘d1 ♖xe1 40.♖xe1 ♖xe1 41.♔xe1 ♗e6 42.c4 ♗f8 43.♗e2 ♗d6 44.♘c3 ♔e5 45.♗g6 ♗b4 46.♘e4 b5 47.♔d3 bxc4+ 0-1**

Justin Sarkar   **6**
James West
Rahway 2010

1.e4 e5 2.♘f3 d6 3.d4 f5 4.exf5 e4 4...♗xf5? 5.dxe5 ♘c6 6.♗b5+−; 4...♕e7 5.dxe5 ♗xf5 6.♘c3 dxe5 7.♗c4+−. **5.♘g5** 5.♘fd2, intending either c2-c4 or ♘c4-e3, is less ambitious, but playable. **5...♘f6**

6.f3! The thematic move in the 4.exf5 line. After 6.♘e6 ♗xe6 7.fxe6 d5± Black has his dream centre and practical play for the relatively weak pawn on e6; 6.♘c3 d5 7.f3 h6! 8.♘e6 ♗xe6 9.fxe6 ♗b4 10.♗e2!±. **6...h6** A better move order to obtain the same position as in the game is 6...d5 7.fxe4 h6 8.♘e6 ♗xe6 9.fxe6 dxe4; 6...♕e7 7.♘c3! (7.♗e2 exf3 8.♘xf3 ♗xf5 Dvoiris-West, New York 2000 – YB/63-145) 7...h6 (7...♗xf5 8.♗c4 transposes to lines discussed under 5...♗xf5 in Game 8) 8.♘e6 ♗xe6 9.fxe6 ♕xe6 10.fxe4+−. **7.♘e6** 7.♘xe4! seems simpler: 7...d5 (7...♘xe4 8.♕e2) 8.♘xf6+ ♕xf6 9.♘c3±. **7...♗xe6 8.fxe6 d5** Black is a pawn down but he's betting on regaining the pawn on e6 and keeping White's pieces somewhat restrained by the black 'Falkbeer' pawn on e4. **9.fxe4** Here or on the next move, 9.♗e2!? came into serious consideration. **9...dxe4 10.♗c4 ♘c6 11.c3 ♗d6 12.♕b3?** This offers Black some counterchances. 12.0-0! looks most natural, after which it's hard to see where Black's compensation must come from, e.g. 12...♕e7 (12...♘a5 13.♗b5+ c6 14.♗e2 threatening 15.b4) 13.♘d2

e3 (13...0-0 14.b4! ♘d8 15.♕e2) 14.♘f3 ♘g4 15.h3 ♘f2 16.♕e2 ♘e4 17.♕c2 ♘g3 18.♕g6+ ♔d8 19.♖e1+−. **12...♖b8!?** Not bad, but Black had a better move: 12...♘e7!± followed by ...0-0 gives Black breathing space and his pieces will soon become active. **13.0-0 ♕e7 14.♗f4?!** Somewhat surprisingly, this natural developing move is wrong. It shows how easy it is for White to go astray in seemingly overwhelming positions. The hard-to-spot 14.♕b5! was White's best way to keep his clear plus. **14...0-0** Black has finished his development and suddenly has counterchances. **15.♘d2 ♘a5** 15...e3!?. **16.♕a4?** 16.♗xd6 cxd6 17.♕b5 ♘xc4. **16...♘xc4 17.♕xc4 b5 18.♕b3 a5 19.♖ae1 a4 20.♕c2 ♕xe6** Black's strategy has miraculously succeeded. White has nothing better than to liquidate into a drawn ending. **21.♗xd6 cxd6 22.♘xe4 ♘xe4 23.♖xf8+ ♖xf8 24.♕xe4 ♕xa2=** ... ½-½ (44)

Stockfish 20200418   **7**
Leela Chess Zero 0.24
Test game 2020

1.e4 e5 2.♘f3 d6 3.d4 f5 4.exf5 e4 5.♘g5 ♗xf5 The traditional move, which Black has been struggling to make work in recent decades.

6.f3 Larsen's preferred move. The alternative 6.♘c3 is discussed in the next game. 6.g4!? is a popular choice at club level. Black should respond 6...h6 (6...♗g6 7.h4!? h6 8.♘e6 ♕e7 was Anand-Garzon, Lladro (simul) 2000, and now 9.d5!± would have been best) 7.gxf5 hxg5 8.♗g2 d5±. **6...♗e7!?** Black sacrifices his pawn on e4, hoping to exploit the weakness

of White's kingside and his somewhat misplaced pieces. It looks like it should be nowhere near enough, but who can argue with an engine?

A) 6...exf3? 7.♕xf3 ♕e7+ 8.♔d1!+– was a disaster for Black in this line (Charbonneau-Nakamura, Lloydminster 2010);

B) 6...♘f6 7.♘c3 ♕e7 (7...d5 8.fxe4 dxe4 9.♗c4+–) 8.♗c4! led to a winning position for White in Rojas Barrero-De Arco, Bucaramanga 2008: 8...exf3+ 9.♔f2 ♘g4+ 10.♔g3 and despite the exposed white king on g3, Black is lost;

C) 6...♕e7 7.♘c3 (Bauer; if 7.fxe4 ♗xe4!? (7...♘f6 8.♗e2!) 8.♘xe4 ♕xe4+ 9.♕e2 ♕xe2+ 10.♗xe2 White has a small edge due to his two bishops but this is the least of Black's worries) 7...exf3+ (7...♘f6 8.♗c4 – see above; 7...e3 8.♘ge4+– Bauer) 8.♔f2 ♘c6 9.♕xf3 ♘h6 10.♗b5 0-0-0 (10...♗d7 11.♘d5 ♘g4+ 12.♔g3 h5 looks tricky but the accurate 13.♕f4! gives White an objectively winning position. These are not lines you want to play without having checked them thoroughly though) 11.♗xc6 bxc6 12.♕xc6 ♔b8 13.♕b5+ ♔a8 14.♕d5+ ♔b8 15.♖f1 should be winning for White, too. Again, handle with care;

D) 6...d5 7.fxe4 dxe4 8.♗c4 ♘h6 9.0-0±; 6...e3 8.♗xe3 ♕e7 8.♔f2 looks a bit tricky from a human perspective but should be good for White. **7.♘xe4** 7.fxe4!? ♗xg5 8.♕h5+ ♗g6 9.♕xg5 ♘c6!? – this may be OK for Black. White's centre is vulnerable and Black has a lead in development. 9...♕xg5 10.♗xg5 h6 11.♗h4 ♘c6 12.♗b5 ♗xe4 13.♘c3 a6 14.♗a4 was a complex endgame but ultimately good for White in Klykow-Wight, cr 2007. **7...d5** Black is a pawn down and he doesn't have any immediate threats. However, he does have a small lead in development, an open f-file and some potential weaknesses on the white kingside to exploit. It's hard

to believe it's sufficient from a human perspective, but the more the engine looks at it, the better it likes Black's chances. **8.♘g3** 8.♘f2 looks a bit passive but the knight could be better placed here. Black should continue in active style: 8...c5!? (8...♘c6 9.♗b5, Avari-Brown, India 1999) 9.dxc5 ♗xc5 10.♗d3 ♘e7 11.0-0 0-0∞ with interesting play for the pawn. **8...♗h4!** A key idea, pinning the knight and restricting the mobility of White's kingside. Black can follow up with ...♕d6 if needed. **9.♘c3** There are many alternatives that need further testing: 9.♗d3!? ♕e7+ (9...♘e7!? 10.0-0 ♗xd3 11.♕xd3± Göller 2012; 9...♗xd3 10.♕xd3 ♘e7±) 10.♔f2 (10.♗e2 ♕d6 11.0-0 ♗xg3 12.hxg3 ♕xg3 13.♕e1 ♖xe1 ♖xe1 ♘e7 15.♗b5+ ♔f7±) 10...♘f6 11.♗xf5 ♕xf5 12.♖e1+ ♘e7 13.♔g1 ♕f7±; 9.♗e2 ♕d6 10.0-0-0± – see 9.♗d3. **9...♘c6 10.♗e3** 10.♗f4 ♘ge7. **10...♘ge7 11.♕d2 ♗g6 12.0-0-0 0-0±**

White is a pawn up but it looks hard to make progress. Black has a lot of activity, as the remainder of the game shows: **13.♔b1 ♘b4 14.♖c1 ♗d7 15.♘ce2 a5 16.a3 h6! 17.♖g1!?** 17.axb4? axb4 18.♕xb4 ♖a4–+. **17...b5 18.♘f4 ♗h7 19.♘fh5 ♖f7 20.b3 ♘c8 21.♔b2 ♘c6 22.♘f4 ♖b8 23.♗d3 ♕d6 24.♗xh7+ ♔xh7 25.♘d3 ♘b6 26.♗a2 a4 27.♕c3 ♖a8 28.b4 ♘c4 29.♖ce1 ♗xg3 30.hxg3 ♕xg3 31.♗c1 ♖f6 32.♖h1 ♖af8 33.♖e2 ♔g8 34.♘e5 ♘6xe5 35.dxe5 ♖e6 36.♖h3 ♕g6 37.f4 ♕g4 38.♖f3 c6 39.♕e1 ♖g6 40.♕f2 ♕f5 41.♕e1 ♖g4 42.g3 ♕e6 43.♕f2 ♕f5 44.♕d4 ♕e6 45.♕f2 ♕f5 ½-½**

Jörg Pape   **8**
Michael Downey
cr 1994

1.e4 e5 2.♘f3 f5 3.exf5 d6 4.d4 e4 5.♘g5 ♗xf5 6.♘c3! d5 6...♘f6 7.f3 ♕e7 8.♗c4! transposes to the notes to 6.f3 ♘f6 in Game 8 above. **7.f3**

7...e3!? Kosten's 1992 suggestion, to make the line viable again for Black. 7...♘f6 8.fxe4 dxe4 9.♗c4 ♘c6 has been tried in several games involving Kalle Gaard, when 10.♘f7 and 10.♗f7+ are not entirely clear. But Stockfish's simple suggestion 10.♗e3! seems very strong, e.g. 10...♘g4 and only now 11.♗f7+ ♔d7 12.♕e2+–; 7...♘c6 8.fxe4 dxe4 9.d5!? ♗b4 10.a3 e3. West's analysis now continues with 11.axb4 but the engines suggest 11.♗b5+! with a near-winning position, Wight-Klykow, cr 2007; 7...♕e7 is a move Black would like to play, analogous to the previous game, but here it runs into 8.fxe4 ♗xg5 9.♕h5+ ♗g6 10.♕xg5 ♕xg5 11.♗xg5 when material is still equal after taking on e4 with the pawn or the bishop, but White is ready to unleash an attack against the black king even without queens. It's doubtful that he will even be able to avoid disaster. **8.♗xe3 ♗e7** Again, simply developing looks natural, but it has a concrete drawback. Kosten's original analysis continued 8...h6 but here Stockfish found the shot 9.♘ge4!! (9.g4!? should also be good but is more complex, e.g. 9...hxg5 10.gxf5 ♗d6 11.♕e2± ♔f8 (Kosten) and now 12.♘xd5! is strong: 12...♗g3+ 13.hxg3 ♖xh1 14.♘c3+–; materially Black is not doing so bad, but White will soon complete his

development and Black's position is in ruins. The engines evaluate it as pretty hopeless) 9...dxe4 (9...♕d7 10.♘g3+) 10.fxe4±. White has two pawns for the piece, a strong centre and a lead in development. Moreover Black's king is still weak. This is not why anyone plays the Philidor Countergambit. **9.♕e2!** A key idea in this line, preparing 0-0-0 and also increasing pressure along the e-file. 9.♘h3? ♗xh3 10.gxh3 ♗h4+⇄; 9.f4!? looks a bit ugly, although after 9...♘c6 10.♗d3 ♕d7 11.0-0 it's hard to believe that Black has full compensation. Then again, these are the kind of positions that advocates of the system tend to still trust for some reason or another! **9...♘c6 10.g4 ♗c8?! ≥ 10...h6 11.♘h3 ♗h7 12.♘f4 ♗b4 13.0-0-0 ♕d7±. 11.0-0-0 ♘f6 12.♗f4 0-0 13.♘e6?!** 13.h4!+−. **13...♗xe6 14.♕xe6+ ♔h8 15.♗g2?** 15.♗g3!. **15...♗b4⇄ 16.♗g5 ♘xc3 17.bxc3 ♖e8 18.♗xf6 gxf6 19.♕f5 ♕d6 20.♖he1 ♕a3+ 21.♔b1?** 21.♔d2±. **21...♕xc3=** 22.♕xf6+ ♔g8 23.♕g5+ ♔h8 24.♖xe8+ ♖xe8 25.♕d2 ♕xd2 26.♖xd2 ♘a5 27.c3 ♘c4 28.♖f2 ½-½

Maurice Ashley   **9**
James West
New York rapid 2002
1.e4 e5 2.♘f3 d6 3.♗c4 f5 4.d4
4.d3 was already mentioned in the Göttingen Manuscript from the early 16th century. Black has many moves at this point, such as 4...f4, 4...♕f6, 4...c6 (intending a later ...b7-b5) and 4...♗e7, played as early as the year 1575, by Ruy Lopez, hence the name 'Lopez Countergambit' for lines starting with this move order. But the engine prefers the natural 4...♘c6!? intending ...♘a5 in some cases. It's hard to imagine this being a better version for White than the text.

4...♘c6!? Morphy's preferred move is probably Black's best try.
A) 4...fxe4? 5.♘xe5! (the refutation, already indicated by Allgaier in 1795) 5...d5 (5...dxe5 6.♕h5+ ♔d7 7.♕f5+ ♔c6 8.♕xe5! and Black won't survive for long) 6.♕h5+ g6 7.♘xg6 ♘f6 8.♕e5+ ♗e7 and now simply 9.♘xe7! ♕xe7 10.♗g5 ♕xe5 11.dxe5+−;
B) 4...b5? is Lev Zilbermintz' creative idea, but it falls short if White stays calm: 5.♗b3! fxe4 and now 6.♘c3! is Stockfish's choice, with the point 6...exf3? 7.♕xf3 and the double threat on f7 and a8 decides;
C) 4...exd4? looks like a sensible move but the simple 5.♘xd4! (5.♘g5 is more complex but ultimately also good for White: 5...♘h6 6.0-0! (6.♗xh7?! was already analysed in the Traitté de Lausanne. In the 1970s, Mestel found a nice way for Black to complicate matters considerably: 6...♘g4!∞) 6...♘c6 7.exf5 ♗xf5 8.♖e1+ ♔d7 9.c3! (opening up the way for the queen to b3, among other threats) 9...♕f6 (9...♘c8 10.♗e6+ ♗xe6 11.♘xe6±; 9...d3 10.♗e6+) 10.♕b3 ♗e7 11.♘e6 ♖ab8 12.cxd4 ♕h4 and now Stockfish suggests the winning 13.g3! (13.♘xg7? ♘xd4! was messy in Adorjan-Mestel, Moscow 1977) 13...♕g4 14.♘c3+−) is very easy to play: 5...fxe4 6.♘c3 ♘f6 7.0-0 c6 (alternatives are hard to find) 8.♘xe4!+− transposes to a position already discussed under 4.♘c3 exd4 (Feetham-Akrill, Great Britain 2017). **5.dxe5** This move, recommended by Jaenisch in the 1840s, leads to an endgame that is doubtlessly better for White, the only question being: how much

better? 5.♘c3!? is seldomly seen but is a healthy alternative. Black's best seems to be 5...♗e7 when exchanging on e5 (not White's only option) leads to similar positions as in the game. **5...dxe5** 5...♘xe5 6.♘xe5 dxe5 7.♗f7+! ♔e7 8.♗g5+ ♘f6 9.♗xf6+ (9.♕h5!?± Bauer) 9...gxf6 10.♕h5±. **6.♕xd8+ ♘xd8** Black will get an isolated e-pawn, but at least the queens are off, which means he has survived the first potential onslaught – a small victory. Having said that, White should be somewhat better in the ensuing endgame. 6...♔xd8 does keep e5 protected, but after 7.♘c3± Black faces a rather bleak endgame.

7.♘c3 7.♘xe5 occurred in the consultation game Löwenthal & Medley-Morphy & Mongredien, London 1858. Now Leela's suggestion 7...♘d6! seems smarter than taking on e4 first. Black is doing relatively OK after e.g. 8.f4 (8.♘d3 fxe4 9.♘f4 ♘f6) 8...fxe4 9.♘c3 ♘f6 10.0-0± Verweij-Moll, Netherlands blitz 2020; 7.exf5 looks strong at first sight, as Black is now a pawn down and still has an isolated e-pawn, but in fact after 7...♘c6 8.♘d3 (8.♘g5 ♗xf5 9.♘f7 ♘d4= West; 8.♗e3 ♗xf5±; 8.♗e6 ♘ge7!) 8...♘ge7 9.♘h4 ♘d4± it turns out he will win back f5 since 10.g4?! h5= (West) is nothing for White. **7...fxe4?!** 7...♘d6±. **8.♘xe4?!** 8.♘xe5! ♗d6 9.♗f4 ♘f6 10.0-0-0 △ ♗e6 11.♗b5+!±. **8...♘f6 9.♘c3 ♗d6 10.0-0 ♗e6 11.♗b5+ c6 12.♗d3 ♘f7 13.♘g5 ♘xg5 14.♗xg5 0-0 15.♗h4 ♗b4** 15...♗c5±. **16.♘e4??** 16.♖fe1±. **16...♘xe4 17.c3** 17.♗xe4 ♖f4-+. **17...♗c5 18.♖ae1 ♘xf2** 18...♘d2 19.♖xe5 ♘xf1 20.♖xe6 g5!. **19.♗xf2**

♖xf2 20.♔xf2 ♖f8 21.♖ee2 ♖xf2 22.♖xf2 ♗xa2–+ ... 0-1 (43)

Johnny Owens   **10**
Michel Aymard
cr 2017
1.e4 e5 2.♘f3 f5 3.♗c4 d6 4.d4 ♘c6 5.♘g5 ♘h6

6.d5! This somewhat paradoxical move (closing off the beautiful diagonal a2-g8) may be White's best chance to demonstrate a forced win in the Philidor Countergambit. Black's pieces lack coordination and he doesn't have much space. Still, since the position is closed White needs to proceed forcefully. 6.♘xh7? **♕h4!** Steinitz; 6.0-0!? ♘xd4 7.f4∞. **6...f4** It's not entirely clear whether closing the centre helps Black, but the alternatives are not very pleasant either: 6...♘b8 might transpose to the text but allows the additional 7.f4!? (7.♘c3 fxe4?! 8.♘cxe4 ♗f5. Steinitz considered this position equal but the engines think White is

almost winning after 9.♘g3! ♗g4 10.♕d3 followed by h2-h3 and/or 0-0, and Black's position falls apart; 7.h4 f4 see 6...f4) 7...fxe4 8.0-0 and according to the engine, White was already close to winning (though he didn't) in a blitz game by a very young Fabiano Caruana vs West, New York 2001; 6...♘e7 7.♘c3. In two postal games from 1893 Kanyurszky lost in this position against the Hungarian legends Charousek (7...f4 8.g3!) and Maroczy (7...a6). If 7...g6 8.h4!± followed by h4-h5, tying Black up further. There's no forced win but even for Philidor Countergambit lovers, this is no picnic. **7.h4** 7.♘e6? ♗xe6 8.dxe6 ♕g5⇄; 7.♘f3?! ♘b8±. **7...♘b8** 7...♘e7 8.g3 is also very unpleasant for Black. It's hard to suggest anything sensible; after 8...fxg3 9.fxg3 Leela comes up with the sad 9...♘eg8± and the engine is somehow holding on for the moment, but who wants to try this as Black? **8.♘e6** 8.g3! is critical: 8...fxg3 (8...♘e7 9.gxf4 exf4 10.♗xf4 0-0 11.♕d2 and Black doesn't have enough compensation) 9.♕h5+! (9.fxg3 ♗g4 10.♗e2 ♕d7 is less clear, although still good for White) 9...g6 10.♕f3 gxf2+ 11.♔xf2 ♕e7 12.♘e6 ♘g4 13.♕f3 ♗xe6 14.dxe6 ♘f6 15.♘c3 c6 16.h5!. With forceful, engine-fuelled play, White has reached an almost winning

position. If Black can't come up with improvements in this line, this may well be the nail to the Philidor Countergambit's coffin. **8...♗xe6 9.dxe6 ♘c6** 9...♕f6 10.♘c3 ♘g6 (10...c6 11.g4!) 11.g3 ♘c6 12.h5 ♘g4 13.♘d5 ♕xd1+ 14.♔xd1 ♘g4 15.♖f1 with a winning endgame for White. **10.♘c3 ♗e7 11.♕h5+ ♔f8**

12.♕d1! White has an overwhelming position. The rest of the game demonstrates the long-term difficulty of playing Black's position. **12...♕e8 13.h5 ♘a5 14.♗b5 c6 15.♗f1 d5 16.g3 d4 17.♘b1 ♗d6 18.♗h3 c5 19.♘c3 g5 20.hxg6 ♕xg6 21.♔f1 ♖g8 22.♘d5 ♕xe4 23.♗g2 ♕g6 24.♕h5 ♕xh5 25.♖xh5 ♔g7 26.b4 cxb4 27.gxf4 exf4 28.♘xf4 ♘c6 29.♘d5 ♘g4 30.♗e4 ♘f8 31.f3 ♘e3+ 32.♘xe3 dxe3 33.♗xe3 ♖e8 34.♔d1 ♖xe6 35.♖xd6 ♖xd6 36.♗c5 ♖g7 37.♗xd6+ ♔e8 38.♗xh7 ♔d7 39.♗f4 ♖f7 40.♗f5+ ♔e7 1-0**

Exercise 1

position after 7...♗f8-c5

White to play.
(solutions on page 248)

Exercise 2

position after 9.♕d1-e2

Black to play.

Exercise 3

position after 7...♘g8-f6

White to play.

A Ponziani piece sacrifice revisited

by Jeroen Bosch

1.	e4	e5
2.	♘f3	♘c6
3.	c3	♘f6
4.	d4	♘xe4
5.	d5	♗c5
6.	dxc6	♗xf2+
7.	♔e2	♗b6
8.	♕d5	♘f2
9.	♖g1	

A brief recap of Yearbook 112

In Yearbook 112 (2014) I reported on a
new idea in an ancient sacrificial line
of the Ponziani (on the basis of my loss
against Peter Lombaers). I will start with
a brief summary of that Survey before we
move on to the reason for this update:
the fact that some two dozen games have
been played in the meantime with my
suggested improvement 9.♖g1!?.

**1.e4 e5 2.♘f3 ♘c6 3.c3 ♘f6 4.d4 ♘xe4
5.d5 ♗c5!?**

First played in Brien-Falkbeer, London
1855, this sacrifices a piece rather than
retreating the knight with 5...♘e7 or
5...♘b8.

6.dxc6 ♗xf2+

6...♘xf2? is bad due to 7.♕d5!.

7.♔e2 ♗b6!

As played by Peter Lombaers against
me in 2014, and an excellent follow-up.
Black plays for long-term compensation
with the vulnerable white king stuck in
the centre.

The old main line starting with 7...bxc6
is met by 8.♕a4! f5 9.♘bd2 0-0 10.♘xe4
fxe4 11.♕xe4! (not 11.♔xf2 d5! which
is dangerous for White) 11...d5 (after
11...♗b6 there is Maroczy's 12.♔d1!±)
12.♕xe5 ♖e8 13.♕xe8+ ♕xe8+ 14.♔xf2
and White should be able to consolidate
his material edge.

8.♕d5! ♘f2

Let's first note that little is promised
White by 9.cxb7 ♗xb7 10.♕xb7 ♘xh1
(see YB 112).

I played 9.♕xe5+?! which I called
White's worst option. After 9...♔f8
10.♖g1 Black obtains excellent play with
10...♘g4! – an improvement I indicated
in YB 112 – 11.♕e4 dxc6 and Black was
winning in Praznik-Pavasovic, Slovenia
tt 2017. My opponent had played
10...dxc6, when after 11.♗e3 ♘g4 12.♗c5+
♔g8 13.♕d4 ♕e8+ White should play
14.♔d1! rather than 14.♔d2 ♗f5 15.♗d3
♗xd3 16.♖e1 ♕d8∓ (Bosch-Lombaers,
Wijchen 2014).

Black also obtains a winning edge with 10...f6(!) 11.♕f4 (11.♕g3 ♕e7+–+) 11...g5 12.♘xg5 dxc6!! 13.♗e3 ♘d3 14.♕f3 ♘e5. This leaves White with one playable move:

9.♖g1!

In 2014 I wrote that nobody had dared to play this rook move so far, and I went on to analyse its consequences. My conclusions were that:

   1) Black gets sufficient compensation, and

   2) the inevitable 'these lines need testing in practice'.

In the in-between years 9.♖g1 has been played quite a few times, and meanwhile the database has also been updated with two correspondence games from before 2014. So let's see how things stand in 2020!

Practical tests with 9.♖g1

After 9.♖g1 Black should be willing to sac another piece and play **9...0-0! 10.cxb7 ♗xb7 11.♕xb7 ♕f6**. For the alternatives see Game 1-3.

The situation is that White is two(!) pieces up (for two pawns), but his king is of course awkwardly placed in the centre. And it will take some time before His Majesty will find a safe haven, if ever. Moreover, Black may cause White significant discomfort with his central pawns, just by pushing them forward.

Black's queen's rook will often get into play via the b-file. And there are of course direct threats like ...e5-e4 and if the f2-knight moves the white rook is hanging on g1 (although Black won't always take it as the bishop is a powerful attacking piece). Nevertheless, two pieces are a considerable investment, and White will often be keen to return one of them if this means safety for his king or being able to finish his development.

In the diagrammed position White faces a choice. In Game 4 we examine the minor lines 12.♕a6 and 12.♘bd2. 12.♗g5? ♕g6! is awkward for White as 13...e4 is a powerful threat. Most often he goes either 12.♘a3 (developing the queenside, whilst keeping control over the c1-h6 diagonal) or 12.♕d5 (centralizing Her Majesty and aiming for a trade of queens – also the queen cannot stay on b7 forever, she may either be cut off from play by ...c7-c6 or attacked by ...♖a8-b8). For the alternatives see the game Gamard-Mosshammer.

Developing the knight

After **12.♘a3**, play continues **12...e4 13.♘c4 ♖ab8** (13...exf3+ is also good for a draw) **14.♕d5**

and here both **14...exf3+** (immediately taking back one piece) and **14...♘g4** have been played. See Games 5-6. I would prefer the former as Black – although the

Javokhir Sindarov

complications are as weird as any you will find in this Survey.

After 14...♘g4 15.♘xb6 ♖xb6 16.♗d2!N White has chances of successfully coordinating his pieces, but in all objectivity, here too Black can achieve a draw – it's only that the path seems narrower and less dangerous for White than in most other lines.

Centralizing the queen

The other attempt for White to make something of his extra two pieces is **12.♕d5**. After **12...c6! 13.♕d2** (for the alternatives see Game 7) **13...e4 14.♘d4 e3** we reach the diagrammed position.

In YB 112 I ended my analysis here with the verdict that Black has compensation. A couple of players have meanwhile gone for this position. See Game 8 in the study material. However, I should like to point out here that in a theoretical sense this

whole line is pretty useless for White. After 14...e3 White is forced to continue with 15.♕c2 when Black if he so wishes can force a draw with 15...♗xd4 16.cxd4 ♘g4 17.♖h1 ♘f2 and so on. In practice Black has (rightly) chosen to play with 15...♖ae8. So we may conclude that **12.♕d5** is mainly dangerous for the first player.

Conclusion

Do try this at home! In YB 112 I concluded that: 'For black players this is a good practical choice versus the Ponziani, more so because the critical position comes about by force after 3.c3.' In the meantime we have seen that 9.♖g1 has been played quite a few times. And while I think that my overall conclusion still stands (White has to play 9.♖g1, and Black has sufficient compensation for the sacrificed material), and that we can speak of a dynamic equilibrium, it definitely makes sense to say something about the practical side of things. As we have seen in the over-the-board games, even very strong players will make a lot of mistakes in such irrational positions. It is therefore no coincidence, I think, that most of the material that we have investigated came from correspondence games. These positions are ideal for elaborate analysis with your silicon friends, and they are very difficult to play without their assistance. So even if there were no coronavirus preventing us from playing over-the-board chess, this is a line most comfortably met in the quiet of your study while playing correspondence chess.

Oh yes, if you like more concrete assessments: 12.♘a3 is the way to go, and a draw is a likely result – if both players are well-prepared, that is.

Practical tests
9.♖g1

Alexander Shabalov 1
Tansel Turgut

Philadelphia 2018 (5)

1.e4 e5 2.♘f3 ♘c6 3.c3 ♘f6 4.d4 ♘xe4 5.d5 ♗c5 6.dxc6 ♗xf2+ 7.♔e2 ♗b6 8.♕d5 ♘f2 9.♖g1

9...bxc6 Black should continue 9...0-0!. Two correspondence games from the noughties went 9...dxc6 10.♕xd8+! (10.♕xe5+ ♔f8 would transpose to Bosch-Lombaers, Wijchen 2014) 10...♔xd8 11.♗e3! ♗xe3 (or 11...♘g4 12.♗xb6 axb6 13.h3 ♘f6 14.c4 ♖e8 15.♘c3 with an artistic pawn configuration on the queenside, Aalderink-Bendig, cr 2007. Black still has all his pawns, which leaves him fairly solid, but it is White whose chances must be preferred) 12.♔xe3± ('the piece is stronger than the three pawns' – YB/112) 12...♘g4+ 13.♔e2 (13.♔d2! e4 14.h3!? exf3 15.hxg4 ♗xg4 16.gxf3 ♗xf3 17.♖g7±) 13...e4 14.♘g5 ♖e8 15.♘xf7+ ♔e7 16.h3! ♔xf7 17.hxg4 ♗xg4+ 18.♔e3 and the knight is far better than the three pawns, Hlavacek-James, cr 2005. There is no point in playing 9...♕f6!? (rather than 9...0-0), for now White has an extra option: 10.♗g5! (10.cxb7 ♗xb7 11.♕xb7 0-0 12.♕a6 transposes to the main line) 10...♕f5 11.♕xe5+ ♕xe5+ 12.♘xe5 – see YB/112. Simply bad was 9...♘g4? 10.cxb7 ♗xb7 11.♕xb7 ♗xg1 12.♕e4 (12.♕xg1; 12.h3) 12...0-0 13.♕xg4+– Liu-Schwartz, Sitges 2017. **10.♕xe5+ ♔f8 11.♘d4!** ♘g4 12.♕f4+ My 2014 conclusion on this position was:

'the two pawns are insufficient compensation here.' However, see what happens next. Also not bad is 12.♕g3 d6 13.♘d1 ♕f6 14.♕f4! ♕g6 15.h3 c5 (Wallgren-Pantzar, Gothenburg 2017) and now best was 16.♘f3 ♘f2+ 17.♔e1 ♘d3+ 18.♗xd3 ♕xd3 19.♔f2 and White consolidates. **12...d5** 12...c5!? 13.♕xg4 (13.♘f5 h5∞) 13...cxd4 14.♘d1 dxc3 15.♖h1 is still sharp although I would prefer the extra piece. **13.♘d1** 13.h3. **13...c5 14.♘f3** Let's face it – in such irrational positions it is hard to play well even for very strong players. Now Black gets excellent counterplay. The engine prefers 14.♘c6 ♕d7 15.♗b5 a6 16.♗a4 ♕f5 17.♕xf5 ♗xf5 18.♖e1±. **14...c4 15.♘d4 h6?!** It's pretty unclear after 15...c5! 16.♘c6 ♕d7 17.♘e5 ♘xe5 18.♕xe5 ♕c7. **16.♗e2 g5 17.♕g3 h5?** 17...c5. **18.h3 h4 19.♕e1 ♘h6 20.♘f1** Black has weakened his own position, while his knight has been pushed back. White is comfortably winning now. **20...♔g7? 21.♘c6 ♕d6 22.♗xg5! ♕xc6 23.♗f6+ ♕xf6 24.♖xf6 ♔xf6 25.♕xh4+ ♔g7 26.g4?!** 26.♗g5+! ♔h7 27.g4+–. **26...f6! 27.♕g3!** 27.g5 ♘g4! 28.gxf6+ ♘xf6∞. **27...♖e8?** 27...♗d7 28.♘d2 ♖ae8. **28.♘a3 ♗d7 29.♘c2 ♗a4 30.♕g2 d4?! 31.cxd4 ♗xd4 32.♔c1 ♗b6 33.♗xc4+– ♖ad8 34.b3 ♗d7 35.♔b2 ♗e6 36.g5 ♘f5 37.gxf6+ ♔xf6 38.♗xe6 ♖xe6 39.♖f1 ♖e5 40.h4 ♖f8 41.h5 ♖f7 42.♕g6+ ♔e7 43.h6 ♘xh6 44.♖d1 ♖e6 45.♕g5+ ♖ff6 46.a4 ♘f7 47.♕d5 ♖d6 48.♖e1+ ♖fe6 49.♖xe6+ ♖xe6 50.♘b4 ♗e5 51.a5 c6 52.axb6! cxd5 53.bxa7 ♘d3+ 54.♘xd3 ♖a6 55.♘b4!** A neat final point! **1-0**

Alexey Pridorozhni 2
Javokhir Sindarov

Voronezh 2018 (9)

1.e4 e5 2.♘f3 ♘c6 3.c3 ♘f6 4.d4 ♘xe4 5.d5 ♗c5 6.dxc6 ♗xf2+ 7.♔e2 ♗b6 8.♕d5 ♘f2 9.♖g1 0-0!

10.♗g5? Also bad is 10.♗e3? bxc6 11.♕c4 d5?! (11...♗xe3! 12.♔xe3 d5 13.♕h4 ♘g4+ 14.♔d2 ♕d6–+) 12.♕xc6? (12.♕h4! (at least getting rid of the queens) 12...♕xh4 13.♘xh4 ♗xe3 14.♔xe3 ♘g4+∓) 12...♗xe3 13.♔xe3 ♘g4+→ Holtman-Mazur, Banska Stiavnica 2017. **10...bxc6 11.♗xd8 cxd5 12.♗h4?!** 12.♗xc7! ♗xc7 13.♔xf2 ♗b6+ 14.♔e1 ♗xg1 15.♘xg1 ♖b8 is better, but the ending still clearly favours Black. **12...♗a6+?!** 12...♘g4! gives White fewer options. After 13.♖h1 ♗a6+ 14.♔d2 ♗xf1 15.♖xf1 f5 Black is winning. **13.♔e1 ♗xf1** Or 13...♘d3+ 14.♗xd3 ♗xd3 15.♗f2 f5∓. **14.♗xf2! ♗a6 15.♗xb6 axb6** The pawn armada will be hard to stop no matter which set-up White adopts. **16.♔f2** 16.a4 f5 17.♘a3∓. **16...e4! 17.♘d4 f5 18.g3?** 18.♘a3∓. **18...c5! 19.♘e2 g5** 19...e3+!–+. **20.h4 h6** 20...e3+!–+. **21.♘a3 ♔f7! 22.hxg5?!** Opening the h-file only helps Black. **22...hxg5 23.♖h1** 23.♖ad1 ♔e6–+. **23...♖h8** 23...e3+!–+. **24.♖ag1 ♔f6 25.♔e3 ♔e5**

White had enough and resigned. The pawn avalanche will inevitably submerge him, like in the prior game Tillyaev-Khoroshev, from the Uzbek Championship, Tashkent 2018: 26.♔d2 d4 27.cxd4+

cxd4 28.♖xh8 ♖xh8 29.b4 e3+
30.♔e1 ♖xe2 31.♔xe2 ♖h2+ 32.♔d3
♖d2+ 33.♔c4 d5+ 34.♔b3 e2 35.♖e1
d3 36.♔c3 ♖d1 37.♘c2 0-1.

Stephane Renard   **3**
Jan Holzer
cr 2018
**1.e4 e5 2.♘f3 ♘c6 3.c3 ♘f6 4.d4
♘xe4 5.d5 ♗c5 6.dxc6 ♗xf2+
7.♔e2 ♗b6 8.♕d5 ♘f2 9.♖g1 0-0
10.cxb7** White is forced to grab
more material, hoping to survive
the attack. **10...♗xb7 11.♕xb7**

So White is up two pieces (against
two pawns), but his king is still
stuck in the centre and he has no
development to speak of. **11...♖b8**
This is not without interest,
although it is probably inferior to
11...♕f6. 11...e4? 12.♘d4 ♕f6 (has
worked well in practice, but is
objectively losing: not 12...♕h4?
13.g3! ♕f6 (13...♕xh2? 14.♖g2+–)
14.♗g2 and Black has lost vital time
and is completely lost, Csonka-
Rechberger, Austria Bundesliga B
2019) 13.♗e3? (13.♕d5! brings back
the queen and threatens 14.♕f5;
after 13...♘d3 14.♗e3□ ♘f4+
15.♗xf4 ♕xf4 16.♖h1 Black has not
enough for his material deficit; e.g.
16...♕c1? does not work on account
of 17.♘b3!) 13...♘g4 14.h3? ♘xe3
15.♔xe3 ♕g5+ 16.♔e2 ♖ab8 17.♕a6
♗xd4 18.cxd4 ♖xb2+–+ Dewenter-
Zude, Bad Wörishofen 2016.
Most often Black plays 11...♕f6!.
12.♕d5 12.♕a6. **12...♕f6** It's
also a mess after 12...c6 but White
appears to have the most attractive
options: 13.♕d6!? (one alternative
is 13.♕d2!? ♕f6 14.g4!?) 13...e4
(and now safest (and best) seems
13...♘g4 14.h3!±; 13...♘e4 14.♕d3
d5 15.♘bd2 ♘d6 16.♕a6±) 14.♔d2!

(after 14.♗g5!? exf3+ 15.gxf3 ♕e8+
16.♗e7 there are weird perpetuals
everwhere: 16...♗c7 (16...f6 17.♕d2
♖f7 18.♗c4 ♗c7! 19.♗xf7+ ♔xf7
20.♕xc7 ♖xb2+ (20...♕d5+ 21.♔c1
♘d3+ 22.♔d2 ♖xb2+ 23.♔e3 ♕e6+
24.♔xd3 ♕e2+ 25.♔d4 ♕f2+
26.♔d3=) 21.♔c1 ♘d3+ 22.♔d1
♘f2+=) 17.♖xg7+ (17.♕f6 ♖xb2+
18.♘d2 g6) 17...♔xg7 18.♕f6+ ♔g8
19.♕xf2 ♖xb2+ 20.♗e2 ♖xe2+
21.♔xe2 ♖d8 22.♕g5+ ♔h8
23.♕f6+=; 14.♘d4 ♘d3! (14...♗c7
15.♘xc6! ♗xd6 16.♘xd8 ♘d3!
17.♔d1±) 15.♔d1 ♗c7 16.♕a3
(16.♕xc6? ♕h4!–+) 16...♘f2+
(16...♕h4? 17.♗xd3 exd3 18.♘d2+–)
17.♔c2 ♗xh2 18.♕xa7 ♗xg1 19.♘e2
♕f6 20.♘xg1 and apparently this
is another crazy perpetual: 20...c5!
(20...♘d3 21.♘d2!) 21.♕xc5 ♘d3!
22.♕xd3 exd3+ 23.♔xd3 ♕g6+
24.♔d2 ♕xg2+ 25.♔d1 ♕g4+!=)
14...exf3 15.gxf3 ♘e4+ 16.fxe4
♗xg1 17.♔c2±. **13.g4** Other lines
to investigate are 13.♘a3 c6 and
13.♗g5 ♕g6 14.♘bd2 c6. **13...e4
14.♘e1** 14.♘d4 ♘d3 15.♕f5 is not
met by 15...♘xc1+ 16.♔d1 ♖xd4
17.♕xf6 ♗xf6 18.♖xc1± but by
15...♕h4! 16.♖g3 (planning ♖xd3)
16...♗xd4! (16...♕xh2+? 17.♗g2 △
♘xc1+?! 18.♔d2 ♕h6+ 19.g5+–)
17.cxd4 (17.♖xd3 ♕xh2+ 18.♔d1
exd3 19.♗xd3 ♕e5∞; 17.♖h3??
♕e1#) 17...g6! 18.♕xe4 (18.♕g5?!
♖xb2+!) 18...♖be8! (18...♖fe8?
19.♕xe8+! ♖xe8+ 20.♗xd3 and
White wins on points) 19.♔xd3!
(19.♕xe8? ♖xc1+) 19...♖xe4
20.♔xe4 ♕xh2 and with the king
in the middle Black apparently has
enough: 21.♔f3□ f5 22.g5□ ♕h1+
23.♔e2 ♖e8+ 24.♖e3 ♕h5+ and
the engine produces only zeroes...
14...♘d3

15.♖g2 Unclear is 15.♘xd3 ♗xg1
(but not 15...exd3+ 16.♔d1 ♗xg1
17.♕g2 and 18.♔xd3 next when
White has consolidated and is
better) 16.♘f4 ♗xh2 17.g5 ♕a6+
(17...♖xb2+ 18.♔d1! ♕b6 19.♕xe4±)
18.c4 ♕b6 19.♘g2 c6 20.♕f5∞.
15...♘xc1+ Black has to take
now, since 16.♗g5 had become
a threat. **16.♔d1 ♕xf1 17.♘d2!
♕a6 18.♖xc1!** 18.♔xc1 is worse
because the rook remains out of
play. In the game White completes
artificial castling on the queenside.
**18...♖be8 19.♔c2 c6 20.♕c4
♕b7 21.♔b1!** Finally things have
normalized. The king has escaped
from the centre, and White is to
be preferred. **21...d5 22.♕a4 c5
23.♖e2 ♕c8** Not 23...d4? 24.cxd4
cxd4 25.♕c6! and if 25...♕xc6
26.♖xc6 e3 27.♘c4 then the passed
pawns are blocked and weak.
**24.h3 f5 25.gxf5 ♗xf5 26.♘c2
♕xh3 27.♖ce1** Prophylaxis. White
is going to destroy the imposing
central pawns by c3-c4, but first
he needs to attack e4 as often as
possible. **27...h5 28.a3 ♖d8 29.c4!
♕d7 30.♕a6 d4 31.♖xe4** Now
White is practically winning. The
passed pawns on the kingside are
not so dangerous as pushing them
weakens the black king. **31...♖f2
32.♖e7 ♕c6 33.♖g1 ♖g2 34.♖xg2
♕xg2 35.♔c1! h4 36.♘e1 ♕c6
37.♘ef3** A beautiful construction
that keeps Black's counterplay in
check. **37...h3 38.♖e1 ♖f8 39.♖h1!
♖xf3 40.♘xf3 ♕xf3 41.♕c8+ ♔f7
42.♖e1** The ending after 42.♕xh3
♕xh3 43.♖xh3 should also win,
but White opts for an attack
which in the end brings about a
similar but even better ending.
**42...♔g6 43.♖g1+ ♔h7 44.♕e6
♕f6 45.♕xf6 gxf6 46.♖h1 ♔g6
47.♖xh3 ♔f5 48.♔d2 1-0**

Michel Aymard   **4**
Michael Mosshammer
cr 2018
**1.e4 e5 2.♘f3 ♘c6 3.c3 ♘f6 4.d4
♘xe4 5.d5 ♗c5 6.dxc6 ♗xf2+
7.♔e2 ♗b6 8.♕d5 ♘f2 9.♖g1 0-0
10.cxb7 ♗xb7 11.♕xb7 ♕f6**

12.♕a6 The move 12.♘bd2 has no independent value and gives Black the extra option 12...e4 (also not bad is 12...♖ab8!? 13.♕a6 e4 14.♘d4 and now 14...♘g4 (Black can also opt for 14...c5 15.♕c2 d5) 15.♔d1 ♘e3+ 16.♔e2 ♘g4 forces a draw) 13.♘d4? (13.♘c4 transposes to 12.♘a3 after 13...♖ab8 14.♕d5) and now Black wins after 13...♗xd4! 14.cxd4 ♘g4! 15.♖d1 (15.♘xe4 ♕xd4–+) 15...♕xd4–+; 12.♗g5? ♕g6! is awkward for White as 13...e4 is a powerful threat. 12.♘a3 and 12.♕d5 are the main tries.

12...e4! 13.♘d4 Not 13.♘e1 ♕d6!, threatening both mate on d1 and to take on h2: 14.♗e3 ♘g4! 15.♗xb6 axb6 16.♕c4 ♕xh2–+.

13...c5 Now the pawns are going fast forward. **14.♘c2 d5 15.♗e3 ♘g4 16.h3 ♘xe3 17.♘xe3 ♖ad8** White still has his two extra pieces, but he is clearly worse off than before. He is undeveloped, his queen is offside and the black pawns are menacing. **18.♘d2 d4 19.♘g4** 19.♘xe4 ♕c6–+.

19...♕g5 20.♘c4 20.♘xe4 ♖fe8–+; 20.♕c4 ♖fe8 21.♖e1 h5–+ and the black position plays itself. **20...h5! 21.♘ge5 d3+ 22.♔d1 ♕g3** 23...♕f2 is the main threat. **23.♗xd3 ♗c7** Even stronger than 23...exd3–+. **24.♕b7 ♖xd3+ 25.♔e2** 25.♘xd3 ♕xd3+ leads to mate. **25...♗xe5 26.♕xe4 ♖dd8** Material is equal again, but Black's attack continues. **27.♕f3** 27.♘xe5 ♖fe8–+. **27...♖fe8! 28.♘e3** 28.♕xg3 ♗xg3+ 29.♔f1 ♖e4–+.

28...♕g6 29.♖gd1 ♗d4! 30.cxd4 ♖d6! 30...cxd4–+. **31.dxc5 ♖f6 32.♕d5 ♕g3 33.♕d4 ♖f4** Winning the queen. **34.♕xf4 ♕xf4 35.♖d3** And Black won:

35...♕g3 36.♖f1 ♕xg2+ 37.♔f2 ♕xh3 38.♖c3 f5 39.b3 g5 40.♔d2 f4 41.♘c4 ♕e6 42.♔c2 ♕f5+ 43.♔b2 ♕xc5 44.♖cf3 h4 45.♖d2 ♕f5 46.♖df2 ♕f6+ 47.♔a3 ♖e4 48.♖d2 g4 49.♖fd3 f3 50.♖d8+ ♔h7 51.♖2d6 ♕e6 52.♖8d7+ ♔g6 53.♖d1 f2 54.♖7d4 g3 55.♖g4+ ♔h5 0-1

Jens Uwe Klügel 5
Marc Schröder
cr 2015
1.e4 e5 2.♘f3 ♘c6 3.c3 ♘f6 4.d4 ♘xe5 5.d5 ♗c5 6.dxc6 ♗xf2+ 7.♔e2 ♗b6 8.♕d5 ♘f2 9.♖g1 0-0 10.cxb7 ♗xb7 11.♕xb7 ♕f6 12.♘a3

12...e4 Also interesting is 12...♖ab8!? 13.♕d5! (13.♕a6 e4 14.♘d4 c5 15.♘dc2 d5♔) 13...c6! (13...e4 14.♘d4 ♘g4 15.♖h1+–; 13...♘g4 14.♗g5) 14.♕d2 (14.♕xd7!? ♕g6!? (14...e4 15.♘d4 ♘d3 16.♕f5! ♕xf5 (16...♘xc1+ 17.♖xc1 ♕xf5 18.♘xf5 ♗xg1 19.♘c4) 17.♘xf5 ♗xg1 18.♘c4) 15.♘c4 ♕c2+ (15...♖bd8? 16.♘xb6!) 16.♕d2 ♕e4+ 17.♘e3 ♖fd8∞) 14...e4 15.♘d4 e3! 16.♕c2 ♗xd4 17.cxd4 ♖fe8 18.g4 d5 (18...♘xg4 19.♖g2!) 19.♔e1 ♖e6 20.♗e2 (20.♖g3 e2 21.♗xe2 ♕h1!) 20...♘h3 21.♖g2 ♕h4+ 22.♖g3 ♘f2 23.♔d1 ♕xh2 24.♖f3 ♗b4 25.♗xe3 ♘xe2? (25...♖xd4+! 26.♗xd4 ♖xe2 27.♖xf4 ♖xc2 28.♘xc2 ♕xf4–+) 26.♕f5! ♗b7 27.♘h5 ♕g2 28.♕h3♔ Reichert-Tyulenko, cr 2015. Also good looks 12...♕f5!?, intending mate in 2!: 13.♕a6 ♖fe8♔. **13.♘c4** 13.♘d4? ♘g4–+. **13...♖ab8** It makes sense to interpose this

move before taking on f3. If Black takes immediately then White can (and must!) take on f3 with the queen: 13...exf3+ 14.♕xf3 (14.gxf3? ♖fe8+ 15.♔d2 ♘e4+ 16.fxe4 ♗xg1–+). However, even here Black can scrape a draw (if he is allowed silicon assistance): 14...♖ae8+ 15.♗e3 ♗xe3 16.♘xe3 ♖xe3+ 17.♕xe3 ♘g4 18.♕xa7 ♖e8+ 19.♔d2 c5! 20.♖e1 (the variation 20.♕xc5 shows why you can only properly play this line in correspondence chess with an engine at your side. Look at the following crazy sequence: 20...♕h6+ 21.♔d3 ♕g6+□ 22.♔d2□ ♕h6+ 23.♔c2 ♘e3+□ 24.♔b3 ♕e6+□ 25.c4 ♖b8+□ 26.♔c3 ♕f6+□ 27.♔d4 (27.♔d3 ♘g4 28.♕d4 ♘f2+ 29.♔c3 ♘e4+ 30.♔d3 ♘f2+=) 27...♕f2□ 28.♔d3 d5!? (28...♖e8=; 28...♖xb2 29.♕xe3+–) 29.cxd5 ♖xb2 30.♖d1 (30.♕xe3? ♕c2+ 31.♔d4 ♖b4+–+ demonstrates the point of 28...d5) 30...♖xa2 and here White can apparently draw with 31.♔e4 and with 31.♕c3) 20...♕f4+ 21.♔c2 ♘e3+ 22.♖xe3 ♕xe3 23.♕xd7 ♕f2+ 24.♔d3 ♔f8 ½-½ Holzer-Renard, cr 2018. Draw agreed because the engine says so: 25.♕d6+ ♔g8 26.♕d7 ♔f8. **14.♕d5 exf3+** 14...♘g4; 14...♘h3!?. **15.gxf3** It's no longer good to take with the queen: 15.♕xf3 ♖fe8+ 16.♗e3 ♕h4!♔. **15...♖fe8+ 16.♔d2 ♘e4+ 17.fxe4 ♗xg1**

In Yearbook 112 I indicated this position in my analysis as '♔'. In a practical over-the-board game I think I would still go along with that assessment. In correspondence chess it's just a draw:

18.♗d3 c6 19.♕f5! ♕xf5 20.exf5 ♗xh2 21.b3 d5 22.♘a5 c5 23.♔d1 Now that the queens have come off, the white king is no longer in danger. Black, on the other hand, has managed to retrieve some material. A rook and two pawns are about equal to two minor pieces here. **23...♗c7!** Or 23...♖b6 24.♗d2 ♗c7 25.c4 ♖a6 26.♘b7 ♗e5 27.♖c1 dxc4 28.♖xc4 ♖xa2 29.♘e4 ♖e7 30.♘xc5 ♗f6 ½-½ Anderskewitz-Ghosh, cr 2016. **24.♘c6 ♖b6 25.♘xa7 ♖g3 26.♗d2 ♖h6! 27.♗xh6** 27.♔c2 ♖h2!. **27...♖e1+ 28.♔c2 ♖xa1 29.♔b2□ ♖g1 30.♗e3 ♖g2+ 31.♔c1!** 31.♔b1 h5. **31...h5** 31...♖xa2 32.♘c6 ♗d6 33.b4⇄. **32.♘c6 ♗d6 33.a4 ♖g3** 33...h4 34.♗f1 ♖g3 35.♔d2! h3 36.♗xh3 ♖xh3 37.a5 ♖h2+ 38.♔d3 ♖a2 39.b4=. **34.♔d2** This move explains the necessity of 31.♔c1. **34...h4 35.♗f1 h3 36.♗xh3 ♖xh3 37.a5** Black is now an exchange up, but White has managed to drum up powerful counterplay on the queenside. **37...♖h2+ 38.♔d3 ♖b2 39.b4 cxb4 40.cxb4 ♗xb4 41.a6 ♖b3+ 42.♔d4 ♗c5+ 43.♔xc5 ♖xe3 44.♔xd5 ♖a3 45.a7 g5 46.fxg6 ♖xa7 ½-½**

Thomas Reichert   6
Alexey Talnis
cr 2015

1.e4 e5 2.♘f3 ♘c6 3.c3 ♘f6 4.d4 ♘xe4 5.d5 ♗c5 6.dxc6 ♗xf2+ 7.♔e2 ♗b6 8.♕d5 ♘f2 9.♖g1 0-0 10.cxb7 ♗xb7 11.♕xb7 ♕f6 12.♘a3 e4 13.♘c4 ♖ab8 14.♕d5 ♘g4

15.♔d2?! 15.♘xb6! ♖xb6 and now according to the engine

there is only one playable move and that is 16.♗d2!N (the game O.Dijkhuis-Ploder, Lüneburg 2019, saw White play 16.♕g5? when 16...exf3+ 17.♔d1 f2 18.♖h1 ♕e6-+ turned out to be good enough, but Black had instead the more spectacular and stronger 16...♖xb2+! at his disposal, which would have finished off White immediately: 17.♗xb2 exf3+-+) 16...exf3+ (16...♖d6 17.♕xe4 ♖e6 18.♕xe6 fxe6 (18...♕xe6+ 19.♔d1 is dangerous for Black only) 19.h3 (19.♔d1 d5♟) 19...♘h2 (19...♘h6 20.♔d1 (20.♖e1 ♕g6 21.♗xh6 gxh6 22.♘f2∞) 20...d5 21.g5 ♕g6 22.♗e3 ♘f5 23.♗c5±; 19...♘e5 20.♔d1 ♘xf3 21.gxf3 ♕xf3+ 22.♔c2 is risky for Black – two bishops and a rook can be very powerful against a lone queen) 20.♔d1 ♘xf1 (20...♘xf3 see 19...♘e5) 21.♖xf1 e5 22.♖e1 and in an over-the-board game I would prefer White (who looks close to achieving piece coordination), but the engine feels that Black has enough counterplay after 22...♕g6 23.♖e2 e4 24.♖e1 ♕e6; 16...♖xb2? 17.♕xe4+-; 16...♖e8 17.♔d1 exf3 18.♕xf3+-) 17.♕xf3 ♕g6! 18.♔d1□ ♖xb2 (18...♗xh2?! 19.♕e3 ♘xf1 20.♖xf1 ♖xb2 21.♖f2 is probably still a draw but it seems easier to play for White, even though Black can obtain more than enough pawns for the bishop: 21...♕c2+?! 22.♔e1 ♖xa2 23.♖xa2 ♕xa2 24.♖e2±) 19.♗d3 ♘f2+! 20.♕xf2 ♕xd3 21.♖c1 and now for full equality Black should play 21...♕a6! rather than 21...♖xa2 22.♖e1!±. **15...exf3 16.♘xb6□ f2! 17.♖h1 ♖xb6 18.♔c2 ♘e5! 19.b3 ♖e8 20.♗a3?!** In the ending after 20.♗d2 ♕g6+ 21.♗d3 ♘xd3 22.♕xd3 ♕xg2 23.♕xd7 ♕e4+ 24.♕d3 ♕xd3+ 25.♔xd3 White still has to display some accuracy to achieve a draw after 25...♖d6+ 26.♔c2 ♖e2 27.♖ad1 g5 28.♔c1 f6 but he should manage after 29.c4!. **20...♕g4 21.♔b2 ♘e3 22.♕d3** 22.♕f3 ♕e5↑. **22...♕c6 23.♖c1**

a5 **24.♔a1** The king has finally achieved a form of 'queenside castling', but his worries are not over... **24...a4 25.b4 ♕f6! 26.b5 ♖be6**

27.h3?! 27.♕xd7 h5 ('luft') and Black threatens to take on f1 and play ...♖e1. 28.♕d4! ♖e5! and the game continues but White is in trouble. **27...♖e5** 27...h5; 27...h6. **28.♕xd7 h6-+** 28...h5. **29.b6 ♕xb6 30.♗d3 c5 31.♕b5 ♕f6! 32.♕a6** 32.♗xc5 ♖d8 33.♗xe3 (33.♗e2 ♕g5-+) 33...♖xb5 34.♗xb5 ♕e5 35.♗xf2 ♕xb5-+. **32...♖5e6!** 32...♕xa6 33.♗xa6 c4-+. **33.♕xa4 c4! 34.♗b1** 34.♗xc4 ♘xc4 35.♕xc4 ♖e1-+. **34...♖b8 35.♕a7 ♖eb6 36.♗b4 f1♕!** More convincing than 36...♖xb4?! 37.♕xe3! ♖xb1+ 38.♖xb1 ♖xb1+ 39.♖xb1 f1♕ 40.♕e8+ ♔h7 41.♖xf1 ♕xf1+ 42.♔b2 ♕xg2+ when the queen ending still needs to be won. **37.♖hxf1 ♘xf1 38.♕e7 ♕xe7 39.♗xe7 ♘e3** Black is an exchange up by now. **40.♗b4 ♘xg2 41.♗c5 ♖e6 42.♗f5 ♖e2 43.a4 ♘e3 44.♖b1 ♖d8 45.♗e4 ♘c2+ 46.♗xc2 ♖xc2 47.♗d4 ♖a8 48.♖b4 f5 49.♔b1 ♖g2 50.♔c1 ♖e8 0-1**

Georges Gamant   7
Stephane Renard
cr 2018

1.e4 e5 2.♘f3 ♘c6 3.c3 ♘f6 4.d4 ♘xe4 5.d5 ♗c5 6.dxc6 ♗xf2+ 7.♔e2 ♗b6 8.♕d5 ♘f2 9.♖g1 0-0 10.cxb7 ♗xb7 11.♕xb7 ♕f6 12.♕d5 c6

13.♕c4? In a high-level blitz game White now 'blundered' with 13.♕xd7? only to win quickly after 13...♘e4? (13...♗g6!–+ is what I indicated in Yearbook 112! White has no defence to the threats of 14...♕e4+ and 14...♖ad8) 14.♕g4!+– ♗xg1 15.♕xe4 ♗b6 16.♘a3 h6 17.♘c4 ♗c7 18.♗f2 ♕e6 19.♗e3 ♔h8 20.♗c4 ♕e7 1-0 Belyakov-Lysyj, Sochi 2019; 13.♕d2 e4 14.♘d4 e3∞. **13...e4!?** 13...d5 14.♕h4 ♕g6 15.♗d2 ♖ae8 (15...♘e4+ 16.♔d1 ♗f2+ 17.♔d2 ♘e4+=; 17...♖ae8!∓) with compensation is what I gave in YB 112 – Black is already better. **14.♘d4 ♗g4** Also good is 14...♖fe8! 15.♘a3 ♗g4 16.♔d1 d5 17.♕a4 (17.♕xc6 ♕f2 18.♖h1 (18.♕e2 d4!–+) 18...♗xd4 19.cxd4 ♕xd4+–+) 17...c5 18.♘db5 c4!, not so much winning the rook, because of 19.♗e2 ♗xg1 20.♘c7, but obtaining a winning attack with an 'octopus' on d3: 20...♘f2+ 21.♔c2 ♘d3! 22.♘xa8 ♖b8! (22...♖xa8–+) 23.♘b5 a6 0-1 Gamant-Mosshammer, cr 2018 24.♘d4 (24.♘bc7 ♕f2) 24...♗xd4 25.cxd4 ♕f2. **15.♔d1 d5 16.♕e2** 16.♕xc6 ♕f2–+. **16...♗xd4 17.cxd4 ♕xd4+ 18.♔e1 ♕xg1 19.♕xg4 e3!**

20.♕f4 Even after 20.♕e2 ♖ae8 21.g3 f5 22.♕g2 ♕xg2 23.♗xg2

White cannot keep Black's attack in check: 23...f4! 24.gxf4 ♖xf4 25.♘c3 ♖f2 – Black has a rook and three pawns versus three minor pieces and an ongoing attack. **20...d4! 21.g4?** The only way to continue was 21.♘c3 dxc3 22.♗xe3 ♖ae8 23.♔e2 ♖e6 24.♔f3! cxb2 25.♖b1 ♕h1 26.♔d3 ♕xb1 27.♗xb1 ♖f6 28.♕xf6 gxf6. **21...♕h1 22.♕g3 f5! 23.♕g2 ♕xg2 24.♗xg2 fxg4!** 24...f4? 25.♗f3±. **25.♗xc6 ♖ac8 26.♗d5+ ♔h8** White cannot develop his queenside in time. **27.♘c3** 27.♘a3 ♖f2. **27...♖f2!** Less clear is 27...dxc3 28.bxc3 ♖xc3. **28.♘b5** 28.♘e4 ♖xh2 29.♘d6 ♖f8 30.♘f7+ ♖xf7 31.♗xf7 g3–+ and there goes another passed pawn! **28...♖c5 29.♘xd4 ♖xd5 30.♗xe3 ♖xh2 31.♘e2 ♖h1+ 32.♗g1 h5 0-1**

Einar Castellano Egea 8
Adrian Jimenez Ruano
Catalunya tt 2020 (2)
1.e4 e5 2.♘f3 ♘c6 3.c3 ♘f6 4.d4 ♘xe4 5.d5 ♗c5 6.dxc6 ♗xf2+ 7.♔e2 ♗b6 8.♕d5 ♘f2 9.♖g1 0-0 10.cxb7 ♗xb7 11.♕xb7 ♕f6 12.♕d5 c6 13.♕d2 e4 14.♘d4 e3 ⌘ YB/112.

15.♕c2 Quite obviously the only move. **15...♖ae8!?** Black can force an immediate draw with 15...♗xd4 16.cxd4 ♘g4 17.♖h1 ♘f2 18.♖g1 ♘g4. Note that 15...♘g4? (without trading on d4 first) is a losing mistake due to 16.♕f5 ♗xd4 and now 17.♕xf6! ♗xf6 18.h3 when White has returned one of his extra pieces for complete safety. **16.g4** White has also tried 16.♘f3 g5!? (16...d5 17.b4 ♖e6 18.♗b2 ♕f4 19.♘a3 ♖fe8? 20.♕b3?) (Karavitaki-

Koutsouraki, Rethymno 2019; 20.g3!±) 20...♖f6!–+ planning ...♘h3) 17.h4 (17.g4 ♘e4 18.♘a3 ♕f4→) 17...gxh4! (now ...♘e4 becomes a threat, combined with ...♘g3+ or ...♕d6) 18.♘a3 d5 19.♘e1 e2! 20.♗xe2 ♘e4 21.♔d1 ♗xg1 22.♘xg1 d4! 23.♘h3 (23.♘f3 ♗f2+ 24.♔e1 d3–+) 23...dxc3 24.♘c4 ♘f2+ 25.♔e1 (25.♘xf2 ♕xf2 26.bxc3 ♕g1+ 27.♔d2 ♖xe2+ 28.♔xe2 ♕xg2+ 29.♔d1 ♕f1+ 30.♔d2 ♖d8+–+) 25...♘xh3 26.gxh3 ♕f3 27.♗e3 ♖xe3 28.♘xe3 ♕xe3–+ 29.♔f1 ♖e8 30.♗g4 h5! 31.♗xh5 ♖e4 32.♖d1 ♕xh3+ 33.♕g2+ ♕xg2+ 34.♔xg2 cxb2–+ Egner-Rimpau, cr 2016. Here 16.♕f5 is met by 16...♕d6!⇄ △ 17.♗xe3? (necessary is 17.♘a3 when Black appears to be better after some typical computer tactics: 17...♗xd4 18.♘c4 ♕xh2 19.cxd4 g6 20.♕xd7 ♘d1!∓) 17...♗xd4 18.cxd4 ♖xe3+! (18...♕xd4 19.♕xf2) 19.♗xe3 ♖e8+! 20.♗xf2 (20.♔f3 ♕xd4–+) 20...♕xd4+ 21.♗g3 ♖e3+ 22.♕f3 ♖xf3+ 23.♔xf3 ♕xb2!–+, even better than 23...♕xg1.

16...♘h3!? 16...♘e4! is also very strong! **17.♗xh3?!** 17.♗g2 ♘f4+?! (17...♘e5!) 18.♔e1 ♗xd4 19.cxd4 ♘xg2+ 20.♕xg2 ♕xd4 21.♘c3 f5! 22.g5 f4 23.♕f3 ♖f5 ½-½ Clough-Grieve, cr 2016. I think a draw was agreed on accord of the perpetual following the (crazy) 24.h4 ♖c5 25.♖b1! ♖xc3 26.bxc3 ♕xc3+ 27.♔d1 ♕d4+□=. **17...♕f2+ 18.♔d3 ♕xg1** 18...e2! appears to win, the main line of the engine is 19.♖g2 e1♕+! 20.♔c4 ♕h4 21.♕f2 ♕xh3 22.♖g3 ♕h4 23.♗e3 and now 23...d5+ 24.♔b3 c5. **19.♘f3 e2□ 20.♘xg1?** 20.♕xe2! ♕xc1 21.♕d2

♖e3+ 22.♔c4 ♕xd2 23.♘bxd2
♗c7∓. **20...e1♕–+** The silicon
verdict is approaching -6 by this
time (but the position is a mess
of course) so the rest of the game
proves that chess is never easy
when you have only your own
head to rely upon. **21.♘e2 ♕h1**
21...d5–+. **22.♘d4 ♕e4+ 23.♔c4**
♕d5+ 24.♔d3 c5? 24...♗xd4
25.cxd4 ♕f3+–+. **25.♕g2! ♕d6**
26.♕g3 ♕e7 26...♕d5?? 27.♗g2+–.
27.♕e3 27.♔c2. **27...♕d8** 27...c4+!.
28.♕f3 cxd4 29.cxd4 ♕c8

30.♗e3? 30.♘c3!. **30...♕a6+**
30...♖xe3+! 31.♕xe3 (31.♔xe3
♕c1+–+) 31...♖e8–+ and ...♕a6+
is coming. **31.♔c2 ♕a4+ 32.♔d3**

♕b4?! 33.♘c3 ♕xb2?! 34.♖b1
♕a3 35.♗f1∞ 35.♖b3. **35...♖e6**
36.♖b3 ♕a5 37.♕f5 ♕a6+?!
38.♔d2 ♕c8 39.♗d3 g6 40.♕g5
♖fe8 41.♗f2 ♕c7? 42.♗g3! ♕c8
43.♕d5 Finally, White is clearly
better. **43...♗c7 44.g5!** Fixing
the f6-square for the knight.
44...♗xg3 45.hxg3 ♖e1? 45...♔g7
46.♘e4 ♕c6 was more stubborn.
46.♗c4 ♖1e6 47.♘e4 ♕d8
48.♘f6++– ♔g7 49.♘xe8+ ♕xe8
50.♖b7 ♕e7 51.♖xd7 ♕b4+
52.♔c2 ♕a4+ 53.♗b3 1-0

Exercise 1

position after 16.♕d5-g5

What is Black's best move
now?

(solutions on page 248)

Exercise 2

position after 13.♕d5xd7

How should Black continue?

Exercise 3

position after 18.c3xd4

Can you accurately calculate
the win for Black?

Looking for material from previous Yearbooks?

Visit our website www.newinchess.com and see under 'Games and Downloads' in the page footer.
Here you can find games, Surveys and contributors from all our Yearbooks.
Surveys are indexed by opening, by author and by Yearbook.

The Chinese Four Knights?

by Glenn Flear

1.	e4	e5
2.	♘f3	♞c6
3.	♘c3	♞f6
4.	♗b5	♞d4
5.	♗c4	♝c5
6.	♘xe5	♛e7
7.	♘f3	d5

This particular variation of the Four Knights has already featured in a couple of Yearbook Surveys (by Lukacs & Hazai in YB/49 and by René Olthof in YB/97, the latter being in 2010).

Since Rubinstein's day, Black's choice of 4...♞d4 has generally been recognized as offering the potential for sharp and lively play. This does however require White to accept the offer of a fair fight by not employing the drawish 5.♘xd4 exd4 6.e5. Assuming that White is a sport and does indeed demonstrate a willingness for a tense struggle by opting for 5.♗c4, then Black can accept the challenge with 5...♝c5. The further moves 6.♘xe5 (grabbing a pawn) 6...♛e7 (inviting complications) 7.♘f3 (coming back to a safe square) 7...d5 (more fuel on the fire) lead us to the diagram position.

Such noble intentions on both sides can yield fascinating play, but there has been a tendency unfortunately for some of the key lines to have been virtually analysed to death, including what I describe as the main line.

Throughout the last decade, a number of elite players have still been willing to employ this variation and not only because they fancy a quick draw. In particular, quite a few of the leading Chinese players have a belief in obtaining positive opportunities, and with both colours!

There are three sections which reflect to a great degree the players' frame of mind:

1) Yu Yangyi's blitz weapon (Games 1-4)

The capture 8.♘xd5 involves White choosing a solid but slightly passive game in a quest to hold onto a pawn advantage. A question of taste perhaps, but Yu Yangyi has demonstrated that (particularly at blitz) Black can easily run out of compensation if he's not careful.

2) Spicing things up (Games 5-9)

After the more common 8.♗xd5, a lot depends on whether one is willing to

Akiba Rubinstein

risk leaving the beaten path. There are several intriguing possibilities which create less well known problems and thus chances to outplay an opponent in the sort of double-edged play which attracted many to the Rubinstein Variation in the first place.

3) The main line (Games 10-13)
Since 2006, the forcing line with 8...♗g4 9.d3 0-0-0 10.♗e3, which I will call the main line here, is 10...♘xd5 11.♘xd5 ♖xd5 12.exd5 ♖e8.

It has been recognized as leading to a draw when White reacts with 13.c3, but there have been developments following 13.0-0.

Conclusions
1) Some choices work better at blitz, especially when an opponent is not particularly familiar with the finer details. Yu Yangyi's choice of 8.♘xd5 perhaps comes into that category. Black seems to be alright if he is precise, but many of his opponents have not found it that easy to keep their 'compensation going' while White slowly consolidates. A good practical choice for pawn grabbers!

2) In some of these early deviations from the main line, the play becomes sharp, whereas in others a sort of 'compensation for a pawn in a simplified endgame' occurs. Both of 8...♘xd5 and 8...c6 don't look too bad although they may not equalize completely (for purists or email players). Best of the bunch could be 9...♘d7, where White can easily go wrong, as was the case in Adhiban-Yu Yangyi (playing Black this time!), but White should then reply with 10.h3 in my opinion.

3) I can't deny that the main line is drawish for those folk who have perfect memories. Nevertheless, after 13.0-0 there are ways to keep the game alive as the complications are not completely worked out, that is, even if email encounters seem to suggest that this whole line should ultimately be drawn.

Yu Yangyi's blitz weapon 8.♘xd5

Nikolas Theodorou   **1**
Grigoriy Oparin
Columbia MO 2019 (2)
1.e4 e5 2.♘f3 ♘c6 3.♘c3 ♘f6 4.♗b5 ♘d4 5.♗c4 ♗c5 6.♘xe5 ♕e7 7.♘f3 d5 8.♘xd5 ♕xe4+ 9.♘e3 ♗g4 10.♗e2 ♘xe2 11.♕xe2 0-0-0! 12.d3 ♕e6!

The best square from where the queen has influence on both wings. 12...♕a4?! 13.c3 (13.♘xg4!? ♘xg4 14.0-0 ♖he8 15.♕d2! leaves Black with very active pieces, but nothing concrete) 13...♖he8 14.d4 ♘d5 15.0-0 ♕c6?? (Cadilhac-Tutsani, Manavgat 2018; 15...♗d6⩲ was better), and now 16.dxc5 ♘f4 17.♕c4+−. The following sequence looks logical: 12...♕e7

13.0-0 (13.♘xg4 is also plausible, as in the main game) **13...♘d5 14.♗d2 ♖he8 15.♖ae1 ♗h5 16.♕d1 ♕d7 17.♘xd5 ♖xd5 18.a3±/=** (Soors-Bergsson, Reykjavik 2015), when the bishop pair is strong, but White nevertheless has chances to consolidate the pawn advantage. **13.♘xg4!?** 13.♗g5!? ♕c6 (13...♕d7!? 14.♘xg4 ♘xg4 15.0-0 ♖he8 16.♕d2∞) 14.♘xg4 ♕xg2 15.♗xf6 ♖xh1+ 16.♕f1 ♕c6 17.♘fe4 ♖he8! (but not 17...♗b4+? 18.c3 f5 19.cxb4 fxe4 20.♘xe4± Yu Yangyi-Sychev, Moscow blitz 2019) 18.♕h3+ ♔b8 19.♗d2 f6 20.♘f3 ♖xe4+ 21.dxe4 ♕xe4+ 22.♔f1 ♖xd2 (22...g5?! 23.♖e1! ♕c4+ 24.♖e2 g4? 25.♕h4±) 23.♘xd2 ♕h1+ 24.♔e2 ♕xa1=; 13.0-0 ♘d5 14.♖e1 (14.♗d2 ♖he8 15.♖ae1 ♘f4 16.♕d1 ♗h5⩲ – it's convenient for Black that the a-pawn is hanging) 14...♘f4 15.♕d1 ♗h5 16.♗d2 ♖he8⩲ Schubert-Henriksen, cr 1957. **13...♕xe2+ 14.♔xe2 ♘xg4 15.♗e3 ♖he8 16.♖he1** 16.♖ae1 ♘xe3 17.fxe3 ♗xe3 (17...♖xe3+ 18.♔d1 ♖de8 19.♖xe3 ♖xe3 20.♖f1 f6 21.♘d2= Betker-Grigoryev, email 2019) 18.♔d1 ♔d7 19.c3 ♔d5 20.b4!?= Betker-Keuter, email 2019. **16...♘xe3 17.fxe3 ♗xe3 18.♔f1 f6** 18...♗e6 19.♖e2 ♖de8 20.♖ae1 h5 21.d4! g5 22.c3∞. **19.♖e2 ♗b6 20.♖ae1 ♖xe2 21.♖xe2 ♗d7 22.g4 c6 23.♖e4 ♖h8 24.h3 h5 25.♔g2 hxg4 ½-½**

Yu Yangyi   **2**
Levon Aronian
St Louis blitz 2019 2019 (14)
1.e4 e5 2.♘f3 ♘c6 3.♘c3 ♘f6 4.♗b5 ♘d4 5.♗c4 ♗c5 6.♘xe5 ♕e7 7.♘f3 d5 8.♘xd5 ♕xe4+ 9.♘e3

9...♗g4 Also reasonable is 9...0-0 10.♘xd4 ♗xd4 11.d3 ♕h4 12.0-0 ♗g4 13.♕d2 ♖ae8 14.c3 ♗e5 (14...♗xe3 15.fxe3 ♗e6!?) 15.f4 ♗d6 16.♕f2 (Hovhannisyan-Wehmeier, Germany tt 2013/14), and now 16...♕xf2+ 17.♖xf2 ♗d7 with gentle but persistent pressure for the pawn. **10.♗e2 ♘xe2 11.♕xe2** ♗xe3 11...♘d7 12.d3 ♕e6 13.♘c4 0-0-0 14.♕xe6 ♗xe6 15.♘e3 (Black would seem to be doing OK, but over the next few moves he runs out of good ideas) 15...h6 (Komodo's line 15...♘d5 16.a3 ♖he8 17.0-0 f6 18.♗d2 ♘xe3 19.fxe3 ♗d7 also feels 'playable' but I would take White) 16.♗d2 ♖he8 17.0-0 g5 18.h3 ♖g8± (Mijovic-Pajkovic, Cetinje 2009) doesn't look like full compensation. 11...0-0-0 is the main move. **12.♕xe3** 12.dxe3?! 0-0-0 13.0-0 ♘d5!∓. **12...0-0-0 13.♕xe4 ♘xe4 14.d3** 14.♘e5 ♗h5 (14...♖he8!? 15.♘xg4 ♘g3+ 16.♘e3 ♘xh1 17.♔f1 f5∞) 15.♘c4 ♖he8 16.♘e3 f5 17.d3 ♗c5 18.f4 ♘e6⩲. **14...♗xf3 15.gxf3 ♘c5 16.♗e3 ♘e6 17.h4** 17.0-0-0!±/= (placing the king out of harm's way) might offer White more chances to set about advancing his pawns. **17...h5 18.♔d2 ♖d5 19.♖ag1 ♖hd8 20.a4 c5!⩲ 21.b3 b6 22.♔e2 ♗b7 23.♔d2 ♔c6 24.♖g3 ♖f5 25.♔e2 g6 26.♔d2 ♗d7 27.♔e2 ½-½** 27...♘d4+!?∓.

Yu Yangyi   **3**
Leinier Dominguez Perez
St Louis blitz 2019 2019 (4)
1.e4 e5 2.♘f3 ♘c6 3.♘c3 ♘f6 4.♗b5 ♘d4 5.♗c4 ♗c5 6.♘xe5 ♕e7 7.♘f3 d5 8.♘xd5 ♕xe4+ 9.♘e3 ♗g4 10.♗e2 ♘xe2 11.♕xe2

11...0-0?! It seems that it's better to 'go long' as that has the additional benefit of bringing the rook to the open d-file: 11...0-0-0! 12.d3 ♕e6∞. **12.d3** 12.♘xg4 ♕xg4 13.0-0 ♖fe8 14.♗b5± Pranav-D. Fischer, Douglas 2017. **12...♕a4** 12...♕e6 13.♘xg4 ♘xg4 14.0-0 ♖fe8 15.♕d1 ♘e6 16.h3 ♘f5 17.♘h4 (17.♖e1 ♖ae8 18.♖xe6 ♕xe6 19.♗d2?! ♕b6!∞) 17...♘d5 18.♕f3± ♖ae8 19.♕xd5 ♖xd5 20.♗d2 ♖e2 21.♘f3 ♗b4 22.d4 ♗d6 23.♗xb4 ♗xb4 24.c3 ♗d6 25.♖fe1± Yu Yangyi-Paravyan, Moscow blitz 2019. **13.♘xg4 ♘xg4 14.0-0 ♖fe8 15.♕d1 h6 16.h3 ♘e5 17.♘xe5 ♖xe5 18.c3 ♕xd1 19.♖xd1 ♖e2 20.d4 ♗d6 21.♗d2 ♖ae8 22.♖e1±** It's flowing so nicely for White. **22...♖8e6 23.♖xe2 ♖xe2 24.♖d1 b5 25.♔f1 ♖e6 26.♖e1 ♖xe1+ 27.♔xe1 f5 28.♔e2 ♔f7 29.♔d3 ♔e6 30.c4 c6** 30...bxc4+ 31.♔xc4 c6 32.♗b4!. **31.d5+ ♔d7 32.dxc6+ ♔xc6 33.cxb5+ ♔xb5**

This looks like a position out of an endgame textbook! **34.b3 h5 35.f3 a6 36.a4+ ♔c5 37.b4+ ♔d5 38.♔c3 g6 39.♗e3 ♗e5+ 40.♔b3 ♗d6 41.b5 axb5 42.axb5 f4** 42...♗g3!? 43.♗b4 ♗e1+ 44.♔a4 ♗c3 45.♔c1 ♗c5 46.♗a3+ ♔b6 (46...♔d5 47.♔b4 ♗e5 48.♔a5) 47.♗b4 ♗d4 48.♔a5+ ♔c5 49.♗d8 ♗c3 (49...♔e3 50.♔a5) 50.♗e7+ ♔b6 51.♔b3 ♗d2 52.♔c4 ♗e3 53.♗d8+ ♔b7 54.♔d5+− and White penetrates to the kingside. **43.♗g1 ♗e5 44.♔b4 ♗d6+ 45.♔a5 ♔c4 46.b6 ♔d3 47.b7 ♔e2 48.♔b6 ♗f1 49.♔c6 ♗b8 50.♗b6 ♔xg2 51.♗c7 ♗a7 52.♔b5! 1-0** The threat of 53.♔a6 is decisive.

Lc0 **4**
Stockfish

CCC final 2020 (43)

1.e4 e5 2.♘c3 ♘f6 3.♘f3 ♘c6
4.♗b5 ♗d4 5.♗c4 ♗c5 6.♘xe5
♕e7 7.♘f3 d5 8.♘xd5 ♕xe4+
9.♘e3 ♗g4 10.♗e2 ♘xe2 11.♕xe2
0-0-0 12.d3 ♕e6 13.♘xg4 ♕xe2+
14.♔xe2 ♘xg4 15.♗g5!?N

15...♖de8+ 16.♔d2 ♗xf2 17.♖af1=
f6 17...h6!?. 18.h3!? fxg5 18...♗e3+
19.♗xe3 ♘xe3 20.♖e1!=. 19.hxg4
♗e3+ 20.♔d1 h6 21.♖e1 ♔d7
22.♖hf1 ♗f4 23.b4!? For queenside
space and influence, I presume.
However, this looks a shade
loosening to me. 23...♖xe1+
24.♖xe1 ♗d6 25.c3 ♖f8 26.a4 ♖f4
27.♖e4 ♖xe4 28.dxe4 ♗e6 28...c5!?
29.bxc5 ♗xc5 is apparently 0.00.
Oh well! 29.♔e2 g6 30.♘d4+ ♔e5
31.♘e3 c6 32.♘b3 ♗c7 33.a5
h5 34.♘d4 The outpost on d4 is
quite handy for White, hence the
idea of an early ...c7-c5 (see move
28) for Black. 34...♔d6 35.♔d3
hxg4 36.♘b3 b6 37.a6 b5 38.♔d4
♗b6+ 39.♔d3 g3 40.c4 bxc4+
41.♔xc4 ♔e5 42.♔d3 g4 43.♘d2
♗d8 44.♘c4+ ♔e6 45.♔d4 ♗e7
46.♘a5 ♔d7 47.♔c4 ♗d8 48.♘b7
♗b6 49.♘c5+ ♔d6 50.e5+ ♔e7!
50...♔xe5? 51.♘d7++-. 51.♘a4 ♗f2
52.♔d3 ♗e1 53.♔c4 ♗f2 54.♘c5
g5 55.♘b7 ♔e6 56.♘d8+ ♔xe5
57.♘xc6+ ♔e4 58.b5 ♗b6 59.♔b4
59...♘e7!? ♗e3!. 60.♘c8 ♗f2! 61.♘xb6
♔xg2!=. 59...♗e3 60.♘xa7! ♗xa7
61.♔a5 ♔f2 62.b6 ♗xb6+ 63.♔xb6
♔xg2 For humans this would be a
curious moment to agree to a draw,
but the engines have access to their
tablebases! 64.a7 ♔f2 (not the only
square, it seems, as 64...♔h2 and
64...♔h3 are also adequate) 65.a8♕
g2 is strangely drawn.

The presence of both additional
pawns on g4 and g5 restricts the
queen's scope sufficiently. The
World's knowledge of queen versus
tripled g-pawns has perhaps been
extended!?
½-½

**Spicing things up
8.♗xd5**

Wei Yi **5**
Li Chao

Xinghua ch-CHN 2013 (3)

1.e4 e5 2.♘f3 ♘c6 3.♗b5 ♘f6
4.♘c3 ♘d4 5.♗c4 ♗c5 6.♘xe5
♕e7 An alternative gambit idea
begins with 6...d5 (first played
by Tkachiev in 1997) 7.♗xd5!
♘xd5 (7...0-0!?N 8.d3 (8.0-0 ♘xd5
9.♘xd5 ♖e8⇄) 8...♘xd5 9.♘xd5
♖e8 10.c3 ♖xe5 11.cxd4 ♗xd4
12.0-0 c6 transposes to 7...♘xd5
etc.) 8.♘xd5 0-0 9.c3 ♖e8 10.cxd4
♗xd4 11.0-0 ♖xe5 12.d3 c6 13.♘f4
(13.♕a4 ♗xf2+ 14.♖xf2 cxd5 15.♗f4
♖e7 16.e5 ♕b6= M.Szabo-Pott,
email 2007) 13...b6 14.♕c2 ♖c5
15.♕e2 ♗a6 16.♗e3 ♕d6 (Shirov-
Kramnik, Cazorla m-6 1998),
with reasonable compensation
for the pawn. The game was soon
drawn, but Obodchuk prefers
White slightly after 17.♗xd4 ♕xd4
18.♖ac1±. 7.♘f3 d5 8.♗xd5

8...c6 Rare, but not bad. Also
worth considering is 8...♘xd5!?
9.♘xd4 (9.♘xd5 ♕xe4+ 10.♘e3
♘xf3+ (10...♗g4?! 11.♘g5! ♗f4
12.♘xg4 ♕xg5 13.c3± Neubauer-
Neumeier, Oberwart 2004) 11.♕xf3
♕xf3 12.gxf3 f6 13.b3 ♗d7 14.♗b2
♔f7⨰ Külaots-Bedouin, France tt
2010) 9...♘xc3! (9...♘f4? 10.♕f3 g5
(Willow-Jarmany, Wakefield 2017)
11.♘b3! ♗d6 12.d4 g4 13.♕g3+-)
10.bxc3 (10.dxc3 ♕xe4+ 11.♕e2
♕xe2+ 12.♔xe2 ♗d7 13.♗e3
0-0-0⨰ Alavkin-Bezgodova, Kazan
2010) and White's extra pawn
is nigh on useless) 10...♕xe4+
11.♕e2 ♕xe2+ 12.♔xe2 ♗g4+ 13.f3
♗d7⨰. In such open positions,
the bishop pair plus a solid
structure generally yield sufficient
compensation for a pawn. 9.♘xd4
9.♗b3 ♗g4 10.d3 ♘d7 transposes
to 8...♗g4. 9...♗xd4 10.♗b3
♗g4 11.♕f3 ♗xf2+ 12.♔e2
♗h4 After 12...♗d4 13.h3 ♘e5
14.♕g3 ♗e6 15.d3 0-0 16.♗g5 f6
17.♗e3 (Kavc-Chatel, email 2014),
I suggest 17...♖ad8!?. 13.h3 ♘e5
14.♕e3 White's whole position
does seem to be somewhat tangled
up, albeit temporarily, but with
the structure being so solid it
might not be possible for Black
to upset the apple-cart. 14...b6
15.d3 ♗a6 16.g3 ♗f6 17.♔f2
0-0-0 18.♔g2± White is gradually
consolidating. 18...♖he8 19.♕f2
♔b7 20.♗f4 ♗xd3? Wild but not
sound. ≥ 20...h5! 21.♖hf1 (21.d4!?
♘g6 22.e5 ♘xf4+ 23.♕xf4 ♗g5
24.♕xf7 ♖xd4 25.♖ad1 ♖xd1
26.♖xd1 ♕xf7 27.♗xf7 ♖xe5
28.♗xh5 ♗f6⨰) 21...♗a8 22.♖ad1±.
21.cxd3 ♘xd3 22.♕e2 ♘xb2
23.♕xb2 g5 24.♗xg5 After
24.♗d2!? ♖d3 25.♖hf1 ♕d6 White
is winning with the astonishing
blow 26.♖xf6!! (hard to believe,
I know...) 26...♕xf6 (26...♕xg3+
27.♔f1 ♗f3+ 28.♖xf3 ♕xf3+
29.♔e1+-; 26...♖xd2+ 27.♔h1+-)
27.♖f1 ♖xg3+ 28.♔xg3 ♕xf1
29.♕c1+-. 24...♗xg5 25.♖ad1 f5
Bluff! 25...♗f6 26.♖hf1. 26.exf5
♗f6 27.♖xd8 ♖xd8 28.♕e2 ♕b4
29.♘e4 ♖d4 30.♗c2 1-0

Nikoloz Chkhaidze 6
Taron Shagbazyan
Marianske Lazne 2019 (5)

1.e4 e5 2.♘f3 ♘c6 3.♘c3 ♘f6
4.♗b5 ♘d4 5.♗c4 ♗c5 6.♘xe5
♕e7 7.♘f3 d5 8.♗xd5 ♗g4 9.d3
c6 First played by none other than
Akiba Rubinstein in 1912. 10.♗b3
♘d7 11.♗e3 ♘e5

12.♘xd4 ♗xd1 13.♘f5 ♕f8
14.♘xc5 ♕xc5 15.d4 ♕a5
16.♖xd1 0-0-0!? 16...♘g6 17.♘xg7+
♔f8 18.♘f5 ♖e8 19.0-0± Vorobiov-
Gerzhoy, Moscow 2010. Two pieces
plus three pawns and the safer
king ensured a durable advantage
for White. **17.dxe5 ♖xd1+**
18.♔xd1 ♕xe5 19.g3 ≤ 19.♗xf7?!
as this hands unnecessary
counterchances to the opponent:
19...g6 20.♘e3 ♕f6⇄. **19...g6**
20.♘e3± Three stable pieces (plus
a pawn), a solid structure and
safe enough king together yield
White the easier game. **20...b5**
21.f4?! Too hasty. 21.♗c1 ♖d8
(21...♕h5 22.♗xf7) 22.a3 a5 23.♖f1±.
21...♕h5+?! 21...♖d8+! 22.♔c1
♕d4⇄. **22.♔c1 b4 23.♘cd1**
♕f3 24.♖f1 ♕xe4 25.♗xf7±
♖f8 26.♗c4 ♔c7 27.♗d3 ♕d4
28.f5! gxf5 29.♘f4 ♕e5 30.♘xf5
♖f7 31.♖e4 More cautious was
31.♔b1! h5 32.♖f1 ♖f8 33.♘de3
♖f6 34.b3±. **31...♕d5** 31...♕xf5
32.♖e7+ ♖xe7 33.♗xf5 ♖e2
34.♗xh7 ♖xh2 35.♗f5±. **32.♘de3**
♕xa2 33.♖xb4 a5 34.♖b3 ♕a1+
35.♔d2 ♕g1 36.♖a3 36.h4±.
36...♕xh2+ 37.♔c3 ♕f2 38.♔b3
♕e1 39.♔a2 ♖f8 40.♖c3+− The
c6-pawn is about to fall. **40...a4**
41.♗b5 ♕b6 42.♖xc6+! ♔a7
42...♔xb5 43.♘d4++−. **43.♖a6+**
♔b8 44.♗xa4 ♖f7 45.♗b3 ♖a7
46.♖xa7 ♔xa7 47.c3 The rest is a

matter of technique, or so they say.
White kept control throughout the
remainder of the game. **47...♔b8**
48.♗d5 ♕d2 49.♔b3 ♕d3
50.♗b4 ♕c7 51.b3 ♕b6 52.♗c4
♕d8 53.♘d5+ ♔c6 54.♘de7+
♔b6 55.♗d5 ♕c7 56.c4 ♕c5+
57.♔c3 ♕a3 58.♗e4 ♔c5 59.♗c2
♕a1+ 60.♔d2 ♕a5+ 61.♔d3
♕e1 62.♘d5 ♕f1+ 63.♔c3 ♕e1+
64.♔b2 ♕e5+ 65.♔a2 ♕e1
66.g4 h6 67.♘fe3 ♕e2 68.b4+
♔d4 69.♔b3 ♕f2 70.♘f5+ ♔e5
71.♘de3 ♕f3 72.b5 h5 73.gxh5
♕xh5 74.♔b4 ♕h1 75.♔c5
♕a8 76.♘g4+ ♔e6 77.♘d4+
♔d7 78.♘e5+ ♔c7 79.b6+ ♔b8
80.♘b5 80.♘ec6+!. **80...♕g2**
81.♘d4 ♕g5 82.♔d6 ♕h6+
83.♘e6 ♕d2+ 84.♗d3 ♔c8 85.c5
♕a5 86.♗e4 ♕d2+ 87.♘d3 ♕e3
88.b7+ ♔b8 89.c6 ♕b6 90.♘dc5
♔a7 91.♘d7 ♕b4+ 92.♘c7 ♕a5+
93.♔c8 ♕a6 94.♘dc5 ♕b5 95.c7
♕e8+ 96.♘d8 ♕d7+ 97.♔xd7 1-0

Bence Korpa 7
Jonas Lampert
Prague tt 2016 (9)

1.e4 e5 2.♘f3 ♘c6 3.♘c3 ♘f6
4.♗b5 ♘d4 5.♗c4 ♗c5 6.♘xe5
♕e7 7.♘f3 d5 8.♗xd5 ♗g4 9.d3
c6 10.♗b3 ♘d7 11.♗e3 11.♗g5?!
♕d6! (11...♕xf3+ 12.gxf3 ♕xg5
13.fxg4 ♘e5⇄, see the analysis of
Drabke-Delchev, St Vincent 2004,
in YB/97) 12.♗b1 ♕g6 13.♗e3 ♗xf3
14.gxf3 ♕g2 15.♘d2 (Bernstein-
Rubinstein, Vilnius 1912)
15...a5!∓; 15...♘e5 (Olthof) 16.♕f1!∞.
11...♘e5 12.♘xd4! ♗xd1 13.♘f5
♕f8 14.♗xc5 ♕xc5 15.d4

15...♕b4 ≥ 15...♕f8!. 16.♖xd1
and now Black seems to have
three plausible ways to obtain an
acceptable game:

A) 16...g6 17.dxe5 gxf5 18.exf5 ♖d8
19.0-0 ♖xd1 20.♖xd1 ♕c5 21.e6
fxe6 22.♗xe6 b5 23.♖d7 ♕e5 24.g3
b4 25.♘d1 ♕e1+ 26.♔g2 ♕e4+
27.♔g1 ♕e1+ G.Müller-Roubaud,
cr 2016. To obtain the 'drawing
counterplay' it was convenient for
Black that White didn't have the
'extra move' a2-a3;
B) 16...♗g4 17.e5 0-0-0 18.♘e2
♔b8 19.h3 ♘xe5 20.dxe5 ♕b4+
21.♘d2 ♕f4 22.♘e3 ♕xe3 23.c3
♕b5 24.♘f3 ♖xd1+ 25.♔xd1 f5∞
Tinture-Zhak, cr 2015;
C) 16...♘g6 17.e5 0-0-0 18.0-0
♘e7!? (18...f6 19.♘d6+ ♖xd6
20.exd6 ♖xd6 21.♘e4 ♕d8= De
La Fuente Alvarez-Chabierski, cr
2018) 19.♘d6+ ♖xd6 20.exd6 ♘f5
21.♘e4 (½-½ Wiersma-Lenaerts,
Belgium tt 2017/18) 21...♘xd6
22.♖fe1 ♘xe4 23.♖xe4 f5 24.♖e6
g6 (24...♔b8 25.c3 g6 26.d5±)
25.c3 ♕h6∞. **16.♖xd1 g6!** 16...♘g6
17.♘xg7+ ♔f8 18.♘f5± Motylev-
Shirov, Bastia rapid 2004. **17.a3**
♕f8 18.dxe5!? 18.♘e3♖ Motylev.
18...gxf5 19.exf5 ♕c5 In the note
to 15...♕f8, Black continues with
...♖d8 in the analogous position
with the pawn on a2 rather than
a3. This doesn't seem to make a
great deal of difference... or does it?
19...♖d8 20.0-0 ♖xd1 21.♖xd1 ♕c5
22.e6 fxe6 23.♗xe6 ♖f8 transposing
to the main game. **20.0-0 ♖d8**
21.e6 fxe6!? 21...f6 22.♘e4∞.
22.♗xe6 ♖xd1 23.♖xd1 ♖f8

24.♖d2 24.♖d3!?. **24...♕e5 25.♖e2**
♕f4? ≥ 25...♕g7±. **26.♖e3 ♔d8**
27.g3 ♕g4 28.♖d3+ ♔e8 29.f3
♕g5 30.f4 30.♘e4! ♕c1+ 31.♔g2
♕xc2+ 32.♖d2 ♕c1 33.♔h3!
(33.g4 h6 34.♖d7 ♕xb2+ 35.♔h3
♖f6 36.♖xb7!±) 33...b6 34.♖d7
♕h6+ 35.♔g2+−. **30...♕h5**

31.h3 ♖f6 31...♕xh3 32.♘e4 ♕h6
33.♖d7+−. **32.♔g2 ♖xe6 33.fxe6
♕f5 34.♖d2± h5 35.♖e2 ♔e7
36.h4 a5 37.b4 axb4 38.axb4
♕f6 39.♖e5 ♔g6 40.♘e4 ♕g4
41.♘f2** 41...♘f6!+−. **41...♕g6 42.f5
♕h6 43.♖e4** 43...♘e4+−. **43...♕f6
44.♖f4 ♔f8 45.♘e4 ♕e5 46.♘g5
♕d5+ 47.f3 ♕d2+ 48.♖f2
♕d5+ 49.♔h2 ♕d4 50.♘h3 ♕e3
51.♔g2** 51.f6! ♕xe6 52.♘g5 ♕e3
53.♔g2+−. **51...♕e4+ 52.♔f1
♕h1+ 53.♘g1 ♕d5 54.♘f3 ♕c4+
55.♖e2 ♕d5 56.♘g5 ♕h1+
57.♔f2 ♕h2+ 58.♔f3 ♕h1+
59.♔f2 ♕h2+ 60.♔f3 ♕h1+**

61.♔e3! 61.♔f2? was threefold
repetition. **61...♕g1+ 62.♔d3?**
62.♖f2! ♕xg3+ (62...♕c1+ 63.♔f3
♕d1+ 64.♔g2 ♕d5+ 65.♔h2 ♕d4
66.♘h3) 63.♖f3 ♕e1+ (63...♕e5+
64.♘e4) 64.♔d4 ♕xb4+ 65.♔e5
♕xh4 66.♘e4! ♕h2+ 67.♖f4 ♕e2
68.♖f2 ♕b5+ 69.♔f6+−; 62.♔e4
♔e7 63.♖e3+−; 62.♔f4 ♕d1 63.♔e3
♕g1+ doesn't help. **62...♕d1+?**
62...♕xg3+!= 63.♖e3 (63.♔d4
♕d6+=; 63.♔c4 ♕g4+ 64.♖e4
♕xf5 and White's winning chances
have evaporated; 63.♔d2 ♕f4+
64.♖e3 ♕f2+ 65.♔d3 ♕xf5+ 66.♖e4
is similar) 63...♕d6+! 64.♔c3
(64.♘e4 ♕xb4+ 65.♔e5 ♕c5+
66.♔f4 ♕d6+!=; 64.♔e2 ♕h2+!
and White cannot make progress)
64...♕f4! and the unfortunate
placement of the white pieces
prevents White from winning.
The black queen is too powerful.
**63.♔e3 ♕g1+ 64.♔d3? ♕d1+?
65.♔e3** Now 65...♕g1+ produces
threefold repetition. According to
Jonas Lampert the mistakes in the
final phase of the game are caused
by mutual time trouble and the
complexity of the position. **½-½**

Adhiban Baskaran   **8**
Yu Yangyi
Gibraltar 2019 (7)
**1.e4 e5 2.♘f3 ♘f6 3.♘c3 ♘c6
4.♗b5 ♘d4 5.♗c4 ♗c5 6.♘xe5 ♕e7
7.♘f3 d5 8.♗xd5 ♗g4 9.d3 ♘d7!?**

10.♗e3 In 2010, the main game
of the Yearbook Survey involved
10.♗xb7 but it has since been
shorn of its terror: 10...♗xf3!
(10...♘e5?! 11.♗xd4! was unpleasant
for Black, see YB/97 p.129-134
for a detailed examination of
B.Muhren-A.Haast, Eindhoven
2010) 11.gxf3 ♕h4! (originally
suggested by Dominguez & Ibarra)
12.f4! ♖b8 13.♗a6 ♘b3 14.♖f1 ♘xa1
15.♗b5 ♕b6!? 16.♘d5 ♖g6 17.♗xd7+
♔xd7 18.♗e3 c6! (this leads to
a break-up of White's pawns)
19.♗xc5 cxd5 20.♕xa1 (20.♗e3!?)
20...dxe4 21.dxe4 (21.b4!?) 21...♕xf4
22.♕d1+ ♔c7 23.♕d3∓ Silva Filho-
Herzog, cr 2011. This game seems
to put 10.♗xb7 under a cloud.
Best seems to be 10.h3! ♗xf3
11.gxf3 c6 (11...♘e5 12.f4 ♘ef3+
13.♔f1 c6 14.♗b3± and after ♗e3
Black's compensation will look a
little vague) 12.f4! ♕h4 (12...cxd5
13.♘xd5 ♕d8 14.c3 ♘e6 15.d4 ♗e7
16.♖g1 g6 17.♕f3∞ Siigur-Gerola,
cr 2011) 13.♗a4 cxd5 14.♘xc5 ♘xc5
15.♗e3 ♘ce6 (15...dxe4 16.♗xd4
♘e6 17.♗e3 ♘xf4 18.♕g4 ♕xg4
19.hxg4 ♘g2+= Rublevsky-A.
Onischuk, Poikovsky 2009) 16.c3
(16.exd5 ♘f5! 17.♕f3 ♘fd4 18.♗xd4
♘xd4 19.♕e4+ ♕e7 20.♔d2 ♘b5
½-½ Nenneman-Henry, cr 2018)
16...♘b5 17.♕a4 a6 18.exd5 ♘ec7
19.♕e4+ (19.c4 0-0 20.cxb5 ♘xd5
21.0-0-0 axb5 22.♕b3 ♖fd8⧩
Olthof) 19...♔d8 20.0-0-0 ♘d6
21.♕e5 ♕h6∞ Privara-Keuter, cr
2017. **10...♘e5**

11.♗xf7+? Surprised by the
opening, Adhiban soon gets into
trouble. Still the alternatives don't
impress either:
  A) 11.♘xd4 ♗xd1 12.♘f5 ♕f6
(12...♕f8 13.♖xd1 ♗xe3 14.♘xe3
0-0-0 15.d4 ♘g6 is given as an
edge by the engines, but in a
practical game the strange material
balance could prove to be tricky
to handle for both sides) 13.♗xc5
♗xc2 14.0-0 0-0-0 (14...c6 15.d4
♘d3 16.♘d6+ ♔d7 17.e5 ♕h4
(Sutovsky-Naiditsch, Wijk aan Zee
2010) 18.♗e4! ♕h5 19.♘xb7∞) 15.d4
♘d3 16.♗e7 (16.♗xa7 ♘f4 17.♗e3
♗d3 18.♖fc1 ♕a6∓ Charpentier-
Volodarsky, cr 2016) 16...♕b6
17.♗a3 ♘f4 18.♖fc1 (Nataf-Baron,
France tt 2013) and now 18...♗d3!
19.g3 ♘e6 retains an advantage for
Black;
  B) 11.♗xd4 ♗xd4 12.♗xb7 ♖b8
13.♘d5 ♗xf3 14.♘xe7 ♗xd1 15.♘c6
♖xb7 16.♘xd4 ♗h5! (16...♗g4 17.f4
c5 18.♘b3 ♗d7 19.♘d2 f6 20.♘a5∞
Oesterman-A.Ponomarev, cr 2008)
17.♔d2 (Oesterman-Dubuc, cr
2006) and now 17...0-0!∓. **11...♘xf7
12.♘d5 ♕d7 13.c3 ♘xf3+**
13...♘e6∓. **14.gxf3**

14...♗xe3 14...♗h5!? is a dangerous
alternative, but by means of
accurate defence White can more
or less stay alive. An illustrative
line is 15.♗xc5 ♘e5 16.♔d2! c6

17.♘f4 ♗xf3 18.♕e1! (defending the pawn on e4) 18...♗xh1 19.♕xh1 0-0-0 20.♗d4 ♕d6 21.♗xe5 ♕xe5 22.♘e3 ♘hf8 23.♘e2 ♖b5 24.d4 ♕xb2 25.♕b1 ♕a3 26.♕b4 ♕xb4 27.cxb4∓. However, the road to reach a draw is still long and arduous. **15.♘xe3?!** 15.fxe3 ♗e6∓. **15...♖h5 16.♘g4 0-0-0 17.d4 ♘g5-+ 18.h4 ♘xf3+ 19.♕xf3 ♖hf8 20.♕e3 ♕xg4 21.♔d2 ♖f3 22.♖ag1 ♕e6 23.♕e1 ♕xa2 24.♔c2 ♗e8 25.♖xg7 ♗a4+ 26.♔c1 ♕a1+ 0-1**

Lu Shanglei 9
Li Chao

China tt 2017 (13)

1.e4 e5 2.♘f3 ♘c6 3.♗b5 ♘f6 4.♘c3 ♘d4 5.♗c4 ♗c5 6.♘xe5 ♕e7 7.♘f3 d5 8.♗xd5 ♗g4 9.d3 0-0-0 10.♗g5!?

10...♗b4 10...♗h5 11.♗b3 (11.♔f1 c6 12.♗c4 h6 13.♗h4 g5 14.♗g3 (Sutovsky-Kramnik, Baku 2010) 14...♘d7!∓) 11...♖he8 12.♔f1 h6 13.♗e3 ♘xf3 14.gxf3 ♗b4 15.♕e2 ♘d7 16.d4 ♗xc3 17.bxc3 ♕f6 18.♖g1 ♗xf3= Turkov-Kharlamov, cr 2013. **11.a3 ♖xd5 12.♗xf6 ♗xc3+** Also possible is 12...♕xf6!? 13.axb4 (13.exd5?? ♘xf3+ 14.gxf3 ♗xc3+ 15.bxc3 ♕xc3+ 16.♔f1 ♗h3+ 17.♔g1 ♕f6-+) 13...♖h5 14.♖xa7 ♘b8 15.♖a3 c6=. **13.bxc3 ♘xf3+ 14.gxf3 ♕xf6 15.fxg4 ♕xc3+ 16.♔e2** 16.♔f1 ♖a5 (16...♖c5=) 17.h4 h5 18.g5 b6 19.♖h3= ½-½ Percze-Hnatovsky, cr 2013. **16...♖c5 17.♕d2 ♕xc2 18.♖hc1 ♕xd2+ 19.♔xd2= ♖g5 20.f3 h5 21.h4 ♖b5 22.g5 ♖b2+ 23.♔c3 ♖h2 24.♖h1 ♖f2 25.♖hf1 ♖h2 26.♖h1 ♖f2 27.♖af1 ♖a2 28.♖a1 ♖f2 29.♖hf1 ♖h2 30.♖h1** ½-½

The main line
10.♗e3

Francisco Vallejo Pons 10
Fabiano Caruana

Karslruhe/Baden-Baden 2019 (6)

1.e4 e5 2.♘f3 ♘c6 3.♘c3 ♘f6 4.♗b5 ♘d4 5.♗c4 ♗c5 6.♘xe5 ♕e7 7.♘f3 d5 8.♗xd5 ♗g4 9.d3 0-0-0 10.♗e3 The 'drawing' line. 10.♗g5!?, **10...♘xd5 11.♘xd5 ♖xd5 12.exd5 ♖e8 13.0-0 ♗xf3 14.gxf3 ♗d6** After 14...♕h4!? it's possible to try 15.♔g2 (hoping to use the rook to help cover the kingside: 15.f4 ♗d6 transposes back to the main game) 15...♗d6 16.♖h1 ♘f5 17.♗c1!? (in 2011 Obodchuk examined 17.♗d2 but it seems that after 17...♘c5! 18.♖f1 ♕h5 Black's attack is certainly strong enough to earn a draw) 17...g5 18.c3 ♕h5 19.h4 ♘xh4+ 20.♔f1 ♕g6 21.♗e3 ♕f5♕ Sazon-Aymard, cr 2014. **15.f4 ♕h4**

16.♗xd4 16.♔g2 ♘xc2 17.♕xc2 ♕g4+ 18.♔h1 ♕f3+ 19.♔g1 ♕g4+ ½-½ Mamedov-Wang Hao, Poikovsky 2019; 16.♔h1 ♕h3 17.♖g1 ♘f3 18.♖g2 g5 and now 19.b4!? (19.c4?! gxf4 20.♕a4 (Motylev-Radjabov, Khanty-Mansiysk ol 2010; 20.♗d2? ♘xd2 21.♕g4+ ♕xg4 22.♖xg4 ♘f3-+ Koscielski-Zwahr, Germany Internet Blitz 2020) 20...c6!∓) as suggested by Olthof, but then 19...h5!∞ when Black's attack is fully worth the exchange. Note how 19...h5 covers the g4-square, thus denying White the possibility of ♕g4+ (trading queens) if the knight were to move. **16...♗xf4 17.♔g2** Six games, all draws from here. **17...♕g5+** 17...♕xh2+ 18.♔f3 ♕h3+ 19.♔xf4 ♕h2+ 20.♔f3

♕h3+ 21.♔f4 ♕h2+ 22.♔f3 ♕h3+ 23.♔f4 ½-½ McShane-So, Douglas 2019. **18.♔h1 ♕h4 19.♔g2 ♕g5+ 20.♔h1 ♕h4 21.♔g2** ½-½

Yasser Quesada Perez 11
Luis Manuel Perez Rodriguez

Havana 2018 (8)

1.e4 e5 2.♘f3 ♘c6 3.♘c3 ♘f6 4.♗b5 ♘d4 5.♗c4 ♗c5 6.♘xe5 ♕e7 7.♘f3 d5 8.♗xd5 ♗g4 9.d3 0-0-0 10.♗e3 ♘xd5 11.♘xd5 ♖xd5 12.exd5 ♖e8 13.0-0 ♗xf3 14.gxf3 ♕h4 15.c3 ♗d6 16.f4 ♗xf4? Black's memory let him down? ≥ 16...g5; ≥ 16...♕h3. **17.♗xf4 ♘e2+ 18.♔h1 ♕xf4 18...♘xf4 19.♕f3+-. 19.f3 ♕e5 20.♕e1 20.♖f2 ♘e3 21.♕f1 ♘f4 22.d4±. 20...♘xc3**

21.♕g3! Now White's material advantage begins to tell. 21.♕xc3?? ♖e2-+. **21...♘xd5 22.♖ae1** 22.♕xg7±. **22...♕g5 23.♕xf4 ♘xf4 24.♖g1 ♖b5?!** 24...♖xg1+ 25.♔xg1 ♗d7 26.♖e4±. **25.♖xg7 ♘xd3 26.♖e7 b6 27.♖gxf7+- ♗c5 28.♖e2 a5 29.♖d2 ♘e5 30.♖f5 ♖c1+ 31.♔g2 ♘c4 32.♖f8+ ♔b7 33.♖e2 a4 34.f4 b5 35.f5 ♘d6 36.f6 ♖c5 37.f7 ♔c6 37...♖f5 38.♖f2+-. 38.♖f2 ♕g5+ 39.♔f1 ♖g7 40.♖f6 ♔d5 41.♖d8 1-0**

Eusebio Huerto Navarro 12
Claudio Cesetti

cr 2016

1.e4 e5 2.♘f3 ♘c6 3.♘c3 ♘f6 4.♗b5 ♘d4 5.♗c4 ♗c5 6.♘xe5 ♕e7 7.♘f3 d5 8.♗xd5 ♗g4 9.d3 0-0-0 10.♗e3 ♘xd5 11.♘xd5 ♖xd5 12.exd5 ♖e8 13.0-0 13.c3 basically forces a draw. **13...♗xf3 14.gxf3 ♗d6 15.c3** 15.f4 ♕h4 16.c3 transposes. **15...♕h4 16.f4**

g5! 16...♕h3 17.cxd4 g5 transposes. **17.cxd4** 17.♔h1?! ♕h3! (17...gxf4? 18.♕a4!) 18.♖g1 (18.f3? ♗xf4 19.♗xf4 ♖e2∓) 18...gxf4 19.♕f1 ♕f3+ 20.♔g2 fxe3 21.cxd4 ♕xg2+ 22.♔xg2 e2=. **17...♕h3 18.♖e1**

18...♖f8! 18...♖g8? 19.♔h1! gxf4 20.♖g1+−. **19.♕e2 gxf4 ½-½** Triay Moll-C.Evans, cr 2019. **20.f3 fxe3 21.♕g2 ♕h6 22.♖e2** ½-½ Gnilka-Hoppenstein, cr 2018. It looks like (at e-mail level) this

line is already considered to be 'drawn' rather than 'equal'. **22... f5 23.♖ae1 ♗f4 24.♔h1 ♖d8 25.♕g1 ♕d6 26.♖xe3 ♗xe3 27.♕xe3 ♕xd5 28.♕e6+ ♕xe6 29.♖xe6 ♖xd4 30.♖e8+ ♔d7 31.♖h8 ♖xd3 32.♖xh7+ ♔d6 33.h4 ♖d2 34.h5 ♖xb2 35.h6 ♖b4** ½-½

Francisco Vallejo Pons   13
Leinier Dominguez Perez
Cuernavaca 2006 (4)
1.e4 e5 2.♘c3 ♘f6 3.♘f3 ♘c6 4.♗b5 ♘d4 5.♗c4 ♗c5 6.♘xe5 ♕e7 7.♘f3 d5 8.♗xd5 ♗g4 9.d3 0-0-0 10.♗e3 ♘xd5 11.♘xd5 ♖xd5 12.exd5 ♖e8 13.c3 13.0-0 is more complex, but best play suggests that there is no route to an advantage. **13...♘xf3+ 14.gxf3**

14...♕h4! 15.♗d2! ♖xe3! 16.fxe3 ♕f2+ 17.♔c1 ♗xf3 18.♕e1 18.♕f1 ♗xe3+ 19.♔b1 ♗xh1 20.♕xh1 transposes. **18...♗xe3+ 19.♔b1 ♗xh1 20.♕xh1 ♕e2 21.a4 ♕xd3+ 22.♔a2 ♕c4+ 23.♔b1** 23.b3?! ♕xc3∓. **23...♕d3+ 24.♔a2 ♕c4+ 25.♔b1** ½-½ Since then this draw has been played out on several occasions.

Exercise 1

position after 17.♘f6-e4

What is Black's best move here?

Exercise 2

position after 11...c7-c6

What should White play here?

Exercise 3

position after 17.♔g1-h1

What is Black's best at this point?

(solutions on page 249)

Rest of the World versus Nakamura

by Michael Adams (special contribution by Anish Giri)

1.	d4	d5
2.	c4	e6
3.	♘c3	♗e7
4.	♘f3	♘f6
5.	♗f4	0-0
6.	e3	♘bd7
7.	c5	c6

This Survey aims to give some general guidance in an important QGD line, and bring things up to date on many new developments, which are occurring daily, or in some cases more frequently than that in the online chess extravaganza.
In the starting position after White opts for the inflexible, but space-gaining 7.c5, Black has three options. Two of them are to head for the complex 7...♘h5, going after the important bishop, or to try the less common 7...♘e4, both of which fall outside the scope of this Survey.
We will focus instead on relying on Black's solid structure to block the c-pawn with 7...c6 and get ready to contest the queenside with ...b7-b6 and ...a7-a5 next. Whilst it's nice to have extra space, and White's impressive pawn chain certainly gels well with the useful bishop on f4, Black's position remains durable, and after development is completed, Black's position will also look harmonious.

This position has become a kind of unofficial 'Rest of the World v Hikaru Nakamura' match-up in various online events, as multiple contenders have attempted to pick holes in his preparation, or find a line he couldn't remember. With varying degrees of success they have attempted to squeeze Hikaru with the extra territory, but he has stuck to his guns, so many top games in such a short time have thrown up some interesting developments.

Black's planned next few moves

Black has a solid but slightly cramped position, which will be alleviated through exchanges. The plan is to challenge White's structure on the queenside, by playing ...b7-b6 and ...a7-a5, making room to swap the problem piece; Black's light-squared bishop on a6. Then Black's queen will move slightly awkwardly to b7 via c8. Longer term, after swapping light-squared bishops and perhaps doubling rooks down the a-file, sometimes ...♗e7-d8-c7, to reduce material further and even eventually planning ...e6-e5, will be desirable. Unfortunately White gets to play some moves as well! In several of the games below White takes disruptive action with tricky finesses to throw spanners into Black's plans at an early stage.
There are few weaknesses on either side. In the very long term the pawn on c6 might become vulnerable, especially in an endgame where Black's

pawn advances to b5 and White's knight arrives on a5, but this is not an immediate concern. Black needs to be permanently alert to tactical tricks involving the b4-b5 pawn break for White on the queenside, and must consider when might be a good moment to shut down that side of the board with ...b6-b5. Generally speaking, Black should have good control of the a-file to make this a good option.

Historical lines

Let's start with some earlier encounters for this line. At one time White used to continue naturally with 8.♗d3, then theory continues 8...b6 9.b4 a5 10.a3. This queenside pawn face off is almost certain to occur through a variety of move-orders to allow the black bishop to emerge. Hence Black now executes his main idea to swap the light-squared bishop with 10...♗a6.

An important tactical line here is 11.♗xa6 ♖xa6 12.b5 cxb5 13.c6, with a massively complex mess, where I included an email game with brief details, which supports the current theoretical assessment of equality. If White continues more calmly with 11.0-0, as in Mamedyarov-Aronian, this allows Black to carry out his strategic ideas of moving the queen to b7, and gradually swapping towards safety. It's notable that at one moment in this game, Black has more useful moves than White, and Mamedyarov has to lose momentum by playing 13.♕c2.

Free drinks and tempo thieves

Everyone likes free things, ideally drinks, but if they are not available, tempi could be worth having too. So White players started to begin scheming to acquire one with 8.h3, when after the traditional 8...b6 9.b4 a5 10.a3 it turns out that after 10...♗a6 11.♗xa6 ♖xa6 12.b5 cxb5 13.c6, the extra move h2-h3 they have obtained might well turn out to be useful. So the stand-off continues, as Black also plays the waiting game, returning the favour with 10...h6.

Sometimes White now accepts it's time to develop the bishop with 11.♗e2 or 11.♗d3 ♗a6 as in some games from our Survey. Here it is worth highlighting another previously unplayed, but not unnoticed idea (see Anish Giri's comments). After 12.0-0 ♕c8, Firouzja tried the unlikely-looking 13.♘a4. The logic behind this naïve-looking move is that losing a little time to fix the structure forever is a fine deal from White's point of view – pawns can't move backwards! It should have paid dividends in its first practical outing, as White gained a highly desirable strategic grip. Anish shows that Black's best response is to sidestep that with

13...♕b7, and outlines the details there in his comments to the stem game. After he wrote those notes, Hikaru gave Anish's recommendation a practical test where they stood up well.

Returning to move 11 alternatives, those who are not easily discouraged have continued to try to search for the elusive extra tempo. They have investigated some tricky queen nudges that insist on gaining a free move. One is 11.♕c1.

Then Black must accept loss in the tempo duel gracefully, and continue developing in slow motion with 11...♗b7 (11...♗a6? 12.♗xa6 ♖xa6 13.b5 is not a good idea here) 12.♗d3 ♕c8 13.0-0 ♗a6, and ask if the extra move ♕c1 is especially useful. So far, it appears to be a fairly minimal gain. Aronian introduced a similar, but typically crafty new idea: 11.♕b1.

He was probably hoping that Black would continue solidly with 11...♗b7 12.♗d3 ♕c8, but then the stolen move ♕b1 looks more useful than ♕c1 in that

Hikaru Nakamura

line, as the king's rook can smoothly transfer to the useful c-file. Instead Hikaru went for the pointed 11...♘e4, which looks like a theoretically sound response, and might even be within his preparation, but the players soon both went badly wrong in the game.

Cutting-edge Caruana

The last word in this Survey has to go to Fabiano Caruana, who has essayed a more aggressive waiting move at an early stage: 8.h4.

I wonder what was the inspiration for this move: Simon Williams videos featuring Harry the h-pawn, Leela, who thinks this is quite reasonable, or was it just a mouse slip? Probably not the latter, if only on the grounds that he repeated it in his next White game, and the fact that it seems to be a good move. A new battle-ground for the line?

In both games so far Hikaru responded with 10...♘e4, but here I am less convinced by this move as Black faces a tricky task to negotiate a path to equality here, although it may be possible with computer help. The question as to how White would respond to 10...h6 against 8.h4 seems a very valid one to me.

Conclusion

If the frequency of online events and Hikaru's penchant for this variation continue, this Survey may outdate fast, but for now Black seems to be hanging on alright, albeit under some pressure in a few different lines.

Postscript

Actually since I wrote those words, about five weeks ago, the online action has tailed off, but I did have a relevant encounter of my own over the board, in the penultimate round in Biel. I have added some notes to this theoretically interesting game in the 'Clever 11.♕c1' section. Earlier in the same tournament I reacted poorly to the third option 11.b5 after 8.♗d3 b6 9.b4 a5 10.a3 ♗a6 in a rapid game against Vincent Keymer.

Natural development
8.♗d3

Shakhriyar Mamedyarov
Levon Aronian
St Louis 2018 (4)
1.d4 ♘f6 2.c4 e6 3.♘f3 d5 4.♘c3 ♗e7 5.♗f4 0-0 6.e3 ♘bd7 7.c5 c6 8.♗d3 b6 9.b4 a5 10.a3 ♗a6

11.0-0 ♕c8 12.h3 ♕b7 Black has achieved his preferred set-up without problems, White doesn't have a very useful move now, and has to lose a little time.
13.♕c2 ♗xd3 14.♕xd3 axb4 I would prefer 14...♖a7 rather than releasing the tension immediately. 15.axb4 ♖xa1 16.♖xa1 ♖a8 17.♕b1 ♖xa1 18.♕xa1 bxc5 19.bxc5 h6 20.♕b1 White could try 20.g4 followed by ♔g2 but Shak decided to call it a day. 20...♕a8 21.♕a2 ♕b7 22.♕b1 ♕a8 23.♕a2 ♕b7 24.♕b1 ½-½

Jorge Eduardo Deforel
Jan Nagel
cr 2018
1.d4 ♘f6 2.♘f3 e6 3.c4 d5 4.♘c3 ♗e7 5.♗f4 0-0 6.e3 ♘bd7 7.c5 c6 8.♗d3 b6 9.b4 a5 10.a3 ♗a6 11.♗xa6 ♖xa6 12.b5 White goes for it, giving up a pawn to create a dangerous passer. 12...cxb5 13.c6 ♕c8 A crucial line both sides need to know in detail, which is less of an issue in an email game, of course. 14.c7 b4 15.♘b5

15...a4 Black shows he also has some trumps in this sharp scenario. 16.♖c1 ♘e4 Covering d6. 17.♘d2 ♘df6 18.♘xe4 dxe4! 18...♘xe4? is a mistake as after 19.f3 Black is in trouble after both Aronian-Adams, Bilbao 2013 and Anand-Carlsen, Sochi Wch m-3 2014. See Anish's 'Lesson in Theory' in Ikonnikov's Survey in Yearbook 114. 19.♘d6 19.♗d6 ♘d5! – it's important Black's knight has access to this square. 19...♗xd6 20.♗xd6 b3 21.♗xf8 ♔xf8 White has won the exchange, but the protected passed pawn on b3 is strong, and the pawn on c7 is likely to be rounded up, so the position is roughly balanced. 22.♕d2 ♘d5 23.0-0 ♖a7 24.f3 The players finished the game as a draw here. 24...♖xc7 25.♖xc7 ♕xc7 26.♖c1 ♕d6 27.♖c8+ ♗e7 28.fxe4 ♕xa3 29.exd5 b2 30.d6+ ♔d7 31.♕c2 ♕xe3+ 32.♔f1 b1♕+ 33.♕xb1 ♔xc8 34.♕c2+ ♔b7 35.♕c7+ ♔a6 36.♕c4+ ♔b7 is one way the game could end. Now 37.♕c7+= but not 37.d7? ♕f4+ 38.♔e2 ♕c7. ½-½

Vincent Keymer
Michael Adams
Biel rapid 2020 (2)
1.d4 ♘f6 2.c4 e6 3.♘f3 d5 4.♘c3 ♗e7 5.♗f4 0-0 6.e3 ♘bd7 7.c5 c6 8.♗d3 b6 9.b4 a5 10.a3 ♗a6 11.b5

11...♗b7 11...cxb5 12.c6 ♕c8 13.♖c1 ♕xc6 14.♘xb5 (14.♘e2? ♘c5 15.dxc5

115

bxc5 16.a4 b4 17.♘ed4 ♕b7 18.♗xa6 ♖xa6 19.♘b5 ♖c8 20.0-0 c4 ½-½ I.Sokolov-Spassky, Malmö 1998. Young Spassky would not have agreed to a draw here! 14...♗xb5 15.♖xc6 ♗xc6 16.♘e5 ♘xe5 17.♗xe5= Miedema-Brandenburg, Netherlands tt 2010/11. **12.cxb6 ♘xb6** 12...♕xb6 13.0-0 a4 14.♘xa4 ♕a5 15.♘c5 ♘xc5 16.bxc6 ♗xc6 17.dxc5 ♗a4 18.♕b1 ♖fc8 19.♖c1 ♖xc5 20.♕h7 ♕a7 21.♕xa7 ♖xa7 22.♖xc5 ♗xc5 with a minimal advantage for Black in Jobava-Lputian, Abu Dhabi 2003. **13.bxc6N ♗xc6 14.♘e5 ♗b7?!N** Black could have improved with 14...♖c8 or 14...♗e8. **15.0-0 ♘fd7 16.♘xd7** 16...♕b1 17.♗xh7+ ♔h8 18.♗xe5 ♘c4 (18...♗a6 19.♗d3 ♖xd3 20.♕xd3±.) 19.♕xb7 ♔xh7 20.a4 ♘xe5 21.dxe5 ♗b4 22.♘b5±. **16...♕xd7 17.♕b1 ♘c4** 17...♖fc8 18.♗xh7+ ♔f8 19.♕xb6 ♖xc3 20.♖fc1 ♘c6 21.♕xc6 ♖xc6 22.♖xc6 ♗xc6 23.♗d3. **18.♗xh7+ ♔h8 19.♗d3 ♘xa3 20.♕d1 ♔g8 21.♕h5 f5 22.g4 ♕e8 23.♕xe8 ♖axe8 24.gxf5 exf5 25.♘a4 ♗b4 26.♖fc1 ♘c4 27.♘c5 ♗c6** ≥ 27...♗xc5 28.dxc5 ♖a8. **28.♘a6 ♖a8 29.♘xb4 axb4 30.♖ab1 ♖a3 31.♗xc4 dxc4 32.♖xb4 ♗d5 33.♖b5 ♗e4** 33...♖d8 34.h4±. **34.♗d6 ♖fa8** A better fighting chance should be 34...♖b3 35.♖xb3 cxb3 36.♗xf8 b2 37.♗a3 bxc1♕+ 38.♗xc1 due to the opposite-coloured bishops. **35.♗xa3 ♖xa3 36.♖c5+– ... 1-0 (52)** Just an awful game on my part.

**Not recommended
11...♗b7**

Magnus Carlsen
Hikaru Nakamura
Carlsen Invitational Prelim 2020 (1.1)
1.d4 ♘f6 2.c4 e6 3.♘f3 d5 4.♘c3 ♗e7 5.♗f4 0-0 6.e3 ♘bd7 7.c5 c6 8.h3 b6 9.b4 a5 10.a3 h6 11.♗d3 ♗b7?! Hikaru totally loses the plot and gifts Magnus a move for no clear reason. He must have confused the lines, perhaps with 11.♕c1. Or did his mouse fall painfully short of 11...♗a6 ? **12.0-0 ♕c8**

13.♖e1 White has many good moves, including 13.♘a4! which is a greatly superior version of games we will see later. Magnus goes for the most enduring edge by preventing the swap of light-squared bishops. **13...♗a6 14.♗c2 ♖e8 15.♖c1** 15.♘d2 was stronger as now 15...♗d8 is met by 16.e4!. **15...axb4 16.axb4 bxc5 17.bxc5 ♗d8 18.♖a1 ♗c7 19.♕d2** Black has done well to get here after the early howler, but eventually succumbed ... **1-0 (67)**

**Typical games
12...♕c8**

Magnus Carlsen
Hikaru Nakamura
Carlsen Invitational Prelim 2020 (1.3)
1.d4 ♘f6 2.c4 e6 3.♘f3 d5 4.♘c3 ♗e7 5.♗f4 0-0 6.e3 ♘bd7 7.c5 c6 8.h3 b6 9.b4 a5 10.a3 h6 11.♗d3 ♗a6 This time Hikaru plays the right bishop move. **12.0-0 ♕c8 13.♕c2 ♗xd3 14.♕xd3 ♕b7**

15.♕c2 Nakamura himself played 15.♘d2 against Topalov in a St Louis Showdown rapid game in 2017. 15...♖fc8 15...♖a7!? looks good to me. **16.♖fb1 axb4 17.axb4 ♗d8 18.♕c1 ♗c7 19.♖xa8 ♖xa8 20.♗xc7 ♕xc7 21.♖a1 ♕b7 22.♖a3 ♘e8** Hikaru is happy to

wait passively. I feel Black should look to play ...e6-e5 as soon as possible, and would have been interested in 22...♘h7!? 23.♕a1 ♖xa3 24.♕xa3 ♗g5 25.♘d2 bxc5 26.bxc5 e5 27.dxe5 ♘e6. **23.♘e2 ♖xa3 24.♕xa3 ♘c7 25.♘f4 ♕a6 26.♕xa6 ♘xa6 27.♘d3** An example where the pawn on c6 remains sensitive, and the play is very one-sided. White's rock-solid pawn chain shouldn't be underestimated. **27...f6** If Black decides on 27...b5, arguing that at least White will be tied to the pawn on b4, he has to be wary that in the long term the white knight might transfer from f3 to a5 via d2 and b3. **28.♘d2** 28.g4 g5 29.♔g2 ♔f7 30.♘d2±. **28...♔f7 28...e5!?. 29.f4 ♘c7 30.♔f2 ♘b5 31.♔f3 ♘c3 32.g4 g5 33.f5 e5** Black is doing alright now but Magnus managed to win in the end: **34.♘c1 e4+ 35.♔f2 ♗e7 36.♘f1 ♘a4 37.♔e2 ♘b2 38.♔d2 ♘c4+ 39.♔c3 ♘b8 40.♘b3 ♘a6 41.cxb6 ♘xb6 42.♘a5 ♗d7 43.♘g3 ♗c7 43...♘c7!. 44.♘h5 ♗d7 45.♘b3 ♔d8 45...♔d6! 46.♘c5 ♘a8 – Giri. 46.♘c5 ♘ab8 47.b5! cxb5 48.♔b4 ♘c6+ 49.♔xb5 ♘a7+ 50.♔a6 ♘xc5+ 51.♔xa7 ♘b3 52.♔b6 ♔d7 53.♘xf6+ ♔d6 54.♘e8+ ♔d7 55.♘c7 ♘xd4 56.exd4 1-0**

Alireza Firouzja
Hikaru Nakamura
Carlsen Invitational Prelim 2020 (3.3)
1.d4 ♘f6 2.c4 e6 3.♘f3 d5 4.♘c3 ♗e7 5.♗f4 0-0 6.e3 ♘bd7 7.c5 c6 8.h3 b6 9.b4 a5 10.a3 h6 11.♗d3 ♗a6 12.0-0 ♕c8 13.♖e1 ♗xd3 14.♕xd3 ♕b7 15.♖eb1 This position usually arises by losing a move with the queen (♕d1-c2xd3) rather than the rook (♖f1-e1-b1). The same applies to 15.♖ec1 ½-½ Van Wely-Kasimdzhanov, Vlissingen 2001. **15...axb4** I like the look of the less committal 15...♖a7. 15...♖fc8, creating the option of playing ...♗e7-d8-c7, is thematic as usual. **16.axb4 ♖fc8 17.♘d2** 17.♕d1, keeping open the option of the other route for the

knight on the kingside: ♘e1-d3, was more precise. **17...♖xa1 18.♖xa1 ♖a8 19.♕b1** Giri: 'White played it a bit clumsy and now Black has a liberating resource.'

19...♗d8 Giri: '?' 19...♖xa1! 20.♕xa1 bxc5 21.bxc5 e5!, as Giri comments, 'would have equalized as after White captures on e5, his c5-pawn is doomed and if he retreats the bishop, Black will have counterplay on the d4-pawn with ...exd4 exd4 and ... ♘d7-f8-♘e6.' I can only endorse these words; Black must be on the lookout for tactical ideas to challenge White's pawn chain when they arise. **20.♖xa8 ♕xa8 21.♕a2 ♕b7 22.♕a4** Giri: 'Threatens 23.b5, so now Black has to take an unpleasant decision.' **22...b5 23.♕a3 ♘e8 24.e4** Giri: 'White could also slowly manoeuvre around, regrouping the knights to d3 and b3, but this is an interesting practical decision.' **24...dxe4 25.♘cxe4 ♘df6 26.♘d6 ♘xd6 27.cxd6** Giri: 'The d6-pawn is quite dangerous and at some point Hikaru was lost, but eventually his blitz skills pulled him through, as Alireza went astray in the time scramble.' **... 0-1 (93)**

Alireza Firouzja
Hikaru Nakamura
Carlsen Invitational Prelim 2020 (3.1)
1.d4 ♘f6 2.c4 e6 3.♘f3 d5 4.♘c3 ♗e7 5.♗f4 0-0 6.e3 ♘bd7 7.c5 c6 8.h3 b6 9.b4 a5 10.a3 h6 11.♗d3 ♗a6 12.0-0 ♕c8 13.♘a4 A new move by Alireza. Actually I wanted

to try it a long time ago already. It sort of provokes ...b6-b5, but Black should be strong and stay away from it.

13...♗xd3?! 13...♕b7! seems to have no refutation, but Black has to know a long forced line here: 14.cxb6 axb4 15.axb4 ♘xb6 16.♘c5 ♗xc5 17.bxc5 ♗xd3 18.♕xd3 ♘c4! 19.♘e5 ♘xe5 20.♗xe5 ♘e4! (the knights have to be active, as Black needs counterplay, when White will regroup and go after the c6-pawn with his major pieces) 21.♖xa8 ♖xa8 22.♖b1 ♕a6 23.♕xa6 ♖xa6 24.f3 ♘d2 25.♖b6 ♖a1+ 26.♔f2 ♘c4 27.♖xc6 ♖a2+. **14.♕xd3 b5?!** This is just not good. In general, it is rare that resolving the b6/c5 tension is good for Black and unless forced to he should try to avoid pushing or trading the b6-pawn. **15.♘c3 ♕b7 16.♘d2 ♗d8 17.♘b3 a4?** It's clear that Hikaru realized this move is no fun and he saw no other way to proceed with his plan of ...♗c7, but the arising position is way too one-sided and sad. **18.♘d2 ♗c7 19.♗xc7 ♕xc7 20.f4!** And Black's only hope is that he may push ...f7-f5 and establish some sort of a fortress, but White has got the e3-e4 push and play on the kingside with g2-g4 as well, so there should be enough resources to keep the game going. The game eventually took a very random course, but as for the opening battle, it didn't go well for Hikaru this time. **20...♔h8 21.♖ae1 ♖ad8 22.g4 ♘g8 23.♘f3 ♗e7 24.♖e2 f6 25.e4 ♘g6 26.exd5 ♘xf4 27.d6 ♕xd6 28.cxd6 ♘xd3 29.♘h4 ♖fe8 30.♖d2 g5 31.♘g2 ♘f4 ... ½-½ (45)**
Giri

Levon Aronian
Hikaru Nakamura
Lindores Abbey Final 8 2020 (1.11)
1.d4 ♘f6 2.c4 e6 3.♘f3 d5 4.♘c3 ♗e7 5.♗f4 0-0 6.e3 ♘bd7 7.c5 c6 8.h3 b6 9.b4 a5 10.a3 h6 11.♗d3 ♗a6 12.0-0 ♕c8 13.♘a4 ♕b7 A practical test for Anish's recommendation. The knight move looks very strange. 13...♗xd3 14.♕xd3 b5 15.♘c3 seems to gain time, however speed is not of the essence here; by defining the queenside structure White has improved his prospects considerably: 15...♕b7 16.♘d2 ♖a6 (16...♖d8 17.♘b3 a4 18.♘d2 didn't work out well in the last game) 17.♘b3 axb4 (17...a4 18.♘d2 leaves White sitting pretty with extra space and no black counterplay) 18.axb4 ♖fa8 19.♕c2 ♖xa1 20.♖xa1 ♖xa1+ 21.♘xa1 ♕a6? 22.♕a2 shows how Black can run into problems with natural moves, e.g. 22...♕xa2? 23.♘xa2 followed by ♘a1-b3-a5 is already winning for White. **14.♕c2 ♗xd3 15.♕xd3**

15...♘e4 15...b5 16.♘c3 ♖a7 17.♘d2 ♖fa8 18.♘b3 ♗d8 works better here. Importantly, Black will choose when to open the a-file. **16.♖fb1 axb4 17.axb4 b5** 17...♖a7!? is also possible. 18.cxb6 ♘xb6 19.♘c5 ♗xc5 20.bxc5 ♖xa1 21.♖xa1 ♘c4 leaves Black in great shape with the two well-placed knights. **18.♘c3 f5** 18...♘df6!? was better. As we have seen, it is dangerous for Black to fix the pawn structure in closed positions where White has a significant space advantage. The advance of the f-pawn creates weaknesses and leaves a permanent outpost on e5. **19.♘e2!±** Although the knight on e4 looks pretty,

White is ready to play ♘e5 followed by f2-f3 to remove it, and the knight on e2 might land on f4 one day ... **1-0 (118)**

Ian Nepomniachtchi
Hikaru Nakamura
Carlsen Invitational Prelim 2020 (4.2)
1.d4 ♘f6 2.c4 e6 3.♘f3 d5 4.♘c3 ♗e7 5.♗f4 0-0 6.e3 ♘bd7 7.c5 c6 8.h3 b6 9.b4 a5 10.a3 h6 11.♕c1

11...♗b7 11...♗a6?. 12.♗xa6 ♖xa6 13.b5 cxb5 14.c6±. **12.♗d3 ♕c8 13.0-0 ♗a6 14.♗xa6 ♖xa6** I once tried 14...♕xa6 15.♕b2 ♖fc8 but after 16.♖fb1 White is pressing. 16.♖fc1!? ♗d8 17.♖ab1 led to a white success in Anton Guijarro-Anand, Leon 2016. **15.♕c2** White accepts that his earlier finesse didn't really pay any dividends as the queen moves again to connect the rooks. **15...♕b7 16.♖ab1 axb4 17.axb4 ♖fa8 18.♖fc1** White argues that his rooks are well placed on the b- and c-files, and that there are no useful entry squares for the black rooks. However, in practice Black getting control of this file gives at the very least considerable annoyance value, and it can sometimes work out even better than that. **18...b5 19.♕b2** 19.♘d2 is met by 19...♗d8 but it is better than the game. **19...♘e4!** Swapping knights creates some possibilities for the black rooks, and if the knight is taken on e4, recapturing gives Black's other knight an important square on d5. **20.♖a1** 20.♘xe4 dxe4 21.♘d2 ♖a2 22.♕c3 ♘f6 and ...♘d5 will chase the white

queen again. **20...♕a7 21.♖xa6 ♕xa6 22.♘xe4 dxe4 23.♘d2 f5 24.♘b3 ♘f6 25.♗d6 ♗d8 26.♖a1 ♕b7 27.♖a3 ♕a4 28.♕a2 ♕a7 29.♖xa4 ♕xa4 30.♕xa4 bxa4** Black is in excellent shape here, but this time it was Hikaru's opponent that proved slippery ... **½-½ (68)**

Ian Nepomniachtchi
Hikaru Nakamura
Nations Cup Online Prelim 2020 (2.1)
1.d4 ♘f6 2.c4 e6 3.♘f3 d5 4.♘c3 ♗e7 5.♗f4 0-0 6.e3 ♘bd7 7.c5 c6 8.h3 b6 9.b4 a5 10.a3 h6 11.♕c1 ♗b7 12.♗d3 ♕c8 13.0-0 ♗a6 14.♗xa6 ♖xa6 15.♕b2 This is a more logical follow-up. White has gained something now, getting the queen to this useful post quickly. **15...♕b7 16.♖fb1**

16...axb4 16...♖a7!? is an interesting idea to keep options open. Black has to be alert, as 16...♖fa8 17.b5 rebounds, leaving his rooks totally blocked out. **17.axb4 ♖xa1 18.♕xa1 ♖a8 19.♕b2 ♘h5** If 19...♗d8, 20.♖a1 prevents Black swapping bishops. I would prefer 19...♘f8 or 19...♘h7 as ways to activate Black's knights. They look better than the move played as the knight will have to retreat from h5 soon. **20.♗h2 ♗d8 21.♖a1 ♘hf6 22.g4 ♘e8 23.♖xa8 ♕xa8 24.♕a2 ♕b7** 24...♕xa2 25.♘xa2 – White's extra space ensures plenty of suffering if queens are swapped too. **25.♕a4 b5** 25...♗c7 seems more logical, following the general rule of avoiding to fix the structure when possible. Hikaru was probably worried by 26.b5 but Black is okay: 26...♗xh2+ 27.♘xh2 (27.♔xh2 cxb5 28.♕xb5

♕c8 29.cxb6 ♘xb6=) 27...cxb5 28.♕xb5 but 28...♕c8! 29.cxb6 (29.c6 ♘b8 30.♕xb6 ♘xc6=) 29...♘xb6=. **26.♕a1 ♗c7 27.♖xc7 ♘xc7 28.♕a5** The drawback to ...b6-b5: White has an extra square available. This is none too pleasant for Black, but again in a long game Hikaru managed to turn things around ... **0-1 (138)**

Levon Aronian
Hikaru Nakamura
Lindores Abbey Final 8 2020 (1.22)
1.d4 ♘f6 2.c4 e6 3.♘f3 d5 4.♘c3 ♗e7 5.♗f4 0-0 6.e3 ♘bd7 7.c5 c6 8.h3 b6 9.b4 a5 10.a3 h6 11.♕c1 ♗b7 12.♗e2 ♕c8 13.0-0 ♗a6 14.♖e1 ♕b7 15.♖b1 axb4 16.axb4 ♗xe2 I once played 16...♖fc8 intending ...♗e7-d8-c7 here, but the simple capture is easier. **17.♖xe2 ♖a7 18.♖c2 b5** Black could have continued 18...♖fa8. Hikaru may have been concerned about 19.cxb6, but then the clever idea 19...♖a6!, waiting for the right moment to recapture on b6, and adding the option to take with the rook, defuses any of White's hopes. **19.♘d2** 19.♖a1, fighting for the a-file, seems logical now. In the game White's rooks have no prospects. **19...♖fa8 20.g4** 20.♘b3 ♗d8 21.♖a1 ♖xa1 22.♘xa1 ♘e4! catches White's pieces disorganized. **20...♗d8 21.♗g3 ♗c7 22.f4** Very ambitious; practically this kind of position seems much easier for Black to handle ... **½-½ (33)**

Noël Studer
Michael Adams
Biel 2020 (6)
1.d4 ♘f6 2.c4 e6 3.♘f3 d5 4.♘c3 ♗e7 5.♗f4 0-0 6.e3 ♘bd7 7.c5 c6 8.h3 b6 9.b4 a5 10.a3 h6 11.♕c1 ♗b7 12.♗e2 ♕c8 13.0-0 ♗a6 14.♕c2 ♗xe2 I had previously played 14...♕b7 15.♖fc1 in a game with Ding Liren, Shenzhen 2017. **15.♕xe2 ♕b7 16.♖fb1** Noel chooses another square for the rook opposite my queen, facilitating b4-b5 ideas.

16...♖a7 It's too early to release the tension: 16...axb4?! 17.axb4 ♖xa1? 18.♖xa1 ♖a8 19.♖xa8+ ♕xa8 20.♕a2 ♕b7 (20...♕xa2? 21.♘xa2 b5 22.♘d2!+−) 21.♕a4 leaves the c6-pawn very vulnerable. 16...♖fc8!? was worth considering.

17.♕c2 It seems more natural to transfer the knight to the queenside immediately, but this move is necessary as 17.♘d2? axb4 18.axb4 ♖xa1 19.♖xa1 bxc5 20.bxc5 ♕b2 is rather embarrassing. My opponent's moves were coming sufficiently quickly that I suspected he was still within preparation. **17...axb4** 17...♖c8!? was interesting; after 18.♘d2 ♖ca8! is good as 19.b5? now no longer works due to 19...bxc5; I didn't like 17...♖fa8 18.b5 a4 19.bxc6 (19.cxb6 ♕xb6 20.♘xa4 ♖xa4 21.bxc6 ♕a6 22.cxd7 ♘xd7=) 19...♕xc6 20.♘e5! ♘xe5 21.♖xb6 ♕e8 22.♘b5! (22.♗xe5 ♘d7) 22...♘c6 23.♘xa7 ♖xa7 24.♕d3 looks more pleasant for White. **18.axb4 ♖fa8 19.♖xa7 ♖xa7** 19...♕xa7 20.b5.

20.♕c1 We both underestimated the dangers after 20.b5!. Black must walk a tightrope to survive: 20...♖a5 (20...bxc5 is very dangerous: 21.dxc5 ♘xc5 22.♘d4 cxb5 23.♘cxb5 ♖a6 24.♘d6 ♕a7 25.♘4b5 ♕d7 26.♕xc5 ♘e4 27.♕c8+ ♕xc8 28.♘xc8) 21.bxc6! (if 21.cxb6 cxb5 22.♘xb5 ♖a6! holds) 21...♕xc6 22.cxb6 (22.♘e5 ♕xe5 23.♖xb6 ♕a8 24.♗xe5 ♘d7) 22...♖a3! 23.b7 g5! hardly an obvious way to play 24.b8♕+ ♕xb8 25.♖xb8+ ♔g7 26.♖b3 gxf4=. **20...♕a8 21.♘d2 ♘e8** I considered the thematic 21...b5 which makes sense with my good control of the a-file. I was worried by 22.f3, aiming

to push the e-pawn, although this strategy has its drawbacks: 22...♘f8 23.e4 dxe4 24.fxe4 ♘g6 25.♗h2 (25.♗d6 ♖xd6 26.cxd6 e5!) 25...e5! 26.dxe5 ♘d7 with good dark-square play. The best is 22.♘b3 ♘e4 23.♘e2! (23.♘xe4 dxe4 with the knight heading to d5 is fine for Black) 23...♖a2 24.♔f1 followed by f2-f3 and ♘c3. **22.♘b3 ♘c7** I thought 22...bxc5 23.bxc5 ♗f6 24.e4 dxe4 25.♘xe4 ♖a4 too risky with my knight on the back rank, but the computer sees it as playable. **23.♗g3** The trickier 23.♖a1!? requires Black to be alert: 23...bxc5! (23...♖xa1 24.♕xa1 ♕xa1+ 25.♘xa1 looks dangerous) 24.♖xa7 (24.♗xc7 c4!∓) 24...♕xa7 25.bxc5 ♗f6, aiming for ...e6-e5. **23...bxc5 24.bxc5 ♗f6 25.e4** 25.♗d6 ♘e8 26.♗g3 was sensible, but hardly fits with White's last move. 25.♖a1 ♖xa1 26.♕xa1 ♕xa1+ 27.♘xa1 ♘a6! creates some problems, the awkward position of the knights mean that the c5-pawn cannot be saved. An unusual occurrence with this pawn structure: 28.♘b3 ♘axc5 29.♘a5. **25...dxe4 26.♘xe4?** 26.♗xc7! ♖xc7 27.♘xe4 ♖a7 was necessary, which the computer regards as equal. I would prefer to be Black. **26...♘b5** Probably my opponent only considered 26...♘d5 although this is also fine for me, but by attacking the pawn on d4, Black claims a clear edge. **27.♕d2 ♖a2 28.♖b2 ♖xb2 29.♕xb2 ♕a4 30.♘c3 ♕b4 31.♘xb5 ♘xc5!∓ 32.♕a2 ♘xb3 33.♕a8+ ♔h7 34.♕xc6 ♕e1+ 35.♔h2 ♘d2 36.♕c2+ g6 37.h4 ♕e2 38.♕c6?** 38.♔h3∓. **38...h5!−+ 39.♘c3 ♘f1+ 40.♔g1 ♕e1 41.♕e4 ♘e3+ 42.♔h2 ♘g4+ 0-1**

New Ideas

Levon Aronian
Hikaru Nakamura
Lindores Abbey Final 8 2020 (1.13)
1.d4 ♘f6 2.c4 e6 3.♘f3 d5 4.♘c3 ♗e7 5.♗f4 0-0 6.e3 ♘bd7 7.c5 c6

8.h3 b6 9.b4 a5 10.a3 h6 11.♕b1 This looks interesting, but Hikaru finds an accurate reply.

11...♘e4! A good response, pointing out that even in this fairly closed position there are limits to how many liberties White can take with development. 11...♗a6? 12.♗xa6 ♖xa6 13.b5 cxb5 14.♕xb5+; 11...♗b7 12.♗d3 ♕c8 13.0-0 ♗a6 14.♖c1± allows White to mobilize very quickly. **12.♘xe4 dxe4 13.♘e5** 13.♘d2? axb4 14.axb4 ♖xa1 15.♕xa1 e5 opens the game before White is ready. After 13.♕xe4?! axb4 Black is doing fine, e.g. 14.♗d3 (14.♕xc6 ♖a7! 15.cxb6? ♘xb6) 14...♘f6! 15.♕xc6 ♕d5! 16.♕xd5 (16.♕xb6? ♕b3! 17.♗e2 (17.0-0 ♕xd3 18.axb4 ♘d5) 17...♘d5) 16...♘xd5 and White will be happy to escape. **13...♘xe5 14.♗xe5 ♕d5 15.♕b2?** 15.♗e2!? ♗a6=; 15.♕c1!? is perhaps best, but this is not really an endorsement for 11.♕b1 instead of 11.♕c1. 15...♗a6 16.♗xa6 ♖xa6 17.0-0 axb4 18.axb4 ♖fa8 is roughly equal. 15.cxb6? axb4 16.a4 b3−+. **15...b5?** Hikaru is bluffed. 15...axb4 16.axb4 ♖xa1+ 17.♕xa1 ♕b3! would have been very embarrassing for Levon, e.g. 18.d5 exd5 19.♗xg7 ♕xb4+ 20.♗c3 ♕xc5 21.♗e2 ♕a3−+. **16.♗e2 a4 17.0-0 ♗d7** Black looks strategically busted, but with typical resilience Hikaru salvaged half a point ... ½-½ (41)

Fabiano Caruana
Hikaru Nakamura
Carlsen Invitational Prelim 2020 (5.3)
1.d4 ♘f6 2.c4 e6 3.♘f3 d5 4.♘c3 ♗e7 5.♗f4 0-0 6.e3 ♘bd7 7.c5 c6 8.h4 A fresh idea by Fabiano.

Similar to 8.h3, but different. Food for thought!

8...b6 9.b4 a5 10.a3 ♘e4 An unusual way of dealing with the problems, but Hikaru probably thought that with the pawn on h4 potentially hanging, this makes sense here. MA: It's hard to understand the difference after 10...♗a6 11.♗xa6 ♖xa6 12.b5 cxb5 13.c6 ♕c8 14.c7 b4 15.♘b5 but I suspect White has reasons for optimism, just like in the related line with the white pawn on h3 instead. 10...h6!? looks pretty logical to me, intending 11.♗d3 ♗a6 12.0-0 ♕c8. **11.♘xe4 dxe4 12.♘e5 ♘xe5 13.♗xe5 ♕d5 14.♗e2 ♗a6 15.♗xa6** Hikaru probably looked up how to hold the position in the previous game, but now Fabi deviates. The first game in the match continued 15.0-0 ♗xe2 16.♕xe2 axb4 17.axb4 bxc5 18.bxc5 ♗xc5 (not wanting to stay passive and worried for

the long-term weakness of the c6-pawn, Hikaru simplifies everything, but the position that ensues is still tricky; 18...♗xh4? 19.♕g4+−) 19.♗xg7! ♔xg7 20.dxc5 ♕e5 21.♖ad1 (the position is more or less equal, due to very limited material, but in practical chess, the difference in the king's safety is striking and eventually Fabiano wins quite nicely; 21.♖ab1!?) 21...♖a5 (MA: 21...♖fd8! – Black can pick off the c5-pawn later, but it is handy to reduce White's attacking potential by challenging the rook) 22.♖d4 ♔h8 23.g3 ♖xc5 24.♖b1 ♖d5 25.♖c4 c5 26.♕c2 f5? (chronically weakening the 7th rank. Black is now doomed to passive defence. 26...♖fd8 27.♖xe4 ♕f5 would have been fine, as it is hard for White to harmonize his major pieces due to all the pins. If he trades the queens the endgame should be very holdable for Black) 27.♖a4 ♖fd8 28.♖b7 ♖5d7 29.♖a8 ♖xb7 30.♖xd8+ ♔g7 31.♔g2 (the kind of move that underlines the essence of the position. Black can't touch the white king at all, nor can he bring his king to any sort of safety, and eventually White gets to the weak e6-pawn) 31...♖c7 32.♕a4 ♕f6 33.♕e8 ♔h6 34.♖d6 ♔g7 35.♕b8 ♖f7 36.♖c6 ♖d7 37.♖c8 ♔h6 38.♖xc5 ♕g7 39.♖c6

♖e7 40.♖c8 ♖f7 41.♖e8 ♖e7 42.♕d8 ♖f7 43.♕d6 ♔h5 44.♖xe6 ♕g7 45.♕f4 ♕f6 46.g4+ ♔xh4 47.g5+ 1-0 Caruana-Nakamura, chess24. com 2020. **15...♖xa6 16.0-0 ♖fa8** MA: What could be more natural than 16...axb4? 17.axb4 ♖fa8 ? Fabiano had prepared a dirty trap here: 18.cxb6 ♖xa1 19.♕xa1 ♖xa1 20.♖xa1 is completely winning, e.g. 20...c5 21.bxc5 f6 22.♖a7 fxe5 (22...♗xc5 23.dxc5 ♕xc5 24.♖a8+ ♔f7 25.b7) 23.b7 ♕b3 24.♖a8+ ♔f7 25.b8♕. Black should consider 16...g6!? or 16...♕d7!? but White is pressing; 16...b5?! 17.a4 axb4 18.axb5 ♖xa1 19.♕xa1 cxb5 20.♕b2±. **17.cxb6 ♖xb6 18.♗c7?** Fabiano probably forgot about his h4-pawn here. 18.♕g4! would win a pawn, e.g. 18...f6 19.♗c7 ♖ba6 (19...♖b7 20.♗xa5 f5 21.♕g3±) 20.♗xa5 f5 21.♕h3 and White is a pawn up and will eventually get the queen back in the game after ♖fc1, g2-g3 and ♕f1. **18...♖ba6 19.♗xa5 ♗xh4** With an unclear position. Eventually the game was drawn after an interesting exchange sac by Fabi. **20.♖c1 ♗e7 21.♖c3 ♗d6 22.♕c2 h5 23.♖c1 ♖c8 24.♕e2 ♖ca8 25.♖c5 ♗xc5 26.♖xc5 ♕b3 27.♕xh5 f5 28.g3 ♕xa3 29.♔g2 ♖f8 30.♕e2 ♕d3 31.♕xd3 exd3 ... ½-½ (42)**

Giri

(solutions on page 249)

Exercise 1

position after 21.b4xc5

How should Black proceed here?

(solutions on page 249)

Exercise 2

position after 19.♕c2-b2

Which thematic move helps Black to exploit his control of the a-file?

Exercise 3

position after 17...♖f8-a8

What idea did Fabiano Caruana have planned for White here, as part of some poisonous preparation?

Taking the bull by the horns – Part I

by Ivan Sokolov (special contribution by Aydin Suleymanli)

1.	d4	d5
2.	c4	e6
3.	♘c3	♗e7
4.	cxd5	exd5
5.	♗f4	♘f6
6.	e3	♗f5
7.	♕b3	♘c6

Aydin Suleymanli

Our main game in this Survey features two of the most promising young players in the world, former World Junior Champion Parham Maghsoodloo and rising Azeri star Aydin Suleymanli. The latter surprised the chess world by winning the last Aeroflot Open. His victory in this game contributed greatly to this success. We have an analysis by the winner, while I have added remarks after 'IS' in some places.

Another second-most common line

The Alatortsev Variation we have here (3...♗e7) is one of the most important in the QGD, and we have seen many of the world greats willing to play it with both colours. In Yearbook 135 I wrote about 5.♗f4 c6 6.♕c2 (the second-most common move behind 6.e3) based on a special contribution by Alireza Firouzja. This time I will examine 5...♘f6 (the

second-most common move) 6.e3 and now the basic idea behind 6...♗f5 is quick development. Its drawback is that Black has not played the move ...c7-c6 yet, so after White's reply 7.♕b3 Black needs to:
 a) be ready to sacrifice a pawn
 b) develop his knight to the not ideal c6-square.
Needless to say, 7.♕b3 is the way for White to exploit the drawbacks of 6...♗f5, and it is White's main line here. White's alternatives will be shown in Part II of this Survey.
After the main move 7.♕b3, Black's reply 7...♘c6 (a pawn sacrifice) is practically forced and here White finds himself at a crossroads.

Accepting the pawn sacrifice

8.♕xb7, accepting the pawn sacrifice, which was Parham's choice in our main game, has a poor track record for White. Black objectively has enough compensation, while in practical play at GM level Black has scored above 50%!

121

White's choices that should worry Black (and which are critical for the assessment of 6...♗f5) are the positional 8.a3 and the rather straightforward 8.g4.

Renewing the threat

There is more than one good reason to play 8.a3.

White now does threaten to take on b7 (so Black's pawn needs to be defended) and also wants to prove that Black's ♘c6 is not well placed (standing in the way of the ...c7-c5-pawn push).

Black's best answer to 8.a3 is 8...♘a5. This may lead to sharp and complicated lines where theoretical knowledge is a must! See Games 2-4.

Black's alternative to 8...♘a5 is 8...♖b8 (Game 5). This leads to less direct play where concrete opening prep is not really needed (and so logic directed me to choose it versus Sadler), however White does have pressure. Black is a bit passive... overall, I did not feel comfortable about my position in that game with Matthew and would advise the reader to opt for 8...♘a5.

The direct approach

White's most direct option ('taking the bull by the horns') is 8.g4, a move which was first employed by Veselin Topalov against Garry Kasparov.

Black's most principled answer is 8...♘xg4, when White's best move is 9.♕xd5 (in the first outing, Topalov did not fare well with 9.♘xd5) after which Black can choose to either play 9...♕c8 (see Game 6) or trade queens (see Game 7). In my opinion, the queen trade favours White, so I would advise Black players to keep the queens on the board with 9...♕c8. As in the game Aronian-Kramnik, this may lead to a piece sacrifice. This sacrifice is interesting, but I could not make it work for Black – and neither could Vladimir, as he lost the game in question.

I suggest here the novel move 10...♘f6!, leading to sharp positions where there is a lot to explore.

As a matter of fact, Black also has sidelines which are worth exploring. Please pay attention to 8...♗xg4 – my 'sidelines analysis' presented in Game 8, 10...♖b8! being a novelty there. 8...♗c8 (Game 9) is little played, and for good reason. But 8...♗g6 is a complicated line and an interesting surprise idea – not easy to handle in human play.

Conclusion

The main line is probably going to remain the straightforward 7.♕b3 ♘c6 8.g4.

Black (in my opinion, and contrary to Suleymanli's) should keep the queens on the board, opting for 9...♕c8 and then either improving on Kramnik's play against Aronian (though I do not see how) or exploring my 10...♘f6 recommendation.

We will show many alternatives to **the queen sortie 7.♕b3** in **Part II** of this Survey, including a hitherto unpublished game by yours truly!

Accepting the pawn sacrifice 8.♕xb7

Parham Maghsoodloo   **1**
Aydin Suleymanli

Moscow 2020 (8)

My win in the previous round had given me a lot of confidence and with my second GM norm in the bag (with two rounds to spare), my morale before this game in the penultimate round was good. Still, another difficult challenge was awaiting me. **1.c4 e6 2.♘c3 d5 3.d4 ♗e7 4.cxd5 exd5 5.♗f4 ♘f6** The alternative is 5...c6, planning to exchange the dark-squared bishops after 6.e3 ♗d6. **6.e3 ♗f5** The most active move. **7.♕b3 ♘c6** I had not prepared this specifically for this game, but I had looked at it for my second-round game against Mustafa Yilmaz. **8.♕xb7** According to the statistics, the most popular move here is 8.a3. But the best move to my mind is 8.g4!, when after 8...♘xg4 9.♕xd5 ♕xd5 (IS: 9...♕c8 is perhaps Black's best – see Game 6) 10.♘xd5 ♗b4+ 11.♘xb4 (IS: 11.♘c3! might be White's best, leading to White's advantage – see Game 7) 11...♘xb4 12.♖c1 chances are equal. On the other hand, the position is also level after 8.a3 ♘a5 9.♕a2 0-0 10.♘f3 ♗e6 (IS: Quite a number of strong players have opted for 10...c5 – see Game 2) 11.♗d3 (IS: It is not clear if Black equalizes in case of 11.♘g5 – see the notes in Game 2) 11...♘h5. **8...♘b4**

9.♖c1 9.♔d1 looks strange, but according to the engine this is the best move: 9...0-0 10.♕xc7 ♕xc7 11.♗xc7 ♖fc8 12.♗g3 a5 (IS: Daniel Fridman, one of the experts on

this line, scored a nice win with 12...♗c2+ 13.♔e1 (13.♔d2 ♘e4+ 14.♘xe4 ♗xe4 15.f3 ♖c2+ 16.♔d1 ♖xb2 17.fxe4 ♘c2 18.♗c1 ♗a3∓) 13...♗f5 14.♖d1?! (14.♔d1! with a likely move repetition is White's best here) 14...♘e4! 15.♘xe4 dxe4 16.a3 (16.d5 ♘xd5 17.♖xd5? (17.a3 ♘b4↑) 17...♖c1+ 18.♔e2 ♗b4 19.f3 ♖ac8–+) 16...♖c2! 17.♗e2 ♘d3+ 18.♔f1 ♘xb2 19.♖e1 ♗xa3 0-1 (34) Lupulescu-Fridman, Khanty-Mansiysk 2011) 13.a3 ♘c2 14.♖c1 ♘xa3. Now, taking on a3 loses immediately, and after 15.f3 ♘c4 the position is balanced. **9...0-0 10.♕xc7** 10.♗xc7 transposes to the game after 10...♕c8 11.♕xc8 ♖fxc8 12.♗f4. **10...♕xc7 11.♗xc7 ♖fc8** More accurate was 11...♖ac8!. In some positions there are ideas for White involving ...♗a6 and then ...♗b7, which is why the rook is not so well placed at a8. **12.♗f4 ♘e4** 12...a5 13.f3 ♘h5 14.♗e5 f6 15.♗c7 ♖xc7 16.g4 guarantees Black a good game too. **13.f3** This is a new move. After 13.a3 ♘xc3 14.bxc3 ♘d3+ 15.♗xd3 ♗xd3 16.♘e2 g5 17.♗g3 a5 White is some material up for the moment, but the position is unclear, because Black has active play. **13...♘xc3 14.bxc3 g5!** The idea of ...g7-g5 is quite simple. Black wants to play ...a7-a5, but without ...g7-g5, White would be able to push e3-e4. After 14...a5 15.e4 dxe4 16.cxb4 ♖xc1+ 17.♗xc1 axb4 18.fxe4 ♗xe4 19.h4 ♖xa2 the only move for White appears to be 20.♖h3, and after 20...♗d5 the position should be more or less equal, since the black b-pawn can become dangerous for White. **15.♗g3 a5!** The key move. Online I read that this was described as the move of the day, which surprised me. I thought it was a normal and easy move and I played it after some two minutes of thinking. In some lines, White wants to go ♗a6 and ♗b7, which would free his play, but this is stopped by this prophylactic move. Less good is 15...♘xa2? 16.♖a1 ♘xc3 17.♗a6 h5 (Black can

move away the rook, but this is stronger) 18.♗xc8 ♖xc8 19.h4 ♗b4 20.♔f2 g4, and although White is an exchange up, his pieces are so passive that the engine assesses this as equal. **16.a4** The only move. Bad is 16.a3? ♘a2 17.♖a1 ♖xc3 18.h4 ♘b1 19.e4 ♘xa3 20.♗d3 ♗d7, and this will not be hard to win for Black with his strong passed a-pawn. **16...♘a2 17.♖a1 ♘xc3 18.♘e2** After 18.h4 ♗c2 19.♗b5 gxh4 20.♗xh4 ♗b4 21.♔f2 ♗xb5 22.axb5 ♖ab8 Black is clearly on top. The two bishops combined with the a-pawn are very dangerous. **18...♗b4** Not the best. After 18...♘xe2 19.♗xe2 ♖c2 20.h4 ♖ac8 21.hxg5 ♖b2 White can easily lose in a couple of moves. He is two pawns up, but that won't be enough. **19.♔f2 ♗c2** After 19...h5 20.h4 ♘xe2 21.♗xe2 ♖c2 22.♖hc1 ♖b2 23.♔f1 ♖e8 24.♗e5 gxh4 both sides have chances, but I'd prefer Black. **20.♘xc3 ♗xc3** 20...♖xc3 21.h4 gxh4 22.♗xh4 ♗g6 23.♗g5 would be slightly better for White, and there is no need for this.

21.♖a2? The losing move. Of course, Maghsoodloo saw that 21.♖a3 ♗b4 22.♖a1 ♗c3 23.♖a3 ♗b4 was a draw, but that was not what he wanted. But he had not seen my 23rd move. **21...♗b1 22.♖e2** White has a lost position after 22.♖a3 ♗b4 23.♗e2 ♗xa3 24.♖xb1. **22...♖c4 23.♖c2?** Missing my reply. **23...♗e1+ 24.♔xe1** 24.♔g1 ♖xc2 25.♗xe1 ♖ac8 leads to an easily winning position for Black, since White is totally paralysed. If White takes the pawn on a5, Black will go ...♖a8, take the a4-pawn and invade with his rooks to the first and second ranks. **24...♖xc2**

25.h4 Rac8 26.Bd6 R8c3 27.hxg5 Rb2 0-1 If he plays 28.Kd1 to avoid the mate, Black will go 28...Ba2 and game over.

M/20-3-71 Suleymanli

Renewing the threat 8.a3

Vasily Ivanchuk   **2**
Rustam Kasimdzhanov
Nalchik 2009 (5)
1.c4 e6 2.Nc3 d5 3.d4 Be7 4.cxd5 exd5 5.Bf4 Nf6 6.e3 Bf5 7.Wb3 Nc6 8.a3 Definitely one of the critical lines here. White wants to prove that Black's knight is not well placed on c6.

8...Na5 Black's main line here. 8...Rb8 is a sideline – see Game 5. **9.Wa2** 9.Wa4+ c6 10.Nf3 Nh5? (a blunder, running into a tactical refutation. Black should have continued 10...0-0 with a good game) 11.Bc7! (White is tactically alert) 11...Wxc7 12.Nxd5 Wd8 13.Nxe7 Kxe7 14.b4 Nc4 15.Bxc4 b5 16.Wd1! (16.Bxb5 cxb5 17.Wxb5 g6 18.Ne5±) 16...bxc4 17.Ne5 and White gets his piece back, remaining a pawn up: 17...Wd5 18.Wxh5 g6 19.Wf3 Be4 20.We2 Bxg2 21.Rg1 f6 22.Nxc4± Gavrikov-Ubilava, Tbilisi 1983. The queen retreat 9.Wd1 should not worry Black: 9...0-0 10.Nf3 c6= (10...Ne4?! 11.Rc1 c6 12.Nxe4 dxe4 13.Nd2± Harikrishna-Kaidanov, Lubbock 2008) 11.Bd3 (11.Be2 Nc4) 11...Bxd3 12.Wxd3 Nc4. **9...0-0 10.Nf3** Black is now on a crossroads, and the decision he now takes will determine the pawn structure and the further type of play. I deem all three

options to be viable here, but the main line I choose looks the most sound to me and, I think, equalizes for Black. In case of 10.b4 Black temporarily sacrifices a pawn with 10...Nc4 11.Bxc4 dxc4 12.Wxc4 and after 12...c6 13.Nf3 a5 will get it back with roughly equal play – we have transposed into the line 10.Nf3 c6 11.b4. **10...c5** Suleymanli in his comments above suggests the little-played 10...Be6:
A) 11.Rd1 Ne4?! (11...Nh5∞) 12.Nxe4! (12.Nb5 Nd6 13.Nxd6 Bxd6 14.Bxd6 Wxd6= Flear-Korneev, Nice 2000) 12...dxe4 13.d5 Bg4 14.h3 Bh5 15.g4 exf3 16.gxh5±;
B) Suleymanli's assessment of 11.Bd3 Nh5 as equal is probably about correct, e.g. 12.Rd1 (White can go for the tactical 12.Be5 f6 13.Wb1 g6 14.Ng5!? but this fancy play actually leads to Black's advantage: 14...fxg5 15.Bxg6 Bf6! (15...Nf6 16.Bxh7+ Kh8∞) 16.Bxh7+ (16.Bxh5 Bxe5 17.dxe5 Nb3∓ 18.Ra2? d4–+) 16...Kh8 17.Wg6 We7 18.Wxh5 Wxh7 19.Wxg5 Wg7∓) 12...Nxf4 13.exf4 Bg4 and we may get tactical exchanges petering out into an equal endgame, e.g. 14.Wxd5 Re8 15.Be2 Wxd5 16.Nxd5 Bd6 17.Ne5 Bxe2 18.Kxe2 f6 19.Nf3 c6 20.Ne3 fxe5 21.fxe5 Bf8 22.b4 Nb3 23.Rd3 Nxd4+ 24.Rxd4 Rxe5 25.Rd7 b5= with 26...a5 or 26...c5 to follow;
C) 11.h3 c5∞;
D) 11.Nb5 should not bother Black, as after simply 11...Ne8 White does not have a good follow-up, e.g. 12.Rc1 (12.Bd3 a6 13.Nc3 c5∞) 12...a6 13.Nc3 c5∞;
E) White's critical reply for the evaluation of this line looks to me to be 11.Ng5!? and it is a pity that Suleymanli does not elaborate on this, as White's chances seem to me to be preferable. White has the threat of 12.b4 (as ...Nc4 is now no longer possible), so Black has to push his c-pawn: 11...c5 (11...Bf5 12.b4±; 11...Nh5 12.Nxe6 fxe6 13.Be5!±; 13.Bg3 c5∞ Kharlov-Belozerov, Tomsk 2004) 12.dxc5

Bxc5 (12...Nh5 13.Nxe6 fxe6 14.Rd1 with White's advantage, e.g. 14...Bxf4 15.exf4 Rxf4? 16.Nxd5+–) 13.b4 Bb6 14.Bd3 Rc8 15.Rc1 and I would evaluate this position as somewhat better for White. Fridman's favoured continuation 10...c6!? has a logical plan behind it: Black wants to push ...b7-b5 and then jump ...Nc4, solving the problem of his stranded knight. This is a serious alternative for Black here. See Game 4. **11.dxc5 Bxc5**

12.Be5 White has to be careful (being behind in development) not to force things here. In my opinion, best is the conservative 12.Be2 – see Game 3.
A) Aggressive attempts like 12.b4 can easily land White in trouble: 12...Bb6 13.Rd1 Rc8 (Black has active play, White has to be careful) 14.Wb2 Re8 15.Bb5 Nc4 16.Bxc4 Rxc4 17.0-0 Bg4! (this is rather unpleasant for White. He is fighting for equality here, while there are many lines in which he may just lose on the spot! The central break 17...d4? turns out to be a blunder: 18.Nb5 dxe3 19.Bxe3 (White was likely counting on 19.Rxd8? exf2+ 20.Kh1 Rxd8∞) 19...Bd3 20.Ne5 1-0 (41) Dreev-Prusikin, Switzerland tt 2011) 18.Ne5 (18.Bg5? shows how easy it is for White to lose in such positions: 18...Bxf3 19.gxf3 h6! 20.Rxd5 Wc8 21.Bxf6 gxf6 and Black has a mating attack: 22.Ne4 (22.Nb1 Wh3–+; 22.Ne2 Rc2 23.Wxf6 Re6 24.Wf5 Rxe2–+) 22...Rxe4 23.fxe4 Wg4+ 24.Kh1 Wf3+ 25.Kg1 Rxe4–+) 18...Rc3 19.Wxc3 (19.Wxg4? does not end well for White either: 19...Nxg4 20.Wxc3 g5! 21.Bg3 (21.h3 gxf4

22.hxg4 fxe3–+) 21...♘xe3♔)
19...♗xd1 20.♖xd1. White's
problem here is that the dynamic
momentum is on Black's side:
20...g5! 21.♗g3 (21.♗xg5? ♘e4
22.♗xd8 ♘xc3 23.♗xb6 ♘xd1
24.♗d4 ♖c8♔) 21...♘e4 22.♕a1 ♕e7
23.♘f3 (23.♘g4 ♕e6♔) 23...♕e6
24.♘d4 ♕f6 25.♘b3 (25.♘f3? ♕xa1
26.♖xa1 h5♔) 25...♕xa1 26.♖xa1 (the
queens are off the board, but Black's
initiative is far from over) 26...f5↑
(in case of 26...h5 White's rook on
c1 is now defended (which was the
reason behind 25.♘b3): 27.♖c1 h4
28.♘c7) 27.♖c1 (27.♖d1 d4♔) 27...d4
28.exd4 f4 29.f3 ♘xg3 30.hxg3 fxg3♔;

C) 12.♖d1 does not look logical:
12...♗c2 13.♖d2 ♗b3 14.♖b1 ♖c8
15.♗e5. Black has an advantage in
development and, with due respect
to Ponomariov, there is no reason
for Black to trade pieces: 15...♕b6
(Black is doing very well here, e.g.
15...♗d6 16.♗xd6 ♕xd6 17.♗e2±
Sasikiran-Ponomariov, Khanty-
Mansiysk 2007) 16.♗e2 (16.♗d4
♘e4; 16.♗xf6 ♕xf6 17.♘xd5 ♕c6
18.♘c3 ♕xa3) 16...♘c4. 12...♗e6
13.♗d4 ♗xd4 14.♘xd4 ♘c6
White is behind in development
and cannot maintain a safe
blockade on d4. 15.♘xe6 In case
of 15.♖d1 ♖c8 16.♗e2 Black has
16...♘xd4 17.♖xd4 ♘e4!↑ 18.♕b3
(18.♘xe4? lands White in trouble
due to 18...♖c1+ 19.♗d1 dxe4)
18...♕a5 and White is fighting for
equality. 15.♗e2 does not equalize
either, e.g. 15...♘xd4 16.exd4 ♘e4
17.0-0 ♖c8 18.♖ac1 ♕g5↑. 15...fxe6

This type of pawn structure
transformation we often see in
isolated pawn positions, and is
mostly fine for Black. 16.♗e2
♕e7 17.0-0 ♖ac8 It is clear that

Black does not have any opening
problems here. 18.♖ac1 ♔h8
19.♖fd1 ♘d7 20.♖d2 ♘de5
21.♕b3 ♕f7 22.♗f1? A slightly
unusual blunder for a player of
Ivanchuk's level. After 22.♖f1
♘a5 23.♕b4 ♘ac4 Black is fine,
but perhaps not more than that.
22...d4–+ 23.♘a2 23.exd4? ♘xd4
24.♕d1 ♘df3+–+. 23...♗g4
24.♖dc2 dxe3 25.fxe3 ♘a5 0-1

Denis Khismatullin   3
Oleg Korneev

Russia tt 2013 (7)

1.d4 d5 2.c4 e6 3.♘c3 ♗e7 4.cxd5
exd5 5.♗f4 ♘f6 6.e3 ♗f5 7.♕b3
♘c6 8.a3 ♘a5 9.♕a2 0-0 10.♘f3
c5 11.dxc5 ♗xc5 12.♗e2

This is likely White's best choice
here. White wants to finish his
development and focus on Black's
isolated pawn. We get the type of
positions often seen in different
QGD lines: White seemingly has
slight pressure due to Black's
isolated pawn, but in reality Black
has no problems holding the
balance. 12...♗e6 12...♘c6 can also
be played, but White has some
pressure: 13.♖d1 ♗e6 14.0-0 ♗d6
(it is not smart to go for a pawn
break here: 14...d4? 15.♗c4 ♗g4
16.exd4 ♗xf3 (16...♗b6 17.♗e2±
White has other good solutions
here too) 17.dxc5 ♗xd1 18.♖xd1
with 19. ♗d6 to follow, with a large
advantage for White) 15.♗xd6
♕xd6 16.♘d4± and Black's
isolated pawn is not really enough
of a target, as Black easily held a
draw in Gustafsson-Baramidze,
Oberhof 2012. 13.♖d1 ♗d6
13...♕e7 leads to a type of position
similar to Gustafsson-Baramidze
above, e.g. 14.♕b1 ♘c6 15.♘a4 ♗d6

16.♗xd6 ♕xd6 17.0-0 ♖ac8 18.♘c3
a6±. In this game, too, Black easily
held a draw, Roiz-Pavlovic, Valjevo
2011. 14.♗xd6 ♕xd6 15.0-0 ♖ac8
16.♘d4 a6! 16...♖fd8 is not precise
due to 17.♘xe6! fxe6 18.e4± ♖xc3
(18...d4?? is a terrible blunder:
19.♘b5 ♕e5 20.♘xd4+–) 19.bxc3
♘xe4 20.♕b2 ♕c5 and now White
missed the opportunity to get a
clear advantage with 21.♗d3! (the
game went 21.c4 d4 22.♗d3 ♘c3
23.♖de1 e5♕ with unclear play,
Sargissian-Bakre, Kavala 2010)
21...♕xc3 (21...♘xc3 22.♖de1±)
22.♕b4±. 17.h3 17.♘xe6 fxe6 18.e4
now does not work for White as
after simply 18...d4 Black has an
excellent game. 17...b5 18.♗d3
♘c4 Here, compared to our
previous isolated pawn examples
in this line, Black has active
counterplay, e.g. 19.♘ce2 ♖fe8
20.♘f4 ♗d7= 21.♖fe1 g6 22.♕a1
♕e7 23.♗e2 ♕d6 24.♗f3 ♘e5
25.b3 ♖c7? 26.♗xd5!± ♘xd5
27.♘de2 ♗e6 28.♘xd5 ♗xd5
29.♘f4 ♖c5 30.b4 ♖c6 31.♘xd5
♘c4 32.♖d4 ♕e5 33.f4 ♕e6
34.e4+– ... 1-0 (54)

Fernando Peralta   4
Daniel Fridman

Rabat blitz 2015 (13)

1.d4 d5 2.c4 e6 3.♘c3 ♗e7 4.cxd5
exd5 5.♗f4 ♘f6 6.e3 ♗f5 7.♕b3
♘c6 8.a3 ♘a5 9.♕a2 c6 10.♘f3
0-0

11.♗e2 Grabbing a pawn with
11.b4 ♘c4 12.♗xc4 dxc4 13.♕xc4
does not seem to lead to an
advantage as Black gets his pawn
back with balanced chances: 13...a5
14.b5 (14.0-0 ♗e6 15.♕d3 axb4
16.axb4 ♗xb4=) 14...♖c8 15.0-0
cxb5 16.♕xb5 ♖xc3 17.♕xf5 ♗xa3∞

Shipov-Marciano, Internet 2001.
11...b5 12.0-0 12.♘e5!?. **12...h6** In his previous game v. Mamedyarov, Fridman went for 12...♘c4 and given that Daniel got a good position, I assume that he did not like White's pawn sacrifice ideas: 13.♖fc1 (13.b3!? looks promising, e.g. 13...♘xa3 14.♖fc1 ♖c8 (14...♘h5? 15.♘e5 ♘xf4 16.♘xc6±) 15.h3♗) 13...♘h5 14.♘e5 (14.b3!? is possible here too, e.g. 14...♘xf4 15.exf4 ♘xa3 16.♘e5 ♗d7 (16...♕e8 17.♘d1 ♗d7 18.♘e3♗) 17.♕b2 b4 18.♘a4♗) 14...f6 15.♗g3 ♘xg3 16.hxg3 ♖b8= Mamedyarov-Fridman, Khanty-Mansiysk 2011. **13.h3 ♖c8 14.♖ac1** Here the sacrificial idea is possible too: 14.♖fc1!? ♘c4 15.b3 ♘xa3 16.♕b2. Black's c6-pawn is weak, and his knight on a3 is stranded. White should have sufficient compensation here. Does he have more? Not easy to say. **14...♘c4** The knight cannot stay on c4. **15.a4 b4** 15...a6 16.b3. **16.♘b1 ♘a5 17.♘bd2 ♕b6 18.♘b3 ♘xb3 19.♕xb3 a5 20.♖fd1 ♖fd8 21.♗d3 ♗e6** Here Black can probably improve with 21...♘e4!?, maintaining the tension while keeping the option of ...c6-c5 – this looks okay for Black. **22.♕c2 c5 23.dxc5 ♗xc5 24.♕e2** White has an advantage. The following trade certainly does not improve Black's situation strategically. **24...♗d6?! 25.♗xd6 ♕xd6 26.♘d4± ♕b6 27.♕d2?! ♘e4 28.♗xe4 dxe4 29.♖xc8 ♖xc8 30.♖c1 ♖xc1+ 31.♕xc1 ♔h7 32.♕c6 ♕xc6 33.♘xc6 ♗d7 34.♘xa5 ♗xa4 35.♘b7 ♔g6 36.♘c5 ♗c2** ≥ 36...♗c6. **37.♔f1 ♔f5 38.♔e1 ♔e5 39.♘a6 b3 40.♘b4 ♗b1 41.♘c6+ ♔d5 42.♘d4 ♔c4**

43.♔d2 43.h4!? g6 44.g4 ♗d3:
A) 45.g5 h5! (crucial! 45...hxg5? 46.hxg5 is actually lost for Black; all his pawns are fixed on light squares) 46.♔d2 ♗f1 47.♘c6 ♗c5 48.♘e5 ♗c4 49.♘d7+ (49.♘c3 ♗e6= the knight has zero manoeuvring space) 49...♔d6 50.♘f6 ♘e5 51.♘c3 ♗e6 52.♔b4 ♔f5 53.♘c5 ♗e5 54.♔c6 ♗c4 55.♔d7 ♔f5 56.♔d6 ♗e6= Black cannot be put into zugzwang!;
B) 45.h5 gxh5 46.gxh5 ♔d5! (the saving retreat) 47.♘xb3 (47.♔d2?! ♗f1! 48.♘c3 ♔e5 49.♘xb3 ♔f6 50.♔c3 ♔g5 51.b4 ♔xh5 52.b5 ♔g4 53.b6 ♔a6=) 47...♔b5 48.♘d4 ♗d7 49.♔f1 ♗g4 50.♔g2 ♔xh5 51.♘f5 ♔c4 52.♘xh6 ♔b3 53.♔g3 ♔xb2 54.♔f4 ♔g6 55.♔g4 ♔c3 56.♘e5 ♗h7 57.♘xf7 ♗d3±. **43...♗d3 44.h4?!** 44.♔e1 makes for a sorry sight but is the only way to retain winning chances. **44...♗f1!= 45.g3 ♗h3 46.♘e2 ♗g4 47.♘c3 ♗f3 48.♘a4 g6 49.♘c3 g5 50.hxg5 hxg5 51.♘a4 f5 52.♘c3 ♗h5 53.♘a4 ♗e8 54.♘c3 ♗c6 55.♘e2 ♗d7 56.♘d4 ♔b4 ½-½**

Matthew Sadler   5
Ivan Sokolov

Maastricht 2017 (7)

1.d4 d5 2.c4 e6 3.♘c3 ♗e7 4.cxd5 exd5 5.♗f4 ♘f6 6.e3 ♗f5 7.♕b3 ♘c6 8.a3 ♖b8 This less popular move is definitely playable – however 8...♘a5 gives Black more dynamic play. Whether or not Black solves his opening problems will depend whether he can either improve or regroup his ♘c6, or create queenside counterplay by pushing his b-pawn. 8...♘a5 is the main line and likely Black's best – see Games 2-4. **9.♘f3 0-0**

10.♖c1 Sadler places his rook on the c-file in order to stop Black's b-pawn push. 10.♗e2 a6 (perhaps best is 10...h6 11.0-0 ♗e6, aiming to trade the dark-squared bishops, regroup and gradually equalize: 12.♘d2 ♗d6 13.♗xd6 ♕xd6 14.♖ac1 a6 15.♕c2 (if White has something here, it is very little) 15...♘e7; my idea during the game was actually 10...b5 but the resulting positions look better for White after 11.♘e5 ♘xe5 12.♗xe5± 11.0-0 b5 12.♘e5 ♘a5 13.♕d1 ♖b6 14.♗d3 ♗xd3 15.♘xd3± Spraggett-Jussupow, Hastings 1989/90. **10...♖e8 11.♗e2 a6** In case of 11...♗d6, 12.♗g5 is annoying for Black. The trade of the dark-squared bishops helps Black to solve the problem of his ♘c6 and in this respect 11...h6! with ...♗d6 to follow was needed. This is definitely an improvement on the game and should gradually equalize for Black, e.g. 12.0-0 (12.♗g3 ♗d6 13.♗h4 g5 14.♗g3 a6 15.0-0 ♔g7=) 12...♗d6 13.♗xd6 (13.♘xd5 ♘xd5 14.♕xd5 ♗e4 15.♕c4 ♗xf4 16.exf4 ♕f6 and Black is at least okay) 13...♕xd6 14.h3 ♘e7 15.♘b5 ♕b6 16.♕c3 c6 17.♘d6 ♖ed8 18.♘xf5 ♘xf5=. **12.0-0** The situation is not easy for Black, and I decided to try to prepare the b-pawn push to create counterplay. **12...h6 13.♗g3** 13.♗e5! was probably more precise, e.g. 13...♗e6 14.♖fd1 ♗d6 15.♕c2 ♖c8 16.h3 and Black has problems to regroup. **13...♗f8** 13...♗e6 14.♘e5± ♘xe5 15.♗xe5 ♗d6 16.f4. **14.♖fe1 ♖e6 15.♘d2** 15.♗e5! was unpleasant for Black, stopping the push of the b-pawn. **15...b5!♗** Now Black has counterplay. **16.♕d1 b4** Another reasonable option was 16...♘a5 when 17.b4 ♘c4 18.e4 ♘xe4 19.♘cxe4 ♗xe4 20.♗xc4 bxc4 21.♘xe4 ♖xe4 22.♖xe4 dxe4 23.♖xc4 ♗d6, though White has a slight pull, looks rather drawish. **17.axb4** How to recapture? **17...♖xb4** The better decision was 17...♘xb4! and after 18.♘a4 ♗d6 my computer engine gives close to 0.00, but it didn't

feel that way during the game.
18.b3 ♗d6 19.♘a4 Black does not
have counterplay to compensate
for his weak queenside pawns.
White is clearly better. **19...♗xg3
20.hxg3 a5 21.♘c5 ♖e7 22.♘d3**
22.♗d3 was also good for White.
**22...♖b6 23.♖c5 ♕d6 24.♕c1
♗xd3 25.♗xd3 ♘b4 26.♕b1 ♘d7
27.♖xa5±**

White is a pawn up and has an
excellent position to boot. For
the purpose of this theoretical
article, the rest of the game is of
no interest. For practical chess
training purposes there are still
quite some twists to come (!), so
I've given a few notes: **27...g6
28.♖c1 ♖e8 29.♗e2 h5 30.♕a1
♘f8 31.♖a8 ♖xa8 32.♕xa8 ♔g7
33.♘f3 ♘c6 34.♗b5 ♘e7 35.♗a4
f6 36.♘c5 c6 37.♗a7 ♘d7 38.♖c2
♔f7 39.♘e1 ♔e8 40.♘d3 ♕b8
41.♕a5 ♔f8 42.♕d2 ♔g7 43.♖c3
♕d6 44.♕d1 ♔f8 45.♖c5 ♘e6
46.♖a5 ♘c7 47.♕e1 ♔f7 48.b4
♕b7 49.♗c2 ♘c8 50.♕a1 ♕c7
51.♗b3 ♘e7 52.♕a2 ♖b7 53.♖a4
♖b5 54.♕e2 ♖b7 55.♕b2 ♘f5
56.♕c3 ♘e7 57.e4! ♖a7 58.♖xa7
58.♖a5+–. 58...♕xa7 59.exd5
cxd5 60.♘c5 ♘c7 61.♗a4 ♘f5
62.♗d7 ♘d6 63.♕c1 ♘e4
64.♘xe4 dxe4 65.♕c6 ♔e7
66.♗c8 f5 67.d5 67.♕xg6 ♕xd4
68.♗xf5+–. 67...♕a1+ 68.♔h2
♕e5 69.♕d7+ ♔f8 70.♕d8+
♔f7 71.♕d7+** 71.d6 ♕d5 72.d7
♘f6 73.♕b6!+– ♘g4+ 74.♔h3
♕a1 75.d8♕+! ♔g7 76.♕c7++–.
71...♔f8 72.♗b7 ♘e8= 72...h4!⇄
73.♕d8+ ♘e8 74.♕xh4 (74.♗c6
hxg3+ 75.fxg3 e3 76.♗xe8 ♕h8+=)
74...♘f6!= 75.f3 (75.♕h6+ ♔f7
76.♕c1 e3 77.fxe3 ♘g4+ 78.♔g1
♕xg3 79.♕d2 ♕h2+ 80.♔f1 ♕h1+

81.♔e2 ♕xg2+∞) 75...exf3 76.gxf3
♕e2+ 77.♔h3 ♕f1+=. **73.♕e6
♕xe6 74.dxe6 ♔e7 75.♗c8 ♘c7
76.f3 e3** 76...♘xe6=77.fxe4 fxe4
78.♗xe6 ♔xe6 79.♔g1 ♔d5 80.♔f2
♔c4 81.♔e3 ♔xb4 82.♔xe4 ♔c3
83.♔f4 ♘d2 84.♔g5 ♔e3 85.♔xg6
♔f2=. **77.♔g1 g5 78.f4 gxf4
79.gxf4 ♘d5 80.b5**

80...♔d8? The decisive mistake.
80...h4 81.♗d7 (81.♔f1 ♔d6
82.♗d7 ♘xf4 83.b6 e2+ 84.♔e1
♘xg2+ 85.♔xe2 ♘f4+ 86.♔f3
♘xe6 87.♗xe6 ♔c6=) 81...♔d6=
(81...♘xf4 82.b6 ♘d3 83.♔f1 ♘c5
84.♔e2 f4=) 82.♗c8 ♘xf4 83.b6 e2
84.♔f2 ♘xg2 85.♔xe2 ♘f4+ 86.♔f3
♘xe6 87.♗xe6 ♔c6=. **81.♗d7+–
h4 82.♔f1 ♘xf4** 82...♔e7
83.♗c6+– ♘xe6 (83...♘b6 84.♔e2)
84.♗xd5+ ♔xd5 85.♔e2. **83.b6
♘d5 84.b7 ♘c7 85.♗c6 ♘e7
86.♗f3+– f4 87.♗e4 ♘g8 88.♔e2
♘e7 89.♔d3 ♔b8 90.♗f3 ♘c7
91.♔c3 ♘f5 92.♔d3 ♘e7 93.♔d4
♘g6 94.♔e4 1-0**

**The direct approach
8.g4**

Levon Aronian   6
Vladimir Kramnik
Monaco rapid 2011 (9)
**1.c4 e6 2.♘c3 d5 3.d4 ♗e7
4.cxd5 exd5 5.♗f4 ♘f6 6.e3 ♗f5
7.♕b3 ♘c6 8.g4** This aggressive
continuation was Veselin Topalov's
idea (v Kasparov). This was
either Veselin's over-the-board
inspiration or some not really
thoroughly worked out opening
preparation, as he soon got into
serious trouble. **8...♘xg4** The main
line for Black. There are perhaps
viable alternatives – see Games 8-9.

9.♕xd5 Topalov's above-
mentioned game went 9.♘xd5?!
0-0 10.♗g2 h4 11.♗g3 ♗e6 and
Black had superior development
and a safer king. Kasparov went
on to win easily in Topalov-
Kasparov, Linares 1997. **9...♕c8!**
Black's best move, in my opinion.
The queen swap 9...♕xd5 is the
main alternative, however, in
my opinion this leads to White's
advantage – see Game 7. **10.♕g2!**
The most consistent. White is
ready to push his central pawns.
10.a3, stopping Black's ...♘b4 jump,
is certainly logical, but likely too
timid to yield White an opening
advantage here, e.g. 10...♘f6
(10...0-0 11.♗e2 ♘f6 12.♕g2 ♖e8
13.♘f3 (13.h4 was probably a better
move, eliminating the possibility
of ...♗h3, but the position looks
unclear) 13...♗h3 and Black was at
least equal in Zhu Chen-Zatonskih,
Beijing blitz 2012) 11.♕g2 0-0
12.♗c4 ♘a5 13.♗a2 c5 14.dxc5
♕xc5=15.♘ge2 ♘c4 16.♗xc4
♕xc4 17.♘d4 ♗g6 18.♕xb7
♖fe8 19.♕b5 ♕c8= Nakamura-
Topalov, St Louis 2017. **10...0-0!?**
An interesting, imaginative piece
sacrifice, which probably does not
entirely work – at least I could not
make it work. Please pay attention,
however, to one important detail
here! Daniel Fridman, one of the
leading experts in this line, was
prepared to enter this tactical mess
as Black and was not willing to
play it with white(!). So if I could
not make Kramnik's 10...0-0!? work
for Black, this does not mean that
it does not work! Perhaps there is
something hidden which I failed
to see, so I definitely encourage
the reader to analyse this line! I

have, however, a quite different idea for Black here: I would advise Black players to investigate the as yet almost untried 10...♘f6! 11.♘f3 (now White cannot push his central pawns, as 11.e4? runs into the tactical refutation 11...♘xe4 12.♘xe4 ♕e6 13.f3 0-0-0∓ 14.♘e2 g5 15.♗g3 g4−+; 11.♕xg7?? ♖g8 12.♕h6 ♖g6 13.♕h4 ♖g4 14.♕h6. Black already has a draw, but obviously he should go for more here: 14...♘xd4 15.exd4 ♖g6 16.♕h4 ♘d5−+) 11...♘h5 12.♗e5 ♗b4∞. This looks to me to be the most precise for Black here. We reach a novel position with no games played at the time I was writing this Survey. The position is dynamic; both sides have their chances. In my opinion Black is not worse. I expect theory to develop in this direction. 12...0-0 13.0-0-0 is also possible, leading to unclear play, though White emerged victorious in Ringoir-Brattain, Charlotte 2018.

11.e4! Forcing Black to sacrifice a piece. 11.f3?? is a strange blunder: 11...♗h4+ 12.♔d2 ♘f2 and White is already completely lost, e.g. 13.♗g5 ♗xg5 14.♕xf2 ♖d8 15.d5 ♘b4 16.f4 ♘f6 17.♗g2 ♖xc3+ 18.bxc3 ♘xd5 19.♔c1 ♘xc3 20.♕d2 ♕f6−+ Geirnaert-Fridman, Belgium tt 2019/20. 11.0-0-0!? was Fridman's idea as White. Black's play can be improved: 11...♘f6 12.f3 (12.e4 ♗g6 13.f3 transposes to the game) 12...♗g6 13.e4 Black's basic idea here is to destroy White's central pawn chain by means of a piece sacrifice! White's king is vulnerable and the tactics are working for Black here: 13...♖d8 (worthy of attention is 13...♘b4!? 14.a3 a5!⇄; 14...c5? 15.d5 ♖d8 16.♕h3!±) 14.♘ge2 (White wants to speed up his development. Further delaying his development is at least risky for White, e.g. 14.♗e3 ♗b4 15.a3 (15.♘h3 c5!∓ 16.d5 ♘fxd5 17.exd5 ♖xd5 18.exd5 ♕f5∓) 17...♕f5∓) 15...c5 16.d5 ♘fxd5! 17.exd5 ♗f6⇆; 14.d5 ♘b4 15.♕h3 ♕b8! 16.a3 a5 16...

b5!? 17.axb4 a5!→). In my opinion this position is easier to play for Black. White's king is weak and he can easily fall under a deadly attack) 14...b5! 15.♗e3 (15.♘xb5 ♖b8 16.♘bc3 ♗b7 17.♖d2 ♕a5→ 18.♕g3 ♗b4∓) 15...b4 16.♘a4. Here Black's play can be improved. He should sacrifice his knight, destroying White's pawn centre: 16...♘xe4! (the actual game went 16...♘a5? 17.♘f4 with advantage for White, though Black managed to survive in Fridman-Prusikin, Bad Wiessee 2012; the non-sacrificing idea 16...♕e6 17.b3 ♘d5∓ also looks good for Black) 17.fxe4 ♕e6 18.d5 (trying to prevent Black's queen getting to a2. After 18.♘f4 ♕xa2 Black has more than just compensation) 18...♖xd5!. Now White is forced into a bad endgame: 19.♖xd5 (19.exd5 ♕xe3+ 20.♖d2 ♕g5−+) 19...♗xe4 20.♘f4 ♗xg2 21.♘xe6 ♗xd5 22.♘xc7 ♗xh1 23.♘xa8 ♗d6 24.h3 ♗e5∓. The smoke has cleared. Black is a pawn up and should win this endgame. **11...♘xe4 12.♘xe4 ♗b4+ 13.♘c3 ♕f5 14.♗e2**

A critical moment! If Kramnik's play can be improved on, it should be somewhere around here. There are many ideas, but I did not manage to really make it work for Black: **14...♖fe8** 14...♖ae8 15.♔f1; 14...h5!? 15.♕g3! ♘xd4 16.♔f1 ♗xc3 (≥ 16...♘e6) 17.bxc3 ♘xe2 18.♔xe2 ♖fe8 (Cvetnic-Sheppard, cr 2015) 19.h3±. **15.♔f1 ♘f6** Aronian plays precisely, and liquidates into a won endgame. **16.♗h6 g6 17.♕g5! ♘xd4 18.♖d1 ♗xc3 19.bxc3 ♘e4 20.♕xf5 ♘xf5 21.♗d2 ♖ad8 22.♗e1 ♖xd1 23.♗xd1** The smoke has cleared.

White has a large advantage, and the game enters the technical execution phase. **23...♖e5 24.♘f3 ♖c5 25.♗b3 ♘xc3 26.♘e5 ♘e4 27.♘xf7 ♔g7 28.f3 ♘f6 29.♗f2 ♖c3 30.♘g5 ♘h5 31.♔e2 ♘f4+ 32.♔d2 ♖d3+ 33.♔c2 ♘h6 34.♘f7+ ♔h5 35.♖g1 h6 36.♘e5 ♘e3+ 37.♔b1 ♖c3 38.♘xg6 ♘h3 39.♘f4+ 1-0**

Radoslaw Wojtaszek   7
James Tarjan
Gibraltar 2016 (2)
1.d4 d5 2.c4 e6 3.♘c3 ♗e7 4.cxd5 exd5 5.♗f4 ♘f6 6.e3 ♗f5 7.♕b3 ♘c6 8.g4 ♘xg4 9.♕xd5 ♕xd5 10.♘xd5 ♗b4+ 10...0-0-0 11.♘xe7+ ♘xe7 12.♖c1 ♘d5 13.h3 ♘gf6 14.♗e5±.

11.♘c3! Probably the most precise. After 11.♘xb4 ♘xb4 12.♖c1 chances are equal according to Suleymanli. I do not agree with this assessment. As long as White's central pawn chain remains intact (and it looks like it will), White should have some advantage. A few practical examples confirm this opinion:

A) 12...♘d5 13.h3 ♘gf6 14.♗e5 0-0 15.♘e2 ♘d7 16.♗h2 (Fridman plays it safe; it was actually possible to be greedy: 16.♗xc7! ♖ac8 17.♗a5 ♖xc1+ 18.♘xc1 ♗e4 19.♖g1 ♖c8 20.♗d2 ♖c2 21.♘d3 and White ends up with a powerful pair of bishops and a large advantage, e.g. 21...♗xd3 (21...♘7f6 22.♗g5±; 22.♔d1±) 22.♗xd3 ♖xb2 23.♖g5 ♘7f6 24.♖e5 and Black is in bad shape: 24...♖xa2 25.e4 ♘b6 26.♖e7 ♘fd7 27.♗b5 ♔f8 28.♗b4 ♖b2 29.♗xd7 ♘xd7 30.♗d6+−) 16...c6 17.♘g3 ♗g6 18.h4 ♘7f6 19.♗e2 h5 20.♔d2 ♖fe8. Fridman now comes

with a nice manoeuvre, advancing his central pawns! 21.♗g1! ♘g4 22.♘f1 (22.e4 ♘f4 23.f3±) 22...♖ad8 23.f3 ♘gf6 24.♘g3 ♖d7 25.a3 ♖de7 26.e4 ♘f4 27.♗c4± and White went on to win in Fridman-Svane, Osterburg 2012. This game nicely shows the dangers for Black if White manages to get his central pawn chain rolling;

B) 12...c6 13.a3 (13.h3 ♘f6 14.a3 ♘bd5 15.♗e5 ♗d7 16.♗d6 ♘7b6 17.b3 ♖d8 18.♗g3 0-0 19.♘e2 ♖fe8 20.♖g1 ♗e6 21.♘d2± Lenderman-Le Quang, Las Vegas 2015) 13...♘d3+ 14.♗xd3 ♗xd3 15.f3 ♘f6 16.♔d2± and White had pressure, though Black managed to survive in Wojtaszek-A.Onischuk, Poikovsky 2012. **11...0-0-0 12.♗g2 ♗d6**

A) 12...♖he8 13.♘ge2 ♘f6 (Black has all his pieces in play, while White's king is still in the centre. Ideally, Black would love to break up White's central pawn chain by means of a piece sacrifice. The problem is it doesn't work: 13...♘xd4 14.exd4 ♗d3 15.0-0 ♖xe2 (now the most precise for White is 15...♗xc3 16.♘xc3 ♗xf1 17.♖xf1 ♖xd4 18.♗xc7±) 16.♘xe2! ♗xe2 17.♖fc1 ♗d6 (17...c6 18.d5+–) 18.♗xd6 ♖xd6 19.♖e1 and White is clearly better, e.g. 19...♗b5 20.♖ac1 ♖xd4 21.♖e7 ♗c4 22.♖e8+ (22.b3? ♔d8) 22...♔d7 23.♖b8 b6 24.b3 ♗e6 25.♖b7±) 14.0-0 ♘h5 15.♗g3 – the engine gives like 0.30 for White, but his position looks pleasant and easier to play;

B) 12...♗a5 is not good for Black either, e.g. 13.♘ge2 ♗b4 14.0-0 ♘d3 15.♗g3↑ and White's pieces are better coordinated, while Black's king is weak: 15...h5 (15...♘xb2 16.e4± ♗e6 17.♖ab1 ♘c4 18.♘b5) 16.h3 ♘f6 17.h4. **13.♗xd6 ♖xd6 14.♘ge2 ♖e8** An important moment! **15.h3** White's play can be improved here. It is a good time to start rolling his central pawn chain: 15.♖d1! ♗b4 (15...♘f6 only delays the process: 16.♘g3! ♗g4 17.f3 ♗d7 18.♘f2±) 16.e4± ♗e6 (16...♘c2+ 17.♔f1 ♗d7 18.h3) 17.h3 ♘h6 18.d5 ♗d7 19.a3±.

15...♘h6? Black refuses to fight for the central squares! 15...♘f6 16.♖d1 ♘b4 17.0-0 ♘bd5 and the position is about equal as White cannot make use of his central pawn chain. **16.♖d1** g5 **17.e4 ♗d7 18.h4!** gxh4 18...g4 was arguably the lesser evil, though White is better after 19.e5. **19.♖xh4**

White has a clear advantage, and Wojtaszek easily brings it home: **19...♖g8 20.♗h1 ♖g4 21.♖h2 ♖g7 22.f3 ♘g8 23.♔f2 ♖h6 24.♖xh6 ♘xh6 25.♗g2 ♘e7 26.♘f4 c6 27.♘ce2 f6 28.♘h5 ♖f7 29.♖h1 ♘hg8 30.f4 f5 31.e5 ♗e6 32.♘c3 ♘h6 33.b3 ♘g4+ 34.♔e2 ♖f8 35.♗f3 ♗c7 36.♘g7 ♗g8 37.d5 cxd5 38.♗b5+ ♔b6 39.♘d4 ♘g6 40.♘h5 ♘4xe5 41.fxe5 ♘xe5 42.♘f4 ♘xf3 43.♔xf3 ♗a5 44.♖c1 ♔b4 45.♘d3+ ♔a3 46.♖a1 1-0**

Sideline analysis   8
8.g4 ♗xg4

1.c4 e6 2.♘c3 d5 3.d4 ♗e7 4.cxd5 exd5 5.♗f4 ♘f6 6.e3 ♗f5 7.♕b3 ♘c6 8.g4 ♗xg4!? This sideline might work for Black and is worth analysing further. **9.♕xb7**

9...♘b4 9...♗d7 10.♗xc7 ♕c8 11.♗a6 ♘b4 12.♕xc8+ ♗xc8 13.♗b5+ ♗d7 14.♔f1±. Black has various ideas here, but he doesn't have enough for the pawn: 14...♖c8 15.♗xd7+ ♔xd7 16.♗e5 ♘e4 17.♘ge2 f6 18.♗g3

h5 19.h4 1-0 (21) Fridman-Azarov, Jurmala rapid 2012. **10.♖c1** 10.♔d2?! ♘e4+ 11.♘xe4 dxe4 12.♗b5+ c6 13.♗xc6+ ♘xc6 14.♕xc6+ ♗d7 15.♕c7 ♗b4+ 16.♔d1 ♕xc7 17.♗xc7 ♖c8 18.♗f4 f6∓. **10...♖b8!N** This novelty might change the verdict on this line.

A) 10...0-0 11.a3 ♖b8 12.♕xc7! (12.♕xa7 ♘c6 13.♕a4 ♖xb2!♔ 14.♕xc6 ♗xa3 15.♘ge2 ♖b6 16.♕a4 ♗xc1 17.♘xc1 ♘f3 18.♖g1 ♘e4♔) 12...♕xc7 13.♗xc7 ♖b7 14.♗e5 ♘c6 15.♗xf6 ♗xf6 16.♘xd5±;

B) 10...♗f5 11.a3!N (11.♗xc7 ♕c8 12.♕xc8+ ♖xc8 13.♗e5 ♘e4! improves on Black's play, with sufficient compensation; after 13...0-0 14.a3 ♘d3+ 15.♗xd3 ♗xd3 16.♔d2 ♗c4 17.♘ge2 Black's compensation is not sufficient, 1-0 (30) Aleksandrov-Dobrowolski, Warsaw 2008) 11...♖b8 12.♕xa7 (12.♕xc7 ♕xc7 13.♗xc7 ♖b7♔) 12...♘c2+ 13.♖xc2 ♗a8 (13...♗xc2 14.♗xc7 ♖a8 15.♗b5+ ♔f8 16.♕b6 ♕c8 17.♘ge2±) 14.♗b5+ ♔f8 15.♗xc7 ♕xc7 (15...♗xc2 16.♘ge2) 16.♗xc7 ♗xc2 17.♘ge2±. **11.♕xc7** 11.♕xa7 ♗d6! 12.♗xd6 cxd6 13.a3 (13.♕a4+ ♗d7 14.♕d1 ♘e4∓) 13...♖a8 14.♕b7 ♖b8=. **11...♕xc7 12.♗xc7 ♖b7 13.♗e5 ♘e4 14.f3** 14.♘xe4? dxe4 15.♗c4 ♘d3+ 16.♗xd3 exd3∓. **14...♗h4+ 15.♗g3 ♘xg3 16.hxg3 ♗xg3+ 17.♔d2 ♗f5 18.♗b5+ ♔d8 19.a3** 19.♘ge2 ♗d6 20.a3 ♗a2 21.♘xa2 ♖xb5 22.b4 ♗e6 looks okay for Black. **19...♘a2 20.♘xa2 ♖xb5 21.b4**

White wins a pawn, however Black keeps counterplay: **21...♗d6** 21...♗e6? 22.f4±. **22.♘c3 ♖b6 23.♘xd5 ♖a6 24.♘c3 ♗e6 25.♘f4 ♗xf4 26.exf4 h5** Black definitely has counterplay thanks to his

dangerous h-pawn. Whether it fully compensates for the pawn deficit is not easy to say.

Alexander Morozevich   9
Alexander Onischuk
Reggio Emilia 2010/11 (6)

1.d4 d5 2.c4 e6 3.♘c3 ♗e7 4.cxd5 exd5 5.♗f4 ♘f6 6.e3 ♗f5 7.♕b3 ♘c6 8.g4 ♗c8?! This is little played, and for good reason. White easily gets an advantage here. 8...♗g6!? is a very interesting line, full of tactics, however probably it doesn't work for Black: 9.g5 (9.♕xb7 ♘b4 10.♗b5+ ♗f8♕) 9...♘e4 (9...♘h5? 10.♕xb7 ♘xd4 (10...♘b4 11.♗xc7 ♕c8 12.♗b5+ ♔f8 13.♗c6 ♘xc6 14.♕xc6+− Lorparizangeneh-Javanbakht, Teheran 2016) 11.0-0-0 ♘xf4 12.♖xd4±) 10.♘xd5! (White's best option, likely leading to an advantage. 10.♕xd5 is far from clear: 10...♘b4 11.♕xd8+ ♖xd8 12.♘xe4 ♗xe4 13.f3 ♗c6 14.♔f2 ♘d5 15.♗e5 ♗xg5 16.e4 ♗e3+ 17.♔g3 ♘f6 18.d5 ♗d7 19.♘h3 h5∞; 10.♘xe4 ♗xe4 11.f3 ♗f5 12.♕xb7 ♘b4 13.♗b5+ ♔f8♕) 10...0-0 11.h4! (11.♗g2 ♗xg5 12.♗xc7 ♕d7 13.♘f3 ♗h5♕) 11...♖e8 (11...♗d6!? may be worth further investigation. We have many possibilities here and I will give just one logical run

of play: 12.♘f3 a5 13.♗xd6 ♕xd6 14.♘f4 a4 15.♕a3 ♕b4+ (15...♘b4 16.♖c1 ♘xa2. This fancy play does not bring the desired result: 17.♕xa2 ♕b4+ 18.♗e2 a3 19.b3 ♕c3 20.♘d3±) 16.♕xb4 ♘xb4 (Black has sufficient compensation here) 17.♔e2 (17.♖c1 ♘xa2∞) 17...a3♕) 12.♘xe7+ ♘xe7 (12...♕xe7 13.♗e2 a5 14.h5 ♗f5 15.♖c1±; 12...♖xe7 13.♖d1+−) 13.f3 ♘d5. Black does not get enough for his sacrificed piece: 14.h5! (14.fxe4?? ♗xe4 15.♖h2 ♘xf4∓) 14...♗xh5 (14...♗f5 15.fxe4 ♗xe4 16.♖h4+−) 15.fxe4 ♘xf4 16.exf4 ♖xe4+ 17.♗e2 ♕xd4 18.♖d1 ♕c5 19.♖d5 ♕c1+ 20.♕d1 ♕xd1+ 21.♖xd1 ♖xe2 22.♘xe2 ♖ae8 23.♖h2 ♖xf4 24.♖d7±. **9.h3**

9...♗d6 9...a5 10.♕c2 c6 11.0-0-0 ♗e6 12.♔b1 ♖c8 13.♗d3 b5 (13...♘c4 14.♘ge2 ♕a5 15.♗g3 b5 16.♘f4±) 14.♘ge2 ♘c4 15.♗g3 (15.♗g3± g6 16.♗xc4 bxc4 17.♗e5) 15...♕a5 16.♘f4 ♗b4 17.♘ce2 c5 18.g5 ♘d7

19.♗xc4 cxd4 (19...bxc4 20.e4 (20.g6±) 20...♘b6 21.dxc5 ♕xc5 22.♘h5±) 20.♘xd4 ♖xc4 21.♕e2+− 0-0 22.♘fxe6 fxe6 23.♘xe6 ♖fc8 24.♕d3 ♘b6 25.g6 1-0 Bocharov-Rychagov, Irkutsk 2010. **10.♗xd6 cxd6** 10...♕xd6 11.♗g2 ♘e7 12.g5 ♘e4 13.♘xe4 dxe4 14.♘e2±; 14.♗xe4±. **11.♘ge2±** White has the better pawn structure and also Black is going to lose his d5-pawn. **11...h5 12.g5 ♘e4 13.h4 0-0 14.♗g2 ♗g4 15.♘f4 ♖c8 16.♕xd5 ♘xc3 17.bxc3 ♘e7 18.♕b3 ♘f5 19.g6?** Instead of 19.♖c1±, and Black emerged victorious after **19...♘xh4! 20.♗d5 ♘f3+ 21.♗xf3 ♗xf3 22.♖h3 ♗g4 23.♖g3 ♖c6⇄ 24.♖c1 d5 25.♕xd5 ♖d6 26.♕xb7 fxg6 27.♕b3+ ♖f7 28.c4 ♖xf4 29.exf4 ♖xd4 30.c5+ ♔h7 31.♔f1 ♖xf4 32.♕e3 ♕f6?! 33.c6! ♗c8 34.♔g1 h4 35.♖g2 ♕d6 36.♕c5** 36.♔h1!? ♖d4 37.f3 h3 38.♖e2±. **36...♕d2 37.♕c2 ♕d6 38.♖d1?** The wrong way forward. **38...♕e6** 38...♕f6! 39.♖d8 h3 40.♕xg6+ ♕xg6 41.♖xg6 ♔xg6 42.♖c8 h2+ 43.♔xh2 ♖xf2+ 44.♔g3=. **39.♕c3** 39.♖c1!±. **39...♖c4= 40.♕a5? ♕xc6 41.♕g5?** White has messed up big time in time pressure. **41...♗h3** 41...h3!. **42.♕d5 ♕xd5 43.♖xd5 ♗xg2 44.♔xg2 ♖a4 45.♔h3 ♔h6 46.f3 g5 47.♖d2 ♔h5 0-1**

Exercise 1

position after 20.♕b2xc3

White is an exchange up. How to evaluate this position?

(solutions on page 249)

Exercise 2

position after 10...♘g4-f6

If White can get his central pawns rolling, this should be good for him. Is it smart to push 11.e4 here?

Exercise 3

position after 20...♖f8-e8

For the time being Black is controlling the central squares, stopping White's pawn roller. Can White get an advantage here?

Tarrasch Defence   Semi-Tarrasch   TD 2.9 (D41)

A highly practical pawn push

by Ivan Saric (special contribution by Peter Heine Nielsen)

1.	d4	d5
2.	c4	e6
3.	♘c3	c5
4.	♘f3	♘f6
5.	cxd5	♘xd5
6.	e4	♘xc3
7.	bxc3	cxd4
8.	cxd4	♗b4+
9.	♗d2	♗xd2+
10.	♕xd2	0-0
11.	♗c4	♘d7
12.	0-0	b6

There are a lot of possible ways for White to break down Black's defences in the Semi-Tarrasch, and one of them recently caught my attention. This was obviously due to the efforts of top player Anish Giri, who has shown its strengths twice so far. Due to the current absence of 'classical' games, both were played with faster time controls, but this doesn't reduce their value.

Personally I have never played the Semi-Tarrasch on either side, but that may actually make this Survey better! It seems strange, but I think it gives me full objectivity, which is a task many authors fail to comply with when writing about openings.

Usually in the Semi-Tarrasch White wants to be flexible with his main trump in the position – his pawn centre. The positional background of the push d4-d5 is that it transforms one advantage, the pawn centre, into another one: a passed pawn. Also, the pawn on d5 often restricts Black's bishop on b7 and gives White a free hand on the kingside (Giri-Ding Liren is a good example). The arising structure with a passed pawn is favourable not only in endgames; it can also be very effective in the middlegame as it gives attacking chances on the kingside and more space for White's pieces.

The main line
The position after 13.♖ad1 ♗b7 14.♖fe1 ♖c8 was already known before World War II and features in hundreds of games.

Our World Champion managed to dispose of Anish Giri in a magnificent game using a novel idea: 16.♖e3 and 17.d5. His second Peter Heine Nielsen explains some of the finer details of this electrifying battle in the first game of the Game Section.

A different square

When White decides to play 13.d5 immediately, which is the main focus point of this Survey, I believe that Black should choose a different square for his bishop than b7 (in the line with 13...♘c5), which happened in some games.

After 13.d5 Black has basically two reasonable choices to fight for equality.

Magnus Carlsen

A) 13...♘f6
B) 13...♘c5

13...exd5 is also possible, but it gives White a small advantage without a fight.

The forcing option

13...♘f6 is less popular, but has one clear plus compared to the main move: it can seriously force matters and drastically simplify the position in the critical line – after 14.♕f4. The drawback is that Black has to react very quickly and concretely to create counterplay. He has two ways of doing this after 14...♗b7 15.♖ad1 exd5 16.exd5:

one with 16...b5 (see the game Henrichs-Remling) and the other with 16...♖c8. In the latter case, the key move which requires further practical tests is 17...♘h5N – see the notes in the game Krishna Teja-Keymer.

The popular choice

13...♘c5 was played more often and has been the choice of the top players.

Here, however, White has a couple of possible set-ups. One of them is 14.♕f4, but now Black at least two decent options, the simplest one being 14...♕f6 (Dreev-Portisch). Two more games with 14.♕f4 are included in this Survey mostly due to their instructional value (Leko-Sarana and Riazantsev-Van Wely). The critical move seems to be 14.♖fe1! when after 14...exd5 White should definitely capture with the pawn because 15.♗xd5 doesn't yield any advantage.

15.exd5 led Giri to a quick victory against Nepomniachtchi with a tactical trick that is definitely worth knowing.

Conclusion

While analysing the numerous positions in this line I have noticed that the engines tend to hold Black's position easily, but in practice Black can quickly end up in trouble. The game Aronian-Matlakov is a good example, as well as the already mentioned game Giri-Nepomniachtchi.

Objectively Black should find a way to equalize (16...♗a6!?N – see the notes to Giri-Nepomniachtchi), but the positions seem easier to play from White's perspective.

The main line
13.♖ad1 ♗b7 14.♖fe1 ♖c8

Magnus Carlsen
Anish Giri

Chessable Masters rapid 2020 (3.21)
Magnus had won the first 'set', but one of the advantages of the set system is that even when ahead, you cannot sit on your lead and cruise to victory. **1.d4 ♘f6 2.c4 e6 3.♘f3 d5 4.♘c3 c5!?** While it was 'only' rapid, clearly the players treated the tournament like a serious event, with opening preparation trying to surprise the opponent. Giri here chooses the Semi-Tarrasch, an opening that has seen a renaissance thanks to Kramnik, who made it into an efficient 'blocking' weapon most recently in the 2018 Candidates, where Anish was his second! **5.cxd5 ♘xd5 6.e4 ♘xc3 7.bxc3 cxd4 8.cxd4 ♗b4+ 9.♗d2 ♗xd2+ 10.♕xd2 0-0 11.♗c4** Recently Magnus tried 11.♗d3, but Giri can be trusted to have solved that problem. **11...♘d7** The modern way. In the old days, 11...♘c6 looked more natural. But while at first sight it appears more active, the knight tends to end up at a5, leaving the black king more exposed, as was illustrated by the beautiful classic Polugaevsky-Tal from the 1969 Soviet Championship. **12.0-0 b6 13.♖ad1 ♗b7 14.♖fe1 ♖c8 15.♗b3 ♖e8** While Magnus earlier had tried a more positional plan with a4-a5, all this is pretty standard. Kramnik has had this position as Black

several times. Black stays flexible and is ready to make exchanges on the e-file after a possible d4-d5, ...exd5 and exd5. Making a useful move for White is not trivial, the most popular choice being 16.h3, passing the move back to Black. **16.♖e3!?** An odd-looking move, as arranging an attack via g3 is certainly not possible. But it has a more subtle hidden point. **16...♘f6** The point of the modern treatment of the Semi-Tarrasch. Instead of at a5 the knight ends up at f6, both attacking the white centre and providing protection for the black kingside (no ♗xh7+ sacrifice!). **17.d5** Technically speaking, only this is the novelty. **17...exd5 18.e5**

18...♘e4 IS: The move in the game looks so logical and tempting that sometimes you wouldn't even consider passive alternatives. Since Black is not really afraid of ♗xd5 (he would like it to happen), the knight on d7 has some sense because it creates pressure on the e5-pawn, it can't be attacked and it can even join the defence with ...♘f8. 18...♘d7!? 19.♕e2 (19.♗xd5 ♗xd5 20.♕xd5 ♘c5= immediately forces the exchange of queens

and puts Black in a more pleasant position; 19.♕e1 ♕c7 20.h4 h6∞) 19...♘c5!? (19...♕c7∞) 20.♘d4 g6∞ might end with an unusual repetition: 21.♕g4 (21.f4 ♘e6= and if we compare this position with the one in the game we can see that the white queen is better on e1 than on e2 in some lines! Here after 22.♘b5 Black not only has 22...♘xf4 with a tempo, but he can also play 22...♗a6) 21...♕d7 22.♕h4 ♕e7 23.♕h6 ♕f8 24.♕h4 ♕e7= (IS). **19.♕e1** This is the point of White's opening concept. At first sight it might look like White is a pawn down and Black has a strong knight on e4, but due to tactics along the e-file White indirectly protects the pawn on e5. He has the unstoppable plan of ♘d4 and f2-f3, which will force the black knight to retreat. **19...♕c7** Giri thought for a while. After the match he said he was aware of the white concept, but obviously he had trouble recalling the right antidote. Black's move is logical, but has the downside that ♘b5 wins a tempo as the knight aims for the d6-square. But something similar could be said of 19...♕e7, then with a possible ♘f5. – IS: The ideal square for Black's knight is e6 and maybe it should go there as fast as it can. The drawback of this move is that Black no longer has pressure on the e5-pawn, but the e5-pawn was untouchable anyway. 19...♘c5 20.♘d4 (20.♗c2 ♘e6∓ looks like losing a pawn without much compensation) 20...♕d7!? (20...♘xb3? is the only

thing Black shouldn't do in this position because the knight is dominating the bishop and this would immediately lead Black into an inferior position: 21.axb3±; 20...g6 (preventing ♘f5) 21.f4≅ (White doesn't have to hurry and I would definitely choose his side here; 21.♘b5 would be great for him, but there is 21...♘xb3! 22.axb3 d4! 23.♖xd4 (23.♘xd4 ♕d5=) 23...♕g5∓ 24.f3 ♗xf3! 25.g4□ (25.♔xf3? ♖xe5–+) 25...♗xg4 26.h4∞) 21...♘e6 22.♘b5; 20...♕g5 21.h4 plays into White's hands) 21.f4 (21.h4 ♘e6 22.♘f5 ♘f4!⇄ 23.♘d6 ♕g4 24.g3 (24.♖g3 ♘e2+) 24...d4! is at least fine for Black) 21...♘e4!?. Now the knight can't be attacked by the f-pawn and the typical 22.♖xe4 dxe4 23.e6 fxe6 24.♘xe6 ♕e7 is good only for a draw (IS). **20.♘d4 a6** Stopping ♘b5. After 20...♕xe5 21.f3 f5 22.fxe4 fxe4 Black has three pawns for the piece. While on the classic scale that is just enough for a knight, modern computers give assessments like 3.1 or 3.2 instead of the traditional 3, more importantly the white knight on d4 makes the position intolerable for Black. – IS: 20...♕c5 is the first choice of the engines, but you have to be prepared for ♖xe4 ideas: 21.e6 (I bet that Magnus would try something like 21.h4!?. Black has many possible moves, but I like 21...b5 with the idea of playing ...a5-a4 and also with a nice defensive point: 22.e6 fxe6 23.♖xe4 dxe4 24.♘xe6 ♕e7 25.♘g5+ ♖c4!= so Black doesn't need to calculate all kinds of white attacks on his king; 21.f3 ♘c3) 21...fxe6 22.♖xe4 dxe4 23.♘xe6 ♕e7□ 24.♘g5+ ♔h8 25.♘f7+ ♔g8. White has a draw in his pocket, but he can also continue a little, although that is not without risk: 26.♕e3!? ♔f8 27.h4. The engines evaluate this around 0.00 but it looks pretty scary – for both sides. (IS) **21.h4!?** Magnus later admitted that his preparation ended around here. 21.f3 was also logical, but, given

the chance: why not stay on brand and add some AlphaZero flavour? **21...♖cd8 22.f3 ♘c5 23.h5** White's position is starting to make sense. The pawn on e5 is now well protected and the h-pawn does a great job discouraging ...g7-g6 (to keep the white knight away from f5), as then, apart from hxg6 and an attack down the h-file, the typical AlphaZero move h5-h6!? becomes very much an option. Black really has his hands full already, not to mention that this was a 15-minute game and that Anish had already spent quite a few of these precious minutes. **23...♘e6 24.♘f5 d4** Giri said that this move gave him hope, as optically the bishop on b7 springs to life, and Black appears to have some activity.

25.♖ed3! A 'slow' looking move, but White now threatens the trivial 26.♘d6 followed by 27.♗xe6 and 28.♖xd4, getting the pawn back while keeping a dominant position. **25...♘c5** Life is not really fair towards Giri here. 25...♗d5 should bring relieving exchanges, but 26.♘d6! ♗xb3 27.♘xe8 works tactically, when, despite Black having a pawn and solidity for the exchange, White's win is just a matter of technique. And it looks like White's e-pawn is en prise after the captures on d4, but back-rank tactics make that an illusion, too. **26.♖xd4 ♖xd4 27.♖xd4 ♘xb3 28.♕g3** With material being equal (when White recaptures on b3) and all Black's pieces being on seemingly optimal squares, it is hard to believe that Black is just lost. However, another AlphaZero theme comes

to mind: Black's king is confined to g8, while White's king has space around it, which makes it easy to escape the black back-rank threats on the safe haven h2, while the black king is caught in a mating net. **28...g6** If 28...f6 then 29.♖g4! immediately wins, with the principal point being 29...♕xe5 30.♖xg7+ ♔h8 31.♖xh7+! and mate on g7 next move. **29.axb3 ♖d8?!** This allows a very beautiful finish, that makes the difference between a great game and a classic. 29...♗xf3 was a better way to muddy the waters, when White has several ways to keep a winning advantage, by far the most convincing being 30.♖c4!, when after 30...♗c6, 31.♘d4 cynically ends the game.

30.e6!! Hitting where it hurts the most. Black's queen is overloaded as 30...♕xg3 is met by 31.♖xd8 mate. **30...♕c1+ 31.♔h2 ♖xd4 32.e7!!** The true moment of beauty. It's the game's least valued piece that breaks Black's resistance. The key idea is that 32...♗c6, stopping the pawn's promotion, fails to the back-rank mate after 33.♕b8+. **32...♕c8 33.♕e5!** Threatening mate on g7, as well as queening the pawn. All that is left for Black is to give a check. **33...♖h4+ 34.♔g3!** A fitting end, illustrating the difference in king's safety. The white monarch safely steps forward, even attacking the rook on h4, while Black's king is trapped on its castling square. If 34...gxf5, White promotes with check, collects the rook on h4 and wins trivially. **1-0**

Peter Heine Nielsen M/20-5-26

(abbr.)

The forcing option
13...♘f6

N Krishna Teja
Vincent Keymer
Sitges 2018 (6)

1.♘f3 d5 2.d4 ♘f6 3.c4 e6 4.♘c3 c5 5.cxd5 ♘xd5 6.e4 ♘xc3 7.bxc3 cxd4 8.cxd4 ♗b4+ 9.♗d2 ♗xd2+ 10.♕xd2 0-0 11.♗c4 ♘d7 12.0-0 b6 13.d5

13...♘f6 13...exd5 14.♗xd5 ♖b8 (14...♗a6?? 15.♗xa8 ♗xf1 16.♗xf1 ♕xa8 17.♕xd7+−) 15.♖fe1 ♗b7 16.♖ad1 ♘c5 17.♕f4±. This position is usually reached via the move-order 13...♘c5 14.♖fe1 exd5 15.♗xd5 ♗b7 16.♖ad1 where Black has a wide choice (16...♖e8= or 16...♕e7=) but nobody would want to play 16...♖b8. **14.♕f4**

A) 14.♖fd1 exd5 15.♕f4 (15.e5 ♗e6 16.exf6 dxc4 17.fxg7 ♔xg7 18.♕c3+ ♕f6∓ Le Tuan Minh-A.Chandra, Lichess blitz 2020) 15...♗b7 16.exd5 (16.♗xd5 ♖b8= Trani-Bujdak, cr 2009) 16...♖c8 17.d6 ♗xf3 is an inferior position for White compared to the one after 14.♕f4 because White needs his rooks on d1 and e1;

B) 14.dxe6 is completely harmless: 14...♗xe6 15.♗xe6 ♕xd2 16.♘xd2 (16.♗xf7+ ♖xf7 17.♘xd2 ♖d8=) 16...fxe6 17.f3 ♖fd8= Huang Qian-Ding Yixin, China tt 2018;

C) 14.♖ad1 can transpose to 14.♕f4, but it also gives Black the extra option of 14...♕c7!?. **14...exd5 15.♖ad1 ♗b7 16.exd5** Strategically speaking, this has been a success for White. He has created a passed pawn, and has control of the d6-square. The d5-pawn can't be taken yet, and d5-d6 is a dangerous threat. Therefore,

Black must react quickly. **16...♖c8** For 16...b5!? see the next game. **17.d6** After 17.♗b3 Black could simply take the pawn: 17...♘xd5= (Dzagnidze-Kosteniuk, Huai'an 2016), because she had ...♖c5 at her disposal. **17...♗xf3** First 17...♘h5! is better, and this is critical for the evaluation of 16...♖c8, and possibly of the whole line starting with 13...♘f6: 18.♕g4 (18.♕d4!? might be better, e.g. 18...♗xf3 19.gxf3 ♕g5+ 20.♔h1∞) 18...♘f6 19.♕d4 ♖c5! (not yet taking the knight; this is the main difference between 17...♘h5 and 17...♗xf3, as here Black has the ...♖d5 idea) 20.♘e5 (20.♖fe1 ♗xf3 (20...♗d5!?) 21.gxf3 ♖c8 22.♗b3 ♖g5+ 23.♔f1 ♕h3+ 24.♔e2∞ – Black should be at least fine here) 20...♗d5=. White can sacrifice the queen, but has enough compensation only to make a draw: 21.♕xc5 bxc5 22.♗xd5 ♘xd5 23.♖xd5 f6 24.♘c6 ♕d7 25.♖a5 ♖d8 26.♖fd1 ♖c8 27.d7 ♕c7 28.♘c4. **18.gxf3± ♘h5** 18...♕d7 (Henneberke-Sosonko, Leeuwarden 1973) 19.♖fe1±. **19.♕g4 ♖c5** 19...♘f6 20.♕d4±. **20.♔h1** 20.h4! is stronger, e.g. 20...♘f6 21.♕d4±. **20...♘f6** 20...♕f6!? 21.d7 g6 is aimed against 22.♖fe1? (when Black has 22.♗b3 ♖d8=) 22...♖xc4! 23.♕xc4 (23.d8♕ ♖xd8 24.♖xd8+ ♔g7!∓) 23...♕xf3+ 24.♔g1 ♘f4. **21.♕f4 ♕c8?!** 21...♘h5=. **22.♖g1 ♖f5??** 22...♘h5 23.♕e4±. **23.♕h6+− g6 24.d7** Followed by 25.d8♕ or 25.♖xg6+. **1-0**

Thomas Henrichs
Christian Remling
Biel 1997 (11)

1.d4 d5 2.c4 c5 3.cxd5 ♘f6 4.♘c3 ♘xd5 5.♘f3 e6 6.e4 ♘xc3 7.bxc3 cxd4 8.cxd4 ♗b4+ 9.♗d2 ♗xd2+ 10.♕xd2 0-0 11.♗c4 ♘d7 12.0-0 ♘f6 A slightly unusual move-order, introduced by Rudolf Spielmann in 1937. 12...b6 is far more common. If 13.d5 ♘f6 14.♕f4 exd5 15.♖ad1 ♗b7 transposes to the game. **13.♕f4 b6 14.♖ad1 ♗b7 15.d5** 15.♖fe1 ♖c8. **15...exd5 16.exd5 b5**

17.♗b3 17.♗xb5 ♗xd5 18.♗c4 looks scary for Black, but there is nothing to be afraid of: 18...♖c8 19.♗xd5 ♘xd5 20.♕e5 ♖c5!, followed by ...♕c7 or ...♕a5, saves the day. **17...a5 18.a3** Keeping the tension. After 18.d6 a4 19.♗c2 ♗d5 20.♘d4 ♗xa2 21.♘xb5 ♗b3 22.♖xb3 axb3 23.♖b1 ♕d7 24.♖xb3 ♖ab8 (or 24...♖fb8) White is a pawn up, but can't really take much advantage of it. The game should end in a draw and might continue 25.♘d4 ♖xb3 26.♘xb3 ♖d8 27.♖d1 ♕b5! 28.♕f3 ♕b6 29.g3 h6 30.♕d3 ♘e8 31.d7 ♘f6=. **18...♕b6** Inserting 18...a4 19.♗a2 is possible, but it's hard to say whether this is better or worse compared to the game: 19...♕b6 20.d6 (20.♘h4 ♖fe8 21.♘f5 ♗c8□ 22.♗b1 (even 22.♘xg7!? ♔xg7 23.d6♚ is possible) 22...b4 23.axb4 a3⇄) 20...♗xf3 (20...♖ad8 21.♘e5! is crushing, e.g. 21...♖xd6 22.♘xf7 ♖xd1 23.♖xd1+−) 21.gxf3 ♖ad8 22.♖fe1. This position is probably crucial for the evaluation of 16...b5: 22...♖c5 23.♖d3 ♖d7 24.♖c1 ♕h5 25.♖d4 ♖fd8 26.♗b1 and White somehow keeps the initiative. **19.♘h4** 19.d6!? might have been better because Black doesn't have anything better than ...a5-a4 and ...♗xf3. **19...♕c5?!** 19...♖fe8! 20.♘f5 ♗c8! is fine for Black, e.g. 21.♘d6 ♖d8 22.♘xf7 ♔xf7 23.d6+ ♔f8 24.♖fe1 ♖a7! and Black has defended. **20.♘f5± ♘h5?! 21.♕g5 a4?! 22.♖c1** 22.d6 also wins, e.g. 22...♔h8 23.♗xf7!+−. **22...♕xa3** Up to this moment White has played perfectly. Now he just needs to finish off: **23.♕xh5?** 23.♗d1!+− f6 24.♕d2! and besides the hanging knight

on h5, suddenly the seventh rank becomes a serious issue for Black: 24...♗c8 (24...g6 25.♖c7+−) 25.♘d4 g6 26.♘xb5 ♕e7 27.d6 is crushing. **23...♕xb3 24.♕g5 ♕b2 25.♖c7 a3 26.♖xb7 a2 27.♖xb5** 27.h4!=. **27...a1♕ 28.♖xb2 ♕xb2∓ 29.h4 g6 30.h5 ♖a1 31.♘e7+ ♔g7 32.♖xa1 ♕xa1+ 33.♔h2 f6 34.♘f5+ ♔g8 35.♘h6+ ♔g7** 35...♔h8! 36.♕f4 ♕d1 (36...gxh5 37.♘f7+! is a surprising perpetual check; 36...♕e5 37.♕xe5 fxe5 38.hxg6! ♔g7 39.♘g4 ♔xg6 40.♘xe5+ ♔f5 41.♘c4 ♔e4 42.d6 ♔d5 43.♘e3+ ♔xd6=.) 37.hxg6 ♕h5+ 38.♔g1 hxg6 39.♘g4 ♔g7 is the last resort to try to win. **36.♘f5+ ♔g8 37.♘h6+ ♔g7 38.♘f5+ ♔g8 39.♘h6+ ♔g7 40.♘f5+ ½-½**

Peter Leko
Alexey Sarana
Moscow rapid 2018 (4)
1.d4 ♘f6 2.c4 e6 3.♘f3 d5 4.♘c3 c5 5.cxd5 ♘xd5 6.e4 ♘xc3 7.bxc3 cxd4 8.cxd4 ♗b4+ 9.♗d2 ♕xd2+ 10.♕xd2 0-0 11.♗c4 ♘d7 12.0-0 b6 13.d5 ♘c5 14.♕f4

This game doesn't have much theoretical importance if we study it move-by-move, but it has instructional importance on the subject of how to handle such a pawn structure as White.
14...exd5 14...♕f6= solves almost all of Black's problems, see the game Dreev-Portisch. 14...♗b7 – Riazantsev-Van Wely. **15.exd5 ♗b7 16.♖ad1 ♕d6** 16...♘d6 looks like the most natural move, but

Black would have to enter into a slightly inferior endgame after ...♕f6 at some point: 17.♗d3 (already ♘g5/♗xh7+ ideas are in the air) 17...♕f6 18.♕xf6 gxf6 19.♘d4±. **17.♕h4 ♘c5 18.♘d4 a6** 19.♗e2 19.♘e6!? is a nice tactical motif worth knowing: 19...♖e8□ (19...fxe6? 20.dxe6+−) 20.♖fe1 ♗b7 21.♘xc5 bxc5±. White's pieces are more active, and his passer is more dangerous. **19...♗d7 20.♗f3** When White can transfer his bishop to f3, he may hope for an advantage. The bishop is safe and is no longer a target on the queenside; it defends the d5-pawn, and can support the knight on c6. **20...♖ae8** 20...♖fe8 looks more logical to me. I really don't see what this rook is doing on f8. **21.♘c6**

21...f6?! Now the real problems start for Black. This weakens the kingside and gives White additional targets, such as the e6-square. 21...f5 with the idea of ...♘e4 would be the only way to justify ...♖ae8, but the problem is 22.♕b4 – or maybe it isn't... 22...g5! (going all in!) 23.g3 f4 24.g4 h5! 25.h3 hxg4 26.hxg4 ♕h6 and Black even managed to create some counterplay. The tactical point is simply amazing: 27.♕xb6 ♗xg4!! 28.♘e7+ (28.♗xg4 ♕h4) 28...♖xe7 29.♕xh6 ♗xf3 30.♖c1 ♖h7 31.♕xh7+ ♔xh7 32.♖xc5 ♖h8 33.♖c3 g4 34.d6 ♔g6 35.♖xf3 gxf3=. **22.♕b4 b5 23.♖c1 ♘b7 24.♕d4 ♖a8?** A blunder, but Black already had a difficult position. 24...♖d8□. **25.♕b6+−** ♖d8 25...♗c8 26.♖fe1 with total domination. **26.♘e7+! ♕xe7 27.d6 ♕e6 28.♗xa8 ♘f7**

29.♕xa6 ♕xd6 30.♕xd6 ♘xd6 31.♗d5+ ♔h8 32.♖c7 ♗f5 33.♖e1 ♖d8 34.h3 g5 35.g4 ♗g6 36.♖ee7 ♘c8 37.♖ed7 ♖xd7 38.♖xd7 ♘b6 39.♖d8+ ♔g7 40.♖g8+ ♔h6 41.♗b3 ♗d7 42.f3 ♘c5 43.♖b8 ♗d3 44.♔f2 ♔g6 45.♔e3 ♗f1 46.♗c2+ ♔g7 47.a3 h5 48.gxh5 ♘e6 49.♖b7+ ♔h8 50.h6 1-0

Alexander Riazantsev
Loek van Wely
France tt 2012 (5)
1.d4 ♘f6 2.c4 e6 3.♘f3 d5 4.♘c3 c5 5.cxd5 ♘xd5 6.e4 ♘xc3 7.bxc3 cxd4 8.cxd4 ♗b4+ 9.♗d2 ♕xd2+ 10.♕xd2 0-0 11.♗c4 ♘d7 12.0-0 b6 13.d5 ♘c5 14.♕f4 ♗b7 15.♖ad1 ♕f6 16.♕xf6 gxf6

17.♘d4 17.dxe6 fxe6 (the paradoxical 17...♘xe6!?N is also possible. It's not clear at all whether the pawn structure e6/f6/h7 is better than f7/f6/h7) 18.♘d4 ♖fe8 19.f3 ♗f8 (19...a6? loses important time and Black was already lost after 20.♘b3, Muse-Tica, Bol 2015) 20.♘b5 ♗a6 21.♘d6 ♗xc4 22.♘xc4= Zhukova-Danielian, Riyadh rapid 2017.
17...♖fc8 18.dxe6 ♘xe6 19.♗b3 19.♘xe6? ♖xc4∓; 19.♗xe6 fxe6 20.♘xe6 ♗a6!? 21.♖fe1 ♗c4⇄. **19...♘xd4 20.♖xd4=** Although Stockfish 'thinks' differently. **20...♗c6** 20...♘c7 21.♖fd1 ♖e8 22.♖d7 ½-½ Giri-Naiditsch, Wijk aan Zee 2010. **21.f3 ♔f8 22.♖d6 ♔e7 23.e5 fxe5 24.♖h6 a5 25.♖e1 a4 26.♖xe5+ ♔f8 27.♗d5 ♗xd5 28.♖xd5 ♖c1+ 29.♔f2 ♖c2+ 30.♔g3 ♖xa2 31.♖d7 ♔g8 32.♖f6 ♖f8 33.♖xb6 a3 34.♖a7 ♖e8 35.♖f6 ♖e6 36.♖axf7 ♖ee2 37.♖f8+ ♔g7 38.♖8f7+ ♔g8**

39.♖f8+ ♔g7 40.♖6f7+ ♔h6 41.♖f6+ ½-½

Alexey Dreev
Lajos Portisch

Zurich 2009 (3)

1.d4 ♘f6 2.c4 e6 3.♘f3 d5 4.♘c3 c5 5.cxd5 ♘xd5 6.e4 ♘xc3 7.bxc3 cxd4 8.cxd4 ♗b4+ 9.♗d2 ♗xd2+ 10.♕xd2 0-0 11.♗c4 ♘d7 12.0-0 b6 13.d5 ♘c5 14.♕f4 ♕f6

15.♕xf6 After 15.♕e3 White is a tempo down compared to the 'normal' position: 15...♗b7 16.e5 ♕g6 17.♖fd1 (Krejci-Sabuk, Czechia tt 2018; 17.d6 f6∓) 17...♗xd5 18.♗xd5 exd5 19.♖xd5 ♖ad8∓. **15...gxf6** This position is perfectly fine for Black, but from here on White showed perfect technique and took advantage of his opponent's inaccuracies: **16.♖fe1 ♗b7 17.dxe6 fxe6 18.♘d4 ♔f7 19.f3 ♖fd8 20.♖ed1 ♖d6** 20...♕e7= or 20...a6= were safer. **21.♘b3! ♖xd1+** 21...♖ad8 22.♖xd6 ♖xd6 23.♘xc5 bxc5 24.♖c1 ♗a6 was probably more practical. The drawing margin in rook endgames is pretty high. **22.♖xd1 ♔e7 23.♘xc5 bxc5** White has made small progress, but the game should definitely have ended in a draw. **24.♔f2 ♗c6 25.♖d3 ♖b8 26.♖a3 ♖b2+ 27.♔e3 ♖xg2 28.♖xa7+± ♔d6 29.♖a6 ♔c7 30.♖a7+ ♔d6 31.h4 ♖c2 32.♔d3 ♖f2 33.♖a6 ♔c7 34.♔e3 ♖h2 35.♗xe6 ♗b7?! 36.♖a7 ♗b6 37.♖a3 ♖xh4 38.♖d3 ♗c6 39.♖d8 ♔c7 40.♖f8 ♔d6 41.♗g8 ♖h6 42.♖f7 ♗e8 43.♖a7 ♗d7 44.♖a6+ ♔e7 45.e5!+− ♗f5 46.♗c4 ♗d7 47.♗g8 ♗f5 48.♗d5 ♖g6 49.♖a7+ ♔f8 50.e6 1-0**

The critical move
14.♖fe1

Anish Giri
Ding Liren

Carlsen Invitational Prelim 2020 (4.4)

1.d4 ♘f6 2.c4 e6 3.♘f3 d5 4.♘c3 c5 5.cxd5 ♘xd5 6.e4 ♘xc3 7.bxc3 cxd4 8.cxd4 ♗b4+ 9.♗d2 ♗xd2+ 10.♕xd2 0-0 11.♗c4 ♘d7 12.0-0 b6 13.d5 ♘c5 14.♖fe1! In my opinion this looks more critical than 14.♕f4. **14...♗b7** Black should be more flexible with his bishop. On b7 it looks natural, but it isn't doing much. 14...exd5 see Giri-Nepomniachtchi. **15.♖ad1±**

15...♖c8 15...♕f6 16.♕e3± was the move order in Alexandrov-Dragnev, Heraklion tt 2017. See the notes to move 19 in the next game. **16.h4** The most typical move in the Semi-Tarrasch, especially nowadays. 16.♘e5!? exd5 17.exd5 ♕d6 18.♖e3± ♘d7 (the exchange of the knights doesn't help Black much) 19.♘xd7 ♕xd7 20.♗b3 ♕d6 21.h4! ♖fe8 22.♖de1 ♔f8 (22...♖xe3? 23.♕xe3 ♔f8 24.h5 might be already strategically lost for Black and shows the dangers in his position. White's follow-up idea of ♕e4/♗c2 looks quite strong) 23.h5±; 16.♕d4!?. **16...♕f6 17.♕e3 exd5 18.exd5 a6 19.h5** Probably White should have kept his bishop on more active squares: 19.a3 b5 20.♗a2, keeping the pressure. **19...b5 20.♗f1 h6 21.♖d4 ♖fd8?** 21...♖cd8! was stronger, but even in a classical game such nuances are very difficult to spot: 22.♖f4 ♕d6 23.♘d4 (23.♘h4 ♗c8!=) 23...♖de8! is the 'trick', e.g. 24.♕xe8 ♕xf4∓. **22.♕d2** 22.♖f4! ♕b2 23.♘d4!

♗xd5 24.♘f5 is crushing, but not at all obvious. **22...♖d6= 23.♖c1 ♕d8 24.♕b4 ♘a4 25.♖xc8 ♗xc8 26.♘e5 ♗b7 27.♗c4 ♕e7 28.♗b3 ♕xe5 29.♖e4 a5 30.♕e1 ♕xh5 31.♖e8+ ♔h7 32.♗c2+ f5 33.♕e5 ♖xd5 34.♕e6 ♘c5 35.♕g8+ ♔g6 36.♖e3 ♖d1+ 37.♗xd1 ♕xd1+ 38.♔h2 f4 39.♖e7 ♕h5+ 40.♔g1 ♕d1+ 41.♔h2 ♕h5+ 42.♔g1 ♕d1+ 43.♔h2 ½-½**

Levon Aronian
Maxim Matlakov

Tbilisi 2017 (3)

1.d4 ♘f6 2.c4 e6 3.♘f3 d5 4.♘c3 c5 5.cxd5 ♘xd5 6.e4 ♘xc3 7.bxc3 cxd4 8.cxd4 ♗b4+ 9.♗d2 ♗xd2+ 10.♕xd2 0-0 11.♗c4 ♘d7 12.0-0 b6 13.d5 ♘c5 14.♖fe1 ♗b7 15.♖ad1 exd5 16.exd5 ♕f6 16...♕d6 17.♘d4 ♕f6 18.♖e3 ♖ad8 19.♖f3 ♕h4? 20.♘f5!+− ♕f6 (20...♕xc4 21.♖g3+−; Black has no defence against the numerous threats on the kingside: ♕h6, ♘xg7, ♖xg7+) 21.♘xg7! 1-0 Timman-Langeweg, Leeuwarden 1979. **17.♕e3±** White has full control on the e-file. **17...♖ad8 18.h4** 18.♘e5!? ♖fe8?? 19.♘g4+−. **18...h6 19.h5** 19.♘d4 b5 20.♗xb5 ♗xd5 21.♘e5 ♕b6 22.♗c4 ♗xc4 23.♖xc4 ♘e6 24.♕xb6 axb6= Alexandrov-Dragnev, Heraklion tt 2017; 19.♘e5!?→. **19...♖d6 20.♖d4 ♕f5 21.♘h4! ♕d7 22.♕g3 ♖f6** 22...♗xd5 23.♖ed1+−. **23.♖g4** 23.d6! was stronger, but 23.♖g4 looks quite tempting and human. **23...♔h8 24.♖xg7?!** 24.♖f4!+− − again, an almost impossible move to make for a human. **24...♗xd5** Surprisingly, White is no longer winning. **25.♘g6+ ♖xg6 26.♖xg6 fxg6 27.♕e5+ ♔g7 28.♕xd5 ♕f6 29.f3 ♖d8= 30.♕f7 ♕xf7 31.♗xf7 gxh5 32.♗xh5 a5 33.♖e8+ ♖xe8 34.♗xe8 ♔g7 35.♔f2 ♔f6 36.♔e3± ♔e5 37.f4+ ♔f5 38.♔f3 ♘d3 39.g4+ ♔e6 40.a3 ♘e1+ 41.♔e4 ♘c2 42.a4 ♘b4 43.♗b5 ♔f6 44.♗e2 ♔e6 45.♗c4+ ♔f6 46.♗f1 ♘a2 47.♔d4 ♘b4 48.♗d3 ♔e6**

49.♔c4 ♘d5 50.g5 ♘xf4 51.gxh6 ♔f6 52.h7 ♔g7 53.♗f5 ♔h8 54.♗e4 ♔g7 55.♗f3 ♘e6 ½-½

Anish Giri
Ian Nepomniachtchi
Chessable Masters rapid 2020 (2.12)

1.d4 ♘f6 2.c4 e6 3.♘f3 d5 4.♘c3 c5 5.cxd5 ♘xd5 6.e4 ♘xc3 7.bxc3 cxd4 8.cxd4 ♗b4+ 9.♗d2 ♗xd2+ 10.♕xd2 0-0 11.♗c4 ♘d7 12.0-0 b6 13.d5 ♘c5 14.♖fe1 exd5 15.exd5 15.♗xd5 ♗b7 16.♖ad1 is an old line which doesn't give White advantage: 16...♖e8= or 16...♕e7!? Shimanov-Dominguez Perez, PRO league rapid 2018. **15...♕d6** Black stops the d-pawn first, so his bishop on c8 can remain flexible.

16.♕d4N Preparing ♖ad1, and also with the idea to counter ...♗d7 with ♘e5.
A) 16.♖ad1 ♗g4=;
B) 16.♘d4 ♗d7 17.♘b5 ♗xb5 18.♗xb5 ♖fd8 19.♖ad1 ♖ac8=;

C) 16.♘e5!? ♖e8 (otherwise White will manage to double rooks on the e-file) 17.♕d4 f6!? (17...♗a6!?) 18.♘c6 ♗d7 19.♖xe8+ ♖xe8 (Black doesn't care about the pawn on a7, because he gets nice counterplay) 20.♘xa7 ♖e4 21.♕c3 ♖h4 22.h3 (after 22.g3 ♕e4! 23.♕c2 ♘g5! White has to be careful to make a draw) 22...♕e4 23.♕e3 ♗xf2! 24.♘b5 ♕b4 (24...♕f4 25.♕xf4 ♖xf4; 24...♕e5 25.♕xe5 fxe5 26.♖c1 ♘e4 27.♘a7 ♔f7 28.♘c6 ♔f6 is a simpler solution) 25.♕xb6 ♘xh3+ 26.gxh3 ♖xc4 27.♕d8+ ♕f8 28.♕xd7 ♕c5+ 29.♔g2 ♖c2+ 30.♔h1 ♖c1+ 31.♖xc1 ♕xc1+ 32.♔g2 ♕d2+ with a perpetual. **16...♗b7** After this move I couldn't find a way for Black to completely equalize, and it seems that White can keep pressure. 16...♗a6!? might be an improvement, trying to swap as many pieces as possible. Black's play is a bit easier after this: 17.♘e5 (17.♗xa6 ♘xa6 18.♖ad1 ♖ad8 19.♘h4 g6 20.♘f3 ♕c7=) 17...♖fe8 18.♖ac1 ♘d7!? (18...h6!?) 19.♘xd7 (19.♗xa6 ♖xe5 20.♖xe5 ♘xe5 and there are some holes in Black's camp, but he should be able to maintain the blockade) 19...♗xc4 20.♘xb6 ♖xe1+ 21.♖xe1 ♕b4! (the point of 18...♘d7) 22.♖c1 axb6 23.♕xc4 ♕xc4 24.♖xc4 ♔f8= and

White can't keep his extra pawn. **17.♖ad1** 17.♕e3 is too artificial to my taste, although later White got some advantage: 17...♖fd8 18.♖ad1 ♖ac8 19.♘d4 ♕f6 20.g4 ♕h4 21.h3 g6 22.♘c6 ♗xc6 23.dxc6 ♖xd1 24.♖xd1 ♕f6 25.♗d5 ♘e6 26.♖d2 ♔f8 27.♗f3 ♖c7 28.♖d6 ♕a1+ 29.♔d1 ♕f6 30.♖d6 ½-½ Dorner-Maurer, cr 2007. **17...♖ae8** 17...a6 18.a3 doesn't change much **18.♘e5 a6 19.a3 ♖e7 20.♖e3**

20...♖fe8?? Inserting 20...b5 was necessary, but Black still has to work for equality, e.g. 21.♗a2 ♖fe8 22.♖de1 (22.♘xf7? ♔xf7 23.♖e6 ♔f8-+ doesn't work due to back-rank issues) 22...h6 23.h4 ♗c8 24.g3±. **21.♘xf7!+- ♔xf7 22.♖e6 ♕d8** 22...♘xe6 23.dxe6+ ♖xe6 24.♕xd6+-. Funnily enough, 22...♕d7 23.♖de1 ♕d6! is a more resilient option for Black. **23.♕f4+! ♔g8 24.♖xe7 ♖xe7 25.d6+ ♖e6 26.d7 g6 27.♖d6 1-0**

Exercise 1

position after 21.♘h4-f5

Black has only one good move against White's threats. Can you find it?

Exercise 2

position after 21...♖f8-d8

How to continue the attack?

Exercise 3

position after 23...♔g8-h8

White is winning here, can you find the best move?

(solutions on page 250)

Carlsen's Way in the Bogo-Catalan

by Viacheslav Ikonnikov

1.	d4	♘f6
2.	c4	e6
3.	g3	d5
4.	♘f3	♗b4+
5.	♗d2	a5
6.	♗g2	dxc4

In this Survey I would like to analyse a new idea in this infrequently encountered version of the Catalan Opening, which is regularly employed by the World Champion, Magnus Carlsen. This line can be called a hybrid between the Bogo-Indian and the Catalan as it includes ideas from both openings. The initial position can also be reached via the proper Bogo-Indian move-order 1.d4 ♘f6 2.c4 e6 3.♘f3 ♗b4+ 4.♗d2 a5 5.g3 d5 (QI 1.4.15 – E11) instead of the more common 5...d6 or 5...b6. This was first played by Mark Taimanov in Wijk aan Zee 1981.
So, 4...♗b4+ in the Catalan prevents White's standard manoeuvre ♕a4+xc4 and the relatively rare move 5...a5 gives Black the opportunity to try and defend the extra pawn by ...b7-b5. The most popular here is Black's idea of holding the pawn by ...♗xd2 and ...b7-b5. Carlsen prefers the fastest development as an alternative.

Another frequently seen move-order, also used by Carlsen, is 4...dxc4 5.♗g2 and only now 5...♗b4+ 6.♗d2 a5. In the diagram position White has two methods of further development. It is worth noting that the most popular move here, 7.0-0, leads in the future to one of the above plans – with some differences.

The plan 7.♕c2

Here, 7...b6 is an attempt to stay away from the long forced variations that arise after 7...♗xd2+ 8.♕xd2. If we follow Carlsen's game against Ding Liren, Black could not fully equalize largely due to problems along the c-file. However, it is too early to give a final assessment without a detailed study of the acceptance of the pawn sacrifice 9...♕xd4.

Black should also be careful in the continuation 8.0-0 ♗b7 9.♗xb4 axb4 10.♕xc4 (see the game Blübaum-Santos Ruiz) where White can get an advantage by combining play against the b4-pawn with pressure on the c-file. Yet, as practice has shown, with the help of the important ...♘d5! manoeuvre, Black maintains the balance.

Alexandra Goryachkina

The best-studied continuation here is 7...♝xd2+ 8.♕xd2 followed by ...b7-b5. Given the opportunity, White has the manoeuvre ♕d2-g5 to restore material equality. An important point is the 13th move, where White has two options.

First, 13.♕xa5. Taking the a5-pawn makes it easiest for Black to achieve a balanced position. After several exchanges, we reach an equal endgame. The other continuation, 13.♕a4, leads to less exchanges and, accordingly, to a more complicated game. In principle, here too the game is equal, but nevertheless, according to the classical interpretation, Black has more pawn weaknesses, which offers White some extra chances.

The plan 7.a3

I think that Carlsen has demonstrated after 7.a3 ♝d6 8.♕a4+ that 8...♝d7 is an even clearer plan to equalize than the older move 8...♘c6. The extra factor of opposite-coloured bishops was seen in his game with Giri. The only drawback is that it is hard to intercept the initiative with black. Therefore, the plan to save the extra pawn with 7.a3 ♝xd2+ 8.♘bxd2 b5 is more popular with black players. As practice has shown, White has very good compensation for the pawn.

White's pressure along the c-file is great. Therefore, Anand's more abstract plan to prepare the ...e6-e5 break (14...♕b8, 15...♖e8) looks very interesting. In a recent game Kasimdzhanov v. Salem, Black came up with the novelty 14...♖c8, which would also be good in connection with a similar plan of preparing ...e6-e5, for example by 15...♕b6 (instead of the game's 15...♘b6), ...♝a8, ...♕b8 and later ...e6-e5.

The plan 7.0-0 0-0

After 7.0-0 0-0 the rare move 8.♘a3!? was tested by So in a recent game

He did not leave Carlsen any choice – he had to play 8...♗xa3 9.bxa3 b5 here, a plan which he usually avoided in other lines. The fact that it was impossible for White to effectively organize counterplay against the array of black pawns by b2-b3 worked in favour of this decision. This same fact obliges White to attack on the kingside. And White, who has an advantage in development, certainly has good chances to succeed in this. I think that the decisive moment was the choice of the wrong plan 12.g4?! (instead, for example, 12.♖e1 with the idea 13.♕c1). Two recent games in the line 7.0-0 0-0 8.♕c2 ♗xd2 9.♘bxd2 b5 (Rozum-Paravyan and Abasov-Piorun) have yielded new information and evaluations. Based on the analysis of these games, it turns out that this plan is less advantageous for White than the similar one in the variation with 7.a3, since here Black gets a reinforced square c3

for the knight. Moreover, the effect is amplified when the d4-pawn is weakened by White's push e2-e4-e5. As the analysis shows, Black could get an advantage by a timely execution of ...c6-c5.

Conclusion

In the variation with 7.a3 Black has no problems, but there is a choice between simple and reliable equalization and the double-edged plan of retaining the pawn. Also, the inclusion of 7.0-0 0-0 rather works in Black's favour. Instead, 7.♕c2 gives White the opportunity to win back the pawn by ♕c2xd2-g5, while after 7.0-0 0-0 8.♕c2 there is no such possibility. Regarding the option 7.♕c2 b6 from the Ding Liren-Carlsen game, it should be noted that White has a slight advantage, but still a more accurate evaluation can be given only after a detailed analysis of the acceptance of the pawn sacrifice.

The plan
7.♕c2 b6

Ding Liren 1
Magnus Carlsen
Lindores Abbey Prelim 2020 (3)
1.d4 ♘f6 2.c4 e6 3.g3 d5 4.♗g2 ♗b4+ 5.♗d2 a5 6.♘f3 dxc4 7.♕c2 b6

8.♘e5 8.0-0 ♗b7 9.♗xb4 axb4 10.♕xc4 is one of the unpleasant plans for Black here. The weakness of the b4-pawn and the pressure along the open c-file create certain problems, e.g. 10...♘c6 11.♘bd2

0-0 12.♖fc1 ♘d5!? (provoking 13.e4 ♘de7, after which the d4-pawn will become a target) 13.e3 ♕d7 14.♕e1 ♖a7 15.♘d3 ♖fa8 16.♘f3 ♘a5 (also possible is 16...♗a6 17.♕c2 ♗xd3 18.♕xd3 ♖xa2 19.♖xa2 ♖xa2 20.♕b3 (not 20.♕c4? ♖xb2 21.♕xc6 ♕xc6 22.♖xc6 b3 23.♖c1 ♖a2–+) 20...♖a7 21.♕c2 ♘ce7 22.♘e5∞ and White has compensation, but not more) 17.♕c2 ♘c6 18.♘fe5 ♘xe5 19.♘xe5 ♕e8?! (losing a pawn; better was 19...♕d8 20.♘c6 ♗xc6 21.♕xc6 g6=) 20.♕b3 h6 21.e4 ♘f6 22.♖xc7 ♗xe4 23.♖xa7 ♖xa7 24.♗xe4 ♘xe4 25.♕xb4± Blübaum-Santos Ruiz, Banter Blitz cup, Chess24. com 2019. 8.♕xc4 does not cause Black any problems: 8...♗a6 9.♕c2 c5 10.♘c3 ♘bd7 11.a3 ♗xc3 (11...♖c8!?) 12.♗xc3 ♖c8 13.0-0 (13.dxc5 ♘xc5 14.0-0 0-0 15.♗g5 ♘cd7 16.♖ad1 ♕e7=) 13...♘d5 14.♗d2 ♘xc3 15.bxc3 0-0 16.♖fe1

♕c7⇄, capturing the c-file after exchanging on d4, which gives Black good counterplay, Thybo-Svane, Riga 2019. **8...♖a7 9.0-0N** Again, interesting for White is 9.♗xb4!? axb4 10.♕xc4 ♕d6 (the typical defensive manoeuvre 10...♘d5!? 11.e4 ♘e7 was worthy of consideration, e.g. 12.♕xb4 ♘bc6 13.♘xc6 ♘xc6 14.♕b5 ♗b7 15.e5 (15.d5 exd5 16.exd5 0-0→) 15...♕a8⩲ and one of White's pawns, a2 or d4, will fall) 11.♘d3 (11.♕b5+ ♘fd7 12.♘d3 c5 13.dxc5 bxc5 14.♘d2 ♗a6 15.♕a4= Scheeren-F.Olafsson, Wijk aan Zee 1983) 11...♗a6!? (again 11...♘d5!? 12.0-0 (12.♗xd5 ♗a6!) 12...♗a6 13.♕c2 ♘c6 14.e3 0-0 15.♘d2 ♖fa8 16.♖fc1 ♗b5∞ would be good enough for Black) 12.♕xb4 ♗xd3 13.♕xd6 cxd6 14.exd3 d5 and Black still has to prove compensation for the pawn, Rozum-Khismatullin, Sochi ch-RUS 2017. **9...♗xd2!**

The most practical solution with limited time. Of course, it is dangerous to accept a 'gift' without a comprehensive analysis of the sacrifice: 9...♕xd4!? 10.♗f4 (10.♘xc4 ♗a6 11.a3 ♗xd2 12.♘bxd2 0-0∓) 10...♗d6 (10...♕d8 11.♘c3 0-0 12.♘b5±) 11.♖d1 (11.♘c3 ♗xe5 12.♘b5 ♕xb2 13.♕xb2 ♗xb2 14.♖ab1 c3 15.♘xa7 ♗a6∓) 11...♕c5 12.♖xd6 cxd6 13.♘xc4 ♗a6 14.♘bd2 ♗d7∞; 9...0-0 10.♖d1!±.
10.♕xd2 ♗b7 11.♗xb7 ♖xb7 12.♘xc4 ♘c6 13.♖d1 0-0 14.♘c3 ♕a8 15.d5!? White's position here is preferable because of Black's problems with the c-file. Perhaps Ding Liren should not have forced things, and should rather have continued to strengthen his position with 15.♖ac1 ♖d8 16.♗f4±. **15...exd5 16.♘xd5 ♘xd5 17.♕xd5 ♖bb8 18.♖ac1** This standard move loses all of White's advantage and allows Carlsen to ease his position by exchanging rooks. Stronger was 18.♘e3! with ideas of attacking the black king with ♕g5 and ♘f5, or exerting pressure on the c-file with ♕c4 and ♘d5. **18...♖fd8 19.♕e4 ♘b4 20.♖xd8+ ♖xd8 21.♕xa8 ♖xa8 22.a3 ♘a6 23.♖d1 ♘c5 24.f3 a4 25.♔f2 f6 26.g4 ♔f7 27.h4 ♔e6 28.h5 g6 29.♘e3 gxh5 30.gxh5 ♖g8?** This move is a mistake. Suddenly the black king gets caught in a mating net. It was interesting to take up an active position with the rook on b5: 30...♖a5!? 31.♖d8 (31.♘d5 ♘d3+ 32.♔xd3 ♖xd5 33.♖c3 ♔d6∓) 31...♖b5 32.♖h8 ♖xb2 33.♔g2∞. **31.♘d5 ♖g7 32.♘f4+ ♔e7** 32...♔e5?? 33.♖d5+ ♔xf4 34.e3#. **33.h6 ♖f7 34.♘d5+ ♔e6 35.♘f4+ ♔e7 36.e4 c6 37.♔e3 ♘d7 38.♘e2?!** Ding Liren, in turn, commits an inaccuracy and allows Black to free himself; 38.♘d3 ♘e5 39.f4±. **38...f5 39.♘d4 fxe4 40.fxe4 ♘e5 41.♘f5+ ♔f6 42.♖d6+ ♔g5 43.♔d4 ♔f4 44.♘g7 ♘f3+ 45.♔c3 ♘e5 46.♔d4 ♘f3+ 47.♔c3 ♘e5 48.♔d4 ½-½**

Santosh Gujrathi Vidit   **2**
Alan Pichot
Khanty-Mansiysk 2019 (1)
1.♘f3 d5 2.d4 ♘f6 3.c4 e6 4.g3 dxc4 5.♗g2 c6 6.a4 ♗b4+ 7.♗d2 a5 8.♕c2 ♗xd2+ 9.♕xd2 b5 10.axb5 cxb5 11.♕g5 White does not have this opportunity after both sides have castled first.
11...0-0 12.♕xb5 ♗a6 13.♕a4 Taking on a5 simplifies Black's task even more, e.g. 13.♕xa5 ♗b7 14.♕xd8 ♖xa1 15.♕xf8+ (forced, as the white queen does not have any good retreat squares) 15...♔xf8 16.0-0 ♖a2 17.♘e5 ♗a6 18.♖c1 (18.♘c3 does not change the character of the position either, e.g. 18...♖xb2 19.♖a1 ♖b3 20.♖c1 ♘bd7 21.♘c6 ♘b6 22.e4 ♗a3 23.f3 ♗a4= Meskovs-S.Pavlov, Voronezh 2019) 18...♖xb2 19.e3 ♘bd7 20.♘xd7+ ♘xd7 21.♘c3 ♖b3 22.♔f1 e5 23.♘e1 exd4 24.exd4 ♘f6= Ju Wenjun-P. Cramling, Lausanne 2020. **13...♕b6**

14.0-0 With the idea of exchanging his weak b2-pawn for the c4-pawn and then utilizing the optimal position of his pieces to win the a5-pawn. 14.♘bd2 has also been seen, e.g. 14...♗b5 (14...♕xb2?? 15.♖b1 ♕c3 16.0-0+−) 15.♕a2 ♖c8 (perhaps Black could have given his pieces more active positions by 15...♕a6!? 16.0-0 ♘c6 17.♖fc1 ♖fc8 18.♘b1 ♕b6∞) 16.0-0 ♘d5 17.♖fc1 ♘d7 18.♘e4 ♘7f6 19.♘c5!? (perhaps, in a position where Black's pawn weaknesses are compensated by the activity of his pieces, exchanging these pieces would have been to White's advantage: 19.♘xf6+ ♘xf6 20.♘d2 ♘d5 21.e3±) 19...♘d7 20.♘e4 (20.♘xd7!? ♗xd7 21.♘e5 ♗b5 22.e3±) 20...♘7f6= Sargsyan-Grachev, Moscow 2019. **14...♕xb2 15.♘bd2**

♗b5 16.♘xc4 ♗xa4 17.♘xb2 ♗b5! The correct solution. In case of the standard 17...♗c6 18.♖fc1 ♖d8 19.e3± Black will not be able to defend the a5-pawn. **18.♘e5 ♖a7 19.♘bc4** 19.♘f3 Kramnik-Topalov, Elista Wch m-1 2006 – YB/81-173; 19.♘bd3 Kir.Georgiev-Pavasovic, Valjevo 2007 – YB/95-158. **19...♘bd7** 19...♘fd7. **20.♘xa5 20.♖fc1. 20...♗xe2N** 20...♘xe5 21.dxe5 ♘d7 22.f4 ♗xe2 23.♖fe1 ♘h5 24.♘c6 ♖c8 25.♖ec1± Gusakov-Klimakovs, cr 2007. **21.♖fe1 ♘h5 22.♘ac6 ♖xa1?!** This only helps White to increase the pressure by ♖a7; 22...♖c7! 23.♖ec1 ♘b6=. **23.♖xa1 ♘xe5 24.dxe5 ♘d7 25.f4 ♖e8 26.♖a7 ♘c5 27.♔f2 ♔f8 28.♔e3 g6 29.g4 ♖c8 30.♘e7** Even stronger was 30.♘d4± with the threats f4-f5 and ♘d4-b5-d6. **30...♖d8 31.f5 exf5 32.gxf5 ♗h5?!** Now White could have played 33.♘d5!±. Black missed the opportunity to give perpetual check: 32...♖d3+ 33.♔f2 ♖d2+ 34.♔f1 ♖d1+ 35.♔e2 ♗h5+= ... **1-0 (43)**

The plan
7.a3 ♗d6

Anish Giri   **3**
Magnus Carlsen
Carlsen Invitational Prelim 2020 (5.1)
1.d4 d5 2.♘f3 ♘f6 3.c4 e6 4.g3 dxc4 5.♗g2 ♗b4+ 6.♗d2 a5 7.a3 ♗d6 8.♕a4+

8...♗d7N A novelty by Carlsen. Though this manoeuvre is widespread in the Catalan, this move hadn't been seen so far in this position. The 'old' plan is also good: 8...♘c6 9.0-0 (9.♕xc4 0-0 10.♗c3 ♕e8 (preparing ...e6-e5 anyway) 11.♘e5 ♘d5 12.♘xc6

---

bxc6 13.♕d3 ♗a6 14.♕c2 c5 15.dxc5 ♗xc5 16.0-0 (entering the complications also leads to equality: 16.♗xg7 ♗xf2+ 17.♔xf2 ♔xg7 18.♘d2 ♕e7 19.♖he1 ♕f6+ 20.♘f3 ♖ab8⇄) 16...♗b6= Wojtaszek-Korobov, Batumi Ech 2018) 9...0-0 10.♕xc4 e5 11.dxe5 (or 11.d5 ♗e7 12.♘c3 h6=) 11...♘xe5 12.♘xe5 ♗xe5 13.♕c2 c6 14.♗c3 ♕e7 15.♖d1 ♖e8 16.♗xe5 ♕xe5 17.♘c3 ♗e6= Fedoseev-Shankland, Danzhou 2018. **9.♕xc4 ♗c6 10.♗g5 ♘bd7 11.0-0 0-0 12.♘c3 h6 13.♗xf6 ♘xf6 14.♖fe1 ♗d5** Black has already planned the exchange on f3, but first prevents the white queen moving to b3 with pressure on the b7-pawn. Also possible was 14...♘e4 15.♖ac1 ♘xc3 16.♕xc3 ♗e4 17.♘d2 ♗xg2 18.♔xg2 c6=. **15.♕d3 ♗xf3 16.♗xf3 c6 17.♕c2 ♕e7 18.♖ed1 ♖fd8 19.♖ac1 g6** Magnus takes his time with ...e6-e5 and first places his pawns favourably. **20.e3 ♔g7 21.♗g2 h5 22.h4 ♖ac8 23.♕a4 ♗c7 24.♕b3 ♖b8 25.♖c2 e5 26.dxe5** 26.d5 offers White nothing, e.g. 26...e4 27.♗e2 c5=. **26...♗xe5= ... ½-½ (41)**

AR Saleh Salem 4
Rustam Kasimdzhanov
Sharjah 2020 (8)

1.d4 ♘f6 2.c4 e6 3.♘f3 d5 4.g3 ♗b4+ 5.♗d2 a5 6.♗g2 0-0 7.0-0 dxc4 8.a3 ♗xd2 9.♘bxd2 b5 10.b3 cxb3 11.♕xb3 c6 12.♖fc1 ♗b7 13.♕b2 ♘bd7

14.♘e1 14.♘b3 leads to main positions by a transposition of moves: 14...♕b6 15.♘e1 a4 16.♘c5 ♘xc5 17.dxc5? (a terrible mistake, now the c5-pawn also becomes weak; 17.♖xc5∞) 17...♕c7 18.♘c2

♖ad8 19.♖d1 ♖xd1+ 20.♖xd1 ♖d8 21.♕c1 ♖xd1+ 22.♕xd1 ♕e7–+ Bosiocic-Santos Ruiz, Moscow Wch blitz 2019.**14...♖c8** 14...♕b8!? returns the extra pawn but gets rid of his bad bishop, e.g. 15.♘d3 (15.♗xc6 ♗xc6 16.♖xc6 ♕b7 17.♖ac1 ♖fc8 18.♕c3 ♖xc6 19.♕xc6 ♕xc6 20.♖xc6 ♔f8=, gradually consolidating his position and obtaining a distant passed pawn in the endgame) 15...♖e8 16.♘b3 ♘d5 17.♘bc5 ♘xc5 18.♘xc5 ♕a7. The strong pressure of White's pieces on the queenside does not allow Black to realize the extra pawn, so Anand prepares a distracting manoeuvre: 19.♖c2 ♖ad8 20.♖ac1 ♗a8 21.♘d3 f6 (preparing ...e6-e5) 22.♘c5?! (obstructing the c-file and only helping Black to carry through ...e6-e5; 22.♖c5!) 22...♘b6! 23.♕c3 e5 24.dxe5 ♘c4 25.♘d3 fxe5 26.♘b2 ♘xb2 27.♕xb2 e4∓ Blübaum-Anand, Germany Bundesliga 2018/19; 14...♕b6 15.♘d3 ♖fc8 (15...♖ac8 – note to move) 16.♘b3 ♗a6 17.♘bc5 ♘xc5 18.♘xc5 Goryachkina-Pogonina, Chita 2015; 14...e5 15.♗xc6 ♗xc6 16.♖xc6 exd4 17.♘df3 ♖b8 18.♘d3 Deac-Bilguun, Changsha 2019; 14...♕b6 15.♗xc6 ♗xc6 16.♖xc6 Giri-Fridman, Rosmalen 2014. **15.♘d3 ♘b6?!** Moving in the wrong direction; the black knight has nothing to do on b6. 15...♕b6!? (with the idea ...♗a8, ...♕b8, ...♖e8 and ...e6-e5) 16.♘b3 ♖fd8 (16...♕a7 17.♕d2 a4 18.♘bc5 ♗a8 19.e4 ♖fd8 20.e5 ♘xc5 21.♘xc5 ♘d7 22.♕e3 ♘xc5 23.♖xc5 ♕e7 24.♕c3♔ ½-½ (42) Goryachkina-Osmak, Mamaia 2016; 16...a4 17.♘bc5 ♘xc5 18.♘xc5 ♖fd8 19.e3 ♕a7 20.♖c2 ♗a8 21.♖ac1 ♘d5 22.♘d3 ♖c7 23.♖c5♔ 1-0 (32) D.Horvath-Subelj, Radenci 2019) 17.♕c3 ♖a8 18.e4 ♖dc8 19.♕d2 ♖d8 20.♕c3 ♖dc8 21.♖ab1 h6 22.h3♔ ½-½ Goryachkina-Airapetian, Sochi tt-2 2018. **16.♘c5 16.a4! b4 17.♘c5± Craciuneanu-E.Jensen, cr 2015. 16...♗a8 17.e3 ♕e7 18.♕c3** 18.a4! b4 19.♘db3 ♕a7 20.♕e2± and it is not easy for Black to

defend the a5-pawn. **18...♕a7 19.♘db3 a4 20.♘d2 ♖fd8 21.♖ab1 h6 22.h3 ♘bd7 23.♘de4 ♘xe4 24.♗xe4 ♘xc5 25.♕xc5 ♕xc5 26.♖xc5 ♗b7 27.h4** Even after the exchange of the two knight pairs and the queens, which in itself is to Black's advantage, White has sufficient compensation for the pawn. **27...♔f8 28.g4 ♗e7 29.f4 ♔d6 30.♔f2 f6 31.h5 ♖e8 32.♔f3?** It was necessary to protect the rook, to be able to take the pawn on e5 with the d-pawn, e.g. 32.♖bc1 e5 33.dxe5+ fxe5 34.♔f3 exf4 35.exf4. **32...e5 33.♗f5 exd4** Now White has a weak pawn on d4. **34.exd4 ♖c7 35.♗g6 ♖ee7 36.♖bc1 ♗c8 37.♖1c3** 37.♗f5 ♗xf5 38.♖xf5 (after 38.gxf5 White will be in zugzwang and will have to allow either ...♔d5 or ...♖e1) 38...♖e6 39.♖fc5 ♔d7∓. **37...♗e6** Now the game is over ... **0-1 (56)**

Wesley So 5
Magnus Carlsen
Lindores Abbey Final 8 2020 (1.23)

1.♘f3 d5 2.d4 ♘f6 3.c4 e6 4.g3 dxc4 5.♗g2 ♗b4+ 6.♗d2 a5 7.0-0 0-0 8.♘a3 A very rare plan. More common here is 8.♕c2 – Game 6. **8...♗xa3 9.bxa3 b5 10.♕b1**

10...c6 Strangely, this logical move is new. Previously, only 10...♗a6 had been seen. **11.e4** Unambiguously threatening 12.e5 and 13.♘g5. **11...h6 12.g4?!** Suddenly, too sharp. It was worth considering 12.♖e1 and 13.♕c1 with the idea of attacking the

black king by ♗h6 and e4-e5, ♖e4, while Black's pieces are stuck on the queenside. **12...♘h7 13.h4** Too optimistic; better was 13.♖d1!?. **13...e5!** Of course; making space for his bishop and other pieces. **14.♘xe5** If 14.d5 ♖e8 15.g5 hxg5 16.hxg5 ♘f8∓ and White's attack stops. **14...♕xd4 15.♗f4 ♖e8 16.♕c1 ♕c5** Of course not 16...♖xe5? 17.♖d1±. **17.♖d1 ♘a6** Even stronger was 17...♘f8! with two threats: 18...♖xe5 and 18...f6 followed by 19...♗xg4. **18.♘xc6 ♕xc6 19.e5 ♕c5 20.♗xa8 ♗xg4 21.♗e3 ♕xe5 22.♖d4 ♘f6** White has managed to win the exchange, but Black has two pawns for it, plus a strong passed pawn on c4. **23.♗c6 ♖e6?** Carlsen misses the hidden threat of a queen exchange, which is not surprising with limited time; 23...♖b8∓. **24.♗g2?** The same thing happens with So; 24.♗b2! ♕c7 25.♖d8+ ♔h7 26.♕xe5 ♖xe5 27.a4 b4 28.♗f4 ♖c5 29.♗xc7 ♖xc6 30.♗xa5 ♗f3∞. **24...♕c5 25.♕c3 ♔h7 26.♕xa5 ♘d3?** It was even better to move the rook to g6, starting with 26...♖fe4!–+. **27.♖b1 ♕f5 28.♖xb5 ♕g6 29.♕a8?!** 29.♔h2=. **29...♘e5?!** 29...♖e8 30.♖b8 ♗f3∓. **30.♖d8 ♗e8?** 30...♕c2 31.♖h8+ ♔g6=. **31.♖xe8??** 31.♔h1±. **31...♖xe8 32.♕xe8 ♘f3+ 33.♔h1 ♕d3 34.♗d2 ♕xd2 0-1**

Ivan Rozum   **6**
David Paravyan
Titled Tuesday Online 2020 (5)
1.d4 ♘f6 2.♘f3 d5 3.c4 e6 4.g3 ♗b4+ 5.♗d2 a5 6.♗g2 0-0 7.0-0 dxc4 8.♕c2 8.♗g5; 8.a3 – Game 4. **8...♗xd2 9.♘bxd2 b5 10.a4 c6 11.b3** 11.e4 ♘a6 12.b3 (12.e5) 12...♘b4 13.♕c3 cxb3 14.♖xb3 ♗a6 Nepomniachtchi-Carlsen, Legends of Chess Online 2020, **11...cxb3 12.♘xb3**

12...b4 12...♗a6; 12...♘d5. **13.♘e5** 13.e4 ♘bd7 14.h4 (14.♕xc6; 14.♖fd1) 14...h6 15.e5?! (a serious inaccuracy. Now the black knight gains access to c3; 15.♖fd1!?) 15...♘d5 16.♘fd2 ♗a6 (good now was 16...c5!? 17.dxc5 (17.♘xc5 ♖xc5 18.dxc5 ♕b7 19.♘c4 ♕c7 20.♘d6 ♗c6∓) 17...♘xe5 18.♖fe1 ♘c6 19.♘c4 ♗d7 20.♖ad1 ♕c7 and Black's chances are not worse? 17.♖fe1 ♘c3?! (allowing White to exchange this strong knight; 17...♖c8! 18.e4 c5 19.♘bxc5 ♘xc5 20.dxc5 ♘c3∓) 18.♘e4 ♘xe4 19.♗xe4 ♖c8 20.♖ac1 ♖e8 21.♕d2?!

(provoking ...c6-c5; it was better to prepare a strengthening of the centre by f2-f4, e.g. 21.♔h2!? ♕b6 22.f4∞) 21...c5! 22.dxc5 ♘xe5 23.♕f4?! (23.♗d6!∞) 23...d3 24.♗xd3 ♖xd3 25.♖cd1?! (25.♕e5 f6 26.♕e3=) 25...♕d5∓ Abasov-Piorun, Khanty-Mansiysk 2019. **13...♘d5 14.e4?** If White wants to push e2-e4, he should do it before ...♘d5 has been played. Now the black knight lands on c3, restricting White; 14.e3∞. **14...♘c3 15.♖fe1 ♗b7?!** Clearly better was 15...c5! 16.dxc5 ♗a6∓ followed by ...f7-f6 and ...e6-e5; or 15...♗a6 16.♕d2 f6 17.♘f3 ♘d7∓. **16.♘c4 ♘d7?!** Missing a tactical refutation of the capture on a5: 16...♗a6! 17.♘cxa5 e5! 18.dxe5 c5∓. **17.e5 ♕c7 18.♘d6 ♖a7 19.♘c5 ♗a8 20.h4 ♕b6 21.♘de4 ♘xe4 22.♗xe4 h6 23.♖ac1 ♖d8** The game is approximately equal; White has sufficient compensation for the pawn. **24.♕b2 ♖c7** Introducing an unnecessary regrouping. Simply good was 24...♘xc5 25.dxc5 ♕c7 26.♖ed1 ♖d5!∞. **25.♗b1 ♕b8 26.♕c2 ♘f8 27.♘a6 ♕b6 28.♘xc7 ♕xc7 29.♕c5 ♖d5 30.♕c4 ♕d8 31.♖ed1 c5 32.♗e4 ♖xd4 33.♖xd4 cxd4 34.♗xa8 ♕xa8 35.♕xd4 h5 36.♖c5 ♘g6 37.♕c4 ♔h7 38.♕e2 ♕d8 39.♕xh5+ ♔g8 40.♕f3 ♘e7 41.♖b5 ♘d5 42.♕d3 ♕c7 43.♕d2?** 43.♕d4+−. **43...♘c3!= ...** **0-1 (81)**

Exercise 1

position after 9.0-0

How can Black circumvent complications and simplify? (*solutions on page 250*)

Exercise 2

position after 15.♕c4-d3

White's threat is 16.e4. Give a simple method of defence.

Exercise 3

position after 13.h2-h4

How can Black start a counter-attack?

The specialist and the holes

by Nikolai Ninov

1.	d4	♘f6
2.	c4	e6
3.	g3	d5
4.	♗g2	♗e7
5.	♘f3	0-0
6.	0-0	dxc4
7.	♕c2	b5
8.	a4	b4
9.	♘fd2	♘d5
10.	♘xc4	c5
11.	dxc5	♗a6

The afternoon of the 4th of July – on chesspro.ru Alexey Korotylev had initially chosen to cover another game than Ding Liren-Carlsen, with short observations of the rest. Perhaps unaware of what the clocks were indicating, his first

Liam Vrolijk

impression from the top-level clash was: 'Carlsen has prepared a line with not just one, but many holes' with the last sentence being 'But for the moment his pieces are successfully covering them.' In fact, a new chapter in the theory had just been opened and the opinion of the commentator naturally changed as soon as his attention turned entirely to the real blockbuster in Zagreb.

Bulgarian school

At the start of the previous decade, the Catalan gained enormously in popularity. The profound works of Avrukh and Bologan had a lot to do with this. Black had to find antidotes and, besides Bukavshin's 7...b6, the riskier 7...b5!? became a frequent guest in practice. According to the databases, it was used for the first time in Benderev-Bardarov, ch-BUL 1947; also the trap 8.a4 c6?! 9.axb5 cxb5 10.♘g5 became famous since then. In the 2010's, several Bulgarian grandmasters – Vladimir Georgiev and his close friends Petkov, Rusev and Arnaudov – made significant new contributions to the line. All these developments were covered by Scherbakov in Yearbook 104.

White desired to prove an advantage after 8...b4 and Bruzon's Survey in Yearbook 125, accompanied by Vigorito's contribution in Yearbook 126, established 9.♘fd2 as the main weapon. For some strange reason it almost disappeared from the scene during the next few years, until 2019, the FIDE Grand Prix in Moscow. After two comfortable draws against 9.♘bd2 in the earlier stages,

Nakamura lost painfully to Grischuk in the semifinals. It looked like 9.♘fd2 had put an end to the fairytale of 7...b5. One month later Carlsen came up with his revolutionary concept of 9...♘d5 10.♘xc4 c5 11.dxc5 ♗a6!.

Analogies

Too many holes? That assumption reminded me of the workers' slogan 'We are plugging up all kinds of gaps!' in the classic Bulgarian comedy *The all-round specialist* with Apostol Karamitev as a dentist graduate who, in order to prolong his stay in the capital, tries various liberal jobs, always with amusing failures. Unlike him, our World Champion is known to be good in many other sports, but he has no need to switch to any of them. Against Ding Liren, Magnus exerted pressure, avoiding several drawish continuations, and scored one of his finest wins. Sielecki wrote: 'this is a fascinating line and great preparation', see Yearbook 133-173. However, it deserved more than an appearance in a book presenting a repertoire for the first player.

Ideas for White

A dozen of games followed the new plan, and White players tried different approaches:

1) The double fianchetto – this set-up has the drawback of weakening the c3-square, which quickly caused big trouble for White in Cordova-Riazantsev (Game 2);

2) Chasing the knight – the advance of the e-pawn to e5 did not bring anything positive in Blübaum-Kuzubov (Game 3). A better version of the plan with b2-b3 was seen in Tsolakidou-Solozhenkina (see analysis in Cordova-Riazantsev),

but White was successful only due to a tactical mistake;

3) Mixing these plans – De Jong-Vrolijk (Game 4) saw 12.♘bd2 ♘d7 at first, but 13.c6 (good in itself as ...♖c8 is not possible) 13...♘c5 14.e4, combined with 16.b3, turned out to favour Black;

4) The real challenge – 14.♘b3!, see Ernst-Vrolijk (Game 5);

5) The 2019 main line (12.♘e3) – it was quickly discovered that 16.c7?!, as in Ding Liren-Carlsen (Game 1), deprives White of any hope for an advantage and he should play 16.♖d1!. Now:

A) 16...♗c4 was not mentioned by Sielecki, but 17.♘d2! ♗xe2 18.♘b3! ♗xd1 19.♖xd1 sets problems for Black. He remains on the defensive side after returning the exchange with 19...♕b6, while 19...♘xb3 can be met by the strong novelty 20.c7!;

B) 16...d4 17.h4 is the recommendation in the book. In Gelfand-Deac (Game 6), 17...♖e8 was played, which does not look like a prepared novelty, since soon after Black made a decisive mistake with 20...♘d3?. On the contrary, the Israeli expert knew well what to do, playing the subtle 20.♖dc1!. Black had to give an exchange for the c-pawn (which is also possible on move 19) and hope for compensation, even though the opponent already had a perfect blockading piece in front of the passed d-pawn.

Sielecki continues with 17...h6 18.♗f3 ♖e8 19.♘d2 d3 20.exd3 ♗xd3 21.♕c1 ♗f8 22.♖e1. Here 22....♕f6! is indisputably the best reply and seems to yield sufficient counterplay.

Conclusion

16.♖d1 is undoubtedly testing, but Black's activity may counterbalance the pawn after 17....h6 or the exchange sacrifice on move 19 or 20 in the line with 17....♖e8. It is also possible to bring the rook to

d1 earlier, intending to capture on d5 with it after exchanging the centralized knight. Once again, Black gets a long-term initiative.

Paradoxically, White's best options are found in games lost by the first player. The knight manoeuvre to b3 seems to offer the best chances for an edge, see Ernst-Vrolijk for the various options on the next move.

For the moment the holes are plugged; more practical examples are needed.

Main game

Ding Liren   1
Magnus Carlsen
Zagreb 2019 (8)
**1.d4 ♘f6 2.c4 e6 3.♘f3 d5
4.g3 ♗e7** I had been scoring very well with the adventurous 4...dxc4 5.♗g2 b5, often from dubious positions. Crucial was my encounter from the Bulgarian team championship in 2010 with Kiril Georgiev, who unleashed Avrukh's recommendation 6.a4 c6 7.axb5 cxb5 8.♘e5 ♘d5 9.♘c3 ♗b4 10.0-0 ♗xc3 11.e4 ♗xb2 12.♗xb2 ♘e7 13.♘xf7! ♔xf7 14.♕h5+ ♔g8 15.♕xb5↑ ♘d7 16.♕xc4 ♕b6 17.♘c3 a5 18.♖fb1 ♕c6 19.♕d3 ♗a6 20.♕d2 ♗c4 21.d5!! (a shocking breakthrough with 5(!) defending pieces) 21...exd5? (White's advantage is unquestionable after the better 21...♘xd5 22.exd5 ♗xd5 23.♗xd5 ♕xd5 24.♕b2) 22.exd5 ♘xd5 23.♕g5 (the beautiful geometrical blow 23.♖a4!!, here or on the next move, was winning on the spot) 23...g6 24.♖d1 h6 25.♗xd5+ ♗xd5 26.♕xd5+ ♕xd5 27.♖xd5 ♖h7 28.♖dxa5 ♖xa5 29.♖xa5 ♖e7 and even though I managed to save this ending and keep my unbeatable record with this variation, it had to be abandoned and for me facing the Catalan was no more fun. **5.♗g2 0-0 6.0-0 dxc4 7.♕c2 b5 8.a4 b4**

9.♘fd2 ♘d5! The regular choice 9...c6 10.♘xc4 ♕d4 wins a pawn, but leaves Black suffering for a long time. The last game at the highest level confirmed this: 11.♖d1 ♕c5 12.♗e3 ♕h5 13.♘bd2 ♘g4 14.♗f3 ♘xe3 15.♘xe3 a5 16.♘d4 (Sielecki's line in YB 133 ended with 16.♘c4≌) 16...♗a6 17.♖ac1 ♖c8 18.♗f3 when 18...♕e5 (18...♕g6 was played, but Black soon succumbed under the pressure in Grischuk-Nakamura, Moscow 2019) 19.♘g4 ♕c7 20.♕b3 ♖a7 21.♗e4! was just part of Grischuk's deep preparation. **10.♘xc4 c5 11.dxc5 ♗a6! 12.♘e3 ♘d7 13.♘xd5 exd5 14.c6 ♖c8**

15.♗f4!
 A) 15.♗xd5 ♘e5 'will win the c6-pawn with active play' – Sielecki in YB 133. In spite of the extra pawn(s) White has to fight for a draw: the main line is 16.♖d1 (a loss of time is 16.♗e4?! ♘xc6! 17.♗xc6 ♗b7 18.♗d1 ♖xc6 19.♖xd8 ♖xc2 20.♖xf8+ ♔xf8 21.♘d2 g5 22.f4 ♗f6∓/–+) 16...♘xc6! and now 17.♗xf7+! (White's position is terrible after

17.♗xc6? ♖xc6 18.♖xd8 ♖xc2 19.♖xf8+ ♔xf8 20.♘d2 ♗f6)
17...♖xf7 18.♖xd8+ ♗xd8 19.♕d1 ♘d4! 20.♗e3 ♘xe2+ 21.♔g2 and the thrilling battle peters out to a draw: 21...♗b6!? (21...♗b7+ 22.♔f1 ♗a6 23.♔g2 ♗b7+=) 22.♘d2 ♗b7+ 23.f3 ♗xe3 24.♕xe2 ♖c2 25.♕xe3 ♖xf3 26.♕e6+ ♖f7+ 27.♔g1 ♖xd2 28.♕e8+ ♖f8 29.♕e6+ ♔h8 30.♕e7 ♖g2+ 31.♔h1 ♖b8 32.♖f1 ♖f2+ 33.♔g1 ♖g2+=;
 B) For 15.♖d1 ♘e5 16.♖xd5 (16.♗xd5 ♘xc6! transposes to the line above) 16...♖xc6 17.♕d1 see the note C1 to Cordova-Riazantsev.
15...♘c5 16.c7?! The acid test for Black is 16.♖d1, see Gelfand-Deac.
16...♕d7 17.♘d2 One move later 17.♖d1 lacks venom – Black is absolutely fine after 17...d4! 18.h4 ♘e6! 19.♗e5 (19.♗h3 ♕d5 20.♘d2 (20.♗g2 ♕a5!) 20...♘xf4 21.gxf4 d3 22.exd3 ♗b7 23.♘e4 f5 24.♖ac1 ♗d6 25.♕c4 ♗xf4; 19.♗c6?! d3! (19...♖xc7 20.♗xc7 ♕xc7≌) 20.exd3 ♕d4 21.♗e3 ♕g4↑ △ 22.♘d2 ♖xc7 23.d4 ♘xd4 24.♕e4?! ♗e2! 25.♖e1 ♘xc6 26.♗f4 ♖d7 27.♕xe2 ♕xe2 28.♖xe2 ♘d4 29.♖e4 f5–+) 19...♗d6! 20.♗xd4 ♖xc7 21.♕d2 ♘xd4 22.♕xd4 ♖d8! 23.♕e4 ♖c4 24.♕f3 ♖c2 25.♘d2 ♖xb2 26.e3 ♕e8∓. **17...g5!** Much stronger than 17...♗xe2 18.♖fe1 ♗d3 19.♕d1 which transposes to 16.♖d1 ♗c4 17.♘d2 ♗xe2 18.c7 ♕d7 19.♖e1 ♗d3 20.♕d1 – see the notes to Gelfand-Deac. **18.♗e5 f6 19.♗d4**

♖xc7 20.♕d1 A later try featured the direct 20.♘b3 ♘xb3 (20...♗e6 with a probable transposition, since 21.♕f5 can be effectively met by 21...♘f4!) 21.♖xb3 ♗e2 22.♗xd5+ ♔g7 23.♖fe1 ♖d8! (the ultimate equalizer) 24.♗e6 ♕xd4 25.♖xe2 ♕d3 26.♖ae1 ♗c5 27.♔g2 ♕xb3 28.♗xb3 ♖dd7 29.♗e6 ♖e7 30.♖e4 ♗d6 31.♖1e2 a5 32.b3 ½-½ Cheparinov-Deac, Douglas 2019. **20...♗e6 21.♘b3 ♗c4 22.♘a5** 22.♗e3 d4 23.♘xd4 ♗xd4 24.♕xd4 ♕xd4 25.♗xd4 ♖d8 26.♗e3 ♗xe2=. **22...♘xd4** As usual, Carlsen creates practical problems without taking too much risk. 22...♗xe2 23.♕xe2 ♘xd4 24.♕d3 ♗c5 25.♘b3 ♘xb3 26.♗xd5+ ♔g7 27.♕xb3. **23.♕xd4 ♗g7 24.♖fc1 ♗xe2 25.♖xc7 ♕xc7 26.♖e1** Probably safer was 26.♕xd5 ♖d8 27.♕e4, relying on the jump to c6. Further simplifications are possible: 27...♖d1+ 28.♖xd1 ♗xd1 29.♘c6 ♗c5 30.♘xb4 (30.♘d4 ♗xd4 31.♕xd4 ♗xa4 32.h4 h6 33.♕xb4 ♗e8=) 30...♗xa4 31.♘d3 ♗b5 32.♘xc5 ♕xc5=. **26...♗c5 27.♕xd5 ♖e8 28.♕b7?!** Missing his last chance to secure the c6-square for the knight: 28.♕c6! ♕xc6 29.♘xc6. **28...♕xb7 29.♘xb7 ♗f8 30.♗c6 ♖e7** Black's pair of bishops is gaining in importance with each move and the coming trade of rooks will just contribute to that tendency. **31.f3** Or 31.♘d6 ♗g4 32.♖xe7+ ♗xe7 33.♘c4 ♗e6 34.♘e3 ♗c5 35.♔f1 f5, expanding like in the game. The rest of it is so aesthetic that we will play on and enjoy Carlsen's supreme technique! **31...♗c4 32.♖xe7+ ♗xe7 33.♔f2 f5 34.♗e3 ♗g8 35.♔d3 g4 36.♘a5 ♗c5 37.♘c4 ♗g1 38.♘e3 ♗e6 39.fxg4 fxg4 40.♔e2 h5 41.♗d5 ♗d7 42.♗b3 ♗xh2 43.♔f2 h4 44.gxh4 ♗e5 45.♘c4 g3+ 46.♔g1 ♗f4 47.♘d1 ♗c6 48.b3 ♔h6 49.a5 ♗e4 50.♔f1 ♔g7 51.♔g1 ♗f6 52.♔f1 ♔e6 53.h5 ♔d5 54.a6 ♔d4 55.♗g4 ♔c3 56.♗e6 ♗c2 57.♘a5 ♗c7 58.♘b7 ♗d3+ 59.♔g1 ♗xa6**

0-1 A fantastic performance by the World Champion from the very beginning! His endgame masterpiece could have been crowned by a picturesque mate: 59...♗e4 60.♗h3 ♗b6+ 61.♔f1 ♔d2! 62.♘d6 g2+ 63.♔xg2 ♗d3#.

Ideas for White

Emilio Cordova   **2**
Alexander Riazantsev
Moscow 2020 (4)

1.♘f3 d5 2.d4 ♘f6 3.c4 e6 4.g3 ♗e7 5.♗g2 0-0 6.0-0 dxc4 7.♕c2 b5 8.a4 b4 9.♘fd2 ♘d5 10.♘xc4 c5 11.dxc5 ♗a6 12.♖d1 ♘d7

13.b3

A) More than risky is 13.♗xd5 exd5 14.♖xd5 when Black's simplest is 14...♗xc5 15.♗f4 (15.♘bd2 ♗b7 16.♖h5 g6 17.♖h4 ♕f6 18.♖f4 ♕c6 19.♘f3 ♖fe8↑) 15...♗c8! 16.♘bd2 ♗b7 17.♖d3 ♘f6 18.♗e3 △ 18...♕h3 19.f3 ♘g4 20.♘f1 ♘xe3 21.♘fxe3 ♗a6 22.♔h1 ♖ac8 23.b3 ♖c6;

B) 13.e4 ♘5f6 (we are going to see more of 13...♘b3 in reply to e2-e4. Here it is playable, though not necessary: 14.♕e2 ♘b4 (somewhat late is 14...♘5f6 15.♘c3 ♗xc4 △ 16.♕xc4 ♗xc5 17.e5 ♕c7 18.♗e3 ♕xe5 19.♕xe5 ♘xe5 20.♗xa8 ♖xa8 21.♔g2) 15.♘ba3 ♗xc5 16.♘b5 ♘c2 17.♖b1 ♗xb5 18.axb5 ♘d4 19.♕d3 e5 20.♗e3 ♕f6 21.♘a5 ♗b6 22.♘xb3 ♗c5 23.♘xc5 ♗xc5♕):

B1) 14.e5 ♘d5 15.♗e3 ♖c8! 16.♘xd5 exd5 with rich counter-play, as shown by 17.♗f4 (17.c6?! ♘xe5 18.♗xd5 ♘xc6 can be achieved via 13.c6 with the e-pawn still on its initial square – its absence is felt at once in the line

19.♗xf7+ ♖xf7 20.♖xd8+ ♗xd8 21.♕d1 ♘d4 22.♗e3 ♘f3+ △ 23.♔g2 ♗b7 24.♔h3 ♗g5! with a decisive attack; for 17.♗xd5 see Exercise 2) 17...♘xc5 18.♖xd5 ♗b6 (18...♗e6 19.♕d1 ♕c7♕) 19.♗e3 ♗b7 20.♖d1 ♗xg2 21.♔xg2 ♗c6+ 22.♔g1 ♕e6 23.♘d2 ♕xe5 24.♘f3 ♕f6 25.♘d4 ♖fd8 26.♖ac1 g6=;

B2) 14.c6 ♖c8 15.♘d6 ♗xd6 16.♖xd6 ♕c7⇄;

B3) 14.♗e3 ♕c7 15.e5 ♘d5 16.♗d4 ♗xc5! 17.♗xd5 exd5 18.♘e3 ♖ac8 19.♗xc5 (after 19.♘xd5 ♕b7 20.♕e4 ♖fe8! White's centre will be destroyed as well) 19...♘xc5 20.f4 ♕b6 21.a5 ♕e6 22.♘xd5 ♗d3 23.♖xd3 ♘xd3 24.♕xd3 ♖fd8–+;

B4) 14.♘d6 ♕c7 15.e5 ♘d5 16.♗xd5 (16.♘f5?! ♗xc5! 17.♗xd5 ♖ac8! (17...exd5 18.♘e7+ ♔h8 19.♗e3) 18.♗f4 exd5 with a dangerous initiative) 16...exd5 17.♗f4 (17.♖xd5? ♘xe5!) 17...♕xc5 18.♕f5! ♖ad8 19.♘d2 g6 (equivalent to a draw offer is 19...♘xe5 20.♗xe5 ♗xd6 21.♗xg7 ♔xg7 22.♕g5+) 20.♕g4 ♘xe5 21.♗xe5 ♗xd6 22.♖ac1 ♕b6 23.♗xd6 ♖xd6 24.♘b3 and here the blockade on d4 and the closest dark squares levels out the d-pawn;

B5) 14.b3?! ♗xc5 15.♗e3 ♗xc4! 16.♕xc4 (16.♗xc5 ♗xb3!) 16...♗xe3 17.fxe3 (Esipenko-Thai Dai Van Nguyen, Tallinn rapid 2019). From this moment on Black started losing the thread of the game; he could have established firm control over the key e5-square in many ways, e.g. 17...♘g4, 17...♕b8, 17...♕e7 or first the solid 17...a5.

C) 13.c6 ♖c8 14.♘e3 (14.e4 ♖xc6) 14...♘e5! and now:

C1) 15.♘xd5 exd5 16.♖xd5 (for 16.♗xd5 ♘xc6! see the notes to

Ding Liren-Carlsen) 16...♖xc6 17.♕d1 ♕c8 (the alternative 17...♖d6 18.♖xd6 ♕xd6 19.♕xd6 ♗xd6 allows 20.♗f4! ♗xe2 21.♘d2±) 18.♘d2 ♖c5! (the most active enemy piece should be eliminated; White will once again be happy to return the pawn for a more active position after 18...♗xe2 19.♕xe2 ♖xc1+ 20.♖xc1 ♕xc1+ 21.♘f1 ♕g6 22.♖d1 ♕c5 23.♘e3). Black has plenty of compensation;

  C2) 15.♕e4 ♘xc6 16.♘xd5 exd5 17.♖xd5 and Black has to find 17...♕xd5! (17...♕b6?! 18.♗e3 ♕b7 19.♘d2 ♗xe2 20.♖c1±) 18.♕xd5 ♖fd8 19.♘c3 (19.♕xd8+ ♘xd8 20.♘d2 ♘e6↑ 21.e3?! ♘c5) 19...bxc3 20.♕e4 ♖d1+ 21.♗f1 ♘d4! 22.bxc3 (22.♕xe7?! ♗xe2 23.bxc3 ♖xf1+ 24.♔g2 ♖e1!; 22.♔g2?! ♘b3 23.♕xe7 ♘xa1 24.bxc3 ♖xc1 25.♕xa7 ♘c4 26.♕b7 ♗e6−+) 22...♘xe2+ 23.♔g2 ♖xf1 24.♕xe7 ♖g1+ 25.♔h3 ♘xc1 26.♕e3 ♘e2 27.♖xg1 ♘xg1+ 28.♔g2 ♘e2 29.♕xa7 ♘c4 30.♕b7 ♗e6 31.a5 ♘xc3 32.f3 ♘a4 33.a6 ♘c5 and a repetition like 34.♕b6 ♘d7 (34...♘d5 35.a7) 35.♕b7 ♘c5 looks sensible.

13...♖c8 A good alternative is 13...♗xc5 14.♗b2 ♖c8 15.♘bd2 ♕e7 16.♖ac1 ♘f6 (16...♘b6!?) 17.♘e4 ♗xc4 (Dragnev-Menezes, Austria Bundesliga 2019/20). White had probably captured automatically (18.bxc4), missing the stronger 18.♘xc5! △ 18...♗xb3 (18...♗xe2? is wrong: 19.♕xe2 ♖xc5 20.♖xc5 ♕xc5 21.♗xd5! exd5□ 22.♗xf6 gxf6 23.♕g4+ ♔h8 24.♕f5+) 19.♕xb3 ♖xc5 20.e4! ♘c3 21.♗xc3 bxc3 22.♖xc3 ♖fc8 23.♕b4 ♔f8 24.♖cd3 ♖c1=. **14.♗b2?** This natural developing move appears to be a serious strategic error. The correct 14.e4 ♘5f6 15.e5 ♘d5 16.♗b2 was played exactly 4 months earlier. Tsolakidou-Solozhenkina, New Delhi 2019, continued 16...♘xc5 17.♘bd2 ♕c7 (17...f5!?) 18.♖ac1 ♖fd8 19.♗f1 ♕b8 20.♗d4 and now instead of 20...♖d7? 21.♘d6!+− Black could continue with 20...♘d7 intending to exploit the vulnerable

c3-square: 21.♕b2 ♗xc4 22.♗xc4 (22.♘xc4 ♗c5! 23.♘d6 ♖xd4 24.♕xd4 ♖c3!) 22...♘c3! 23.♗xc3 bxc3 24.♖xc3 ♘xe5. **14...♘xc5!** **15.♘bd2** The justification of the last move is revealed by 15.e4 ♘xb3! 16.♕xb3 ♗xc4 17.♕f3 (17.♕c2 b3 18.♘d2 ♘b4) 17...♗f6! – from here on, to his misfortune, White got tactically outplayed as well. **15...♗f6∓ 16.♘e4** 16.♗xf6 ♕xf6 17.♘d6 runs into 17...♘d3! 18.♘2e4! (18.♘6e4 ♕xa1 19.♘c4 ♕b2; 18.♘xc8 ♕xf2+ 19.♔h1 ♖xc8 20.♘c4 ♘e3−+) 18...♕xa1 (Black will also be a pawn up after 18...♖xc2 19.♘xf6+ gxf6 20.♗xd5 ♖xe2 21.♗f3 ♖b2 22.♖ab1 ♖xb1 23.♖xb1 ♘c5∓) 19.♘xc8 ♕b2 20.♕xb2 ♘xb2 21.♘e7+ (21.♖d2?! ♖xc8 22.♖xb2 ♖c1+ 23.♗f1 ♘c3−+) 21...♘xe7 22.♖d2 ♕xa4 23.bxa4 ♖b8 24.♘c5 ♘c4 25.♖c2 ♘d5 26.♗xd5 exd5!∓. **16...♗xb2**

17.♖xc5?! An act of desperation. 17.♕xb2 ♘xb3; 17.♘xb2 could have maintained the material balance, though this is no fun after 17...♘xe4 (or 17...♘b7!? 18.♘c4 f5 19.♘ed2 ♘c3 20.♖e1 ♘a5) 18.♕xe4 ♕f6 19.♖d2 ♘c3 20.♕e3 ♖fd8. **17...♗xa1** In combination with the next moves the game turned into a reminder of what happened or could have happened in Ernst-Vrolijk, with many pieces on the same squares! 17...♖xc5 18.♕xb2 ♗xc4 19.bxc4 ♕f6 20.♕xf6 ♘xf6 is (only) better for Black. **18.♘xa6 ♕f6 19.a5 ♗d4−+ 20.e4 ♖xc4!** The start of a clever operation, based on the hanging f2-pawn. **21.bxc4 b3! 22.♕d2 ♘c3 23.♖f1 e5** A solid move to fix the advantage, but it was also possible to prolong at

once the path for the b-pawn with 23...♕h6! 24.♕d3 ♖d8 25.♔h1 ♗f6! 26.♕f3 b2−+. **24.♘c5?!** 24.♘b4 was more stubborn, though the result would not be in doubt after 24...♕d8 25.a6 (25.♘d5 ♕xa5) 25...♕c7 26.♘d5 ♕xc4 27.♘xc3 ♕xc3 28.♕xc3 ♗xc3 29.♖b1 b2 △ 30.♗f1 ♖c8 31.♔g2 ♗d4 32.♗d3 ♖c1. **24...b2!−+** 24...♘xc5 25.♕xc3 ♖b8 should also win, but why not take a piece? **25.♕xb2** 25.♘d7 ♕d6 26.♘xf8 b1♕ 27.♖xb1 ♘xb1. **25...♘a4 26.♕xd4 exd4 27.♘xa4 0-1**

Matthias Blübaum   **3**
Yuriy Kuzubov
Batumi Ech tt 2019 (8)

1.d4 ♘f6 2.c4 e6 3.♘f3 d5 4.g3 ♗e7 5.♗g2 0-0 6.0-0 dxc4 7.♕c2 b5 8.a4 b4 9.♘fd2 ♘d5 10.♘xc4 c5 11.dxc5 ♗a6 12.e4 ♘f6

13.e5 13.♖d1 ♘bd7 – 13.e4 ♘5f6 in Cordova-Riazantsev. **13...♘d5 14.♘bd2** 14.♖d1 ♘d7 15.b3 transposes to Tsolakidou-Solozhenkina. **14...♗xc5** A reliable alternative is 14...♕c7 15.♖d1 ♘d7 16.♘b3 ♘xc5 17.♘d6 ♘xb3 18.♕xb3 ♗xd6 19.exd6 ♕xd6 20.♗xd5 exd5= while 14...♘d7?! is never advisable when 15.c6 cannot be countered with ....♖c8. **15.♘e4 ♘d7 16.♘xc5** The knight has moved to the centre, but the access to the g5-square does not promise much: 16.♗g5 (his prospects are even worse in case of 16.♘g5 g6 17.♖e1 ♖c8) 16...♗e7 17.♗xe7 ♕xe7 and White can only hope to compensate the loss of his central pawn: 18.♖fc1 ♖ac8 19.♘ed6 ♗xc4 20.♘xc4 ♘5b6 (20...♘xe5 21.♕e2 ♘xc4 22.♖xc4 ♕d6) 21.♕e4 ♖xc4 22.♖xc4 ♘xc4 23.♕xc4 ♘xe5

24.♕d4 f6. **16...♘xc5 17.♖d1 b3 18.♕e2**

18...♖b8 It is difficult to explain why Black preferred the text to 18...♖c8. White's best seems to be 19.♗f1 (19.♕g4 might be the reason for Kuzubov's decision, but White has to fight for equality after 19...h5! 20.♕d4 ♘b4!, e.g. 21.♕xd8 ♖cxd8 22.♗e3 ♖xd1+ (22...♘cd3 23.♗a5 ♘c2 24.♖ab1 ♘xe3 25.fxe3 ♘xe5 26.♘xb3 ♘g4) 23.♖xd1 ♘xa4 24.♘d6 ♗xb2 25.♖b1 ♘4d3 26.♗xa7 ♘c4 27.♖xb3 ♘dxe5∓), e.g. 19...♘d3 20.♗a3 ♘3b4 21.♘b5 ♘c2 22.♕e1 (22.♕e4 ♕b6 23.♕d4 ♖fc8) 22...♕b8 23.♗a3 ♖xc1 24.♖xc1 ♗xb5 25.axb5 ♘c2 26.♕a5 ♘xa3 27.♕xa3 ♕xe5 28.♕xb3 ♖d8 29.♖c6 with approximate equality. **19.♖d4 ♖b4 20.a5 ♘a4** Natural was 20...♗d7 21.♗d2 ♖xc4 22.♖xc4 ♘xe5 23.♕xe5 ♗xc4 24.♖c1⩲ △ 24...♗b5! 25.♖c5 a6 26.♗xd5 exd5 27.♘c3 f6 28.♕xd5+ ♕xd5 29.♖xd5=. **21.♕d2?!** This square belongs to the bishop: 21.♗f1! ♕c7 22.♗d2 ♗xc4 23.♖xc4 ♕xc4 24.♕xc4 ♖xc4 25.♗xc4 ♘xb2 26.♗xb3 ♘d3 27.♗xd5 exd5 28.♗e3 a6 29.♖d1 ♘xe5 30.♖xd5⩲. **21.♖xc4 22.♖xc4 ♗xc4 23.♖xa4 ♕c7 24.♕d4 ♗d3! 25.♖a1 ♕c2 26.♗f3 a6** 26...♖c8 27.h3 (27.♗g5?! drops material after 27...♖c4! 28.♕xa7 h6 29.♗d1 ♕xb2 30.♕b8+ ♔h7 31.♕xb3 ♕xa1 32.♕xd3+ ♔g8 33.♖xc4 ♕xd1+ 34.♔g2 hxg5) 27...a6 28.♗xd5 exd5 29.♗e3 △ 29...♗e4 30.e6 fxe6 31.♕e5 ♕c6 32.f3! ♗c2 (32...♗xf3 33.♖c1) 33.♗d4 ♕d7 34.♖e1 ♖c6 35.♕b8+ ♖c8 36.♕b6 ♖c6=. **27.♗g5 ♘c3!? 28.♖c1** A bit safer was 28.♖e1 h6 29.♗e3 ♘e2+ 30.♗xe2 ♗xe2 31.♖c1 ♕f5 32.♕f4. **28...♘e2+ 29.♗xe2**

♕xe2 30.♕e3 ♕xe3 31.♗xe3 ♗c2 32.♖b6 The position with an active rook after 32.♖a1 ♖d8 33.♖a4 would have been easier to handle. **32...♖c8 33.f3 ♖c4 34.♖a1 h5 35.♗e3** ≤ 35.♔f2 ♗f5 36.♖e1 ♖a4. **35...♔f8 36.♔f2 ♗e7 37.♔e2 ♗d7 38.♔d2 ♗c6 39.♗b6 ♔d5 40.♖e1 ♗f5 41.♖c1 ♗c2 42.♖e1 g5 43.♖e3 g4 44.fxg4** A radical solution, based on the drawish tendencies of the opposite-coloured bishops. Instead of 44.f4 h4 White forces an exchange of the rooks. **44...hxg4 45.♖c3!** ♖xc3 45...♖a4 46.♖c5+ ♔e4 47.♖c7 ♗xe5 48.♖xf7. **46.♔xc3 ♗xe5 47.♔d2 ♗e4 48.♗a7 ♗f3** In spite of all the efforts, which brought an extra pawn, the draw seems inevitable: 48...e5 49.♗b8 f6 50.♗d6 ♔d4 51.♗e7 f5 52.♗f6 ♗e4 53.♗g7 f4 54.gxf4 exf4 55.♔e2 g3 56.hxg3 fxg3 57.♔f1. **49.♗d4 ♗e4 50.♗f6 ♗c6 51.♗d4 f5 52.♗e5 ♔g2 53.♔e3 ♔xh2 54.♔f2 ♗d5 ½-½**

**Migchiel de Jong   4
Liam Vrolijk**

Hoogeveen 2019 (3)

1.♘f3 d5 2.d4 ♘f6 3.c4 e6 4.g3 ♗e7 5.♗g2 0-0 6.0-0 dxc4 7.♕c2 b5 8.a4 b4 9.♘fd2 ♘d5 10.♘xc4 c5 11.dxc5 ♗a6 12.♘bd2 ♘d7

13.e4 13.c6 ♘c5

A) 14.♖d1?! b3! 15.♘xb3 ♘b4 16.♖xd8 ♘xc2 17.♖xa8 ♖xa8 18.♘xc5 ♗xc5 (18...♗xc4?! 19.♗g5! ♗xg5 20.♖d1 ♖d8 21.♗d7!) 19.c7 ♖c8 20.♖b1 ♗xc4 21.♗f4 ♘d4!∓/∓;

B) Once again the plan with 14.b3 ♖c8 15.♗b2 does not disturb Black: 15...♖xc6 16.♖fd1 (it is too late for 16.e4?! because of 16...♘b6) 16...♕c8 17.♖ac1 ♖d8 with comfortable play;

C) Too optimistic is 14.♘e5 ♕c7! 15.♘df3 b3! 16.♕d1 ♖fd8 △ 17.♗d2 ♖ac8 18.♖e1 ♘e4!;

D) 14.e4?! b3! 15.♘xb3 ♘b4 16.♕c3 ♘xb3 17.♕xb3 ♕d4∓;

E) For the best reply 14.♘b3! see Ernst-Vrolijk.

13...♘5f6?! In my view, 13...b3! 14.♘xb3 (14.♕xb3 ♘xc5 15.♕f3 ♘b4≙) 14...♘b4 has to be played. Black will eliminate the c5-pawn and seems to have decent compensation. **14.c6 ♘c5 15.e5** 15.♖d1!? deserves serious attention when urgent measures like 15...♕d4 (Black does not have time for the usual 15...♖c8?! in view of 16.♘b3! ♕c7 17.e5! ♘d5 18.♘xc5 ♗xc5 19.♗e3±) 16.♗f1 ♗g4 are not everyone's cup of tea. The line can go on with 17.♘f3 ♕xe4 18.♕xe4 ♘xe4 19.♖d4 and the engines are assuring that Black can fearlessly go for 19...♘gxf2 20.♘ce5 ♗xf1 21.♔xf1 f6 22.♘g4 e5 23.♘xf2 ♗xf2 24.♖d7 ♗c5 25.c7 ♖ac8 26.♗d2 ♘e4 27.♖c1 with a repetition after 27...♖f7 28.♖d8+ ♖f8 29.♖d7 ♖f7=. **15...♘d5**

16.b3 Not the best way to use the advanced e5-pawn. White had the stronger 16.♘b3! (once again 16.♖d1 allows the thematic blow 16...b3! 17.♘xb3 ♘b4) 16...♖c8 17.♘d4!, e.g. 17...♕c7 18.♖d1 b3 19.♕e2 ♗xc4 20.♕xc4 ♕xe5 21.♗xd5 ♕xd5 (21...exd5 22.♕c3 ♘e6 23.♗e3 ♗f6 24.♕xb3 ♕d6 and White can fix his advantage in many ways, the most forcing of which is 25.♘b5 ♕xc6 26.♘xa7 ♕c2 27.♕xc2 ♖xc2 28.♖xd5 ♖xb2 29.a5! ♖a8 30.♖a4) 22.♕xd5 exd5 23.♗e3 ♗f6 24.♘b5! ♖xc6 25.♖ac1 a6 26.♖xd5 axb5 27.axb5 ♖b6 28.♖cxc5 ♗xb2 29.♖c4 ♖b7

30.♖b4±/+−. **16...♖c8 17.♗b2
♖xc6 18.♖ac1 ♕c7 19.♖fd1
♖c8 20.♗f1** Remarkably, all
White's pieces and pawns took the
same squares on the next day in
Tsolakidou's game after her 19th
move! **20...♗g5!** A clever attempt
to profit from the improved
location of Black's major pieces
and the relevant tactical motifs.
Black could already pull the
trigger with 20...♘xa4 21.bxa4
♗b6 22.♗g2 ♗xc4 and enjoy great
compensation for the exchange.
21.♘d6? Sometimes tiny details
are incredibly significant. This
jump decided the aforementioned
game, while here it falls into a
crafty trap! 21.f4 was obligatory –
after 21...♗e7 White is surprisingly
short of useful moves. The
solidity of his set-up is fictitious;
besides the tactical blows on a4
and b3 now he must also take
care of the weakened e3-square:
22.♗d4 (Black can react to 22.♖e1
by regrouping to the d-file by
22...♕d8 23.♕d1 (the pressure
is mounting after 23.♖cd1 ♗c7
24.f5 ♖d7; the same manoeuvre
can be used with 23.♔f2) 23...♘b6
24.♘a5 ♗c7 25.♗xa6 ♘xa6
26.♖xc7 (26.♘e4 ♘xa4) 26...♕xc7
27.♘c4 ♖d8 28.♕f3 ♘c5) and
now the multifunctional move
22...♘b7!? is probably the best one.
The knight is going to disturb the
vulnerable b3-pawn from aside
and even the positional threat of
23...♗c5 is annoying, as well as the
immediate access to the c3-square
after 23.♗xa7 ♘c5 24.♗xc5 ♗xc5+
25.♔h1 ♘c3. **21...♗xf1 22.♔xf1
♗xd2! 23.♖xd2 ♘xb3!−+ 24.♕xb3
♖xc1+ 25.♔g2** 25.♗xc1 ♕xc1+
26.♖d1 ♕c2. **25...♖c2 26.♖d3 ♖f8
27.♗d4 ♖c1 28.♖f3 ♕c2 29.♕xc2
♖xc2 30.♗xa7 ♖c3 31.♘b5 ♖xf3
32.♔xf3 b3 33.a5 ♖a8 0-1**

**Sipke Ernst   5
Liam Vrolijk**
Amstelveen ch-NED blitz 2019 (30)

**1.d4 ♘f6 2.c4 e6 3.g3 d5 4.♘f3
♗e7 5.♗g2 0-0 6.0-0 dxc4 7.♕c2
b5 8.a4 b4 9.♘fd2 ♘d5 10.♘xc4**
c5 11.dxc5 ♗a6 12.♘bd2 ♘d7
12...♗xc5. **13.c6 ♘c5**

14.♘b3! A logical novelty,
introduced in practice 15 days
before the featured game by
Vincent Tsay. **14...♖c8 15.♘xc5**
   A) One of the most testing
continuations is 15.♘e3!?:
   A1) 15...♖xc6 16.♘xd5 exd5
17.♗e3 and after the relatively
best 17...♘xb3 18.♗xc6 ♗c4!
19.♗xa7 Black has to accept a small
material deficit: 19...♘xa1 (19...♕a8
20.♕xa8 (Black is holding in
the line 20.♕xc4 dxc4 21.♗xa8
♖xa8 22.♗e3 ♘xa1 23.♖xa1 ♗f6
24.♖c1 ♖c8 25.b3 due to 25...♗b2!)
20...♖xa8 21.♗b6 (21.♗e3 ♘xa1
22.♖xa1 ♗f6 23.♗c1 ♗a5 24.♗d2
♗xb2 25.♗xb4 ♖a8 26.♖b1 ♗e5
suddenly transposes to the leading
line after the alternative 19...♘xa1)
21...♘xa1 22.♖xa1 ♗f6 23.a5 ♗xb2
24.♖d1 ♗f6 25.♗xd5 ♗xd5 26.♖xd5
b3 27.♖b5 b2 28.♔g2 ♔f8 29.e4
♗c3 will lead to an ending with 4
against 3 pawns on the kingside)
20.♖xa1 ♗f6 21.♗c5 ♕a8 22.♕xa8
♖xa8 23.♗xb4 ♗xb2 24.♖b1
♗e5 25.♖c1 ♖xa4 26.♗xd5 ♖xb4
27.♗xc4 g6 and Black still has to
work for the draw, putting his
hopes on the opposite-coloured
bishops;
   A2) The courageous 15...♗xe2!?
may well be the best reply. White
has several tempting options, I
will just mention them without
going into detail: 16.♘xc5 ♗xf1
17.♘xd5 (17.♗xd5!? exd5 18.♘b7
♕e8 19.♗xf1 ♖xc6 20.♕f5 g6
21.♕e5 ♕d7 22.♘a5 ♖d6 23.♕d4;
17.♘b7!? ♘xe3 18.♗xe3 ♕d3
19.♕xd3 ♗xd3 20.♗xa7 ♗f6
21.♗c5 ♗xb2 22.♖d1 ♗c2 23.♖d7
♗e5 24.♗xb4 ♗xa4 25.♗xf8 ♔xf8
26.♘d8!) 17...exd5 18.♘b7 ♕b6
19.a5! ♖xc6 (suspicious is 19...♕xb7
20.cxb7 ♖xc2 21.♗xf1 ♗c5 22.♗f4
♖xf2 23.♔h1 ♖xf4 24.gxf4 ♗e3
25.♖d1) 20.axb6 ♖xc2 21.♗xf1 axb6
22.♗xd5 and once again Black
must prove that a rook and a pawn
are worth two minor pieces, which
does not look easy after, let's say,
22...♖fc8 23.♗e3 ♖xb2 24.♗xb6
♖d2 25.♖a5!;
   A3) 15...♘xb3 16.♕xb3 leaves
Black searching for compensation
for the lost pawn: 16...♘f6!?
transposes to Tsay-Nestorovic,
New York 2019, which continued
17.♗f3 (perhaps 17.♕c2 is the
proper way to defend the e-pawn;
worth a try is 17.♖d1 ♕b6 18.♘c2!?
△ 18...♗xe2 19.♖e1 ♗a6 20.♗e3
♕c7 21.♘d4 ♕a5 22.♘b5!) 17...♕a5
18.♗d2 ♖fd8 19.♖fd1 e5.

White has played logically, but
suddenly faces the task of stopping
...e5-e4. Now, instead of the game
move 20.♘f5, White's best bet
is 20.♕c2! e4 21.♗xe4 ♗xe2 (if
21...♖xd2!? 22.♖xd2 b3 23.♕d1 ♘xe4
24.♖d7 ♕e5 White has the brilliant
25.♕d5!! ♕xb2 26.♘f5!! ♕xa1+
27.♔g2 ♔h8 (27...♗f6 28.♘h6+
with a smothered mate) 28.♘xe7 g6
29.♕xe4! ♖f8 30.♖xa7, trapping the
bishop, while the opponent is not
able to advance his passed pawn:
30...b2 31.♕d4+ f6 32.♘xg6+!+−)
22.♖e1 ♕h5 23.♘f5 ♗f8 24.♗xb4
♘xe4 25.♕xe2 (an amusing line
is 25.♖xe2!? ♖xc6 26.♕xe4 ♖e6
27.♖d2! ♖xe4 28.♖xd8 h6 29.♘d4
♔h7 30.♗xf8 but 30...♕a5! wins
the bishop!) 25...♕xf5 26.♕xe4
♕xe4 27.♖xe4 ♖xc6 28.♗c3 and
White keeps a healthy extra pawn.
   B) Even 15.♖d1 ♘xb3 16.♕xb3
♖xc6 17.♘e3 (17.♘e5 ♖d6□)

17...♗xe2 18.♖e1 is not that innocuous. Black needs to be patient, e.g. 18...♗a6 19.♗xd5!? exd5 20.♘xd5 ♗d6 21.♗f4 h6! 22.♗xd6 ♖xd6 23.♘e7+ ♔h7 24.♕xb4 g6! 25.♖ac1 ♖e8 26.♘c6 ♖xe1+ 27.♖xe1 ♕f6♚;

C) 15.♘e5!? ♗xb3 16.♕xb3 deserves attention: 16...♗d6!? (16...♕d6 is highly rated by the engines, but I dislike the resulting position after 17.♗f4! ♘xf4 18.gxf4 ♗xe2 19.♖fe1 ♗h5 20.♕e3! ♕c7 21.♖ac1 and the c6-pawn is a big asset) 17.♘d7 ♖e8 18.♗xd5 exd5 19.♕xd5 ♕c7 20.♗e3 ♕xc6 and Black can expect sufficient counterplay thanks to his active pieces, combined with the odd-looking knight, e.g. 21.♖fd1 ♕xd5 22.♖xd5 ♗e7 23.♗xa7 ♖c2♚ (23...f6);

D) 15.♘ba5!? cannot be easily neutralized either: 15...b3! 16.♕d1 ♗f6 17.♖e1 ♕c7 18.♗xd5 exd5 (now 18...♕xc4!? is a promising alternative: 19.♘xc4 exd5 20.♕xd5 ♕xc6 21.♕xc6 ♖xc6 and White's queenside is about to collapse, but it is actually made of solid material: 22.♗e3! ♘b7 23.♖ac1 ♖fc8 24.♘a3!! (an ingenious resource – the b2-pawn is hanging, but it is currently more poisoned than in the Najdorf) 24...♘f8 25.♖xc6 ♖xc6 26.♖d1 ♗xb2 27.♖b1 ♗xa3 28.♖xb3 ♗c5 29.♖xb7 ♗xe3 30.fxe3 ♖a6 31.♖b4 ♔e7 and Black should be able to hold) 19.♕xd5 ♗e6 20.♗e3 ♖fd8 21.♕e4 ♗xb2! 22.♘xb2 ♕xa5♚;

E) 15.e4 ♘xb3 16.♕xb3 ♘b6! (16...♖xc6? 17.♘e5) 17.♘xb6 ♕xb6 18.♗e3 ♕xc6 19.♖fc1 ♗c4 20.♕c2 ♕a8 21.e5 ♕b8 22.♕e4 ♗d5 23.♕d4 ♗xg2 24.♔xg2 ♕b7+ 25.♔g1 a6=.

15...♗xc5 16.♘e5

16...♗d4 An interesting thought, albeit, objectively speaking, not entirely correct. This tense, and very important for theory, blitz game now enters a dramatic phase, in which I will indicate the improvements as briefly as possible:

A) 16...♕d6! is definitely the best. Now, critical is 17.♗f4! g5! 18.♘d7 gxf4 19.♕xc5 ♕xc5 20.♘xc5 ♗xe2 21.♖fe1 f3 22.♘d7 ♖fd8 23.♘e5 ♗d6 24.♖ac1 ♔g7 25.♖c5 ♗f6 26.♘xf3 ♗xf3 27.♗xf3 ♖cxc6 28.♖b5 ♖c2 29.♗xd5 ♖xd5 30.♖xb4 ♗f5 31.♖f1 a5 32.♖b7 ♖d5♚ △ 33.b4 ♖a2!=;

B) 16...♗d6 – the engines are happy with this retreat compared to the text, though 17.♘f3! is hard to meet: 17...♕b6 and a true Catalan devotee will be happy to switch to the kingside by 18.♘g5 g6 19.♕e4!↑.

17.♘d3

A) The most testing continuation is 17.♗f4! b3 (17...g5 is not so effective here in view of 18.♖ad1) 18.♕xb3 (or 18.♕c1 ♗xe5 19.♗xe5 ♕b6 20.♕d2 ♕xc6 21.♖fc1 △ 21...♕d7 22.e4 ♘b6 23.♕xd7 ♘xd7 24.♗c7) 18...♘xf4 19.gxf4 ♗xe2 20.♖fc1! ♕h4 (20...♖b8 looks strong, but White remains on top due to the witty 21.♕a3! ♕h4 22.♕c2 ♕xf2+ 23.♔h1 ♕xf4 24.♘d7) 21.♕c2 ♕xf4 (21...♗xf2+ 22.♔h1±) 22.♘d7 ♕xf2+ 23.♔h1 ♖fd8 24.♖f1 ♗xf1 25.♖xf2 ♗xf2 26.♕xf1 ♖xc6 27.♕f3 ♖c1 28.♕xf2 ♖xd7 29.♔g2 a5 with some hope to eliminate the queenside pawns and to build a fortress;

B) 17.♕e4 ♗xe5 18.♕xe5 ♖xc6 19.♖d1 is posing problems, but Black's resources to meet 20.e4 are far from exhausted: 19...♖c5!? (19...♖c2 △ 20.e4 ♕f6 21.♕xf6 ♘xf6 22.♗e3 b3!⇄) 20.♗f3 (20.♗e3 ♘xe3 21.♕xe3 ♕e7 22.♗f3 g6; 20.e4?! ♘e3! 21.♖xd8 ♖xd8) 20...♕c8 △ 21.♗xd5 ♖d8!;

C) Black is doing much better after 17.♘f3 ♗f6 18.e4!? b3! (he should avoid 18...♕b6 19.a5! ♗xf1 20.♗xf1) 19.♕xb3 ♖b8 20.♕d1 ♗xf1 21.♗xf1 ♘b4 22.♗f4 ♘xc6

23.♗xb8 ♕xb8 24.♖b1 ♖d8 25.♕c2 ♘d4 26.♘xd4 ♖xd4 27.♖c1 g6♚;

D) 17.♗g4 ♕d6 18.♖d1 ♖xc6 19.♕e4 ♗c5 20.♗f4 ♕e7 21.♘e3 ♘xe2 22.♗xe3 ♕c7 23.♖ac1 ♗xe3 24.♕xe3 ♖d8=.

17...♕d6 Safer was 17...♕b6 18.a5 ♕b5 19.♗xd5 exd5 20.♕a4 ♖fe8 21.♗xb4 ♖xe2 22.♕xd4 ♕xd3 23.♕xd3 ♗xd3 24.♗e3 ♖xb2 (24...a6 25.♖fd1 ♗c4 26.b3 ♗xb3 27.♖db1) 25.♖fc1 ♗c4 (25...a6 26.♗b6 f6) 26.♗xa7 ♖xc6 with a likely draw. **18.♗xd5!?** Here too, 18.♗f4 would have been challenging. **18...exd5** Black has difficulties in reaching equality with the alternatives:

A) 18...♗xd3 19.♕xd3 ♕xd5 20.♖d1 ♖fd8 21.♗e3 e5 (21...♗xb2 22.♕a6!) 22.♗xd4 exd4 (22...♕xc6 23.♕b3 xb4) 23.♖dc1 ♖xc6 24.♕b5!; or

B) 18...♕xd5 19.♘xb4 ♕c4 20.♕xc4 ♗xc4 21.♗e3!.

19.♗f4 ♕e7 For 19...♗xd3 20.♕xd3 ♕f6 see the next note.

20.♖fe1?! This natural move surprisingly appears to be inaccurate. White has the upper hand after 20.♕d2! ♗xd3 21.♕xd3 ♕f6 (21...♗xb2 22.♖ab1 ♗c3 23.♕xd5 ♕xe2 24.c7) 22.c7 ♗xb2 (22...♗e5 23.♗xe5 ♕xe5 24.♖fc1 ♖xc7 25.♖xc7 ♕xc7 26.♕d2 ♕b6 27.♖c1) 23.♖ab1 ♗e5 24.♗xe5 ♕xe5 25.♖fc1 ♖xc7 26.♖xc7 ♕xc7 27.♖xb4. **20...♗c4?!** Black could have taken over the initiative by 20...g5! 21.♗d2 ♕f6 22.♗xb4 ♖xc6 23.♗c3 (23.♕d2 ♖fc8) 23...♗xc3 24.bxc3 ♖xc3 25.♕d2 d4. **21.b3?!** ≥ 21.♕d2. **21...♗a6** The rook could and had to be taken: 21...♗xa1! 22.♖xa1 (22.bxc4?! ♗c3 △ 23.cxd5 ♗xe1 24.d6 (24.♘xe1 g5 25.♗e3 b3

26.♕xb3 ♖fd8) 24...♕d7!), when 22...♖xc6! 23.bxc4 dxc4 24.♘e5 ♗c5 is quite promising. **22.♗d2?** 22.♖ac1 ♗c3 23.♗d2 d4 (23...♖xc6 24.♘xb4 ♕xb4 25.♗xc3 ♖fc8 26.♗xb4 ♖xc2 27.♖cd1) 24.e3! ♖xc6 25.exd4 ♕f6 26.♘e5! ♗xd4 27.♕xc6 ♗xf2+ 28.♔g2 ♗xe1 29.♕xf6 gxf6 30.♖xe1 fxe5 31.♖xe5. **22...♗xa1** Missing the opportunity to get to the weakened f2-pawn by 22...♗xd3! 23.exd3 ♕f6! 24.♗xb4 ♗xa1 25.c7 ♗d4−+. **23.♘xb4?!** 23.♖xa1 △ 23...♕e4 24.♘xb4 ♕xc2 25.♘xc2 ♖xc6 26.♘d4≌. **23...♗d4! 24.♘xa6** ≥ 24.e3 ♗c5 25.♘xa6 ♖xc6 26.♘xc5 ♖xc5 27.♕d3 ♕b7. **24...♕f6** The similarity with Cordova-Riazantsev is really striking! **25.♘b4?** 25.e3 ♖xc6 26.♕d3 ♗c3! (26...♖xa6 27.exd4 ♖e6) 27.♘b4 ♗xb4 28.♗xb4 ♖b8 29.♗d2 ♕f3∓. **25...♗xf2+ 26.♔g2 ♗xe1 27.♗xe1 ♖fe8−+ 28.♗f2 a5 29.♘xd5 ♕xc6 30.♕d3 ♕e6 31.♔f3 ♖cd8 32.e4 f5 0-1**

Main line
12.♘e3

Boris Gelfand   **6**
Bogdan-Daniel Deac
Bucharest rapid m 2019 (2)
1.d4 ♘f6 2.c4 e6 3.♘f3 d5 4.g3 ♗e7 5.♗g2 0-0 6.0-0 dxc4 7.♕c2 b5 8.a4 b4 9.♘fd2 ♗d5 10.♘xc4 c5 11.dxc5 ♗a6 12.♘e3 ♘d7 13.♘xd5 exd5 14.c6 ♖c8 15.♗f4 ♘c5 16.♖d1!

16...d4 The alternative 16...♗c4 was not mentioned in YB 133: 17.♘d2! ♗xe2 and now:

A) It is a bit early for 18.c7 ♕d7 (18...♖xc7!? 19.♗xc7 ♕xc7 20.♖e1 and Black can exploit the fact that

his pawn is still on d5 by 20...♗d3 21.♕d1 ♗f6 22.♘b3 ♗c4 23.♘xc5 ♕xc5 24.♖b1 b3♞) 19.♘b3 (19.♖e1 ♗d3 (19...♗a6!? △ ...♗d3) 20.♕d1 (the same position arises after 17...♗xe2 in Ding Liren-Carlsen) 20...g5 21.♘b3 gxf4 22.♘xc5 ♗xc5 23.♕xd3 ♕xc7 24.♖ad1 fxg3 25.hxg3 ♔h8 with a slightly worse, but defensible position) 19...♘xb3! (19...♖xd1 20.♖xd1 is more problematic for Black: 20...♕xa4! 21.♗xd5 ♘e6 22.♗xe6 fxe6 23.♕c4 ♗f6! (initiates timely counterplay against the b-pawn). The position is dynamically balanced, e.g. 24.♕xe6+ ♔h8 25.♖d2 ♕b5 26.♖d5 ♕e8 27.♕xe8 ♖fxe8 28.♖b5 ♗xb2 29.♘a5 a6 30.♖b8 (30.♖xb4?! g5! 31.♗xg5 ♗c3 32.♖a4 ♖xc7) 30...g5! 31.♗d6 ♗g7 32.♘c4 ♗f8 33.♗e5+ ♗g7=) 20.♖xd5 ♘a1 21.♕xe2 ♕e8! 22.♗h3 ♗c6! (the key to equality!) 23.♗xc8 ♕xd5 24.♗a6 ♕c5 25.c8♕ ♖xc8 26.♗xc8 and the draw is inevitable after 26...g5! 27.♗b8 (27.♗d2 ♘b3 28.♗b7 ♘xd2 29.♕xd2=) 27...♕xc8 28.♕xe7 ♕xb8 29.♕xg5+ ♔h8 30.♕f6+ ♔g8 31.♕g5+=;

B) 18.♘b3!. To his credit, GM Korotylev managed in limited time to determine this best move order. 18...♗xd1 (it is wrong to start with 18...♘xb3?! because of 19.♕xe2 ♘xa1 20.♖xd5 ♕b6 (20...♕e8?! 21.♗e5 ♖c7 22.♖e3) 21.♕xe7±) 19.♖xd1 and now:

B1) 19...♘xb3 20.c7! (a big improvement upon the line on chesspro.ru, 20.♕xb3 ♖xc6 21.♗xd5 ♖d6 22.♗xd6 ♗xd6 23.♕d3. Indeed, Black needs a few more precise moves: 23...♕f6 24.♕a6 ♗c7! △ 25.♕xf6 gxf6 26.♗c4 ♖d8, to rule out the last doubts about the inevitable draw) 20...♕e8!? (the natural 20...♕d7?! transposes to the aforementioned unfavourable line, in which White has the luxury of choice how to take on d5; returning the material by 20...♖xc7 21.♗xc7 ♕c8 22.♗xd5 ♘c5 does not solve Black's problems after the precise 23.♗a5!) 21.♕xb3 g5! leads to

exciting complications: 22.♕xd5! gxf4 23.♕f5! (an incredible idea!) 23...♔g7 24.♗e4 ♖g8! (24...♔h8? 25.♕g4+ ♔f8 26.♗c6! ♖xc6 27.♕xc8+ ♔g7 28.♕g4+ ♔h6 29.♕xf4+ ♔g6 30.♕g4+ ♔h6 31.♖d7+−) 25.♕xh7+ ♔f8 26.♕h6+ ♖g7 27.♗c6 ♗g5□ 28.♖d8!! ♖xd8 29.♗xe8 ♖d1+ 30.♔g2 ♗xh6 31.c8♕ ♖g6 and Black is surviving, though his troubles are not over;

B2) 19...♕b6 20.♗xd5 ♘xb3 21.♕xb3 ♖xc6 22.♗xc6 ♕xc6 23.♖c1 eliminates the annoying pawn and avoids the danger of a quick catastrophe, but Black will have to take care of his queenside, where his pawns are permanent targets.

17.h4! ♖e8 A logical novelty, but unexpectedly the rook appears to be exposed here.

A) The lesser alternative 17...♘e6 18.♗e5 was examined by Sielecki: 18...d3 19.exd3 ♗d6 20.d4 ♗xe5 21.dxe5 ♘d4 22.♕d2 when his assessment of 'huge advantage' has yet to be proven after 22...♘b3 23.♕e1 ♕a5 24.♘a3 or 24.e6 − not as simple as the title of the book may suppose, but, due to the mighty c-pawn, White's chances are better;

B) Sielecki's main line is 17...h6! 18.♗f3 ♖e8 19.♘d2 d3 20.exd3 ♗xd3 21.♕c1 ♗f8 (21...♗d6?! 22.♘e4! ♗xe4 23.♖xd6) 22.♖e1.

So far Yearbook 133 − with an exception of the subtleties on move 17, the rest of the line is understandable without a thorough examination. The board is full and the c6-pawn is still alive and kicking, while Black's pieces are so active that the tactics are now working for

him – especially after the precise 22...♕f6!, e.g. 23.♖xe8 ♖xe8 24.c7 (a rare combination with a double deflection can be realized after 24.♗e3 ♖xe3! 25.fxe3 ♘b3! 26.c7 ♘xc1 27.c8♕ ♘b3! (from the same square!) 28.♖d1 ♘xd2 29.♖xd2 ♕xf3 30.♖xd3 ♕e2! (a beautiful way to secure a perpetual) 31.♖d8 ♕xe3+ 32.♔h1 ♕f3+=) 24...♖c8 25.♕e1 ♗d6 26.♗xd6 ♖xd6 27.♖c1 a5! (there is no need to allow 27...♖xc7 28.♕e8+ ♔h7 29.♕e3 △ 29...a5? 30.♗b3!+−) 28.♗e3 ♖xc7 29.♘c4 ♗xc4 30.♖xc4 ♔f8 with roughly equal play.

18.♘d2 18.c7 ♕d7 19.♘d2 will normally transpose to the text. **18...♗xe2 19.c7 ♕d7** Essential is 19...♖xc7 20.♗xc7 ♕xc7

and we are arriving at the critical position for the assessment of 17....♖e8 after 21.♖e1. Black can

look for compensation in several directions:

A) 21...♕d8!? 22.♗f1 b3 23.♕b1 (23.♘xb3 d3 24.♕c3 ♘xb3 25.♕xb3 ♗c5 26.♗xe2 ♕d4! 27.♖xd3 ♕xf2+ 28.♔h1 ♖e3 29.♕d8+ ♗f8 30.♕d4 ♕xg3 31.♕g4 ♕e5!! (31...♕f2?! 32.♖f1! ♕xe2 33.♕xe2 ♖xe2 34.♖ac1!) and White's king is too exposed: 32.♖ac1 (32.♔g2 h5) 32...♖e4 33.♕g5 ♕e6 34.♕g3 ♖xe2 35.♖xe2 ♕xe2 36.b3 ♕e4+ 37.♔h2 g6 38.♖c4 ♕e2+=; 23.♕f5 g6 24.♕h3 ♗xf1 25.♕xf1 d3♔) 23...♗xf1 24.♔xf1 (24.♘xf1 ♕d7 25.♕d1 d3 26.♖c1 ♗f8) 24...♕d7! (24...d3 25.♕d1) 25.♕d1 (25.♔g1 ♖d8 26.♕d1 d3) 25...♘d3! 26.♖e4 ♘c5 27.♖e2 ♖b8 28.♔g1 ♗xh4!;

B) 21...♗f8 22.♗f1! (Black had prepared a nasty surprise after 22.♗f3: 22...♖e3!! with a forced draw: 23.♗xe2 (23.fxe3 ♕xg3+ 24.♔g2 d3 25.♕c1 ♕xe3+ 26.♔h1 ♕g3=) 23...♖xg3+ 24.fxg3 ♕xg3+ 25.♔f1 ♕h3+ 26.♔f2 ♕h2+ 27.♔f3 ♕h3+) 22...d3 23.♕c4 ♕e5 24.♕xb4 ♘a6 25.♕c4! ♘c5! 26.♔g2 ♗xf2! (26...♕f6 27.f4! ♕xb2?! 28.♖ad1!!) 27.♔xf2 ♕e3+ 28.♔g2 ♕xd2 29.♕c3 (29.♗xe2 ♖xe2+ 30.♖xe2 ♕xe2+ 31.♔h3 h5! 32.♖g1 ♕f2⇄) 29...♕xc3 30.bxc3 ♘c5 and

Black has decent chances to save this ending;

C) 21...d3 22.♕c4 ♕e5 23.♗f1 ♕xb2 24.♗xe2 dxe2 (or 24...♕xd2 25.♖ad1 ♕c2 26.♗xd3 ♕xc4 27.♗xc4 ♗f8) 25.♕xe2 ♘e6 26.♘f3 ♕xe2 27.♖xe2 ♖c8.

20.♖dc1! A clear sign that Gelfand had not arrived at the board empty-handed. **20...♘d3?** A tempting idea, but its refutation is easy.

A) The big point behind 20.♖dc1 is revealed after 20...♘g4 21.♗c6 ♗d3 and here comes a splendid queen sacrifice: 22.♕xc5!! ♗xc5 23.♖xc5. White is going to win the blockading rook and the pawn should decide the issue. We can take it for granted that this line had been worked out to victory in Gelfand's files;

B) Black is practically left with 20...♖xc7 21.♗xc7 ♕xc7 22.♖e1 – 19...♖xc7.

21.♗c6 ♕h3 22.♗xe8 ♘xf4 22...♘xf2 23.♕c6. **23.♕e4!+−** The rest is child's play for a player of Gelfand's calibre. **23...♖xe8 24.♕xf4 ♗a6 25.♕f3 ♕c8 26.♔h2 ♗b7 27.♕f4 ♕d7 28.♖c4 ♗f6 29.♖c5 ♗e7 30.♕f5! ♕c8 31.♕xc8 ♖xc8 32.♖c4 ♗d5 33.♖xd4 1-0**

(solutions on page 250)

Exercise 1

position after 14.♗c1-b2

White has just played the inaccurate 14.♗b2. How can Black punish it?

Exercise 2

Position after 16...e6xd5

Why is 17.♗xd5 worse than 17.♗f4 ♘xc5 18.♖xd5 ?

Exercise 3

position after 15...♘f6-d5

16.♘f5 appears to be inferior to the immediate 16.♗xd5. Why?

Digging holes in opening theory

by Ruslan Ponomariov

1.	d4	♘f6
2.	c4	e6
3.	♘c3	♗b4
4.	♕c2	0-0
5.	e4	

Maxime Vachier-Lagrave

The Nimzo-Indian with 4.♕c2 is a very popular choice even among players who don't play 1.d4 regularly, because it's kind of easy to include it in your opening repertoire. With this move-order you don't need to learn all these fancy Ragozin and Vienna variations. Also, White will have some extra options if Black wants to play the Queen's Gambit or the Accelerated Tarrasch.

I started playing this line from time to time with white in 2001 because it was fashionable thanks to Garry Kasparov. But most of the time I was on the opposite side – Black. I really hated it when I needed to play for a win versus lower-rated opponents because if White wants, he can minimize all the risks already at home. I remember in 2013 we had a brainstorm when Carlsen needed to beat Radjabov at the Candidates tournament. In the end we couldn't find anything better to suggest to Magnus than 4...d6. Which is a dubious move, but at least you can avoid many forced lines and try to get a long game.

Very aggressive

In this Survey we will discuss the less popular, but very aggressive set-up for White with 5.e4, which featured in a Survey by Jan-Willem de Jong in Yearbook 91 and twice in Alexey Kuzmin's Harvest column, in Yearbooks 103 and 108. This approach received a fresh look on the top level recently. It is much more concrete, and precise play is required from both sides. At the same time, I was surprised how deeply theory proceeds here. Novelties only started to appear from move 23 onwards!

It's really hard to say something general about plans and manoeuvres. What you need here is to have a good memory. I have tried to check all the possible options from Black's perspective, and I think the second player should be fine in all lines. If Black needs to play for a win, or if he doesn't like very forced lines, I recommend to try 5...d6.

Conclusion

Trying to win by preparation, without really making your own moves over the board, is a popular concept. But I believe White needs to look for new ideas after 5.a3 in this line. As Mikhail Gurevich said about the evaluation of this position, after smoking one cigarette: 'I've got a pair of bishops already.'

Anish Giri
Fabiano Caruana
Wijk aan Zee 2020 (2)

1.d4 ♘f6 2.c4 e6 3.♘c3 ♗b4 4.♕c2 0-0 5.e4 d5 6.e5 ♘e4 7.♗d3 c5 8.♘f3 cxd4 9.♘xd4

9...♘d7 Nowadays, almost everyone plays this logical developing move, and I guess not without reason. In 2012 my compatriot Andrei Volokitin had some success with the sharp 9...♘c5 10.♗xh7+ ♔h8. I believe it worked well for him in the first games as a surprise weapon. But now everyone can turn on an engine and see different ways to find good play for White: 11.♘f3!? (the most ambitious, but 11.♗e3 also poses Black some problems, e.g. 11...dxc4 12.0-0-0 ♕h4 13.♗e4! ♗xc3 14.♘f3! ♕xe4 15.♗xc5 ♕xc2+ 16.♔xc2 ♖e8 17.♗xc3 b6 18.♗d6±. Material is equal, but the white pieces are much more active and even without queens White can try to create an attack on the kingside) 11...d4 (now it looks like every

move is good for White!) 12.0-0 (12.♗g5 f6 13.exf6? (White should play 13.0-0-0 fxg5 14.h4 g4 15.♖xd4 ♕e7 16.♖xg4→) 13...gxf6 14.♗f4 d3 15.♕d1 ♗xh7–+ Jones-Volokitin, Plovdiv 2012 – see Yearbook 103, Kuzmin's Harvest, page 37; also tempting looks 12.♘g5!? g6 (12...dxc3 13.bxc3 ♗a5 14.0-0) 13.0-0 dxc3 14.bxc3 ♕d3 15.♕xd3 ♘xd3 16.cxb4 ♘c6 17.f4. I am not sure that there is a way to win the bishop on h7. Otherwise White has some extra material and a healthy position) 12...d3 13.♕d1 d2 14.♗c2 dxc1♕ 15.♕xc1 ♗xc3 16.♕f4 ♔g8. A complicated position has arisen, where precise play is required from both sides. 17.♖ad1? (better was 17.♘g5 f5 18.♕h4 ♕xg5 19.♕xg5 ♗xb2 20.♖ad1 ♗xe5 21.♕e7 ♘ba6 22.♗xf5 exf5 (22...♖xf5 23.♖d8+ ♔h7 24.♕h4+ ♔g6 25.g4) 23.♕xe5 ♗e6 – I think White's queen should be stronger here, especially with a black knight on a6) 17...♗xe5 18.♕xe5 ♕e7? (now Black could defend and keep an extra piece with 18...♘bd7 19.♕h5 f5∓ △ 20.♘g5 ♘f6) 19.♗h7+ ♔xh7 20.♕h5+ ♔g8 21.♘g5 ♕xg5 22.♕xg5 ♘bd7 23.♕e7 a5 24.♖fe1 and White is winning because Black has trouble coordinating his pieces. But after many adventures, the result was the opposite and Black won: 0-1 (49) Baramidze-Volokitin, Austria Bundesliga 2011/12. **10.♗f4 ♕h4** In Yearbook 108, Kuzmin mentioned the rare 10...♕b6, played by Kramnik.

There has not been much development here: 11.♘b3 ♕c7 12.0-0 ♘xe5. Here I suspect that White can improve with 13.♘xe4!? (13.♗xe4 dxe4 14.♕xe4 ♗xc3 15.bxc3 f6 16.♖fe1 ♕xc4 17.♗xe5 ♕xe4 18.♖xe4 fxe5 19.♖xe5 b6 and Black solved all his problems in Anand-Kramnik, Moscow 2013) 13...dxe4 14.♗xe4 f5 15.c5! fxe4 16.♗g3 and Black has trouble to save both the bishop on b4 and the knight on e5: 16...♖f5 17.♕xe4 a5 (17...♗xc5 18.♖ac1) 18.♘d4 ♗g5 19.♖ac1 ♗d7 20.a3 ♗xc5 21.♘b3 ♗c6 22.♖xc5 ♗xe4 23.♖xc7 ♘d3 24.♘d4± – there are still some problems for Black even without the queens. 10...♘dc5 11.0-0 ♗xc3 (11...♘xd3 12.♕xd3 ♘xc3 13.bxc3 ♗e7) 12.bxc3 ♘xd3 13.♕xd3 b6 14.cxd5 exd5 (or 14...♕xd5) is the other main line. **11.g3 ♕h5 12.0-0 g5!?** This concrete move looks scary when you play it for the first time. But nowadays such forced play can be easily evaluated by computers, you just need to have a good memory to reproduce it over the board. **13.cxd5 gxf4 14.dxe6 ♘xc3 15.exd7 ♗xd7 16.bxc3**

16...⌶ac8?! An inaccurate move. **17.♕d1!** Probably Fabiano forgot about this move and thought White should play 17.♗f5 anyway. **17...♕xd1 18.⌶axd1 ♗xc3** 18...⌶xc3 19.♘e2 now loses the pawn on f4. **19.♗f5 ⌶cd8** Unfortunately there is no more time to exchange pawns, e.g. 19...⌶c4 20.♗xd7 ⌶xd4 21.⌶xd4 ♗xd4 22.gxf4 and White wins a pawn. Maybe Black can still hold with active play, e.g. 22...⌶d8 23.♗f5 ♗b6 24.♔g2 ⌶d2, but you don't want to take such unnecessary risks. 19...♗xf5 20.♘xf5 ♗xe5 21.♘e7+. **20.♗xd7 ⌶xd7 21.♘f5 ⌶xd1 22.⌶xd1** Now White has a knight instead of a bishop, which is kind of a different story. The endgame is a bit unpleasant for Black. **22...fxg3** Technically this natural move can be called a novelty. In another game, after 22...♗xe5 23.⌶d7 Black decided to keep the a-pawn instead: 23...a5 (23...b6 24.⌶xa7 could transpose to Caruana's game) 24.⌶xb7 fxg3 25.hxg3 ⌶b8 26.⌶a7 ♗c3 27.♘h6+?! (more patient was 27.♔g2±) 27...♔g7 28.♘xf7 ♗d4. Now more pieces were exchanged, which made Black's defence easier: 29.⌶d7 ♗xf2+ 30.♔xf2 ⌶f8 31.⌶d5 ⌶xf7+ 32.♔g2 ⌶a7 33.a4 ⌶a6 and now Black holds this rook ending without any big problems, ½-½ Li Chao-Ni Hua, China tt 2017.

23.hxg3 A very natural move, which I think 99% of players would make without much thinking. But according to my engine, much stronger was 23.f4!, sacrificing a pawn for activity: 23...gxh2+ 24.♔xh2 b5 25.⌶d7 a5 26.♘e7+ ♔h8 27.♔g3 b4 28.♔g4 a4

29.♘d5. The position looks very unpleasant for Black. I am kind of wondering: with deep analysis, is this endgame still holdable or already lost for Black? It can be a nice position for an analytical test. **23...♗xe5 24.⌶d7 b6** This move looks more logical than 24...a5 because with the asymmetrical pawn structure it will be easier for Black to exchange pawns. **25.⌶xa7 h5 26.⌶a6 ⌶b8 27.♔g2**

White is slightly better. But since it was a game with a long time control, Black had enough time to think. I believe that Black still should not have many problems to hold the draw, even if you're playing versus Carlsen. **27...♔h7 28.♔f3 ♗c3 29.⌶a7 ♔g6 30.♘e7+ ♔g7 31.♘c7 ♗f6 32.♘f5+ ♔g6 33.♘e3 ♗d4 34.♘d5 ⌶a8 35.♘f4+ ♔f6?!** Slight panic before reaching the 40-move limit. Simpler was 35...♔h6 36.⌶xf7 (36.⌶c6+ ♔g5) 36...⌶a3+ 37.♔g2 ⌶xa2 38.♘e6 ♔g6, keeping equal material. **36.♘xh5+ ♔g5 37.♘f4 ⌶a3+ 38.♔e4 ⌶a4** Probably Black blundered in his previous calculations: 38...♗xf2? 39.♘h3+ ♔g4 40.♘xf2+ ♔xg3 41.⌶c2! and White saves the last pawn. **39.♔d5 ♔g4 40.⌶c2 ♗c5** Luckily for Black, his position is solid enough even with one pawn less. **41.⌶d2 ♔f5 42.♘g2** 42.♘d3 ⌶d4+ 43.♔c6 ⌶d6+ 44.♔b5 ⌶d4 45.f3 f6 and it's not so clear how White is going to unpin his knight. **42...⌶a5 43.♔c6 ♔e4 44.♘e1 ⌶a3 45.⌶c2 f5 46.♔d7 f4 47.gxf4 ♔xf4 48.♔e6 ♔g5 49.♔d5 ♔f5 50.⌶e2 ⌶a4 51.♔c6 ⌶a3 52.♘c2 ⌶f3 53.♘e3+ ♔e4 54.♔b5 ♔d3 55.⌶b2 ♗d4 56.⌶b3+ ♔e4 57.♘d1 ⌶f5+ 58.♔c4 ⌶c5+ 59.♔b4**

⌶a5 60.f3+ ♔f4 61.♘c3 ♗xc3+ 62.♔xc3 ⌶xa2 63.⌶xb6 ♔xf3 ½-½

Nikita Vitiugov
Fabiano Caruana
Wijk aan Zee 2020 (9)
1.d4 ♘f6 2.c4 e6 3.♘c3 ♗b4 4.♕c2 0-0 5.e4 d5 6.e5 ♘e4 7.♗d3 c5 8.♘f3 cxd4 9.♘xd4 ♘d7 10.♗f4 ♕h4 11.g3 ♕h5 12.0-0 g5 13.cxd5 gxf4 14.dxe6 ♘xc3 15.exd7 ♗xd7 16.bxc3 fxg3! An improvement.

17.hxg3 Actually White can try to improve as well: 17.♗xh7+!?

A) Now after 17...♔h8?! I will play 18.hxg3!;

B) 17...♔g7 and now:

B1) Bad is 18.hxg3?! because Black can start an attack on the h-file: 18...⌶h8 (18...♗c5!? 19.♗e4 ⌶h8 20.⌶fe1 ⌶ae8; 18...⌶ac8!?) and White should be very careful to hold this position: 19.♘f5+! ♔xh7 20.♘h4+ ♔g7 21.cxb4 ♕g4 22.f3 ♕xg3+ 23.♕g2 ♕xg2+ 24.♘xg2 a5 25.a3 ⌶h5⇄;

B2) 18.fxg3! ⌶ac8 19.e6! fxe6 (19...♗xe6 20.♘xe6+ fxe6 21.⌶xf8 ♗xf8 22.⌶f1 ♗c5+ 23.♔h1±; 19...♗xc3? 20.♘f5+ ♔xh7 21.♘e3+ (covering the d4-g1 diagonal) 21...♕g6 22.exd7+−) 20.⌶xf8 ♗xf8 21.♗e4 ♗c5 22.♔h1 ♗xd4 23.♕d3! and Black is still suffering to make a draw.

C) 17...♕xh7 18.♕xh7+ ♔xh7 19.cxb4 gxh2+ (or 19...gxf2+!? 20.♔xf2 a5 21.b5 ⌶fe8 22.♔g3 ⌶e7 23.⌶f4 ⌶g8+ 24.♔f2 ⌶xe5 25.⌶xf7+ ⌶g7 26.⌶xg7+ ♔xg7∓) 20.♔xh2 ⌶g8 21.⌶g1 ⌶xg1 22.⌶xg1 a5± looks very close to a draw, but Black doesn't need to enter all these complications and it's simpler to play 15...fxg3 earlier, as in the next

game. After the pawns have been exchanged it's OK for Black to play **17...♖ac8**. The difference is that now the pawn on f4 is not hanging. **18.♗f5** Now in case of 18.♕d1 ♕xd1 19.♖axd1 Black has an extra option: 19...♖xc3!? (19...♗xc3 20.♗f5 ♖c4 is a transposition to the 18.♗f5 line) 20.♘e2 ♖c7 21.♘f4 ♗c6. I believe that with the pair of bishops Black should be fine, e.g. 22.♗c4 ♗f3 23.♖d3 ♖xc4 24.♖xf3 ♖e8 25.♖d1 ♖xe5 26.♖d7 ♖f5 27.♖xb7 ♗d2=. **18...♗xc3**

19.♕d1 White has also tried to play with the queens on: 19.♗xd7 ♕xa1 20.♗xc8 ♗xd4 when there is some small hope for White that Black's king is slightly exposed and maybe with the opposite-coloured bishops it's possible to create some attack. But as tournament practice shows, Black's activity fully compensates the weaknesses near his king: 21.♗xb7 (21.♗f5 ♕f3 (21...♖e8!?) 22.♗xh7+ ♔g7 23.♕d3 ♕xd3 24.♗xd3 ♗xe5= Nesterov-Yilmaz, Moscow 2020) 21...♕xe5 22.♔g2 ♖b8 23.♖h1 (trying to improve on an old game, or was MVL just improvising over the monitor, since he played online? 23.♖b1 ♔g7 24.♕d3 ♕f6 25.♕e2 ♖e8 26.♕g4+ ♔f8 27.♗f3 ♕g6 28.♕xd4 ♕xb1 29.♕h8+ ♔e7 30.♕e5+ ♔f8 31.♕h8+ ♔e7 32.♕e5+ (Leko-Dominguez Perez, Tashkent 2012) was old known theory. I even played in this tournament myself) 23...h5 24.♖h4 ♔g7 25.♖e4?! (≥ 25.♕b3 f6 26.♕f3 ♗xf2! 27.♖xh5 ♕xg3+ 28.♕xg3+ ♗xg3 29.♗e4 ♗e5 30.♖h7+ ♔f8 31.♖xa7=) 25...♕f5 26.♕d2 ♕xf2+ 27.♕xf2 ♗xf2 28.♔xf2 ♖xb7 and Black was even nominally slightly

better, but the draw was never in doubt: ½-½ (40) Vachier-Lagrave-Ding Liren, Nations Cup Online 2020. **19...♕xd1 20.♖axd1 ♖c4 21.♗xd7 ♖xd4 22.♖xd4 ♗xd4 23.♖b1 ½-½**

I guess such short draws can be expained by the psychological factor. Fabiano was leading in the tournament, meanwhile Nikita was suffering without a single victory so far.

Maxime Vachier-Lagrave
Anish Giri

Magnus Carlsen Invitational 2020 (2.1)

1.d4 ♘f6 2.c4 e6 3.♘c3 ♗b4 4.♕c2 0-0 5.e4 d5 6.e5 ♘e4 7.♗d3 c5 8.♘f3 cxd4 9.♘xd4 ♘d7 10.♗f4 ♕h4 11.g3 ♕h5 12.0-0 g5 13.cxd5 gxf4 14.dxe6 ♘xc3 15.exd7 fxg3! Probably the most precise move order. **16.hxg3** The difference is that now in case of 16.fxg3 ♗xd7 17.bxc3 ♖ac8 18.♗xh7+ Black has 18...♔h8! (see the previous game for more details on the 16th move) △ 19.e6 ♗xc3! 20.♕e4 ♗c6 21.♘xc6 ♕xh7. **16...♗xd7 17.bxc3 ♖ac8 18.♕d1 ♕xd1 19.♖axd1 ♗xc3 20.♗f5 ♖c4 21.♗xd7 ♖xd4 22.♖xd4 ♗xd4**

23.♖e1!? A small idea prepared by Maxime. **23...♖d8 24.♗a4**. It's kind of surprising that with such limited material White can have any winning chances. But Maxime managed to squeeze water from the stone! I guess Giri was just overconfident: how can you beat me with a line I played myself not so long ago?! **24...♖d5** I guess it was more accurate to play 24...♔f8!? 25.♔g2 (25.e6 ♗f6 26.exf7 ♔xf7 27.♖e2 h5) 25...b5 26.e6 (26.♗xb5 ♖d5) 26...fxe6

27.♗xb5 e5 and Black should not have many problems here. **25.e6 fxe6 26.♖xe6 ♖e5 27.♖d6 ♗c5 28.♖d2 ♗g7 29.♔g2 b6 30.♗b3 h6 31.f4 ♗e3 32.♖d7+ ♔e7 33.♖d8 ♗b4 34.♔f3 ♗e1 35.g4 ♗c3 36.♖d6 ♗f6 37.♗e6 ♖c7 38.♔e4 ♗e7 39.♖d3 ♔f6 40.♗b3 b5 41.♖d5 ♖c5?** 41...♗c5 was still very close to a draw. **42.♖d7** Suddenly Black is in big trouble. **42...a5**

43.♖a7? Decisive is 43.♔d4! which wins the bishop after 43...♗c1 44.g5+ hxg5 45.fxg5+ ♔xg5 46.♖xe7 a4 47.♗d5 b4 48.♗c4+−. White should win without much trouble because Black can't eliminate White's last pawn. If 48...b3 49.♗xb3! axb3 50.axb3 is mate in 35 according to the Nalimov tablebase. **43...a4 44.♗d5 ♖c1 45.♖a6+ ♔g7 46.♔f5 ♖c7 47.♖a5 ♖c5?** Again leaving the 7th rank unjustifiably; 47...a3! 48.♖xb5? ♖c5= Reinderman. **48.♔e6 ♗d8 49.♖a8 ♗h4 50.♖a7+ ♔f8 51.♖h7 ♗g3 52.f5 ♖c7 53.♖xh6 ♖e7+ 54.♔f6 ♗e5+ 55.♔g5 ♖g7+ 56.♖g6 ♔e7 57.♖xg7+ ♗xg7 58.♗c6 a3 59.♗xb5 1-0**

When I prepared this Survey, another elite game was played online.

Maxime Vachier-Lagrave
Wesley So

St Louis Clutch QF 2020 (1.2)

1.d4 ♘f6 2.c4 e6 3.♘c3 ♗b4 4.♕c2 0-0 5.e4 d5 6.e5 ♘e4 7.♘f3 c5 8.♗d3 cxd4 9.♘xd4 ♘d7 10.♗f4 ♕h4 11.g3 ♕h5 12.0-0 g5 Another common move-order is 12...♗xc3 13.bxc3 g5! (13...♘ec5!? 14.♗e2! ♕g6 (14...♕h3!? 15.♕d1!+−) 15.♕xg6 hxg6 16.cxd5! exd5

(Lombaers-Umudova, Utrecht 2020) 17.♘b5!±; 13...♘dc5? 14.♗e2! ♕g6 15.f3 ♘g5 16.♕xg6 ♘h3+ 17.♔h1 hxg6 18.♗e3+− Alinasab-Pichot, chess.com blitz 2020) 14.cxd5 transposes to the text game. **13.cxd5 ♗xc3** Numerically this move is played far more often than 13...gxf4, but the character of play is very similar. **14.bxc3 exd5**

15.♗e3 15.♗xe4 dxe4 16.e6 gxf4 17.exd7 ♗xd7 18.♕xe4 fxg3 19.fxg3 b6 20.♘f5 ♖ae8; 15.e6 fxe6 (15...gxf4 16.exd7 ♗xd7 17.♗xe4 dxe4 – 15.♗xe4) 16.♗c7 ♖f7 17.f3 ♘ec5 18.♗e2; 15.♗e2 ♕h3 16.♗e3 ♘xe5 17.f3 ♘xg3 18.hxg3 ♕xg3+ 19.♔h1 ♕h3+ 20.♔g1 ♕g3+ ½-½ Jovanic-A.Saric, Vinkovci ch-CRO 2020. **15...♘xe5 16.f3 ♘xd3** 16...♘c5. **17.♕xd3 ♘d6 18.g4** 18.♖f2 ♕g6 19.♕xg6+ fxg6 (19...hxg6!?) 20.♗xg5 ♘c4 21.♘b5 ♖f7 22.♗f4 ♘h3 23.♖d1 ♖d7?! 24.♗e2 a6 25.♘c7 ♖ad8 26.♔f2 d4? (26...h6±) 27.cxd4 ♖xd4? 28.♖e8+ ♖xe8 29.♖xd4 1-0 Mamedyarov-Gelfand, Moscow rapid 2019. **18...♕g6 19.♕xg6+ hxg6 20.♗xg5 f6** Once again we have an endgame with opposite-coloured bishops. White is slightly more active, but with some accurate play I think Black should hold. **21.♗f4** 21.♗h6 ♖f7 22.♗f4 ♘c4 23.h4 ♗d7 24.♔f2 ♘e5 25.♔g3 ♖c8 26.g5?! ♖xc3 27.gxf6 ♘g4 28.♘e2 ♘d3 29.♘c1 ♖a3 30.♗d6 ♘e3?! 31.♗xa3 ♘xf1+ 32.♔f2 ♖xf6 33.♗b2 ♖b6 34.♗d4 ♖b4 35.♗c3 ♖c4 36.♘e2 d4 37.♗xd4 (1-0 (46) Burg-Wiedenkeller, Budva 2019) 37...♘h2! 38.♗xa7 ♖xh4 39.♗b8 ♗c6 40.♔g3 ♖h5 41.♘d4 ♗d5 although the knight remains terribly off-side. **21...♘c4**

22.♘b5 A novelty, but not a great improvement on the previous efforts: 22.h4 ♗d7 23.♔f2 ♔f7 24.♖h1 ♖ac8 25.♖ac1 ♘b2 26.♖c2 ♘d3+ 27.♔e3 ♘e5 28.♔f2 ♘d3+ 29.♔e3 ♘e5 30.♔f2 ♘d3+ ½-½ Mamedyarov-So, Bucharest blitz 2019; 22.♖fe1 ♗d7 23.h4 ♖fe8 24.♔f2 ♔f7 25.♖xe8 ♖xe8 26.♖e1 ♘a3 27.♖xe8 ♗xe8 28.♔e3 ♗a4 29.♗b8 a6 30.♔d3 ♗d1 31.♔d2 ♗a4 32.♔d3 ♗d1 33.♔d2 ♗a4 ½-½ Santos Ruiz-Kryvoruchko, Germany Bundesliga 2019/20. **22...♗d7 23.♘c7 ♖ac8 24.♘xd5 ♖c5 25.♖ad1 ♗e6 26.♘b4 g5 27.♖fe1 ♗xg4 28.fxg4 gxf4 29.♘d3 ♖a5 30.♘xf4 ♖xa2= 31.♘g6 ♖f7 32.h4 ♔g7 33.h5 ♔h6 34.♖d4 b5 35.♖e8 f5 36.♖h8+ ♔g5 37.♖g8 ♔h6 38.♖h8+ ♔g5 39.♖g8 ♔h6 40.g5+ ♔xh5 41.♘f4+ ♔g4 42.g6 ♖b7**

43.♖f8? ♘e5∓ **44.♘h5+ ♔xh5 45.♖xf5+ ♔xg6 46.♖xe5 a5 47.♖d6+ ♔g7 48.♖g5+ ♔f8 49.♖f6+ ♔e7 50.♖a6 ♔f7 51.♖ag6 ♖e8** 51...♖d7 52.♖g7+ ♔e8 53.♖xd7 ♔xd7 54.♖xb5=. **52.♖g8+ ♔d7 53.♖8g7+ ♔c8 54.♖xb7 ♔xb7 55.♖xb5+ ♔a6 56.♖b8 a4 57.c4 a3 58.c5 ♔a5 59.♖a8+ ♔b4 60.♖b8+ ♔a4 61.♖a8+ ♔b4 62.♖b8+ ♔xc5 63.♖b3 ♖a1+ 64.♔h2 ♔c4 65.♖g3 ♖a2+ 66.♔h1 ♖a1+ 67.♔h2**

♔d4 68.♖g4+ ♔e3 69.♖g3+ ♔f4 70.♖b3 ♔e4 71.♖g3 ♔d4 72.♖g4+ ♔c3 73.♖g3+ ♔c4 ½-½

**Main line
9.♘xd4 & 12.h4**

**Maxim Chigaev
Mustafa Yilmaz**
Douglas 2019 (4)

1.d4 ♘f6 2.c4 e6 3.♘c3 ♗b4 4.♕c2 0-0 5.e4 d5 6.e5 ♘e4 7.♗d3 c5 8.♘f3 8.♘e2 may just transpose to the same lines, e.g. 8...cxd4 9.♘xd4 ♘d7 etc. **8...cxd4 9.♘xd4 ♘d7 10.♗f4 ♕h4 11.g3 ♕h5 12.h4**

This move became popular thanks to the efforts of Paco Vallejo. The play after 12.0-0 g5 looks very forced, with lots of piece exchanges. So let's check some other options for White. **12...♘xe5** This is the most popular move, probably because it has been played by the top players. But actually I don't see anything wrong with the rarely played 12...f6!? 13.cxd5 exd5 14.exf6 ♖xf6 15.f3 ♘ec5⇄. This looks playable for Black, and it's nice to have more options just in case. **13.♗e2 ♘g4** Once again Black had another option: 13...♕g6!?, temporarily sacrificing a knight. But the material will be returned pretty quickly after 14.♗xe5 f6 15.h5 (15.♗f4 e5) 15...♕f7 16.♗f4 e5 17.cxd5 ♕xd5 18.0-0-0 (18.0-0 ♗xc3 19.bxc3 exf4 20.gxf4 ♘h8) 18...♘xc3 19.bxc3 ♗a3+ 20.♔b1 exd4 21.♕a4 ♗f5+ 22.♔a1 d3 23.♕xa3 ♖fe8 24.♗e3 (24.g4 ♕c4 25.♗f3 ♕xf4 26.♗d5+ ♗e6) 24...♕c6 25.♗xd3 ♗xd3. No-one

has played this yet, but it looks fine for Black. **14.♗xg4 ♕xg4 15.f3 ♕h5 16.g4 ♕g6 17.fxe4 e5!** A very concrete position where you need to calculate well – or better, check the lines beforehand at home. When Paco played this line for the first time, his opponent was caught by surprise and immediately made a mistake: 17...♕f6? 18.♘de2 e5 (18...d4 19.e5) 19.♗g5 f3 20.0-0-0 and here White just has an extra piece without any compensation (1-0 (36) Vallejo Pons-So, Leon 2018). To defend the black player, I should mention that this game was played in rapid chess where the probability to make a mistake is much higher.

18.♗xe5 White doesn't get an advantage with 18.0-0-0 ♗xc3 19.♘f5 ♗xf5 20.gxf5 ♕g4 (probably simpler is 20...♕a6 21.♕xc3 d4 22.♕d3 exf4 23.♔b1 ♖ac8 24.b3 ♖fd8 25.e5 when White has some activity for the pawn, but Black's pieces are well placed and I doubt that he should be very much afraid for his king) 21.♗e3 ♗d4 (probably Black could also play 21...d4!? 22.♗h6 (22.♖dg1 ♕h5 23.♗g5 ♗b4) 22...♕h5 23.♗xg7 ♗xb2+ 24.♔xb2 ♕xg7 25.♕g2+ ♔f6!? (25...♔h8 26.♕g5 ♕xg5 27.hxg5 ♖g8 28.♖h5 ♗g7 29.♖g1 f6 30.gxf6+ ♔xf6 31.♖h6+ ♔f7 32.♖xh7+ ♔f6). It looks a bit scary, but I don't see any refutation: 26.♖xd4 ♖ad8 (26...exd4? 27.e5+ ♔e7 (27...♔xf5 28.♖f1+) 28.♕xb7+) 27.♖d5 ♖g8 28.♕d2 ♖xd5 29.♕xd5 ♕e2+ 30.♔a1 ♖g2 31.♕d6+ ♔g7 32.♕xe5+ ♔g8 33.♕e8+ ♔g7 34.♕e5+=) 22.♗xd4 exd4 23.exd5 ♖ac8 24.♔b1 b5 25.c5 ♖fd8 26.♖hg1

♕xh4? (probably only this greedy move was the decisive mistake. Correct was 26...♕f3! 27.♖xd4 (27.d6 ♖xd6) 27...♖xd5 28.♖xd5 (28.♖dg4 ♖cxc5 29.♖xg7+ ♔f8 30.f6 ♕xf6 31.♕g2 ♕e7) 28...♖xd5 29.♖d1 ♕c6 30.b4; it's more pleasant to play with white here from the practical aspect, but still a lot of play is ahead) 27.c6 g6 (27...♖xd5 28.♕g2+−) 28.fxg6 hxg6 29.♕f5 ♔g7 30.c7 ♖e8 31.d6 ♖e6 32.♖df1 ♖f8 33.c8♕ 1-0 Howell-Adair, Hull 2018. In the end the better player prevailed. But I feel that if we changed sides the result might have turned out different. **18...♗xg4!** I think this is the simplest solution. White has an extra piece. There is no comfortable way to keep it, although it's also possible to play 18...♖e8 19.0-0-0 ♗xc3. But now the position is messier:

20.exd5 (20.bxc3 ♗xg4 21.♖dg1 ♖xe5 22.exd5 f5 23.♖e1 ♖ae8 24.♖xe5 ♖xe5∞; 20.♗xg7!? ♕xg7 (20...♗xg4!? 21.♕xc3 ♖xe4) 21.bxc3 dxe4 and both kings are exposed) 20...♖xe5 21.♕xc3 ♗xg4. Both sides have their chances here. In the end, the better player benefits more from such complicated play: 22.♖de1 ♖ae8 (22...♖xe1+!? 23.♖xe1 ♕h6+ 24.♔b1 ♕xh4) 23.b3 h5 24.♖xe5 ♖xe5 25.♖e1 ♖e4 26.♔b2 ♖xe1 27.♕xe1 ♕f6 28.♔c3 g5 29.hxg5 ♕xg5 30.d6 ♗d7 31.♕e4 ♕g3+ 32.♕f3 ♕xf3+ (32...♕xd6 33.♕xh5 ♕g3+=) 33.♘xf3 ♗g7? (a blunder) 34.♘e5 h4 35.♘xd7 h3 36.♘c5 h2 (36...♔f6 37.♘e4+ ♔e6 38.♘f2 h2 39.c5+−) 37.d7 h1♕ 38.d8♕ 1-0 (53) Vallejo Pons-Sebenik, chess.com 2019. **19.exd5 ♖ae8 20.♕xg6 fxg6N** I played

in the same tournament, and I remember that both players were blitzing out the opening moves with a lot of confidence. But it seems that Black was ready for this psychological bluff.

21.♘e6?! The knight is actually more useful here with passed pawns than a bishop. Better was 21.♔d2 ♖xe5 22.♖ae1 ♖f2+ 23.♔d3 ♖xe1 24.♖xe1 ♖xb2 25.♖e8+ ♔f7 26.♖a8 a6 27.♘e4 and White's activity compensates for the sacrificed pawn: 27...♗f5 28.♖b8 ♗xe4+ (28...♗d6? 29.♖xb7+ ♖xb7 30.♘xf5+−) 29.♔xe4 ♗d6 30.♖d8 ♔e7 31.♖g8 ♔f7=. **21...♗xe6 22.0-0-0 ♗g4 23.♖de1 ♖c8** As happened many times, Black is happy to have easily solved his opening problems. But now he could have played more ambitiously with 23...♗c5!? 24.♗c3 (24.♗g3 ♖xe1+ 25.♖xe1 ♖f3 26.♗c7 ♗f5 27.d6 ♔f8) 24...♖xe1+ 25.♖xe1 ♗f2 26.♖h1 ♖f3. White's passed pawn won't go far, while Black's bishops are really powerful: 27.d6 ♔f7. **24.a3 ♗xc3 25.♗xc3 ♖xc4 26.♖e7 ♖f7 27.♖he1 ♗d7 28.d6 ♖cf4 29.♖e8+ ♖f8 30.♖8e7 ♖8f7 31.♖e8+ ♖f8 32.♖8e7 ♖8f7 ½-½** It seems Black has more than one good option in this line, but some precise play is required.

**Minor lines
7.♗d3**

Francisco Vallejo Pons
Jorden van Foreest

PRO League Stage 2019 (10)

1.d4 ♘f6 2.c4 e6 3.♘c3 ♗b4 4.♕c2 0-0 5.e4 d5 6.cxd5 The more normal move-order is 6.e5

♞e4 7.♝d3 c5 and now after 8.cxd5 exd5 9.a3 we reach our game.
6...exd5 7.e5 ♞e4 8.♝d3 c5 9.a3!?

A new attempt by Paco to find new ideas in this line for White. The old classical move is 9.♞e2 cxd4 10.♞xd4 ♞d7 11.f4 ♛h4+ 12.g3 ♛h3 13.♝f1 ♛h5 (later Black improved with 13...♛h6!? 14. ♝g2 ♛a6⇄ and White had some problems with his king in the centre) 14.♝g2 ♞b6 15.0-0 ♝xc3 16.bxc3 ♛h3 17.f5 ♝xg2 18.♛xg2 ♞c4 19.g4 ♛h4 20.f6↑ Kramnik-Adams, Cologne 1998. It's hard to believe, but this game was played more than 20 years ago! **9...♝xc3+** Probably the biggest problem when you face something unexpected is the big choice between the different options. Which way to go? I guess in case of 9...♝a5 White can play similarly: 10.♞e2 cxd4 11.♞xd4 ♞d7 12.f4 ♛h4+ 13.g3 ♛h3 14.♝f1 ♛h6 15.♝g2 ♛a6 but now, with the moves a2-a3 and ...♝a5 included, he has 16.b4!? ♝xb4 17.axb4 ♛xa1 18.♝xe4 dxe4 19.0-0 ♛a6 20.♞xe4 with nice active play for the sacrificed exchange. One good GM immediately made a huge tactical mistake: 9...♛a5? (Simutowe-Ehlvest, Reno 2005) and now White could have punished him with 10.axb4! ♛xa1 11.♞xd5+−; Black's knight is trapped in the centre and White wins some material. Probably simple play was possible with 9...cxd4 10.axb4 dxc3 11.bxc3 ♞c6 12.♞f3 ♜e8 13.0-0 (13.♝f4 ♝g4) 13...♞xe5 14.♞xe5 ♜xe5. Black wins a pawn and in general doesn't have problems to develop his pieces on good squares: 15.♝e3 a6 16.♝d4 ♜e8 17.f3 ♞f6 18.g4⇄, although White's bishops

are pretty active and so far the extra pawn doesn't play a big role here. **10.bxc3**

If White manages to finish his development, he will be left with a nice pawn structure and the bishop pair. So Black should try to play energetically in such situations. **10...♞c6** After 10...f6 11.f3 once again Black's knight is trapped in the centre: 11...c4 12.♝e2 ♝f5 13.♛b2 fxe5 14.fxe4 ♛h4+ (very aggressive play by Black) 15.♔d1 ♛xe4 but probably he doesn't have enough compensation for the sacrificed material, e.g. 16.♞f3 exd4 17.♞xd4 ♝d7 18.♝f3 ♝a4+ 19.♔d2 ♛d3+ (19...♛h4 20.g3) 20.♔e1 and White's king escapes to the safe zone. Smarter was 10...♝f5!? 11.♞e2 (if now 11.f3 then 11...♛h4+ 12.♔f1 ♞g3+ 13.hxg3 ♝xd3+ 14.♛xd3 ♛xh1 15.♛f5 cxd4 16.cxd4 ♞c6 17.♝e3 ♜ac8, and I don't think White has time to trap Black's queen in the corner; 11.♛b2 ♞c6 12.♞e2 cxd4 13.cxd4 ♛a5+ 14.♔f1 f6∓) 11...c4 12.♝xe4 ♝xe4 13.♛b2 ♝xg2 14.♜g1 ♝e4. It looks like the previous moves were more or less forced. White's king is stuck in the centre, and the opposite-coloured bishops give both sides chances to create an initiative. 15.♝h6 (15.♛xb7 ♞d7; 15.f3 ♝g6 16.♛xb7 ♞d7 17.♔f1 (17.♛xd5 ♛h4+ 18.♜g3 ♞b6) 17...♞b6 18.♝f4∞) 15...♝g6 16.♛xb7 ♞d7!? (I like to try to keep the queens on; if 16...♛d7 17.♛xd7 ♞xd7 18.h4 gxh6 19.h5 ♜ab8 20.♝f4∞) 17.♝g5 ♛e8 18.♛xd5 ♞b6 19.♛g2 f6. Frankly speaking, I feel this is easier to play for Black. Maybe Vallejo was just bluffing? Although with some

precise moves White can probably keep the balance: 20.♝xf6 gxf6 21.h4 fxe5 22.h5 ♜f6 23.♜d1 etc. Also interesting is 10...♛a5!? △ 11.♞e2 (I am not sure White has something better) 11...cxd4 with a transposition to the line that we will check in the game Wang Hao-Wei Yi below. **11.♞e2**

11...♝f5? But now the same move is bad. Black should play 11...f6 and now 12.f3 does not win the knight in the centre because of 12...fxe5 13.fxe4 c4. Another tricky option was 11...cxd4 12.cxd4 ♝g4!? 13.f3 (13.0-0 ♝xe2 14.♛xe2 ♞xd4) 13...♝xf3 14.gxf3 ♛h4+ 15.♞g3 ♞xd4 (15...♞xg3 16.♛f2) 16.♛g2 ♞c5 with a messy position. But it looks like Black should be fine: 17.♝b1 ♞cb3 18.♝b2 ♜xa1 19.♝xa1 f6!↑ and White always lacks one tempo to castle. **12.f3 cxd4** Black could have saved the knight with 12...c4 13.♝xe4 dxe4 14.fxe4 ♝g6 15.0-0 but from a practical point of view his position looks hopeless. **13.0-0!** Maybe this move had been missed by Black. Chess is not checkers and you don't need to recapture material immediately. It's never to late make a mistake: 13.cxd4?! ♜c8 and now Black is fine after 14.♛b2 ♛h4+. **13...♞xe5** Trying to complicate things in a bad position, but without much success. 13...♜c8 14.fxe4 dxe4 15.♜xf5+−. Black could have saved material; I think more stubborn was 13...♝g6 14.cxd4 ♞g5 (14...♜c8 15.fxe4 dxe4 16.♝b5 ♞xd4 17.♛b2) 15.♝xg5 ♛xg5 16.f4 ♝xd3 17.♛xd3 ♛g4 18.♜ab1± although it's not much fun to defend so many weaknesses without any real counterplay.

14.♘xd4 ♘xd3 15.♕xd3 ♘g3 16.♕xf5 ♘xf1 17.♔xf1 Rook and pawn can be approximately equal to a bishop and knight. But this is not the case here. Having two pieces in the attack against one in defence is a huge factor in this position. **17...♕f6 18.♗e3 ♕e5 19.♕xd5** I think more in the spirit of the position was 19.♗d4!? ♕xh2 20.♗xg7 intending to give mate with the queens on the board, e.g. 20...♕h1+ 21.♔f2 ♕xa1 22.♕d4 ♕a2+ 23.♔g3 f6 24.♕g4 ♔f7 25.♗xf8 ♖xf8 26.♕g7+ ♔e6 27.♘d4++−. **19...♖fe8 20.♕xe5 ♖xe5 21.g4 f6 22.♗d4 ♖e6 23.a4** Now White slowly converted his advantage in the endgame: **23...♖d8 24.♔f2 h5 25.h3 ♔f7 26.♘e3 ♖d7 27.gxh5 ♖a6 28.♖g1 ♖a5 29.h6 gxh6 30.♘g4 h5 31.♘h6+ ♔e6 32.♖e1+ ♔d5 33.♖g8 ♗c4 34.♘xf6 ♖f7 35.♘e4 ♖f8 36.♘d6+ ♔b3 37.♘xb7 ♖af8 38.♘c5+ ♔c4 39.♘e3 ♖xc5 40.♗xc5 ♔xc5 41.♖e5+ ♔c4 42.♖xh5 ♔xc3 43.♖a5 ♖f7 44.h4 ♔d4 45.h5 ♖g7 46.h6 ♖h7 47.♖h5 a5 48.♔g3 ♔c4 49.♖h4+ ♔d5 50.♔g4 ♔e6 51.♔g5 ♔e7 1-0**

Wang Hao
Wei Yi
Danzhou 2019 (1)

1.d4 ♘f6 2.c4 e6 3.♘c3 ♗b4 4.♕c2 0-0 5.e4 d5 6.e5 ♘e4 7.a3 The same position as in the game can occur after 7.♗d3 c5 8.a3 ♗xc3+ 9.bxc3. **7...♗xc3+ 8.bxc3 c5 9.♗d3** This looks very similar to what Vallejo played. The only difference is that the c- and e-pawns have not been exchanged. There is more tension in the centre, but also it's harder for Black to develop the bishop. **9...♕a5!?** I like the way Black by very concrete moves solved all his problems in this game. More frequently played is 9...cxd4 10.cxd4 ♕a5+ 11.♔f1 ♘c6 12.♘e2 or 9...♘c6 10.♘e2 cxd4 11.cxd4 ♕a5+ 12.♔f1 which is the same position: 12...f6 13.♗xe4 dxe4 14.exf6 ♖xf6 (14...♕f5 15.♗e3

♕xf6 16.♖d1 b6 17.♕xe4 ♗b7 18.♔g1 ♘a5 19.d5 ♖ae8 20.♕d4 ♕xd4 21.♘xd4 (Grigore-Korneev, Manresa 2004) 21...e5!∓) 15.♗e3. In general Black has done okay here in practice. But the play is not so forced, and maybe White can look for improvements, to get at least interesting play: 15...b6 16.h4 (16...♘g3!?) 16...♗b7 17.♖h3 (or now 17.♔g1 ♘e7 18.♘g3!?) 17...♘e7 18.♔g1 ♖c8 19.♗g5 ♖f7 20.♖c3 ♘f5 21.♖b1 h6 22.♖b5 a6 23.♖b4 ♗c6 24.d5 exd5 25.cxd5 ♗d7 26.♖xc8+ ♕xc8 27.♕xc8+ ½-½ Bartel-Tomashevsky, Moscow 2012. **10.♘e2** I tried to check the following unusual idea: 10.♗xe4 dxe4 11.♗d2 ♕a6 12.♕xe4 ♕xc4 and since many of Black's pieces are still on the queenside, maybe with the pawn on e5 White can create an attack on the kingside... 13.♘e2 (13.♘f3 ♗d7 14.♗g5 f5) 13...♗d7 14.0-0 ♗b5 15.♖fe1 (15.♘f4 ♘c6 16.♘h5 ♕e2) 15...♕d3 16.♕f4 ♘c6 but probably this just doesn't work if Black plays carefully. **10...cxd4 11.cxd5 exd5** Black should not react to the small provocation: 11...♘xc3?! 12.♗d2 ♕xd5 13.♗xc3 dxc3 14.♗xc3 h6 15.0-0 ♘c6 16.♖fd1 ♕c5 17.♗h7+ ♔h8 18.♗e4± and Black has won a pawn, but now he will struggle to finish his development. **12.f3** 12.♘xd4 ♗xc3+ 13.♕xc3 ♘xc3 14.♗e3 ♘a4 and the knight goes to c4. Black doesn't have any problems. **12...♗xc3 13.♘xd4**

13...♗e4+! The most precise. It looks as if White will not get rid of this knight so easily. In case of the 'softer' 13...♗b5+ 14.♗d2 ♘xd4 15.♗xh7+ ♔h8 16.♗xa5 ♘xc2+ 17.♗xc2 ♘c6 maybe White

can hope for some small edge thanks to the pair of bishops: 18.♗c7!? (18.♗b4 ♖e8 19.f4 f6) 18...♗e6 19.♗d6 ♖fc8 20.♗d3. **14.♔e2 f5!** Once again, the most ambitious. After 14...♕c3 15.♗e3 (15.♗xe4 ♕xa1 16.♗xh7+ ♔h8 17.♖d1 ♘c6 18.♗b2 (18.♘xc6 bxc6 19.♗b2 ♕a2 20.♘d4 ♖b8 21.h4 ♕xb2 22.♗g6+ ♔g8 23.♗h7+=) 18...♘xd4+ 19.♖xd4 ♕h1 20.♖h4 ♕xg2+ 21.♔e1 ♕xc2 22.♗xc2+ ♔g8 23.♗h7+=) 15...♕xc2+ 16.♗xc2 ♘c5 17.♘b5 ♗a6 Black has an extra pawn in the endgame but his pieces are slightly passive: 18.♖hd1 (18.♔f2!? ♗d7 19.♘d6 ♗c6 20.♗g5 ♘e6 21.♗e7 ♖fb8 22.♘f5 ♘ac7 23.♗d6±) 18...♗d7 19.♘c3 (19.♘d6 ♗c6 20.♖ac1 ♖ad8 21.♗xc5 ♘xc5 22.♗xh7+ ♔xh7 23.♖xc5 f6⇄) 19...♖ac8 20.♖xd5 (20.♘xd5 ♖fe8) 20...♗e6 21.♖d2 ♘b3 22.♗xb3 ♗xb3 23.♘e4 and this may still be slightly better for White.

15.e6!? A slightly surprising idea with the king in the centre. I guess White's intention is not to promote this pawn, but rather to create problems for Black to develop his queenside. Of course it's not possible to take the knight: 15.fxe4 fxe4 16.♗b5 ♗g4+ 17.♔e3 ♕b6 18.e6 ♘d8 19.h4 ♕f6, threatening 20...♕h6 or 20...♕f4 mate. Young Paco of course played 15.♗e3 ♘c6 16.♘xc6 bxc6 17.♖hc1 ♖b8 but ended up without material with a bad king in the centre: 18.♔d1 ♖d8 19.♗d4 ♗e6 20.♖ab1 ♖xb1 21.♖xb1 c5 22.♗b5 ♕xa3 23.♗b2 ♕a2 24.♔e2 ♗d7 25.fxe4 ♗xb5 26.♗xb5 ♖b8 27.♘c6 ♕xb2−+ Vallejo Pons-Leko, Morelia/Linares 2006. **15...♘c6 16.♘xc6 bxc6 17.e7 ♖e8 18.♕xc6**

♖xe7 19.♕xa8 Similar play ensues after 19.fxe4 fxe4 20.♗c4 dxc4 21.♕xa8 ♖e8 22.♕c6 ♗g4+ 23.♔f2 ♕e5 24.♖e1 ♖f8+ 25.♔g1 ♕xa1 26.♕xc4+ ♔h8 27.♕xe4 ♕c3 28.♕e3 ♕xe3+ ½-½ Braun-Meier, Saarbrücken 2009. **19...♘g3+ 20.♔d1 ♕c3** 20...♕a4+ 21.♔d2 ♕f4+ 22.♔c2 ♕a4+=. **21.♗d2 ♕xa1+ 22.♗c1 ♕c3** 22...♘xh1? 23.♕xc8+ ♗f7 24.♕xf5+ ♕f6 25.♕xd5+ ♕e6 26.♕xe6+ ♔xe6 27.♗e3±. **23.♗d2 ♕a1+ 24.♗c1 ♕c3 25.♗d2 ½-½** It looks like both players demonstrated good knowledge of theory and the game finished without any independent human moves over the board.

Minor lines
7.a3

Yu Yangyi
Levon Aronian

Riga 2019 (1)

1.d4 ♘f6 2.c4 e6 3.♘c3 ♗b4 4.♕c2 0-0 5.e4 d5 I can recommend 5...d6!? for Black if he needs to play for a win, or if he doesn't like very forced lines. **6.♗d3** (the aggressive move 6.e5 was recently analysed in great detail by José Vilela in Yearbook 132. My general feeling is that Black should be fine here; 6.a3 ♗xc3+ 7.bxc3 is the most common line) 6...e5 7.a3 exd4!? 8.axb4 dxc3 was my concept when I prepared 5...d6 15 years ago against Vallejo Pons, Cuernavaca 2006. My modern engine suggests the novelty 9.♘e2!?, sacrificing a pawn for quick development. **6.e5 ♘e4 7.a3 ♗xc3+ 8.bxc3 c5**

9.♗b2?! A very risky way of playing which is hard to recommend. But in view of the match situation Yu Yangyi had to win at any cost, and somehow it worked for him. When I had almost finished the Survey the following game was played: 9.f3!? (a move which is hard to evaluate. Is it a bluff or did White miss something during preparation? Please keep in mind that the time control was 10 min+10 sec and the game was played online) 9...♕h4+ 10.g3 ♘xg3 11.hxg3 ♕xh1 12.♕f2 ♕h5 13.♗d3 f6! (a wise decision. Wesley opens up the position for his rook on f8 – Ramirez) 14.exf6 ♖xf6 15.g4 ♕f7 16.♕h4 g6 17.♗g5 ♘d7 18.♔f2 dxc4 19.♗xc4 cxd4 20.cxd4 b5 (before, Fabiano was blitzing, but now he took a long think: 4.5 minutes) 21.♗xb5?! (the engine suggests 21.♗a2 ♗b7 22.♗xf6 ♘xf6 23.♖e1 but the position looks totally fine for Black and it's White who tries to survive a pawn down: 23...♖e8 24.♘h3 ♕c7 25.♕xf6 ♕h2+ 26.♔f1 ♕xh3+ 27.♔g1 ♕g3+ 28.♔f1) 21...♗b7 (material is equal, but White's king looks much weaker) 22.♕g3?! ♖f8?! (22...e5! 23.♗xf6 ♘xf6∓) 23.♗xf6?! (23.♗e1!=) 23...♘xf6 24.♔g2 h5?! (24...♕d5∓) 25.gxh5? (25.♖c1! ♕d5 25...♕xg4 26.♖c7! 'is a cute trap' – Ramirez) 26.gxh5 ♘f4+ 27.♔h2 ♕h7 28.♘h3 ♕xh5 29.♖c5 ♕h6 30.♗c4=) 25...♘xh5–+ 26.♕g4 ♘f4+ 27.♔f2 e5? 28.♘e2? (28.♕d7!∓) 28...♗xf3–+ 29.♔xf3 ♕b3+ 30.♔f2 ♕xb5 31.♖e1 ♔g7 32.♘g3 ♕b2 0-1 Caruana-So, Clutch Chess International 2020. **9...♘c6** Not a bad move. But the most unpleasant for White might be 9...cxd4 10.cxd4 ♗d7! (not immediately 10...♕a5+ because after 11.♔e2 ♗d7 12.f3 the knight is trapped in the centre) 11.♘e2 (not possible was 11.f3 ♕h4+ which was one of the points of not playing ...♕a5 too early; 11.♗d3 ♕a5+ 12.♔e2 ♗a4 13.♖c1 ♘c6 14.f3 f5 also looks bad for White; 11.0-0-0 ♕a5). Now it's not so clear how

White can properly finish his development. Meanwhile Black can involve his pieces directly in the attack: 11...♘c6 12.♖d1 (12.f3 ♕a5+ 13.♘c3 ♘xd4 14.♕d3 ♘b3 15.fxe4 ♘xa1 16.♗xa1 ♕xa3–+) 12...f6! (the most energetic move) 13.♘c3 (13.f3 ♕a5+). Now Black can simply play 13...♕a5 with an attacking position for free, or the more adventurous 13...♘xf2!? 14.♕xf2 fxe5↑. **10.♗d3?!** I would say thst more in the spirit of the previous move was 10.0-0-0. At least now White's king is temporarily safe and Black's knight on e4 is in danger:

A) 10...cxd4 11.cxd4 f5 12.f3 ♘g5 13.h4 ♘f7 14.♔b1 ♕a5 15.cxd5 exd5 16.♘h3 may actually be good for White because Black is not in time to create counterplay, e.g. 16...♗d7 17.♘f4 ♖c8 18.♕f2 ♕b6 (18...♗a4 19.♖c1 ♖xc1+ 20.♗xc1 ♕b6+ 21.♕b2) 19.♘xd5 ♕e6 20.♘f4 ♕b6 21.♕e1 ♗a4 22.♖c1 ♘b3 23.♖c4 ♖xc4 24.♗xc4 ♖c8 25.♗e6 ♖c1+ 26.♕xc1 ♘xc1 27.♖xc1 g6 28.♖c8+ ♔g7 29.♗xf7 ♗d7 30.♘d5 ♕b5 31.♖c7 ♔xf7 32.♘f6. Very powerful play by the white player! 1-0 Feller-Sethuraman, Paris 2010;

B) 10...♗d7 11.f3 ♘xc3! 12.♕xc3 cxd4 13.♕e1 (13.♕d2 ♕a5 14.♗b4 ♖c8 15.♔b1 dxc4 16.♗xd4 (16.♖xd4 ♘c6) 16...♗c6∞; 13.♖xd4 ♘xd4 14.♕xd4 dxc4) 13...dxc4 14.♗xc4 b5↑. I think in general it's much easier to attack than to defend. **10...f5 11.♘e2 dxc4**

12.♗xe4?! I don't like the idea of keeping the dead bishop on b2. More principled was 12.♗xc4 although with some simple play: 12...cxd4 13.cxd4 ♕a5+ 14.♗c3 ♘xc3 15.♕xc3 ♕xc3+ 16.♘xc3 ♗d7! (16...♘xd4 17.0-0-0! ♘c6 18.f4 and

White has some dominance for the sacrificed pawn) 17.♗a2 ♖fd8 (17...♘xd4 18.0-0-0) 18.0-0-0 ♘e7 19.f4 ♔f7 20.d5 exd5 21.♘xd5 ♗e6 22.♘xe7 ♔xe7 23.♗xe6 ♔xe6, it should be fine for Black. 12...b5!? also deserved attention, but after 13.♗a2 (13.♗xb5 cxd4 14.♗xc6 d3 or 14.cxd4 ♕a5+) some precise play is required from Black: 13...cxd4 14.cxd4 ♕a5+ 15.♔f1 ♕b6 (15...♗d7 16.d5 ♘d8∞) 16.f3 b4! 17.fxe4 b3 18.♕xb3 (18.♗xb3 ♖b8) 18...♕xb3 19.♗xb3 ♖b8 20.♗a4 ♖xb2 21.♗xc6 ♗a6⇄. **12...fxe4 13.0-0 b5 14.♕xe4 ♗b7** Black has an excellent position, but Aronian couldn't quite control his nerves in the final stage of this game: **15.♕g4 ♕d5 16.f3 a5 17.♘f4 ♖xf4!?** Sacrificing an exchange in the style of Tigran Petrosian. **18.♕xf4 cxd4 19.cxd4 b4 20.axb4**

axb4 21.♖xa8+ ♗xa8 22.♖c1 ♗b7 23.♔f2 c3?! Making White's life much easier because now he can finally gets rid of this bad bishop on b2 and doesn't need to worry so much about the passed pawns. Something like 23...h6 24.h4 ♘e7 might have been a more practical decision, because White doesn't have any active play while Black can play ...c4-c3 at a better moment. **24.♗xc3 bxc3 25.♖xc3 h6 26.h4**

26...♗a6?! If Aronian only needed a draw I can't imagine why he didn't play 26...♕xd4+ 27.♕xd4 ♘xd4 28.♖d3 ♘c6 when with all the pawns on the same side it should be a simple draw. **27.♖a3 ♕b5 28.♔g3 ♘e7 29.♔h2 ♕b6 30.h5 ♗b7 31.♖d3 ♗d5 32.♖c3 ♘f5** Another not very practical decision. **33.♖c8+ ♔h7 34.♕g4** Probably this was a blunder in mutual time-trouble. **34...♘e7?** In fact it was still okay for Black after 34...g5 35.hxg6+ ♔g7 because White's queen cannot join the attack. **35.♖e8 ♕c7 36.♖f8 ♕c1 37.♖e8 ♕c7 38.♕g3 ♗b3 39.♖f8!+−** Now because of the threat of 40.♖f7 it's over. **39...♕c1 40.♖f7 ♘f5 41.♕g6+ ♔g8 42.♖b7 ♕f4+ 43.g3 ♕d2+ 44.♔h3 1-0**

Exercise 1

position after 18...♖a8-c8

White to move.

(solutions on page 251)

Exercise 2

position after 26.♕b3-f3

Black's king looks weak. How would you play?

Exercise 3

position after 9...♕d8-a5

Black is increasing the pressure on the pinned knight. How to deal with it?

Tough choices for Black

by Yu Yangyi

1.	d4	♘f6
2.	c4	e6
3.	♘c3	♗b4
4.	♘f3	d5
5.	♕b3	c5
6.	dxc5	

Yu Yangyi

This line has been played by some well-known grandmasters like Radjabov (against Leko in 2013), Andreikin, Fedoseev and Rapport, and also the Chinese grandmasters Wang Hao, Bu Xiangzhi and Xu Yinglun. Top players on the black side are Anand, Leko, Wojtaszek, Harikrishna and Vidit. Here Black has three options:

Complex play

A) 6...♘c6 is the most complicated. Play usually continues 7.♗g5 dxc4 8.♕xc4 ♕a5.

After White's attempt to expose Black's king with 9.♗xf6 gxf6 10.♖c1 ♕c5 11.♕h4 ♔e7, he continued with 12.g3 in Radjabov-Leko (2013) and Rapport-Gajewski (2014). If instead White plays 12.e3 then 12...♗xc3+ 13.♖xc3 ♕b4 or 13...♕b6 leads to an equal position with enough counterchances for Black. Instead of 8...♕a5, 8...h6! was a novelty Anand played against me at the Tata Steel tournament in 2020. I replied with 9.♗xf6 ♕xf6 10.e3 but couldn't get any advantage. If 9.♗h4 ♕e7 or 9...♕a5 Black should also be equal.

More solid

B) 6...♘a6

This move entered into the limelight in recent years. It was played first in 1994. Later, after Bartel-Gajewski (2011), several Polish players more often chose this line with black. After opening expert Peter Leko played it in 2016, 6...♘a6 became popular and was deeply analysed. Usually White continues 7.a3 ♗xc3+ 8.♕xc3 ♘xc5 9.cxd5 ♕xd5, see the game Bu Xiangzhi-Leko, Danzhou 2016. 7.cxd5 is an interesting idea. I first tried this against Harikrishna in the Chinese League in 2019, and gained a memorable victory with it against Wesley So in the final of the 2020 Online Nations Cup, allowing me to level the score in the match with USA, earning China the title.

A rare line

C) 6...♕a5

This is a rare line. Usually White replies 7.♗d2 and now follows 7...dxc4 8.♕xc4 ♕xc5, see the game Wang Hao-Mamedyarov (2017).

7.cxd5 is an interesting alternative also here: 7...♘xd5 8.♗d2 ♘xc3 9.a3 ♘c6 10.♖c1 was seen in the game Demuth-Lazarev (2015).

Conclusion

Most players opt for 6...♘c6, which leads to more complex play compared with the other two variations. In some variations Black seems to be in danger when his king is on e7, but White's queenside pawns are also weak, and Black gets more active pieces in compensation.

6...♘a6 has become popular in recent years. It is a more solid option, usually leading to an exchange of queens and a transfer to an endgame, where basically Black can achieve equality.

6...♕a5 is the rarest option. There are not many games in the database here, so we need to analyse it by ourselves.

I hope my article will help the reader to find his way in this interesting line.

**Complex play
6...♘c6**

**Teimour Radjabov
Peter Leko**
Zug 2013 (4)
1.d4 ♘f6 2.c4 e6 3.♘f3 d5 4.♘c3 ♗b4 5.♕b3 c5 6.dxc5 ♘c6 The first outing of this move in a top tournament was in Stahlberg-Wade, Saltsjöbaden izt 1952. 7.♗g5 ♕a5 8.♗xf6 dxc4 9.♕xc4 gxf6 10.♖c1 ♕xc5 11.♕h4 ♔e7 12.g3 ♗xc3+ 13.bxc3 b6 14.♗g2 ♗b7! I prefer this move because it is relatively safer, guarding the knight on c6. If

Black plays 14...♗a6, White can play ♘f3-d2-e4 to attack the black queen and the f6-pawn, when Black's position is uncomfortable. 15.0-0 h5 16.♘d4 ♖ac8 17.♖b1

17...♖c7?! Maybe Black should have played 17...♖hd8!? 18.♖fd1 (18.♖b5? is met by 18...♖xd4–+) 18...♘a5! 19.♘b3 (19.♗xb7 ♘xb7 20.♕f4 (20.♖d3 ♕g5!=) 20...♕xc3 21.♖b3 ♕c7 22.♕h6 ♘c5 23.♖e3 ♖d5∓) 19...♘xb3 20.♗xb7 ♘d2=. 18.♖fd1 ♘xd4 19.cxd4 ♕g5 20.d5± White is slightly better, but not enough to win. 20...♕xh4 21.d6+ ♔e8 22.dxc7 ♕c4 23.♖bc1 ♕xc1 24.♖xc1 ♗c8 25.♖d1 ♔e7 26.h4 e5 27.♗f3 27.f4!?± 27...♗e6 28.♖c1 ♗c8 29.♖d1 ♗e6 30.♗b7 ♗c8 31.♗xc8 ♖xc8 32.♖c1 b5 33.f3 b4 33...f5!? 34.♖c5

♔d6 35.♖xb5 ♖xc7 36.♔f2 f6
37.♖a5 ♔e6=. **34.g4 hxg4 35.fxg4**
a5 36.♖c4 a4 37.♖xb4 ♖xc7
38.♖xa4 ♔f8 39.♔f2 ♖c3 40.e3
♔g7 41.♖a8 ♖c2+ 42.♔f3 ♖h2
43.h5 ♖h3+ 44.♔f2 f5 45.gxf5
♖xh5 46.e4 ♖h3 47.♖a6 ♖d3
48.a4 ♖d4 49.♔e3 ♖b4 50.a5
♖a4 51.♔f3 ♖a3+ 52.♔g4 ♖a1
53.♖a8 ♔f6 54.♖a6+ ♔g7 55.♖b6
♖xa5 56.♔g5 ♖a1 57.f6+ ♔h7
58.♖b8 ♖h1 59.♖b7 ♖g1+ 60.♔f5
♖f1+ 61.♔xe5 ♔g6 62.♖b2 ♖g1
63.♖f2 ♖g5+ 64.♔d6 ♖a5 65.e5
♖a6+ 66.♔d5 ♖a5+ 67.♔d4
♖a4+ 68.♔d3 ♖a3+ 69.♔e4
♖a4+ 70.♔e3 ♖a3+ 71.♔d4
♖a4+ 72.♔c5 ♖a5+ 73.♔d6 ♖a6+
74.♔d7 ♖e6 75.♖g2+ ♔f5 76.♖g7
♔xe5 77.♖xf7 ♖xf6 78.♖xf6 ♔xf6
½-½

Richard Rapport
Grzegorz Gajewski
Budapest HUN-POL m 2014 (2)
1.♘f3 d5 2.d4 ♘f6 3.c4 e6 4.♘c3
♗b4 5.♕b3 c5 6.dxc5 ♘c6 7.♗g5
♕a5 8.♗xf6 dxc4 9.♕xc4 gxf6
10.♖c1 ♕xc5 11.♕h4 ♔e7 12.g3
♗xc3+ 13.bxc3 b6 14.♗g2 ♖a6?!
Usually Black plays 14...♗b7!? here.
15.♘d2! As mentioned in the
previous game, now the threat
of 16.♘e4 is very uncomfortable
for Black. **15...♖ac8** Here Black
should have preferred 15...♖ad8
16.♘e4 (16.♕xf6+ ♔xf6 17.♘e4+
♔g7 18.♘xc5 bxc5 19.♗xc6 ♖d6
20.♗e4 ♖b8=) 16...♕e5 17.f4 ♕f5
18.♘xf6±. **16.♘e4! ♕f5** If 16...♕e5
White keeps harassing Black
with 17.f4 ♕f5 18.♖d1→. **17.g4**
♕g6 18.f4 18.♕g3!?± with the
idea of h2-h4 or if 18...♘e5 19.g5!.
18...♘d4? 18...♗b7!? 19.0-0 ♘a5
20.f5→. **19.♖d1!** ♘c2+ 20.♔f2+−
♖hd8 21.♗f3 h6 22.♘g3! A very
strategic move, planning to play
♘h5. Of course the initial threat
is 23.♗e4. **22...♖xd1 23.♖xd1 ♖c4**
24.♘h5! ♗b5 25.♕g3!+− A nice
move, which I believe was White's
idea when he played 22.♘g3. Now
the threat is 26.f5, attacking the
black queen as well as the king
with ♕d6+ and mate. **25...♕g8**

26.f5 e5 27.♘xf6! A beautiful
tactic. **27...♗xf6 28.♖d6+ ♔g7**
29.♕h4 ♕f8 30.♕xh6+ ♔g8
31.♖g6+ 1-0 Accurate calculation
by Rapport.

Wang Hao
Santosh Gujrathi Vidit
Chengdu Ach 2017 (5)
1.d4 ♘f6 2.c4 e6 3.♘f3 d5 4.♘c3
♗b4 5.♕b3 c5 6.dxc5 ♘c6 7.♗g5
♕a5 8.♗xf6 dxc4 9.♕xc4 gxf6
10.♖c1 ♕xc5 11.♕f4

This is another option here. The
queen is closer to the centre,
controlling the diagonal f4-c7, but
the disadvantage of the move is
that Black can later play ...e6-e5
with tempo, followed by ...♘d4,
and equalize. **11...♔e7 12.g3 e5**
12...♗xc3+ 13.bxc3 (13.♖xc3 ♕b6
14.♗g2 ♕xb2 15.♕e3 ♕b1+ 16.♖c1
♕b6=) 13...b6 (13...h5!?∞) 14.♗g2
♗b7. **13.♕h6 ♗xc3+?!** If 13...♗e6
White replies 14.♗h3 to exchange
the bishops. Because the black
king is in the centre, his pieces do
not cooperate effectively enough
to attack White, and the white
king is safer. White is slightly
better, but this is not so easy to
prove: 14...♗xh3 15.♕xh3 ♘d4
16.0-0 (16.♔f1 ♗xc3 17.♖xc3 ♕d5
18.♖g1∞) 16...♗xc3 17.♘xd4 exd4
18.bxc3 (18.e3 ♕a5 19.♕g2 ♔f8
(19...♗b4?? 20.♕xb7++−) 20.♕xb7
♔g7 21.bxc3 dxc3=) 18...dxc3 19.♕g2
♖ac8 20.♕xb7+ ♖c7 21.♕e4+
♕e5= Bruzon Batista-Lenderman,
Tsakhkadzor Wch-tt 2015.
13...♖d8!N is a very important
novelty, intending to equalize
quickly with ...♘d4: 14.♗h3 ♗xh3
15.♕xh3 ♘d4= or 14.♗g2 ♘d4 15.0-0
♗xc3 16.♘xd4 exd4 17.bxc3 dxc3=.
14.bxc3 ♗e6 14...♘a5!? 15.♗g2

♘c4 16.0-0 ♗e6 17.♘h4±. **15.♗h3**
e4 15...♖ag8 16.♗xe6 fxe6 17.0-0
(17.♘d2!?±) 17...e4 (17...♕c4) 18.♘d4
♕g5=. **16.♗xe6 exf3 17.♗g4 fxe2**
18.♖c2 ♘e5?! 18...♘d4 19.♕e3+
♘e6 20.♕xc5+ ♘xc5 21.♖xe2+±;
18...♖ag8 19.♘f3 ♘e5 20.♗xe2 ♗g6
(20...♔d8 – game) 21.0-0±. **19.♗xe2**
♖ad8 20.0-0 ♖d6 21.♖e1 21.♔h5!?.
21...♖e6 22.♖d1 ♖d6 23.♖xd6
♕xd6 24.♕e3 ♕f8 25.♕xa7 ♕c6
26.f4 ♘d7?! 26...♘c4! 27.♕d4 b5
28.a4 ♗g7 29.axb5 ♕xb5± is possible
because of the check on b1; 26...♘f3+
27.♔f2 ♘xh2 28.♖b2 ♗g7 29.♖xb7
♖f8+−. **27.♕b2!+− b6 28.♖d2 ♔e7**
29.a4 ♖c8 30.♗b5 ♖c7 31.♗xc6
♖xa7 32.♗xd7 ♖xd7 33.♖xd7+
♔xd7 34.♔f2 ♔c6 35.♔e3 ♔c5
36.♔e4 ♔c4 37.♔f5 ♔xc3 38.♔xf6
♔b4 39.♔xf7 ♔xa4 40.f5 b5 41.f6
b4 42.♔g7 1-0

Yu Yangyi
Viswanathan Anand
Wijk aan Zee 2020 (4)
1.d4 ♘f6 2.c4 e6 3.♘c3 ♗b4
4.♘f3 d5 5.♕b3 c5 6.dxc5 ♘c6
7.♗g5 dxc4 There are scores of
games with 7...h6 8.♗xf6 (8.♗h4N
dxc4 9.♕xc4 ♕a5; 9...♕e7!?)
8...♕xf6 9.cxd5 exd5 10.e3, e.g.
10...0-0 (10...♗e6 11.♗b5 ♗xc5
12.♘xd5 ♗xd5 13.♕xd5 ♗b4+
14.♔f1 0-0±) 11.♗b5 d4 12.♗xc6
dxc3 13.♕xb4 cxb2 14.♖b1. **8.♕xc4**

8...h6!N A new idea by former
World Champion Anand! Now if
White replies 9.♗h4, Black has a
choice between 9...♕e7 or 9...♕a5.
In the line with 9...♕a5, Black's
pawn is better on h6 because in
some cases the white queen can't
come to h6. 8...♕a5 9.♗xf6 gxf6
transposes to the line 7...♕a5
examined before. **9.♗xf6** 9.♗h4

♕e7!? (9...♕a5 10.♗xf6 gxf6 11.♖c1 ♕xc5 12.♘h4 (12.♕f4 ♗e7 13.g3 e5) 12...♗e7) 10.♘e5 ♕xc5 11.♕xc5 ♗xc5 12.♘xc6 bxc6 13.0-0-0 e5 14.♘e4 (14.e3 ♗e6=) 14...♗e7 15.♘d6+ ♗xd6 16.♖xd6 ♗e6 17.♖xc6 ♔e7 18.b3 a5=. **9...♕xf6 10.e3 ♕e7 11.♖c1 ♕xc5 12.b3** In the queenless middlegame after 12.♕xc5 ♗xc5 13.♗b5 ♗d7 14.♔e2 ♗e7 15.♖hd1 a6 Black has no problems. **12...♗b6 13.a3 ♗xc3+ 14.♕xc3 0-0 15.♗d3 ♘e7 16.0-0** Because the pawn structure is symmetrical, the position is equal. **16...♘d5 17.♕c2** 17.♕c5 ♕xc5 18.♖xc5 b6 19.♖c2 ♗b7 20.♖fc1 ♖fc8 21.♘e5 ♖xc2 22.♖xc2 ♖d8=. **17...♗d7 18.♘e5 ♗b5= 19.♖fd1 ♗xd3** The pseudo-sacrifice 19...♘xe3? 20.fxe3 ♕xe3+ does lose a piece after 21.♔f2 ♕xe5 22.♖c5+−. **20.♖xd3 ♕d6 21.♘f3 ♕e7 22.h3 ♘b6 23.♕c7 ♕f6 24.♕xb7 ♖fb8 25.♕a6 ♖xb2 26.♖dc3 ♘d5 27.♖3c2 ♕b7 28.♖c6 ♕xa6 29.♖xa6 ♖b6 30.♖a5 a6 31.♘d4 ♖ab8 32.g3 ½-½**

More solid 6...♘a6

Mateusz Bartel
Grzegorz Gajewski
Warsaw ch-POL 2011 (3)

1.d4 ♘f6 2.c4 e6 3.♘f3 d5 4.♘c3 ♗b4 5.♕b3 c5 6.dxc5 ♘a6 This was the first game in the 21st century in which this move was played. The premiere was in 1994, in the game Golla-Groeger at the U.S. Open. **7.e3?!** Here White should prefer either 7.a3 or 7.cxd5, because now Black gets time to equalize easily. **7...♕a5 8.♗d2 ♘xc5 9.♕c2 ♘ce4=**

**10.♖c1 ♘xd2 11.♘xd2 ♗d7=
12.a3 ♗xc3 13.♕xc3 ♕xc3
14.♖xc3 ♔e7 15.♗d3 ♖hc8
16.♔e2 dxc4 17.♖xc4 ♗b5
18.♖cc1 ♖xd3+ 19.♔xd3 ♖d8+
20.♔e2 ♖ac8 21.♘b3 ♘e4 22.f3
♘d6 23.♘a5 ♔d7 24.♖hd1 ♖xc1
25.♖xc1 ♖c8 26.♖xc8 ♔xc8
27.♔d3 ♔c7 28.e4 e5 29.♘c4
♘xc4 30.♔xc4 ♔c6 31.b4 ½-½**

Yu Yangyi
Pentala Harikrishna
China tt 2019 (15)

**1.d4 ♘f6 2.c4 e6 3.♘c3 ♗b4
4.♘f3 d5 5.♕b3 c5 6.dxc5 ♘a6
7.cxd5 ♕a5** Black needs to watch out for traps. **8.♗d2 ♘xc5 9.♕c2 ♘xd5 10.a3**

10...♘d7! 10...♗xc3?! 11.♗xc3 ♘xc3 12.b4! ♕b6 13.bxc5 ♕a5 14.♕d2! b6 15.♖c1±. **11.♘xd5± ♗xd2+
12.♕xd2 ♕xd5 13.♕xd5 exd5**
With just a slight edge for White due to Black's isolated d-pawn.
**14.♖c1 ♘b6 15.e3 ♗d7 16.♗d3 ♔e7 17.♔d2 ♖ac8 18.b3 ♖xc1
19.♖xc1 ♖c8 20.♖b1 ♗e6 21.♘d4
♘d7 22.h4 h6 23.f3 ♘e5 24.♗b5
♗d7 25.♗xd7 ♘xd7 26.h5 ♘c6
27.♘f5 ♘e7 28.♘d4 ♘c6 29.♘f5
♘e7 30.♘d4 ♘c6 ½-½**

Yu Yangyi
Wesley So
Nations Cup final 2020 (1)

During this special period, I was very happy to participate in the online Nations Cup organized by FIDE. My teammates and I played very well and were ranked 1st in the preliminaries, but then in the last round of the preliminaries we lost to the U.S. team 1½-2½. After Round 9, the European team had been ranked 2nd and I had

no idea which team we would play against in the final. I hadn't watched my teammates' games in the other rounds, but now they suggested that I better watch their games since our team had already qualified for the final. Which I kept in mind in the last round of the preliminaries in our encounter with the USA when I played Wesley So. I planned to go for the Berlin Defence so I could make a draw and get myself some sleep. But when I saw that my teammates' games were all in so-so positions, I suddenly realized that I had to play for a win. However, I missed a couple of chances and my opponent played very well and managed to attack my king, and so I lost in the end. And then our team had to play the USA again in the final, and again my opponent was Wesley So. **1.d4 ♘f6 2.c4 e6 3.♘c3 ♗b4 4.♘f3 d5** He goes for the Ragozin Defence. **5.♕b3** I had played this before in classical games. **5...c5 6.dxc5 ♘a6** This year in Wijk aan Zee, Vishy Anand played 6...♘c6 against me (½-½, 32). **7.cxd5 ♘xd5** Last year, Pentala Harikrisha played the variation with 7...♕a5 against me (½-½, 30). **8.c6!** A new move and a new idea. I wanted to fracture the black queenside pawn structure, hoping to leave the a6-knight in an awkward position.

8...♕a5?! This will cause Black small problems. Perhaps 8...0-0!? or 8...bxc6 9.♕c2 were better continuations for Black. **9.♗d2 bxc6 10.g3!** I chose to move the bishop to g2, to control the h1-a8 diagonal, rather than the f1-a6 diagonal. After both 10.e4 ♘xc3

11.bxc3 ♗e7 and 10...♘c5 11.♕c2 ♘xc3 12.bxc3 ♗a3 the position is equal. **10...♘xc3 11.bxc3 ♗e7 12.♗g2 0-0 13.0-0** Interesting was 13.♘d4!? ♗d7 14.♗xc6 ♘c5 when Black should have compensation for the pawn. **13...e5 14.♕c2!?** I had planned to play 14.♕c4 but then I saw that Black could play 16...f6 and I was not impressed by my position: 14...♗e6 15.♕xc6 ♖ac8 16.♕e4 f6 17.♘d4!, but I had missed that I could in fact go for 16...♗f6, giving Black counterchances. **14...♕c7 15.♕e4! f6 16.♕c4+ ♔h8 17.♗e3!** At this point I felt my position was a bit better, because my queen on c4 controlled Black's bishop and the a6-knight. **17...♘b8 18.♖fd1!** Here I faced a dilemma, because Black is about to play ...♗a6 and attack my pawn on e2 and then ...♘d7 next. Therefore I decided to sacrifice a pawn. **18...♗a6 19.♕e6** After 19.♕g4 f5 20.♕h5 ♗xe2 21.♖d2 g6 22.♕h6 ♗xf3 23.♗xf3 ♘d7 White has enough compensation for the pawn. Another good square for the queen is 19.♕e4 ♘d7 (19...♗xe2 20.♖d2 ♗a6 21.♘h4 also favours White) 20.♘h4 and White is better. **19...♗xe2?!** Risky. An interesting alternative was 19...♗c8!? 20.♕c4 ♗a6 when I was thinking of 21.♕e4 anyway. **20.♖d2** Here 20.♘h4!? was a very powerful exchange sacrifice: 20...♗xd1 21.♖xd1 and now:
A) 21...♖d8 22.♖xd8+ ♕xd8 23.♗e4! g6 (23...♘d7 24.♗xc6 ♘f8 25.♕f7 and the threat of 26.♘f5 is killing) 24.♕f7 with a strong attack;
B) 21...♗a3 22.♕h3 and here too White's attack is strong.
20...♗a6 20...♗xf3 21.♗xf3 is really bad for Black. **21.♘h4!?** I was calculating 21.♖ad1!? but I thought Black could free himself after 21...♗c8 22.♕c4 ♘d7 (also after 22...♗a6 23.♕h4 ♗c8 24.♗f1! ♗f5 25.g4 ♗e4 26.♕h3 White should be better); however, I missed 23.♘g5! and White is much better. **21...♗c8 22.♕c4 f5 23.♘f3!** Eyeing the g5-square.

I was looking at 23.♖ad1, but I was afraid that after 23...e4 my knight on h4 and my bishop on g2 would be blocked. **23...h6!?** I had not considered this, as I spent a lot of time calculating the variations after 23...♘d7!? 24.♘g5!, for example 24...♗xg5 25.♗xg5 ♗b7 26.a4!? ♘b6 27.♘c5 h6 28.♗e7 ♖fe8 29.♗d6 ♕f7 and White should have enough compensation for the pawn. **24.♖ad1 ♔h7!** The best defence, as 24...♘d7 loses to 25.♕e6, and 24...♖f6 to 25.♘xe5 ♕xe5 26.♖d8+ ♗xd8 27.♖xd8+ ♔h7 28.♕g8+ ♔g6 29.♖xc8.

25.h4!! Very strong, preparing h4-h5 and ♘h4. I also calculated 25.♗c5!? but this only leaves White with a minimal plus after 25...e4 26.♘h4 (26.♘d4 ♗xc5 27.♕xc5 ♖f6 is even better for Black as the b8-knight will come to e5) 26...♖f6 27.♗xe7 ♕xe7 28.g4. **25...♖f6** Now Black is ready to go ...♗e6 followed by ...♘d7. I started calculating both 26.♗g5 and 26.♘g5 and after three minutes I decided on: **26.♘g5+!! hxg5** If the king moves away (26...♔h8), White continues 27.♗c5! ♗f8 (also losing are 27...hxg5 28.hxg5 ♖f8 29.♕h4+ ♔g8 30.♗d6 ♕b7 31.♕h5 and 27...♘a6 28.♕b4 ♗xc5 29.♖d8+) 28.♗d6 ♗xd6 29.♖xd6 and now Black is lost after both 29...hxg5 30.hxg5 f4 (30...e4 31.♕e2) 31.♗e4 and 29...♕e7 30.♕c5 ♔g8 31.♗f1. **27.hxg5 ♖g6** While Black was thinking, I quickly calculated the variations after 27...♖g6 and 27...♖a6. After 27...♖a6 28.♕b3 ♖f8 (28...♖g6 loses to 29.♕f7 ♗c8 30.♖d4 exd4 31.♖xd4) White wins with 29.f4!! e4 30.♔f2 ♗c8 31.♖h1+ ♔g6 32.♕d1 ♖h8 33.♖d6+ ♗xd6

34.♕xd6+ ♔f7 35.♖xh8 ♕xh8 36.g6+ ♔e8 37.♗c5 and mate soon. During the game I didn't realize that actually Black's best defence is 27...♖e6!, but analysing afterwards I found that White wins with 28.g4!! f4, for instance 29.♗d5 fxe3 30.♗xe6 exd2 31.♕e4+ g6 32.♕h1+ ♔g7 33.♕h6 mate. **28.♗d5!!**

I had the feeling that this was crushing, as there is no way Black can stop the combined threats of 29.♗g8+ and 29.♔g2, vacating the h-file. Short of time, my opponent immediately replied: **28...f4 29.♗e4!** I felt that this was winning, because of the threats 30.♕f7 and 30.♔g2. In the meantime, Black's queenside pieces are stuck on their original squares. **29...♗xg5 30.♖d6!** ♗f6 **31.♔g2!** A very nice move, allowing the rook to go to h1 with check. **31...f3+ 32.♔xf3 ♗g4+ 33.♔g2 ♗xd1 34.♖xd1 1-0** I was very happy to win this game, because So is a very competitive player. I felt I had been playing at a high level and I was nervous all the time. It was not until I realized that my victory turned the score into 2-1 that I had secured the championship point, as a tie would bring us the title. This game made me feel like a good artist painting an unforgettable picture!

M/20-4-67

Bu Xiangzhi
Peter Leko
Danzhou 2016 (7)
1.d4 ♘f6 2.c4 e6 3.♘c3 ♗b4 4.♘f3 d5 5.♕b3 c5 6.dxc5 ♘a6 7.a3 The most played option. **7...♗xc3+ 8.♕xc3 ♘xc5**

9.cxd5 If White plays 9.♗g5, Black can immediately force an equal ending with 9...♘ce4 10.♗xf6 ♕xf6 11.♕xf6 ♘xf6.

9...♕xd5 9...♘ce4 10.♕e5 ♕xd5 11.g3 (11.♗e3 – game; 11.g4!?) 11...0-0 12.♗g2 b6 13.♕xd5 ♘xd5±.
10.♗e3 ♘ce4 11.♕e5 There are two other options here, both of them basically equal as well: 11.♕d4 0-0 12.g3 b6 13.♗g2 ♗a6=; 11.♕b4 ♗d7!? (11...a5 12.♕d4 0-0=) 12.g3 ♗g4 13.♕d4 ♗c6 14.♗g2 0-0=. **11...♕xe5 12.♘xe5 ♘d5 13.♗c1 ♗d7** Quickly developing. After 13...♘c5 14.♖b1 f6 15.♘c4 e5 16.f3 ♗e7 17.e4 ♘f4 18.♗e3 ♘cd3+ 19.♗xd3 ♘xd3+ 20.♔e2 ♘f4+ 21.♗xf4 exf4 22.♘a5! White retains some pressure. **14.f3 ♘c5 15.e4 ♘b3 16.♖b1 ♘b6 17.♗e3 ♖c8 18.♘xd7** A very interesting idea here is 18.g4!? ♗a4 19.g5 ♗e7 20.♖g1 ♖hd8 21.♖g4 (21.♖g2!? ♘d4= Vallejo Pons-Wojtaszek, Batumi Ech tt 2019) 21...♘d7 22.♘xd7 ♖xd7 23.♖h4 ♖c2∞ Vitiugov-Inarkiev, Russia tt 2017; 18.♗xb6 axb6 19.♘c4 ♖c6 20.♖d1 f6 21.♘e3 ♗c7 22.♔f2 ♗e7=; Black has organized his defences.
18...♗xd7 19.♗e2 ♗e7 20.0-0 ♖hd8 21.♖fd1 e5 Some time after this game, I improved on the text with 21...♖xd1+!?, which is more clear-cut: 22.♗xd1 ♘c4 23.♗xb3 ♘xe3 24.♔f2 ♘c4 25.♖c1 b5 26.a4 a6 27.axb5 axb5 28.♔e2 ♔d6 29.♖c3 ♖b8 30.♗xc4 bxc4 31.♖xc4 ♖xb2+ 32.♔f1 ♔e5 ½-½ Bu Xiangzhi-Yu Yangyi, China tt 2016. **22.♖xd8 ♖xd8 23.♗d1 ♘d4 24.♖c1 ♖c8 25.♖xc8 ♘xc8 26.♗xd4 exd4 27.♔f2 ♔d6 28.♗b3 ♘f6 29.♔e2 ♔e5 30.♔d3 g5 31.g3 f5 32.exf5 ♘xf5 33.♗f7 b6 34.a4 h6 35.♗e8**

♘g7 36.♗d7 ♘h5 37.♗c8 ♔d5 38.b4 a5 39.♗b7+ ♔e5 40.bxa5 bxa5 41.♔c4 ♘f6 42.♗c6 ♔d6 43.♗b5 ♔e5 44.♗c5 ♘d5 45.♗c4 ♘e3 46.♗d3 ♘d1 47.f4+ gxf4 48.gxf4+ ♔xf4 49.♔xd4 ♘b2 50.♗c2 ♔g4 51.♗c3 ♘xa4+ 52.♗xa4 ♘h3 53.♗d1 ♔xh2 54.♔b3 ♔g3 55.♔a4 ½-½

Vladimir Fedoseev
Maxim Matlakov
Moscow 2017 (8)

1.d4 ♘f6 2.♘f3 d5 3.c4 e6 4.♘c3 ♗b4 5.♕b3 c5 6.dxc5 ♗a6 7.a3 ♗xc3+ 8.♕xc3 ♘c5 9.cxd5 ♕xd5 10.♗e3 ♘ce4 11.♕e5 ♕xe5 12.♘xe5 ♘d5 13.♗c1! ♘c5 As I showed in the above game, I prefer to play 13...♗d7. Of course, if Black's analysis is good, I think he can keep the balance. After the third option, 13...f6 14.♘d3 ♔f7 15.f3 ♘d6 16.e4 ♘e7 17.♗e3±, White's position is still more pleasant to play, with the two bishops and several targets in Black's camp. **14.♖b1** White doesn't achieve much with 14.b4 ♘b3 15.♖b1 ♘xc1 16.♖xc1 ♔e7 17.e4 ♘b6 18.♖c7+ ♔d6 19.♖c5 ♖f8=. **14...f6 15.♘c4 e5 16.f3!** ♔e7 17.e4 ♘f4 18.♗e3 ♘cd3+ **19.♗xd3 ♘xd3+ 20.♔e2 ♘f4+** 20...♖d8 21.♖hd1 (21.a5 ♗e6 22.b4 b6=) 21...♘f4+ (21...♗e6 22.♘a5 ♘f4+ 23.♗xf4 exf4 24.♘xb7 ♖d1 25.♔xd1 ♖c8 26.♔d2±) 22.♗xf4 exf4 23.♖xd8 ♔xd8 24.♘a5 and as we saw earlier, White retains some pressure also here. **21.♗xf4 exf4 22.♘a5!**

22...b6?! More active was 22...f5! 23.♖hc1 (23.e5 ♖d8 24.♖hd1 ♖xd1 25.♖xd1 ♗d7=; 23.exf5 ♗xf5 24.♖bc1 ♖hc8) 23...fxe4 24.♖c7+

♔f6. **23.♘c6+ ♔d6? 24.♖bc1 ♗a6+ 25.♔f2 ♖hc8 26.♖hd1+ ♔e6 27.g3!±** A good move, expanding White's advantage by creating a second front. **27...fxg3+ 28.hxg3 g6 29.f4 ♗b7?** 29...h5 30.♔e3 ♖e8 31.f5+ gxf5 32.♘d4+ ♔f7 33.♘xf5±. **30.f5+!** Winning material as with the bishop on b7, 30...♔f7 is impossible. **1-0**

A rare line
6...♕a5

Wang Hao
Shakhriyar Mamedyarov
Huai'an rapid 2017 (2)

1.d4 ♘f6 2.c4 e6 3.♘f3 d5 4.♘c3 ♗b4 5.♕b3 c5 6.dxc5 ♕a5!? A rare line. **7.♗d2** Maybe because it was a rapid game, White chose to play this safe move, but now the position soon becomes close to equal because of the symmetrical pawn structure. **7...dxc4 8.♕xc4 ♕xc5**

9.♕xc5 9.♕d3!?; 9.♕h4!?; 9.♕b3!?; 9.e3 ♕xc4 10.♗xc4=. **9...♗xc5 10.♖c1** 10.g3 ♘c6 11.♗g2 0-0 12.0-0 ♗d7 13.♖ac1 ♗e7 14.♖fd1 ♖fd8 15.h3 ♗e8 16.♘f1 ♖ac8 17.g4 h6 18.♔e1 ♘f8 19.♗e3 ♖xd1+ 20.♖xd1 a6 21.♘d4 ½-½ Adhiban-Sargissian, Moscow 2019. **10...0-0 11.e3** If White wants to play more actively, maybe he should prefer 11.g3!?, after which his bishop controls the g2-b7 diagonal, e.g. 11...♘c6 12.♗g2 ♗d7 13.0-0 ♖ac8 14.♗f4 ♖fd5 15.♖fd1 ♗e8=. **11...♘c6 12.♗e2 ♗d7 13.0-0 ♖fd8 14.♖fd1 ♗e8 15.♗e1= ♖xd1 16.♖xd1 ♖d8 17.♖xd8 ♘xd8 18.♔f1 ♔f8 19.♘d2 ♗c6 20.♘b3 ♗b6 21.♘b5 ♗d5 22.♗d2 f5 23.♘a5**

♗d7 24.♘d6 ♗xa5 25.♗xa5 ♔e7 26.♘c4 ♘c6 27.♗d2 e5 28.a3 e4 29.♘a5 ♘xa5 30.♗xa5 g5 31.♗c4 ♗e6 32.♗xd5 ♗xd5 33.♗c3 ♔e6 34.♗d4 a5 35.♗b6 a4 36.♗d8 h6 37.h4 gxh4 38.♗xh4 ♗c4+ 39.♔e1 ♗d5 40.♔f1 ♗c4+ 41.♔e1 ♗d5 ½-½

Vlad-Cristian Jianu
Ni Hua
Bazna ROM-CHN m 2014 (3)
1.♘f3 ♘f6 2.c4 e6 3.d4 d5 4.♘c3 ♗b4 5.♕b3 c5 6.dxc5 ♕a5 7.♗d2 ♕xc5 8.cxd5 ♘xd5 9.♘xd5 ♖c1!?. 9...♗xd2+ 10.♔xd2±

10...♕xd5+ 10...♕d6!? 11.e4 (11.g3!?) 11...exd5 12.♗b5+ ♘c6 13.♕xd5 ♕f4+ 14.♔c3 0-0 15.♗xc6 bxc6 16.♕e5 ♕g4≅ S.Ernst-Landa, Germany Bundesliga 2012/13. 11.♕xd5 exd5 12.e3± ♔e7 13.♖c1 ♘c6 14.♗b5 ♗d6 15.♖c3 ♘e7 16.♖hc1 ♗e6 17.♘d4 ♖hc8 18.♖xc8 ♗xc8 19.♗d3 ♗d7 20.♖c3 h6 21.h4 g5 22.♖c1 22.h5!?. 22...gxh4! 23.♖h1 h3

24.g3 h5 25.♗f1 h4! 26.gxh4 ♖h8 27.♗xh3 ♖xh4 28.♗g2 ♖xh1 29.♗xh1 ♘c6 30.♔c3 ♘xd4 31.♔xd4 ♗e6 White's advantage is structural but simply too small to convert into something tangible. 32.b4 b6 33.b5 f6 34.♗f3 ♗d7 35.a4 ♗e6 36.♗d1 ♗f5 37.f3 ♗c8 38.♗b3 ♗b7 39.♗a2 ♗a8 40.♗b3 ♗b7 41.♗a2 ♗a8 42.♗b1 ♗b7 43.♗f5 a6 44.♗g4 axb5 45.axb5 ♔e7 46.♗h5 ♗a8 47.♗g4 ♗b7 48.♗f5 ♔d6 49.f4 ♔e7 50.♗h7 ♔f7 51.♗b1 ♗e6 52.♗h7 ♔f7 53.♗f5 ♔e7 54.♗g6 ♗a8 55.♗h7 ♔f7 56.♗f5 ♔e7 57.♗h7 ♔f7 58.♗f5 ♔e7 59.♗h7 ♔f7 ½-½

Adrien Demuth
Vladimir Lazarev
Sables d'Olonne 2015 (8)
1.d4 ♘f6 2.c4 e6 3.♘f3 d5 4.♘c3 ♗b4 5.♕b3 c5 6.dxc5 ♕a5 7.cxd5!?N An interesting choice, more positive and more complicated than the alternative 7.♗d2.

7...♘xd5 7...♘a6 see Yu Yangyi-Harikrishna, China tt 2019, above. 8.♗d2 ♘xc3 8...♗xc3 9.bxc3 ♕xc5 10.c4 ♘f6 11.g3 ♘c6 12.♗g2 0-0 13.♗b5±. 9.a3! 9.bxc3 ♗xc5 10.g3 ♕b6=. 9...♘c6 Also here Black needed to be careful: 9...♘a6? 10.♖c1! ♘xe2 11.♗xe2 ♗xd2+ 12.♘xd2 ♕xc5 13.♕c2! ♘d7 14.♕xc8+ ♖xc8 15.♖xc8+ ♔e7 16.♖xh8+−. 10.♖c1 ♘xe2 11.♗xe2 ♗xd2+ 12.♘xd2± ♘d4 12...0-0 13.♕e3! ♖d8 14.b4± and White has more space. 13.♕e3 ♘xe2 14.♕xe2 ♗d7 15.0-0 0-0 16.♕e3±

16...♗c6?! 16...♗b5 gives more counterplay: 17.♖fd1 ♖fd8 18.♘e4 ♖xd1+ 19.♖xd1 ♕a4 20.♘d2±. 17.♘c4 ♕c7 18.b4 ♗d5 19.♖fd1 ♖fd8 20.♘d6 a6 21.♖c3 b6 22.h4! bxc5 23.bxc5 ♖ab8 24.h5 h6 25.♖d4 ♗d7 26.♖g4 ♔h8 27.♕d4 f6 28.♖cg3 ♕d8 29.♖g6 ♕f8 30.♔h2 ♖c7 31.♕f4 e5 32.♕e3 ♖b3 33.♕d2 ♖xg3 34.♖xg3 ♗e6 35.♕a5 ♖c6 36.♕b4 f5 37.♖g6 ♕d8 38.♖xe6 ♔h7 39.♖xe5 1-0

Exercise 1

position after 26...e6-e5

How to attack Black's king?

(solutions on page 251)

Exercise 2

position after 25...♖c8-d8

How can White exploit Black's king still being in the centre?

Exercise 3

position after 26...♔d6-e6

How can White expand his advantage here?

Shamkovich's old move back into the limelight – Part I

by Jan Timman (special contribution by Anish Giri)

1.	d4	♘f6	
2.	c4	e6	
3.	♘c3	♗b4	
4.	♘f3	d5	
5.	cxd5	exd5	
6.	♗f4		

Both in the Classical Queen's Gambit and in the Ragozin, it used to be an automatic reaction to develop the bishop to g5. Nowadays the trend is different: in the QGD the main line is 5.♗f4, and in the Ragozin we can see a shift as well. After White has swapped pawns, the move 6.♗f4 has become quite common in recent years.

In fact it is an old move: it was first played in Shamkovich-Taimanov, 1951, about half a year before I was born. For decades the move was leading a dormant existence till Eljanov used it to beat Saric in a surprisingly easy way. The move 6.♗f4 became popular on top level. This year we saw Caruana-Anand in Wijk aan Zee apart from the Online games Carlsen-Firouzja and Carlsen-Giri. 6.♗f4 has an advantage over 6.♗g5: if the bishop is on g5, it can immediately

be questioned by 6...h6. Swapping on f6 doesn't guarantee a tangible edge, and retreating to h4 gives Black the opportunity to create direct counterplay by 7...g5 followed by 8...♘e4.

With the bishop on f4 Black doesn't have this counterplay. On the other hand, the bishop development doesn't contribute to any influence in the centre, so Black has several ways to counter the move: 6...c5, 6...♘e4, 6...c6 and 6...0-0. It is a large theoretical subject that I have cut into two. In this first part of the Survey I will deal with Black's moves that immediately put pressure in the centre: 6...c5 and 6...♘e4.

Pressure with the c-pawn push

To 6...c5, White reacts with 7.g3!.

At first sight, the preparation for the fianchetto seems odd, since it is White's second move that does nothing to increase his influence in the centre. Still, it is a strong move. White aims for a Tarrasch Defence set-up with the black bishop on b4. In the stem game Eljanov-Saric, Black just castled and was

Anish Giri

in trouble after one inaccuracy later on (Game 1).

In Dorfman-Sanikidze, Black opted for a much more active and ambitious plan and got away with it. White could have gotten a huge advantage though (Game 2).

In general, practice has shown that Black has no way to get an early initiative, so White is guaranteed an excellent middlegame from a positional point of view.

The knight jump

The 6...♘e4 jump is the obvious move that is considered crucial these days. White has to go 7.♖c1 and now Black has different options again.

In Xiong-Swiercz, Black opted for 7...♘d7. The knight move is linked with an interesting plan: Black wants to bring the knight to b6 to control the

queenside. It is not easy for White to obtain a clear advantage here (Game 3).

In Javakhishvili-Ju Wenjun, the World Champion opted for a risky plan: she went 7...g5 8.♗e3 f5, followed by 9...♖f8. It worked out well, but White could have gotten a clear edge (Game 4).

By far the most common move is 7...♘c6, more or less forcing White to play 8.♘d2, otherwise he loses the initiative. Black now continues 8...g5, leaving White with a choice.

In Moiseenko-Sadzikowski, White was successful with 9.♗g3, although this is not very consistent and shouldn't have given him an edge (Game 5).

The key move is 9.♗e3, leading to sharp and unusual positions. In the fight for the initiative, Black has to swap on c3 now. After 9...♘xc3 10.bxc3 ♗d6 White has 11.h4 with good chances for an advantage (see Schoppen-D.Horvath, Game 6). Firouzja came up with a known improvement on Black's play against Carlsen by inserting 10...♗a3, a move that was first played by the Swiss GM Georgiadis. The idea is 11.♖b1 f5! and now White doesn't have the break h2-h4 so he has to go for the more modest 12.g3. Now Firouzja castled – an inaccuracy which was, however, not the cause of his defeat (Game 7).

One week later in the same online tournament, Giri improved on Black's play by 12...♗d6, threatening to win a

piece. Carlsen ignored the threat by lashing out with 13.♖g1!?. Giri eventually won the game and explains all the intricacies in his comments (Game 8).

Conclusion

Shamkovich's move 6.♗f4 leads to very interesting play, both from a tactical and a strategic point of view. The reaction 6...c5 seems logical, but here White's kingside fianchetto is very strong. He gets a superior version of the Tarrasch Defence, so the push of the c-pawn has not occurred on top level for years.

On the other hand, 6...♘e4 is very popular nowadays. After 7.♖c1, Swiercz' move 7...♘d7 is quite interesting, although I feel that White should have a way to get an edge.
The focus is on 7...♘c6. The positions that arise are unusual and sharp. An interesting question is whether Carlsen's piece sac was serious and sound, or just an experiment for a rapid game.

> In the **second part** of this Survey we will take a look at two more reserved options for Black: **6...0-0 and 6...c6**.

Pressure with the c-pawn push 6...c5

Pavel Eljanov   **1**
Ivan Saric
Jerusalem Ech 2015 (9)
1.d4 d5 2.c4 e6 3.♘f3 ♘f6 4.♘c3 ♗b4 5.cxd5 exd5 6.♗f4 c5 7.g3 ♘c6 8.♗g2 0-0 9.0-0

9...c4 A bad mistake, because Black's d-pawn will become very weak. Better was 9...h6 to keep the white bishop from g5. **10.♗g5!** The best reaction. Black has problems to maintain the centre. **10...♗xc3** If Black protects the d-pawn by 10...♗e6, White has 11.♘e5 with a big advantage. The situation is much more favourable for White than in the Tarrasch Defence. **11.bxc3 h6 12.♗xf6 ♕xf6 13.♘d2 ♘e7** The only move was 13...♕d8, since the queen is badly placed on f6. White still keeps an edge after 14.e4 ♘e7 15.♖e1. In a rapid game Harika-Tan Zhongyi, China 2016, Black tried 13...♖d8 but after

14.e4 ♘e7 15.♖e1 White had a big plus. **14.e4 ♗e6 15.♕a4** Increases the pressure. **15...♖fd8 16.♖ab1** Even stronger was 16.♕b4 with a double threat: the black b-pawn is hanging, while Black's knight would be lost if White pushes his e-pawn to e5. **16...b6 17.♕a3 ♘c6 18.exd5 ♗xd5 19.♗xd5 ♖xd5 20.♘xc4 ♖ad8** Slightly better was 20...♖c8. **21.♕b2 b5** Desperation. Black could still fight with 21...♘a5. **22.♘e3 b4 23.♘xd5 ♖xd5 24.♖fd1** Now White remains an exchange up for no compensation at all. **24...bxc3 25.♕xc3 ♘xd4 26.♔g2 ♕e5 27.♕e3 ♕d6 28.♖bc1 ♕d7 29.♕c3 ♔h7 30.♕d3+ g6 31.♖c4 ♖h5 32.♖xd4 ♕h3+ 33.♔f3 ♖f5+ 34.♖f4 1-0**

Iosif Dorfman   **2**
Tornika Sanikidze
France tt 2015 (6)
1.d4 d5 2.c4 e6 3.♘f3 ♘f6 4.♘c3 ♗b4 5.cxd5 exd5 6.♗f4 c5 7.g3 ♘e4 8.♖c1

8...♘c6 In Chandra-Hracek, Paleochora 2019, Black tried 8...♕a5. The game continued 9.♗g2! ♘xc3 (in a rapid game Shankland-Hou Yifan, Hawaii 2015, Black varied with 9...♘c6 but after 10.0-0 ♗xc3 11.bxc3 c4 12.♕c2 0-0 13.♘d2 White was clearly better) 10.bxc3 ♗xc3+ 11.♗d2 ♗xd2+ 12.♕xd2 ♕xd2+ 13.♔xd2 ♘d7 14.dxc5 b6 and now White could have gotten a clear edge by 15.c6! ♘c5 16.♘d4. The passed c-pawn is quite strong. **9.♗g2 ♗f5** The introduction of a sharp, ambitious plan that is however not really sound. **10.0-0 ♘xc3 11.bxc3 ♗a3** That was the idea. Black wins an exchange. But at what price? **12.♕b3** Much stronger was 12.♖a1! with the idea 12...♗b2 13.♖b1 and Black is forced to take the rook with the other bishop. Meanwhile White gains important time. After 13...♗xb1 14.♕xb1 ♗xc3 15.dxc5! White is almost winning, e.g. 15...0-0 16.♗d6 ♖e8 17.♕xb7 and the black queenside falls apart. **12...♗xc1 13.♖xc1 0-0 14.♕xb7** White has obtained a pawn for the exchange, but has lost the initiative. **14...♕b6** Forcing a favourable endgame for Black. **15.♕xb6 axb6 16.♗d6 ♖fc8 17.dxc5 bxc5 18.♗xc5 ♖xa2 19.♘d4** Now White can probably just hold the endgame. **19...♗e4**

20.♗h3 ♘xd4 21.♗xd4 ♖b8 22.f3 ♖b1 23.♖xb1 ♗xb1 24.♗f1 ♗c2 25.g4 ♗d1 More accurate was 25...♗b3 immediately, winning a tempo. 26.♔f2 ♗b3 27.h4 g6 And here 27...h6 offered more practical chances. 28.g5 ♔f8 29.f4 ♔e7 30.♗h3 ♔d6 31.♗g4 ♗c4 32.h5 ♗d3 33.hxg6 hxg6 34.♔e3 ♗c4 35.♗e5+ ♔c5 36.♗g7 ♔c6 37.♗f8 ♖a8 38.♗g7 ♖a2 39.♗f8 ♖a8 40.♗g7 ♖a2 ½-½

The knight jump 6...♘e4

Jeffery Xiong   **3**
Dariusz Swiercz
St Louis 2019 (10)

1.d4 ♘f6 2.c4 e6 3.♘c3 ♗b4 4.♘f3 d5 5.cxd5 exd5 6.♗f4 ♘e4 7.♖c1 In Svidler-Mamedyarov, Wijk aan Zee 2018, White played 7.♕a4+ but this is a waste of time. After 7...♘c6 8.♖c1 0-0 9.g3 g5 10.♗e3 f5 Black had a strong initiative. 7...♘d7 In Girya-Ju Wenjun, China tt 2019, Black played 7...♕e7 and after 8.♘d2 ♘xc3 9.bxc3 ♗a3 10.♖b1 0-0 White should just have continued 11.e3 with the idea 11...g5 12.♗g3 f5 13.♗e5! ♘c6 14.f4 and White is better. 8.♘d2 An important alternative is 8.♕b3, forcing Black to cede the bishop pair. After 8...♗xc3+ 9.bxc3 ♘b6 10.e3 White has a slight plus. 8...♘xc3 9.bxc3 ♗a3 10.♖b1 ♘b6

The main idea of the 7th move. Black wants to keep control on the queenside. 11.♕c2 Keeps the black bishop from f5. After 11.e3 ♗f5 12.♖b3 ♗d6 Black has no opening problems. 11...♗d7 Black

follows an interesting strategy: he postpones castling to get even more control on the queenside. After 11...0-0 12.e3 ♗d6 13.♗g3 White would get an edge. 12.e3 The alternative is 12.e4. Black's best answer is 12...♕e7 13.e5 c5 to generate counterplay on the c-file. 12...♕e7 He still delays castling. 13.♗b5 It was not very good to take the c-pawn. After 13.♗xc7 ♗a4 14.♗b5+ ♗xb5 15.♗xb6 ♕d7 Black has sufficient compensation for the pawn. 13...c6 It seems to me that the exchange of bishops was a better way to fight for equality. After 13...♗xb5 14.♖xb5 ♕d7 15.♖b3 ♗e7 Black's position is reasonably solid. 14.♗d3 c5 15.dxc5 ♗xc5 16.♘b3 ♗d6 17.0-0 ♖c8 Safer was 17...g6 to prepare castling. 18.♘d4 g6 19.♘b5 It was also possible to keep the knight in its central position and go for 19.a4. The idea is 19...♗xa4 20.♕a2! and Black is in trouble. 19...♗xb5 20.♗xb5+ ♔f8

21.♗xd6 White could have continued the fight for the initiative by 21.♗h6+ ♔g8 22.g3. He must be ready to sac the c-pawn. After 22...♗e5 23.a4 ♖xc3 (better is 23...♗g7) 24.♕d2 Black is in serious trouble. 21...♕xd6 22.a4 ♔g7 Now Black has solved all problems. 23.♕d2 ♖c7 Stronger was 23...a5 to keep the stronghold for the knight. 24.a5 Now White is better. 24...♘c8 25.♕d4+ This check leads to the exchange of queens and diminishes White's advantage. He could have kept pressure by 25.♖fd1 ♖d8 26.♗e2. 25...♕f6 26.♗e2 ♖d8 27.♗g4 ♖c4 The equalizer. 28.♕xf6+ ♔xf6

29.♗xc8 ♖dxc8 30.♖xb7 ♖8c7 ½-½

Lela Javakhishvili   **4**
Ju Wenjun
Khanty-Mansiysk 2016 (2)
1.d4 ♘f6 2.c4 e6 3.♘f3 d5 4.♘c3 ♗b4 5.cxd5 exd5 6.♗f4 ♘e4 7.♖c1 g5 8.♗e3 f5 9.g3

9...♖f8 An interesting but risky strategy. Black is going to castle queenside, but it is a long way to go. In a rapid game Sjugirov-Ni Hua, Riyadh 2017, Black swapped on c3 first and was fine after 9...♗xc3+ 10.bxc3 (10.♖xc3!?) 10...♖f8 11.♕b3 f4. White could improve by 11.♗d2 f4 12.g3 with an edge. 10.♗d2 The right reaction. By unpinning the knight White forces Black to show her cards. 10...♗xc3 11.♗xc3 White could have taken with the pawn, but under these circumstances this is even better. 11...♘c6 12.e3 In itself, an understandable move. White wants to develop her bishop to b5 and sometimes the queen has the chance to go to h5, after moving the knight. Still, the text is not the best, since it allows Black to get good counterplay on the kingside. The natural developing move 12.♗g2 is White's best. It is not easy for Black to justify her strategy, e.g. 12...f4 13.0-0 ♕d6 14.♘e5 ♗d7 15.♕b3 and White has a strong initiative. 12...f4 Of course. 13.exf4 Crucial was 13.♘d2 when Black has the following options: 13...♘xf2!? (13...♗f5 14.♘xe4 ♗xe4 15.f3 ♗g6 16.exf4 gxf4 17.♗h3 (better than 17.♔f2 ♕g5 18.♗h3 ♗e4! and Black has good counterplay)

17...♕d6 18.♘f2 and White has a slight plus) 14.♕h5+! ♖f7 15.♘xf2 fxe3+ 16.♔e2 exd2 17.♔xd2 ♗f5 18.♖e1+ with some advantage for White. **13...♕e7** The idea of this move is to force the white bishop to e2, but White has a different option. Stronger was 13...♗g4 14.♗g2 gxf4 15.0-0 ♕d6 followed by queenside castling. Black has an excellent game. **14.♗e2** After this timid move, Black gets her way. White had to go for 14.♘e5. In fact she would have been a little better after 14...♘xe5 15.dxe5 c6 16.♕h5+. **14...gxf4 15.0-0 ♗h3** Now Black gets a crushing attack. **16.♖e1 fxg3 17.fxg3 0-0-0 18.♗f1 ♕d7 19.♖e3 ♖f6 20.♗b5 ♕f5 21.♗e1 ♖df8** The last piece is brought to the attack. **22.♗e2 ♕h5 23.b4 ♘g5 24.♖cc3 ♕g4 25.♖cd3 a6 26.a4 ♘xd4 27.♖xd4 ♘xf3+ 28.♖xf3 ♕xf3!** Attractive and accurate. **29.♗xf3 ♖xf3 30.♕xf3 ♖xf3 31.♖f4** The only move, but the ensuing bishop ending is won for Black. It will take a long time, since the World Champion is not in a hurry. **31...♖xf4 32.gxf4 b6−+**

33.♔f2 ♔d7 34.♔e3 ♔d6 35.♔h4 ♗d7 36.♔g3 ♗f5 37.♗h4 c5 38.♗d8 d4+ 39.♔d2 ♔c6 40.a5 cxb4 41.axb6 b3 42.♗c1 d3 43.b7 ♔xb7 44.♗a5 ♗c6 45.♗b2 ♗b5 46.♗d2 ♗c4 47.h4 h5 48.♗a5 ♔d4 49.♗d2 ♔e4 50.♔xb3 ♔f3 51.♗b2 ♔g3 52.♗e1+ ♔xf4 53.♔c1 ♔e4 54.♔b2 ♔d4 55.♔d2 ♔c4 56.♗e1 ♔b5 57.♔c3 a5 58.♗d2 a4 59.♔c1 ♔c5 60.♗a3+ ♔d5 61.♔e7 ♔e4 62.♗c5 ♗g6 63.♔d2 ♔d5 64.♗a3 ♔c4 65.♔e7 ♗b3 66.♗f6 a3 67.♔c1 ♔a2 68.♗g5

♗f7 69.♗h6 ♗e6 70.♔g5 ♔b3 71.♗f6 ♗f5 72.♗g7 ♗d7 73.♗f6 ♔a2 74.♔g5 ♗b5 75.♗h6 ♔b3 76.♗g7 ♗c4 77.♔d2 ♔d5 78.♔e3 ♗e6 79.♗c3 ♔f5 80.♔f3 a2 81.♔e3 ♔g4 82.♗f6 ♔g3 83.♔d2 ♔f3 84.♗c3 ♔g4 85.♗f6 a1♕ 86.♗xa1 ♔xh4 87.♔e3 ♔g4 88.♗c3 h4 89.♗b4 ♗a6 90.♗a5 h3 91.♗c7 ♔f5 92.♗h2 ♔e6 93.♔g3 ♔d5 94.♗h2 ♔c4 95.♔e5 ♗b5 96.♔f2 ♔b3 0-1**

Alexander Moiseenko — Daniel Sadzikowski   5

Turkey tt 2016 (8)

1.d4 ♘f6 2.c4 e6 3.♘f3 d5 4.♘c3 ♗b4 5.cxd5 exd5 6.♗f4 ♘e4 7.♖c1 ♘c6

8.♘d2 In Martirosyan-Ganguly, Pro Chess League 2020, White played the careless move 8.e3. After 8...g5 9.♗g3 h5! Black had a strong initiative. The same applies to inserting 9.♗e5 f6 10.♗g3 h5 11.h4 (11.h3 ♗xc3+ (11...♘xg3 12.fxg3 ♕d6 13.♔f2 ♗xc3 14.♖xc3!?) 12.bxc3 ♘xg3 13.fxg3 ♕d6 14.♔f2 h4 15.gxh4 gxh4∓) 11...♗xc3+ 12.bxc3 ♘xg3 13.fxg3 ♕d6 14.♔f2 ♗g4 15.♗b5 gxh4 16.♖xh4 (Baikov-Vasiukov, Moscow 1972) 16...0-0-0∓. **8...g5 9.♗g3 ♘xg3 10.hxg3 ♘xd4 11.e3 ♗xc3 12.bxc3 ♘c6** The alternative was 12...♘e6. After 13.♕f3 ♕e7 14.♕xd5 c6 15.♕c4 ♘c5 chances are approximately equal. **13.♗b5 ♕f6** Black neglects his development. He had to play 13...♗f5 or 13...♗d7. White has sufficient compensation for the pawn, but not more. **14.c4** Of course. White opens up the position and gets a strong initiative. **14...♗e6 15.cxd5** Probably, 15.♗xc6+ was

more accurate, with the idea 15...bxc6 16.cxd5 ♗xd5 17.♕c2 and Black can't castle yet, so White will push his e-pawn with even more vigour than in the game. **15...♗xd5 16.e4 ♗e6 17.♖xc6!?** An attractive move, but not better than the normal 17.♗xc6+ bxc6 18.♖xc6 with a slight edge. **17...bxc6 18.♗xc6+ ♔e7 19.♕c1 ♕e5 20.♗xa8 ♖xa8 21.0-0 g4!** A strong push, keeping the white knight from f3. **22.♘b3 c5** Better was the simple 22...♗xb3 23.axb3 ♖d8 when Black has little to fear. **23.♕a3 ♗c8** A passive move that allows White to build up pressure. A stronger defence was 23...♕c3 with the idea 24.♖c1 ♕b4 and Black is safe. White can keep a small edge by 24.♕a6. **24.♖c1 ♗xb3 25.axb3 ♖c7 26.♖c4 h5 27.♕a5**

27...♔f6 It is a good idea to bring the king to the kingside, but 27...♔f8 was better, with the idea 28.b4 h4! 29.gxh4 g3 with sufficient counterplay. White can keep his advantage by 28.♖c1. **28.♕d2** Much stronger was 28.b4 and White simply wins a pawn, since Black's counterplay doesn't work with the king on f6: 28...h4 29.gxh4 g3 30.fxg3 ♕xg3 31.bxc5 ♖d7 32.♕c3+ and wins. **28...♔e7** Very inconsistent. The obvious 28...♔g6 was much better. Black has good chances to hold. **29.♕e3 ♔d8 30.♖c1 ♔e7 31.♕d3 ♖b7** And now 31...♔f6 was obligatory. **32.♖d1 ♔f6** Too late. White gets a decisive attack now. **33.♕e3 ♔g6 34.♖d5 ♕e7 35.♖xc5 ♖b6 36.♖a5 f6 37.♕f4 ♖xb3 38.♕f5+ ♔g7 39.e5 ♖b7 40.♕xh5 fxe5 41.♖xe5 ♕b4 42.♖g5+ ♔f8 43.♕h6+ 1-0**

Casper Schoppen 6
Dominik Horvath

Pardubice Ech tt U18 2019 (5)

1.d4 ♘f6 2.c4 e6 3.♘f3 d5 4.♘c3 ♗b4 5.cxd5 exd5 6.♗f4 ♘e4 7.♖c1 ♘c6 8.♘d2 g5 In the game Farago-G.Szabo, Zalakaros 2016, there followed 8...♗xc3 9.bxc3 ♘xf2 10.♔xf2 ♕f6 11.e3 g5 12.♕f3 gxf4 and now White took with the queen on f4. He could have gotten a clear edge by 13.exf4. **9.♗e3**

9...♘xc3 In Wojtaszek-Zelbel, Germany Bundesliga 2017/18, Black played the immediate 9...f5 which is not very good because White could have gotten a clear edge with 10.♘dxe4 fxe4 11.a3 ♗a5 12.b4 ♗b6 13.♕d2. **10.bxc3 ♗d6 11.h4 ♗f4** The only way to stop White from building up a substantial strategic advantage. In Svane-Socko, Germany Bundesliga 2015/16, White was better after 11...gxh4 12.♘f3 ♗e7 13.♗f4 ♗f5 14.e3. **12.c4** The sharpest move, leading to unusual positions. The alternative is 12.♗xf4 gxf4 13.e3. The game Xiong-Burke, Philadelphia 2019, continued 13...fxe3 14.♕e2 0-0 15.fxe3 ♘e7 16.♕f3. Also 12.♕c2 has been played, but it is certainly not stronger than the text. **12...♗xe3 13.fxe3 ♕d6** And White was clearly better. Black's 15th move was too passive. It was better to bring the queen to e7, with counterplay. The alternative is 13...dxc4. Probably it is best now to take back with the rook. After 14.♖xc4 gxh4 15.♕b1! White has the initiative. **14.♕b3!** An excellent move. White vacates square d1 for the king and pressurizes the black queenside.

14...♗e6 15.♕xb7 The most principled, but a bit risky. White could have gotten a slight plus by taking on d5 first: 15.cxd5 ♗xd5 16.♕xb7 ♘xd4 17.♕xc7 ♕xc7 18.♖xc7 ♘e6 19.♖c3. It is not easy for Black to equalize here. **15...♖b8 16.♕a6 ♖b6** There was no need to drive the queen away. 16...0-0 was quite strong. After 17.♔f2 g4 Black has excellent compensation for the pawn. **17.♕a4 ♕g3+ 18.♔d1 ♕xe3 19.cxd5 ♗xd5 20.♖h3 ♕f4 21.e3 ♕f2** Also 21...♕g4+ was possible, e.g. 22.♔e1 (if 22.♖f3 Black has 22...0-0) 22...♗xg2 23.♗xg2 ♕xg2 24.♖f3 ♕h1+ 25.♔f1 ♕xh4+ 26.♔d1 ♕h5+ with a draw. **22.hxg5 ♗xg2?** A bad mistake. Black exchanges his excellent centralized bishop for White's undeveloped bishop. He could have forced a draw by 22...♖b2 23.♖c2 ♖b1+ and White can't avoid the repetition of moves. **23.♗xg2 ♕xg2 24.♖f3 ♕g1+ 25.♖f1 ♕g4+ 26.♔e1 ♕g3+ 27.♔d1 ♕g4+ 28.♔e1 ♕g3+ 29.♖f2** Black has no more checks and will lose material. **29...0-0 30.♘f1 ♕d6 31.♖f6 ♕d5** This just loses a piece. The only chance was 31...♕b4+, although the ending should be winning for White after 32.♕xb4 ♘xb4 33.♖xc7. **32.♖fxc6 ♖b2 33.♖6c2 ♖xc2 34.♕xc2 ♖e8 35.♕c6 ♕a5+ 36.♔f2 ♖e6 37.♕xc7 ♕xa2+ 38.♔g1 1-0**

Magnus Carlsen 7
Alireza Firouzja

Magnus Carlsen Invitational 2020 (2.1)

1.d4 ♘f6 2.c4 e6 3.♘f3 d5 4.♘c3 ♗b4 5.cxd5 exd5 6.♗f4 ♘c6 7.♖c1 ♘e4 8.♘d2 g5 9.♗e3 ♘xc3 10.bxc3 ♗a3 11.♖b1 f5 12.g3

12...0-0?! 13.♕b3 It was stronger to play 13.f4! immediately, e.g. 13...♖e8 14.♗f2 gxf4 15.gxf4 ♗d6 16.e3 ♗xf4 17.♕f3 ♕d6 18.♔d1 with a complex position that offers White the better prospects. The text gives Black the opportunity to regroup his pieces in an efficient way. **13...♗e7 14.f4 ♘a5** Taking control of the queenside, while winning a tempo. **15.♕c2 c6 16.♗g2 ♗d6** Black has equalized. RR: '16...g4!? doesn't look bad to me, stopping ♘f3-e5 once and for all. After h2-h3, ...h7-h5, White can't really use the open h-file, while c3-c4 can always be met with ...♗e6, c4xd5 c6xd5 and Black holds the fort' – Giri. **17.c4 gxf4** It is not a bad idea to open the g-file, but 17...♕e7 was a good alternative. After 18.♗f2 ♗e6 19.c5 ♗c7 chances are even. **18.gxf4 ♗e6 19.cxd5 cxd5 20.0-0 ♔h8 21.♘f3** The knight is heading for e5. **21...♘c4 22.♕d3 b6 23.♔h1**

23...♕e7 More accurate was 23...♖c8. Black can decide where to put his queen later on. **24.♘e5 ♗xe5** Dubious from a strategic point of view; now White gets a strong protected passed pawn. Apart from that, the black f-pawn may become weak. Black had to keep the tension with 24...♖ac8 and the game is still balanced. **25.fxe5 ♖g8** And here it was necessary to swap on e3. After 25...♘xe3 26.♕xe3 ♖g8 27.♖bc1 White is better, but Black keeps chances for a successful defence. **26.♗f4!** An excellent move. Play will be on the kingside, so White preserves his bishop which is now much stronger than Black's knight. **26...♖g6 27.♗h3** RR: 'Magnus goes

after the f5-pawn and it works in the game, but it could have been not so clear. 27.♕h3! is an even better regrouping: 27...♖ag8 28.♗f3' – Giri. **27...♖f8 28.♗f3 ♕h4 29.♖bf1 ♕h5 30.♗c1**

White has conducted the game in a classical way. The black f-pawn cannot be protected anymore. **30...♖fg8** RR: 'Black tries to indirectly protect the f5-pawn, which he could have done with the sophisticated 30...♖f7!, when f5 is taboo because of 31.♗xf5 ♗xf5 32.♖xf5 ♕g4! and now the point of 30...♖f7 is revealed here: the rook can still be captured but no longer with check, while 33...♕g2 mate comes first' – Giri. **31.♗xf5 ♖g2 32.♗h3!** Stopping all of Black's counterplay. **32...♖xe2 33.♕xe2 ♗xh3 34.♖g1 1-0**

Magnus Carlsen   8
Anish Giri
Magnus Carlsen Invitational 2020 (5.2)
1.d4 ♘f6 2.c4 e6 3.♘f3 d5 4.♘c3 ♗b4 5.cxd5 exd5 6.♗f4 Magnus played this system against the Ragozin twice, against Firouzja and against me. Basically he would play it forever, until someone would fall into the 13.♖g1 novelty. **6...♘e4 7.♖c1 ♘c6 8.♘d2 g5 9.♗e3 ♘xc3 10.bxc3 ♗a3 11.♖b1 f5 12.g3 ♗d6** An easy improvement over Firouzja's game, ready to meet 13.f4 with capturing and 14...♕h4+!. This had actually already been played before, in a game Gähwiler-Georgiadis, Swiss Championship, Leukerbad 2019. **13.♖g1!?** A peculiar novelty and a rather deep one too. Now obviously the critical response is ...f5-f4, winning a piece, but the arising position did

not seem like the most practical choice. This being a rapid game I didn't have much time to weigh all the options, but I did spend half of my time here to make sure the game took a reasonable course. 13.♘f3 f4 14.♗c1 ♕f6 is how the Georgiadis game went. 14...0-0! is not a difficult improvement.

13...0-0!? After this extremely natural move Magnus sank into thought. It is the unavoidable consequence of preparing with the computer, that sometimes the most natural moves, if they don't enter the engine tab, are dismissed. No matter how much we (chess professionals) try to avoid that and analyse the human moves, they still slip away. No-one is immune to that.
A) After 13...f4 14.gxf4 gxf4 15.♗xf4 ♗xf4 16.e3 ♕e7! is an important move to see, but here it continues: 17.♕h5+ ♔d8 18.♕xd5+ ♗d6 when Black has won a piece for two pawns and has a reasonably stable position, but being unprepared, I didn't fancy the difference in the kings' safety;
B) 13...♕e7 is met with 14.♘f3 when the queen is somewhat misplaced on e7 and would rather stand on f6;
C) 13...♕f6 14.f4! gxf4 15.gxf4 ♕h4+ is a fat tempo for White, compared to 13.f4.
14.h4! Nevertheless, Magnus found the best reply. Frankly it didn't enter my radar when I played 13...0-0 and once I saw it I immediately realized that, of course, it was the one.
A) 14.♘f3 can be met with 14...g4, or 14...h6 first, which was what I had intended;

B) 14.♕b3? was tempting, but here I had a strong reply ready: 14...♔h8!;
C) 14.f4 was the most obvious move, but here I have 14...♕e7! 15.♗f2 ♘a5!? 16.e3 with a very unclear position. Black doesn't have to fear ♘d2-f3-e5 that much, because of play on the light squares with ...♘c4 and so on. Very messy. **14...f4!** The choice between 14...f4 and 14...g4 was a good test. I am glad I passed it. After 14...g4 15.♗g5 White's kingside structure is a rock and he will sooner rather than later break Black's centre with c3-c4, so unless a miracle happens here, Black is doomed. **15.gxf4 g4**

With the king still on g8 this felt at the very least as dubious as it felt cool. In fact, while White has many interesting options, the position remains balanced, so surprisingly my reaction to the novelty seems to have been very fine, also from the objective point of view.
16.♖b5? This doesn't feel like the best practical decision. In some sense it is logical though. White wants to meet ...♗xf4 with takes and e3, c4, while he intends to meet ...♘e7 with the flashy ...f7-f5!?.
A) 16.c4 felt very right. Here I saw the right idea, but it is the engine that sees the right execution:
A1) 16...♗f5 followed by ...♘b4 looks tempting, but the computer points out the flaw here: 17.♗g2!, when taking the exchange is a sin, with all the light squares gaping and as then it's not clear what ...♗f5 was for;
A2) 16...♔h8!, keeping all options open: ...♗xf4, as well as ...♘b4 and

...♘e7. 17.cxd5 (after 17.♗g2!? ♗xf4 18.♗xf4 ♖xf4 19.e3 ♖f8 20.cxd5 ♘e7 Black eventually holds, but this would be possibly the most testing) 17...♘b4!?. Probably, 17...♘e7 also has some merits, but this gives fine counterchances. The position is insane, but more or less balanced.

B) 16.♗g2 is nicely met with 16...♘e7! which is even stronger than capturing on f4 immediately;

C) 16.♘f3 is also very testing, when after 16...♗xf4 17.♗xf4 ♖xf4 18.e3 ♖f7 19.c4 ♖g7 20.cxd5 ♕xd5 21.♘d2 ♔h8 Black's position looks strategically suspect, having lost the fight for the pawn centre, but White's potentially weak king ensures that Black has adequate counterplay. **16...♘e7** Again, my choice wasn't too hard. One doesn't want White to rid himself of the ugly e3-bishop and give him easy play. Therefore 16...♗xf4 wasn't an attractive alternative. **17.f5!?**

Spectacular and clever. Here I started feeling the time pressure a little, because of an abundance of options and all of them being highly vague. **17...h5!?**

A) Instead, 17...♘xf5 was simplest, and pretty strong, but I wanted to have none of the ♖xd5xd6 sacrifice: 18.♖xg4+ (18.♗g5!? bothered me, but after 18...♕e8 19.♖xd5 ♕f7 the exchange sac is a fine version for Black, because he has kept the g4-pawn and gets a tempo as f2 is hanging. Still very double-edged, of course) 18...♔h8 19.♗g5 ♘e3!! (of course I didn't see this trick. 19...♕e8 20.♖xd5 ♗e6 21.♖xd6 seemed like something I should really be trying to avoid) 20.♕b1!!. Stockfish says -0.20. I'm outta here;

B) 17...g3 is a flashy move which, combined with the fact that it was the first line of a weak engine on the website, prompted some to ask me why I didn't play it. Many reasons, starting with that I didn't see it was possible. And frankly, many more. 18.♗h6 ♘xf5 19.♗xf8 ♔xf8 20.♘f3 gxf2+ 21.♔xf2 ♗f4 22.♗h3 with a mess, which is objectively balanced;

C) I also seriously considered 17...♔h8!?, I don't even remember with what point, but at some point I realized I should stop with all the creative nonsense and just make a move. **18.♗g5** 18.f6!? could have transposed to the game, but could also have not: 18...♖xf6 19.♗g5 ♖f5 (19...♕f8!? is another cool way to sac the exchange) 20.e4 ♖xg5 21.hxg5 c6 22.♖b2 and we've transposed to the game. **18...c6** Again, the time factor made me pick this one. I was very much into 18...♕e8 at this point, but this seemed more direct and spirited. 18...♕e8!? 19.e4 (19.♗xe7 ♕xe7 20.♖xd5 ♗xf5) is total chaos: 19...c6 20.♖b2 ♘xf5 21.♕e2. Black is doing quite well, he can for example sac a piece with 21...♕g6!? but after the obvious 22.♔d1 the fight continues. **19.♖b2**

19...♖xf5 Intending the exchange sac. 19...♗xf5!? is strong apparently: 20.e4! (20.♖xb7 ♗c8 21.♖b2 ♕c7 is suddenly very good for Black. Indeed the knight will go to g6, the bishop to f5, Black can take the b-file or break the g5-bishop by offering a trade. White's queenside is yet to be developed and his rook on g1 has no future, because trying to open the g-file with f2-f3 will only backfire on his own king) 20...dxe4 21.♖xb7 ♖b8 22.♗c4+ ♔h8

23.♖xa7 ♕e8 24.♗h6 and Black can choose to repeat with 24...♖f6 or sac the exchange with, for example, 24...♗g6!?. **20.e4! ♖xg5!** The point, otherwise the last 5 moves would have made no sense. **21.hxg5** Premoved☺. **21...♘g6**

I honestly had no idea how to evaluate this position in the heat of the battle, but I thought that for sure, practically speaking, I am very much in the game. Which might have been a modest assessment in hindsight. White was of course not thrilled having to be on the defensive side after unleashing a strong opening novelty. **22.e5 ♗f8** I was well aware of the fact that it is possible to spend half an hour thinking here choosing between ...♗a3, ...♗c7, ...♗e7 and ...♗f8 (not sure if ...♗b8 has some merit, but time can be spent thinking about that philosophical question too). Enough is enough, however, and with the clock ticking I played this move instantly. **23.♗d3?!** This actually felt wrong, inviting 23...♘f4, but I suspect already at this point Magnus had the ♘f1, f2-f3 idea in mind, which while positionally sound has a minor tactical flaw. 23.c4 ♕xg5 24.♕b3 is natural, trying to get to the d5-pawn, though it is a little loose. Black has many interesting options, for example 24...♔h8!? when White is better off trying to trade queens (25.♕e3) than actually grabbing that central pawn: 25.cxd5 cxd5 26.♕xd5 ♗f5 and with the a8-rook joining, Black will develop a very dangerous initiative. My personal favourite here is 23.♘f3!, an absolutely sick move,

offering the knight for just one pawn. Black in fact should ignore it: 23...b5 (23...gxf3 24.♕xf3 is simply very dangerous. ...♗g4 will be chopped off too and then White will just enter on the weak light squares: 24...♗g4 25.♖xg4 hxg4 26.♕f5 ♕e8 27.♖xb7 etc.) 24.♗d3 ♘f4 25.♕d2!? (White insists on the piece sac) 25...♘xd3+ 26.♕xd3 gxf3 27.♕xf3 ♗g4 28.♖xg4 hxg4 29.♕xg4 and here the computer maintains the balance thanks to some ...b5-b4!? idea with counterplay, but I would take White any day: 29.♕c8 30.e6 b4 31.cxb4 ♖b8. **23...♘f4! 24.♘f1 ♕xg5**

25.f3?? This blunder is in a way the logical consequence of White's play, but on the other hand it would all still make some sense if he had first withdrawn the d3-bishop to b1. 25.♘e3 b5 is just good for Black, who is now in time with ...a7-a5 and ...♖a7. 25...♗a3!? 26.♖b3 ♗c1! is another strong resource. Also cool.

25.♔h1!? was best; 25...♘h3 (just one of the moves. The engine also suggests activating the bishop with 25...♗h6 or 25...♗a3. 25...b5 26.f3 a5 27.fxg4 ♖a7 is mayhem. If I would see this idea, I would likely be tempted to go for it) 26.♖h1 ♗h6 27.♘e3 g3 28.♕f3 ♘xf2 29.♖xf2 gxf2+ 30.♔xf2 ♗g4 31.♘xg4 hxg4 32.♕d3 ♕d2+ 33.♕xd2 ♗xd2. This is one of the random ways how the computer makes sense of this position. Here White ends up a pawn down, but should hold due to the rest of the position being

good. **25...♘xd3+! 26.♕xd3 ♕c1+ 27.♔f2 ♕xb2+ 28.♘d2 ♗f5**

In the heat of the battle I didn't immediately realize how completely winning this is, but the moment I saw that the incoming check on g6 is just a check, it became clear. **29.♕xf5 ♕xd2+ 30.♔g3 ♕xc3** It may seem like a perpetual is on the cards, but White only has two checks, whether he starts from e6 or from g6, and so he is just dead lost here. **31.♔h4 ♕xd4 32.♖g3 ♗g7 33.f4 ♖f8 0-1**

Giri M/20-4-34

Exercise 1

position after 14...h4-h3

Black has just pushed his h-pawn to h3. How should White react?

(solutions on page 251)

Exercise 2

position after 13...f7-f5

Black has just pushed his f-pawn to f5, which was not very good. How should White have profited from this?

Exercise 3

position after 14.♗e3-c1

How should Black continue?

Bullets whining past my king's head? I don't care! – Part II

by Alojzije Jankovic

1.	d4	♞f6
2.	c4	g6
3.	♞c3	♝g7
4.	e4	d6
5.	♞f3	0-0
6.	♝e2	e5
7.	0-0	♞c6
8.	d5	♞e7
9.	♞e1	♞d7 (or ♞e8)
10.	♞d3	f5
11.	♝d2	

In the first instalment of this Survey in Yearbook 135 we focused on the sidelines of the Mar del Plata Variation (11...♞b6, 11...fxe4, 11...♚h8 and 11...♞f6 12.f3 c5/c6).

Genna Sosonko

In this part we will take a detailed look into what I call the Sosonko-Kozul Variation: **11...♞f6 12.f3 f4 13.c5 g5 14.cxd6 cxd6 15.♞f2.**

Later White will play ♛c2 followed by ♜fc1, instead of playing the other rook to c1, and this will be the subject of this article. Like in most Mar del Plata lines, White plays on the queenside while Black is launching his kingside assault. Black is not forced to go all-in, there are several alternatives which I will cover as well.

As I explained in Part I, Sosonko in the late 1970s till the 1990s and Kozul from the 1990s made special contributions to the development of the line, both exclusively placing their kingside rook on c1.

When Kozul became my coach (replacing GM Hulak) I started to play this line myself, and in general it has served me well, especially in blitz and rapid. If White knows what to do, he can gain a considerable time advantage on the clock. My games in rapid and blitz against weaker players would mostly

follow the scenario of the game Jankovic-Berbatov, and that one was even played with a classical tempo! It completely took off-guard even the strong King's Indian specialist Etienne Bacrot, in our rapid game where I achieved a huge advantage right after the opening (see the notes to Jankovic-Berbatov).

The Sosonko-Kozul Variation

11...♘f6 is the main move. After **12.f3** Black can respond with 12...♔h8 (see Part I), but more straightforward is **12...f4** when after **13.c5 g5 14.cxd6 cxd6 15.♘f2 ♘g6 16.♕c2 ♖f7 17.♖fc1 h5 18.h3**

a very double-edged position arises with many interesting games like Kozul-Jovanovic (see Game Section), Kekelidze-Baklan, Sosonko-Fedorowicz, Lalic-McShane (these three games are included in Kozul-Freitag), Fier-Flores (included in Kozul-Jovanovic) etc.

Conclusion

This line requires nerves of steel from white players, but isn't that the way things are meant to be in the Mar del Plata Variation? My nerves badly betrayed me once (see Jankovic-Pavlidis), and I'm not the only one, however if White is not afraid of Black's kingside assault and knows how to defend against it, then he can start asking questions on the queenside. If you are a black player entering the Mar del Plata Variation, then I advise you to read this article carefully, so as not to end up in a dubious position right after the opening, as many players already have...

White postpones h2-h3

Levon Aronian
Hikaru Nakamura
Bursa Wch-tt 2010 (8)

1.d4 ♘f6 2.♘f3 g6 3.c4 ♗g7 4.♘c3 d6 5.e4 0-0 6.♗e2 e5 7.0-0 ♘c6 8.d5 ♘e7 9.♘e1 ♘d7 10.♘d3 f5 11.♗d2 ♘f6 12.f3 f4 13.c5 g5 14.cxd6 cxd6 15.♘f2 ♘g6 16.♕c2 ♖f7 17.♖fc1

This game will show that White is not forced to react to ...h7-h5 with

the move h2-h3, if Black postpones it for too long. **17...♘e8**

A) 17...♘f8 18.a4 h5 19.♘b5 ♘e8 20.a5 ♗g7 21.♖a3 g4 (21...♘h4 22.h3 ♕f6? 23.♕xc8! ♖xc8 24.♖xc8+– ♕g6 25.♘xa7 ♘f6 26.♘b5 g4 27.fxg4 hxg4 28.hxg4 ♘h5 29.♘c7 ♘g3 30.♗d1 ♖xc7 31.♖xc7 ♕e8 32.♖b3 ♕a4 33.♖xg3 1-0 Kozul-Miroshnichenko, Bled 1999; 21...a6 22.♖c3 ♗d7 23.♘c7±. Now there is no ...♗a4!) 22.fxg4 hxg4 23.♘xg4 (23.♖c3!? ♗d7 24.♘xg4 ♘h4 25.h3 ♘f6 26.♗e1 ♘xg4 27.hxg4 ♗xg4 28.♗xg4 ♖xg4 29.♘xh4±) 23...♘h4 24.♕d1 a6! 25.♘c3? ♘xg2! 26.♔xg2 ♗xg4 27.♗xg4 ♘f6 28.h3 ♘xg4 29.hxg4 ♕h4 30.♕f3 ♖xg4+ 31.♔f1 ♖g3 32.♕f2 ♗e7 33.♘e2 ♕h3+ 34.♔e1 ♖xa3 35.bxa3 ♘h4 0-1 A.Saric-Vedmediuc, Budva 2009;

B) 17...♗d7 18.a4 h5 19.♘b5 ♘e8 20.♕d1 ♗f8 21.♖c3 a6 22.♘a3

b5 23.axb5 (23.♘c2!?±) 23...axb5 24.♖b3 ♘f6 25.♗xb5 g4 26.♗xd7 ♕xd7 27.♘c4 ♖xa1 28.♕xa1 ♘h4⇄ 29.fxg4 hxg4 30.♕a6 ♘h5? 31.♘b6 ♕c7 32.♖c3 ♕d8 33.♘xg4 ♗g7 34.h3 ♘g3 35.♖c8 ♕e7 36.♘d7 ♖xg4 37.♘xf8 ♕e2+ 38.♕xe2 ♕a7+ 39.♗e3 ♕a1+ 40.♖c1 1-0 Kozul-Heinatz, Germany Bundesliga B 2016/17.

18.a4 h5 19.♘cd1!? For a broad audience that was not familiar with the nuances of the variation, this move came as a big surprise! **19...♗f8 20.♖a3 a6 21.♕c3!?** Another uncommon idea, trying to provoke a weakening of the c6-square. **21...♗d7 22.♕a5 b6 23.♕b4 ♖g7 24.♖ac3 ♘h4 25.h3 ♗e7 26.♗e1± ♕b8 27.♔f1 ♗d8** Nakamura knows very well how to play solidly and keep the tension in the King's Indian! **28.♖b3 ♗c7**

29.♕a3 ♕d8 30.♖bc3 ♗b8 31.b4 ♖a7 32.♖c6! Aronian decides he is ready for this known motif! **32...b5 33.axb5 axb5 34.♖a6 ♗b7 35.♖cc6! ♗xc6 36.dxc6⩲** A very unpleasant position to play with black. **36...♖a7?** 36...♗bf7! 37.♘c3 ♘c7 was the only way to defend. **37.♘c3 d5 38.♘xd5+– ... 1-0 (53)**

Main line
18...♗f8

Alojzije Jankovic
Kiprian Berbatov
Budva Ech 2009 (8)

1.d4 ♘f6 2.c4 g6 3.♘c3 ♗g7 4.e4 d6 5.♘f3 0-0 6.♗e2 e5 7.0-0 ♘c6 8.d5 ♘e7 9.♘e1 ♘d7 10.♘d3 f5 11.♗d2 ♘f6 12.f3 f4 13.c5 g5 14.cxd6 cxd6 15.♘f2 ♘g6 16.♕c2 ♖f7 17.♖fc1 h5

18.h3 It's possible to play immediately 18.♘b5!? ♘e8 19.a4:
A) 19...♘h4 20.♘xa7!? (20.♖a3†) 20...♗d7 (20...♖c7 21.♗a5 ♖xc2 22.♗xd8†) 21.♘b5∞;
B) 19...♗d7 20.h3 ♗f6 21.♖a3 a6 (21...♕b8 22.a5 ♗d8 23.♘c3 ♘f6 (23...♖g7 24.♗b5 ♗xb5 25.♘xb5 a6 26.♘c3 ♕a7 27.♘a4 ♘h4 28.♔f1 ♘f6 29.♕d1 ♕h7 30.♖b3⩱ Matlakov-Baryshpolets, Chotowa 2010) 24.♗b5 ♗xb5 (24...♗c8 25.♘a4†) 25.♘xb5 a6 26.♘c3 ♕a7 27.♔f1 b5 28.♗a2±) 22.♘c3∞ – White's knight won't be able to execute the b5-a3-c4 route now, but b5-c3-a4 can also be dangerous for Black;
C) 19...♗f6 20.♖a3 a6 21.♖c3! ♗d7 22.♘a3. This regrouping is a very important resource for White!
C1) 22...♖b8 23.♕d1 (after doubling the rooks, the queen is ready to fight against the ...g5-g4

break) 23...♘h4 24.♗e1! (this is also an important resource for White to fight against the knight on h4. After Black's ...g5-g4 push, White sometimes liquidates everything on g4 and then exchanges on h4 to remain with a knight against the bishop!) 24...♗g7 25.h3 ♕b6 26.♘c4 ♕a7 27.a5±;
C2) 22...♕b8 23.♘c4 ♕a7 24.a5 ♗d8 25.♔f1 ♖c8 26.♕b3 ♗b5 27.♕a3†; 27.♗e1!?;
C3) 22...b5 23.axb5 (23.♖c6!? – the well-known motif; even Aronian executed it at some stage against Nakamura! Yet, Black is not obliged to take: 23...g4!∓; 23...♗xc6 24.dxc6⩱) 23...axb5 24.♖b3 b4! (24...g4 25.fxg4 ♘h4 26.gxh5? (26. g3!±) 26...♗xf2+ 27.♔xf2 ♘h4∓ Bogdanovich-Golubev, Odessa 2010) 25.♖xb4 g4∞.
18...♗f8 18...a6 19.a4 see Kozul-Freitag. **19.♘b5**

19...♘e8 19...♗d7? 20.♕c7± – Jankovic-Bacrot, Villandry rapid 2012. **20.a4** 20.♘xa7? ♗d7 (20...♖c7? 21.♗a5 ♖xc2 22.♗xd8 ♖xe2 23.♘xc8±) 21.♘b5 g4 22.fxg4 hxg4 23.hxg4 (23.♘xg4?? ♗xb5 24.♗xb5 ♕b6+–+) 23...f3 24.gxf3 ♗xb5 25.♗xb5 ♖xf3 26.♕d1 (26.♗xe8? ♕h4–+; 26.♗e2? ♖g3+ 27.♔f1 ♕h4–+) 26...♖xf2 27.♔xf2 ♕b6+ 28.♗e3 ♕xb5= Stean-Hjartarson, Luzern 1982. **20...♗g7**
A) 20...♗d7 and now:
A1) 21.a5? is a move which, in general, White should think twice to make, since it leaves the knight unprotected and the question is whether a5-a6 is a threat: 21...g4 22.fxg4 hxg4 23.hxg4 (if 23.♘xg4? now 23...f3∓ is even more powerful) 23...f3 24.gxf3 ♖h7 (24...♕f6!?) 25.♔g2 ♘h4+ 26.♔g3 ♕f6⇄;

A2) 21.♕b3 ♘h4 22.♘c3 a6 23.♘a3 ♖g7 24.♘c4 b5 (24...g4!⇄) 25.axb5 ♗xb5 26.♕d1 ♘f6 27.♗e1 ♕e8 28.♘a5± Neverov-Akopian, Minsk 1990;
A3) 21.♖a3 a6 (21...♘h4 22.♖c3 a6 23.♘a3 ♖g7 – 20...♖g7 21.♖a3 a6 22.♖c3 ♗d7 23.♘a3 ♘h4) 22.♘c3 ♘h4 23.♕d1 ♘f6 (23...♖b8 24.♗e1 b5 25.axb5 axb5 26.♘a2†) 24.a5 b5 25.♘a2 ♕e8 (25...♖b8 26.♘b4 ♕a7 27.♔f1 g4 28.hxg4 hxg4 29.fxg4 f3 30.♗xf3 ♘xg4 31.♕e1!±) 26.♘b4 ♖h7 27.♗e1 ♕g6 28.♖ac3±.
B) 20...a6?! 21.♘a3 ♘h4 22.♘c4 g4 23.fxg4 f3 24.gxf3 ♘xf3+ 25.♗xf3 ♖xf3 26.♖a3! ♖xa3 27.bxa3 hxg4 28.hxg4±. **21.♖a3** 21.♘xa7!? ♖c7 (21...♗d7 22.♘b5 g4?! (now the knight on b5 is defended so this idea is no longer effective!) 23.fxg4±) 22.♗a5 ♖xc2 23.♗xd8 ♖xc1+ 24.♖xc1 ♗d7 25.♗b6 ♗xa4±. **21...♗d7** 21...a6 22.♘c3 ♗d7 23.♘a3 (23.♘c7 ♗xa4 (23...♖xc7 24.♖xc7±) 24.♕xa4 ♖xc7 25.♖xc7 ♘xc7 26.♗a5 ♕e8!⇄) 23...g4 (23...♘h4 24.♗e1± – this move is more useful than ♕d1 and should be played first) 24.fxg4 ♘h4 25.♗e1 ♘f6 26.♕d1 hxg4 27.hxg4 ♘h5 28.♘h1? (28.♖h3; of course the knight is taboo, yet for a clear advantage it was important to control the f4-square: 28.♘h3!±) 28...f3! 29.♗xf3 (29.gxf3 ♘f4∓) 29...♘f4 30.♘c4? (usually mistakes come in pairs) 30...♘hxg2 31.♗xg2 ♘xg4 32.♕d2 ♗h3 33.♖xh3 ♘xh3+ 34.♔h2? ♘f4 35.♗g3 ♕g5 36.♗xf4 exf4 37.♗h3 ♗e7 38.♕g2? 0-1 Kozul-Cigan, Yugoslavia tt 1988. **22.♖c3 ♔h8 23.♗e1 a6 24.♘a3 ♕b8 25.a5 b5 26.axb6 ♕xb6 27.♘c4 ♕a7 28.♘a5 ♘e7 29.♔f1 ♖b8 30.♖a1 b5 31.♗xb5 ♖xb5 32.♘c6 ♕b6 33.b4 ♘g8 34.♘d3+– ... 1-0 (43)**

Plan with ...♔h8

Alojzije Jankovic
Antonios Pavlidis
Kavala 2012 (6)

1.d4 ♘f6 2.c4 g6 3.♘c3 ♗g7 4.e4 d6 5.♘f3 0-0 6.♗e2 e5 7.0-0 ♘c6

**8.d5 ♘e7 9.♘e1 ♘d7 10.♘d3 f5
11.♗d2 ♘f6 12.f3 f4 13.c5 g5
14.cxd6 cxd6 15.♘f2 h5 16.h3
♔h8!?**

This moved surprised me, and actually, as later analyses show, it's one of the sharpest lines!

17.♕c2?! Black is playing for the ...g5-g4 push, which is why it might be useful for the queen to stay on d1 for a while: 17.a4!

A) 17...a6 18.a5 ♖g8 (18...g4 19.fxg4 hxg4 20.♘xg4 ♖g8 21.♖a3±) 19.♘a4 g4 20.fxg4 hxg4 21.hxg4±;

B) 17...♘g6 18.♘b5 ♖f7 (18...♘h4 19.♘c2 g4 20.hxg4 hxg4 21.fxg4 ♘e8 22.♖fc1 ♗d7 23.♕d1 ♗h6 24.♖c3 ♖g8 25.♖ac1±; 18...a6 19.♘a3±) 19.♕c2↑ and now the combination of ...♔h8 and ...♖f7 makes no sense;

C) 17...♖g8 18.♘b5 ♗h6 19.♘b4 ♘e8 20.♕b3 a6 21.♘a3± 19.♘a3 ♘g6 20.♘c4 ♘h4 21.♘a5±;

D) 17...♘eg8! 18.♘b5! (18.a5 ♗h6 19.a6 bxa6 20.♗xa6 g4⇄) 18...♘e8 19.♕c2 ♖f7 20.♖fc1 and now:

D1) 20...♖f8 21.♗xa7! ♗h6 ♗xc2 23.♗xd8 ♖xc1+ 24.♖xc1 ♗d7 25.♗b6 ♗xa4 26.h4!? gxh4 (26...♗h6!?) 27.♘h3 ♗d7 (27...♗e7 28.♖c4± – the advantage of the move 26.h4 is that the bishop can come to f2 with tempo!) 28.♗f2 ♘e7 29.♘g5 (29.b4 ♗c8=) 29...♔g8 30.♖c3 (30.♘e6!?) 30...b6 31.♘c6±;

D2) 20...♘h6 21.♗xa7 ♖c7 (21...♗xh3 22.♘xh3 ♖c7 23.♘f2±) 22.♗a5 ♖xc2 23.♗xd8 ♖xc1+ 24.♖xc1 ♗d7 25.♗b6 ♗xa4 26.♘b5 ♗f6 27.♖a1 ♖a6 28.♘c3 ♖xb6 29.♖xa4+–;

D3) After 20...♗d7! there are many options, it's a matter of taste:

D31) 21.♗b4 ♗f8 22.♕c3 a6 (22...a5∞) 23.♘c7 ♖c8 24.♗a5 ♘xc7 25.♗xc7 ♕e7∞;

D32) 21.♖a3 ♘h6 (21...a6 22.♘c3 ♘h6 23.a5 g4 24.fxg4 hxg4 25.hxg4 ♗f6 26.♘cd1 (26.♘a4 ♖c8↑ with ...♗h4-g3 to follow) 26...♖g7 27.♖h3 ♗h4 28.♕b3 ♔g8 29.♕b6±) 22.♖c3 ♗f6 (22...♖f8 23.♘c7 ♘xc7 24.♖xc7 ♗xa4 25.♕c3 ♖xc7 26.♕xc7 ♕xc7 27.♖xc7 ♖b8 28.h4 gxh4 (28...♔g8 29.hxg5±) 29.♘h3 ♔g8 30.♘g5 ♗e8 31.♘e6 ♗f7 32.♗b4 a6 33.♔h2±) 23.b3 (now ♘c7 is the next threat; 23.♔f1 ♖g7↑; 23.♕d1 ♖g7 24.b3 g4 25.fxg4 ♗h4!) 23...g4 24.fxg4 ♗h4! 25.gxh5 a6 (25...♖g7 26.♗f3±) 26.♘a3 (26.♘c7 ♘xc7 27.♖xc7 ♗xf2+ 28.♔xf2 ♕h4+ 29.♔g1 ♗xh3→) 26...♖g7 27.♗f3 b5∞;

D33) 21.♕c3 ♘h6 22.♕a5 b6 23.♕b4 (23.♕c3 a6 24.♘a3 ♗xa4 25.♕b4 ♗d7 26.♘c4 ♗b5∞) 23...♗f8∞;

D34) 21.♕b3 ♗f8 22.♘a3 (22.♗c3 ♖g7⇄) 22...♘h6 23.♗xb7 (23.♗b5 g4 24.♗xd7 (24.fxg4 hxg4 25.hxg4 ♕g5 26.♗xd7 ♖xd7 27.♕f3 ♖g7⇄) 24...♘xd7 25.♔f1 (25.hxg4 hxg4 26.♔f1 ♘f6↗) 25...gxf3 26.gxf3 ♖g7⇄ with ...♖g3 to follow; 23.♘c4 b6 24.♘d3 ♖g7⇄) 23...♗xh3 (23...g4? 24.♗a5±) 24.♗a6 g4 25.gxh3 ♕h4 26.hxg4 hxg4 27.♔g2 ♗g3+↑;

D35) 21.a5 g4 (21...a6 22.♘a3± is just an easy game for White; 21...♘h6 22.a6 b6 (22...bxa6 23.♖xa6±) 23.♖a3 ♗f8 24.♘c7 ♘xc7 25.♖xc7 ♖f6 26.♕b7±) 22.fxg4 hxg4 23.♘xg4∞.

17...a6 18.a4 18.♖fc1!?∞ might be an interesting idea, like in Aronian-Nakamura. **18...♖g8 19.a5 ♗h6 20.♘a4 g4 21.fxg4** 21.hxg4 hxg4 22.♘b6? g3–+ 23.♘h3 ♗xh3 24.gxh3 ♘g6↑. **21...hxg4 22.hxg4 ♘xg4**

23.♘b6? 23.♗xg4□ ♗xg4 24.♘xg4 (24.♖a3 ♗d7∓) 24...♖xg4 25.♘b6 ♕g8!→ (25...♘g6 26.♗e1∞) – this possibility is the advantage of the move ...♔h8 over the ...♖f8-f7-g7 manoeuvre! **23...♘e3 24.♗xe3 fxe3 25.♕xa8 exf2+?** 25...♘g6!! 26.♘g4 (26.♘d3 ♘h4 27.♗f3 ♕g5–+; 26.♘b6 ♕h4 27.♘xc8 exf2+ 28.♗xf2 ♗e3 29.♗f3 ♗f4–+) 26...♗f4–+. **26.♖xf2** 26.♔xf2 ♘f5–+; 26...♖xd5–+. **26...♗e3 27.♘b6 ♘g6 28.♕xc8??** After 28.♖a3! many moves lead to a draw, e.g. 28...♗xf2↑ 29.♔xf2 ♕h4+ 30.g3 ♕h2+ 31.♔e1 ♗g4 32.♖c3 ♘h4 33.gxh4 ♕xh4+ 34.♔d2 ♗xe2 35.♖c8 ♗f2 36.♖xg8+ ♔xg8 37.♕c8+ ♔g7 38.♕d7+ ♔g8 39.♕e8+ ♔g7 40.♕e7+ ♔g8=. **28...♗xf2+! 29.♔f1** 29.♔xf2 ♕h4+–+. **29...♗xb6 30.♕h3+ ♔g7 31.axb6 ♖h8 32.♗h5 ♘f4 33.♕g4+ ♔h6 34.♗f7 ♖f8 ... 0-1 (39)**

**Zdenko Kozul
Manfred Freitag**
Austria Bundesliga B 2010/11 (3)
**1.d4 ♘f6 2.♘f3 g6 3.c4 ♗g7
4.♘c3 0-0 5.e4 d6 6.♗e2 e5 7.0-0
♘c6 8.d5 ♘e7 9.♘e1 ♘d7 10.♘d3
f5 11.♗d2 ♘f6 12.f3 f4 13.c5 g5
14.cxd6 cxd6 15.♘f2 h5** 15...♘g6
16.♕c2 ♖f7 17.♖fc1 a6 (Black can also play without ...a7-a6) 18.a4 h5 (18...♗f8 19.a5 ♗d7 20.♘a4 ♖c8 21.♕b3 ♖xc1+ 22.♖xc1 ♗xa4 23.♕xa4± White has a free ride, yet it's not easy to convert: 23...♖c8 24.♖c4 (24.♖b1!) 24...♖xc4 25.♕xc4 ♗e7 26.♗e1 ♔g7 27.♔f1 h5 28.♗d1 (28.b4±) 28...♘h8 29.h3 ♘f7 30.♗e2 ♕b8 31.♔d3 ♗d8 32.♔c2 ♕a7 33.b4 b6= Kozul-Weiss, Austria Bundesliga B 2009/10) 19.h3

A) 19...♘h4!?

A1) 20.♕d1!? – prophylaxis against ... g5-g4, however Black can push the pawn anyway: 20...g4 (20...♗f8 21.a5 b5 22.axb6 ♕xb6 23.♘a4 ♕a7 24.♗a5 ♖b8 25.♗b6±; 20...♖h6 21.a5±) 21.hxg4 hxg4 22.fxg4 ♕h7 (22...f3 (22...♗d7!?) 23.♗xf3 ♘h7 (23...♘xf3+ 24.gxf3 ♘h7 25.♔g2 ♕g5 26.♗xg5 ♕xg5 27.♕d3 ♗d7 28.♖h1 ♖af8 29.♖h3+–) 24.♖a3 ♘g5 25.♗xg5 ♕xg5 26.♘e2 ♘xf3+ 27.gxf3 ♗h6 28.♔g2 ♗d7 29.♖cc3±) 23.a5 ♘g5 (23...f3 24.♗xf3 (24.gxf3? ♘g5∓) 24...♗f8 25.♖a3 (25.♘a4!? ♘xf3+ 26.gxf3 ♖xf3 27.♕e2 ♗d7 28.♔g2 ♖f7 29.♘b6 ♗b5 30.♕d3±; 30.♕e3? ♗h6!–+) 25...♘xf3 (25...♘xf3+ 26.gxf3 ♖xf3 27.♕e2±; 25...♖h6? 26.♘a4+–) 26.gxf3 ♖xf3 27.♕xf3 ♘xf3+ 28.♔g2 ♘xd2 29.♘a4 ♗d7 30.♘b6 ♖d8 31.♖c2 ♖h6 32.♖d3 ♘f6 33.♖xd7 ♖xd7 34.♖dxd2 ♗xd2 35.♖xd2±) 24.♗f1! (nice prophylaxis! The bishop moves away from the ...f4-f3 tempo, to which White will now react with g2-g3, and then after 23...♘g5 it's harder for Black to attack the g4-pawn, which is less well defended after 24.♗f1) 24...♕f6 (24...b5? 25.axb6 ♕xb6 26.♘a4 ♕a7 27.♗a5 ♗b7 (27...♖b8 28.♗b6±) 28.♖c6 (28.♗d8!? △ 28...♘xe4 29.♗xh4 ♗f6 30.♘c5!+–) 28...♖ab8 29.♗b6 ♖xb6 30.♘xb6 ♗b7 31.♖b3!+– ♗e6 32.♘d7 ♖a8 33.♖cxa6 ♗xa6 34.♖xa6 ♕xd7 35.dxe6 ♕c8 36.e7+ ♔h7 37.♖xa8 ♕xa8 38.♕f7 1-0 Lalic-McShane, Southend 2000) 25.♘a4 f3 26.g3 ♗xg4 27.♖c4±;

A2) 20.a5 g4

21.fxg4 (21.♘a4? g3! 22.♘d3. Now comes the typical Mar del Plata sac 22...♗xh3! 23.gxh3 ♕d7–+) 21...f3

(21...hxg4 22.hxg4 b5 23.axb6 ♕xb6 24.♘a4 ♕a7 25.♗a5 f3? (25...♖b7!∞) 26.♗xf3 ♗xg4?! 27.♗xg4 ♘xg4 28.♗b6 ♖xf2 29.♕xf2+– Kozul-Arapovic, Porec 1998) 22.♗g5! (22.♗xf3 (22.gxf3 ♘h7∞) 22...♘xg4 23.hxg4 ♘xf3+ 24.gxf3 ♕h4 25.♘cd1?? (25.♔g2, with the idea of ♖h1: 25...♗xg4! 26.f4!∞) 25...♕g3+! 26.♔f1 ♗d7!–+ 27.♗e3 ♖xf3 28.♖a3 ♗b5+ 29.♔e1 hxg4 30.♖b3 ♖af8 31.♖xb5 ♖xe3+ 32.♘xe3 ♕xe3+ 33.♔f1 g3 34.♖b3 ♖xf2+ 35.♔g1 ♕h6 36.♕c8+ ♔h7 0-1 Kekelidze-Baklan, Batumi 2002) 22...♘xg2 23.♗xf3 ♘f4∞.

B) 19...♗f8 20.a5 and now:
B1) 20...♗d7 21.♘a4 ♖c8 22.♕b3 ♖xc1+ 23.♖xc1 g4 24.fxg4 hxg4 25.hxg4 ♗xa4 26.♕xa4± Kozul-Gislason, Kallithea 2008;
B2) 20...b5 21.axb6 ♕xb6 22.♘a4 (22.♘b5! g4 23.♗a5↑) 22...♕a7 23.♗a5 ♗b7 24.♔f1 ♗d7 25.♖a3 (25.♕d1±) 25...♗e7 26.♖c3 ♗d8 27.b4 ♕b8 28.♖c6! ♗xa5 29.bxa5 ♖xc6 30.dxc6 ♘c7 31.♘b6 ♖aa7 32.♘d5 ♗g7 33.♘xc7 ♕xc7 34.♘d3 g4 35.hxg4 hxg4 36.♘b4 ♗c8 37.fxg4 ♗f8 38.g5 ♘e8 39.♘d5 ♔g6 40.c7 ♗xg5 41.♖c6 f3 42.♗xf3 1-0 Sosonko-Fedorowicz, Cannes 1992;
B3) 20...g4 21.fxg4 hxg4 22.hxg4 transposes to 19...g4 20.fxg4 hxg4 21.hxg4 ♗f8 22.a5;
B4) 20...♘h4 21.♘a4 g4 22.hxg4 hxg4 23.fxg4 ♖g7 24.♕d1 ♗d7 (24...♘xg2 25.♖xc8 ♖xc8 26.♔xg2 ♘h5 27.♘h1 (27.♖a3; 27.♘b6 ♖cc7 28.♖a3 ♘g3 29.♘c3) 27...♕h4) 25.♘b6 ♖b8 26.♘xd7 ♕xd7 27.♖a3 ♕e8 (27...♗e7 28.g3 fxg3 29.♖xg3 1-0 Jankovic-Makaj, Cakovec 2011) 28.♖h3 ♖h7 29.g5 ♘d7 30.♗g4 ♖c8 31.♗e6+ ♔g7 32.♖xc8 ♕xc8 33.♕g4 ♕c2 34.♖xh4 1-0 Mekhitarian-Lucci, Maringa 2012.
C) 19...g4 20.fxg4 hxg4 21.hxg4 ♗f8 22.a5 b5 23.axb6 ♕xb6 24.♘a4 ♕a7 25.♗a5 ♖b8 (25...♖b7 26.g5 ♘h7 27.h5 ♘h4 28.♕d1? (28.♗b6! ♖xb6 29.♘xb6 ♕xb6 30.♕c7±) 28...♘xg5 29.♖xc8 ♖xc8 30.♕g4 ♘hf3+ 31.gxf3 ♖g7 32.♔f1 ♖c2 33.♗b6 ♕b7 34.♕f5 ♖c4 35.♘g4

♖xa4 36.♖xa4 ♕xb6 37.♘h6+ ♔h8 38.♕xf8+ ♔h7 39.♘g4 ♕b5+ 40.♔e1 ♖xa4 41.♕f5+ ♔h8 42.♕f8+ ♔h7 43.♕f5+ ♔h8 ½-½ Grigoryan-Andriasyan, Martuni 2013) and now:
C1) 26.g5? ♘g4! (26...f3? 27.♗xf3 ♘g4 28.♕d2± Spassov-Danailov, Pamporovo 1981) 27.♗xg4 (27.♗f3? ♘e3? (27...♖h7! 28.♗xg4 ♗xg4 29.♘b6 ♖xb6 30.♘xb6 ♕xb6∓) 28.♕e2 ♖fb7 29.♖c6± ♖g7 30.♖ac1 ♗d7 31.♖xa6 ♕d4 32.♘b6 ♘h4 33.♘xd7 ♘xf3+ 34.♕xf3 ♖xd7 35.♗c3 ♗c4 36.♖c6 ♗b5 37.♘g4 ♘xg4 38.♕xg4 ♗g7 39.♕e6+ ♔h7 40.♗f2 1-0 Kozul-Schekachev, Linares 1996) 27...♗xg4 28.♖a3? (28.♕d3 f3 29.♗c7! ♖xc7 30.♗xc7 ♕xc7 31.♘xg4 fxg2 32.♘f6+ ♔f7 33.♘h5=) 28...f3 29.g3 ♖h7∓ 30.♕d2 ♖h3 31.♖c7 ♖xg3+ 32.♔f1 ♖b7 33.♗b6 ♕b8 34.♕c3 ♖xb6 35.♘xb6 ♕xb6 36.♖b3 ♕d4 37.♕xd4 exd4 38.♘xg4 ♖xg4 39.♖xf3 ♖xg5 40.♖c8 ♔g7 41.♖d3 ♖h6 42.♖xd4 ♗g7 43.♖a4 ♗xb2 44.♖xa6 ♗e5 45.♖d8 ½-½ Azmaiparashvili-Cvitan, Tilburg 1993;
C2) 26.♗c7! ♗b4 (26...♗b7 27.♗xd6 ♗xd6 28.♕xc8+± Sosonko-Rogic, Bled 1997) 27.♗xd6 ♗xd6 (27...♘xe4 28.♗c5+–) 28.♕xc8+ ♘f8 29.♕xa6 (29.♗f3 ♘xe4 30.♗xe4 ♖xe4 31.♘c3 ♖b4 32.♖xa6 ♗c5 33.♖xa7 ♖xa7 34.♖c2 ♗d4± S.Romanov-Mehlhorn, cr 2010) 29...♘xe4 30.♕xa7 ♖xa7 31.♘xe4 ♖xe4 32.♗d1±.

16.h3 ♘g6 17.♕c2 ♖f7 18.♖fc1 g4! 18...a6 19.a4 transposes to 15.♘g6.

19.fxg4 hxg4 20.hxg4 ♘e8!? 21.a4?! Since Black has already shown his cards on the kingside

this move might be a waste of time; 21.♘cd1! ♗f6 22.♕b3 ♗h4 23.♖c3 ♗f6 (23...a6? 24.♖ac1 ♗f6 25.♕a3 1-0 Kozul-Nataf, Istanbul 2003; 23...♗g3?! 24.♖xg3! fxg3 25.♕xg3± is the way for White to take the initiative!) 24.♖ac1 ♗h7! (the best regrouping! If 24...♗f8? 25.♖h3 ♗g6±; 25...♗g3?! 26.♖xg3 fxg3 27.♕xg3±) 25.♖h3 (25.♕a3 ♘h8 26.♖c4 (26.♖h3!?; 26.g3 fxg3 27.♖xg3 ♗xg3 28.♕xg3∞) 26...♘f7 (26...♗g3 27.g5∞) 27.♗a5 (27.♗c7!?) 27...♕f8 (27...b6 28.♗xb6↑) 28.♖c7 ♗g3 (28...♗d7 29.♖xb7∞) 29.♖c3=) 25...♘h8 26.♖cc3 (26.♖xh4 ♖xh4 27.g3∞) 26...♘f7 27.g3!↑ △ 27...fxg3 28.♖cxg3 ♗xg3 29.♖xg3±. **21...♗f6 22.♘cd1 ♗h4 23.♖a3** 23.♘h3!?.

23...♗g3 Black should not be in a hurry to put the bishop on g3, because White sometimes has the idea ♘h1 with ♘df2 to follow. Actually the knight has better perspectives on h1 than the other one on d1! Black should put the bishop on h4 and the knight on f6. **24.♖c3** 24.♘h3!? ♕h4 25.♘df2 ♗f6 26.♕d1 ♗d7 27.a5 ♖af8 28.♗e1 f3 29.♖xf3 ♘f4 30.♖xf4 ½-½ Sosonko-Hellers, Wijk aan Zee 1986. **24...♗d7** Now when Black plays ...♘f6, ♖c7 again is still not a threat due to ...♗xa4!. **25.♗b5?** 25.♘h3! ♕h4 26.♘df2 ♘f6=; 25.♕b3? ♕h4 26.♕xb7 ♕h2+ 27.♔f1 ♘h4 28.♗f3 ♖d8 29.♕b3 ♖g7∓. **25...♗xb5?** 25...♕h4! 26.♘h3 ♗xg4 27.♘df2 ♘f6–+. **26.axb5 ♕h4 27.♘h3 ♘f6 28.♖c8+?** 28.♘df2! was still equal. Kozul, true to his fighting style, didn't want a draw and later ended up on the verge of defeat, but still managed to draw on move 63.
½-½

Zdenko Kozul
Zoran Jovanovic
Otocac ch-CRO 2010 (3)
1.d4 d6 2.♘f3 g6 3.c4 ♗g7 4.♘c3 ♘f6 5.e4 0-0 6.♗e2 e5 7.0-0 ♘c6 8.d5 ♘e7 9.♘e1 ♘d7 10.♘d3 f5 11.♗d2 ♘f6 12.f3 f4 13.c5 h5 14.cxd6 cxd6 15.♘f2 g5 16.h3 ♘g6 17.♕c2 ♖f7 18.♖fc1 g4 19.fxg4 hxg4 19...f3? 20.♗xf3 hxg4 21.hxg4 ♘h7 22.♘h5 ♘h4 23.♘c7 (23.♗e2+–) 23...♘xf3+ 24.gxf3 ♕h4? 25.♔g2 ♖xf3 26.♗xf3 ♗xg4+ 27.♘xg4 ♖f8+ 28.♗e2 ♕xg4+ 29.♔d3+– Fier-Flores, Campinas 2010. **20.hxg4 ♘h4!?**

This move is very sharp and White needs to be very precise. **21.a4?** Again, White doesn't have time to start his play on the queenside.
A) 21.♘cd1?! ♗h6 22.♕b3 (22.♗f3 ♖g7–+) 22...♖g7 23.♗e1 ♘h5!→ (23...♗xg4? 24.♗xg4 ♘xg4 25.♘xg4 ♖xg4 26.♕h3⇄);
B) 21.♘b5!? is the most forcing move, but probably it yields no more than a draw: 21...♘xg4! (21...♕b6? 22.a4 ♘xg4 23.♕xc8+ ♖xc8 24.♖xc8+ ♖f8 25.♖xf8+ ♗xf8 26.♗xg4 a6 27.♘c3±; 21...♘xg4?? 22.♘xg4+–; 21...♘e8!? 22.♕d3 ♗d7 (22...a6 23.♘a3±) 23.♘a3 ♘f6 24.♘c4∞) and now:

B1) 22.♘xa7? ♕b6 23.♖xc8+ ♖xc8 24.♖xc8+ ♔h7 25.♗xg4 ♕xb2 26.♖d1 ♕a3 27.♘b5 ♕g3–+;

B2) 22.♘xd6?! ♕xd6 23.♕xc8+ ♖xc8 24.♖xc8+ ♗f8 25.♗xg4 (25.♘xg4 ♕g6 26.♗f3 ♕g6+ 27.♔f1 ♘xf3 28.gxf3 ♖g7∓) 25...♕b6∓;

B3) 22.♗xg4!? ♗xg4 23.♘xg4 ♕b6+ 24.♔h1 (24.♗e3!? – a spectacular move! Yet Black is still in the driving seat: 24...♕xb5 (24...fxe3 25.♕e2 ♖af8 26.♖f1∞) 25.♗f2 ♕d7 26.♘h2 ♗f6∓; 24.♘f2 ♕xh5 25.♕d1 ♗f6∓; 25...f3?! 26.g3±) 24...♕xb5 25.♗e1 ♕d7 26.♘h2 ♗f6 27.♕b3 ♗h7 28.♕h3 ♕xh3 29.gxh3 ♗d8 30.♖c4 ♗b6 31.♖ac1 ♖f8 32.♘c8 ♘g6⇄;

B4) 22.♘xg4 f3 and now:

B41) 23.♘h6+? ♗xh6 24.♗xh6 ♕b6+! (24...fxe2? 25.♗xe2±; 24...♔h7 25.♕d2 fxe2 26.♕e3=; strange that in a correspondence game in 2012 Black was not able to find the winning move: 24...♗g4? 25.♕d2 ♗xg2 26.♗g5+ ♕xg5 27.♗xg5 fxe2 28.♔xg2 ♖g7 29.♘xd6 ♖xg5 30.♗f2 ♖f8+ 31.♘f5 ♗xf5 32.exf5 ♖fxf5+ ½-½ Oortwijn-Volkov, cr 2012) 25.♔h2 ♗h7!! 26.♗g5 (26.♗xf3 ♗xh6–+) 26...♗d7 27.♗xh4 f4! 28.♗g3 ♖h8!–+;

B42) 23.♗xf3 ♖xf3! (23...♘xf3+ 24.gxf3 ♗xg4 25.fxg4 ♕b6+ (25...♖f3 26.♗e1 ♕b6+ 27.♔g2 ♖af8 (threatening 28...♖f1) 28.♕d2!! (a fantastic defensive move! 28.♗g3 ♕e3–+) 28...♕xb5 (28...♖f1 29.♘d4! is the point!) 29.♗g3 ♕d7 30.♕g5 ♕b5 31.♕d2=) 26.♔h1 ♕xb5=) 24.♕c7 (24.gxf3?? ♘xf3+ 25.♔g2 ♗xg4–+) 24...♗xg4 25.♕xd8+ ♖xd8 26.♗g5 ♘xg2 27.♗xd8 ♘f4= with a perpetual.

C) 21.♕d1 ♗h6 (21...♗f8 22.a4 ♖g7 23.♖a3 ♘h5→; 23...♘xg2?! 24.♔xg2 ♘xg4 25.♗xg4 ♗xg4 26.♕xg4! (this motif is important to know! 26.♘xg4? ♕h4∓)

26...♖xg4+ 27.♘xg4± 22.a4 (22.♗f3 ♖g7→) 22...♖g7∓ △ 23.♖a3 ♘xg2 24.♔xg2 ♘xg4–+;

D) 21.♗e1 f3 22.♗xf3 (22.gxf3 ♘h5–+) 22...♘xf3+ 23.gxf3 ♘h7 24.♘h3 (24.♗d2 ♖xf3 25.♔g2 ♕f6! 26.♖f1 ♗d7 27.g5 ♕f7 28.g6 ♕f6–+) 24...♖xf3 25.♔g2 ♖f7 26.♘d1 (26.♗d2 ♕h4†) 26...♗h6 27.♖c3 ♖g7→;

E) 21.♕b3!? might be White's best try to take a risk and play for a win. Engines tend to overestimate Black's prospects: 21...♗f8 (21...♗h6!? 22.♘cd1∞) 22.♘cd1 ♖g7 23.♗e1 (23.♕h3!?) 23...♘h5 (23...♖xg4 24.♖xc8 ♕xc8 25.♗xg4 ♖xg4 26.♘xg4 ♕xg4 27.♗xh4 ♕xh4 28.♘f2±) 24.♖c3 ♗d7 25.♖ac1 ♘g3 26.♖xg3 fxg3 27.♕xg3∞.

21...♗f8? 21...♗h6? (21...♘xg4! 22.♘xg4 f3∓) 22.♘b5 ♖g7 23.♘c7± △ 23...♘xg4? 24.♘xa8 ♘xf2 25.♕xc8+–.

An important position. If the bishop were on f8 Black would win with 25...♕g5!. Sometimes this is important when Black chooses whether to play ...♗f8 or ...♗h6. **22.♕d1 ♖g7!? 23.♗e1** 23.♖a3!?. **23...♕b6 24.a5?** 24.♔f1 ♕e3 25.♗f3 (25.♕d3 ♘xg2 26.♔xg2 ♗xg4 27.♗xg4 f3+ 28.♔h1 ♘xg4 29.♕xe3 ♘xe3 30.♘cd1 ♖h7+ 31.♔g1 ♖g7+=) 25...♘xf3 26.gxf3 ♘xg4 27.fxg4 ♗xg4 28.♘xg4 ♕h3+ 29.♔e2 ♕xg4 30.♔f2 ♖g2 31.♖c2 ♕e3+ 32.♔f1 ♕h3=. **24...♕e3–+ 25.♕d3 ♘xg4 26.♗xg4 ♖xg4 27.♕xe3 ♖xg2+ 28.♔h1 fxe3 29.♖fd1 ♖g6?** 29...♗h6! 30.♗xh4 ♖g4 31.♗e1 (31.♗e7 ♖g6 32.♘e2 ♗g4–+) 31...♖g7 32.♘c2 ♗g4–+. **30.♗xh4 ♖h6 31.♔g2 ♖xh4 32.♘xe3 ♗h6 33.♖e1 ♗f4 34.♘f5 ♗xf5 35.exf5 ♖f8 36.♖h1 ♖g4+ 37.♔f3 ♖g3+ 38.♔f2 ♖xf5 39.♖hg1 ♖xg1 40.♖xg1+ ♔f7 41.♔e2 ♖h5 42.♘e4 ♖h2+ 43.♔d3 ♖xb2 44.♘xd6+ ♔f8 45.♔e4 ♖d2 46.♘f5 ♖e2+ 47.♔f3 ♖d2 48.♔e4 ♖e2+ 49.♔f3 ½-½**

Karpov's lessons

The variation also suited Karpov's style:

Anatoly Karpov
John van der Wiel

Brussels 1987 (4)

1.d4 ♘f6 2.c4 g6 3.♘c3 ♗g7 4.e4 d6 5.♘f3 0-0 6.♗e2 e5 7.0-0 ♘c6 8.d5 ♘e7 9.♘e1 ♘d7 10.♘d3 f5 11.♗d2 ♘f6 12.f3 f4 13.c5 g5 14.cxd6 cxd6 15.♘f2 h5 16.h3 ♘g6 17.♕c2 ♘e8

The main line is 17...♖f7 18.♖fc1 and now:

A) 18...♗f8 (Jankovic-Berbatov);

B) 18...a6 (comments in Kozul-Freitag);

C) 18...g4 (Kozul-Freitag & Kozul-Jovanovic).

18.a4 ♗f6 19.♖a3 ♕c7 20.♖c1 ♗d8 21.♘b5 ♕b8 22.a5 a6 23.♘c3 b6 24.♘cd1 ♖f7 25.♕b3 b5 26.♘d3 ♗f6 27.♘1f2 ♖c7 28.♖c3 ♖xc3 29.bxc3 ♘d7 30.c4 White is clearly better now. Karpov was not at his best in this game since he failed to convert the advantage ... ½-½ **(61)**

Exercise 1

position after 25.♘a4-b6

How should Black proceed with his attack?

Exercise 2

position after 27.♗g5xh4

Black to move.

Exercise 3

position after 25.♗e2-b5

Black to move.

(*solutions on page 252*)

A revelation in the main line KID – Part II

by Nikolaos Ntirlis

1.	d4	♘f6
2.	c4	g6
3.	♘c3	♗g7
4.	e4	d6
5.	♘f3	0-0
6.	♗e2	e5
7.	0-0	exd4
8.	♘xd4	♖e8
9.	f3	c6

In the previous part of this Survey, we went through the main theoretical continuations of what may well become the new big trend in the Classical KID: 7...exd4! 8.♘xd4 ♖e8 9.f3 and now the soundest move 9...♘c6!.

Herman Pilnik

In that installment, I briefly mentioned the alternative **9...c6!?**, a move designed to help Black to blast open the centre with ...d6-d5. As I wrote in the introduction to the previous Survey, the analysis engines don't like 9...c6 that much, but in this rich position there are unexplored possibilities which, in my opinion, make the whole line playable, even at the highest levels of correspondence play.

The practical advantages of playing both 9...♘c6 and 9...c6!?

One of the main attractions of the 7...exd4 line is that Black chooses how to dictate the play. In the traditional main line after 7...♘c6 8.d5 ♘e7, White is the side with several good options: 9.♘e1!?, 9.♘d2!?, 9.b4! as well as some other moves which are not silly at all, for example 9.a4!?.

After 7...exd4 8.♘xd4 ♖e8 9.f3, if we want to play a somewhat closed but solid position, then 9...♘c6 can serve us pretty well. If we want to play with an open centre, where the value of each choice for White up until move 25 is sometimes very high, then 9...c6 is excellent. Imagine a White player, having a couple of hours to prepare against you, realizing that he needs to prepare two totally different types of positions, in a line which at the end of the day doesn't look bad at all for Black! I am predicting that a lot of players will end up playing the London against you more and more often!

A new weapon

After **10.♔h1** the move **10...d5** has been considered unplayable for decades, but I hope that I'll overturn this assessment in this Survey. **11.cxd5 cxd5 12.♗g5 ♘c6 13.♗b5** is the critical line.

Now comes **13...h6!N**, a crucial novelty which seems to be giving Black excellent practical chances: **14.♘xc6 bxc6 15.♗xc6 hxg5 16.♗xa8 d4** and the fun starts! Black is down an exchange and a pawn but this is far from the whole story in the position. White has to play very

well to keep whatever edge he has in the position and Black is still within the drawing zone.

That being said, the traditional and well-tested 10...♘bd7!? is not that bad either, as we will see in Game 1, while any other 10th move for White is not at all critical.

Conclusion

I hope that in the previous part of this Survey I convinced you that 9...♘c6 is equal. My aim in this Survey is not to do the same with 9...c6 as I am not 100% confident that Black equalizes. But honestly, nobody should care about that. The resulting positions are super-exciting and fresh (especially after 10.♔h1 d5!) and White should play on a very high level in order to keep winning chances in some objectively drawn endgames. My main point is that if you combine 9...♘c6 and 9...c6 in your preparation, you'll become a fearful KID player!

Minor lines
10.♔h1

Hans Galjé
David R Cumming
cr 2014

1.d4 ♘f6 2.c4 g6 3.♘c3 ♗g7 4.e4 d6 5.♘f3 0-0 6.♗e2 e5 7.0-0 exd4 8.♘xd4 ♖e8 9.f3 c6 10.♔h1!

When the Argentinean grandmaster Herman Pilnik introduced this concept in the early 1950s, it took the players ot the time a few years to realize how strong this prophylactic king

move is. According to my database, Taimanov was the first to play this move, against Geller in 1957. Since then, this is the main line for White, so it is natural to start our study of Black's system here. **10...♘bd7!?** This is the move Black players have based their hopes on for decades. In 2014, Bulgarian grandmaster Dejan Bojkov wrote a book that was ahead of its time: 'Modernized: The King's Indian Defense', after which more and more Black players burnt a lot of electric power to analyse this line deeply. One of these players was the Scottish Correspondence Master David Cumming, who played a few nice games here.

A) 10...♘h5!? became a huge trend a few years ago, until White players discovered the way to deal with it: 11.g4! (otherwise ...f7-f5) 11...♘f6 (now ...h7-h5 comes) 12.♗f4! h5 13.♘f5!!. This

was mentioned by Dejan Antic in 2013 in his Survey in Yearbook 107. It's the only way to challenge Black's set-up. Some strong correspondence players have defended this position recently and scored a few draws, but OTB this is scary;

B) 10...d5!? is the move White is supposed to have stopped with his king's move! Nevertheless, this is my main suggestion, please check the next game.

11.♗e3! This is the only line which threatens Black's life.

A) 11.♗g5!? ♕b6 12.♘b3 (12.♘a4!? is more rare. 12...♕c7 13.♕d2 ♘c5 14.♘c3 a5 was a bit better for White in Dubov-Kokarev, Sochi 2017, but nothing too worrying for Black. He has seen worse in this line) 12...a5 13.♕d2 a4 14.♗e3 ♕d8 15.♘d4 ♘c5 seems to be OK for Black. A possible plan is ...♕e7-♘fd7-♘f8 where Black is flexible to meet whatever White

will throw at him, while he has counterplay ideas like ...f7-f5, ...♘fe6, ...♗e5 etc... if White is better here, it is only slightly; nothing to lose sleep about;

B) 11.♗f4 has a nice story behind it which I followed for some time after the publication of the Bojkov book. Article after article was published (for example, by Kaufman, Watson and others) and game after game was played where both sides defended their ground with passion. It seems to me that the final verdict should be that Black is fine. The main line runs 11...♘h5 12.♗xd6 ♕f6 13.♘b3 ♘f4 14.c5 a5 15.♗xf4 ♕xf4 16.♘a4 ♕c7 17.♕d2 b5 18.cxb6 ♘xb6 19.♘xb6 ♕xb6 20.♘c4 ♕b4 21.a3 ♕e7⇄. Here Black has proven in a series of correspondence games that his bishops provide enough counterchances for his broken structure.

11...a6! If you want to play 10...♘bd7, this is the move. I am sure about it. 11...♘b6?! is recommended by FM Kamil Plichta in his Chessable course, based on the practical consideration that in order for White to get a slight edge he should know the 'weird' 12.♕c1!. I appreciate the idea, but I believe that also 12.♕d2!? d5 13.c5 gives White an advantage. So, I cannot recommend 11...♘b6?!. **12.♘c2!** Otherwise 12...d5 comes; 12.♘b3N is an alternative worth mentioning, e.g. 12...♘e5 (12...♕e7!? is OK as well, with ...d6-d5 coming next) 13.f4 ♘eg4 14.♗g1 h5 15.♗f3 ♗e6⇄ with a much improved version of our main line. **12...♘e5 13.f4 ♘eg4** 13...♘ed7 has also been

tried in correspondence chess, but I cannot believe it. **14.♗g1 h5** I spent a lot of time trying to make the move 14...♘h6 work. It might not be that bad, but it doesn't make that much sense for humans either, so let's go for the more exciting main line. **15.♗f3 ♗e6**

16.♕d3! This move was proposed after the super-GM encounter Kramnik-Ponomariov, Dortmund 2011, where White played another move: 16.b3, but after 16...♕a5! Black is doing very well in the complications:

A) 17.♕d2?! ♘d5! 18.♘b1 ♕xd2 19.♘xd2 ♘xf4 20.♗xg4 hxg4 21.♖xf4 ♗xa1 22.♘xa1 d5⇄. Black is at least equal here. White's pieces are discoordinated. A sample line: 23.cxd5 cxd5 24.♘c2 ♖ac8 25.♘d4 f5 26.exf5 ♗xf5 and the black rooks will penetrate to the second rank;

B) 17.♕e1?! ♗f5! (17...b5⇄ was seen instead in the stem game Kramnik-Ponomariov, Dortmund 2011, which was not bad) 18.♘d4 ♕d8 19.♖d1 ♗xe4 20.♘xe4 ♘xe4 21.♗xe4 d5∓ De Oliveira-Rook, cr 2014;

C) 17.♘e2!? ♘xe4 18.♗xe4 ♗xa1 19.♘xa1 ♗xc4 20.bxc4 ♖xe4 21.♘b3 ♕b4 22.♘g3 ♖xc4 23.h3 ♖c3 24.♘xh5 gxh5 25.hxg4 ♕e4 26.gxh5 ♖g3 27.♔f2 ♖h3+ 28.♗h2 ♖h4 and Black was doing well in Leelenstein-Stockfish, chess.com 2019. White has a few weaknesses and Black's central pawns are dangerous. **16...b5! 17.cxb5 axb5 18.♖fd1! d5! 19.e5** 19.♕f1 has been seen in another Cumming game, but I recommend Black to follow another course: 19...♘d7!N (19...♕c7 was seen in Mende-Cumming, cr 2014, and

I could really spend a few more pages analysing the details here. I think that my alternative is more practical) 20.exd5 c5! 21.♗xc5 ♕c7 22.♗d4 ♕xf4 23.♗xg4 ♕xf1+ 24.♖xf1 ♘xg4 25.♗xg7 ♔xg7. Black has enough compensation for his pawn here. His main counterplay idea is ...♘g4-e5-...d3/c4. If you need more evidence that Black is fine, allow me to follow the main line of the top engines a bit further: 26.♔g1 ♘e5 27.♘b4 h4 28.h3 ♖ac8 (an alternative which potentially keeps more life in the position is 28...♘c4!? 29.b3 ♘d6⇄ followed by ...g6-g5 and ...f7-f5) 29.♖ae1 f6 30.d6 ♖e6 31.♘bd5 ♖xd6 32.♘xf6 ♖xf6 33.♖xe5 ♖xf1+ 34.♔xf1 ♘f6 35.♖e4 g5=. This position might not exactly look exciting, but it seems to be a fortress. For example, Black can put his bishop on c6 and his rook on the 5th rank (e.g., e5) and wait forever. **19...♘d7!?** 19...♘f5!?N is a move which I'll let the interested reader analyse on his own. My conclusion is that if White has any edge after this, it is certainly quite small. If you don't fancy Black's prospects after 23.♗e2! in the main line below, then this is the place to investigate. **20.♘d4 ♘gxe5! 21.fxe5 ♘xe5**

22.♕c2 When I prepared this line for the first time 4-5 years ago, I chickened out with 22.♘xe6!?N ♖xe6 23.♕f1, stopping here and claiming 'a small edge for White'. This was quite lazy of me, of course, and I should have analysed the position further: 23...♘xf3 24.♕xf3 b4 25.♘e2 ♗xb2 26.♖ab1 ♗g7. This is a type of position which arises quite often,

for example in the QGD (in the Exchange Variation, or in some lines of the Tarrasch Defence). What I have in mind actually is the position with the a2- and b4-pawns exchanged. Here is one line (which is the top line of the engines) where this comes on the board: 27.♘c1 ♕e7 28.♘d3 ♖xa2 29.♘xb4 ♖b2 30.♖xb2 ♗xb2. My experience tells me that although engines tend to prefer White, in an OTB game Black is quite safe and actually he is the one playing for the full point. I won't provide any further lines to back up my claim, but I did indeed spend some time checking this to be sure. So, I ask you to have faith in me and not in my older and lazier self! **22...♗d7**

It is obvious that in practical terms, Black has tremendous compensation for the piece. His threat is 23...b4, followed by 24...c5 and 25...♗xf3, while ...h5-h4-h3 is in the air. In the old days, an 'unclear' symbol (or 'compensation for the material') would be attached and we would move on. In the silicon era of chess (of which I am a proud representative) we need to go deeper and provide more evidence of the above claim. So please bear with me a little longer. **23.a3** I think that there are two alternatives which are objectively better:

A) 23.b4!?N ♘xf3 24.♘xf3 ♗g4 25.♖f1 d4 26.♖ad1 ♗f5 27.♕f2 dxc3 28.♖xd8 ♖axd8⧏ is a sample line in this rich position. I believe that Black is fine here;

B) I think 23.♗e2!N is White's best and at the moment of writing this article I haven't found a completely satisfactory solution

for Black. I think best is 23...♘c4! 24.♗xc4 (24.a4?! b4! 25.♗xc4 bxc3! gives Black strong counterplay) 24...bxc4 25.♘f3! (otherwise 25...c5) 25...♗g4. Stockfish thinks that White holds a large advantage while Lc0 thinks that Black is only a bit worse. I cannot say that I have exhausted all the possibilities of the position in my analysis, but I think White retains an advantage. That being said, in a practical OTB game things are much less clear. Typical moves that give Black plenty of counterplay are ...♗xf3, ...h5-h4-h3, ...♖b8 or ...♕f6 and ...♗e6-♖ae8 etc. I wouldn't be 100% confident that I wouldn't lose this position in a correspondence game, but I would have fun in an OTB game. **23...c5 24.♗xd5** 24.♘b3 b4!⇄ keeps the equilibrium for Black with the main point being 25.axb4 ♖xa1 26.♖xa1 ♗f5, followed by taking on f3 and taking on b4. **24...cxd4 25.♗xa8 d3! 26.♖xd3 ♕xa8 27.♖xd7** This bishop has to leave the board, otherwise, after ...♗c6 and ...h5-h4-h3, White will feel a lot of pressure on the long diagonal. **27...♕xd7 28.♘xb5 ♖c8 29.♕e2 h4!⧏**

Black's compensation is obvious. All his pieces are active and he has the initiative. The threat is now 30...h3, so... **30.h3 ♘f6!** Now the knight goes to h5. In an OTB game I would be worried as White, but in a correspondence game, with the help of the engines, White held comfortably: **31.♘d6 ♘h5 32.♗f2 ♖d8 33.♘e4 ♗xb2 34.♕xb2 ♕xe4 35.♕b4 ♕e5 36.♖e1 ♘g3+ 37.♗xg3 ♕xg3 38.a4 ♕f2 39.♕c3 ♔h7 40.a5 ½-½**

Analysis
1.d4 ♘f6 2.c4 g6 3.♘c3 ♗g7 4.e4 d6 5.♘f3 0-0 6.♗e2 e5 7.0-0 exd4 8.♘xd4 ♖e8 9.f3 c6 10.♔h1 d5! If there is a consistent move, then this is it! For decades, White believed that with 10.♔h1 he stopped 10...d5 and we needed a new KID on the block, Lc0, to show us that Black's resources haven't been exhausted! **11.cxd5 cxd5 12.♗g5 ♘c6 13.♗b5**

This is the main line (we are going to look at a couple of alternatives later), and now comes the new move **13...h6!N**. This is the start of an exchange sacrifice, after which Black's pair of bishops seem to provide adequate compensation: **14.♘xc6 bxc6 15.♗xc6 hxg5 16.♗xa8 d4** Black is a pawn an an exchange down and already Stockfish screams that White is much better! We need to dig much deeper into the position to see if indeed Black's counterplay is enough. **17.♘e2** I think this is the strongest move; 17.♗c6 is not dangerous, e.g. 17...dxc3 18.♗xe8 ♕xe8 19.bxc3 ♗e6⇄ and White is the one who will feel the pressure after ...g5-g4 next; 17.♘d5 ♗a6! 18.♖e1 (18.♘xf6+ ♕xf6 19.♗d5 ♗xf1 20.♕xf1 ♖c8⇄ and Black's counterplay ideas down the c-file and the ...g5-g4 break, as well as the opposite-coloured bishops, make him safe here) 18...♕xa8 19.♘c7 ♕b7 20.♘xe8 ♘xe8 with a rare material configuration on the board. White has two rooks and a pawn for three pieces, but Black has the two bishops and a

dangerous pawn on d4. After 21.e5 ♕d7∞ or 21...♕d5∞ I couldn't prove an advantage for White in my analysis. **17...d3!** I consider this to be the most dangerous move in practice. I had fun analysing 17...♗a6 18.♗c6! ♖e6 19.♗a4 ♘h5 with the idea ...♗e5. Unfortunately, it seems to me that White defends and ends up being better, but in an OTB game wouldn't bet that White will find all the best moves. Especially tempting is 20.♗b3!? (most probably, better is 20.♕d2) 20...♖e8 21.♕d2 ♗e5 22.g3 and now after 22...♔g7!⇄ the rook goes to h8 and White definitely feels the heat from Black's pieces! 17...♗d7 18.♗d5 ♘xd5 19.exd5 ♖e5 is another critical line. My analysis indicates that best for both sides is 20.♘c1 ♗b5 21.♖e1 ♕xd5 when after 22.♖xe5 (another line runs 22.♗b3!? d3 23.♕d2 ♖f5 24.♖e4 ♕d6 25.♘a5 and now 25...g4! 26.fxg4 (26.♖xg4 ♖h5!⇄) 26...♖e5⇄) 22...♕xe5 23.♘d3 ♗c7 I think Black is not worse, or at least I couldn't break his positional fortress in my analysis as the two bishops prove to fight well against the rook and knight. A sample line goes 24.♖c1 ♕d6 25.g3 g4 26.a4 ♗c6 27.♘e5 ♗b7 28.♘xg4 d3 29.♔g2 ♗b6 followed by ...♕d4 with strong counterplay (petering out in equality deeper down the line). In a correspondence game, I would most probably choose 17...♗d7 as it seems to be the most 'correct' one among Black's alternatives, but in an OTB game, 17... d3! seems to pose more practical problems to White. **18.♘g3!** 18.♘c3 g4! can become dangerous for White, e.g. 19.♕d2 (19.♗c6 ♖e5⇄) 19...g3!⇄. **18...♗a6 19.♗c6 ♖e6**

20.♗a4! 20.♖c1 d2! 21.♖c2 ♗xf1 22.♔xf1 g4 23.♖xd2 ♕e7 24.♗a4 ♗h6 and Black has strong counterplay on the kingside in this opposite-coloured bishops scenario, which makes his two-pawn deficit irrelevant for the time being. His play is simple with ...gxf3, ...♘h5, ...♗f4 coming. 20.♕a4 ♕b6 21.♗d5 ♘xd5 22.exd5 ♖d6 is another unclear middlegame, where Black will get the d5-pawn and claim compensation with his strong bishops and the d3-pawn. According to my analysis, he is not worse at all. **20...♘d7** It is clear that Black's initiative continues. Next comes ...♘c5. **21.♗xd7** Another critical decision White has to make: 21.♕d2 ♘c5! 22.♗b3 ♖b6 23.♖fd1 ♕e7⇄. **21...♕xd7 22.♕d2 ♕d8! 23.♖fd1 ♗e5 24.♘f1** This is the most critical line in my analysis. In an OTB game I would be scared as White as ...♗f4-♕f6 and ...g5-g4 are coming and my king feels the pressure, but analysis indicates that there is nothing concrete which is that scary. **24...♕f6** 24...♗f4!? 25.♕f2 g4! 26.fxg4 ♖xe4 is another line where Black has enough counterplay to draw, but a well-prepared White player will find a way to exert some pressure. For example: 27.♖e1! ♕d4 28.♔g1! ♕xf2+ 29.♔xf2 ♖b4 30.b3 ♗d6 and Black will get the g4-pawn, as 31.h3 ♗f4+ 32.♔g1 ♗c5+ 33.♔h1 ♗f2 gives Black dangerous counterplay. **25.♖ab1 g4 26.fxg4 ♗f4 27.♕c3 ♕h4 28.♖xd3** The logical human reaction, and among the engines' top choices. Of course, 28.h3 is very greedy and after 28...♖xe4 White can win another pawn with 29.♕c6 ♖e6 30.♕a8+ ♔g7 31.♕xa7 but Black has excellent counterplay on the weak dark squares, for example: 31...♕f6⇄ followed by ...♖e2. **28...♗xd3 29.♕xd3 ♕xg4** Black will soon win the e4-pawn and have good compensation for his remaining missing pawn.

Objectively, we could say that White holds a small edge, but it is of the kind that produces draws in correspondence chess with all three possible results on the table for OTB chess. This analysis is far from conclusive, but I hope that I unearthed some key points so that you can play this interesting novelty (13...h6!) with confidence.

Ding Liren
Magnus Carlsen
Chessable Masters rapid 2020 (2.14)
1.d4 ♘f6 2.c4 g6 3.♘c3 ♗g7 4.e4 d6 5.♘f3 0-0 6.♗e2 e5 7.0-0 exd4 8.♘xd4 ♖e8 9.f3 c6 10.♔h1 d5 11.cxd5 cxd5 12.♗g5 ♘c6 13.♗b5 h6 When I delivered my Survey to New In Chess, this move was a novelty. Only a few days after that, Carlsen played it in this game. I'd be naive to claim that I knew about this novelty and others didn't. The reason is simple: after 10.♔h1, this line with the exchange sacrifice is the main line of Lc0! **14.♘xc6 bxc6 15.♗xc6 hxg5 16.♗xa8 d4 17.♘d5 ♗a6**

18.♗c6!? This was Ding's reaction to Carlsen's novelty, but what actually impressed me was that GM Shankland, watching and commentating the game live, also gave this move as his main line very quickly. I am assuming that moving the bishop away from the attack with tempo, while possibly misplacing the rook, is attractive and comes to mind immediately. That being said, this is not the best move, simply because not only is the rook not misplaced on e6, but actually it

has improved its position, while White hasn't won any time as his bishop will need to move again anyway. **18...♖e6 19.♖c1** For example, 19.♘xf6+ ♖xf6 20.♗d5 ♗xf1 21.♕xf1 g4 shows why the rook on e6 is not bad. It has the whole 6th rank to operate on, and Black's counterplay is more than enough for equality. **19...♗xf1 20.♕xf1** Both Shankland and Seirawan pointed out how drawish this position seems to the human eye, as we will (most probably) soon have opposite-coloured bishops on the board. In the game, Ding tried his best to avoid this scenario, showing his fighting spirit. **20...g4!?** Black's move is thematic and he is fine after this anyway, but maybe there was an even better way to play: 20...♕b8! wins a tempo on b2 and after 21.b3 g4= the knight cannot go to f4 as in the game. **21.♘f4!** Not exchanging knights and putting this horse on d3 to blockade the dangerous passer. Still, this is not enough for an edge, but kudos to Ding for finding a great way to keep the game going and finding a line which I hadn't analysed at all when I delivered my first draft of this Survey to New In Chess! **21...♖e7 22.♘d3 gxf3 23.♕xf3 ♘d7!**

We can see now why Ding's concept cannot succeed. If this knight reaches e5, then Black has nothing to fear. White can stop this with ♗xd7, but then, as Shankland points out, ...♗h6-♘e3 comes and the e4-pawn remains very weak. So, no problems for Black here. **24.♗d5** 24.♗xd7 ♕xd7 25.b3 (other moves don't change

the character of the position) and now 25...♕b7!⇄ is most probably Black's most accurate move. The queen does an excellent job defending f7, attacking e4 and getting ready for ...♕a6 at the right moment. The engines give as best 24.g3 but this will transpose to the game after 24...♘e5. **24...♘e5 25.♘xe5 ♗xe5 26.g3 ♔g7 27.♔g2 ♖c7 28.♖c4 d3! 29.♕xd3** If White tries to get ambitious with 29.b4 then after 29...d2 he might actually lose if he is not careful. **29...♖xc4 30.♕xc4 ♗xb2 31.♗xf7 ♕d2+ 32.♔h3 ♕h6+ 33.♔g2 ♕d2+** Draw agreed. If 34.♔f3 both 34...♕xh2 and 34...♕d1+ keep the equilibrium.

A solid start for 'my' novelty then! Nothing too spectacular, but with sensible and not difficult moves, Black was never in any danger. Not every KID needs to contain fireworks!

Analysis
1.d4 ♘f6 2.c4 g6 3.♘c3 ♗g7 4.e4 d6 5.♘f3 0-0 6.♗e2 e5 7.0-0 exd4 8.♘xd4 ♖e8 9.f3 c6 10.♔h1 d5 11.cxd5 11.exd5?! cxd5 12.♗g5 (12.c5) 12...♘c6 is fine for Black, e.g. 13.♘xc6 bxc6 14.cxd5 cxd5 15.♗b5 ♖e6⇄. **11...cxd5 12.♗g5 ♘c6 13.♗b5!** 13.exd5 ♘xd4 14.♕xd4 ♘xd5= 15.♕xd5 ½-½ Sosonko-Kaplan, Amsterdam 1974. **13...h6!N** We saw that here 14.♘xc6 is the best move for White. Let's check some alternatives: **14.♗xf6!?** 14.♗h4 g5 15.♘xc6 bxc6 16.♗xc6 ♗a6! 17.♗xe8 ♕xe8⇄ – due to the double attack on the rook and bishop, Black wins back material and stands fine. For example: 18.e5 ♘h5 19.f4 d4 20.♕xh5 dxc3=. **14...♗xf6 15.exd5 a6!** The other line starts with 15...♕xd4 and is slightly less comfortable for Black. **16.♗a4** 16.♗xc6 ♖d8! is an important nuance to remember! **16...♕xd4 17.dxc6**

17...♖f8 17...♕xd1 18.♖axd1 ♖f8 transposes to the main line; 17...b5!? 18.♗b3 ♗f5 keeps a bit more life in the position, but I'm afraid that White is better here. **18.♕xd4 ♗xd4 19.♖ad1 ♗g7 20.♘d5 bxc6 21.♗xc6 ♖a7♕** The point of 15...a6 ! Black has enough compensation for his pawn due to his strong bishops: ...♗e6, ...a6-a5 and ...♖b8 or ...♖c8 are coming.

Ioan Bucsa
Tolgay Pekin
cr 2018
1.d4 ♘f6 2.c4 g6 3.♘c3 ♗g7 4.e4 d6 5.♘f3 0-0 6.♗e2 e5 7.0-0 exd4 8.♘xd4 ♖e8 9.f3 c6 10.♗f4

If White checks your games in the database after 9...c6 and wants to prepare a surprise, most probably this is what he will choose. This line has been played by GMs that are well known for their dangerous preparation like Vitiugov, Ragger, Lenderman, A.S.Rasmussen and Mads Andersen, to name a few. **10...♘h5! 11.♗e3 f5! 12.♕d2 f4 13.♗f2 ♘e5! 14.♖fd1 ♘d7⇄** This line has been tested in a few high-level correspondence games and has been proved reliable. **15.♖ac1**

15.♘a4 ♕f6 16.♖ac1 ♘c5⇄ 17.♕a5?! was seen in Andersen-Nilsen, Oslo 2014, and now excellent for Black would have been 17...♘g3!N 18.♗f1 ♘e6↑ with Black having the initiative on the kingside (for example, ...h7-h5-h4-h3 is not a stupid idea) while White's pieces are misplaced on the other side of the board.

15.♘c2 ♕e7 16.♘e1 g5⇄ and Black was the one with all the fun in MacTilstra-Cumming, cr 2015.

15...♘g7!? 16.♗f1 h5 16...♕f6!? 17.b4 ♘f8 is another way to play for Black. A sample line goes 18.♘a4 ♖d8, stopping c4-c5, and if 19.♕e1 ♘ge6! 20.♘b3 b6!, stopping c4-c5 once and for all and now going after White's king with 21.♘c3 g5 etc. Obviously, there are many ways to play this rich position. In the game, Black played on the queenside: **17.b4 h4 18.♘a4 a5! 19.c5 axb4 20.♕xb4 ♕a5 21.♕xa5 ♖xa5= 22.♘b2 dxc5 23.♘c4 ♖a8 24.♘xe5 ♘xe5 25.♖xc5 h3 26.gxh3 ♗h7 27.♖c2 ♖d8 28.♔g2 ♘e6 29.♗e2 ♘g5 30.h4 ♗h3+ 31.♔h1 ♘gf7 32.♖b1 ♖a4 33.♘b3 b5 34.♗b6 ♖da8** Draw agreed. In an OTB game, Black would mostly be the one pressing for the full point.

Jan Hansen
Frantisek Tunega
cr 2016

1.♘f3 ♘f6 2.c4 g6 3.d4 d6 4.♘c3 ♗g7 5.e4 0-0 6.♗e2 e5 7.0-0 exd4 8.♘xd4 ♖e8 9.f3 c6 10.♘c2!? The second most popular move after 10.♔h1, but here it has more or less been proved that Black is fine: **10...♘a6!** Black has the simple idea of ...♘c7 and ...d6-d5.

11.♔h1 11.♗e3 d5!⇄ 12.exd5 (12.cxd5 cxd5 13.exd5 ♗f5 (13...♘b4!?) 14.♗f2 ♗xc2 (14...♘xd5 15.♘xd5 ♗xc2 16.♕xc2 ♕xd5 17.♗c4) 15.♕xc2 ♘xd5 (Benko-Pilnik, Budapest 1952) 16.♘e4!±) 12...cxd5 13.♗f2 (13.c5 ♘b4⇄) 13...dxc4 (13...♘c7!?) 14.♗xc4 (Kuljasevic-Skoberne, Meissen 2013) 14...♕c7N followed by ...♗e6 etc. **11...♘c7 12.♗g5!** This is the only line where White might pretend to play for something. Here though, there is a concrete solution. 12.♗e3 allows 12...d5. **12...♘e6! 13.♗e3** After 13.♗h4N Black can play 13...♘f4!? and take on e2, or 13...a5!? intending ...a5-a4, waiting for White to blunder with the natural 14.♕d2? ♘xe4!. I know about this trap because I once fell for it myself in an online game! **13...♘h5** Insisting on putting a knight on f4, before or after the move ...♕h4 (if White allows it). **14.g3** 14.f4?! was seen in Spasov-Mathe, cr 2008. White is a bit over-extended and Black can take advantage of this with 14...♗xc3!N 15.bxc3 ♘eg7⇄; 14.♕d2 ♕h4 15.♗f2 ♕f4 16.♖fd1 (Drazic-Nadj Hedjesi, Senta 2019) 16...a5! – once again this move, intending ...a5-a4, and if 17.g3 ♕xd2 18.♖xd2 a4!⇄ with the point 19.♖xd6? a3 20.♖xa3 ♗xc3. **14...♗e5** 14...b6!? 15.♕d2 ♗b7⇄. **15.♕d2 b6! 16.f4 ♗xc3 17.♕xc3 ♕f6 18.♕d3 ♕xb2!?** 18...♘c5!?⇄. **19.g4 ♘hg7 20.♖ab1 ♕f6 21.♕xd6 ♗b7 22.f5 c5 23.♗f3 ♖ed8 24.♕g3 ♘g5⇄**

Black is not worse in this rich position. **25.♗xg5 ♕xg5 26.♖be1 gxf5 27.♕c7 ♗xe4 28.♗xe4 fxe4 29.♕xf7+ ♔h8 30.♖xe4 ♖g8 31.♘e1 ♕g6 32.♕xg6**

hxg6 33.♘f3 ♖ge8 34.♘e5 ♔g8 35.♖fe1 ♖e6 36.♔g2 ♖d8 37.♖1e2 ♖d4 38.♔f3 ♖d8 39.h4 ♖ed6 40.♔g3 ♖e8 41.♖4e3 ♖de6 42.♖e4 ♖d6 43.♖4e3 ♖e7 44.♔h3 ♖ee6 45.♔g2 a6 46.a4 ♖d4 47.♔f3 ♖f6+ 48.♔g3 ♖e6 49.♖e1 ♖dd6 50.♔f4 ♖e8 51.♘f3 ♖f8+ 52.♔g3 ♖b8 53.♘g5 b5 54.axb5 axb5 55.cxb5 ♖xb5 56.♖c3 ♖bb6 57.♖xc5 ♗e6 58.♘xe6 ♖xe6 59.♖c8+ ♔h7 ½-½

We are going to wrap up by taking a look at some sidelines.

Jan Gustafsson
Vladimir Kramnik
Dortmund 2012 (2)

1.d4 ♘f6 2.c4 g6 3.♘c3 ♗g7 4.e4 d6 5.♘f3 0-0 6.♗e2 e5 7.0-0 The actual move order of the game was 7.♗e3 c6 8.0-0 exd4 9.♘xd4 ♖e8 10.f3 etc. **7...exd4 8.♘xd4 ♖e8 9.f3 c6**

10.♗e3?! I consider this move to be dubious despite the fact that it has been seen in the practice of many amazing players like Eljanov, Fridman etc. My reasoning is that it allows Black comfortable equality.

Let's check a few alternatives:

A) 10.♗g5 ♕b6! 11.♔h1 d5!⇄ and once again White didn't manage to prevent Black from opening the centre;

B) 10.♘b3 a5!, threatening to push the pawn further. There are two ways to stop it:

B1) 11.a4?! ♕b6+ 12.♔h1 ♘a6∓ followed by ...♗e6 and ...♘fd7; White's queenside is chronically weak;

B2) 11.♘a4 d5! and Black is fine, but at least here my analysis says

that White is not worse after 12.♗f4N ♘bd7 13.cxd5 cxd5 14.♗b5 dxe4 15.fxe4 ♘h5⇄;

C) 10.♖e1 d5! 11.cxd5 cxd5 12.♗b5 ♘c6 and Black is already better. One recent example: 13.♗e3 ♗d7 14.♗xc6 ♗xc6 15.exd5 ♘xd5 16.♘xc6 bxc6 17.♘xd5 (Afanasiev-Kokarev, Khanty-Mansiysk 2018) 17...cxd5! 18.♕d2 d4 19.♗f2 ♕b6∓.

10...d5! 11.cxd5 ♘xd5 12.♘xd5 cxd5 The centre has been opened and our KID bishop is a wonderful piece. **13.♖c1** 13.♕b3 ♘c6= Lisitsin-Taimanov, Kiev ch-URS 1954. **13...a5!** A beautiful move with the idea to stop ♕b3 but also to push this pawn all the way to a3 if allowed. Looking at the alternatives gives us a better idea why this move is important: if 13...dxe4 14.fxe4 ♗xd4! (14...♖xe4?

loses to 15.♘e6! ♕d7 16.♘xg7 ♔xg7 17.♕b3 threatening 18.♕c3+ as well as 18.♗f3) 15.♗xd4 ♘c6 16.♗f6. Black is a bit under pressure here. It might be a draw with perfect play, but it is not that attractive. **14.♕b3 a4 15.♕xd5** 15.♕a3 dxe4 16.♖cd1 has been suggested as a safer way to play for White, but among other lines, Black is fine after 16...♗f8 17.♕c3 ♕a5⇄. **15...♕xd5 16.exd5 a3 17.b3 ♘c6! 18.♘c2 ♖xe3! 19.♘xe3 ♘b4** Black is an exchange and a pawn down, but already White has to find an incredible defence to stay alive: **20.♖c4?** That was not it! Correct was 20.♖c7! ♗d4 21.♖e7! ♘xd5 22.♖e8+ ♔g7 23.♔h1 ♘xe3 24.♖c1 ♘d5 25.♖cxc8 ♖xc8 26.♖xc8 ♘c3 27.♖xc3 ♗xc3 28.♔g1 and White should survive

in this opposite-coloured bishops endgame. Who can blame the German GM for not finding this? **20...♘xa2 21.♖a4 ♖xa4 22.bxa4 ♗d4∓**

Black is better as the pawn on a3 and his bishops are more than enough compensation for the exchange. Kramnik won in style: **23.♔f2 ♘b4 24.♖c1 a2 25.♖xc8+ ♔g7 26.♖c1 ♘xd5 27.♖d1 ♘xe3 0-1**

Exercise 1

position after 16.♗b5xc6

Which is the key move for Black here?

(solutions on page 252)

Exercise 2

position after 12.♗c1-g5

Black has a concrete way to gain counterplay.

Exercise 3

position after 13.♖a1-c1

What was Kramnik's star move here?

Looking for material from previous Yearbooks?

Visit our website www.newinchess.com and see under 'Games and Downloads' in the page footer. Here you can find games, Surveys and contributors from all our Yearbooks. Surveys are indexed by opening, by author and by Yearbook.

The fashionable Makogonov

by Krisztian Szabo (special contribution by Jan Timman)

1.	d4	♘f6
2.	c4	g6
3.	♘c3	♗g7
4.	c4	d6
5.	h3	0-0
6.	♗e3	♘c6
7.	d5	♘e5

Alireza Firouzja

This is one of the most fashionable lines against the King's Indian nowadays. The idea of 5.h3 is not just to protect White against ...♘g4 and ...♗g4 sorties, but also to prepare the ambitious expansion g2-g4. This can be a very effective prophylactic measure against Black's typical kingside play, as well as a springboard to a kingside attack by White.

The theme I will present in this Survey is based on the cunning move-order with 6.♗e3, which allows White to improve on several important aspects of the move-order with 6.♘f3, while still achieving the same strategic goals. By keeping the knight on g1, White keeps flexibility on the kingside.

6...♘c6 is an interesting but rather rare idea. The topic of the current Survey is the 6...♘c6 7.d5 ♘e5 variation. The replies ...♘b8 and ...♘b4 are just less

common. Compared to them, in the line under scrutiny Black hopes to lure his opponent into overextending with f2-f4 and g2-g4 after his knight jumps. Firouzja is an expert on this line; he plays it with both colours.

Too optimistic?
In Repka-Manik, Banska Stiavnica 2018, White continued with **8.♕d2**.

White keeps the option of f2-f4. **8...e6** This is a natural move. Black should open the centre, otherwise he doesn't have any counterplay against f2-f4 and g2-g4. **9.f4 ♘ed7 10.dxe6 fxe6 11.g4!** At first sight this move is too optimistic, but

White needed to prevent ...♘h5. **11...b5!** and Black gets great dynamic play for the sacrificed pawn.

The restrained approach

8.♗e2 is a restrained approach, which maintains the options of both f2-f4 and ♘f3.

8...e6 9.♘f3 The solid continuation; the alternative is 9.f4. **9...♘xf3+ 10.♗xf3 exd5** occurred in Ponkratov-Shimanov, PRO League 2020. **11.cxd5 ♘d7** The knight goes to c5 or e5 and it opens the diagonal of the g7-bishop. **12.0-0** and here 12...♘c5 would have been the accurate reply, with good chances for Black to equalize.

An alternative on move 10 is the immediate **10...♘d7**. As in the previous game, Black improves his knight, but he keeps the possibility of closing the position with ...e7-e5. **11.0-0** 11.dxe6 was also an option, to open the position. **11...♗xc3 12.bxc3 e5** was played in Can-Adhiban, Moscow rapid 2019. Black exchanges his g7-bishop for the knight, so he should close the centre as much as possible. **13.♗h6 ♖e8 14.♕d2 b6** with a balanced position.

The principled approach

The game Studer-Cheparinov, Gibraltar 2020, went **8.f4**. This is the most principled approach.

Probably White is to be preferred here, but the position becomes extremely double-edged: **8...♘ed7** Black has lost several tempi with this knight, but he is still okay as White's centre has become a bit shaky. **9.♗d3** By keeping the knight on g1, White still has the possibility of ♘ge2. Nevertheless, 9.♘f3 is the most straightforward continuation. **9...e5 10.dxe6 fxe6 11.♘ge2 b6** It is rare in the King's Indian for the c8-bishop to develop to b7, but in this structure it has no prospects on the c8-h3 diagonal. **12.0-0 ♕e7** Obviously, 12...♗b7 was the alternative choice. **13.♕d2 ♗b7** with a playable middlegame for both sides. 9.g4 is the most aggressive reaction!

White doesn't continue his development, and instead continues the attack with another pawn. The position is closed enough, so White has time to play this. **9...c6** Obviously, Black tries to open the centre. **10.♘f3!** occurred in Caruana-Firouzja, Wijk aan Zee 2020. This move is more accurate than 10.♗g2, because the

bishop should control the f1-a6 diagonal to avoid the ...b7-b5 break. **10...cxd5 11.cxd5 b6** Making room for the bishop and also preparing ...♞c5. **12.♞d4 ♞c5 13.♕f3 ♗b7** with huge complications.

Conclusion

The modern way of fighting the King's Indian involves the little move h2-h3. White has traditionally used the combination of ♞f3 and h2-h3 on moves 5 and 6 to achieve this set-up. One of the main points is that after the likely ...e7-e5 White will play d4-d5 and will be quick to continue with g2-g4,

discouraging Black's typical counterplay with ...f7-f5. One of the reasons why White waits with the development of the g1-knight for a while is that we can often execute the manoeuvre ♞g1-e2-g3, which is not available in case of 6.♞f3 when the knight is usually forced to retreat to d2 to protect the e4-pawn.

Theoretical knowledge is obviously important here, because the middle-games can become very sharp and complex. In summary, the Makogonov with first 5.h3 and then 6.♗e3 is a rare line, but a powerful weapon against the King's Indian.

Christopher Repka 1
Mikulas Manik
Banska Stiavnica ch-SVK 2018 (6)
1.d4 ♞f6 2.c4 g6 3.♞c3 ♗g7 4.e4 d6 5.h3 0-0 6.♗e3 ♞c6 7.d5 ♞e5 8.♕d2 8.♞f3 ♞xf3+ 9.♕xf3 ♞d7 (9...c6?! 10.♗d3 (the move 10.♕d1?! is a bit early. The queen was not badly placed on f3, so developing was more important: 10...e6 (10...♕a5?! 11.♕d2 ♗d7 12.♗d3 cxd5 13.cxd5 ♖fc8 14.0-0± H.Andersen-Mittelbachert, Germany tt 2010/11) 11.♗e2 cxd5 12.cxd5 exd5 13.exd5 a6 14.0-0 ♖e8=) 10...♞d7 11.♕e2 (11.♗c2?! (Parkhov-Asadli, Poprad jr 2016) 11...b5!. White has some space advantage, however Black has great counterplay on the queenside: 12.dxc6 (12.cxb5 cxb5 13.0-0 b4 14.♞a4 ♗a6 15.♖fc1 ♗b5∓) 12...♞e5 13.♕e2 bxc4 14.0-0 ♗a6↑ and Black looks nicely placed) 11...♞e5 12.♗c2±; 9...♞e6!?) 10.♗e2 ♞c5 11.0-0 e6∞. **8...e6** 8...♖e8!? 9.0-0-0 (9.g4 (Nadarzynski-Gorski, cr 1993) 9...e6! 10.f4 ♞ed7 11.dxe6 ♖xe6∞; 9.f4 ♞ed7 10.♞f3 e5!∞) 9...e6 (9...c5 10.f4 ♞ed7 11.♞f3 (11.♗d3!?) 11...b5! 12.cxb5 (Kizilkus-Molla, Konya tt 2018) 12...a6!⇄; 9...c6!? 10.f4 ♞ed7 11.♞f3 cxd5 12.cxd5 a6 13.♔b1 b5∞) 10.f4

♞ed7 11.♞f3 exd5 12.exd5 b5! 13.cxb5 ♞b6⇄. **9.f4 ♞ed7 10.dxe6 fxe6**

11.g4! 11.♞f3?! ♞h5⇄. **11...b5! 12.cxb5 a6?!** 12...♗b7! 13.♗g2 a6 14.bxa6 ♖xa6 15.♞ge2 ♕a8⯑. **13.♞f3 axb5 14.♗xb5 ♗b7 15.♕c2 d5?!** 15...c6 16.♗e2±. **16.e5 d4 17.♞xd4! ♗xh1 18.♞xe6 ♕e7 19.♗c4!+− ♔h8 20.0-0-0 ♗b7 21.♞xg7 ♞b6 22.♗b3 ♞fd5 23.♞xd5 ♕xg7 24.e6 ♞xd5 25.♗d4 1-0**

Pavel Ponkratov 2
Alexander Shimanov
PRO League KO Stage 2020 (1)
1.d4 ♞f6 2.c4 g6 3.♞c3 ♗g7 4.e4 d6 5.♗e2 5.h3 is our basic move-order: 5...0-0 6.♗e3 ♞c6 7.d5 ♞e5 8.♗e2 transposes to the game. **5...0-0 6.♗e3 ♞c6 7.d5 ♞e5 8.h3**

8...e6 8...c5?! is not logical now, because Black should open the centre instead of closing it: 9.f4 ♞ed7 10.♞f3 ♞h5 11.♗f2! (11.0-0 ♞g3⇄) 11...a6 12.g4 ♞hf6 13.a4 ♞e8 14.h4 e6 15.h5 exd5 16.cxd5 ♞df6 17.♞d2± Bacrot-Claverie, Paris blitz 2009; 8...♞ed7 9.♞f3 e6 10.0-0 ♖e8 11.♕c2 a6 12.♖fe1 ♕e7 13.♗d3± T.Fodor-Vakhidov, Hampstead 2014; 8...c6 9.♞f3 ♞xf3+ 10.♗xf3 ♞d7 11.0-0 (11.♗e2 ♕a5 (11...♞c5!?) 12.♗d4 ♞h6 13.f3 c5 14.♗f2 f5 (14...b5?!) 15.cxb5 a6 16.0-0 axb5 17.♗xb5± Ganguly-Guseinov, Moscow blitz 2019) 15.exf5 gxf5 16.0-0 f4∞) 11...a6 12.♗e2 (12.♕d2!?) 12...cxd5 13.cxd5 b5 14.♗d4 (14.♖c1±) 14...♞xd4 15.♕xd4 ♕b6 16.♕xb6 ♞xb6 17.a4 ♞xa4 (17...b4?! 18.a5! bxc3 19.axb6 cxb2 20.♖a2± Tsvetkov-Utegaliev, Moscow blitz 2019) 18.♞xa4 bxa4 19.♖xa4 ♖b8=. **9.♞f3** 9.g4?! exd5 10.cxd5

c5 (10...♕e7 11.♕c2 (11.g5?! ♘fd7 12.♕d2 ♘b6 13.b3 (Bates-Pein, Hove 1997) 13...f5!↑) 11...c6⇄) 11.a4 (11.♕d2? (Steadman-Goldenberg, Cammeray 2015) 11...b5! 12.f3 (12.♗xb5? ♘xe4–+; 12.f4? b4! 13.fxe5 bxc3–+; 12.♗xb5 c4!∓) 12...b4 13.♘d1 ♕a5∓ followed by ...♗a6) 11...♖e8∞; 9.f4 ♘ed7 10.dxe6 fxe6 11.g4 ♕e7 (11...b6 12.♕c2 ♗b7 13.♗f3 (Djurhuus-Hoi, Copenhagen 1998) 13...♘c5!∞; 11...b5!? 12.cxb5 ♗b7⇄) 12.♕c2 (12.♕d2?! b5! (a strong tactical blow! Black sacrifices a pawn for quick development with ...♗b7) 13.cxb5 (Tahbaz-Nyazi, Dubai 2018; 13.♘xb5? ♘xe4–+) 13...♗b7! 14.♗f3 (14.♗f3 ♘b6↑) 14...♘xe4 15.♘xe4 ♗xe4∓ and White can't solve the problem of his king) 12...♘c5 13.♘f3 b6∞.
9...♘xf3+ 10.♗xf3 exd5 10...♘d7 see Game 3. **11.cxd5 ♘d7 12.0-0 ♘e5?!** 12...♘c5 13.♗d4 a5 14.♗xg7 ♔xg7 15.♕d4+ ♕f6 16.♕e3 ♗d7 17.♗e2 ♖ae8 18.f4 ♔h8 (18...b6!?) 19.♗g4 ♗xg4 20.hxg4 ♕h4 21.g5 f6 22.gxf6 ♖xf6 23.♖ae1 g5! (½-½ Mende-Telepnev, cr 2017) 24.fxg5 ♖g6 25.♖f5 h6!⇄. **13.♗e2 f5 14.f4 ♘f7 15.exf5** 15.♗d4!?± **15...♗xf5 16.♕d2** 16.♗d4±. **16...♖e8?!** 16...c5! 17.dxc6 bxc6 18.♗f3 d5∞. **17.♗f3 ♖e7 18.♗d4 ♕f8 19.g4 ♗d7 20.♘e4±♘h6 21.♖ae1 ♖ae8 22.♗xg7 ♕xg7 23.g5+–♘f7 24.♘f6+ ♔f8 25.♗g4 ♗b5 26.♘xe8 ♗xe8 27.♖xe7+ ♔xe7 28.♖e1+ ♔f8 29.♖c1 c5 30.dxc6 ♗xc6 31.♕c3 ♕xc3 32.♖xc3 d5 33.♔f2 ♘d6 34.♖d3 ♔e7 35.b3 ♘e4+ 36.♔e3 ♔d6 37.♔d4 ♗b5 38.♖e3 a5 39.♗f3 ♘g3 40.♖e5 ♘f5+ 41.♖xf5 gxf5 42.♗xd5 b6 43.♗g8 ♗e8 44.♗xh7 ♔e6 45.♗g8+ 1-0**

Emre Can 3
Adhiban Baskaran
Moscow Wch rapid 2019 (3)
1.d4 ♘f6 2.c4 g6 3.♘c3 ♗g7 4.e4 d6 5.♗e2 0-0 6.♗e3 ♘c6 7.d5 ♘e5 8.h3 e6 9.♘f3 ♘xf3+ 10.♗xf3 ♘d7

11.0-0 11.dxe6 fxe6 (11...♘e5!?) A) 12.0-0 ♗xc3!?. This is always an interesting question in the King's Indian: when should Black take the knight on c3? Black gives up his important king's bishop, but White's pawn structure will be really bad: in my view, 12...a5!?, to prepare ...♘c5, was more accurate, e.g. 13.bxc3 ♕h4 14.♗g4 ♘e5 15.c5! (15.g3 ♕e7 16.♗e2 b6 17.f4 ♘d7 18.♗d3 ♗b7 19.♕c2 ♘c5∞ Vrolijk-Warmerdam, Netherlands tt 2017/18) 15...♘xg4 16.♕xg4 ♕xg4 17.hxg4±; B) 12.♕d2 b6!? (12...a6?! 13.h4!→; 13.0-0 b6 14.♗g5 (V.Stefansson-V.Ivic, Konya tt 2018) 14...♕e8∞ 15.e5? ♖xf3! (a great exchange sacrifice to crush White's kingside!) 16.gxf3 ♘xe5 17.♕e2 ♗b7–+ and Black is winning); 11.♖c1 f5 (11...♕e7?! 12.0-0 ♘e5 13.♗e2 c6 (Viloria-D.Zilberstein, New York jr 1998) 14.♕d2±; 11...a5!?) 12.♕d2 e5 13.♗g5 ♗f6 (13...♕e8?! 14.♘b5! fxe4 15.♗xe4 ♕f7 16.0-0 ♘c5 17.♕c2± Avalyan-Rahul, Paracin 2018) 14.♗h6 ♗g7∞. **11...♗xc3** 11...e5!?. **12.bxc3 e5 13.♗h6 ♖e8 14.♕d2 b6** 14...♘c5!?. **15.♗d1 ♗a6 16.♗b3 f6 17.h4 ♘c5 18.♖ae1 ♗c8?!** 18...♕d7 19.f4 ♕g4⇄. **19.f4 ♕g4?!** 19...exf4 20.♕d4↑. **20.♗c2 ♕e7 21.♕f2** 21.fxe5! fxe5 22.♕f2±. **21...♗d7 22.fxe5 ♕xe5 23.♕xf6?** 23.♗f4 ♕xc3 24.h5±. **23...♕xf6 24.♖xf6 ♗f5! 25.g4 ♘d7 26.♖xf5 gxf5 27.♗a4?** 27.gxf5∞. **27...♘e5 28.♗xe8 ♖xe8 29.♔g2 ♘xg4 30.♗g5 h6 31.♗d2 ♖xe4 32.♖xe4 fxe4 33.♔g3 e3 34.♗c1 h5 34...e2 35.♗d2 ♘e5–+. 35.♔f3 ♔f7 36.♗xe3 ♘e5+?! 36...♔f6. 37.♔e4 ♘xc4 38.♗g5 ♘e5 39.a4?** 39.♔f5 still held the draw. **39...a5–+**

40.♗d8 b5 41.♗xc7 bxa4 42.♗xa5 ♘c4 43.♗b4 a3 44.♗xa3 ♘xa3 45.♔f5 ♘b5 46.c4 ♘a3 0-1

The principled approach 8.f4

Noel Studer 4
Ivan Cheparinov
Gibraltar 2020 (8)
1.d4 ♘f6 2.c4 g6 3.♘c3 ♗g7 4.e4 d6 5.h3 0-0 6.♗e3 ♘c6 7.d5 ♘e5 8.f4 ♘ed7

9.♗d3 9.♘f3 e6 (9...e5 (Kumaran-Finkel, Bratislava jr 1993) 10.f5! ♘xe4!? 11.♘xe4 gxf5 12.♘c3 f4 13.♗f2 e4 14.♗h4! ♕e8 15.♘h2 and Black has some compensation, but White's chances are better) 10.♗d3 (in case of 10.dxe6 fxe6 11.♗d3, 11...♘h5∓ is a main difference when g2-g4 has not been played yet) 10...exd5 11.cxd5 ♕e7! (11...♖e8 (A.Mikhalevski-Finkel, Ramat Gan 1992) 12.0-0! ♘xe4 13.♘xe4 f5 14.♘fg5! fxe4 15.♘e6!? 12.♔f2 (12.0-0 ♘xe4! 13.♘xe4 f5⇄) 12...c6∞; the position is very complex and Black's chances are not worse. For 9.g4 see Game 5. **9...e5** 9...♖e8?! is too slow and too passive: 10.♘f3 e5 11.fxe5 ♘xe5 12.♘xe5 ♖xe5 13.0-0 ♘d7 14.♕d2 a6 15.♖f2 ♕f8 16.♖af1↑ Fedorovsky-Krstic, Austria Bundesliga B 2014/15. **10.dxe6 fxe6 11.♘ge2** 11.g4!? b6 12.♕c2 ♗b7 (12...♘c5!?) 13.0-0-0 ♕e7 14.♘ge2 ♘c5 15.♗xc5 (15.♔g3?! ♘xd3+ 16.♖xd3 (Koneru-Zhang Xiaowen, China tt 2013) 16...♘d7! 17.h4 ♘c5↑) 15...bxc5 16.♖hg1 ♗c6∞. **11...b6 12.0-0 ♕e7** 12...♗b7 13.♕d2 (13.f5?! ♕e7! 14.♕d2 (14.♗g5?! (Colin-Slobodjan, Cappelle-la-Grande

2002) 14...h6! 15.♗h4 exf5 16.exf5 ♖ae8∓) 14...♘e5∓) 13...♘c5∞.
13.♕d2 ♗b7 14.♗c2 ♘c5 15.♘g3 a5 16.♖ae1 ♘fd7 17.b3 ♕h4 18.♘ge2 ♘f6 19.♗f2 ♕h6 20.♗e3 ♘cxe4 20...♕h4=. 21.♘xe4 ♘xe4 22.♗xe4 ♗xe4 23.f5 ♕h5 24.♘g3 ♕h4 25.♘xe4 ♕xe4 26.♖f4 ♕c6 27.fxe6 ♖xf4 28.♗xf4 ♕c5+ 29.♗e3 ♕f5?! 29...♗h6∞. **30.♕d5 ♖e8 31.♕c6?** 31.g4! ♕e5 (31...♕xe6? 32.♗xb6! ♕xd5 33.♖xe8+ ♔f7 34.cxd5 ♔xe8 35.♖xc7+) 32.♗f2 ♕f6 33.e7+ ♕f7 34.♖e6±. **31...♖xe6∓ 32.♕xc7?** 32.♖f1 ♕e4 33.♕xe4 ♖xe4∓. **32...♗d4!–+ 33.♕c8+ ♔f7 34.♕d7+ ♖e7 35.♕xe7+ ♔xe7 36.♗xd4+ ♔d7 37.♗xb6 ♕c2 38.♖a1 a4 39.bxa4 ♕b2 0-1**

Fabiano Caruana   **5**
Alireza Firouzja
Wijk aan Zee 2020 (10)
1.d4 ♘f6 2.c4 g6 3.♘c3 ♗g7 4.e4 d6 5.h3 0-0 6.♗e3 ♘c6 A rather unusual way to fight the Makogonov System. Black is trying to provoke pawn moves in hopes of attacking the strong white centre later. **7.d5 ♘e5 8.f4 ♘ed7 9.g4** More or less forced expansion, since Black was threatening to play his king's knight to h5.

9...c6 KS: Now 9...e6?! (Peng Li Min-Sokolovsky, Petah Tikva 2020) does not work so well in view of 10.dxe6! fxe6 11.♗g2 ♘b6 12.♕e2± and White has an attractive position. **10.♘f3!** KS: 10.♗g2 ♘b6 (10...cxd5 11.cxd5 b5! (as we saw in the previous games, this is one of Black's typical counterplay ideas) 12.♘ge2 (12.♘xb5? ♕a5+ 13.♘c3 ♖b8

14.♕d2 ♘xg4! (a strong tactical blow!) 15.hxg4 ♖xb2! and this is the point, suddenly Black is winning!; 12.a3 (Studer-N.Petrov, Bad Ragaz 2020) 12...♘b6!⇄) 12...b4 13.♘a4±) 11.♕d3 e6⇄. **10...cxd5 11.cxd5 b6** A novelty that was not hard to find as it is the computer's first suggestion. Interestingly, Black does not have to worry much about the weakness of square c6. The position is dynamic, and in many cases White will not have time to effectively occupy it with a knight. The text is stronger than 11...♘c5, as in Jones-Pavlidis, Hersonissos 2017. After 12.♗xc5 dxc5 13.e5 ♘d7 14.♕c2 White had a clear advantage. **12.♘d4** White can also go for the set-up 12.♗g2 ♘c5 13.♕c2, when I really don't see how Black will get sufficient counterplay. He has two ways to develop his queen's bishop:
A) 13...♗b7 14.0-0 e6 15.♘d4 exd5 (15...♖c8 is met strongly by 16.f5) 16.exd5 ♖e8 17.♗f2, with a positional plus for White;
B) 13...♗a6 14.0-0-0 ♘cxe4!? (an interesting piece sacrifice that is more or less forced, since 14...♖c8 15.♘d4 would leave White in charge) 15.♘xe4 ♖c8 16.♘c3 ♗c4 17.♘d4 ♘xd5 18.♗xd5 ♗xd5 19.♖h2 ♗xa2 20.♕a4 ♗c4 21.♖c2, and White is better, although things are not completely clear. It is quite possible that Firouzja had planned this piece sacrifice. **12...♘c5** KS: 12...♗b7 is not flexible enough, as White can now play 13.♗g2 and the bishop on a6 doesn't make so much sense anymore. **13.♕f3** I suspect that Caruana wanted to go for a set-up that Firouzja had not particularly prepared for. An obvious move was 13.♘c6, after which the game could continue as follows: 13...♕e8 14.♗g2 ♗a6 15.♗xc5 bxc5 16.♕d2 ♘d7 17.0-0-0 ♘b6 18.e5, and the computer indicates that White is better. But it is risky to go for this without preparation. **13...♗b7 14.g5**

14...♘fxe4!? The most interesting continuation. Black will end up with enough pawns for the piece. The alternative 14...♘h5 did not look bad either. White has two options: 15.0-0-0 (15.f5 ♖c8 16.♖d1 ♗e5 17.♗b5 e6 18.0-0 a6, and Black is OK) 15...e5 16.fxe5 ♗xe5 17.♖g1 f6, and Black has sufficient counterplay; **15.♘xe4 ♗xd5 16.♘f6+ exf6 17.♕xd5 ♖e8 18.♘c2** The alternative was 18.♕f3, when Black has two options: 18...♕e7 (18...fxg5 19.0-0-0 gxf4 20.♕xf4 ♖c8 (or 20...♖e4 first) 21.♔b1 ♖e4, and Black has sufficient counterplay) 19.♘c2 fxg5 20.0-0-0 ♕f6 21.♗d4 ♕xf4+ 22.♕xf4 gxf4 23.♗b5 ♖e7, and the endgame is tenable for Black. **18...fxg5 19.0-0-0 gxf4 20.♗d4 ♗xd4 21.♕xd4** We can take stock here. Black has four pawns for the piece, but his majority is on the kingside, which makes it hard to advance with the queens on the board. So White should avoid the exchange of the queens. With both players having many squares to play on, the position is probably dynamically balanced, although White's is slightly easier to play. **21...♘e6** The alternative 21...♕h4 was probably less accurate. After 22.♔b1 ♖ac8 23.♖g1! ♘e4 24.♗d3 White is slightly better. The text secures square f6 for Black's queen. **22.♕d2** The computer has a slight preference for 22.♕f2, but the text looks more natural. **22...♕f6 23.♔b1 ♖ac8 24.♗b5** Caruana shows a deep understanding of the position. He takes his bishop to the most active outpost on which it will be able to maintain itself. **24...♖ed8 25.♘b4**

d5 This pawn move is a tactical turn to prevent the white knight landing on d5. Black could also have played 25...♖c5, seeing that 26.♘d5? would fail to 26...♕f5+ 27.♔a1 ♕xd5 28.♕xd5 ♖xd5 29.♖xd5 ♘c7, and Black is better. **26.♖hf1** Certainly not 26.♘xd5?, in view of 26...♕f5+ 27.♔a1 ♖xd5 28.♕xd5 ♖c1+, and wins. **26...♖c5 27.a4!** The consequence of move 24. White protects his bishop on its strong outpost, sharply calculating that this does not weaken his kingside.

27...d4 This advance has a clear aim: Black wants to take his rook to f5 to support the foremost f-pawn. It looks plausible and is the computer's first move at first – but it is not correct. It is, in fact, Firouzja's first mistake after excellent play so far, despite the difficult positional problems. The

drawback of the text is that it loses black squares. A good move was 27...♔g7, quietly reinforcing the position. Play could then develop as follows: 28.♘d3 (obvious but not so good. Black will be better after 28.♖f2 h5 29.♖df1 g5 30.h4 g4 31.♖xf4 ♘xf4 32.♘d3 ♖xb5! 33.axb5 ♕g6 34.♖xf4 d4, and the position is equal; 28.♕g2 ♕f5+ 29.♔a2 ♖dc8, and Black has sufficient counterplay) 28...♖c4!. The rook is strongly positioned on the fourth rank. **28.♘d3** An excellent square for the knight, given the circumstances. **28...♖f5 29.♖f3!** A rook is normally not a very effective blocking piece, but it's different here. White is preparing an attack. **29...g5** KS: 29...h5!? 30.♗c4 ♖c8 31.♗xe6 ♕xe6∞. **30.♖g1**

30...♔f8 The move absolutely called for was 30...h5, to prevent

the breaking move h3-h4. White remains better, especially because of the extra squares for his bishop. With 31.♗c6 he can transfer it to e4. It remains a pitched battle, as witness 31...♔f8 32.♗e4 ♖a5 33.♖gf1 h4 34.b4 ♖xa4 35.♘b2 b5 36.♘xa4 bxa4 37.♖c1, and White is better. But things are not completely clear. Black has three strong pawns for the rook, and White's king is not entirely safe. **31.h4!+–** Breaking open the h-file. **31...h6 32.hxg5 hxg5 33.♖h3 f3 34.♗c4** An illustration of my comment after Black's 27th move. Square c4 has become available to the bishop. **34...♔e7** Now things do downhill fast, but after 34...f2 35.♖f1 ♖c8 36.b3 Black's situation would also have been hopeless. **35.♗xe6** The simplest solution. White's major pieces are going to win the attack. **35...♔xe6 36.♕h2 f2 37.♖f1 ♔d7 38.♖h6 ♕e7 39.♖xf2 ♖xf2 40.♕xf2 ♔c8** The black king has reached the queenside, but it is anything but safe there, too. **41.a5 bxa5 42.♕c2+ ♔b8 43.♘c5 ♖d6 44.♖h8+ ♖d8 45.♕b3+ ♔c7 46.♕b7+ ♔d6 47.♖h6+ f6 48.♘e4+ 1-0**

Timman M/20-2-100

Exercise 1

position after 11.♗d3-c2

White has a space advantage, however Black can start great counterplay on the queenside. How?

Exercise 2

position after 12.♕d1-d2

What is the strongest continuation for Black?

Exercise 3

position after 15.e4-e5

White's last move was the tempting 15.e5?. How should Black reply?

(solutions on page 252)

Edouard's creative pawn sac

by Andrea Stella

1.	d4	♘f6
2.	c4	g6
3.	g3	♗g7
4.	♗g2	0-0
5.	♘c3	d6
6.	♘f3	♘c6
7.	0-0	e5
8.	dxe5	♘xe5

Romain Edouard

The position after **1.d4 ♘f6 2.c4 g6 3.g3 ♗g7 4.♗g2 0-0 5.♘c3 d6 6.♘f3 ♘c6 7.0-0 e5** is one of the main ones in the Fianchetto Variation of the King's Indian Defence. Here my favourite approach is **8.dxe5**, with which White aims to neutralize Black's counterplay and plays for a small but long-term positional advantage.

This variation has been discussed by two distinguished authors: Boris Avrukh in his book *Grandmaster Repertoire 2A – King's Indian & Grünfeld* and Michael Roiz in his opening database *Complete Repertoire for White after 1.d4 ♘f6 2.c4 g6 3.g3 – Part 2*.

Playable is 8.d5, but after 8...♘b8! (rather than the far more common 8...♘e7 which was examined in Yearbooks 34 and 50) Black gets a more complex game, where it is possible to play for three results.

In reply to the capture, **8...♘xe5!?** is a fashionable attempt to simplify the position and equalize. Although by transposition from 6...♘bd7 it's the oldest reply, dating back to the 1920s, in my opinion it hasn't been properly taken into account by theory. So, since this move is very serious and increasingly popular, I want to offer an antidote in this Survey, showing a path for White to play for a long-term advantage with a minimal risk of losing.

8...dxe5 is the main reply, and it has been very well analysed. Generally White can play for a risk-free advantage, he can easily force a draw against stronger opponents or try to put less experienced players under pressure. For example, in my case in this variation I forced a quick draw against super-GM Etienne Bacrot (2698) and gradually converted a small advantage into a victory against the promising IM Thore Perske (2445). I will not analyse this continuation, as the reader can find satisfactory analysis in many chess books, whose advices do not

contradict what I claim here. After 9.♗g5 ♗e6 White can play for the advantage with 10.♕c1, as recommended by Avrukh and Roiz, but also with other moves like 10.♕a4!? or 10.♘d2!?.

9.♘xe5!? is my favourite move, and it is the most straightforward way to fight for a secure advantage. Recent chess books don't analyse this move and prefer the sideline 9.b3; anyway Avrukh states that 'White keeps an edge here, too, and can definitely press for a while'.

9.b3 is suggested by both Avrukh and Roiz. In fact, after the forced variation 9...♘xf3+ 10.♗xf3 ♘e4 11.♘xe4 (11.♗xe4 ♗xc3= simplifies the position too much) 11...♗xa1 12.♗g5 (in order to win back the exchange) 12...f6 13.♗h6 ♗e5 14.♗xf8 ♕xf8 we reach a position where White has a temporary advantage due to the better coordination between his pieces, but Black has a very solid position without weaknesses and with the bishop pair. This means that if White is not able to do something soon, he may even get in trouble. After 15.♗g2 f5 16.♘g5, white players won two times out of two against opponents with much lower ratings, but I am firmly of the opinion that after some precise moves Black has no problems at all. See the Internet game Grandelius-Kukk, chess.com 2018. Not satisfied with my analysis after 9.♘g5, I once improvised with 16.♘c5, but

my opponent didn't face any problems and his position even turned out to be easier to play, see the game Stella-Möhn, Barcelona 2019.

9...dxe5 10.♕xd8 Less effective seems 10.♗g5 ♕xd1 11.♖fxd1 c6 followed by moves like ...♗e6; ...♖fe8; ...h7-h6; ...♗f8; ...♘d7, where Black has a very solid position, although even here White might have some chances to create some pressure.

10...♖xd8 11.♗g5

This pin is very important. The threats of 12.♘d5, 12.♘e4 or 12.♗xf6 followed by 13.♘d5 allow White to win an important tempo.

11...♖d4! is the most popular and critical move in this variation. Black counterattacks the c4-pawn, trying to win a tempo as well. This move seems very strong, and White's score against it is only 51% according to my database. 11...♖d7!? is the most reliable alternative. Anyway here White has a higher score (57%) and has various attempts to fight for an advantage. My favourite move is 12.♗h3 (see the game Predojevic-Draskovic, Bihac 2016) but also interesting is 12.♘a4 when the ♘ points to c5 – see the game Jones-Theodorou, Heraklion 2017. Other moves, like 11...♗e6 or 11...♖e8 or 11...♖f8, are inferior, see the game Bukal-Livaja, Plovdiv 2012.

I was about to give up and stop investigating this position, but then I noticed an interesting online blitz game played by the very strong and creative French GM Romain Edouard.

12.♗e3!? The key move in this Survey. Instead of losing time protecting the c4-pawn, White attacks Black's rooks. 12.b3!? is the main move and it's ten times more popular than 12.♗e3. But if Black plays accurately, he will be able to gradually extinguish White's initiative.

12...♖xc4 More cautious but also passive is 12...♖d7, which gives White some advantage. See the Internet game Edouard-Kollars, chess.com 2017.
Taking the pawn is the critical test of the variation.

Here, with 13.♖fd1!, taking control of the only open file, White starts a vigorous initiative, which more than compensates

for the sacrificed pawn. Even here, White can play for a risk-free advantage (see the analysis part in the Game Section)

Conclusion

In the Fianchetto Variation of the King's Indian with 6...♘c6 and 7...e5, after 8.dxe5 then 8...♘xe5 is a solid and fashionable alternative, whose popularity has been growing recently. Here the suggestions by recent chess publications are, in my opinion, not completely satisfactory; they lead to very solid and easy-to-play positions for Black, where White gives up the bishop pair which can be dangerous in the endgame.

I instead recommend the more straightforward move 9.♘xe5, looking for positions where White, in the spirit of the variation, can exert pressure and at the same time minimize any risk of losing. Theory agrees that White's position is slightly more comfortable except for the critical line 9...dxe5 10.♕xd8 ♖xd8 11.♗g5 ♖d4. Here the majority of white players haven't managed to prove an advantage after the principled 12.b3. But the lesser-known and relatively unexplored 12.♗e3 seems to promise White a small and long-term advantage, breathing new life into this line.

The standard way 9.b3

Andrea Stella
Hans Möhn
Barcelona Sants 2019 (9)
1.d4 ♘f6 2.c4 g6 3.g3 ♗g7 4.♗g2 0-0 5.♘c3 d6 6.♘f3 ♘c6 7.0-0 e5 8.dxe5 ♘xe5 9.b3 When this game was played, I hadn't yet studied this variation seriously, so I played in the standard way.

9...♘xf3+ 10.♗xf3 ♘e4 10...♗h3 was played in Arkell-Durao,

Cappelle-la-Grande 1992, the stem game for 9.b3. **11.♘xe4 ♗xa1 12.♗g5 f6 13.♗h6 ♗e5 14.♗xf8 ♕xf8 15.♗g2 f5 16.♘c5** I didn't check the theory of this variation before the game, but I remembered that I was not satisfied by 16.♘g5. For this reason, I tried this novelty, in order to play an unexplored position and take my opponent out of book. Unfortunately, Black's position is very solid and easy

to play. **16...c6** Of course not 16...dxc5? 17.♕d5+±. **17.♘d3 ♗f6 18.♕d2** The d6-pawn is Black's only weakness. Unfortunately, it is quite easy to defend. Black's bishop pair is an important positional factor in his favour. **18...♗e6 19.♖d1** Stockfish suggests 19.♘f4 ♗f7 20.h4 but I cannot see any problem for Black after a solid move like 20...♔g7=. **19...♗f7 20.♕a5 ♕d8** Followed by a draw offer. Influenced by external factors (I was White and I was facing a lower-rated player), I declined. An unbiased evaluation of the position would suggest White accept. **21.♕a3 ♕c7 22.♘c1 ♗e7 23.♕b2** It was difficult to find a productive plan here. **23...a5!** Creating practical problems. **24.a4** I prevented ...a5-a4, but now my structure is more rigid, and might become weak. **24...♖d8 25.♕d4 ♖d7 26.h4** I felt the need to 'do something', but I didn't know exactly what. It is difficult to find a plan and White might suddenly lose the plot. **26...♕d8 27.♘d3** 27.♗h3!? d5 28.e4 b6!?∞. **27...♗f6 28.♕e3 ♖e7 29.♕d2 ♕b6 30.♘c1 ♖d7 31.h5 31.♕c2=. 31...♔g7 32.hxg6 hxg6**

33.e4?! Sometimes it is psycho-logically difficult to wait; 33.e3=. **33...fxe4 34.♗xe4 d5!⇄** Black did nothing in the whole game but now suddenly he gets the initiative. Might this mean that his position after the opening is simply healthier? **35.cxd5 cxd5 36.♗f3 ♕b4 36...d4!?↑. 37.♕xb4 axb4 38.♘d3 ♗c3 39.♔g2 d4?** A mistake in mutual time trouble. 39...b6∓ followed by ...♔f6 and ...g6-g5, gradually improving

Black's position, would have given him a small advantage. **40.♘e5! ♖e7 41.♘xf7 ♔xf7 42.♗d5+ ♔g7 43.♔f3** We reach an endgame which is slightly more pleasant for White, but Black can easily defend thanks to the opposite-coloured bishops. **43...b6 44.♗c4 ♖e8 45.♗d3 ♖f8+ 46.♔g2 ♖h8 47.♖h1 ♖xh1 48.♔xh1 ♔f6 49.♔g2 g5 50.♔f3 ♔e5 51.♔e2 ♗b2 52.♗b1 ♗a1 53.♔d3 ♗c3**

54.♗c2 54.♔c4 ♗e1! 55.♗d3 ♗xf2 56.♔b5 ♗xg3 57.♔xb6 g4 58.a5 ♗e1 (58...♗f2? seems good but after 59.a6 g3 60.a7 g2 61.a8♕ g1♕ 62.♕e4+ ♔f6 63.♕f5+ ♔g7 64.♕h7+ ♔f6 65.♕h6+ ♔e7 66.♗c4, incredibly, White has a decisive attack. The bishop is terribly in the way on f2 as evidenced by 66...d3+ 67.♔c6 ♕g2+ 68.♗d5; 58...♔f6 59.a6 ♗b8 60.♔b7 g3 61.♗e4 d3! 62.♔xb8 d2 63.♗f3 g2 64.a7 g1♕ 65.a8♕ d1♕=) 59.a6 g3 60.a7 g2 61.a8♕ g1♕ 62.♕e4+ ♔f6 63.♕f5+ ♔g7 64.♕h7+ ♔f6 65.♕h6+ ♔e7 66.♗c4 d3+! 67.♔c6 (67.♔a6 d2=) 67...♕g2+! 68.♗d5 ♕c2+ is what makes the difference. **54...♗e1 55.♔e2 ♗c3 56.♔f3 ♗e1 57.♗d3 ♔d5 58.♔e2 ♗c3 59.f4 gxf4 60.gxf4 ♗b2 61.♔f3 ♗c1 62.♗c4+ ♔d6 63.♔e4 d3!** A wise move. 63...♗e3 64.♗d3± would have created some practical problems for Black. **64.♗xd3 ♗b2 ½-½** White cannot win this endgame.

Nils Grandelius
Sander Kukk
PRO League Stage 2018 (9)
1.d4 g6 2.c4 ♗g7 3.g3 d6 4.♗g2 ♘f6 5.♘f3 0-0 6.♘c3 ♘c6 7.0-0 e5 8.dxe5 ♘xe5 9.b3 ♘xf3+ 10.♗xf3

♘e4 11.♘xe4 ♗xa1 12.♗g5 f6 13.♗h6 ♗e5 14.♗xf8 ♕xf8 15.♗g2 f5 16.♘g5**

In his book, Avrukh states: 'despite Black's bishop pair, he still faces some difficulties in developing his queenside pieces'. The author seems to suggest that White has a momentary development advantage, but if Black solves this temporary problems, he is in good shape. **16...c6**

A) Inferior is 16...♕e7?! because the queen is badly placed here: 17.♕d2 ♗f6?! 18.h4! a5 19.e4!± Avrukh-Liang, Chicago 2017, and White has a good initiative;

B) A reliable move might be 16...♕f6!? 17.♘f3 (17.♕d2 c6 18.♖d1 a5=; 17.h4 a5=) 17...♗c3!? (also possible is 17...c6 18.♘xe5 dxe5 19.♕d2 ♗e6, when engines slightly prefer White, but it seems difficult to find a plan to improve White's position and get a tangible advantage) 18.c5 (18.♘e1 f4!?∞; 18.♕d3 a5 19.♖d1 ♗b4=; 19...c6!? transposes to a position analysed in the sub-variation 17...♕f6) 18...dxc5 19.♕d5+ ♕f7 20.♕xc5 ♗f6 21.e4 ♕e7! 22.♕d5+ ♕e6 23.♕xe6+ (23.♕d1 fxe4 24.♘d2 e3 25.♘e4 ♗e7∞. White has compensation but no advantage, e.g. 26.♕d4 exf2+ 27.♖xf2 c6 28.♗f1 b5 29.♘f6+ ♗xf6 30.♖xf6 ♕e8 31.♖d6 ♗f5=) 23...♗xe6 24.e5 ♗e7 25.♘d4 ♗c8 26.♗d5+ ♔f8, and the bishop pair counterbalances the passed pawn. **17.♕d2** Avrukh suggests 17.♕d3, but I cannot see any problems for Black after 17...a5 18.♖d1 (18.a4 ♕f6=) 18...♗b2!?, planning ...♗a3-b2-c5 and ...♕f8-f6, with a good position for Black,

e.g. 19.♕xd6 ♕xd6 20.♖xd6 ♗a3 21.♖d8+ ♔g7 22.♘f3 (...♗a3-e7 with a double attack was threatened) 22...a4!, and Black's strong bishop pair gives him at least full positional compensation for the sacrificed pawn. Black is absolutely not worse. **17...h6?!** This move weakens Black's kingside. Better was 17...♘f6! 18.♖d1 a5!? 19.♘f3 (19.a4 ♗b2 20.♕f4 ♗e5 21.♕h4 ♕g7 22.♘f3 ♘f6 23.♕f4 ♗e7 is still very solid for Black) 19...♘c3 20.♕xd6 ♕xd6 21.♖xd6 a4. Once again the bishop pair offers full long-term strategic compensation for the pawn. **18.♘h3** 18.♘f3±. **18...♗e6 19.♖d1 ♖d8?!** Leaves the a7-pawn unprotected and allows White to create a double attack. After a move like 19...a6 it is not easy for White to prove an advantage. **20.♕e3!±** With the double threat 21.♕xa7 and 21.f4. **20...♖e8 21.♕xa7±**

White is a pawn up and Black has no compensation. Grandelius converted his advantage into victory, showing excellent technique, but the rest of the game is not of opening-theoretical interest: **21...♕e7 22.♕e3 ♗g7 23.♘f4 ♗f7 24.♕xe7 ♖xe7 25.♔f1 g5 26.♘d3 ♔f8 27.♗b4 ♖d7 28.♘c2 ♔e7 29.e4 f4 30.gxf4 gxf4 31.♘d4 ♗xd4 32.♖xd4 ♔f6 33.♖d3 ♖d8 34.♔e2 ♗e5 35.c5 d5 36.exd5 cxd5 37.a4 ♖g8 38.♔f1 ♗e6 39.a5 ♖g7 40.♗f3 ♖c7 41.b4 d4 42.♗e2 ♗c4 43.♖h3 ♗xe2+ 44.♔xe2 ♔e4 45.f3+ ♔d5 46.♔d3 ♖e7 47.♖h5+ ♔c6 48.♖xh6+ ♔c7 49.b5 ♖e3+ 50.♔xd4 ♖xf3 51.♖h7+ ♔c8 52.a6 bxa6 53.b6 ♖b3 54.♔d5 f3 55.♔c6 ♖d8 56.b7 f2 57.♖f7 ♖b2 58.♖xf2 1-0**

The most reliable alternative 9.♘xe5 dxe5 10.♕xd8 ♖xd8

Borki Predojevic
Luka Draskovic

Bosnia/Hercegovina tt 2016 (4)

1.♘f3 ♘f6 2.c4 g6 3.g3 ♗g7 4.♗g2 0-0 5.0-0 d6 6.♘c3 e5 7.d4 ♘c6 8.dxe5 ♘xe5 9.♘xe5 dxe5 10.♕xd8 ♖xd8 11.♗g5 ♖d7

12.♗h3!? A strategic idea I really like! Soon or later Black will play ...c7-c6, limiting the 'operating range' of the ♗g2, which might become passive. So it makes sense to exchange it! Moreover, in the future White's dark-squared bishop might be stronger than Black's one, which is limited by the e5-pawn. I consider the same idea when analysing the game Edouard-Kollars, in the sub-variation after White's 13th move. **12...♖d4** 12...♖d6 was played by Theodorou against Fridman, but Black suffered throughout this game, and White had many chances to increase his advantage: 13.♗xc8 ♖xc8 14.♖ad1 ♘e8 (worse is 14...♖cd8 15.♖xd6 ♖xd6 (15...cxd6 16.♘d5+−) 16.♘b5 ♖c6 (16...♖d7 17.♘xa7±) 17.♖d1! and although few pieces are left on the board, White can still generate a dangerous initiative: 17...♔f8 18.♖d8+ ♔e7 19.♖b8 b6 (19...♖xc4 20.♖xb7 with a better pawn structure) 20.b3 with a huge positional advantage for White) 15.b3 (it was possible to start centralizing the king with 15.♔g2 followed by e2-e4 and ♗e3, with a small advantage) 15...♗f8 16.♖xd6 (16.♘b5) 16...♗xd6 17.♖d1 f5 18.♗e3 (18.e4!?, fixing the opponent's pawns on the dark squares, gave

White a small technical advantage in the endgame) 18...a6 19.c5 ♗f8 (½-½ (47) Fridman-Theodorou, Heraklion 2017) and now 20.c6!? was a promising opportunity, e.g. 20...bxc6 (20...b6 21.♖d7±) 21.♘a4 followed by ♖d1-c1, and his better pawn structure gives White a pleasant advantage in the endgame. **13.♗xc8 ♖xc8 14.b3 a6 15.f3 h6 16.♗e3 ♖dd8 17.♖fd1 e4 18.♖ac1 exf3 19.exf3** The position still slightly favours White. **19...♗f8** 19...♖e8 (J. Christiansen-Al Sayed, Doha 2016) 20.♔f2 ♖cd8 (planning to double rooks on the d-file) 21.♘d5 (21.g4!?) 21...♘xd5 22.♖xd5±. **20.♔f2 ♗a3 21.♖b1 ♗b4**

22.♘a4! Finally White plays the typical manoeuvre to bring the knight to c5. **22...♔g7** It was necessary to protect h6. **23.♘c5** The knight is so strong that Black must exchange it. **23...♗xc5 24.♗xc5** In such positions, with pawns on both wings, the bishop is usually slightly better than the knight. Furthermore it coordinates better with rooks, and White can activate his king more easily. Predojevic managed to convert his advantage into a win, showing wonderful technical skills: **24...♖d7 25.♗b4 ♖cd8 26.♖xd7 ♖xd7 27.♖e1 g5 28.♖e5 ♖d1 29.♖e7 ♖d7 30.♔e3 ♖xe7+ 31.♗xe7 ♘d7 32.♔e4! ♔g6 33.f4 gxf4 34.♔xf4** Both White's pieces are more active than his opponent's. **34...h5 35.♔e4** White waits for Black to exhaust his pawn moves, and tries to create some zugzwangs. **35...c6** 35...♘b6? 36.♗d8 ♘a8 37.♔e5+−; here the bishop dominates the knight;

35...♘f6+ 36.♗xf6 ♔xf6 37.♔f4 and the pawn endgame is winning for White, thanks to his more active king and the possibility to create a distant passed pawn on the h-file (e.g. after h2-h4 and g2-g4 at the appropriate moment). **36.♔f4 f6 37.♗d6 f5** 37...♘b6 38.a4 ♘d7 39.a5 b6 40.b4 bxa5 41.bxa5 f5 42.♗b4 ♔f6 (42...♘f6 43.♔e5+−) 43.♗c3+ ♔g6 44.♗d4 c5 45.♗c3 and Black is in zugzwang. Any move would worsen the position of one of his pieces, allowing the white king to penetrate. **38.♗e7 ♔f7 39.♗d8 ♔g6 40.b4 b6 41.a3 c5 42.b5 axb5 43.cxb5** Zugzwang. Black has to move and worsen his position. **43...c4** This pawn will go nowhere. Actually it will fall. **44.♔e3 1-0**

Gawain Jones
Nikolas Theodorou

Hersonissos Ech tt 2017 (5)

1.d4 ♘f6 2.c4 g6 3.♘f3 d6 4.g3 ♗g7 5.♗g2 0-0 6.0-0 ♘c6 7.♘c3 e5 8.dxe5 ♘xe5!? 9.♘xe5 dxe5 10.♕xd8 ♖xd8 11.♗g5 ♖d7 12.♘a4!? White's knight is directed to the c5-square, from where it exerts pressure on the enemy queenside. This is a typical manoeuvre in this kind of position, and is a good way to play for an advantage. I prefer Predojevic's idea 12.♗h3, but this is just a matter of taste. **12...h6 13.♗e3**

13...c6 An alternative is 13...♘g4. Instead of retreating the bishop to c1, as was seen in Martinovic-Smirin, Hersonissos 2017, I prefer 14.♘c5!? (or 14.♗c5 f5 15.e4±) 14...♘xe3 15.fxe3 ♗e7 (15...♖d2 16.♖ad1! ♖xd1 17.♖xd1↑) 16.♖ad1±, reaching a position in which White has given up the bishop pair

and worsened his pawn structure in return for enormous activity. Now there is pressure against b7 and along the d-file. 16...♗e8?! fails to 17.♘a6!±. **14.♘c5 ♖c7** Or 14...♗e7 15.♖fd1 ♖e8 16.h3!? with ideas like g3-g4, a2-a4-a5, ♖d1-d2 and ♖a1-d1, where White has a small edge and can keep improving his position. **15.♖fd1** Now it is not easy for Black to protect the d-file. **15...b6** 15...♗f5 allows 16.♘xb7!? ♖xb7 17.♗xc6±, forcing an endgame where the rook and two pawns are clearly better than two minor pieces. **16.♖d8+ ♔h7 17.♘a6!?** 17.♗e4 ♘xe4 18.♗xe4 f5 19.♗c2 was also somewhat better for White. **17...♖d7 18.♖xd7 ♗xd7 19.a4!?** By advancing his a-pawn, White looks for a possible break on the queenside, on a5 or c5. 19.♖d1!?↑ was a possible alternative. **19...e4 20.♖d1** 20.a5!? was slightly better for White, e.g. 20...♗g4 21.♔f1 ♖d8 22.♔e1 and Black is under unpleasant positional pressure. Premature would be 22.axb6 axb6 23.♗xb6 ♖d2⇄. **20...♗g4 21.♖d2 ♖e8 22.b4?!** Slow and pointless. There was still time to attack Black's pawn chain with 22.a5!±. **22...♗c8 23.b5 ♘g4 24.♗f4 cxb5?!** 24...g5!⇄. **25.♘c7!** 25.cxb5 g5!∓. **25...♖e7** 25...♖g8 26.♘xb5±; 25...♖h8 26.♘xb5 g5 27.♗b8!±. **26.♘d5** 26.axb5±. **26...♖e8?!** 26...♖d7 27.axb5 f5 28.f3↑. **27.axb5±** Now the a7-pawn is a potential target. **27...g5 28.♗b8 e3** 28...a6 29.♗c7±. **29.fxe3 ♘e5** 29...♘xe3 30.♘xe3 ♖xe3 31.♗xa7+−. **30.♗xe5** 30.♖d4 ♘d7 31.♘e4!+−. **30...♗xe5 31.♖a2 ♔g7** 31...♗b8 32.♘f6+−. **32.♖xa7+−** And White went on to win: **32...♗d6 33.♘xb6 ♗c5 34.♘xc8 ♖xc8 35.♖a4 ♗xe3+ 36.♔f1 ♖c7 37.♖a3 ♗c5 38.♖b3 ♖a7 39.♖b1 ♗b6 40.c5! ♗xc5 41.b6 ♖a6 42.b7 ♖f6+ 43.♔e1 ♗f2+ 44.♔d2 ♖a7 45.b8♕ ♗xb8 46.♖xb8 ♖f2 47.♖d5 ♖xh2 48.♔e1 f5 49.♖b6 h5 50.♗e6 ♖g2 51.♗xf5 ♖xg3 52.♔f2 h4 53.♖d6 ♖a3 54.♖g6+ ♔h8 55.♖xg5 1-0**

Vladimir Bukal Jr
Mario Livaja

Plovdiv 2012 (9)

1.d4 ♘f6 2.c4 g6 3.g3 ♗g7 4.♗g2 0-0 5.♘c3 d6 6.♘f3 ♘c6 7.0-0 e5 8.dxe5 ♘xe5 9.♘xe5 dxe5 10.♕xd8 ♖xd8 11.♗g5 ♖f8

A) 11...h6?! 12.♗xf6 ♗xf6 13.♘d5 ♗g7 14.♘xc7, winning a pawn, with a clear advantage;

B) 11...♗e6?! is a dubious move. Strangely, the strongest reply has not been played yet:

B1) 12.♘d5 ♗xd5 13.cxd5 (H.Ramirez-Posada, Pereira 1958) 13...h6! 14.♗xf6 ♗xf6 might give White a small advantage, due to the weak c7-pawn, but Black should be able to hold thanks to the opposite-coloured bishops;

B2) 12.♘e4 is tempting, since is seems to win an exchange. Unfortunately Black has 12...♘xe4! 13.♗xd8 (13.♗xe4 f6 14.♗e3 c6⇄) 13...♘d2 14.♘xc7 (14.♖fd1? ♖xd8−+) 14...♘xf1 15.♔xf1 ♖c8 16.♗a5 (16.♗d6 ♖xc4 17.♗xb7 ♖c2 18.b3 e4⇄) 16...b6 17.♗c3 ♗xc4= Edouard-L.van Foreest, chess24. com 2019;

B3) 12.♗xb7! ♖ab8 13.♗g2± when White is a pawn up and Black cannot take on b2 because of the threat ♘c3-e4; 13.♗d5!?±;

C) 11...♖e8 exposes Black's rooks to a possible knight fork and allows 12.♘b5! ♖e7 13.♖fd1! when Black is forced to protect his back rank by developing his bishop, at the price of the b7-pawn: 13...♗e6 (even worse would be 13...h6 14.♖d8+ ♔h7 15.♗xf6 ♗xf6 16.♗h3 and White wins) 14.♗xb7 ♖b8 15.♗g2 a6 (15...c6 16.♘d6±; 15...♗xc4 16.♘xa7±, and now 16...♖xb2? is not possible in view of 17.♖d8+ ♖e8 18.♗xf6+−) 16.♗a7 ♖ee8 (16...♖xb2 17.♖d8++−) 17.b3 and White was clearly better in Shinkevich-Averin, Izhevsk 2009. **12.♘b5!** Activating the knight. **12...c6 13.♘d6** The d6-square is a strong outpost. However, the knight may be exchanged for the ♗c8 in order to get the technical advantage of the bishop pair.

13...h6 14.♗e3 ♘g4 14...♖d8 15.♘xc8 (15.♖ad1!?↑ ♗f8 (Ihonen-Jouhki, Vantaa 1988) 16.♘e4! ♘d7 (16...♗e7 17.♘c5! ♖xe4 18.♗xe7 ♖e8 19.♗xe4 ♖xe7 20.♖d8+ ♔g7 21.♖fd1±) 17.♘f6+ ♔g7 (17...♔h8 18.♗h3+−) 18.♕g4±) 15...♖dxc8 16.♖fd1 ♘g4 17.♗d2 ♖e8 18.h3 ♘f6 19.♗e3 when the bishop pair gives White a better endgame, Mirzoyan-Amartuvshin, Ahmedabad 2017. **15.♗c5 f5** Trying to gain space on the kingside. **16.e4!** With such active pieces, White wants to open the position. **16...b6** 16...f4? 17.♗xc8 ♖axc8 18.♗h3 h5 19.f3+−; 16...fxe4 17.♘xe4 and his better pawn structure, control of the e4-square and higher activity give White a clear positional advantage. **17.♗a3 ♗d7 18.♖ad1** Bringing the last piece into play and intensifying the pressure. **18...f4 19.♘f5!** White has multiple threats. **19...♖fd8 20.♘xg7 c5** Black wants to close off the ♗a3 and only later take the ♘g7, which has no squares to escape, but this idea is too slow. 20...♔xg7 21.♗e7 and White wins the exchange. **21.♖d6!** Pinning and winning. **21...♔xg7 22.♖fd1 ♘f6 23.gxf4 1-0** 24.fxe5 or 24.e5 will follow, and Black's position will fall apart.

The critical variation 11...♖d4

Leandro Krysa
Maximiliano Perez
Neuquen 2017 (4)

1.d4 ♘f6 2.c4 g6 3.♘f3 ♗g7 4.g3 0-0 5.♗g2 d6 6.0-0 ♘c6 7.♘c3 e5 8.dxe5 ♘xe5 9.♘xe5 dxe5

10.♕xd8 ♖xd8 11.♗g5 ♖d4 The critical variation. **12.b3** White believes Black and protects the c4-pawn. This shy move has been played more than 90 times, but it is probably not enough to get an advantage. **12...c6 13.♘a4** This typical manoeuvre to bring the knight to c5 is the only reliable attempt to get something; 13.♖fd1 ♗e6=. **13...h6!** Driving away White's pieces. **14.♗e3 ♖d8 15.♖fd1**

15...♖e8! Very well played. By keeping all the rooks on the board, Black gives White no dangerous entry squares on the d-file. Worse would be 15...♖xd1+?! 16.♖xd1 and White is threatening to invade the back rank, e.g. 16...♗f5 17.♘c5↑ with an initiative on the queenside. **16.h3** A useful move, aimed to prevent ...♘f6-g4 followed by ...f7-f5. **16...♘h7!** A strong plan! Black doesn't hurry with the development of his light-squared bishop, which is more useful defending the b7-pawn at the moment! Instead, Black wants to advance his f-pawn, in order to expand on the kingside. Bad would be 16...♗f5?! 17.♘c5↑. Another playable idea is 16...♘d7 17.♖d2 ♘f8 (I like 17...f5!?⇄) 18.♖ad1 (18.♘c5 f5 19.♖ad1 ♗e6 20.♘xe6 ♗xe6= Fridman-E.Zude, Port Erin 2005) 18...♘e6 (18...f5!? was still possible). Now the c5-square is under control and Black should no longer be worrying about possible raids of the opponent's knight to that square: 19.♘c5 ♘xc5 20.♗xc5 ♗e6 (20...♗f8!?=) 21.a4 ♗f8 22.♗xf8 ♔xf8 23.a5 a6 24.f4 exf4 25.gxf4 ♔e7 with a balanced position, Fridman-Ivic, Skopje 2018. **17.♘c5 f5 18.♖d6?!** A careless move.

Stockfish suggests 18.♘a6!?, but it probably leads nowhere after 18...♗e7 (18...bxa6 19.♗xc6 ♗e6 20.♗xa8 ♖xa8 21.♖d6 is slightly more pleasant for White) 19.♗c5 ♖f7 20.♖d8+ ♗f8= and White cannot scratch Black's position. **18...♘f8** 18...e4 (closing in the ♗g2) 19.♖ad1 leads to an approximately equal position. 18...f4!? was Black's chance to play for an advantage. White's pieces turn out to be uncoordinated, e.g. 19.gxf4 (19.♗d2 ♗f8 (winning an exchange) 20.♘e4 ♗xd6 21.♘xd6 gives White some positional compensation, which is probably not enough) 19...exf4 20.♗d4 ♗f8 21.♘xb7!? (21.♖xg6+ ♔f7−+ and White's rook is trapped!) 21...♗xb7 (21...♖xd6 22.♘xd6 ♖e6 23.♘e4± with more than enough compensation) 22.♖xg6+ ♔f7 23.♖g4∓ and White has some compensation for the sacrificed piece, but not enough. **19.♖ad1 ½-½** White got no advantage after the opening, so he offered a draw, which was accepted.

Romain Edouard
Dmitrij Kollars
PRO League Stage 2017 (7)

1.d4 ♘f6 2.c4 g6 3.g3 ♗g7 4.♗g2 0-0 5.♘c3 d6 6.♘f3 ♘c6 7.0-0 e5 8.dxe5 ♘xe5 9.♘xe5 dxe5 10.♕xd8 ♖xd8 11.♗g5 ♖d4 12.♗e3!

A great idea! It is not necessary to protect c4. The black rook is driven away from this active square. **12...♖d7** The most logical retreat. 12...♖xc4 is the critical test, and it will be covered in the 'analysis' section below. 12...♖d8 is weaker than the text move. After 13.♖ad1± White easily takes control of the d-file, as Black

cannot develop his light-squared bishop without losing b7. **13.♘b5** The most direct move. 13.♗h3!? is the same strategic idea as was implemented by Petrojevic in his game against Draskovic. White probably gets a slightly better position also here, e.g. 13...♖d8 14.♗xc8 ♖dxc8 (14...♖axc8?! is even worse as White can take on a7: 15.♗xa7 b6 16.c5!±) 15.♖ad1±. **13...♘g4** 13...a6 14.♘a7± and ♘a7xc8, winning the bishop pair, is a positional gain but can also be followed by tactical ideas like ♗g2xb7 or ♗g2-h3. **14.♗c5 ♗f8** Black tries unsuccessfully to reduce White's initiative by exchanging pieces. 14...a6 is still met by 15.♘a7±. **15.♗xf8 ♔xf8 16.♖fd1** 16.c5!, threatening c5-c6, would have been even stronger, e.g. 16...c6 17.♘d6± and White seizes this strong outpost. He can now attack on the queenside by pushing his a- and b-pawns. **16...c6 17.♘d6** This knight is powerful. **17...♖c7** 17...♘f6 18.c5 ♘e8 is an attempt to exchange White's strong knight. Anyway White can create problems on the light squares by playing 19.♗h3! f5 20.♘xc8 ♖xd1+ 21.♖xd1 ♖xc8 22.e4! ♘f6 (22...♘g7 23.♖d7+−; the rook is too strong on the seventh rank) 23.exf5 g5 24.♖d6 ♘g7 25.♗f1+− Tilicheev-Zlatanovic, Ohrid 2019. Although Black miraculously managed to save this endgame, White has a decisive technical advantage. **18.c5 ♗e6 19.♖d3** 19.b4!?± followed by a2-a4-a5 or a2-a4 and b4-b5. ♘xb7, aiming for an endgame with rook and two pawns against two minor pieces, is also threatened. **19...♘f6 20.b4 ♘d5 21.b5** 21.a3±. **21...♘b4 22.♖d2 cxb5 23.a3** ♘c6 24.♘xb5 ♖d7 **25.♖d6** 25.♖xd7 ♗xd7 26.♘d6±. **25...♘d8 26.♖xd7 ♗xd7 27.♘d6 ♖b8 28.♖b1** White's pressure on the queenside is annoying. 28...♔e7 29.♔f1 b5 30.cxb6 ♗e6 31.♘b7 axb6 32.♖xb6 e4?! 32...f5 gave some compensation for the pawn, but White keeps a small

advantage after 33.♖b4; 32...♗c8? 33.♘d6+−. **33.♖xe4 ♗c8**

34.a4! The passed a-pawn is simply too strong. The temporarily loss of a piece is not a problem. 34.♘d6? ♗h3+!−+. **34...♗xb7** 34...♘xb7 35.a5+−. **35.a5 ♔d7** 35...♖a8 36.♗xb7 ♖xa5 37.♗e4±. **36.♗xb7! ♔c7** 36...♖xb7 runs into 37.♖xb7+ ♔xb7 38.a6! ♔c7 39.a7!+−. A typical pattern in endgames. The knight is awkward when fighting against a rook pawn. **37.♗d5!** From this square the bishop dominates the knight. **37...♖xb6 38.axb6+ ♔xb6 39.e4** Due to the domination of the knight, we can assess this position like a pawn endgame. Black will be put in zugzwang soon. **39...♔c5 40.♔e2 ♔d4 41.h4 h6 42.f3 g5 43.h5 f5 44.g4 fxg4 45.fxg4 ♔e5 46.♔e3 ♔f6 47.♔d4 1-0**

Analysis

1.d4 ♘f6 2.c4 g6 3.g3 ♗g7 4.♗g2 0-0 5.♘c3 d6 6.♘f3 ♘c6 7.0-0 e5 8.dxe5 ♘xe5 9.♘xe5 dxe5 10.♕xd8 ♖xd8 11.♗g5 ♖d4 12.♗e3! ♖xc4 Here Black accepts the pawn, but White can take control of the important d-file. **13.♖fd1!** White is threatening a devastating invasion on the back rank.

13...♗f5N This is one of the best squares for the bishop, since it controls b1. The importance of controlling this square will become clear at move 20.

A) 13...♗f8 14.♖d8 ♗g7 (it was necessary to parry ♗h6; 14...♘g4? 15.♗d5 ♖b4 16.♗c5+−) 15.♗h3! ♘g4 (relatively better was 15...♗xh3 but after 16.♖xa8± Black does not have enough compensation for the exchange) 16.♗xg4 ♗xg4 17.♘d5! with a winning initiative, e.g. 17...♖c4 (17...c6 18.♘c7 ♖b8 19.♗xa7+−; 19.♘e8+!? ♔h8 20.♘f6+−; 17...♗d6 18.♖c1 c6 (18...f6 19.♘xc7 ♖b8 20.♘e8++−) 19.f3! ♖a4 20.♘c3!+−, winning material) 18.♗g5! 19.♗f6 or 19.♗e7 is threatened. White's pieces are just too active: 18...f5 (18...♖c6 19.♗e7 ♗xe7 20.♘xe7+−; 18...♗d6 19.♘f6 (threatening 20. ♖g8 mate!) 19...♗f8 20.♘e8+ ♔g8 21.♘xc7 ♖xc7 22.♗h6+−; 18...f6 19.♗xf6+ ♔f7 20.♗xe5+−) 19.♗e7 ♗xe7 20.♘xe7+−;

B) After 13...♗d7, first seen in Baburin-Gullaksen, Port Erin 1998, White's strongest move is 14.♖ac1!, protecting the ♘c3. The threat is 15.b3 ♖b4 16.♗c5, exploiting the fact that Black's rook has almost no mobility: 14...e4 (giving back the pawn, in order to let the rook escape to c6, seems the only way to stay in the game; if 14...♗f8 15.♗g5, winning a piece) 15.b3 ♖c6 16.♘xe4 ♖xc1 17.♗xc1! and Black has to reckon with tactical threats against his bishop and his queenside pawns, e.g. 17...♗c6 (17...♘xe4 18.♖xd7+−; 17...♗b5 18.♘xf6+ ♗xf6 19.♗xb7 ♖e8 20.♗e3 ♗xe2 21.♖d7+−) 18.♘xf6+ ♗xf6 19.♗xc6 bxc6 20.♗f4 with a decisive technical advantage;

C) 13...♗e6 is worse than the main move, as the bishop does not control b1. In a few moves the reason will become evident: 14.♗xb7 ♖b8 15.♗a6! (thanks to this retreat Black has no time to take on b2) 15...♖c6 (15...♖cb4 16.b3 simply leads to an awful position for Black, due to his weak pawn

structure on the queenside, e.g. 16...♗f8 17.f3 (17.♘a4± was even better, preparing moves like ♖ac1 or ♘c5) 17...c5 18.♖ac1 h6 19.♔f2 e4 (Edouard-Moranda, chess. com 2019) and now the simple 20.♘xe4 would have secured White a huge advantage) 16.♗b5! (White is not afraid to trade two minor pieces for the rook, as the invasion of the back rank will be decisive) 16...♖xc3 (16...♖d6 17.♗xa7 is hopeless for Black) 17.bxc3 ♖xb5 18.♖d8+ ♗f8 19.♗h6 ♘d7 20.♖d1! and Black cannot parry ♖d1xd7 followed by mate on f8. Note that if Black's light-squared bishop had been on f5, Black would have been able to play 20...♖b5-b1, pinning White's rook and avoiding immediate defeat. 20...♖b8 is useless as White still plays 21.♖1xd7+−. **14.♗xb7 ♖b8 15.♗a6!** The most forcing move. As his rook is attacked, Black has no time to take on b2 with the other rook. **15...♖c6** 15...♖cb4 16.b3 leads to a much better endgame for White, thanks to his superior pawn structure. **16.♗b5!** Forcing Black to trade the rook for two pieces. White's rooks will be very strong in the resulting position.

16...♖xc3 16...♖d6 17.♗xa7+−. **17.bxc3 ♖xb5 18.♖d8+ ♗f8 19.♗h6 ♘d7 20.♖d1**

Threatening to eliminate the defender of f8. **20...♖b1!** We can now understand why it was important for Black to develop the bishop to f5, in order to control the b1-square. Unfortunately for Black, even if he manages to survive, his position is still difficult. **21.♖xb1 ♗xb1 22.a4** Black's queenside pawns can be easily attacked by white rook. **22...♗a2** 22...♗e4 23.a5± (23.♖xd7 ♗xh6 24.♖xc7±) 23...♗c6 (23...f5 24.♖xd7 ♗xh6 25.a6+− followed by 26.♖xc7 and 27.♖xa7) 24.c4 a6 (24...f5 25.♖c8+−) 25.f3 (White simply prepares the centralization of his king while Black is doomed to passivity) 25...f5 26.♗xf8 ♘xf8

27.♖c8+−; 22...a5 23.♗xf8 ♘xf8 24.♖a8±. **23.♗xf8** Simplifying the position. Various moves give White a slight pull, for example, 23.♖xd7 ♗xh6 24.♖xc7; 23.♖c8±; 23.a5!?±; or 23.f3!?±. **23...♘xf8 24.♖a8 ♗c4 25.♖xa7 ♘e6** 25...♘xe2 26.♖xc7± and White's queenside pawns will soon become a nightmare for Black. **26.a5 ♔g7** 26...♗c2? 27.♖a8 ♔g7 28.a6+−; the a-pawn will soon cost Black a piece. **27.♔f1±**

This endgame is very unpleasant for Black. White can centralize his king or push his a-pawn (a5-a6, ♖a8, a6-a7).
We can establish that even if Black challenges the 12.♗a3 variation by taking the c4-pawn, White can still play for the advantage in a risk-free position, if he knows what to do.

Exercise 1

position after 19.♘g5-f3

What should Black play here?

(solutions on page 253)

Exercise 2

position after 13...♗c8-d7

What is White's strongest move here?

Exercise 3

position after 15...♖c4-c6

White has the better pawn structure but both his ♗a6 and his b2-pawn are under attack. How can he solve this?

The Polish Benoni

by Bogdan Lalic

1.	d4	♘f6
2.	c4	c5
3.	d5	e6
4.	♘c3	exd5
5.	cxd5	d6
6.	e4	g6
7.	♘f3	♗g7
8.	h3	a6
9.	a4	♘bd7
10.	♗d3	♘h5

Some 10 years ago this line of the Benoni, where Black saves a tempo on castling kingside, became all the rage due to some wins by Polish grandmaster Radoslaw Wojtaszek. In fact, in the big database I found that it was the late Polish/American grandmaster Alexander Wojtkiewicz who adopted it, so perhaps it would be more fair to christen this line as the Polish Variation of the Benoni. Between 2005 and 2012 Black was scoring excellently with this line, mostly due to the fact that it had a surprise value (as was also mentioned in the book *Dangerous Weapons: the Benoni and Benko* by Palliser, Emms, Ward and Jones from 2008). But recently White had found various ways to pose problems against Black's set-up. Recently I played an online blitz

tournament in which with black I played two games which I also include in this Survey. In one of them, my opponent played one of the most challenging plans, obtaining an advantage, and in the end I was lucky to save a draw.

Driving away the knight

In the games Hertneck-Naiditsch, Nebolsina-Zhukova and Enchev-Vernacki White immediately drives away Black's knight with 11.g4. By doing so White gains space on the kingside but also this pawn can later become weak and exposed after Black plays ...h7-h5. I quite like the plan from the game Nebolsina-Zhukova, where Black played ...h7-h5 before defending her pawn on d6, which in my opinion grants Black full counterplay.

The bishop thrust

In the games Goganov-Indjic and Krasenkow-Kurmann we see one of the main lines in this system: 11.♗g5. In the game Goganov-Indjic, Black exchanged the bishops with 14...♗g5!? which is more active than 14...♘g7 and which equalized easily. In fact, later Black overplayed his opponent in the endgame using the pressure along the f-file. Quite interesting is the game Krasenkow-Kurmann in which White gets compensation for the sacrificed pawn. But I think the position is still quite balanced (the same type of structure as already seen in the game Fridman-Eljanov which I discussed earlier in the commentary).

Alexander Wojtkiewicz

In a recent Internet game between Shoshin and Fier, White surprisingly castled queenside and went for a kingside attack (see the analysis of the game Goganov-Indjic). Later Black won, but accurate computer analysis shows that he is under serious pressure here.

Black is in trouble

The game Zakhartsov-Zeller (included in Dard-Lovakovic) follows the main line 11.0-0 ♘e5 12.♗e2 ♘xf3+ 13.♗xf3 ♕h4 14.♗xh5 gxh5.

In the Forum Section of Yearbook 126 (page 15), the Russian grandmaster Viacheslav Zakhartsov analysed his game from the Dresden Open 2017. I have not found any new examples in this line, and the position after 20.♗d2! looks quite bad for Black; in fact the computer gives plus 1.5 for White at this point. This is because Black's threats along the g-file

are parried, while the most important issue of the position is the insecurity of Black's king in the centre. White has an easy plan with f2-f4 and e4-e5, also sometimes exchanging the bishops with ♗c1-d2-c3. Black's counterplay could be ...♗c8-d7 and ...♖a8-c8, using some tricks to promote the b2-pawn. This is exactly what happened in the game Zakhartsov-Zeller, in which, despite having two queens on the board, Black could not avoid defeat. However hard I tried to find an improvement for Black on this key game from 2017 I just could not! The endgame which arises after 11.0-0 ♘e5 12.♘xe5 ♗xe5 13.f4 ♗d4+ 14.♔h2 ♕h4 15.♕e1! is also quite nice for White. He will soon gain important space on the kingside by attacking the knight with g2-g4 and Black's bishop will have to lose more time after White attacks it with ♘c3-e2. Perhaps with the best play Black can hold this endgame (if he plays a well-timed ...f7-f5 break) but unfortunately this is the best Black can hope for.

Conclusion

The Benoni aficionado should also go back to studying the old lines in which Black castles kingside, since the game Zakhartsov-Zeller looks very convincing for White. Also if White plays the prophylactic 11.♗e2 from Jakovenko-Dubov which I mentioned in the notes to the game Krasenkow-Kurmann, then this can often lead to lines where Black has already castled kingside. I have included the game Navara-Ivanchuk (see the notes in Krasenkow-Kurmann), in which Black also castled kingside. I hope that after this article black players will be more aware of the dangers which face them when playing this line against a well-booked opponent.

Driving away the knight 11.g4

Gerald Hertneck
Arkadij Naiditsch
Germany Bundesliga 2008/09 (4)

1.d4 ♘f6 2.c4 e6 3.♘f3 c5 4.d5 exd5 5.cxd5 d6 6.♘c3 g6 7.h3 ♗g7 8.e4 a6 9.a4 ♘bd7 10.♗d3 ♘h5 11.g4 11.a5 with the idea to prevent ...b7-b5 is a rare move. After 11...♘e5 12.♗e2 in the game Bendana Guerrero-Brooks, cr 2006, Black could have continued simply with 12...♘xf3+ 13.♗xf3 ♘f6; the trade of one pair of minor pieces usually gives Black a comfortable game in the Benoni; he should be fine and close to equality. **11...♘hf6 12.♗e3 0-0**

13.♘d2 Planning f2-f4 and going for the expansion on the kingside. Less logical is 13.0-0 h5 14.g5 ♘e8!. The knight is much better placed on e8 than on h7. Here it defends the weakened pawn on d6 while at the same time preparing the thrust ...b7-b5. If 15.a5 ♖b8 16.♕e2 ♘c7 17.♔g2 b5 18.axb6 ♖xb6 the game is still balanced but with full dynamic play for Black, due to his counterplay along the b-file added to pressure along the a1-h8 diagonal. Later Black went on to win in the correspondence game Ferre Perez-Martin Gonzalez, 2010. **13...♘e8?!** This turns out to be a faulty plan. The correct plan was 13...♖b8 14.0-0 ♕e7!?, for the time being exerting pressure in the centre because 15.f4 can be answered well with the tactical resource 15...♘xe4! 16.♘dxe4 f5 with equal play. **14.f4 ♖b8 15.0-0 ♗d4?!** The continuation of the plan started on the 13th move,

but later the pawn on d4 will be weak. **16.♗xd4** Even stronger looks 16.♕f3 ♕f6 17.♔g2! and if 17...♗xc3 18.bxc3 ♕xc3 19.♕e2♕ ♕g7 20.♔h2→. White's strong pawn centre added to his pair of bishops give White more than sufficient compensation for the sacrificed pawn. **16...cxd4 17.♘e2 ♘c5** Worthy of attention was 17...h5!? in order to search counterplay against White's extended and somewhat weakened kingside, e.g. 18.gxh5 ♘c5 19.♖f3 ♕h4 20.♕f1 ♘xd3 21.♖xd3 ♕xh5 22.♕g2 ♘f6 23.♖f1±. However, in that case also Black has zero compensation for his sacrificed (lost) pawn. **18.♖f3 ♘f6**

19.♘xd4? The pinned knight will get into all sorts of trouble along the a7-g1 diagonal; 19.b4! ♘xd3 20.♖xd3 h5 21.g5 ♘d7 22.♖xd4 f6 23.gxf6 (avoiding 23.h4? fxg5 24.hxg5 ♘e5!⇄ with the idea ...♗c8-g4, when in case of 25.fxe5?? ♕xg5+ 26.♔h1 ♖f2 White suddenly gets mated) 23...♕xf6 24.♖a3±. **19...♖e8 20.♕c2 ♕b6?** After this Black gets the pawn back but enters a very passive endgame. Much stronger was 20...♗d7! 21.b4 ♘xa4! 22.♖xa4 ♖c8 23.♕d1 ♗xa4 24.♕xa4 ♕b6 25.b5 axb5 26.♗xb5 ♖a8 27.♕b4 ♘xe4 with a rather chaotic position and chances for both sides. **21.♘c4 ♕b4 22.♕c3! ♘xd3 23.♖xd3 ♕xc3 24.bxc3 ♘xe4 25.♖e3 ♗d7 26.a5! ♘f6 27.♖xe8+ ♗xe8 28.♘b6± ♘e4?** The knight on b6 was paralysing Black's position, so 28...♘d7 just had to be played, e.g. 29.♘c4 ♘f6. **29.c4 ♘c5 30.♖b1 ♗f8 31.♘b3 ♘a4 32.♔f2 ♖d8 33.♔e3 ♘xb6 34.axb6 ♗d7 35.♔d4 ♖e8 36.♘a5**

♗c8 37.♖c1! White has a decisive space advantage and the threat of the c4-c5 break is impossible to meet. The rest was easy ... **1-0 (46)**

Vera Nebolsina
Natalia Zhukova
Russia tt W 2012 (2)

1.d4 ♘f6 2.c4 e6 3.♘c3 c5 4.d5 exd5 5.cxd5 d6 6.e4 g6 7.♘f3 ♗g7 8.h3 a6 9.a4 ♘bd7 10.♗d3 ♘h5 11.g4 ♘hf6 12.♗f4 12.♔f1!? deserves attention, with the idea to transfer the king to g2 in order to protect the pawn on h3 better after Black undermines it with the standard ...h7-h5: 12...♕e7 13.♔g2 h6?! (the wrong plan. Better is to play the standard ...h7-h5 either immediately or after first castling kingside) 14.♖e1 g5 15.e5 dxe5 16.♗c4 ♕d6 17.♘d2 0-0 18.♘de4 ♘xe4 19.♘xe4 ♕b8 20.♗e3 b6 (Van Wely-Youssoupov, France tt 2017), and now best was 21.h4!→ and if 21...gxh4, 22.g5 hxg5 23.♗xg5 b5□ 24.axb5 axb5 25.♖xa8 ♕xa8 26.♗xb5 f5 27.♘d6 ♘f6 28.♘xc8 ♕xc8 29.♗xh4 with a clear advantage for White.

12...h5!? Rather than defending d6, Black undermines White on the kingside, looking for counterplay. Besides, the ♗xd6 threat can always be answered with ...♕b6, hitting both the bishop on d6 and the pawn on b2. **13.♗xd6?!** This leads to some wild positions but I think that objectively White should settle for 13.g5 ♘h7 14.♕d2 ♕e7 with chances for both sides. **13...hxg4 14.♘g5 ♘h5** This looks very tempting for Black but stronger is the calm retreat 14...♘h7! 15.♘xh7 ♖xh7 16.♗g3 ♗d4 17.h4 ♘e5

18.&e2 f5 19.&d2 fxe4 20.&xe4
&f5↑ and Black is very active.
15.&xf7? This piece sacrifice is
easily refuted. Correct was 15.hxg4
&xg5 16.gxh5 &xh5 17.&xh5
gxh5 18.&d2! &g4 (≤ 18...&g1+
19.&f1) 19.&f4 with probably still
balanced play. **15...&xf7 16.hxg4
&f6** 16...&f4!?∓ was also very good
for Black. **17.gxh5 &xd6 18.f4
&g8?!** 18...c4! was even stronger
and if 19.&xc4 (or 19.&c2 &xh5
20.&xh5 &xf4!! 21.&e2 &d6 22.&h1
&e5 23.&a3 &g4 24.&f1+ &e7
25.&d2 &h8 26.&g3 &f6! 27.&xg4
&xg4 28.&f4 &h4 29.&xd6+
&xd6–+. What a sudden change
of scenery! Material is equal but
due to his complete domination
over the dark squares (which is
by the way a common theme in
the Benoni) Black has a winning
advantage in this endgame!),
19...&c5 20.&e2 &b6 21.hxg6+
&f8 22.&xh8+ &xh8 23.&h5 &g7
24.&h4 &d7 25.d6 &xc4 26.&e7+
&g8 with a win for Black. **19.&f3**
Or 19.e5 &xe5 20.fxe5 &xe5+
21.&e2 &xh5 22.&xh5 &xh5
23.&e8+? &h7 when White's king
is more exposed than Black's, for
example 24.&d2 c4 25.&e4 &h2+
26.&e2 &xe2+! 27.&xe2 &g4+ and
Black wins. **19...c4! 20.&xc4?!** ≥
20.&e2∓. **20...&b4 21.&e2 &xc3+
22.bxc3 &xc3+ 23.&f2 &f6?!**
Often in such messy positions
there is just no time for normal
developing moves! 23...b5! 24.axb5
&f6∓ would have followed lines
similar to the game but in case
White continues with &ag1, as in
the game, then the subsequent
opening of the a-file would prove
to be decisively in Black's favour.
24.&ag1 &d4+?! 24...&h6! 25.d6+
&g7 26.&d3 (necessary because
Black was threatening to land on
g4 with a minor piece) 26...&b2+
27.&e3 b5 28.&d5 &b8–+; Black
has activated all his dormant
pieces and now the extra material
is bound to tell. **25.&f1?** 25.&f3!
&g4+ 26.&xg4 &xg4 27.d6+□ (in
order to free square d5 for the
bishop after Black attacks it with

...&a8-c8) 27...&g7 28.&xg4 &xh5
29.&xh5 gxh5+ 30.&f3∓. **25...&xe4
26.&xg6+ &f8 27.&g2 &f5** Now
Black is clearly winning. **28.d6
&xd6 29.&g5T &xf4+ 0-1**

Ivaylo Enchev
Srdjan Vernacki
Zagreb 2018 (9)

**1.d4 &f6 2.c4 c5 3.d5 e6 4.&c3
exd5 5.cxd5 d6 6.&f3 g6 7.h3
&g7 8.e4 a6 9.a4 &bd7 10.&d3
&h5 11.g4** 11.&e3!? is very rarely
played but is a refined way to meet
Black's set-up. Anticipating Black's
next move ...&e5, White waits with
kingside castling so that ...&h4
after the eventual exchange on h5
will have less effect: 11...&e5 12.&e2
&xf3+ 13.&xf3 0-0!? (the problem
with 13...&f6 is that White has the
strong central break 14.e5! dxe5
15.&xc5+) 14.&xh5 gxh5 15.&xh5
f5 (maybe Black should try to
insert 15...&b6!? 16.&c1 f5) 16.&h6
and in the game Siebrecht-Reich,
Germany Bundesliga 2009/10,
instead of 16...&e8?! 17.&g5 &g6
18.&xg6 hxg6 19.&xg7 &xg7
20.0-0±, when Black had nothing
to show for his lost pawn in the
ensuing endgame, he should have
opted for a middlegame with
16...&f6 17.&xg7 &xg7 18.0-0
&d7, planning to harass White's
queen after ...&f8-f6...&a8-f8,
...&f6-h6(g6). White is still
better but Black has practical
counterchances. **11...&hf6 12.&f4
&e7**

13.0-0
A) Or 13.&d2 &e5 14.&xe5 &xe5
15.&c4 &e7 16.f4 &d7 17.&f3 0-0
18.0-0 &b8 19.&fe1?! (the wrong
rook! ≥ 19.&g2! with next &ae1

with chances for both sides)
19...&d4+ 20.&g2 b6 21.&e2 &b7
22.g5? (the losing move, after
which White's kingside gets
overextended) 22...f6 23.h4 fxg5
24.hxg5 &e5! 25.&xe5 &xe5–+
26.f5 &xg5+ 27.&f1 &be8 28.&g2
&f6 29.&e2 &xc3 30.bxc3 &xc3
31.&h1 c4 0-1 Liu Yi-P.Karthikeyan,
Sydney 2012;
B) After 13.&f1 0-0 14.&g2?
(Van Wely-Roberson, chess.
com rapid 2018) Black should
go for 14...h5 15.g5 (15.&g5 &e8
16.&f4 &e7 leads to a draw by
move repetition) 15...&e8!? with a
set-up already seen by IM Martin
Gonzalez Angel in the previous
correspondence game.
13...h5 Black should go for this
break before castling with the
h-file still open; ≤ 13...0-0. **14.g5**
A) 14.&e1?! with the threat e4-e5
is easily parried with 14...0-0
15.e5 &xe5 16.&xe5 dxe5 17.&xe5
(Melone-Piscopo, Bratto 2010)
17...&d6!?∓;
B) 14.e5!? is a direct attempt to
refute Black's set-up. In fact it
occurred in the first game where
the Accelerated Benoni set-up was
played by the late Polish/American
GM Wojtkiewicz. After 14...dxe5
15.d6 Wojo played 15...&d8 and
later went on to win but after
16.&e1 0-0 17.&g5! hxg4 18.hxg4
White has more than sufficient
compensation for the sacrificed
pawn, e.g. 18...&b6 19.&e4 &xg4?
20.a5 &c6 21.&c4 &gf6 22.&xf6+
&xf6 23.&xe5+− is one example
showing the strength of White's
set-up. Critical is 15...&xd6
16.&xe5 &xe5 17.&xe5 &c6 18.&e4
(18.g5? &xh3 19.f3 &xf1 20.&xf1
&f8! 21.gxf6 &xf6 is obviously
excellent for Black) 18...&xe4
19.&xg7 &xc3 20.&e1+. Most
probably Wojo had calculated
until this position and rejected it
so he went for 15...&d8 instead
of 15...&xd6, but in reality Black
is fine after the calm 20...&e4!
21.&xh8 hxg4 22.hxg4 &e6 23.f3
0-0-0= and if 24.&xe4 &xe4
25.fxe4 &xh8≌.

14...♘h7 15.h4 0-0 16.♗g3

White's minor pieces get exposed down the f-file after the superficial 16.♕d2?, which was played in the game Koelmans-Kuck, Maastricht 2012, and now 16...f6!∓ would have been a big problem for White.

16...f6? But now this move loses by force! ≥ 16...♘e5 17.♘xe5 ♗xe5 18.f4 (18.♗xe5 dxe5!∞ and White has to be careful about a possible sacrifice on g5) 18...♗d4+ 19.♔g2 f6 20.♕d2 fxg5 21.hxg5 ♗g4 22.♘e2 ♗g7 23.♖ae1 ♕d7 24.♘g1 ♕xa4 and one fascinating line could be 25.f5 ♕d4!⇄ when 26.f6?! is answered strongly with 26...c4!. **17.e5!** Black simply cracks on g6. **17...♘xe5 18.♘xe5 fxe5 19.♗xg6+– ... 1-0 (40)**

The bishop thrust 11.♗g5

Aleksey Goganov
Aleksandar Indjic
Yerevan 2014 (3)

1.d4 ♘f6 2.c4 c5 3.d5 e6 4.♘c3 exd5 5.cxd5 d6 6.e4 g6 7.h3 ♗g7 8.♘f3 a6 9.a4 ♘bd7 10.♗d3 ♘h5 11.♗g5 ♗f6 12.♗h6 Harmless is 12.♗xf6 which strengthens Black's control over the dark squares (f4): 12...♕xf6 13.0-0 0-0 14.♖e1 ♘e5 15.♘xe5 ♕xe5 16.♗f1 ♖b8 17.♕c2. We are following the game Mörling-Hillarp Persson, Tylosand 2015. Black could have continued with 17...♘f6!? 18.g3 g5 19.♕d2 ♗d7 with solid play because after 20.f4 gxf4 21.gxf4 Black always has 21...♕d4+. **12...♘e5**

13.♗e2
A) The sharp alternative is 13.g4 ♘g7 (or 13...♘xf3+ 14.♕xf3 ♘g7

15.♕g3 0-0 16.♗f4 ♘e8 17.0-0 ♖b8 18.♖fe1 g5!? 19.♗d2 ♗e5 20.f4 gxf4 21.♗xf4 f6 as in the game Landa-Yilmaz, Baku 2012, and here best would have been 22.♗xe5 fxe5 23.♖f1 ♘g7 24.♖xf8+ ♕xf8 25.♕h4 ♗d7 26.♗e2 ♕d8 27.♕xd8+ ♖xd8 28.♖a3! ♗c8 29.♖b3 with a small but lasting initiative for White in the arisen endgame) 14.0-0 0-0 15.♔g2 ♘xf3 16.♕xf3 ♗e5 17.♗f4 (on 17.♕e3 Black would continue with 17...f5∞) 17...f6 18.a5 ♗d7 (Black has fully equalized) 19.♗xe5? (opening the f-file and leaving a weak square on f4 will have dire consequences for White) 19...fxe5 20.♕e2 ♕g5 21.♔h2T (or 21.♕e3 ♖f4 22.♘e2 h5 23.♘xf4 exf4 24.♕c1□ (immediately losing was 24.♕e2? hxg4 25.hxg4 ♗xg4 26.f3 ♗xf3+! 27.♔xf3 ♕g3#) 24...hxg4 25.h4 ♕f6 when Black's attack should prevail) 21...h5→ (worthy of attention was 21...♘h5!? 22.gxh5 ♗xh3 23.f4□ (23.♔xh3? ♖f4 with mate to follow) 23...♖xf4 24.♖xf4 exf4 25.♕f3 ♗g4 26.♕f2 ♕xh5+ 27.♔g1 ♖f8 and due to his strong kingside pawn avalanche Black is clearly better) 22.f3 ♖f4 23.♘d1? (the losing move; more resilient was 23.♕g2 ♖af8 24.♗e2∓) 23...hxg4 24.hxg4 ♗xg4! 25.fxg4 ♕h4+ 0-1 Garrido Legarreta-Lalic, Bilbao 2013;

B) 13.♘xe5 ♗xe5 14.♕d2!

is at the moment the greatest concern for Black in this set-up:
   B1) The problem with 14...♕f6 is that White can embark on a very promising pawn sacrifice with 15.♘e2!? ♗xb2 16.♖a2 ♗e5 17.♗g5 ♕g7 18.g4± with f2-f4 to follow;
   B2) So far 14...♘g7 had been Black's more reliable plan,

---

followed by castling kingside and ...f7-f5, but the recent online game Shoshin-Fier, Sunway Sitges 2020, had casted doubt on Black's set-up; White castled queenside and started a kingside attack with 15.0-0-0! (the normal plan is connected with kingside castling. Rather important is the following game: 15.0-0-0 14.f4 ♗d4+ 17.♔h2 ♗d7 18.♘e2 ♗f6 19.g4 ♕b6 20.g5 ♕xb2 21.♕xb2 ♗xb2 22.♖ab1 ♗a3 23.♖xb7 ♖fd8 24.f5, Krasenkow-Indjic, Warsaw 2014, in which one possible line is 24...♖ab8! 25.♗xa6 gxf5!? 26.exf5 ♗b2 27.f6 ♘f5 28.a5 ♖xb7 29.♗xb7 ♖e8 30.♖f2 ♗e3 31.a6 ♖a3 32.♗c6 ♗c8 33.♗b7 ♗d7 with move repetition in this rather picturesque position where the activity of Black's pieces saves the day) 15...0-0 16.f4 ♗f6 17.g4→ b5⇄ and now White should have continued with 18.e5! dxe5 19.g5 ♗e7 20.fxe5 b4 21.♘e4 ♕xd5 22.♘f6+ ♗xf6 23.gxf6. Black loses material while his attack on the queenside does not seem sufficient. One possible line is 23...♖e8 24.♗xg7 ♕a2 25.♗f8! ♕a1+ 26.♔c2 ♗c2 b3+ 27.♔c3 ♕xa4 28.♗xc5 ♗b7 29.♗c4 ♗xh1 30.♖xh1 ♕a5+ 31.♔b4 ♕xe5+ 32.♔xb3 ♖ab8 33.♔a2+– and after these enormous complications White's two bishops are clearly stronger than Black's rook;
   B3) 14...f5 also seems insufficient after 15.exf5 ♗xf5 16.♗xf5 gxf5 17.g4 f4 (thanks to the tactical cheapo of trapping the bishop on h6, by a miracle Black stays alive) 18.♘e4! (18.gxh5 ♕f6 is equal; 18.h4 ♕f6 19.♗g5 ♕f7 20.gxh5 h6 21.♘e4 ♔d7!= (21...hxg5? 22.hxg5 ♖xh5 23.♘xd6+! ♗xd6 24.♕e2++–)) 18...♕f6 19.♘g5 ♕b6 20.♗g7 ♖g8 21.♗xf6 ♗xf6 22.♘e6 ♕xb2 23.♕xb2 ♗xb2 24.♖b1☒ ♗c3+ 25.♔e2 ♖b8 26.♖hc1 ♗e5 27.a5±. Black is temporarily a pawn up, but this endgame is no fun for him to play. The pawn on f4 is weak while White's knight on e6 is a monster piece. Also the

pawn on b7 is weak, and White has the clear plan of ♖b1-b6 and ♖c1-b1.

13...♘xf3+ 14.♗xf3 ♗g5!? This newer attempt seems more active to me than the more often played solid 14...♗g7 15.0-0 0-0 16.♕d2 ♖b8, against which White can continue with the usual nagging plan 17.♖ab1! b5 18.axb5 axb5 19.b4 c4 20.♖d1±. Black has a passed c-pawn which is however well-blocked, while White continues with the usual pressure along the a-file with ♖a1-a5, ♖fa1 etc.

15.♗xg5 ♕xg5 16.♕d2

A) Or 16.♗xh5 gxh5 17.♕f3 0-0 18.0-0 ♗d7 19.♖fe1 f6 20.a5 ♖ae8 21.♗e3 h4 22.♖ae1 ♘e5= and Black has nothing to complain of, Semcesen-Hillarp Persson, Sunne 2015;

B) 16.h4 ♕e5 17.♗xh5 gxh5 18.0-0 ♖g8 19.f4 ♕g7 20.♕c2 ♗h3 21.♖f2 0-0-0 led to a quite murky position in the game Kunin-Kislinsky, Orlova 2015, in which White had the better pawn structure but Black had some counterplay along the g-file.

16...♘f4 17.0-0-0 ♘d3+ 18.♔b1 ♕xd2 19.♖xd2 ♘e5 20.♗e2 g5 21.a5 ♗d7 22.h4 g4!= By keeping the knight on e5 Black has nothing to worry about in this endgame. The position is about equal, but after... **23.h5?!** This pawn was rather exposed and weak, and Black eventually won on move 70.

0-1

Michal Krasenkow
Oliver Kurmann
Germany Bundesliga B 2012/13 (3)

1.♘f3 ♘f6 2.d4 e6 3.c4 c5 4.d5 exd5 5.cxd5 g6 6.♘c3 d6 7.h3 a6

8.a4 ♗g7 9.e4 ♘bd7 10.♗d3 ♘h5 11.♗g5 11.♗e2!?.

This prophylactic move has recently been scoring excellently for White. In anticipation of Black's next move ...♘e5 White retreats the bishop.

A) Black faces some problems after 11...0-0 12.0-0 ♖e8 13.♗g5! ♗f6 (although possible, 13...♕b6 14.♕c2 doesn't look trustworthy because White has the clear plan of ♘f3-d2-c4 etc.) 14.♗h6±. Practice has shown that White keeps a small but lasting advantage and if Black tries to win a pawn after 14...♗xc3 15.bxc3 ♘hf6 16.♗d3 ♘xe4 17.c4, later he will suffer along the a1-h8 diagonal and White has more than sufficient compensation for the sacrificed pawn;

B) After 11...h6 12.0-0 ♕f6 White should go for 13.g3!N (instead of the already played 13.e5), followed by ♔g2, after which Black's queen will have to sadly retreat to either d8 or e7. White is clearly better;

C) 11...♘e5!? 12.♘xe5 ♗xe5 13.♗xh5 gxh5 14.♕xh5 ♕f6 15.♕f3 (I think more natural is 15.0-0 ♕g6! 16.♖xg6 hxg6 after which Black's pair of bishops should be enough compensation to hold this endgame. Of course it is clear that Black's winning chances in this line are close to zero but as a drawing weapon I think it is quite okay!) 15...♕xf3 16.gxf3 f5 17.♘d1 (Jakovenko-Dubov, Satka 2018) and now best for Black seems to be 17...♗d7! 18.♘e3 (against 18.♗d2 Black continues 18...fxe4 19.fxe4 ♖f8 because if 20.♗c3, Black has a strong reply in 20...♖f4!=, recovering the pawn with good play) 18...fxe4 19.fxe4 b5 20.axb5

♗xb5 21.♘f5 ♗d7 – Black has definite compensation and is not worse. **11...♗f6 12.♗e3 ♘e5** 12...0-0 13.0-0 ♖e8 is the other main option for Black, but the text is more in the spirit of the Accelerated Benoni where Black plays a quick ...♘e5 before castling kingside. The most successful plan for White was 14.♘d2, intending f2 f4 (11.a5 led to equal play after 14...♖b8 15.♕c2 ♘e5 16.♗e2 ♘xf3+ 17.♗xf3 ♘g7 18.♗f4 b5 19.axb6 ♖xb6 20.♖a2 ♗d4 21.♘e2 ♗e5 22.♗xe5 ♖xe5 23.♘f4 ♗d7 24.♖fa1 ♗b5 25.♗e2 ♕f6 26.♗xb5 ♕xf4 27.♗d3 f5= in Navara-Ivanchuk, Wijk aan Zee 2012), 14...♘d4!? 15.♖e1 ♘e5 16.♘f3 ♗xe3 17.♖xe3 ♖b8 18.♗f1 and now in the game Kholopov-Kurmann, Sitges 2015, the simple 18...♗d7, intending ...b7-b5, would have equalized. **13.♗e2 ♘xf3+ 14.♗xf3 ♘g7 15.0-0 0-0 16.♕d2**

16...♗e5! Black is looking for some counterplay by means of ...f7-f5. 16...♗d7 was seen in the game Blagojevic-Ivanisevic, Podgorica 2011, which continued 17.♖ab1 b5 18.axb5?! (there was no need to help Black by opening the a-file. White wrongly feared the loss of an exchange for a pawn after 18.b4!↑ cxb4 19.♖xb4 a5 but then rather strong is 20.♖xb5□ ♗xb5 (or 20...♗xc3 21.♕xc3 ♗xb5 22.axb5 f5 23.b6± when White's passed b-pawn becomes a rather annoying factor) 21.♘xb5 ♗e5 22.♘a7! followed by the transfer of the knight to c6, which leaves White very comfortable) 18...axb5 19.b4 ♖a3 20.♖fc1 c4 21.♗g4 ♗xg4 22.hxg4 ♕d7 23.♗d4 ♗xd4 24.♕xd4 ♖fa8 (24...h5!? with the

idea to immediately activate the knight on g7 was interesting too) 25.♕b6? (25.e5! dxe5 26.♕xe5 ♕xg4 27.♘xb5∞) 25...♕xg4 26.♘xb5 ♘h5!→ (suddenly Black's dormant knight springs to life with devastating effect) 27.♘xa3 ♘f4! 28.g3 ♖xa3−+.

17.♗d1

A) The alternative is 17.♗f4 f6 (or 17...♕e7 18.♖fe1 ♗d7 19.a5 ♖ab8 20.♗e2 f6 21.♗e3 f5 22.f4 ♗xc3 23.bxc3 fxe4 24.g4♗ ♘e8 25.♖ab1 ♘f6 26.♔h2 h5 27.♔g3 ♔f7 28.♖f1 ♖h8 (Fridman-Eljanov, Natanya rapid 2009) and here White had to play 29.g5∞) 18.♖fe1 ♗d7 19.♗g4 ♗xg4 20.hxg4 h5!⇄ (activating Black's knight on g7!) 21.gxh5 ♘xh5 22.♗e2 ♖f7 23.♖a3 ♖h7 24.♖h3 ♘xf4 25.♘xf4 ♗xf4 26.♕xf4 ♖xh3 27.gxh3 ♕e7 28.♖e3 ½-½ Sundararajan-Asis Gargatagli, Montcada y Reixac 2009;

B) 17.♗e2 f5 18.f4 ♗xc3 19.♕xc3 fxe4 20.b4?! (20.g4□, restricting Black's knight on g7) 20...b6?! (20... cxb4! 21.♕xb4 ♘f5↑) 21.a5? (21. g4□) 21...♘f5! 22.axb6 cxb4 23.♕b3 ♘xe3 24.♕xe3 ♖b8−+ and Black later converted his advantage into a win in Savola-Mertanen, Jyväskylä 2010.

17...f5 18.f4 ♗xc3 19.bxc3 fxe4 20.g4♗

Restricting the knight on g7. The pair of bishops gives White the usual compensation for a sacrificed pawn but hardly more than that. **20...♗d7 21.a5 ♗b5** 21...♖b8!? with the idea ...b7-b5. **22.♗e2 ♗xe2 23.♕xe2 b5 24.axb6 ♕xb6 25.♖fb1 ♕a7 26.♖a4 ♖fb8 27.♖ba1 ♖b6?** Too passive. Correct was 27...♕b7!, attacking the pawn on d5, thus forcing White to

play c3-c4, which helps Black because the 3rd rank is opened after Black's rook lands on b3, e.g. 28.c4 h5⇄ 29.♗f2 ♕e7 30.♖xa6 ♖xa6 31.♖xa6 ♖b3∞. **28.♖xe4 ♕b7 29.♕d3 ♖b8 30.♖e1 ♕f7 31.♗d2 ♖e8 32.♖xe8+ ♘xe8 33.c4** White has recovered the sacrificed pawn and stands clearly better now because his bishop is dominating Black's knight **... 1-0 (45)**

**Michel Dard
Franjo Lovakovic**
cr 2010

1.d4 ♘f6 2.c4 c5 3.d5 e6 4.♘c3 exd5 5.cxd5 d6 6.e4 g6 7.♗d3 ♗g7 8.h3 a6 9.a4 ♘bd7 10.♘f3 ♘h5!? 11.0-0 ♘e5 12.♗e2 12.♘xe5 ♗xe5 13.f4 (or 13.♘e2 ♕h4 14.f4 ♗g7 15.♕e1 ♕xe1 16.♖xe1 0-0 17.♖b1?! (≥ 17.g4!) 17...♗d7 (≥ 17... f5!⇄) 18.a5? ♗b5! 19.♗xb5 axb5 20.♗d2 b4 21.g4 ♘f6 22.♘g3 ♖xa5 with an extra pawn for Black and a winning position endgame, Stepanyan-Lalic, Lichess blitz 2020) 13...♗d4+ 14.♔h2 ♕h4

15.♕e1!. This computer recommendation seems at the moment to be the main problem for Black in this line. I even had to face it in a recent online blitz tournament (3 minutes plus 2 extra seconds per move) in which I was lucky to escape with a draw from a much inferior position. 15...♕xe1 16.♖xe1 and now:

A) 16...♗d7?!, planning queenside castling, backfired in the game Ipatov-Indjic, Kochaeli 2013, which continued 17.g4

♘f6 18.♗e3 0-0-0? 19.♗xd4 cxd4 20.♗e2 ♖de8 21.♘xd4 ♖e7 22.♘e2 followed by ♘c3, with a clear pawn up which White later converted into a win;

B) 16...♗f2!? 17.♖f1 ♗g3+ 18.♔g1 0-0± might be Black's best bet in this endgame (18...f5? 19.e5 dxe5 20.fxe5 b6 21.♗d2± ♔d7? (21...♗b7 22.♗c4 0-0-0 23.e6±) 22.♗xf5+! gxf5 23.♖xf5 ♘g7 24.♖g5 ♗xe5 25.♖xe5 and White soon won in Sobek-Klima, Karvina 2012) 19.♘e2 f5? (≥ 19...♖e8! and if 20.♘xg3 ♘xg3 21.♖e1 ♗f5 22.♖e3 ♘xe4 23.g4 it looks as if Black is losing material, but he has a fantastic tactical resource which saves him from defeat: 23...♘d2!! 24.♖xe8+ ♖xe8 25.gxf5 ♘b3! followed by ...♖e1+) 20.e5! dxe5 21.♘xg3 ♘xg3 22.fxe5 ♘xf1 23.♗xf1.

Another picturesque position. White has sacrificed a full exchange for the pawn duo on d5 and e5 which completely restricts Black's bishop on c8. The late World Champion Petrosian would have been quite excited! 23...f4 24.e6 ♖b8 25.a5! g5 26.♗c4 ♖f6 (Black is completely tied up) 27.b3 b5 28.axb6 ♖xb6 29.♗a3 ♖b5 (desperation) 30.♖e1 ♔f8 31.d6 1-0 Shen Yue-Garcia Perez, Salobrena 2012;

C) 16...0-0 17.g4 ♘g7 18.♔g3 (also very good for White is 18.♘e2!?) 18...♖e8 (stronger was 18...f5!? in order to get some breathing space because if 19.e5?! dxe5 20.fxe5 fxg4 Black is threatening 21...♗f2+) 19.♘e2 ♗f6 20.g5?! (too impatient; ≥ 20.♘g1!± with the idea ♘f3) 20...♗d8 21.♗d2 f5! 22.♘c3 fxe4 23.♘xe4 ♗f5+ 24.♔g2 ♗d7 25.♗c3 ♖c8= Barceloski-Lalic, Lichess blitz 2020.

12...♘xf3+ 13.♗xf3 ♕h4!

14.♗e3 14.♗xh5 gxh5↑ 15.♘e2! (15.♕d3? ♖g8 16.♔h1 ♗d7 17.f4 c4 18.♕f3 ♗d4 19.♗e3 (19.♘e2 ♗g4 20.♕g3 ♖xg3 21.♘xg3 ♗xh3! 22.♔h2 ♗xg2 23.♔xg2 h4–+) 19...♖g3 20.♗xd4 (Dziuba-Wojtaszek, Warsaw rapid 2005) 20...♗xh3 21.♔g1 ♗xg2 22.♕xg2 0-0-0 23.♖f2 ♖dg8 24.♘e2 ♖3g4!–+ with the idea ...♕h3!) 15...♖g8 16.♖a3 ♗e5 17.♕d3 (17.♔h1? ♕xe4 18.♘f4 (18.♘g3? from the well-known game Skembris-Wojtaszek, Greece tt 2006, could have lost on the spot after 18...♗xh3! 19.♘xe4 ♗xg2+ 20.♔g1 ♗f3+ 21.♗g5 ♗xd1–+) 18...♗f5 19.♖e1 ♕c2 20.♕xc2 ♗xc2∓ due to his strong bishop pair, Van Hoolandt-A.Kovacevic, Khanty-Mansiysk 2010) 17...c4 (17...f5? 18.f4 fxe4 (Lazarev-Oleksienko, Al-Ain rapid 2014) and White missed an easy win with 19.♕xe4 ♗xh3 20.♖xh3 ♕xh3 21.fxe5 0-0-0 22.e6+– etc.) 18.♕e3 c3

19.♔h1! (19.♖xc3?! ♗xc3 20.bxc3 ♗xh3□ (20...♕xh3? 21.♘g3!N (21.♘f4? ♕xe3 22.♗xe3⩲ Gouchard-Marzolo, France tt 2009) 21...♕g4 22.e5 ♗d7 23.exd6+ ♔d8 24.♕b6+ ♔e8□ 25.♖e1+ ♔f8 26.♗h6++–) 21.♘f4 ♗xg2 22.♘xg2 ♕g4N 23.♕g3 ♕xg3 24.fxg3 ♖xg3 25.♗f4 (25.♗e3!?±) 25...♖xc3 26.♗xd6 ♖ac8= with the idea ...♖c1. Due to the reduced material, Black should be able to hold this endgame) 19...cxb2 20.♗d2!± and as was already shown in the Forum Section of Yearbook 126 (page 15) in the comments to Vi.Zhakhartsov-Zeller, Dresden 2017, Black is indeed in great peril due to the unsafe position of his monarch. **14...♘f4!** 14...♗e5?! 15.♖e1! ♘f4 16.g3! ♘xh3+ 17.♔g2 ♕d8 18.♗g4 ♘g5 19.♗d2! ♗xc3 (19...f6 20.f4 ♗xc3 21.♗xc3 ♘f7 22.♗e6↑) 20.bxc3 f6 (20...h6 21.c4±) 21.♗xg5 fxg5 22.e5 0-0 23.e6 ♕e7±. **15.♖e1!?**
A) 15.♕d2!?;

B) 15.♗g4?! ♗xg4 16.♕xg4 (16.hxg4 g5!∓) 16...♕xg4 17.hxg4 ♘d3∓;
C) 15.g3 ♘xh3+ 16.♔h2!? (16.♔g2 ♕d8∓) 16...♗e5 17.♔g2 ♗e7 18.♗g4 ♗xc3! 19.♗xc8 (19.bxc3!? ♘g5 20.♗xg5 ♕xg5 21.♗xc8 ♖xc8 22.f4 ♕d8∓) 19...♗xc8 20.♕g4 f5! 21.exf5 ♗e5 22.♕xh3 (22.fxg6 ♕d7∓) 22...0-0 23.fxg6 hxg6∞.
15...0-0 16.♕d2 16.♗g4? ♘xg2! 17.♔xg2 f5–+ 16.♗g5!? Or 16...♗e5 17.♘e2 ♘xe2+ (or 17...g5 18.♗g3 (18.♖a3!?) 18...♖b8= 19.♘f5 ♗xf5 20.exf5 ♖fe8=) 18.♖xe2 ♗e7 19.♗g5 (19.♖c1 b5=) 19...f6∞ and again Black is solid. **17.♘e2 ♘xe2+** 17...♗e5 18.♘g3 ♖b8= 19.♘f5 ♗xf5 20.exf5 ♖fe8∞ deserved attention. **18.♖xe2** Black is also fine after 18.♗xe2 h6 19.f4 ♖e8! 20.e5!? gxf4 21.♗f2 ♕g5! 22.h4!? (22.exd6?! ♗xh3 23.♗f3 ♗e5 24.♗xc5 ♖ac8 25.♗b4 ♗d7∓) 22...♕d8 23.exd6 ♕xd6 24.♖ac1 ♗d7 25.♗xc5 ♕f6∞. **18...h6 19.e5** After 19.♖c1 Black should prevent White's queenside minority attack with the thematic 19...a5!∞. If 19.a5!? ♗e5 20.♖c1 ♗d7 21.b4 c4! 22.♗d4 ♗f4 23.♗e3 (23.♕e1 ♖xc1 24.♕xc1 f6∞) 23...♗e5=. **19...♗xe5 20.♗xc5 ♗f4 21.♗e3 ♗e5∞ 22.♗b6 ♗f5 23.♖xe5!? dxe5 24.d6♕ e4 25.♕d4** 25.♗g4 ♗xg4 26.hxg4 ♕xg4 27.d7 ♖fd8=. **25...♖fe8!** Now the greedy 25...exf3? loses to 26.♕f6! and 27.♗d4. **26.♗e2 ♗d7=** ... ½-½ **(35)**

Exercise 1

position after 32.♘e3-c2

How can Black convert his initiative?
(*solutions on page 253*)

Exercise 2

position after 26.♘c3xb5

How should Black react to the attack on the a3-rook?

Exercise 3

position after 27.♖b1-a1

How can Black organize counterplay?

Benoni Defence   Benko/Volga Gambit   BI 25.3 (A58)

Is it all over for the Perunovic Benko? – Part II

by Tibor Karolyi

1.	d4	♘f6
2.	c4	c5
3.	d5	b5
4.	cxb5	a6
5.	bxa6	g6
6.	♘c3	♗g7
7.	e4	0-0
8.	♘f3	

In Part I of this mini-series in Yearbook 135 we covered the very ambitious 8.e5 and Blübaum's 8.a7 ♖xa7 9.♘f3 against the Perunovic Benko. However, White's main move by far is 8.♘f3, continuing his kingside development.

Jan Willem van de Griendt

Early divergences
Here Black rarely plays anything else than 8...♛a5.
8...e6 is a rare bird indeed, although there is certainly logic behind opening the centre. White failed to find the right solution to the central problems after 9.♗e3 exd5.

In Game 1, played in the Dutch club cup, 10.e5? was refuted by 10...d4! 11.exf6 ♛xf6. White should choose between 10.exd5, 10.♘xd5 and the intermediate move 10.a7!?.
Instead, 8...d6 just gives a few more options to White for free (Game 2). Sometimes the queen is also placed on b6, which works all right in several Benko lines, but not here. For example Nguyen was able to build up on outpost on b5 against Bartholomew and obtained a nice advantage. If Black delays ...♛a5, White can do without ♗d2 and this means he can play for e4-e5, which seems to give him an edge, as Atalik nicely demonstrated against Swapnil. In other games Black players have scored all right, but their White opponents had chances to obtain an advantage.

On 8...♕a5 White should close the diagonal, as after 9.♗d3?! ♘xd5! 10.exd5 ♗xc3+ White has to be very careful. Gelfand took the bishop and lost in a blitzkrieg way to Carlsen in a rapid event. Even Jack Rudd's improvement 15.♗b1! is not enough to equalize after the novelty 15...♕b3!. 11.♗d2 or 11.♘d2 (Game 3) is indicated, but still more pleasant for Black.

White blocks the diagonal with his knight
9.♘d2 was Karpov's choice in his rapid match versus Vaisser in 2017 (Game 4).

After 9...♗xa6 10.♗xa6 ♕xa6, 11.a4 does not look quick enough. The 12th World Champion played 11.♕e2 twice. In the first game, Vaisser took, and was beaten fairly convincingly. 11...e6 was Vaisser's improvement. This line looks pleasant for Black.
White can also play 10.♗e2 (Game 5). Here Black has several choices: 10...♘h5 is interesting, but 10...♗xe2 11.♕xe2 ♕a6 is dubious. The standard 10...e6 doesn't work well for Black as he has no play against the d5-pawn.
Black can play conventionally with 10...d6 (Game 6). After 11.0-0, 10...♗xe2 helps White develop. On 11...♘bd7, 12.♘c4 seems pretty simple as it is likely to get White the bishop pair.
11.a4 aims to block the queenside on b5, and Black has not found a fully adequate

answer to this yet. Black players more often play 11...♘fd7, which works fine against 12.♗xa6. However White can play the awkward 12.♘db1, when it is not clear what is Black's best reply. The moves that have been tried do not look nice; maybe my 12th move suggestion should be tested. Playing for the b5-square with 12.a4 doesn't look dangerous for Black, as in the game Ipatov-Tregubov.

White blocks the diagonal with his bishop
White more often blocks the diagonal with 9.♗d2.

After 9...♗xa6 10.♗xa6?! ♕xa6 11.♕e2 e6 White has to be careful not to get into trouble (Game 7). Black can also employ 11...d6. Game 8 shows there is nothing wrong with this.
Now White can just develop with 10.♗e2 and after 10...d6 11.0-0 ♘bd7 he has several options.

On 12.♖e1, 12...♖fb8 looks the better choice; this looks fine for Black. 12.♗xa6

♕xa6 13.h3 followed by slowly gaining space on the queenside seems to give White a small edge. Kazhgaleyev played 12.a4 against Ponomariov in 2017 and got a clear edge (Game 9). One year later, Novikov deviated against Levin, but his idea also doesn't equalize.
Black can play 11...♗xe2 12.♕xe2 ♕a6.

Here, 13.♘b5 or 13.♕xa6 offers White little hope for an advantage, while on 13.♖fe1 both 13...♘bd7 and 13...♕xe2 provide even chances for Black (Game 10). White can try 13.♕d1; on 13...♘bd7 Batchuluun played 14.h3 against Batchimeg in 2016 and got an edge by concentrating on the queenside. In 2019, Castrillon Gomez tried to improve against Nechaeva, but he also failed to equalize. Black can play 13...♕d3 as well and after 14.♘e1 ♕a6 15.♕c2 ♘bd7 16.♘f3 choose between 16...♖fb8 and 16...♘g4. On first 17.h3, 17...♘h5 with ...♘e5 is very interesting, while 17...♘e8 looks worse for Black. After 17.a4, 17...♖b4 looks the best. In Moradiabadi-Zaragatski (2016) Black did fine in the game; the line depends on this move. I suggest an improvement for White. Bologan tried 16...♘g4 against Wojtaszek (Game 11), but he failed to equalize.

Conclusion
On the one hand, 8.♘f3 is by far the most common reply against the set-up with an early kingside castling in the Benko Gambit, but the success rate of this move is the only one below 50 per cent! This is hard to explain.
White has to choose between blocking the diagonal by putting his knight on d2 (Karpov's preference in 2017!) or the bishop. White may retain some advantage in either line.

Enrico van Egmond   **1**
Jan Willem van de Griendt
Netherlands tt 2019/20 (3)
1.d4 ♘f6 2.c4 c5 3.d5 b5 4.cxb5 a6 5.bxa6 g6 6.♘c3 ♗g7 7.e4 0-0 8.♘f3 White decides not to refute Black's set-up, but to calmly develop his pieces. **8...e6 9.♗e3** 9.♗e2 ♗xa6 (9...exd5 10.exd5 ♗xa6 11.♗xa6 ♘xa6 12.0-0 d6 was slightly better for White in Cvitan-Sydoryka, Internet blitz 2020) 10.0-0 exd5 11.exd5 ♖e8 12.♗e3?! (12.♖e1±) 12...♘g4! 13.♗xa6 ♘xe3 14.fxe3 ♖xa6♕ (Kolasinski-Duda, Zgierz rapid 2018) 15.d6!?. **9...exd5**

10.e5? A poor solution to the central problems. 10.a7!? d4 (10...♖xa7 11.e5 (11.♗xc5?! is risky because of the tactical shot 11...♘xe4! 12.♘xe4 dxe4 13.♘d2 (13.♗xa7? exf3 14.♕d2 ♖e8+ 15.♗e3 d5 16.gxf3 ♘c6−+) 13...♘c6 14.♗xa7 ♘xa7 with tremendous compensation) 11...d4 12.♘xd4 cxd4 13.♗xd4 ♖b7 (13...♖a6 14.♗xa6

♗xa6 15.exf6 ♖e8+ 16.♗e3 ♗xf6 17.♕b3 ♗xc3+ 18.bxc3± and Black's compensation is not quite enough) 14.exf6 ♗xf6 15.♗xf6 ♕xf6 16.♕d2 d5 17.♗e2 d4 18.♘d5 ♕e5 19.♘f4 ♖e8 20.0-0 d3 21.♗xd3 ♖xb2 22.♕e1±) 11.axb8♕ ♖xb8 12.♘xd4 cxd4 13.♗xd4 ♘xe4 (alternatively, Black may investigate 13...♖e8; 13...♖xb2; or 13...d5) 14.♗xg7 (14.♘xe4 ♖b4 15.♗xg7 ♖xe4+ 16.♗e2 ♗a6 17.♗xf8 ♗xe2 18.♕xe2 ♕a5+=) 14...♖e8 15.♗e2 ♔xg7 16.0-0 ♖xb2 17.♕c1=; 10.exd5 ♘g4!?∞; 10.♘xd5 ♘xe4 11.♗d3 ♘f6 12.♘xf6+ ♗xf6 13.0-0-0∞. **10...d4! 11.exf6 ♕xf6 12.♘d5** 12.♖c1 ♗xa6 13.♘d5 ♕d6 14.♗xa6 ♘xa6 15.♘f4 ♕e7 16.0-0 dxe3 17.♘d5 exf2+ 18.♖xf2 ♕d8∓ **12...♕d6 13.♘f4**

♕e7 14.♘d5 ♕e4 Cementing Black's central superiority. **15.♕b3** 15.♗c4 ♗xa6 (15...dxe3 16.♘xe3 ♗xa6∓) 16.♘g5 ♕e5 17.f4 ♕e8∓. **15...dxe3 16.♗d3** The only way to get his kingside development going. **16...exf2+ 17.♔xf2 ♗d4+ 18.♔g3 ♗e5+ 19.♔f2 ♗d4+ 20.♔g3 ♕e6!** Obviously Black is not interested in a repetition of moves! **21.♘xd4 cxd4** 21...♕d6+!? 22.♘f4 ♕xd4 23.♕d5 ♘c6 24.♕xd4 ♘xd4∓. **22.♖hf1 ♕e5+** Perhaps slightly inaccurate, because it invites White to occupy the open e-file with tempo. With 22...♘xa6 23.♗c4 ♕d6+ 24.♔f2 ♖b8 25.♕a3 ♕xa3 26.bxa3 ♖b2+ 27.♔g1 ♗b7 (27...♘c5!?) 28.♖ab1 ♖xb1 29.♖xb1 ♗xd5 30.♗xd5 ♘c5∓. Black continues to call the shots. **23.♔f2 ♗xa6?** The wrong capture altogether. 23...♘xa6! 24.♖ae1 ♕d6 25.♗c4 (25.♔g1 would have allowed the effective jump 25...♘c5! 26.♘f6+ (26.♖f6 ♘e6∓) 26...♕xf6 27.♖xf6 ♘xb3 28.axb3 d5∓ with a pawn-up ending) and with the rook on e1 rather than a1, 25...♖b8 26.♕d3 ♘c7 loses most of its power due to 27.♘xc7 (27.♘e7+ ♔g7 28.♘xc8 ♖fxc8 29.♔g1 ♘e6 30.b3∓) 27...♖xb2+ 28.♔g1 ♗b7 and suddenly there is 29.♗xf7+! ♖xf7 30.♖e8+ ♔g7 31.♖xf7+ ♔xf7 32.♕c4+ ♔f6 33.♖e6+ ♕xe6 34.♘xe6 ♖xg2+ 35.♔f1 dxe6 36.♕xd4+ ♔f5 and White can still try. **24.♖ae1!** A crucial gain of time. The cautious 24.♔g1 allows for an undesirable exchange of queens. After 24...♗xd3 25.♘f6+ ♔g7 26.♕xd3 ♕e3+ 27.♕xe3 dxe3 28.♘d5= the e-pawn will fall. **24...♕xh2** The black king won't survive after the retreat 24...♕d6 25.♔g1 ♗xd3 26.♘f6+ e.g. 26...♔h8 (now 26...♔g7 can be met by 27.♘e8+! ♖xe8 28.♖xf7+ ♔h6 29.♖xe8) 27.♕xd3 ♘c6 28.♕h3! (a characteristic geometrical motif) 28...h5 29.g4 ♔g7 30.gxh5 ♖h8 31.♕f3 ♖hf8 32.♖e8! (a nice touch; inverting the moves does not work in view of 32.♘e8+? ♖axe8 33.♖xe8 ♘e5!= and White has to return

the exchange) 32...d3 33.♖xa8 ♖xa8 34.♘e8+! (the final solution) 34...♖xe8 35.♕xf7+ ♔h6 36.♕xe8 ♕d4+ 37.♖f2 and White wins. **25.♖h1 ♕d6**

26.♗xg6?? Flashy but unsound. 26.♗e4! (this option makes all the difference!) 26...♘c6 (26...♗b7 27.♕xb7 ♖a5 28.b4 (or 28.♘b4, retaining all the trump cards) 28...♖xa2+ 29.♔g1± and the extra piece counts for much more than the extra pawns) 27.♕h3 h5 28.♕xd7 (the typical petite combinaison) 28...♕xd7 29.♘f6+ ♔g7 30.♘xd7 ♘b4 31.♘xf8 ♖xf8 32.a3 f5 33.♖b1 ♘d5 34.♖e6 ♗c4 35.♖d6 with a technical win. **26...fxg6+!** Not afraid of ghosts. 26...hxg6?? 27.♕h3, mating; 26...♘c6 27.♖xh7+ ♔g7 28.♕f3+−. **27.♘f6+** Remember White was in check! **27...♔g7 28.♖xh7+ ♔xf6 29.♔g1 ♕f4?** The right defensive approach is 29...♘c6!, since there is no concrete threat. g5 is a relatively safe place for the black king with e5, e7 and f1 covered by the minor pieces. **30.♖ee7** 30.♕d5 ♘c6 31.♖xd7 ♘e5 32.♖d6+ ♔g7 33.♕xe5+ ♕xe5 34.♖xe5 ♖f1+ 35.♔h2 ♖f2−+; 30.♖h3! and Black has to return in his tracks (30...♕d6!), otherwise he loses a significant portion of his material advantage: 30...♕g5 (30...♘c6 31.♖f3) 31.♕f3+ ♔g7 32.♕xa8 and has to start winning all over again. **30...♔g5 31.♕d5+ ♖f5 32.♕xa8** One. **32...♕f1+** 32...♕g3−+; 32...d3−+. **33.♔h2 ♕f4+ 34.♔g1** Two. **34...♕c1+ 35.♔h2 ♕f4+ 36.♔g1** Three. **36...♕f2+ 37.♔h2 ♕f4+ 38.♔g1** Four. **38...♕f1+ 39.♔h2 ♕f4+ ½-½** 40.♔g1 would be five-fold repetition.

1.d4 ♘f6 2.c4 c5 3.d5 b5 4.cxb5 a6 5.bxa6 g6 6.♘c3 ♗g7 7.e4 0-0 8.♘f3 d6 8...♕b6 9.e5!? (9.♗e2 see Alvarez-Esquivias below) 9...♘g4 (9...♘e8 10.♕b3±) 10.♘d2 d6 11.e6±. **9.♗e2**

9...♕a5 Other moves are not appetizing:

A) 9...♘xa6 10.0-0 ♘c7 11.h3 ♖b8 12.♖e1 ♗b7 (Vallejo Pons-Cordova, Baku 2016) 13.a4 ♘d7 14.♗f4 ♗a6 15.♕d2 ♖b4 16.♗h6±;

B) 9...♗xa6 is the main move. Now 10.0-0:

B1) 10...♘bd7 11.♖b1 ♕a5 12.♗d2 (12.♗xa6 ♖xa6 13.♗d2 ♘g4 14.h3 ♘ge5 15.b3 ♗xf3+ 16.♗xf3 ♖b8±) 12...♖fb8 13.b3 ♖xe2 14.♕xe2 ♘e8 (14...♕a6 – exchanging queens allows Black to get closer to White's pawns: 15.♕xa6 ♖xa6 16.♖fc1 ♖a3 (16...♘g4 17.a4) 17.♖c2 ♘e8=) 15.♘a4 (15.♕e3!?) 15...♕a6 16.♕xa6 (16.♕e3!? ♘c7 (16...♘e5 17.♘xe5 ♗xe5 18.♗c3±) 17.♗c3 ♘b5 18.♗xg7 ♗xg7 19.e5 ♘d4 20.♘xd4 cxd4 21.♕xd4 dxe5 22.♕d2±) 16...♖xa6 17.♖bc1 ♘c7 18.♗c3 ♗h6 19.♗d2 ♗g7 (Oganian-M.Novikov, Kolomna 2016) 20.♖fe1 ♘b5 21.g3 h6=;

B2) 10...♕b6 11.♖b1 (11.h3 ♘bd7 12.♖b1 (12.♖e1 ♘e8 13.♗xa6 (13.a4 ♘c7 14.♖a3±) 13...♖xa6 14.♖e2 ♘c7 15.♗g5 e6 16.♕d3 ♗b7 17.♖d1±) 12...♖fb8 13.♗c2 (White is ready to lose a tempo by making two queen moves; 13.♗d2!?; 13.♖e1!?±) 13...♗xe2 14.♕xe2 ♘e8 15.♗d2 ♕a6 (15...♗xc3 16.♗xc3 ♖xa2 17.♕e3 ♘ef6 18.♘d2 ♗b5 19.b3±) 16.♕e3 ♘c7 17.a4 (17.b3 ♗xc3 18.♗xc3 ♕xa2 19.♘d2∞) 17...♖b3

18.♕g5 ♗f6 19.♕g4 ♘e5 20.♘xe5 ♗xe5= Alvarez Marquez-Esquivias Quintero, Seville 2017) 11...♘bd7 12.b3 ♗b4 13.♗xa6 ♖xa6 14.♕e2 ♖fa8 15.♗d2 ♕b7 (Black starts moving back; 15...♖a3 16.♕d3 ♖b8 17.♖fc1 ♖b7 18.♖e1±) 16.a4 ♘e8 17.♘b5± P.Nguyen-Bartholomew, London 2015. **10.0-0 ♗xa6** 10...♘bd7. **11.♖e1** White gets prepared to play e4-e5. With 11.e5! White acts at once: 11...dxe5 12.♘xe5 ♖d8? (this is not just an inaccuracy: 12...♕c7! 13.♖e1 ♘e4 14.♗f4±) 13.♗xa6 ♕xa6 14.♕f3! ♖a7 15.♗e3 ♗c7 16.♖ad1 ♖f8 17.♗g5± Atalik-Swapnil, PRO League rapid 2018; 11.♗d2, by transposition from 8...♕a5 9.♗d2, leads to the most common position of this line. See Games 9-11. **11...♘bd7** 11...♘fd7 12.♗g5 (12.♗f4 ♗xc3 13.bxc3 ♕xc3 14.e5±) 12...♖e8 13.♕d2 ♗xe2 14.♖xe2 ♘a6 (14...♘b6 15.♖c1 ♗xc3 16.bxc3 ♕a4 17.e5±) 15.♗f4 (15.♗h6 ♗f6 16.♗f4 ♗xc3 17.bxc3 f6 18.h4 ♕a4±) 15...♘b4 16.e5 dxe5 (16...c4! 17.exd6 exd6 18.♖xe8+ ♖xe8 19.♗xd6 ♘d3⊠) 17.♘xe5 ♖ad8 18.♘xd7 ♖xd7 19.d6± Shishkin-Bekasovs, Berlin 2018. **12.h3 ♘b6** The knight may go to c4, and it vacates the d7-square. 12...♖fb8 13.♗xa6 ♕xa6 14.e5 (Black is well developed for this move; 14.♕c2 ♘e8 15.a4 ♕b7 16.♖a2 ♗b4 17.♗g5 ♘e5 18.♘xe5 ♗xe5 19.♗d2±) 14...dxe5 15.♘xe5 ♘xe5 16.♖xe5 ♖b7 17.♕e2 ♗f8 18.♗xa6 ♖xa6 19.♖e2 ♖d7= E.Levin-Ponkratov, St Petersburg 2015. **13.e5 ♘fd7 14.exd6** 14.e6!? (White wants to play against the e7-pawn) 14...fxe6 15.♗xa6 ♖xa6 16.♖xe6+. **14...exd6 15.♗f4** 15.♗xa6 ♖xa6 16.♕e2 c4 17.♗d2±. **15...♖fe8 16.♗xa6 ♕xa6 17.♖xe8+ ♖xe8 18.♗xd6 ♘c4 19.♕d3 ♖a8 20.♗f4** 20.♗c7 ♘xb2 21.♕xa6 ♖xa6 22.♗b5±. **20...♘xb2∓ 21.♕xa6 ♖xa6 22.♗d2 ♘c4** 22...♘a4 23.♖c1 ♘xc3 24.♗xc3 ♗xc3 25.♖xc3 ♖xa2∓. **23.♖c1 f5 24.♗e1 ♘b2 25.♖c2 ♘d3 26.♗e2 ♖b6 27.♘c1 ♘f4 28.♗d2 ♘xd5 29.♘d3 ♖b1+**

30.♔h2 ♗f8 31.g3 ♗d6 32.♔g2 ♖b7 33.♗c1 ♖a7 34.♘d2 ♖a4 35.♘c4 ♗f8 36.♔f3 ♗g7 37.a3 ♘c3 38.♘db2 ♖a6 39.♘d3 ♘b5 40.♗b2 ♘d4+ 41.♗xd4 ♗xd4 42.♔e2 ♔f7 43.h4 h6 44.♖a2 g5 45.hxg5 hxg5 46.f4 g4 47.♘de5+? 47.a4 ♔e6 48.a5 ♔d5 49.♘de5 ♘xe5 50.♘xe5 c4 51.♖a4 ♗xe5 52.fxe5 ♔xe5 53.♖xc4 ♖xa5=. 47...♘xe5 48.fxe5 48.♘xe5+ ♗xe5 49.fxe5 ♖a4-+. 48...♖h6 49.♔f1 ♖h1+ 50.♔g2 ♖g1+ 51.♔h2 ♖c1 52.♘d6+ ♔e6 53.♘b5 ♗xe5 54.a4 c4 55.a5 c3 56.a6 c2 57.a7 ♖h1+ 58.♔xh1 c1♕+ 59.♔h2 ♕h6+ 60.♔g1 ♕e3+ 0-1

Daniel Gormally 3
Thorben Koop
Douglas 2015 (7)

1.d4 ♘f6 2.c4 c5 3.d5 b5 4.cxb5 a6 5.bxa6 g6 6.♘c3 ♗g7 7.e4 0-0 8.♘f3 ♕a5 Black creates a threat on the diagonal quickly, already setting up a trick. **9.♗d3?!** A blunder, though not a losing one; it only costs the d5-pawn. Even a great player like Gelfand fell for it. **9...♘xd5! 10.exd5!** 10.0-0? results in a position with a pawn down for nothing: 10...♘xc3 11.bxc3 ♕xc3 12.♖b1 ♗xa6 13.♗xa6 ♖xa6 14.♗b2 (≥ 14.♗g5∓) 14...♕c4 15.♖c1 ♕b4 16.♗xg7 ♔xg7 17.♕d5 d6 18.e5 ♘d7 19.♖b1 (≥ 19.♖fe1∓) 19...♕a4 20.♖b7 e6-+ Stern-Van Wely, Berlin 2015. **10...♗xc3+**

11.♘d2 11.♗d2 is the most played move and 11...♗xd2+ 12.♕xd2 ♕xd2+ leads to a happy ending for Black; 11.bxc3?! ♕xc3+ 12.♗d2 ♕xa1 13.0-0 ♗xa6! 14.♗b2 ♕xa2 15.♗b1! (Rudd's big improvement over 15.♖a1 ♕b3-+ Gelfand-Carlsen, Zurich rapid 2014)

15...♕b3! (other moves simply lose) 16.♖e1 d6! 17.♗a1 ♕a3! 18.♗b2 ♕b4! (18...♕b3 only repeats) 19.♗c3 ♕c4 20.♗a1 f6! (20...♖a7?! 21.♗xg6! (21.♕h6?! f6 – 20...f6) 21...hxg6 22.♕h6 e5 23.♗xe5!? (23.dxe6?! f6 24.♘d2 ♕g4∓ – 20...f6) 23...dxe5 24.♘g5 ♖d8!? (24...f6 and 24...f5 are both instantly perpetual check) 25.♕h7+ ♔f8 26.♕h8+ ♔e7 27.♕xe5+ ♔d7 28.♗xf7 ♔c8 29.♕e6+ ♔b7 30.♘xd8+ ♔a8 31.♘c6 ♘xc6 32.♕xc6+ ♖b7 and Black has stopped the checks. A sharp but equal ending has arisen) 21.♕h6 ♖a7 22.♗xg6 (22.♘g5 e5 23.♘e6 ♖e8 24.♗xg6 ♖xe6 25.dxe6 ♕xe6 26.♗e4 ♖g7∓) 22...e5! (22...hxg6? 23.♕xg6+ ♔h8 24.♘g5 ♕d3 25.♘f7+ ♖xf7 26.♕xf7 ♕f5 27.h3!±) 23.dxe6 hxg6 24.♘d2! (the only chance) 24...♕g4! (24...♖h7 25.♕xg6+ ♖g7 26.e7 ♖xg6 27.♘xc4 ♗xc4 28.e8♕ ♖xe8 29.♖xe8+ ♔f7 30.♖xb8∓) 25.♘e4 ♗b5! 26.♘xf6+ ♖xf6 27.♗xf6 ♕h5∓. **11...♗g7 12.0-0 ♗xa6** 12...♘xa6 13.♘c4 ♕d8 14.d6 e6 15.♗e4 ♖b8 16.a3 ♕h4 17.♕e2 ♗b7 18.♗xb7 ♖xb7= Onischuk-Perunovic, Berlin 2015. **13.♘c4 ♕c7** 13...♕b4 14.♕g4 ♗d4∓. **14.d6** White is looking for a draw. **14...exd6 15.♗f4 ♗e5** 15...♕c6!? 16.♘xd6 (16.♘a5 ♕b6 17.♘c4 ♕b5 18.♘xd6 ♖e8 19.♖e1) 16...♗xd3 17.♕xd3 ♘a6; 15...♖a7 16.♗xd6 ♖e8 17.♖e1 ♘c6 18.♖xe8+ ♖xe8 19.♘d2=. **16.♗h6 ♗g7** 16...♖d8!? would avoid the repetition, but would give a no more than playable position after 17.♖e1. **17.♗f4 ♗e5 18.♗h6 ♗g7 19.♗f4 ♗e5 ½-½**

Blocking with the knight 8...♕a5 9.♘d2

Anatoly Karpov 4
Anatoli Vaisser
Cap d'Agde m 2017 (2)

1.d4 ♘f6 2.c4 c5 3.d5 b5 4.cxb5 a6 5.bxa6 g6 6.♘c3 ♗g7 7.e4 0-0 8.♘f3 ♕a5 9.♘d2 The knight blocks two diagonals, making

it harder for the c1-bishop to develop, but on the other hand it can help on the queenside. **9...♗xa6 10.♗xa6 ♕xa6** The queen stands better on a6 than the knight: 10...♘xa6 11.0-0 d6 12.♘c4 ♕b4 13.♕e2 ♗d7 14.♗f4 ♘b6 15.♘xb6 ♕xb6 16.e5 ♖fb8 17.♖ab1 ♘c7 18.♖fe1± Li Shilong-Zhu Hengyi, China tt-2 2017.

11.♕e2 White can consider keeping his king in the centre after exchanging the queens. It is early to play for the knight outpost on b5: 11.a4 e6 12.♘b5 (12.dxe6 fxe6 13.♘b5 ♕c6 14.♕e2 d5 15.0-0 ♘bd7 16.♖a3 (Flear-Gormally, Hastings 2015/16) 16...c4=) 12...♕b7 13.0-0 (13.dxe6 fxe6 14.♕e2 d5 15.0-0 ♘a6 16.exd5 exd5 17.♕e6+ ♕f7 18.♕xf7+ ♖xf7= Naumkin-R.Golubev, Moscow 2015) 13...exd5 14.exd5 ♘xd5 15.♘c4 ♘b4 (15...♘a6=; 15...♘b6=) 16.♘bd6 ♕c6 17.♗f4 ♘8a6 (Chatalbashev-Mihok, Vaujany 2016) 18.♗e5±. **11...♕xe2+** 11...d6 12.♘c4 (maybe 12.♘b5!? is an improvement: 12...♘bd7 13.a4!?) 12...♘bd7 13.0-0 ♖fb8 14.♖e1 ♖b4 15.♘a3 ♗e8 (15...♘e5∓) 16.♘c2 ♖b7 17.a4 ♕xe2 18.♖xe2 ♘b6 19.♘e3 ♘ba7= Klekowski-Heberla, Poland tt 2015; 11...e6!? is the principled decision. One feels the undermining comes in time: 12.dxe6 (12.♘c4 ♖e8 13.d6 (13.♘e3 ♘xe4 14.♘xe4 exd5 15.♘xc5 ♕a5+ 16.♕d2 ♕xc5∓ Kotanjian-Salman, Moscow 2017) 13...♘c6 14.0-0 ♘d5 15.exd5 exd5 16.♘e3 ♕e2 17.♘xe2 d4 18.♗f4 dxe3 19.♗xe3∓ Kanarek-Chr.Bauer, Cappelle-la-Grande 2016; 12.♕xa6 ♘xa6 13.d6? (13.0-0=) 13...♘b4 14.0-0 ♖fb8 15.a3 ♘d3 16.♘c4 ♗g4

17.♖a2 ♘gxf2–+ Quesada Perez-Soto Hernandez, Santa Maria del Mar 2017) 12...fxe6 13.♘b3 ♕xe2+ (13...c4 14.♘d4 ♕g4=) 14.♔xe2 c4 (14...♘a6 15.♗e3 ♖fc8 (15...♘g4 16.♘d2 ♖fd8=) 16.♖hd1 c4 17.♘d2 d5 18.exd5 exd5= Grischenko-Milevich, Orsha blitz 2018) 15.♘c5 ♖c8 16.♘b7 ♗e8 17.♖d1 ♖c7 18.♘d6 ♘xd6 19.♖xd6 ♘c6 20.f4 (Karpov-Vaisser, Cap d'Agde m rapid 2017) 20...e5 21.g3 ♘d4+=. **12.♔xe2** Karpov had a superb, magic feeling for when a king was vulnerable in a queenless position and when it was not. **12...d6** 12...e6 13.♘c4±. **13.♘c4 ♘fd7** 13...♘bd7. **14.♗g5 f6 15.♗d2 f5 16.♗g5** 16.a4 looks fine as well. **16...♘e5 17.♘xe5 ♗xe5 18.f4 ♗xc3 19.bxc3 ♖a4 20.e5±** 20.♖he1 would also have been strong. **20...dxe5 21.♗xe7 ♖e8 22.♗xc5 ♘a6 23.♗b6 ♔f7 24.♖hd1 ♖e4+ 25.♔d3 ♖c8 26.♖e1 ♖b8 27.♗g1 ♖xf4 28.♖xe5 ♖c8 29.♖b1 ♘c5+ 30.♗xc5 ♖xc5 31.♖b4 ♖f2 32.c4 ♖xa2 33.♖b7+ ♔f6 34.♖e6+ ♔g5 35.♔d4 ♖c8 36.♖c6 ♖d8 37.♖xh7 ♖xg2 38.h4+ ♔f4 39.♖h6 g5 40.hxg5 ♖xg5 41.♖cg6 ♖g3 42.♖xg3 ♔xg3 43.♖g6+ ♔f3 44.c5 1-0**

Alexey Goganov   5
Konstantin Novikov
Samara 2019 (5)

1.d4 ♘f6 2.c4 c5 3.d5 b5 4.cxb5 a6 5.bxa6 g6 6.♘c3 ♗g7 7.e4 0-0 8.♘f3 ♕a5 9.♘d2 ♗xa6 10.♗e2 White just develops the bishop.

10...e6 10...♘h5!? is a surprising idea. Black instantly puts pressure on c3: 11.0-0 (11.♘db1!? d6 12.0-0 ♘d7 13.a4 ♖fb8 14.♖a3 ♗xe2! (14...♖b4 15.♘b5!) 15.♕xe2 ♖b4! 16.b3 c4=; 16...♗xc3 17.♘xc3

c4=) 11...♘f4 (11...♗xc3 12.♘b3!±) 12.♗xa6 ♕xa6 13.a4 ♗xc3 14.bxc3 ♘e2+ 15.♔h1 ♗xc3 16.♕c2 ♘e2 17.♕xc5 d6 18.♕e3 ♘xc1 19.♖fxc1 ♘d7 20.♘b3±; 10...♗xe2 11.♕xe2 ♕a6 (11...♘h5 12.0-0 ♘xc3 13.♘b3 ♕a6 14.♕xa6 ♖xa6 15.bxc3 c4 (Polugaevsky-Kholmov, Tbilisi ch-URS 1967) 16.♘d4±. This is the oldest recorded game I could find with 8...♕a5, although I have to admit that it did not feature the regular Benko/Volga move order) 12.e5 (12.♘c4 d6 13.a4±) 12...♕xe2+ (12...♗e8 13.♘c4±) 13.♔xe2 ♗g4 14.f4 (14.h3 ♘h6 15.g4±) 14...f6 15.♗f3 h5 16.h3± fxe5? 17.hxg4 ♖xf4+ 18.♗e2+– Vorobiov-Garcia Gata, La Roda 2017. **11.0-0 exd5** 11...♗xe2 12.♕xe2 exd5 13.exd5 ♕a6 (13...♖e8 14.♕f3 ♕b4 (14...♘a6 15.♘c4 ♕b4 16.b3 ♗g4 17.♕xg4 f5 18.♕d1± Campos Moreno-Alvarez Pedraza, Barcelona 2018) 15.a3 ♕h4 16.g3 ♕h3 17.♘de4 (17.♘c4±) 17...♘xe4 18.♘xe4± Campos Moreno-Prié, Barcelona 2019) 14.♘c4 d6 (14...♖e8 15.♕d3 d6 16.♗f4 ♘bd7 17.♖ad1 ♘h5 18.♗xd6 d4?! (18...♗xc3 19.♕xc3 ♖e4 20.♘d2 ♖d4 21.♗xc5 ♘f4 22.♗xd4 ♘e2+ 23.♔h1 ♘xc3 24.♗xc3±) 19.a4?! (19.b3!) 19...♕b6?! 20.♘b5!+– Naumann-Koop, Austria Bundesliga 2016) 15.♗f4 (15.a4±) 15...♘bd7 16.♗xd6 (16.♖fe1 ♖fe8 17.♕f1 ♕b6 18.♗xd6±) 16...♖fe8 17.♕d3 ♕b6 18.♘e5 ♘c5 19.♕xa6= Tran Tuan Minh-Shyam, New Delhi 2018. **12.e5** 12.exd5 d6 13.♘c4±. **12...♘h5 13.♗xh5** 13.♘xd5 ♗xe2 14.♕xe2 ♖e8 15.♘c4+–. **13...♗xf1 14.♘xf1**

14...d4? There is no time for this. 14...gxh5! 15.♘xd5± ♘c6 **15.d5! ♘c6 16.♘f6+ ♔h8** 16...♗xf6 17.exf6

♖fe8 18.♗e2 d5 19.b3 is equally unattractive due to the bishop pair. **17.♗f3 ♘xe5** 17...♕c7 18.♗g5 h6 19.♗h4 ♖a7 20.♘d5 ♕xe5 21.♘g3+−. **18.♗xa8 ♖xa8 19.♘g4 ♘xg4 20.♕xg4+− ♕e1 21.♕xd7 c4 22.♕c6 ♖f8 23.♕xc4 h5 24.a4 d3 25.♕xd3 ♖c8 26.♕d2 ♕e4 1-0**

Alexander Ipatov 6
Pavel Tregubov
France tt 2016 (3)

1.d4 ♘f6 2.c4 c5 3.d5 b5 4.cxb5 a6 5.bxa6 g6 6.♘c3 ♗g7 7.e4 0-0 8.♘f3 ♕a5 9.♘d2 ♗xa6 10.♗e2 d6 Black plays conventionally. Now White has to choose a plan. He can prepare e4-e5 or build the outpost on b5. **11.0-0**

11...♘fd7 Black combines improving the knight and hitting c3.
  A) 11...♗xe2 12.♕xe2 ♕a6 13.♘c4 (13.♘b5 ♘bd7 14.a4 ♖fc8 15.♘c4±) 13...♘bd7 14.a4 (14.♖e1 ♖fb8 15.♖b1 ♗g4! (in time!) 16.♗d2 ♘ge5 17.♘xe5 ♘xe5 18.b3 ♘d3= Arkhipov-Pugachev, Moscow tt 2015) 14...♖fb8 15.♖a3 ♖b4 16.♘b5 ♘b6 17.b3 ♗e8 (17...♕xc4 18.bxc4 ♖xa4 19.♘c7+) 18.♗g5 ♗f8 19.e5 dxe5 20.f4± Ponkratov-Mertanen, Budva tt 2019;
  B) 11...♘bd7 and now:
  B1) 12.♘c4 (if White gets the two bishops, it is good news for him) 12...♗xc4 (12...♕b4 13.a3 ♕b7 14.♖b1 ♘b6 15.♘xb6 ♕xb6 16.b4 ♗xe2 17.♕xe2 ♘d7 18.bxc5 ♕xc5 19.♘b5± Antonsen-Von Bahr, Gothenburg 2017) 13.♗xc4 ♖fb8 (13...♘b6 14.♗d3 c4 15.♗c2 ♘fd7 16.♗e3±) 14.♕c2 ♗e8 (14...♘b6 15.♗e2 ♘a4 16.♘d1 ♕b4 17.f3 ♘d7 18.♖b1±) 15.♗d2 ♕c7 16.a4 (16.♘b5 ♕b6 17.a4±) 16...♘b6 17.♘b5 ♘e5 18.♗e2 c4 19.♗e3 (19.♘xc7

♕xc7 20.b4±) 19...♕a5 (Rozum-M.Novikov, Sochi rapid 2017) 20.♘d4±;
  B2) 12.a4 ♖fb8 13.♖a3 and now:
  B21) 13...♖b4 14.b3!? (building up play on the queenside is more promising: 14.♖e1 ♘e5 15.♗xa6 ♕xa6 16.♘b5 ♗e8 17.f4 ♘d7 (17...♘d3 18.♖xd3 ♖xa4 19.♖b3 c4 20.♖xc4 ♖xc4 21.♖a3=) 18.b3 ♘b6 (Akesson-Risting, Graz 2017) 19.♘f3∞) 14...♕b6 (14...♘e5 15.♗b5±; 14...♗xe2 15.♕xe2 ♘e8 16.♘b5 ♘b6 17.♘b1 ♘c4 18.bxc4± Leko-Artemiev, Moscow rapid 2015) 15.♗xa6 ♕xa6 16.♕c2 ♘e8 17.♗b2 (17.♘b5 ♘b6) 17...♘c7 (17...♗d4 18.♘a2±) 18.♗a1 ♖ab8 19.♘a2±;
  B22) 13...♗xe2 14.♕xe2 ♘b6 15.♘db1!? (this move is a bit awkward, but the b6-knight is slightly in Black's way) 15...c4 (15...♕a6 16.♕xa6 ♖xa6 17.b3 c4 (17...♘bd7 18.♗e3 ♘e5 19.f3 ♘fd7 20.♘b5±) 18.b4 ♘xa4 (Banikas-Markos, Hersonissos 2017) 19.♖xa4±) 16.♕c2 (16.♘b5 ♘xa4 17.♘d4 ♕a6 18.♘c3±) 16...♗g4 17.♗d2 (17.♘b5 ♖c8 18.♗g5 ♗f8 19.♘1c3±) 17...♕c5 18.h3 ♘e5 19.♗e3± Avrukh-Dobrov, Chicago 2015. **12.a4** 12.♗xa6 ♕xa6 (12...♘xa6 13.♘c4 ♕b4 14.♕e2 ♘e5 15.♘xe5 ♗xe5 16.♗g5 ♖fb8 17.♘d1 ♘c7 18.♖e1 ♘b5= Sammalvuo-Rasmussen, Sweden tt 2015/16) 13.a4 ♕d3?? (a horrible blunder; 13...c4 14.♘f3 ♘c5∞; 13...♖c8 14.♕c2 c4 15.♘f3∞) 14.♘b5 ♕xb5 15.axb5 ♖xa1 16.♘c4+− Ulybin-Kadric, Sarajevo 2014; 12.♘db1 is a very weird move, but it strengthens the queenside. White hopes to gradually push Black back: 12...♖c8 (it is not so simple for Black to create play: 12...♘e5 13.a4 ♗xe2 14.♕xe2 ♘a6 (14...♕b4 15.♗g5 ♖e8 16.♘a3 c4 17.♖fb1 ♘a6 18.♘c2±) 15.♗g5 ♖fe8 16.♘a3 ♘b4 17.♖ad1 h6 18.♗e3 ♖ec8 19.f4± E.Levin-Mesropov, Voronezh 2015; 12...♖e8 13.a4 c4 14.♖a3 ♘e5 15.♘b5±; maybe 12...c4!? should be tried, e.g. 13.♕c2 ♘e5 14.♗g5 (14.♗d2 ♘bd7 15.♘a4 ♕c7 16.♗e3∞) 14...♖e8 15.a4

♘bd7 16.♘a3∞) 13.♖e1 (13.a4 ♕b4≅; 13.♗g5 ♖e8 14.♕c2 ♘e5 15.a4±) 13...♗xe2 14.♖xe2 ♘a6 15.♗g5 ♘b4 (15...♖e8=) 16.♗xe7 ♕a6 17.a4 ♘d3 18.♗xd6± Bocharov-Dubov, Sochi rapid 2016. **12...♗xc3** Black can take the pawn, but it is not everyone's cup of tea as it reduces Black's pressure. 12...♗xe2 13.♕xe2 ♘b6 14.♖a3 ♘8d7 15.h3 ♖fb8 16.♖e1∞. **13.bxc3 ♕xc3 14.♖a3 ♕b4 15.a5** 15.♖b3 ♕xa4 16.♖xb8 ♕xd1 17.♖xf8+ ♔xf8 18.♖xd1 ♖xf1 19.♔xf1 ♖a1 20.♘b3=. **15...♘f6** 15...♘e5 16.f4 ♘ed7 17.♗xa6 ♖xa6 18.♕e2 c4=; 15...♗xe2 16.♕xe2 ♖xa5 17.♖b3 ♕a4 18.♗b2 ♘f6 19.h3≅. **16.♗xa6 ♖xa6 17.♖a4 ♕b5 18.♘c4± ♘bd7 19.f3 ♖b8 20.♗d2 ♕b3 21.♕xb3 ♖xb3 22.♖aa1 e6 23.♖ab1 ♖xb1 24.♖xb1 exd5 25.exd5 ♘f8** 25...♘xd5 26.♖b7 ♘7f6 27.♖b8+ ♔g7 28.g4!±. **26.♗f4 ♘xd5 27.♗xd6+ ♔g7** 27...♔e8±. **28.♖b7+− ♘e3 29.♘b6 ♘xb6 30.axb6 ♖a2 31.♗e5+ ♔f8 32.♗f6 1-0**

Blocking with the bishop
8...♕a5 9.♗d2

Ognjen Jovanic 7
Ante Brkic
Bjelovar ch-CRO 2019 (7)

1.d4 ♘f6 2.c4 c5 3.d5 b5 4.cxb5 a6 5.bxa6 g6 6.♘c3 ♗g7 7.e4 0-0 8.♘f3 ♕a5 9.♗d2 Blocking the diagonal with the bishop is more popular. **9...♗xa6**

10.♗xa6?! Exchanging pieces often helps Black as it becomes easier for him to get closer to White's pawns. It is a bit paradoxical, as White has a material advantage, but these are

the things that make chess such a wonderful game. **10...♕xa6 11.♕e2 e6** Black is not at all unhappy to exchange queens as well. He starts undermining the centre at once. **12.♕xa6** 12.h3 (White overestimates the time he has to develop) 12...exd5 13.e5 ♖e8 14.♗e3 d4 15.exf6 ♗xf6 16.♘d5 ♗g7 17.♕xa6 ♘xa6 18.0-0-0 dxe3∓ Belous-Larson, Chicago 2017; 12.♗e3 exd5 13.exd5 d6 14.♕xa6 ♘xa6 15.0-0 ♖fb8 16.♗f4 ♖xb2 17.♗xd6 ♘d7 18.♖ac1 ♘b4 19.♖fd1 ♖a6∓ Espinosa Veloz-Ortiz Suarez, Oaxtepec 2016; 12.dxe6 fxe6 13.♗g5 ♘c6 14.♕xa6 ♖xa6 15.♖d1 ♖b8 (15...d5=) 16.♖d2 d5 (all of Black's pieces work) 17.exd5 ♘xd5 18.♗xd5 exd5 19.♖xd5 ♘b4 20.♖d2 ♖xa2= Tenikashvili-R.Golubev, Sochi tt-2 2019. **12...♘xa6 13.dxe6 fxe6** The fluent play of Black's pieces easily offers him equality. **14.0-0** The king will not be safe in the centre: 14.♔e2 ♖fb8 15.b3 d5 16.exd5 exd5 17.♖hc1 ♘b4 18.♘a4 ♘e4∓ Debashis-J.S.Christiansen, Doha Wch blitz 2016. **14...♘b4** White can do several things, but nothing is dangerous for Black: 14...d5 15.exd5 exd5 16.♗g5 d4 17.♗xf6 ♖xf6 18.♘e4 ♖e6 19.♘ed2 ♘b4= Martirosyan-Zubov, Yerevan 2016. **15.a4** 15.♖fd1 ♘d3 16.♖ab1 ♘g4! 17.♖f1 ♘d4 18.♘xd4 cxd4 19.♘b5 ♖xf2∓ Urkedal-Lokander, Stockholm 2014/15; 15.b3 ♖fc8 16.a4 ♘c2 17.♖ab1 ♘a3 18.♖a1 ♘c2 19.♖ab1 ♖ab8 20.♖b2= Sharafiev-Dubov, Sochi tt 2015. **15...♘d3 16.b3** 16.♖ab1 d5 17.exd5 ♘xd5 (17...exd5∓) 18.♗g5 ♖fe8 19.♘ge4 ♘xc3 20.bxc3± Zhao Xue-Javakhishvili, Chengdu 2016. **16...d5 17.exd5 ♘xd5 18.♖ad1 ♘b2 19.♖c1 ♘d3 20.♖cd1 ♘b2 21.♖c1 ♘d3 ½-½**

Valeriy Grinev   **8**
Nikita Meskovs
Voronezh 2019 (3)

1.d4 ♘f6 2.c4 c5 3.d5 b5 4.cxb5 a6 5.bxa6 g6 6.♘c3 ♗g7 7.e4 0-0 8.♘f3 ♕a5 9.♗d2 ♗xa6 10.♗xa6 ♕xa6 11.♕e2 d6 Black just

develops and wants to build the usual play on the two files on the queenside.

12.h3
A) 12.♖c1 ♘bd7 13.♕xa6 ♖xa6 14.♖c2 ♘g4 15.♗e2 ♗xc3 16.♗xc3 ♖xa2 17.h3 ♘gf6= Sambuev-Avila Pavas, Havana 2018;
B) 12.♕xa6 ♘xa6 13.♔e2 ♖fb8 14.♖ab1 ♖b4 15.e5 ♘g4 (15...♘d7=) 16.exd6 exd6 17.♖hd1 ♘c7 18.h3 ♘e5 19.♘xe5 ♗xe5= Schenk-Mihok, Germany Bundesliga 2015/16;
C) 12.♖b1 ♘bd7 (12...♘fd7 (Black intends to undermine the centre with ...f7-f5) 13.b3 f5 (13...♕xe2+ 14.♔xe2 f5 15.a4 ♗xc3 16.♗xc3 fxe4=) 14.a4 (14.♕e3 ♘e5=) 14...♗xc3 15.♗xc3 ♕xe2+ 16.♔xe2 fxe4= 17.♘g5 ♘b6 18.♖hd1 ♖f5 19.♘xe4 ♘xd5= Quintiliano Pinto-Shabalov, Medellin 2017) 13.♕xa6 ♖xa6 14.0-0 ♘g4 15.a3 ♖b8 16.♖fd1 c4 (Black's play comes fluently) 17.h3 ♘ge5 18.♘d4 ♘d3 19.♘c6 ♖xb2 20.♖xb2 ♘xb2= Akesson-De Haan, Gibraltar 2018;
D) 12.a4 ♘fd7 (12...♘bd7 13.♘b5 ♖fb8 14.0-0 ♘e8 15.♗c3 ♘c7 16.♗xg7 ♔xg7 17.h4? (17.♖a3 ♘xb5 18.axb5 ♕b6=) 17...♘xb5 18.axb5 ♕xa1∓ Capone-Hauchard, Dieppe 2015) 13.b3 ♖c8 (undermining the centre with 13...f5! is simple and effective: 14.exf5 (14.♕e3 ♘e5) 14...♗xf5=) 14.♖c1 (14.♖b1 ♕xe2+ 15.♔xe2 f5 17.♘e3 fxe4 18.♘g5∞) 16.a5 cxb3 17.axb6±) 15...c4 (15...♕xe2+ 16.♔xe2 f5 17.♘e3 fxe4 18.♘g5∞) 16.a5 cxb3 17.axb6±) 15...c4 (15...♘8d7 16.♕xa6 ♖xa6 17.♘b5±) 16.b4 ♗xc3 17.♗xc3 (17.b5!? ♕xa4 18.♗xc3 ♕xb5

19.♕e3 and White's compensation is really dangerous) 17...♘xa4 18.♗d4 ♕b5 (Gähwiler-Jaksland, Porto Carras 2018) 19.♕e3±.
12...♘bd7 12...♘fd7 13.♗g5 (13.a4 ♘e5 14.♘xe5 ♗xe5 15.♖a2 ♘d7 16.♕xa6 ♖xa6 17.♔e2 f5 18.a5±) 13...♖e8 (13...h6 14.♗f4 ♘b6=) 14.♕xa6 ♖xa6 15.♔d2 c4 16.♗e3 ♘ac5 17.♗d4 ♘d3 18.♖ab1 ♘7c5= Baryshpolets-Langer, Dallas 2016. **13.♕xa6 ♖xa6 14.♖b1** 14.0-0 ♖b8 15.♖ab1 ♘e8 16.♖fe1 ♘c7 17.♗f4 ♘b6 18.g3 ♘c4 19.e5 ♖xb2 20.♖xb2 ♖xb2 21.♖b1 ♖b6= Nybäck-Van Wely, Puhajarve rapid 2015. **14...♖b8** 14...♘b6 15.0-0 (15.b3 ♘fd7∓) 15...♘a4∓. **15.♔d1** An original idea; the king is rarely placed on the queenside. Yet, equalizing is not a problem for Black here. **15...♘e8 16.♔c2 ♘c7 17.♖he1 ♘b6 18.b3?** Giving back the pawn hands over the initiative. 18.a3 ♘c4 19.♗c1=. **18...♗xc3 19.♗xc3 ♖xa2+ 20.♖b2∓ ♖a3 21.♖bb1 f5 22.exf5 ♘bxd5 23.fxg6 hxg6 24.♗d2 e5 25.♖b2 ♘e6 26.h4 ♘f6 27.♗c3 ♘g4 28.♖e2 ♘f4 29.♖d2 ♖b6 30.♘g5 ♘xg2 31.♘e4 d5 32.♖xd5 ♘2e3+ 33.fxe3 ♘xe3+ 34.♔d3 ♘xd5 35.♘xc5 ♖b5 0-1**

Murtas Kazhgaleyev   **9**
Ruslan Ponomariov
PRO League Central 2017 (3)

1.d4 ♘f6 2.c4 c5 3.d5 b5 4.cxb5 a6 5.bxa6 g6 6.♘c3 ♗g7 7.e4 0-0 8.♘f3 ♕a5 9.♗d2 ♗xa6 10.♗e2 White develops and gets ready to castle. **10...d6 11.0-0**

11...♘bd7 11...♘fd7?! is slow this time: 12.♕c2 (12.a4 ♕b4 13.♖e1 c4 14.♘b5 ♕xb2 15.♖b1 ♕a2 16.♗g5±) 12...♗xe2 13.♘xe2 ♕a4 14.b3 ♕a6

15.♗c3 ♘f6 16.a4 ♘bd7 (Dubrovin-Vaisser, St Petersburg 2018) 17.h3 ♖fb8 18.♖fb1±. **12.a4** White starts building the outpost on b5 at once. 12.a3 ♖fb8 13.♖b1 ♕c7 (13...♗xe2 14.♕xe2 ♕a6=) 14.♗xa6 (14.b3 ♘h5 15.a4 ♘b6 16.♘b5 ♕d7 17.♕c2 e6 18.dxe6 fxe6 19.♖bd1+− Laurusas-Narmontas, Plateliai 2015) 14...♖xa6 15.a4 ♕b7 16.♕e2±; 12.♖e1 ♗g4 (12...♖fb8!? 13.♕c2 ♗xe2 14.♖xe2 ♗g4 15.b3 ♕a6 (15...c4 16.♖b1 cxb3 17.axb3=) 16.♖b1 ♘ge5 17.♘xe5 ♘xe5 18.a4 ♕d3= Kaczmarczyk-Chr. Bauer, Switzerland tt 2015) 13.h3 (13.♕c2 c4 14.♘d1 ♘c5 15.♖b1 ♖fc8 16.♘e3 ♘ge5 17.♘xe5 ♘xe5 18.b4 cxb3= Potpara-Kapnisis, Skopje 2015) 13...♘ge5 14.♘xe5 ♘xe5 15.♘b5 ♕b6 16.a4 ♗xb5 17.♗xb5 c4 18.♗e3 ♕a5 19.♖e2 ♕d3?! 20.♖b1! △ 21.b3+− Koziak-Oglaza, Police 2016; 12.♗xa6 ♕xa6 13.h3 (13.♕c2 c4 14.♘d4 ♘c5 15.♘c6 e6∓ Zoler-Schnepp, Biel 2018) 13...♖fb8 14.♕c2 ♘e8 15.♖ab1 (15.a4 ♘c7 16.♖fb1 ♕b7 17.♖a3 ♘e5 18.♘xe5 ♗xe5 19.♘d1±) 15...♘c7 16.b3 ♗xc3 17.♕xc3 ♘b5 18.♕e3 ♕xa2= Suleymenov-Maneluk, Voronezh 2019. **12...♖fb8** 12...♕b6 13.♗xa6 (13.b3!?) 13...♖xa6 14.♕c2 (14.♕e2 ♕b7 15.♘b5 ♖fa8±) 14...♖b8 (14...c4 15.♘b5 ♘c5 16.♕xc4 ♘fxe4 17.♗e3±) 15.♘b5 e6 16.dxe6 fxe6 17.b3± E.Levin-K.Novikov, Sochi tt-2 2018. **13.♘b5 ♕b6 14.♕c2 ♘e8 15.♗c3 ♘c7 16.♘xc7 ♕xc7 17.♗xa6 ♖xa6 18.♘d2 ♕b7 19.♗xg7 ♔xg7 20.b3± ♕b4 21.♖fc1 ♘e5 22.♕c3 ♕xc3 23.♖xc3 ♖b4 24.h3 g5 25.♔f1 ♔g6 26.♔e2 f5 27.exf5+ ♔xf5 28.♘f1 ♔g6 29.♘e3 h5 30.f3 ♖a8 31.♘c2 ♖b6 32.♖a3 ♖b4 33.♘c2 ♖b6 34.♘a3 ♖b4 35.♘c2 ♖b6 ½-½**

Milan Pacher   **10**
Christoph Natsidis
Lviv 2018 (2)
1.d4 ♘f6 2.c4 c5 3.d5 b5 4.cxb5 a6 5.bxa6 g6 6.♘c3 ♗g7 7.e4 0-0 8.♘f3 ♕a5 9.♗d2 ♗xa6 10.♗e2 d6 11.0-0 ♗xe2 12.♕xe2 ♕a6

White is a tempo up compared with the game Grinev-Meskovs.

13.♖fe1 13.♕d1 – Wojtaszek-Bologan; 13.♕xa6 ♘xa6 14.b3 (14.e5 dxe5 15.♘xe5 ♘b4 16.♖fd1 ♘fxd5 17.♘xd5 ½-½ Miljkovic-Marinkovic, Ruma 2017) 14...♘d7 15.♖ab1 ♘c7 16.a4 ♖fb8 17.♖fe1 ♖b7 (17...e6 18.dxe6 fxe6± Zubov-Moingt, Paris 2017) 18.♘a2 ♘b5 19.♘c1 ♘d4= Garcia Palermo-Collutiis, Gallipoli 2018; 13.♘b5 ♘xe4 14.♕xe4 ♕xb5 15.♗c3 (15.♕xe7 ♕d7 16.♖fe1 (16.♕h4 ♖a4 17.♕g3 ♗xb2 18.♖ae1 ♗g4 19.♕h3 (Tari-Adair, England 4NCL 2014/15) 19...♖a4∓) 16...♗xb2 17.♖ab1 ♖xa2 18.♗h6 ♗xe7 19.♖xe7 ♗g7= Raykhman-D.Sebastian, Germany Bundesliga 2017/18) 15...♕b7 (15...♖e8!? 16.a4 ♕b7∞; 15...♘d7 16.♕xe7 ♗xc3 17.bxc3 ♘b6 18.♕xd6±) 16.♖fe1 ♖a7 17.♖ad1 ♖e8 18.♗g5! (Greenfeld-Enkhtuul, Paramaribo 2014) 18...♗xc3 19.bxc3 ♘d7∓. **13...♕xe2** Exchanging queens works here as well. 13...♘fd7 is slow this time: 14.♗f4 (14.b3 ♕xe2 15.♖xe2 ♘a6 16.♖b1 ♖fb8 17.♘d1 ♘b4 18.♗xb4 ♖xb4 19.♘c1 ♘b6 20.♖cc2 c4= Schandorff-Risting, Helsingor 2015) 14...♗xc3 (14...♕xe2 15.♖xe2 ♗xc3 16.bxc3 ♘b6 17.♖b1±) 15.bxc3 f6 16.c4± Kantor-Kozak, Budapest 2016; 13...♘bd7 (Black can do well just playing standard Benko Gambit moves) 14.e5 (14.h3 ♖fb8 15.♕xa6 ♖xa6 16.♖ab1 ♘e8 17.♗f4 ♖ab6 18.♘a4 ♖b4 19.b3 f5= Teplyi-S.Kasparov, Aarhus 2015; 14.♕xa6 ♖xa6 15.e5 ♘g4 16.exd6 exd6 17.h3 ♘ge5 18.♘xe5 ♘xe5 19.b3 ♘d3= Makhmutov-Shimanov, Moscow 2015) 14...♘g4 (14...♕xe2 15.♖xe2 ♘xe5 16.♘xe5

dxe5 17.♖d1 ♘e8=) 15.exd6 exd6 16.h3 ♘ge5 17.♘xe5 ♕xe2 18.♖xe2 (Koziak-Hnydiuk, Police 2016) 18...♗xe5 19.♗h6 ♖fb8 20.♖d1 ♖b4=. **14.♖xe2 ♘bd7 15.e5** 15.h3 ♖fb8 16.♗e1 ♘e8 17.♖c1 ♗xc3 18.bxc3 f6 19.♖cc2 ♖a4= Cori-Alsina Leal, Badalona 2015. **15...dxe5 16.♘xe5 ♘xe5 17.♖xe5 ♖fb8 18.♖xe7 ♖xb2 19.♖d1 ♘e8= 20.♘e4 ♗f8 21.♖d7 ♘f6 21...♖bxa2=. 22.♘xf6 ♗xf6 23.d6 ♖bxa2 24.g4 ♖a1 25.♖xa1 ♖xa1+ 26.♔g2 ♖a2 27.♗f4 g5 28.♗g3 c4 29.♖c7 c3 30.♔f3 ♖d2 ½-½**

Radoslaw Wojtaszek   **11**
Viktor Bologan
Poikovsky 2016 (9)
1.d4 ♘f6 2.c4 c5 3.d5 b5 4.cxb5 a6 5.bxa6 g6 6.♘c3 ♗g7 7.e4 0-0 8.♗e2 ♕a5 9.♗d2 d6 10.a7 10.♘f3 ♗xa6 11.0-0 ♗xe2 12.♕xe2 ♕a6 13.♕d1 ♘bd7 14.♕c2 is the diagram position at move 17.
10...♖xa7 This way the players reach the same position with an extra move on each side. **11.♘f3 ♗a6 12.0-0 ♗xe2 13.♕xe2 ♕a6 14.♕d1** The most common move. For 14.♕xa6 see the notes to move 13 in Pacher-Natsidis; for 14.♘b5 see the notes to move 13 in Pacher-Natsidis; 14.♖fe1 – Pacher-Natsidis.

14...♕d3 A very rare insertion. 14...♘bd7 15.h3!? (White spends a tempo on stopping the standard move ...♘g4; for 15.♕c2 see move 17 below) 15...♘b6 (15...♖fb8 16.♕c2 ♘e8 (16...♘h5) 17.a4 ♘c7 18.♖fb1±) 16.b3 ♖fb8 (16...♘xe4 17.♘xe4 ♖xa1 18.♕xa1 ♕xa2 19.♕d1 ♖a3 20.♗g5±) 17.♕c2 (17.a4!?) 17...c4 (17...♘e8 18.a4 ♘c7 19.a5 ♘d7 20.♖a4 ♕b7 21.♖b1 ♖a6 22.♘a2± Batchuluun-Batchimeg,

Ulaanbaatar 2016) 18.b4 ♕a3 19.♘d4 ♘a4 (19...♘fxd5 20.♘cb5 ♕a4 21.♕xa4 ♖xa4 22.exd5±) 20.♘c6 ♖b7 21.♖fc1± Nechaeva-Castrillon Gomez, Moscow 2019. **15.♘e1** 15.♖e1 ♘bd7 16.h3 ♖fb8 17.b3± makes a good impression. **15...♕a6 16.♕c2 ♘bd7 17.♘f3** The players have reached a standard position with some extra moves.

17...♘g4 Again Bologan leaves the trodden paths. Two novelties in one game! 17...♖fb8 18.a4 (pushing the a-pawn can be effective but also premature; 18.♖fe1 ♘g4 19.a4 ♕c4 20.h3 ♘ge5= Santiago-Kazhgaleyev, Skopje 2015; 18.h3 ♘h5!? (an interesting idea, Black plans to play ...♘e5; 18...♘e8 19.♖fb1 (the rook strengthens the queenside; with 19.♖fe1 White aims to play in the centre: 19...♘c7 20.♗f4 (20.a4 ♘e5 21.♘xe5 ♗xe5 22.♖a3±) 20...b5 21.a4 ♘xc3 (21...♘d4 22.♘xd4 cxd4 23.♘b5 d3 24.♕c6±) 22.bxc3 ♘b6 23.a5

c4 24.e5± Jianu-Pisu, Arad 2017) 19...♘c7 20.a4 (White has no more piece to improve, therefore he advances a pawn) 20...e6 21.dxe6 fxe6 (Korchmar-Nebolsina, Kazan 2016) 22.♘d1±) 19.♖fb1 (19.g4 ♘hf6 20.a4 (20.♔g2 c4∞) 20...♘e8 21.♔g2 (21.♘b5 ♘b6) 21...♘c7 22.a5 ♘b7 23.♖fb1 ♖ab8 24.♖a3±; 19.a4 ♘e5 20.♘xe5 ♗xe5 21.g3 ♖b4 22.♖fe1 (22.♖fb1 ♘f6= see Kashlinskaya-Zhukova) 22...♗d4 23.♔g2±) 19...♘e5 20.♘xe5 (20.♘e1 ♘c4 21.♗c1 ♘a5 22.a4 ♗xc3 23.bxc3 ♖xb1=) 20...♗xe5 puts the ball in White's court. It is not easy to make progress for White, a small edge is the most he can hope for: 21.g3 (21.a4 ♘f4 (21...♖b4 (Kashlinskaya-Zhukova, Kragujevac 2016) 22.♖a3 ♗f4 23.♗e1±) 22.♗xf4 ♗xf4 23.g3 ♗e5 24.♘b5∞) 21...♕c4 22.b3 ♕d4 23.♔g2 c4 (Sammalvuo-Karttunen, Helsinki 2017) 24.bxc4 ♕xc4 25.♖xb8+ ♖xb8 26.a4±) 18...♖b4 (18...♕b7 19.♘b5 ♘b6 20.♗c3 ♘xa4 21.♘xd6±; 18...♘c4 19.♖a3 (19.♖fb1 ♕b3 20.♕d3 ♘g4 21.♖a3±) 19...♖b7 20.♗c1!? ♖ab8 21.♘d2 ♕a6 22.♘b5 ♘e8 23.♘c4±; 18...♘e8 19.♖a3 (19.♘b5 ♘b6⇄) 19...♘c7 20.♖b1 ♘e5 21.♘xe5 ♗xe5 22.♘d1 (22.h3 ♗d4 23.♘d1±) 22...♕e2 23.♗e3±) 19.♖fe1 (19.♖a2 ♘g4 20.♖fa1 ♕c4 21.h3 ♘ge5 22.♘e1 ♕b3 23.a5±)

19...♕c4 20.♖a3 (20.h3 ♕b3 21.♕xb3 ♖xb3 22.♖a2 (22.♗c1!?) 22...♘b6 23.a5 ♘c4 24.a6 ♘d7=) 20...♖ab8 21.♗c1 ♘g4 22.♘d2 ♕d4? (Moradiabadi-Zaragatski, Port of Spain 2016; 22...♕a6=) 23.♖f1±. **18.a4! ♕c4 19.b3 ♕a6 20.h3 ♘ge5 21.♘xe5 ♗xe5**

22.♖fb1 22.♖ab1 (White wants to place the knight on b5) 22...♖fc8 23.♖fc1±. **22...f5!? 23.a5 fxe4 24.♕xe4 ♘f6 25.♕c4± ♗d4 26.♗e1 ♖fb8 27.♖a4 ♗xc3 28.♕xc3 ♘xd5 28...♕e2 29.♖b2 ♕h5 30.♖d2 ♘xd5 31.♕c4 e6±. 29.♕f3 e6 30.♖e4 ♕c8 30...♖f8 31.♕g4 ♖ae8±. 31.♖d1 ♕d7 32.♕g4 ♕c7 33.b4 cxb4 34.♗xb4 d5 34...♖a6±. 35.♗c3 ♘b5 36.♗b2 ♘d6 37.♖xe6 ♘f5 38.♖b6 ♖xb6 39.axb6 ♕b5 40.♕f3 ♖d8 41.♗f6 ♖d7 42.♕c3 d4 43.♕c8+ ♔f7 44.♗g5 h6 45.♗f4 ♖e7 46.♗c7 ♕c6 47.♖b1 h5 48.♕a6 ♘h4 49.♕f1 d3 50.b7 d2 51.b8♕ ♖e1 52.♕b3+ ♔f6 53.♗d8+ 1-0**

Exercise 1

position after 25.♕b3-d3

White's last move was a mistake. How can it be refuted?

Exercise 2

position after 16...♗a6-b7

White to play.

Exercise 3

position after 12...♗g7xc3

Would you recapture on c3 or rather play something else?

(solutions on page 253)

English Opening   Reversed Sicilian   EO 24.7 (A20)

What to do with the knight on d4?

by Jacek Ilczuk and Krzysztof Panczyk

1.	c4	e5
2.	g3	c6
3.	♘f3	e4
4.	♘d4	d5
5.	cxd5	♛xd5

1.c4 e5

In the Reversed Sicilian, by playing
2.g3

White avoids variations with ...♗b4.
However, Black has an interesting
possibility here:

2...c6

The idea is to push ...d7-d5.

3.♘f3

This move provokes Black to push
his e-pawn further, with the idea to
undermine Black's centre in the future.
The position resembles the Alapin
Variation in the Sicilian Defence,
however with the extra tempo g2-g3.
This determines the development of the
light-squared bishop on g2.

3...e4 4.♘d4 d5 5.cxd5 ♛xd5

Black attacks the knight and forces
White to either withdraw it or defend
it. This position may also arise with the
insertion of the moves 2...♘f6 and 3.♗g2.
If we were to analyse all Black's possible
ideas here, we would definitely have

too much material for a single Survey.
Therefore we will focus on the lines
where after ♘c3, Black plays ...♛e5 and
...♘f6. In Yearbook 80, back in 2006, IM
Kick Langeweg examined the option
...♛h5, while the sister variation 1.c4
e5 2.g3 ♘f6 3.♗g2 c6 4.♘f3 e4 5.♘d4
♛b6 and 5...d5 6.d3 were both touched
upon more recently by Jan Timman in
Yearbooks 124 and 127.

The unpopular knight retreat
6.♘b3 is currently the least popular
move, however probably not quite
rightly.

After **6...♘f6 7.♘c3 ♛e5 8.♗g2 ♗e7 9.d4
exd3 10.♛xd3 0-0**, now the immediate
11.♛e3 can be met by 11...0-0 with a
transposition to 11.0-0. Black can also
fight for the d-file by withdrawing his
queen to c7 and following up with ...♖d8.
The less popular **11.♗f4** also has to be
considered (comments to Popov-Anand,
St Petersburg 2018).

Light-square issues
The second-most popular line is **6.e3**
♘f6 7.♘c3 ♛e5 8.♗g2. However, the
weakness of the light squares and

problems with the dark-squared bishop cause some problems to White, which is reflected in the statistics.

Jon Ludvig Hammer

Definitely the best idea is **8...♗c5**. Black hasn't the slightest problem achieving equality after **9.d3 exd3 10.♕xd3 0-0** (Svidler-Vidit, chess24.com 2020) while **9.♘b3** does not give White great chances of obtaining an advantage either. **9...♗b6** is the best reply (Liang-Sadhwani, Sitges 2018).

The other knight retreat

Lastly, we look at the knight retreat to c2. The knight's position on c2 seems to be passive but it has good prospects to reach the e3-square, e.g. **6.♘c2 ♘f6 7.♘c3 ♕e5 8.♗g2**.

In this case, **8...♗c5** is inaccurate. Other than in the 6.e3 line, the black bishop does not attack anything here. Moreover, White can finish his development by 9.b4 followed by ♗b2 with a small edge (Shtembuliak-Zierk, St Louis 2019).

White can count on a small advantage after **8...♗f5 9.0-0** (Hemant-Dvirnyy, Gibraltar 2018).

However, the main theoretical discussion currently revolves around the moves ...♘a6 and ...♗e7. After **8...♗e7** White can castle, which leads to variations that also arise after 8...♘a6. The line **9.♘e3 ♘a6** has independent meaning as long as White doesn't castle. Now, **10.a3** is a continuation that is not without venom, after which Black should castle, preserving the option for the a6-knight to jump to c5, as the inaccurate **10...♘c7** will be met with **11.♕a4** (Buchaillot-Vertiz Gutierrez, cr 2017). The other separate possibility is the provocative **10.♕c2 ♘b4 11.♕b1** with slightly better play for White (Hammer-Navara, Novy Bor 2016).
The most accurate move is the immediate **8...♘a6**.

White will not obtain an advantage after **9.♖b1 ♘b4** (Ganguly-Yu Yangyi, Douglas 2019). The main path of the theoretical discussion is **9.0-0 ♗e7**.

Here, the safe move is **10.♘e3** (Giri-Grischuk, Yekaterinburg ct 2020), however this does not offer White serious chances of obtaining an advantage. Also after the more ambitious **10.d4** White does not have an advantage: **10...exd3 11.♕xd3** (the less popular 11.exd3 ♗g4 brings White nothing, Janssen-Nikolic, Netherlands tt 2018/19) **11...0-0** (Black can also play 11...♘c5 and after 12.♕d4 ♕xd4 13.♘xd4 0-0 the

position was equal in Tomashevsky-Grischuk, Moscow 2019; however, White can try other retreats) **12.♕e3** and now the best move is **12...♕c7**, as after 12...♗d6 13.♖d1 White has slightly better chances (Hammer-Giri, Moscow 2017).

Conclusion

Definitely the worst idea for White on move 6 is to support the knight by 6.e3. This move only weakens the light squares in White's camp, and it is the first player who has to fight for a draw. The knight retreat to b3 looks good, however we have dealt only with the positions where Black plays ...♕e5. The most popular, however, is the move 6.♘c2, and undoubtedly rightly so. The position is sufficiently complex to create interesting play, and White's chances of gaining a slight advantage are quite good. Of course, if Black plays accurately enough, he should be able to equalize. However, it is White who plays first fiddle here.

The unpopular knight retreat 6.♘b3

Valery Popov
Viswanathan Anand
St Petersburg Wch blitz 2018 (16)
1.c4 e5 2.g3 ♘f6 3.♗g2 c6 4.♘f3 e4 5.♘d4 d5 6.cxd5 ♕xd5 7.♘b3 ♕e5 8.♘c3

8...♗e7 8...♗f5 9.d3 (9.0-0 ♘a6 10.d4 ♕e6 11.f3 (11.♗g5!? ♘d5 12.f3 ♘xc3 13.bxc3 f6±; 11.a3

(E.Larsen-J.Pedersen, Aarhus 1972) 11...♘c7 in order to block the d4-pawn with the c7-knight and after 12.d5 ♘cxd5 13.♘d4 ♕d7 14.♘xd5 ♘xd5 15.♘xf5 ♕xf5 16.♕c2 ♘f6 17.♕b3 ♕c8 18.♗e3 White only has compensation for the pawn) 11...exf3 12.♖xf3 ♕d7 13.♗g5±) 9...♗b4 10.0-0 0-0 11.♗f4 ♕e7 12.♘xe4 ♘xe4 13.a3†; 8...♘a6 9.0-0 ♗e6 10.d4 exd3 11.exd3 0-0-0 12.♗e3±. **9.d4 exd3 10.♕xd3 0-0** 10...♘a6 11.♗f4 ♕h5 with good equalizing chances for Black. **11.0-0** 11.♕e3 ♕c7 12.0-0 ♖e8 (a good square for the rook is d8. Black could have played 12...♖d8 or 12...♘a6 followed by 12...♖d8 with equality) 13.♖d1 ♘a6 (13...♗g4 (V.Popov-S.Zhigalko, St Petersburg 2018) 14.♕f4†) 14.♕f4 ♗f8 15.a3 ♗g4=; 11.♗f4 ♕h5 12.h3

♘a6 13.g4 ♕g6 14.♕xg6 fxg6 (14...hxg6 15.0-0-0± Strikovic-Huerga Leache, Pontevedra 2017) 15.♗g3 h5 16.g5 ♘e8 17.♘e4 with only minimally better chances for White. **11...♖d8** 11...♘a6!? 12.♗f4 ♕h5 (Fernandes-Sokolin, ICC 2009) 13.♖ad1=. **12.♕e3 ♕xe3?!** As the position of the queen on e3 is a little unnatural, Black should rather have played 12...♕c7 13.♗d2 (13.♕f4 ♘a6 14.♗d2 ♗d6 15.♕a4 ♘c5 16.♘xc5 ♗xc5 17.♖ad1 ♗e6=) 13...♘a6 14.♖fd1 ♗e6=. **13.♗xe3 ♗g4** 13...h6±. **14.♘c5 ♗f8 15.♖fd1 ♘d7 16.♗d6?!** Now White could have obtained a solid advantage after 16.♘xe7+ ♔xe7 17.♘a5. **16...♘gf6 17.♘a5 ♖e8 18.♘xc6??** A difficult-to-understand move. Black can easily untie. 18.b4±; 18.e4±. **18...♗xd6 19.♖xd6 bxc6**

20.♗xc6 ♖b8–+ White has insufficient compensation for the piece. Black won on the 55th move. **0-1**

**Awonder Liang
Raunak Sadhwani**
Sitges 2018 (4)
1.c4 e5 2.g3 c6 3.♘f3 e4 4.♘d4 d5 5.cxd5 ♕xd5 6.e3?! ♘f6 7.♘c3 ♕e5 8.♗g2 ♗c5! 9.♘b3 9.d3 exd3 10.♕xd3 ♗xd4 (10...0-0 11.0-0 ♖d8 12.♕c2 Svidler-Vidit, Pepe Cuenca Online 2020; 12.♘ce2 Svidler-Giri, Legends of Chess Online 2020) 11.♕xd4 ♕xd4 12.exd4 ♗e6 13.♗g5 ♘bd7 14.0-0-0 0-0 15.d5 cxd5 16.♘xd5 ♘xd5 17.♗xd5 ♗xd5 (17...♖ac8+ 18.♔b1 ♗f5+ 19.♔a1 b6=) 18.♖xd5 (Donchenko-Burri, Vandoeuvre 2018) and now 18...f6 is the simplest way to equalize.

9...♗b6 9...♗d6 10.0-0 0-0 11.d4 exd3 (Risdon-Asquith, cr 1997) 12.e4 ♖d8 13.♕xd3 ♕h5 14.♖d1±; 9...♘a6 10.0-0 (10.a3 0-0 11.0-0 ♗b6 (Perez Guerra-Alsina Leal, Marbella 2019) 12.f3 exf3 13.d4 ♕e7 14.♗xf3 ♗h3 15.♖e1∓; 10.d4 exd3 11.♕xd3 0-0 12.0-0 ♗b6 transposes to 10.0-0 ♗b6) 10...♗b6 (10...0-0 11.♘xe4 ♘xe4 12.d4 ♕e7 (Skotheim-Vorobiov, Fagernes 2019) 13.dxc5 ♘axc5 14.♘d4 ♘a6±) 11.d4 exd3 12.♕xd3 0-0 13.♘a4 ♖d8 14.♕c3=; 9...♗b4 10.d4 exd3 11.♕xd3 ♗f5 12.♕d4. **10.d4** 10.0-0 0-0 11.f3 (11.d4 exd3 12.♕xd3 ♖d8 13.♕c2 ♘a6 14.a3 ♗f5 15.e4 ♗e6∓) 11...exf3 12.d4 (12.♕xf3 ♗g4 (Vlad.Zakhartsov-Balashov, Kolomna rapid 2018) 13.♕f4 ♘bd7∓) 12...fxg2!? (12...♕e7

13.♕xf3 ♗e6 14.♘d2 ♖e8∓ Brekke-Benko, Gausdal 1984) 13.dxe5 gxf1♕+ 14.♕xf1 ♘g4∓; 10.f3 exf3 11.♕xf3 ♗f5 (leaving the queens on the board with 11...0-0!? deserved serious attention, e.g. 12.0-0 ♗g4 13.♕f4 ♘bd7 14.d4 ♕h5∓) 12.♘a4 ♘a6!? (12...0-0 (Hübner-Kortchnoi, Solingen 1973) 13.♕xf3 ♗xf5 14.♘bc5 ♗c8 15.0-0-0=) 13.♕xf5 ♗xf5 14.0-0 ♕e4∓; 10.d3 exd3 11.♕xd3 – game. **10...exd3 11.♕xd3 0-0 12.♕e2** 12.0-0 ♖d8!? (12...♘a6 (Efimov-Berelowitsch, Yalta 1996) 13.♘a4!?, with the idea to prepare the c3-square for the queen after 13...♖d8, is close to equal, e.g. 13...♗c7 14.♘d2 ♕h5 15.♖fe1=) 13.♕c2 ♘a6 14.a3 ♗e6 (14...♗f5 15.e4 ♗e6 16.♗f4 ♕h5∓) 15.♘d2 ♘c5 16.♘f3?! (16.b4=) 16...♕h5! 17.b4 ♗f5 18.♕a2 ♘d3∓ Belous-Fedoseev, PNWCC Online Masters 2020; 12.♘a4 ♗c7 13.♕e2 ♖e8 14.♘c3 ♗f5 15.0-0 ♘bd7 with excellent play for Black. **12...a5** 12...♘a6!?; 12...♗g4∓. **13.0-0** 13.h3!? ♖d8 14.0-0 ♘a6 15.♘a4 ♗c7 16.♘d2 ♘e4 17.♖fd1 ♘xd2 18.♘xd2 ♗e6∓/=. **13...♗g4** 13...a4!?. **14.♕c2** 14.f3!?. **14...♘bd7 15.h3 ♗e6?!** 15...♗f5 16.♕e2 (16.e4? ♗xh3!) 16...♖fe8∓. **16.♕e2** 16.♖d1 △ 17.♘d4=. **16...a4 17.♘d2 a3 18.♔h2** 18.♘c4!?. **18...♘d5?!** 18...♖fd8∓. **19.♘d1?** 19.♘xd5 ♗xd5 20.♗xd5 cxd5=. **19...♘b4 20.f4 ♕c5 21.bxa3 ♘c2 22.f5 ♘xa1** 22...♘d5 23.♗xd5 cxd5 24.♖b1 ♖fe8∓. **23.fxe6 ♕xc1 24.exd7 ♕c2 25.♘f2** 25.♗e4 ♕xa2 26.♘c3 ♕b2 27.♘c4 ♕xc3 28.♘xb6 ♖ad8∓. **25...♗a5?** 25...♕xa2 26.♖b1 ♗d8 27.♖xb7 ♖xa3 28.♘d3 ♕e6∓. **26.♘fe4 ♕xa2 27.♕g4** 27.♕c4 ♕xa3 28.♘f6+ gxf6 29.♕g4+ ♔h8 30.♕f5 ♕xe3 31.♕xf6+ ♔g8 32.♖f4 ♕e6 33.♖g4+ ♕xg4 34.hxg4 ♗xd2 35.♗e4=. **27...♗xd2 28.♘f6+** 28.♖f2 f5 29.♘h4 ♕xa3 30.♖xd2 fxe4 31.d8♕ ♖axd8 32.♖xd8 ♘b3 33.♗xe4 h6 34.♗f5=. **28...♔h8 29.♕f5 ♕c2 30.♗e4 g6 31.♕g4 ♕b2 32.♖f2 ♕e5??** 32...♔g7 with a draw by 33.♘h5+ ♔h8 34.♘f6 ♔g7. **33.♕h4! h5 34.♖f5!** Ouch!

34...♕xf5 35.♗xf5 ♖fd8? 35...♗xe3 36.♕e4+–. **36.♕d4 ♘b3 37.♕e5 ♔g7 38.♗c2 ♖a5 39.♕e7 1-0**

**Evgeny Shtembuliak
Steven Zierk**
St Louis 2019 (5)
1.c4 e5 2.g3 c6 3.♘f3 e4 4.♘d4 d5 5.cxd5 ♕xd5 6.♘c2 ♘f6 7.♘c3 ♕e5 8.♗g2

8...♗c5 8...h5 is premature. Black cannot neglect his development: 9.d3 exd3 (after 9...♗f5? Black loses a tempo and has to open the e-file: 10.♗f4 ♕a5 11.0-0 exd3 12.exd3 ♗e7 13.♖e1 ♖d8 14.♘e3 with a huge advantage for White, Braga-Nogueira, Sao Paulo 1991) 10.♕xd3. After 10...♘a6!? (10...♗f5 11.e4 and White has a clear advantage in all variations, e.g. 11...♗e6 (11...♗g6 12.♗f4 ♕e7 13.0-0-0+– Maletin-Balashov, Sochi 2018; 11...♗g6 12.♗f4 ♗c5 13.♖d1 ♘bd7 14.b4) 12.♗f4 ♕a5 13.♘d4 ♘bd7 14.♘xe6±) White's advantage is not so big, e.g. 11.♗f4 ♕e7 12.♘e3 ♘c5 13.♕c2 ♗e6 14.♘f5 ♕b4. **9.b4** 9.0-0 ♕e7 (more accurate looks 9...0-0 10.b4 ♗b6 11.♗b2 ♕e7 12.a3 ♘a6 13.♘e3±) 10.b4!? (10.♘e3 0-0 11.♕c2 ♖e8 12.♘xe4 ♘xe4 13.♗xe4 ♕xe4 14.♕xc5 b6 15.♕c3 (15.♕d6!?±) 15...c5 and Black has some compensation for the pawn due to the opposite-coloured bishops and his space advantage, Grandelius-Semcesen, Uppsala 2016) 10...♗xb4 11.♘xb4 ♕xb4 12.♖b1 ♕e7 13.♕a4 with a very strong initiative for the pawn. Or 9.♘e3 0-0 10.♕c2 ♖e8

(this is more ambitious than 10...♗xe3 11.fxe3 ♗f5 12.0-0 ♘bd7 13.b3 ♖fe8 14.♗b2 ♘e6 15.♖f4 ♗g6 16.♖af1 ♖ad8 17.♖a1 ♘d5 18.♖xd5 ♕xd5 19.♘c3 f6 20.♖c1 ♗e6 ½-½ Sebastian-Naumann, Germany Bundesliga 2017/18) 11.a3 ♗d4 12.0-0 ♘a6 with excellent play for Black. **9...♗b6** 9...♗d6 10.♗b2 ♕e7 11.0-0 0-0 (11...♗f5 12.d3 exd3 13.exd3 0-0 14.♖e1 ♖d8 15.♘e4 ♗e7 16.♕f3 ♗g6 (16...♘xe4!? 17.dxe4 ♗e6 18.a3 a5 19.♖ad1 ♕c7 20.♕c3±) 17.♘xf6+ ♗xf6 18.♗xf6 ♕xf6 19.♕xf6 gxf6 20.♖e7! with a much better ending for White, Adams-Christiansen, Gibraltar 2018) 12.a3 ♘a6 13.d3 exd3 14.♕xd3 ♖d8 15.♖fd1 ♘c7 16.♘d4± **10.♗b2 ♕e7 11.♘a4 ♗f5** 11...0-0 12.♘xb6 axb6 13.0-0 ♘a6 14.a3 ♘c7 15.d3 ♖d8±. **12.♘xb6 axb6 13.♘e3 ♗g6 14.♕b3** 14.b5±, here or on the next move. **14...0-0** 14...♘a6!?. **15.g4 ♖d8 16.h4 h5 17.♗h3 ♘a6** 17...♘bd7 18.♖g1 ♔h7 19.gxh5 ♘xh5 20.♗f5 ♘df6 21.♖g5 ♕f8 22.♗xf6 ♕xf6 23.h5 ♗xf5 24.♘xf5 ♘e8 25.♕e3↑; 17...hxg4 18.♖g1 gxh3 19.♖xg6 ♔f8 20.♖xg7 h2 21.0-0-0 c5 22.b5 ♘bd7 23.♖h1 ♕e6 24.♕xe6 fxe6 25.♖g5±; 17...♘d6 18.♖g1 hxg4 19.♗xg4 ♔f8 20.♘c4 ♕h2 21.0-0-0±. **18.♖g1 ♔h7 19.gxh5 ♘xh5 20.♗g4** 20.a3!? ♘c7 21.♗g4 ♖g8 22.♘f5 ♕e6± **20...♘f4?** 20...♖g8 21.a3 f6 22.♗e6 ♖ge8 23.♗h3± **21.h5 ♗xh5 22.♗xh5 ♘xh5 23.♘f5 ♕d7 24.♕h3?** 24.♘xg7! ♕xd2+ 25.♔f1 ♘f4 26.♖e1+−. **24...♕xd2+ 25.♔f1 g6 26.♗c3 ♖d3** 26...♕d7?? 27.♖g5+−. **27.♕xd3 exd3 28.♗xd2 gxf5 29.♖g5** 29.a4!?; 29.f3!?. **29...♗g7 30.exd3** White still should win after 30.♖g3!? or 30.a4. **30...♘c7** and after many inaccuracies the game ended in a draw on the 55th move. ½-½

Sharma Hemant
Daniyyl Dvirnyy
Gibraltar 2018 (9)

1.c4 e5 2.g3 ♘f6 3.♗g2 c6 4.♘f3 e4 5.♘d4 d5 6.cxd5 ♕xd5 7.♘c2 ♕e5 8.♘c3 ♗f5

9.♘e3 Or 9.0-0 and now:
A) 9...♗e7 10.♖e1 0-0 11.d3 ♖d8 12.♗f4 ♕e6 13.♘e3 ♗g6 (Haack-Enchev, Heusenstamm 2019) 14.♕a4±;
B) 9...♘a6 10.d4 (a serious inaccuracy is 10.♘e3 ♗g6 11.d4 exd3 12.exd3 (Donchenko-Hambleton, London 2017) 12...0-0-0 with excellent play for Black) 10...♕e6 (10...exd3 11.exd3 0-0-0 12.d4 ♕a5 (12...♗xc2 13.♕xc2 ♕xd4 14.♗f4 with a fierce initiative for White) 13.d5±) 11.♘e3 ♗g6 12.d5 cxd5 13.♘cxd5 ♘xd5 14.♕xd5±;
C) 9...♘bd7 10.♘e3 (10.d3±) 10...♗g6 (Forintos-Enklaar, Nice 1974; after 10...♗e6 11.♕c2 Black loses a pawn as after 11...♗d5 12.♘exd5 cxd5 13.d3 he will face unsolvable problems, e.g. 13...♖c8 14.♕a4) 11.d4 ♕e7 (11...exd3 12.exd3 ♕h5 13.♗f3 ♕h3 14.♘c4+) 12.♕b3 ♕b4 13.♖d1±. **9...♗g6** 9...♗c5 10.♘xf5 ♕xf5 11.0-0 0-0 12.♕b3 ♗b6 13.a4±. **10.b3** 10.♘c4 ♕e6 11.♕b3 b5 12.♘e3 ♕xb3 13.axb3 b4 14.♘a4 ♘bd7∞. **10...♘a6** 10...h5!?∞. **11.♗b2** 11.a3 h5∞. **11...♖d8 12.♕b1 ♕e6 13.h4 h5 14.♘h3 ♗g4 15.♗g2** 15.♘cd1 ♘c7∓. **15...♗b4** The idea of exchanging the excellent dark-squared bishop for the c3-knight cannot be good. Black could have solved the problem of the defence of the e4-pawn by 15...♘xe3 16.dxe3 f5 17.0-0 ♗e7 18.♖d1 0-0; or 15...f5 16.♕c2 ♘xe3 17.dxe3 ♘b4 18.♕c1 ♗e7, or even 15...♗c5 16.♕c2 (16.♗xe4? ♖xd2 17.♔xd2 ♘xf2−+; 16.♘xe4 ♘xe3 17.fxe3 ♗b4 18.0-0 0-0 19.d3 f5∓) 16...0-0 17.a3 ♗d4 with better chances for Black in all variations.

16.a3 ♘xe3?! Black could still turn back from the wrong path by 16...♗e7 17.♗xe4 ♘c5 18.♗xg6 fxg6 19.b4 ♘b3 (19...♘xf2 20.♔xf2 ♖xd2 21.♖c1 ♘d3+ 22.♔g2 ♕xe3 23.♗xd2 ♕f2+ 24.♔h3 with a perpetual check) 20.♘xg4 hxg4 21.♘e4 ♘xa1 22.♗xa1 ♕f7∓. **17.dxe3 ♗xc3+ 18.♗xc3 0-0 19.♕b2 f6 20.0-0 ♖d5 21.b4 b6 22.♖fd1 ♖fd8 23.♖d4 ♘c7** and the game ended in a draw on the 39th move. ½-½

Luis Mario Buchaillot
Pedro Vertíz Gutiérrez
cr 2017

1.c4 e5 2.g3 c6 3.♘f3 e4 4.♘d4 d5 5.cxd5 ♕xd5 6.♘c2 ♘f6 7.♘c3 ♕e5 8.♗g2 ♗e7

9.♘e3 9.0-0 0-0 10.f4 exf3 (Grandelius-Giri, Stavanger 2016) 11.♗xf3 ♗h3 12.d4 ♕e6 13.♖e1 ♘a6 14.e4 ♖ad8=. **9...♘a6 10.a3** 10.♕a4 ♘c5 11.♕c2 0-0 12.b3 ♘e6 13.♗b2 ♘d4 14.♕b1 ♗e6 15.♘xe4 ♖ad8 16.♕d3 ♘xe4 17.♕xe4 ♘f3+ 18.♗xf3 ♕xb2∓. **10...♘c7** An inaccuracy. Now Black will have problems with the e4-pawn. 10...0-0 11.b4 ♘d5 (11...♕h5 12.♕c2 ♗h3 13.♗xe4 ♘xe4 14.♕xe4 ♗e6 15.♗b2 ♖fe8 16.h4 Black has some compensation for the pawn) 12.♘cxd5 cxd5 13.♖b1 ♕h5 14.0-0 ♗e6 15.d3± **11.♕a4** After 11.♕c2 0-0 12.♘xe4 ♘b5 Black has compensation for the pawn, e.g. 13.f4 (13.♘c4 ♕h5 14.e3 ♘xe4 15.♕xe4 ♗e6 16.♕c2 ♗f5 17.♕b3 ♖ad8) 13...♕h5 14.b4 ♘xe4 15.♗xe4 ♘d4 16.♕d3 ♖d8 17.♗b2 ♗f6. **11...0-0** After the weakening move 11...b5 the situation has changed: 12.♕c2 ♘e6 13.♘xe4 ♘d4 14.♕d3 ♘xe4 15.♘c2!±. **12.♘xe4 ♘xe4** 12...♘b5!?. **13.♕xe4 ♕f6** 13...♕xe4

14.♘xe4 ♘e6 15.d3 (15.♖b1!?)
**15...♘d4 16.♗d2 f5 17.♗g2 ♗e6
18.♘c3 ♖ad8 19.♖c1** (19.♖b1!?)
**19...♘b3 20.♕c2 ♘d4 21.♖d2 ♘b3
22.♖d1 ♘d4 23.♖b1** and White is
a pawn up, which is difficult to
convert, Bhattacharjea-Lund, cr
2019. **14.0-0 ♘b5 15.♖b1 ♖d8
16.d3 ♗e6 17.♗d2 ♖a2 18.♖a1
♗e6** 18...♕xb2 19.♕xe7 ♕xd2
20.♕xb7 ♗e6±. **19.♘d1** 19.♘c4!?.
**19...♘d4 20.♕e3 ♖d7 21.♗c3
♘d4 22.b4 h5 23.♖b1 h4 24.♗xd4
♕xd4 25.♕xd4 ♖xd4 26.b5 cxb5
27.♖xb5 ♖b8 28.♖xb7 ♖xb7
29.♗xb7 ♗xa3 30.♘e3 ♗b2
31.♖b1 ♗b4 32.♗a6 ♖a2 33.♖e1
h3 34.♔f1 ♖a4 35.♗b5 ♖b4** ½-½

**Jon Ludvig Hammer
David Navara**
Novy Bor 2016 (4)

**1.c4 e5 2.g3 c6 3.♘f3 e4 4.♘d4
d5 5.cxd5 ♕xd5 6.♘c2 ♘f6
7.♘c3 ♕e5 8.♗g2 ♗e7 9.♘e3
♘a6 10.♕c2 ♗b4** Less accurate
is 10...♗c5 11.b3 ♘e6 12.♗b2
♘d4 13.♕b1 ♗e6 14.♘xe4 ♘xe4
15.♕xe4 ♘f3+ 16.♗xf3 ♕xb2 17.0-0
♕xd2 18.♖ad1±. **11.♕b1**

11...♗e6 11...♘bd5 12.♘xe4 ♘xe3
13.dxe3 (13.fxe3 ♘xe4 14.♕xe4
♕h5 15.♗f3 ♕g6 16.♕xg6 hxg6
17.d3 ♗f6 18.♖b1 a5 Vidit-Wang
Hao, Nations Cup Online 2020)
13...♗f5 14.♘xf6+ ♗xf6 (after
14...♕xf6 15.e4 ♗b4+ 16.♔f1
(Navara-Cs.Balogh, Achaea tt 2016)
16...♗e6 17.♘e3 ♗a5 18.♕c2 Black
does not have full compensation
for the pawn) 15.e4 0-0-0 16.f4
♕a5+ 17.♔f2 ♕b6+ 18.♗e3=
(18.♔f3 ♗e6 19.♕c2 g5 20.f5 h5
21.♗e3 g4+ 22.♔f2 ♗d4 23.♕c1
♗xf5 24.exf5 ♖he8 25.♗xd4
♕xd4+ 26.♔f1 ♖xe2 27.♗xe2 ♕d3+

28.♔f2 ♕d4+=) 18...♘d4 19.♕d3
♖he8 20.♖hd1 ♗xe3+ 21.♕xe3
♗xe4 22.♕xb6 axb6 23.♖xd8+
♔xd8 with an equal ending. **12.b3**
More forcing play arises after 12.a3
♘bd5 13.♘xe4 (13.♘exd5 cxd5
14.d3 (Orlovtsev-Zolochevsky, cr
2018) 14...0-0 15.♗f4 ♕h5 16.dxe4
dxe4 17.♘xe4 ♗h3 18.0-0 ♗xg2
19.♔xg2 ♕xe2 20.♖e1 ♕a6=)
13...♘xe3 14.dxe3 0-0-0 15.♗d2
(15.♗d2 h5 16.♘f3 ♕d5☒) 15...♘xe4
16.♗xe4 ♖xd2 17.♔xd2 (Parushev-
Spasov, cr 2018) 17...♘f6 18.a4
(18.♖c1 ♘b3 19.♗c2 ♗e6 20.♗d3
♗b3=) 18...♘d5=. **12...♘bd5
13.♗b2 ♘xe3 14.fxe3 ♗f5 15.0-0
♕e6 16.♖f4 ♗d6?!** 16...♗g6
17.♕c2 (17.♘xe4?! ♘h5 18.♖f2 f5
(Tanner-Fric, cr 2019) 19.g4 fxg4
20.♕c2 0-0-0∓) 17...0-0-0 18.♖af1
♔b8 19.♘xe4 ♖he8=. **17.♖xf5
♕xf5 18.♘xe4 ♘xe4 19.♗xe4
♕g5 20.♕c2**

20...f5?! White's initiative for
the exchange is very strong, e.g.
20...h6?! 21.♖f1! (21.♗xc6+ bxc6
22.♖xc6+ ♔e7 23.♕b7+ ♔e6
24.♕e4+=) 21...0-0 22.♖f5 ♕e7
(22...♕g4 23.♕c4 (threatening
24.♖xf7) 23...h5 (there is no other
defence) 24.♕c2 ♖ad8 25.♗f3
♕g6 26.♗xh5 ♕h6 27.♕e4±)
23.♖d3?! g6 24.♖h5 ♔h7 25.g4
26.♕b1 ♕e6 27.h3 ♗e7 28.♖f5=,
but 23.♖h5!± looks frightening
for Black: 23...♖fe8 24.♗h7+ ♔f8
25.♕c3. **21.♗xf5 0-0?!** 21...♖d8
22.♖f1 ♖f8 23.♗xh7 ♖xf1+ 24.♔xf1
♔c7 25.♕g6 ♖f8+ 26.♔g1±.
**22.♗xh7+ ♔h8 23.♕g6 ♕xg6
24.♗xg6 a5 25.♖c1** 25.a4!? was
more precise. **25...a4 26.♖c4 axb3
27.axb3 ♖a2 28.♗c3 ♗e7 29.♖e4
♗f6 30.♗xf6 gxf6 31.♖d4 ♖b2
32.b4 ♖a8 33.♗f5 ♖a4 34.♖d8+**

**♔g7 35.♖d7+ ♔f8 36.♖d8+
♔e7 37.♖d7+ ♔f8 38.♖xb7**
38.h4!?+−. **38...♖xd2** 38...♖axb4
39.♖d7±. **39.♔f2 ♖b2 40.♖b6
♖axb4 41.♖xc6 ♖b6 42.♖c8+
♔g7 43.♖c7+ ♔f8 44.♗e4 ♖e6
45.♔f3 ♖e7 46.♖c6 ♔g7 47.g4?!**
47.♗f5 ♖d2 48.♗c4 ♖a2 49.e4±.
**47...♖b8 48.h4 ♖h8 49.h5 ♖he8
50.h6+ ♔xh6 51.♖xf6+ ♔g7
52.♖f4 ♖e5 53.♘d3 ♖xe3+ 54.♔f2
♔h6 55.♖f5 ♖3e5 56.♔f3 ♖xf5+
57.gxf5 ♔g5 58.e4 ♖d8 59.♔e3
♔f6** ½-½

**Surya Shekhar Ganguly
Yu Yangyi**
Douglas 2019 (4)

**1.c4 e5 2.g3 c6 3.♘f3 e4 4.♘d4
d5 5.cxd5 ♕xd5 6.♘c2 ♘f6 7.♘c3
♕e5 8.♗g2 ♘a6**

9.♖b1 9.♘e3 ♗c5 10.a4
(10.♕c2 ♘b4 11.♕b1 ♗xe3 12.fxe3
(12.dxe3!?) 12...♗f5 13.b3 0-0
14.0-0 (Puranik-Prithu, Moscow
2019) 14...♖ad8∞; 10.a3 0-0 11.♕c2
♖e8 12.b3 (12.0-0 ♗d4 13.b4 ♗d7
14.♗b2 ♖ad8 15.♖ab1=) 12...♗d4
13.♗b2 ♘c5 (13...b5!?) 14.b4
(A.Marjanovic-Kashlinskaya, Ruma
2017) 14...♘cd7!?∞ ∆ ...♘b6, ...♗e6)
10...♗xe3 11.fxe3 ♗f5=; 9.a3 ♗c5
(9...♘c5 10.b4 ♘b3 11.♖b1 ♘xc1
12.♕xc1 g6=; 9...h5!?) 10.b4 ♗b6
11.♗b2 0-0 (Bicer-Tarun, Antalya
2019) 12.0-0 ♗e7 13.♘e3±. **9...♘b4**
9...♗e7!?=; 9...♗d6!?. **10.♘xb4
♗xb4 11.♕a4 a5** 11...♕d4!?
12.e3 ♕c5 13.a3 ♗xc3 14.bxc3 0-0
15.c4 ♕e7 16.♗b2 ♘d7=. **12.a3
♗xc3 13.dxc3 0-0 14.♗e3 ♗f5?!**
14...♕h5=. **15.♖d1 ♕e6 16.0-0
♗h3 17.♗d4 ♗xg2 18.♔xg2 b5
19.♕c2 ♘d5 20.c4 bxc4 21.♖c1
♕g4 22.e3 ♕f3+ 23.♔g1 ♘c7
24.♕d1 ♕f5 25.♖xc4 ♘e6**

26.♖xc6 26.h4!?. **26...♖fd8 27.♕c2 h5 28.f3 ♘xd4 29.exd4 ♖xd4 30.fxe4 ♕xe4 31.♖c8+ ♖xc8 32.♕xc8+ ♔h7 33.♕f5+ ♕xf5 34.♖xf5 ♔g6 35.♖xa5 ♖d1+ 36.♔f2 ♖d2+ 37.♔f3 ♖xb2 ½-½**

Anish Giri
Alexander Grischuk
Yekaterinburg ct 2020 (7)

1.c4 e5 2.g3 c6 3.♘f3 e4 4.♘d4 d5 5.cxd5 ♕xd5 6.♘c2 ♘f6 7.♘c3 ♕e5 8.♗g2 ♘a6 9.0-0

9...♗e7 9...h5 is premature, e.g. 10.d4 (10.d3!?) 10...exd3 (10...♕e6 11.♗g5 ♗e7 (11...h4?! looks like a desperate try: 12.♗xh4 ♖xh4 13.gxh4 ♕g4 14.♘xe4 ♘xe4 15.f3+− Martinez Alcantara-Vitiugov, Riga 2019) 12.♘e3±) 11.exd3 ♗e6 12.♗f4 ♕a5 13.♖e1 h4 14.♘d4 0-0-0 15.♘xe6 fxe6 16.♖xe6±. **10.♘e3** A safe move which does not give White serious chances of obtaining an advantage. However, other continuations do not offer much either:

A) 10.f3 exf3 11.♗xf3 ♗g4 (also good is 11...♗h3 12.d4 ♕e6 13.♖e1 0-0 14.e4 ♖ad8=) 12.d4 ♕h5 13.e4 ♖d8 (Lagarde-Prithu, Porticcio 2019) 14.♗xg4 ♘xg4 15.♕e2 ♕g6=;

B) 10.♖e1 ♗e6 11.d3 exd3 12.exd3 ♕d6 13.d4 0-0 14.d5 ♘xd5 15.♘xd5 ♗xd5 16.♗xd5 cxd5 17.♘e3 ♖fe8 18.♘xd5 ♘f8 19.♖xe8 ♖xe8 20.♗f4 ♕e6 21.♕f3 ♕e2 22.♕xe2 ♖xe2 23.♖b1 f6 24.♔f1 ♖c2 25.♗e3 ½-½ Henry-Zaas, cr 2019. **10...h5** After the insertion of the moves ♘e3 and ...♗e7 this flank thrust is not bad. **11.d4 exd3 12.exd3 ♕d4 13.♘c2 ♕g4 14.♗f4 ♕xd1 15.♖axd1 ♗g4 16.♖d2 0-0-0 17.d4 ♕c7 18.♘e3 ♗e6 19.d5= ♘cxd5 20.♘cxd5 ♘xd5 21.♘xd5**

♗xd5 **22.♖xd5 ♖xd5 23.♗xd5 cxd5 24.♖c1+ ♔d7 25.♖c7+ ♔e6 26.♖xb7 ♖c8 27.♖xa7 ♖c2 28.♗e3 ♘f6 29.♖a4 ♗xb2 30.♔g2 d4 31.♗xd4 ♗xd4 32.♖xd4 ♖xa2 33.♖e4+ ♔f6 34.♖f4+ ♔e6 35.♖e4+ ♔f6 36.♖f4+ ♔e6 37.♖e4+ ♔f6 38.♖f4+ ♔e6 39.h4 g6 40.♖e4+ ♔f6 ½-½**

Ruud Janssen
Predrag Nikolic
Netherlands tt 2018/19 (7)

1.c4 e5 2.g3 ♘f6 3.♗g2 c6 4.♘f3 e4 5.♘d4 d5 6.cxd5 ♕xd5 7.♘c2 ♕e5 8.♘c3 ♘a6 9.0-0 ♗e7 10.d4 exd3 11.exd3

11...♗g4 This move causes some problems. White has to play f2-f3, closing the h1-a8 diagonal for his active light-squared bishop, or move the queen to a square which is not the best. 11...♗e6?! 12.♗f4 (12.♖e1 ♕d6 13.d4 0-0 transposes to Henry-Zaas, cr 2019, see the previous game) 12...♕h5 13.♘d4 ♖d8 14.♘xe6 fxe6 15.♖e1 ♕xd1 16.♖axd1±. **12.♕d2** 12.f3 ♗e6 (12...♗c8 13.f4 ♕c7 14.f5 0-0=) 13.f4 ♕a5 14.♕e2 (14.♘e3!?∞) 14...♖d8 15.♗d2 ♕f5 (15...♕b6+!?) 16.♗e4 ♘xe4 17.dxe4 ♕g4 18.♕g2 ♗c5+ 19.♗e3 0-0 20.f5 ♗c8 21.♔f2 b6 22.♖ad1 ♖fe8 23.a3 ♗b7 24.♖d2 ♗f8 25.♖fd1 ½-½ Kutlu-Doronkin, cr 2019. **12...0-0 13.♖e1?!** 13.♘e3 ♕h5 14.♘xg4 ♕xg4 15.♕d1 ♕f5 16.d4 ♖ad8=; 13.d4 ♕c7 14.♘e3 ♗e6 15.♖d1 ♘b4=. **13...♕c7 14.♕g5** 14.h3!?. **14...♕d7 15.♗f4?** 15.d4 ♖fe8 16.a3 ♗e6∓. **15...♘d5 16.♖xe7** 16.♕e5 ♗f6 17.♕d6 ♘xc3−+. **16...♘xe7 17.♘e3 ♗e6 18.♘e4 ♘g6** and Black realized his extra exchange on the 36th move. **0-1**

Evgeny Tomashevsky
Alexander Grischuk
Moscow Wch blitz 2019 (6)

1.c4 e5 2.g3 c6 3.♘f3 e4 4.♘d4 d5 5.cxd5 ♕xd5 6.♘c2 ♘f6 7.♘c3 ♕e5 8.♗g2 ♘a6 9.0-0 ♗e7 10.d3 exd3 11.♕xd3

11...♘c5 11...♗f5? 12.♗xc6+ (12.e4± Iturrizaga-Narayanan, chess24. com 2020) 12...bxc6 13.♖xa6 0-0 (13...♕c7 14.♘d4±) 14.♗f4 ♕c5 15.♗e3 ♕d6±; 11...♗e6 12.♗xc6+ (12.♗f4 (Iturrizaga-Narayanan, chess24.com 2020) 12...♕a5 13.♘d4 ♖d8 14.♖ad1 ♗c5 15.♘b3 ♗xb3 16.♕xd8+ ♕xd8 17.♖xd8+ ♔xd8 18.axb3 ♗e7=) 12...bxc6 13.♖xa6 0-0 14.♗f4 ♕h5 (14...♕c5 15.♖fd1±) 15.♕xc6±. **12.♕d4** Other queen retreats do not give White much either, e.g. 12.♕f3 0-0 13.♖d1 ♕f5 14.♘d4 ♕xf3 15.♘xf3 ♘fe4=; 12.♗e3 ♕h5 13.♕g5 ♕g6=. **12...♕xd4?!** Black has a good position after 12...♕h5 13.♖d1 ♗h3 14.♗xh3 ♕xh3 15.f3 0-0 16.♕f2 ♖ad8 17.♗e3 b6=. **13.♘xd4 0-0 14.♗f4** White's pieces are a little more active. **14...g6?!** 14...♖d8 15.♖fd1 a5 16.h3 ♖e8 17.e3 ♘e6 18.♗e5 ♘xd4 19.♗xd4 ♗e6 20.b3 ♖ad8=. **15.b4 ♘e6 16.♘xe6 ♗xe6 17.b5 ♘d5** 17...♖ac8 18.♖fd1 ♖fd8 19.♖xd8+ ♖xd8 20.bxc6 bxc6 21.♖b1 c5 22.♔f1 ♕h5 23.♗e3±. **18.♘xd5 cxd5 19.♖fd1 ♖fd8 20.♖ac1 ♖d7 21.♗e5 f5 22.♗d4 ♔f7 23.e3 ♗d8 24.♖c2 ♗b6 25.a4 ♔e7 26.f4** 26.♗xb6 axb6 27.♖d4 ♔d6 28.♔f1±. **26...♖ad8** Black should have exchanged one pair of rooks: 26...♖c7! 27.♖xc7+ ♗xc7 28.♖c1 ♔d7 29.♔f2±. **27.♔f2 ♖a8 28.♖dc1 ♖ad8** Here or later, 28...♖xd4!? 29.exd4 ♔d6± and White would have

had to find a way to realize his advantage. **29.♔e2 ♖a8 30.♔d3 ♖ad8 31.♔e2 ♖a8 32.♔d3 ♖ad8 33.♖c8 ♖xc8 34.♖xc8 ♔d6 35.♗xb6** 35.a5 ♗xd4 36.♔xd4+−. **35...axb6 36.♔d4 ♗f7 37.♖f8 h5 38.h4 ♖c7 39.♖d8+ ♔e7 40.♖b8 ♔d6 41.♖d8+ ♔e7 42.♖b8 ♔d6 43.♗xd5 ♗xd5 44.♖d8+ ♔e6 45.♖xd5 ♖c1 46.♖e5+**

46...♔d6? The black king chooses the wrong side. 46...♔f6 47.♖e8!; 46...♔f7! 47.e4 ♖d1+± was the most resilient defence. **47.e4! fxe4** 47...♖d1+ 48.♔e3! ♖e1+ 49.♔d3 fxe4+ 50.♔d4 and the white rook has gained entry to the kingside via g5. The pawn on g6 will fall sooner or later. **48.♔xe4 ♖e1+ 49.♔d4 ♖d1+ 50.♔c4 ♖c1+ 51.♔b3 ♖b1+ 52.♔c3 ♖a1 53.♖g5** and White realized his advantage on the 64th move. **1-0**

Jon Ludvig Hammer
Anish Giri
Moscow 2017 (4)
1.c4 e5 2.g3 c6 3.♘f3 e4 4.♘d4 d5 5.cxd5 ♕xd5 6.♘c2 ♘f6 7.♘c3 ♕e5 8.♗g2 ♘a6 9.0-0 ♗e7 10.d4 exd3 11.♕xd3 0-0

12.♕e3 12.♖d1 ♖e8 13.e4 ♕h5 14.f3 ♘c5 15.♕f1 b6 16.♕e1 ♗a6 17.♘b4 ♗b7= Lorenz-Conde Poderoso, cr 2020; 12.e4 ♕h5 13.♕d1 ♗g4 14.f3 ♖ad8 15.♕e2 (Ju Wenjun-Goryachkina, Skolkovo 2019) 15...♗e6 16.♗e3 ♘c5=. **12...♗d6?!** After 12...♕c7 Black has equal play in all lines, e.g. 13.♖d1 (13.♕f4 ♗d6 (13...♖d8 14.♕xc7 ♘xc7 15.e4 ♗e6 16.♗f4 ♘a6 17.♖ad1 ♘b4) 14.♕h4 ♗e7 15.♕f4 ♗d6) 13...♗f5 14.♘d4 ♗g6 15.♕f3 ♖ad8. **13.♖d1 ♖e8 14.♕d4** 14.♕xe5 was good now or on the next move, e.g. 14...♗xe5 15.e4 ♘c5 16.f3 ♘fd7 17.♘d4±. **14...♗c7** After 14...♕xd4

15.♘xd4 any move with d6-bishop will be met by ♘xc6 with a better ending for White. **15.♗f4?!** 15.♕xe5 ♖xe5 16.e4±. **15...♕h5** 15...♕xd4!? 16.♖xd4 ♗b6 17.♖d2 ♘c5=. **16.♗xc7 ♘xc7 17.f3** 17.♘e3 ♘b5 18.♘xb5 ♕xb5 19.♗f3 ♗e6=. **17...♗e6** 17...♘b5 18.♘xb5 ♕xb5 19.e4 ♗e6 20.a4 ♕b3 21.♗e3. **18.♕f2 ♘g5 19.g4** 19.♖d3 ♕h3+ 20.♗xh3 ♗xh3 21.♖ad1. **19...♕g6 20.♘e3 h5** 20...♗e6!? 21.h4 ♘f4 22.♖d4±. **21.h4 ♘e6 22.g5 ♘f4 23.♖d4 ♘6d5 24.♘cxd5 ♘xd5 25.♘xd5 cxd5 26.♖xd5 ♗e6 27.♖d2 ♖ad8 28.e4 f5?!** Black loses another pawn. Nevertheless, the realization of this material advantage is not easy due to White's exposed kingside pawns. 28...♖xd2 29.♕xd2 ♗c8 30.♔h2 ♕b6 31.♖d1±. **29.♖xd8 ♖xd8 30.♕xa7 ♕f7** 30...fxe4 31.fxe4 ♕e8 32.♕e3 ♗c4±. **31.♕a5?!** 31.♕b6 ♖d3 32.♖e1+−. **31...♕d7 32.♕e5 fxe4 33.fxe4 ♗h3** 33...b5!?. **34.♕d5+** More chances of a win were given by 34.♗f3, e.g. 34...♕d7 35.♕h2 ♕d4+ 36.♕f2 ♕e5 37.♗xh5 ♖f8 38.♕e3. **34...♕xd5 35.exd5 ♗xg2 36.♗xg2 ♖xd5 37.♗f1 ♖d4** White did not manage to realize his extra pawn and the game ended in a draw on the 79th move. **½-½**

Exercise 1

position after 10.d2-d3

Black took the d-pawn. Was that his best option?

(solutions on page 254)

Exercise 2

position after 23...♕e7-d7

White played the inaccurate 24.♕h3 and after 24...♕xd2+ 25.♔f1 g6 26.♗c3 ♖d3! Black was still in the game. What should White have played?

Exercise 3

position after 15.h2-h3

Here Black played 15...♗e6, which was not the best. Which move was better?

VIEWS

Featuring
Reviews
Solutions to Exercises

The joy of finding wisdom

by Glenn Flear

Englishman Glenn Flear lives in the south of France. For every Yearbook he reviews a selection of new chess opening books. A grandmaster and a prolific chess author himself, Flear's judgment is severe but sincere, and always constructive.

I recently saw a fascinating mini-documentary on the BBC. Amateur researchers had discovered some amazing truths about the curious disposition of some large rocks. It seems that ancient people from 5000 years ago(!) had moved and shaped these boulders in order to create a very precise calendar generated by the sun's apparition. A Japanese lady commented on her implication by explaining there was no pecuniary benefit from spending countless days measuring and observing, just 'the joy of finding wisdom from the bottom of my heart'. That's such a beautiful thing to say! In the chess world there is always something new to learn, like the latest trends expanded on by an opening book. Despite the extensive powers of modern technology, I like to imagine (just like the great masters of yesteryear) an author poring over his chess set, moving a few pieces around and ultimately having his Eureka moment. It's sort of a noble human way of uncovering (or rediscovering) something special that, once shared, can offer knowledge and pleasure to many chess adventurers.

Semko Semkov
The Modern Triangle
Chess Stars 2020

Bulgarian IM Semko Semkov sets out a repertoire for

Black based around playing ...d7-d5, ...e7-e6 and ...c7-c6, essentially in this order. For the uninitiated, it's a sort of hybrid with features of the Slav, Semi-Slav and Queen's Gambit. He explains his typical game plan which involves a timely capture on c4 and then a willingness to return the pawn to open up play and liberate his game. So, for example, he embraces the Noteboom and Meran, but avoids any sort of Stonewall.

A whole career's worth of experience has enabled him to point out the salient features of the early move order trickery and jostling. He explains what is at stake when meeting White's various attempts, and is willing to steer the game into certain forms of the Semi-Slav (such as the Moscow Variation), the Queen's Gambit Declined (Exchange Variation) or the Catalan (with ...dxc4), depending on circumstances.

So his approach is a chameleon-like one, seeking the better versions of related openings and avoiding certain problematic alternatives. He has aimed to make the work as pragmatic as possible, both in terms of a well-defined repertoire and (for the reader's comfort!) by sticking to essentials has kept the book to a manageable size.

Although I thought I knew this subject quite well, I kept getting surprised with his ideas:

1.d4 d5 2.c4 e6 3.♘f3 c6 4.♘bd2

Against other non-critical moves, he generally replies with 4...♘f6, e.g. 4.♕c2 ♘f6 5.g3 (after 5.♗g5 the repertoire suggestion is 5...h6, possibly heading towards a Moscow Variation) 5...dxc4 6.♕xc4 b5; or 4.♕b3 ♘f6 5.♘c3 dxc4 6.♕xc4 b5 etc.

4...♘f6 5.g3 b6 6.♗g2 ♗b7 7.0-0 ♗e7 8.♕c2 0-0 9.e4 ♘a6!

This does seem to solve a number of problems for Black for meeting such Catalan-style move orders. I didn't know this particular move order idea, although Semkov gives the impression that it's been well-known for years (where have I been all this time?).

10.a3

10.e5 ♘d7 11.cxd5 is neatly met with 11...♘b4! 12.♕b3 ♘xd5.

10...c5

The fact that the book is conveniently thin gives the impression that a reader isn't going to get overwhelmed with sub-variations and sub-plots! Even so, he still addresses the critical lines and allocates them ample space:

1.d4 d5 2.c4 e6 3.♘c3 c6 4.e4 dxe4

4...♗b4?! 'is not worth the pain' – SS.

5.♘xe4 ♗b4+ 6.♗d2 ♕xd4 7.♗xb4 ♕xe4+ 8.♗e2

In the other main line 8.♘e2 ♘a6 9.♗a5, the author opts for the surprising 9...♕h4 (despite there being only one practical example) 10.♕d2 ♘h6 11.0-0-0 0-0 12.♘g3 (Utnasunov-Kezin, Sochi rapid 2017), and now Semkov prefers Black after two different ways: 12...f6, with ...e6-e5 and ...♘f7 in mind, as well as 12...b6 13.♗c3 ♗b7.

8...♘a6 9.♗d6

Following 9.♗c3, SS argues the case for 9...f6, the 'more challenging' option, in a murky web of variations; whereas another critical line is 9.♗a5 b6 10.♕d6 ♗d7 11.♗c3 f6 12.♘f3 ♘h6 13.♖d1 ♖d8 14.♕a3 ♗c8 15.♘d2 ♕f4 where recent e-mail games suggest that Black is fine here as well.

9...♕xg2 10.♕d2 e5!?

This 'liberating' move has hardly been discussed before with, for example, leading

expert Scherbakov just mentioning in passing that it might be playable.

The main move here has been 10...♘f6.

11.♗xe5 ♗f5

The book also examines 11...♘e7 which, SS describes, 'is more tangled, yet also more risky'.

12.♗f3 ♕g6 13.0-0-0 ♘c5 14.♕e3 ♗b1 15.♖d2 ♗xa2 16.♗d6+ ♘e6 17.♗e4 ♕h6 18.f4

'This position looks critical for 11...♗f5' – SS.

18...♘f6 19.♘f3 ♗xc4

Although Etienne Bacrot (playing White) actually beat Alexander Morozevich (Biel 2012) from this position, that was due to a blunder from his opponent. Evidence since then suggests that Black is holding his own here.

As an alternative, 19...♘xe4 20.♕xe4 0-0-0 21.♘e5 ♖he8 is 'a simpler solution' according to the author but it still looks quite tense!

There has been a conscious effort to discuss and emphasize the plans, aims and potential drawbacks whilst offering the reader easy-to-understand advice. In this domain, the benchmark until now was Scherbakov's noticeably heavier *The Triangle System* (Everyman Chess, 2012), which was a sort of 'complete' work, whereas the present 'repertoire' edition is only half the size. *The Modern Triangle* fits into the reasoning that if someone is telling a good tale, you don't want it to go on for too long, or it won't be any good any more!

Still, Semkov also found the space for a bonus chapter looking at how to cope with the Réti and King's Indian Attack.

Of course, each chapter follows the Chess Stars' pet formula of dividing material into three distinct sub-chapters: 'Main ideas', 'Step-by-step' and then 'Annotated games'. Well, it's probably Semkov who formulated this method in the first place! It works very well here, as it does so often, as everybody can satisfy their quest for information to the desired degree. It's also worth noting that, compared to other publications emanating from Bulgaria, the use of English was rather good here. Of all the review books from this quarter's selection, this is the one that best fits into the traditional formula of what one expects from an opening monograph.

Summing up: it's always a pleasure to read what a knowledgeable expert has to offer. Someone who plays an opening himself, points you in the right direction and cuts out all the 'less desirable variations'. In terms of obtaining a dynamic and credible opening repertoire against 1.d4, most of the hard work has been done for you, all that's left to do is buy the book and then start turning pages.

Daniel Hausrath
Double Fianchetto
Thinkers Publishing 2020

A new author and a novel subject, but the two-word title is sufficient to give you a good idea as to what it's all about. It turns out that the *Double Fianchetto* examines the relevant scenarios in several openings, but the main area of struggle is generally later on. It's an opening book where theory is kept to a minimum.

A glance at any bookstall will perhaps confirm to you that all sorts of creative middlegame strategy books are available these days. This trend of weaving a striking theme throughout a work is spilling over into literature dealing with the opening phase. So here we essentially have a gentle preamble through 62 games where various set-ups are tried out. A decent selection with a great deal of fighting chess, general principles, practical advice and some psychology, can be found, but no real theory at all! The only thing that links the whole project together is that at some point at least one of the players will fianchetto both bishops. The *Introduction* indicates that the main purpose of the author is to explain the structures arising, but I didn't find a great deal of this in these pages (there is just too much flexibility!). Instead, it came across as more of a 'selection of games that illustrate how play can pan out' in various openings, that is, after at least one of the players decides to place both his bishops on the long diagonals. There are quite a few of the German GM's own games, so the reader is treated to a fair serving of anecdotes that often help put the 'at the board' decisions into context. The annotations are light but with plenty of instructive text in straightforward English, as if a school teacher is showing a pupil how it works.

I suppose the subtitle *The Modern Chess Lifestyle* may help clarify the author's philosophy, and Hausrath does seem to be one of those players who seem to make a living from fianchettoing his bishops as quickly and often

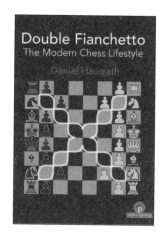

as possible! Still, I wonder if the message can come across and help the average reader. Is it possible to change 'lifestyle' from being a 'classical theory buff' to a 'get your pieces out and see what happens later' person? If someone has played concrete forcing variations all their life, how will they adapt to the vagueness of general principles, even when largely well founded?

Here is one of the lines where a bit of real theory does actually creep in:

1.♘f3 ♘f6 2.g3 g6 3.b3 ♗g7 4.♗b2 c5 5.♗g2 0-0 6.c4 d6 7.d4 ♘e4 8.0-0 ♘c6

The author is something of a specialist of the less common **9.a3!?**,
discussing some alternatives: 9.♘bd2 ♘xd2 10.♕xd2 e5∞. Or 9.h3 ♗f5 10.e3 ♘f6 (the author instead suggests 10...♖c8 with ...d6-d5 often

coming quickly) 11.♘c3 (11.d5 ♘b4 12.a3 ♘a6 13.♕e2 'with ♘bd2 and e3-e4 coming' – DH) 11...cxd4 12.♘xd4 ♗d7 13.♕e2 'Now we have a normal position where Black has lost time' DH (Kramnik-Caruana, Zurich 2015).

9...d5

The author mentions that he once had 9...♗g4 10.♕c2 ♗f5? 11.g4 and went on to win. Otherwise, 9...♗f5 10.♖a2 (one of the features behind his ninth move choice) 10...cxd4 11.♘xd4 ♘xf2?! (11...♗xd4 12.♗xd4 ♘xg3 13.♗xc6 ♘xf1 14.♗g2 e5 15.♗c3 ♗xh2 16.♔xh2 ♕h4+ 17.♔g1 ♗h3 18.♕f1 ♕g4=) 12.♖xf2 ♗xd4 13.♗xd4 ♗xb1 (Hausrath-Cheparinov, Dos Hermanas blitz 2004), and now the author points out 14.♗xc6! ♗xa2 15.♗d5 with a crushing position.

10.cxd5 ♕xd5 11.♘fd2 f5 12.♘c3 ♕xd4 13.♘dxe4 ♕xd1 14.♖fxd1 fxe4 15.♗xe4 ♗e6=

I suppose these lines show that even when development seems sedate, matters can soon come to a head. Of course, it's also clear that even when a non-theoretical approach is sought after, theory will develop in due course anyway!

Although I found it to be entertaining at times, I'm personally too set in my ways to be tempted by this lifestyle change. It's more suitable for those who want something completely different which involves a minimum of memory work.

Ilya Odessky
Winning Quickly with 1.b3 and 1...b6
New In Chess 2020

I'm going to start by quoting the author: 'How are we

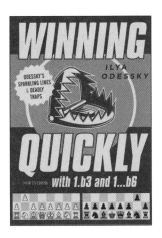

going to win by starting the game with second-rate moves such as 1.b3 or 1...b6?' The answer it seems is 'We are prepared to set traps!'. Such is how the author Ilya Odessky sets out his store. It soon becomes apparent that he is an original writer and thinker in many ways! A case in point is that the Foreword has been replaced with a series of twelve exercises in rather sharp positions. Not easy these! I think that the idea is to inspire the reader with the amazing ideas that can be found herein, but there is a risk of putting people off who might already feel out of their depth. His text is full of wit, pithy comments, barbed leading questions, some political incorrectness and many dramatic turns of phrase. In these pages, success relies on the fact that 'to err is human', as in a stressful situation (i.e. limited time, lack of opening knowledge) strong players have a tendency to go astray. Maybe this aspect of the book is more important than the content itself. So if you are tempted to open up these pages, be prepared for calculated gambles, psychological ploys, and sheer

bravado! If you have recently become an adept of online blitz, and want to develop the traits that this involves, then this book could be a godsend. Here is an example amongst many others that you can find in the work:

1.b3 d5 2.♗b2 ♗g4 3.f3 ♗h5 4.e4

'The gambit is unsound, but it is fresh and interesting and analyzing it is a pleasure.' – IO. Well, now you know where he stands! By the way, I have to admit that I did once get mated (and quite prettily) by a lower-rated player in this gambit.

4...dxe4 5.♕e2 c6 6.♘c3 exf3 7.♘xf3 e6 8.0-0-0 ♘f6 9.h3 ♘bd7 10.g4 ♗g6 11.h4 h5 12.g5 ♘g4

'White's counterplay is insufficient' – IO. The book demonstrates that 12...♘d5 is also quite decent.

13.♗h3 ♕a5 14.♔b1 0-0-0

The author, in an online game, followed his own home-brewed analysis and played the remarkable move
15.♘e4,
'which looks like an oversight' – IO, and ultimately went on to win after
15...♗xe4 16.♕xe4 ♘f2 17.♕f4 ♘xd1 18.♖xd1,
when White has pressure on the kingside and great bishops for the exchange. As the author concludes, 'If such fantasy as 15.♘e4

can give results, who knows what else one may be able to dream up'.

There is perhaps a point to all this. Isn't the author reminding us of those days of old where we used to just play and analyse to our heart's content without a worry in the world? Did we care back then what the authoritative experts thought about the quality of our games and tricky ideas? If a child keeps winning with a dubious opening, why try and persuade him to play something else? Odessky mentions the traditional Botvinnik-era-inspired teaching books that he describes as reading like 'military didactic manuals'. I suppose that he means Soviet-era treatises where Chess is thought of in a largely scientific, rather than sporting, manner.

As he never quite fitted in there, he himself has since embraced a counter-current of seeking practical, tricky play to bamboozle an opponent – something which was perhaps frowned upon by a previous generation of coaches!

Even so, if a purported opening work (even a little offbeat) can earn its place on many a chess-lover's bookshelf then it needs to offer plausible opening ideas that are going to work more often than not:

1.b3 e5 2.♗b2 ♘c6 3.e3 d5 4.♗b5 ♗d6 5.f4 ♕e7

Unfortunately, there is not a word on 5...♕h4+ which is an important alternative. I was looking forward to seeing what he had in mind, but my hopes were dashed.

6.♘f3 f6 7.♘c3 ♗e6

8.e4!?

'Formally, this is a novelty, but at the same time it is not new' – IO. His point is that this theme arises with reversed colours (with the difference being that the c-pawn is still on c7 here, rather than two squares forward)!

In fact I (GCF) have noticed that there have actually been a couple of games (from 2016 and 2017), both of which White won.

The inferior 8.♕e2?! is refuted by 8...a6 9.♗xc6+ bxc6 10.0-0-0 ♘h6. Otherwise, 8.0-0 ♘h6 9.fxe5 fxe5 10.e4 d4 11.♘d5 ♕d7 is examined, the author discussing briefly 12.c3, 12.c4, and 12.♘g5, before summarizing that 'the position is very complicated and I hesitate to give a categorical assessment'.

8...exf4

Here are those games that I mentioned: 8...dxe4 9.♘xe4 ♗f5 10.♘xd6+ cxd6 11.0-0 0-0-0? (11...♘h6±) 12.♗xc6 bxc6 13.fxe5 dxe5 14.♘xe5± Repkova-Cvitan, Balatonszarszo 2017; and 8...d4 9.♘d5 ♕d7 10.0-0 a6 11.♗xc6 (11.fxe5 axb5 12.exd6 ♕xd6 13.♗xd4? (13.♕e2!↑) 13...♗xd5 14.exd5 ♕xd5 15.♖e1+ ♘ge7 16.♗f2 K.Holm-R.Holm, Tylosand 2016, was only about equal) 11...bxc6 12.fxe5± is strong in view of 12...fxe5? 13.♘xe5!+− ♗xe5 14.♕h5+ etc.

9.0-0 dxe4 10.♘xe4 0-0-0 11.♗xc6 bxc6 12.♘d4

'White regains the pawn and in all variations retains the more pleasant game' – IO.

This example perhaps shows the positive and negative side of the Odessky odyssey: something new and lively with back-up analysis, but an important and critical alternative missed out completely.

I just wonder if the author's mind works in the same way as his organization. There are 450 pages of chess games, discussion and analysis, and yet only four chapters! One idea follows another without a clear break and the reader is invited to follow this helter-skelter cascade of thoughts until he is breathless! The indices at the end try and give some clue (sanity?) as to how one can navigate such a work, but they only partially allay the sentiment that it's impossible. Odessky's enthusiasm takes him in several directions at once and it's hard trying to stay on the same wavelength.

Despite all the confusion, the mischievous almost anti-establishment joy in all this trickery is contagious. What tremendous fun! Still, coming back to earth, just as with another of Odessky's books from 2008 (*The English Defence*, Russian Chess House, see my review in YB/87) there are plenty of variations missing (i.e. those where you don't get too many chances to win quickly!).

So it's far from being a rigorous textbook on 1.b3 and 1...b6, more a personal journey showing the appeal as well as the trials and tribulations of going your own way.

Erwin l'Ami
The Benko Gambit Explained
ChessBase DVD 2020

As a general rule, DVDs and video presentations are particularly attractive to those for whom modern technology is a way of life. I'm thinking of young players in particular, who also seem to be drawn to the Benko Gambit, as this pawn offer is associated with seizing the initiative early without having that much theory to learn. So Erwin l'Ami's *The Benko Gambit Explained* may well be compelling for some. I haven't seen any of the previous ones, but the Dutch GM has already been the author/presenter in several ChessBase DVDs on openings. In this case, I think that the word explained in the title hints that the level is largely for an amateur club player who wants to get to know a new opening. After reviewing the content, I think that the ChessBase advertising, suggesting that it's also for Advanced and Professional level players, is perhaps pushing their luck a little. Despite having a fairly strong accent, l'Ami's use of English is perfectly understandable and his way of expressing himself is rather good and fairly lively. His manner of laying out the key elements generally works quite well, as he uses model games to point out the general set-ups whilst not being afraid of pointing out any 'issues'. In fact, he was quite honest about those lines where he couldn't find equality or where he felt that Black players might have some practical difficulties. Naturally, with just one game to illustrate each principal

variation it isn't going to be as detailed as most books on the market. So many sidelines only receive a passing comment, if that. However, in order to become aware of the main ideas that drive both players' thinking, a DVD can certainly help focus one's attention. For those who relish in the interactive experience, there are questions throughout the presentations to test and further stimulate the reader, plus a set of exercises is available. Other regular features of the ChessBase DVDs are repertoire training, practice positions and the like. There are all sorts of advantages to a DVD over a book, especially if you need a training partner (here, Fritz is your helper) or just find that having the information presented in several ways is quite handy.

I found some sticking points. In the section on 4.♘d2, the narrator features the game Kramnik-Leko, Dortmund 1998, and plays through the endgame despite it being normally outside the scope of an opening work. His conclusion that Kramnik (two pawns down) was drawing easily surprised me as I recognized the double-rook endgame from specialized literature where there has been some discussion about whether there is indeed a win or not. Leko certainly felt that he was winning. Granted, in an opening work, an author might not have the inclination to study the resulting endgame, but I still wasn't impressed. Unfortunately, there is an annoying 'oversight' in the opening phase as well:

1.d4 ♘f6 2.c4 c5 3.d5 b5 4.cxb5 a6 5.♘c3 axb5
Here, 6.e4 b4 7.♘b5 is the Zaitsev Variation, which is known to be tricky and is discussed by l'Ami in a main game.
6.♘xb5!?

Erwin l'Ami is troubled by this move and seems to be unaware of the standard response
6...♗a6,
after which
7.♘c3
transposes to the traditional main line (A59) which he is recommending in his repertoire.
The Dutch GM instead examines 6...♕a5 and also mentions 6...e6, but he doesn't think that they equalize. For the record, the maverick Serbian GM Milos Perunovic recently analysed and recommended the weird-looking 6...♘e4!?,

which has almost never been played.

Curious, perhaps, but Erwin l'Ami's own playing experience in the Benko Gambit is solely with the white pieces. His protégé Anish Giri only seems to have one example on the database with black (his game against Demuth from 2015 which happens to be featured in the video). In that particular encounter, Giri played the 'modern' way (i.e. where Black delays capturing on a6, preferring instead quick kingside development), against which the move order mentioned above might indeed be a nuisance. So in this case, unless any player with black doesn't mind being move-ordered, he might need to find an alternative to 6...♝a6 that 'feels right for him'.

I was wondering if up-and-coming folk and amateurs generally prefer an inter-active experience, or is it that they just want to glean their information without having the bother of turning pages? In the bonuses section there are additional model games, and this component is actually quite substantial as these encounters do contain notes at times. It's like someone has sifted through Megabase for you and picked out a few gems (although some of them turn out to be rather uninteresting short draws).

I'm a lover of the printed page, so I'm not the ideal person to review this sort of work. Still, it's true that listening to a high-rated GM can be uplifting, especially when they point out some neat little subtleties, some of which hadn't occurred to

you in the past. A bit of GM reasoning here and there never does any harm! On the other hand, it can be frustrating when they don't deal with something that you feel should be addressed. Alas, there is only so much you can fit into six-and-a-half hours! So, whether you choose a book or a DVD as your tool, there is no real short-cut to learning an opening properly. You have to put some hard work in yourself, either way.

Overall, a useful club player's guide to the Benko, but with a few rough edges.

Rustam Kasimdzhanov
The Benoni is back in business
ChessBase DVD 2020

It's interesting to see such a high-profile GM put his mind to a serious investigation of Black's chances in this sharp but unfashionable opening. Rustam Kasimdzhanov has plenty of experience as a DVD frontman (I'm not sure which of presenter, author, narrator or analyst fits best, perhaps a bit of each!) and one of his earlier ones was on the Nimzo-Indian (1.d4 ♘f6 2.c4 e6 where one meets 3.♘c3 with 3...♝b4). So to some extent this can be considered a sister work, in that he is heading towards the Benoni via 1.d4 ♘f6 2.c4 e6 3.♘f3 and only now 3...c5. The advantage of this move order is that it avoids a number of troublesome variations where White has opportunities to benefit from not committing the king's knight to f3 early.

Will this DVD, with its clever title, induce people to turn their attention once again in this direction?

First of all, Kasimdzhanov has a strong accent which might take some time to get used to, but his use of English is excellent and, despite his calm studious manner, the DVD has its share of deadpan humour. The content however is deadly serious with the analysis often turning highly complex, so will better suit stronger or tactically-minded players.

There is always a measure of risk involved in the Benoni, but frankly it's a great choice if you want to develop your creative side. Just viewing this production might get you going, especially as you could easily find yourself almost spoilt for choice with lots of dramatic novelties suggested by the author.

Here are a few examples in the Classical Variation.

1.d4 ♘f6 2.c4 e6 3.♘f3 c5 4.d5 exd5 5.cxd5 d6 6.♘c3 g6 7.♘d2 ♝g7 8.e4 0-0 9.♝e2 ♜e8 10.0-0 ♘bd7

A complex struggle lies ahead, where all sorts of Benoni ideas are possible. White is often objectively better, but for 'real tournament practice the struggle remains unclear' – RK. Anyway, the author continues, 'if all else fails then Black can always play with ...g6-g5'.

11.♕c2

After 11.a4 a6 12.f4, Kasimdzhanov suggests a remarkable idea: 12...♖b8 13.♔h1 c4 14.e5 b5!?. 'You won't see anything like this every day!' – RK. This looks like a novelty! 15.axb5 axb5 16.exf6 ♘xf6♔. 'I have a good feeling about this' – RK.

11...♘e5 12.a4

Following 12.b3 ♗g4 13.♗xg4 ♘fxg4 14.♗b2 (Aronian-Caruana, Moscow 2016), another new idea of the author is 14...c4!? 15.bxc4 ♖c8; 'this pawn sac has some sort of potential' – RK.

12...a6 13.a5 ♗d7 14.♖a3 c4!?

RK again proposes a sacrificial idea.

15.f4 ♘eg4 16.♘xc4 ♗b5

'I have a feeling that Black will have a lot of dynamic resources' – RK.

17.♘b6 ♖c8!?

Summing up, he says he's looking forward to playing this line, but suggests to the reader that one shouldn't perhaps play it in a World Championship match just yet!

Some of these suggestions are so outrageous, and yet imagine an opponent facing them with no prior knowledge! Even when the engine doesn't totally approve, these adrenaline-stoked Benonis are rarely easy for White to keep control.

Another line that I decided might be problematic for Black is the following. It turns out that the former FIDE World Champion has some suggestions here that certainly muddy the waters (even further!).

1.d4 ♘f6 2.c4 e6 3.♘f3 c5 4.d5 exd5 5.cxd5 d6 6.♘c3 g6 7.♗f4 ♗g7

Kasimdzhanov recommends the provocative text move, whereas for many years 7...a6 8.a4 and only now 8...♗g7 was the consensus continuation. That's another story, but the author wants to keep open the possibility of the black knight being able to use the a6-square.

8.♕a4+ ♗d7 9.♕b3 b5 10.♗xd6 ♕b6 11.♗e5 0-0 12.e3 c4 13.♕d1 b4

It's no secret that this leads to a complicated struggle!

14.♘e2

After 14.♘b1 then 14...♖c8 (after 14...♗b5, RK mentions that 15.a3 'is not so easy to meet') 15.♘bd2 Kasimdzhanov opts for the rare move 15...c3 which leads to 16.♘c4 ♕c5 17.bxc3 ♘xd5 18.♗xg7 ♔xg7 19.♕d4+ and although the engines suggest a small white pull, the author's analysis suggests that Black has 'enough for dynamic equality'.

14...♖c8

His recommended line, despite Black not having scored well from here.

15.♘f4

Alternatively, 15.♖c1!? ♕a5 16.♕d4 is well met by 16...♘xd5! 17.♗xg7 ♘c6∞.

15...c3 16.♗d3 ♕a5 17.0-0 ♗a4

'Now White either has to allow the recapture of the pawn or start taking risks' – RK.

18.b3 ♗b5!♔

Indeed, some email games seem to confirm this assessment.

I found the lines to be fascinating and could well induce a like-minded reader to start making the Benoni a more regular feature of his tournament play. For further detail, the analysis section at the end contains more game segments and analysis input from the author, but the rough-cut mass of variations haven't been edited or typeset to make them particularly presentable. These will perhaps be mainly of use for stronger spectators, but it's easy to lose one's way by unfortunately clicking in the wrong place! It might be easier to scroll through the model games however, some of which (presumably from ChessBase's own files) contain annotations.

I'm still a beginner when it comes to using some of the aspects of chess DVDs, but these few days have been a voyage of discovery for me. Overall, I was surprised that there were so many facets to gleaning the information, and that such videos could be so useful for higher-ranking players. So I've been converted!

Solutions to Exercises

Demchenko-Gajewski
Moscow Wch rapid 2019 (3)

25...♗xb5 26.cxb5 ♘g4! 27.♕f3
♕c2 0-1

Harikrishna-Navara (analysis)
Prague m rapid 2018 (10)

18.♘d4! ♕a3 18...♘d7 19.♖a1
♕b2 20.♘c3, trapping the
queen. **19.c5! dxc5 20.♘c6 ♖fe8
21.e5+-**

**Vaibhav-Deepan Chakkravarthy
(analysis)**
Jammu ch-IND 2018 (12)

17...e5! 17...♘xd5 18.exd5 ♖e8.
18.♘xc7 18.c4 ♘xd5 19.cxd5 f5
with loads of counterplay on the
kingside. **18...♕xc7 19.c4 ♘f6
20.f3 ♘h5 21.♖bd2 ♖cd8 22.♗f1
♘g3 23.♗d3 ♘h5 24.♗f1** With a
very weird repetition.

Adams-Giri
Batumi Ech tt 2019 (4)

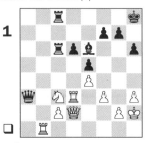

33.♘d1! Heading to e3, where
the knight keeps everything
in check. **33...♕a7=** 33...♕a2
34.♖b2!=.

Karjakin-Giri
Riga rapid 2019 (1)

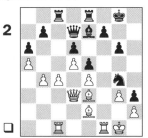

25.♗d2! would have kept Black's
counterplay within the minimum.
The game saw 25.♗b6 ♗g5
26.♖c3 ♖f8 27.c5 dxc5 28.♗xc5
♖xc5 29.bxc5 ♗e3+ 30.♔h1 ♘f2+
31.♖xf2 ♗xf2 32.c6 bxc6 33.dxc6
and now 33...♕xd3! 34.♖xd3 ♗e1
35.♖d5 ♖c8 36.♖c5 is ±.

Nepomniachtchi-Wojtaszek
Moscow 2019 (3)

24...♖f8!= 25.♕f4 ♗d8 26.h3
½-½

Mamedov-Nevednichy (analysis)
Turkey tt 2013 (7)

15...f6! 16.♗e3 16.exf6? ♕xg3+
is the key point. **16...♗xe3
17.♕xe3 ♘dxe5 18.♖ad1∞**

**Predojevic-Bukal
(analysis)**
Zadar 2019 (4)

15.♕xe6+! fxe6 16.♗g6+ ♔e7
17.♗g5+ ♘f6 18.♗xf6+ ♔d7
19.♗xd8±

**Jones-Camus de Solliers
(analysis)**
England 4NCL 2012/13 (4)

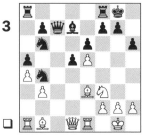

19.♕d4! ♘c8 20.♗xh6! gxh6
21.♕g4+ ♔h8 22.♕h4+− Black
is defenceless, i.e. **22...♔g7
23.♕f6+ ♔g8 24.♘g5! hxg5
25.♕xg5+ ♔h8 26.♕h6+ ♔g8
27.♕h7#**

page 62 — CK 2.8
Caruana-Thavandiran (analysis)
PRO League Stage 2019 (3)

1

9...♘h5!? 9...h5 10.f3 h4 11.fxg4 hxg3 12.h3±; 9...♗d6 10.♖e1 0-0 11.h3 ♗xg3 12.fxg3 ♗f5. **10.h3 ♘xg3 11.fxg3 ♗h5∞**

Ganguly-Eljanov
Wijk aan Zee B 2020 (12)

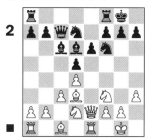

2

13...♘h5!? This move is very risky but it's the only real try for Black to create some play. **14.♗xh7+** Very interesting and tempting. Other moves offer no advantage: 14.♘b3 ♘f4=; 14.♘g5 ♘hf6. **14...♔xh7 15.♘g5+ ♔g6∞**

Tukhaev-Mchedlishvili (analysis)
Turkey tt 2018 (3)

3

13...0-0-0! is already very bad for White, Black will take on e5 next. 13...♘dxe5 was Safarli-Postny, Moscow Wch rapid 2019. **14.♕xf7 ♘cxe5 15.♘xe5 ♕xe5+ 16.♗e3 ♕e4!** White's position collapses.

page 69 — CK 4.7
Najer-Popov
St Petersburg-Moscow m 2011 (2)

1

20.♘b4! ♕b3 21.♘a6 ♖b7 22.♘h4 ♕b2 23.♘xf5 exf5 24.♘b4! ♕xa1 25.♖xa1 ♖xa1 26.♗f3+−

Sutovsky-Ruck
Bosnia i Herzegovina tt 2004 (8)

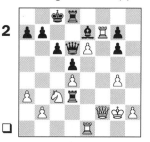

2

23.♘b5! cxb5 24.♕c2+ ♔b8 25.♕xd3 ♗h4 26.e7 1-0

Petrov-Byron
Cardiff 2014 (1)

3

36.♘xb6 ♘xb6 37.♗xb6+ ♔xb6 38.♘c8+ ♔c7 39.♘xe7 ♔d7 40.♖a4 ♔xe7 41.♖a7+ ♔f8 42.♖a8+ 1-0

page 76 — CK 11.1
Matanovic-Pomar
Palma de Mallorca 1966 (1)

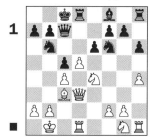

1

15...♘bxd5! Black played 15...♗e7 and the game was very soon drawn. **16.♗xf6** 16.♘xf6 ♘xc3+−+; 16.cxd5 ♖xd5 17.♕c2 ♖xd1+ 18.♕xd1 ♘xe4−+. **16...♘xf6 17.♕xd8+ ♕xd8 18.♖xd8+ ♔xd8−+**

Leupold-Ruggieri
cr 2014

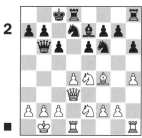

2

14...♕b5! Other moves allow White to fight for an advantage. **15.♕xb5** After 15.c4 ♕f5 16.f3 ♘xe4 17.fxe4 ♕g4 Black is not worse. **15...cxb5 16.♘xf6 ♘xf6 17.♖d3 ♘d5=**

J.van Foreest-Dziuba
Germany Bundesliga 2019/20 (7)

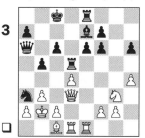

3

23.♕h7!+− 23.c3 ♖h8±; 23.♗xh6 ♖h8 24.♗f4 c5∞. Now Black can't defend everything. The game continued **23...♖f8 24.♖xe6!**.

Perunovic-Fridman

Skopje Ech blitz 2018 (17)

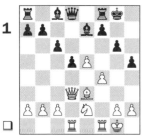

No! The move ...h7-h5 has weakened Black's kingside too heavily, so **14.f5! ♗xf5 15.♖xf5 gxf5 16.♕xf5** and White simply has a crushing attack.

Adams-Sandipan

Gibraltar 2018 (8)

Exchanging of all minor pieces reduces the pressure: **17...a5!** Not allowing White to install a knight on d4. **18.♖d2 ♗a6 19.♕f3 ♗e7 20.♗xe7 ♕xe7 21.♖fd1 ♗xe2 22.♕xe2** And Black is doing fine.

Tkachiev-Giri

France tt 2010 (3)

White should try to play on his stronger side. Mobilizing the kingside majority is key. Hence, **16.g4!?** does lead to a very sharp position, in which I would certainly prefer to be White.

Van Keulen-Moll

Barcelona rapid 2019

8.♘xe4! ♗e7 9.♘g5! A key motif for White in the Philidor Countergambit. If the knight on g5 is taken, White has 10.♕h5+ and 11.♕xg5, liquidating into an endgame with the two bishops.

Green-Strautins

cr 2017

9...♕d5! An important defensive manoeuvre for Black in positions with the 'hanging pawns' on e5 and f6 is to bring the queen over to the kingside. **10.♘c3 ♕f7 11.0-0-0 c6** followed by ...♗e6, ...♘d7 and ...0-0-0.

Rojas Barrero-De Arco

Bucaramanga 2008 (5)

8.♗c4! White ignores the discovered check and continues with quick development. **8... exf3+ 9.♔f2 ♘g4+ 10.♔g3+−**

Dijkhuis-Ploder

Lüneburg 2019 (6)

In the game Black played 16... exf3+ 17.♔d1 f2 18.♖h1 ♕e6 which turned out to be good enough. Best is the spectacular **16...♖xb2+! 17.♗xb2 exf3+−+**.

Belyakov-Lysyj

Sochi ch-RUS blitz 2019 (3)

13...♕g6! is winning as White has no defence to the threats of 14...♕e4+ and 14...♖ad8. Instead the game went 13...♘e4? 14.♕g4!+−.

Castellano Egea-Jimenez Ruano (analysis)

Catalunya tt 2020 (2)

18...♖xe3+! 18...♕xd4 19.♕xf2 f5 20.♘c3 f4 21.♔e1 fxe3 22.♕e2±. **19.♔xe3 ♖e8+!** 20.♗xf2 20.♔f3 ♕xd4−+. **20...♕xd4+ 21.♔g3 ♖e3+ 22.♕f3 ♖xf3+ 23.♔xf3 ♕xb2!−+** Even better than 23...♕xg1.

page 111   KP 11.3
Yu Yangyi-Sychev
Moscow Wch blitz 2019 (3)

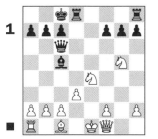

Correct is **17...♖he8!**. Instead, if 17...♗b4+? 18.c3. **18.♕h3+ ♚b8 19.♗d2 f6 20.♘f3 ♖xe4+** leads to equality.

Siigur-Gerola
cr 2011

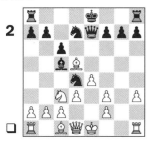

It's best to sacrifice the piece: **12.f4!** 12.♗b3? ♕h4!−+ and 12.♗c4?! b5!∓ are dangerous for White. **12...cxd5 13.♘xd5 ♕d8 14.c3 ♘e6 15.d4 ♗e7 16.♖g1** And White has three pawns and the centre for his piece.

Huerto Navarro-Cesetti (analysis)
cr 2016

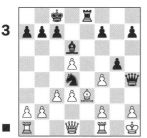

17...♕h3! 17...gxf4? is scuppered by 18.♕a4!. **18.♖g1 gxf4** 18...♘f3 19.♖g2 b5!? 20.♕f1 gxf4 21.♗xa7∞. **19.♕f1!** 19.♗xd4 f3 20.♖g3 ♗xg3∓. **19...♕f3+ 20.♕g2 fxe3 21.cxd4 ♕xg2+ 22.♔xg2 e2=**

page 120   QO 1.5
Firouzja-Nakamura (analysis)
Carlsen Invitational Online 2020 (3.3)

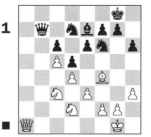

Black should seize the moment to break the white pawn chain with **21...e5!**, activating his minor pieces. He will regain the pawn on c5, and one of Black's knights will head towards the e6-square.

Nepomniachtchi-Nakamura
Carlsen Invitational Online 2020 (4.2)

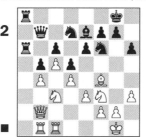

Black should play **19...♘e4!**, aiming to create entry squares for the rooks on the open file. If the knight is swapped on e4 Black's other knight has a handy square on d5 available to head towards.

Caruana-Nakamura (analysis)
Carlsen Invitational Online 2020 (5.3)

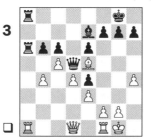

After **18.cxb6 ♖xa1 19.♕xa1 ♖xa1 20.♖xa1** Black is so beset with back-rank troubles that he can't prevent the white pawn on b6 from queening.

page 130   QO 11.3
Dreev-Prusikin
Switzerland tt 2011 (6)

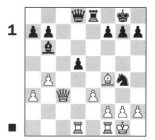

Black is better: **20...g5! 21.♗g3** 21.h3 gxf4 22.hxg4 fxe3−+. **21...♘xe3∓**

Ringoir-Brattain
Charlotte 2018 (4)

No it is not, as it runs into a tactical refutation: **11.e4? ♘xe4! 12.♘xe4 ♕e6 13.f3 0-0-0∓ 14.♘e2 g5 15.♗g3 g4−+**.

Fridman-Svane
Osterburg ch-GER 2012 (3)

Yes, he can: **21.♗g1! ♘g4 22.♘f1! ♖ad8 23.f3 ♘gf6 24.♘g3 ♖d7 25.a3 ♖de7 26.e4 ♘f4 27.♗c4±** White managed to get his central pawn chain rolling and went on to win.

Henrichs-Remling (analysis)
Biel 1997 (11)

21...♗c8! 21...♖ad8? 22.d6+−; 21...♖e4? 22.♕g5+−. **22.♘d6** 22.d6 ♗xf5 23.♕xf5 ♖ad8=. **22...♖d8=**

Giri-Ding Liren
Carlsen Invitational Online 2020 (4.4)

22.♖f4! 22.♕d2= was played in the game. **22...♕b2 23.♘d4!** Or 23.♘h4!. **23...♗xd5 24.♘f5±** ♖e8 25.♕xe8+ ♖xe8 26.♖xe8+ ♔h7 27.♖g4 ♘e6 28.♘e7! ♗c4 29.♘g6!

Aronian-Matlakov
Tbilisi 2017 (3)

24.♖f4! 24.♖xg7 ♗xd5 25.♘g6+ ♖xg6 26.♖xg6 fxg6 27.♕e5+± was the game continuation. **24...♖xf4 25.♕xf4 ♗xd5** 25...♖d8 26.♘f5+−; 25...♖e8 26.♖xe8+ ♕xe8 27.d6+−. **26.♘g6+−**

Ding Liren-Carlsen
Lindores Abbey Prelim 2020 (3)

9...♗xd2! The most practical solution with limited time. Of course, it is dangerous to accept the 'gift' with 9...♘xd4!? without a comprehensive analysis. **10.♕xd2 ♗b7 11.♗xb7 ♖xb7 12.♘xc4 ♘c6 13.♖d1 0-0 14.♘c3 ♕a8 15.d5!?** White's position here is preferable because of Black's problems with the c-file.

Giri-Carlsen
Carlsen Invitational Prelim 2020 (5.1)

15...♗xf3 16.♗xf3 c6

So-Carlsen
Lindores Abbey Final 8 2020 (1.23)

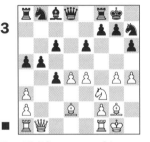

13...e5! Of course; making space for his bishop and other pieces.

Cordova-Riazantsev
Moscow 2020 (4)

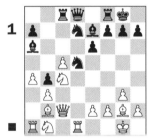

14...♘xc5! with the tactical justification **15.e4** (15.♘bd2 ♗f6∓ was played in the game) **15...♘xb3! 16.♕xb3 ♗xc4 17.♕f3** (17.♕c2 b3 18.♕d2 ♘b4) **17...♗f6!−+.**

Cordova-Riazantsev (analysis)
Moscow 2020 (4)

17.♗xd5 is worse because of **17...♖xc5 18.♕e4 ♘xe5!!** and Black has the initiative after the relatively best **19.♗e3 ♗d3! 20.♖xd3 ♘xd3 21.♗xc5 ♘xc5.**

Goluch-Pulpan
Bohumin 2020 (9)

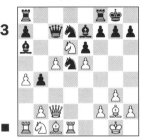

16.♘f5 16.♘b5 was played in the game. **16...♘xc5! 17.♗xd5 ♖ac8!** A great move to avoid 17...exd5 18.♘e7+ ♔h8 19.♗e3. **18.♗f4 exd5** With a dangerous initiative.

page 164   NI 24.13

Vitiugov-Caruana (analysis)
Wijk aan Zee 2020 (9)

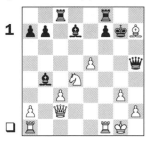

19.e6! An unexpected intermediate move. **19...fxe6** 19...♖xc3 20.♕e4 fxe6 21.♕xb7 ♗c5 22.♕xd7+ ♖f7 23.♖xf7+ ♕xf7 24.♕xf7+ ♔xf7 25.♔g2 ♗xd4 26.♖d1±. **20.♖xf8 ♗xf8 21.♗e4** And Black doesn't have enough compensation for the pawn.

Vachier-Lagrave-Ding Liren (analysis)
Nations Cup Online Prelim 2020 (2.1)

26...♗xf2! creates counterplay just in time – otherwise Black would be in big trouble: **27.♖xh5 ♕xg3+ 28.♕xg3+ ♗xg3=**

Umstead-Ozgur
Internet blitz 2009 (9)

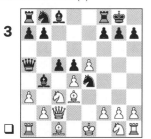

10.axb4! ♕xa1 and now 11.♘xd5! ♘c6 12.♗xe4 ♘xd4 13.♗xh7+ ♔h8 14.♕b1 and White's material advantage is decisive.

page 171   NI 27.1

Rapport-Gajewski
Budapest HUN-POL m 2014 (2)

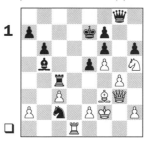

27.♘xf6! A beautiful tactic. **27...♔xf6 28.♖d6+ ♔g7 29.♕h4 ♕f8 30.♕xh6+ ♔g8 31.♖g6+** 31.♕g5+ ♔h7 32.♕h4+ ♔g8 33.♖d8 ♗e8 34.f6 and 31.♕f6 also win. **1-0** If 31...fxg6 32.♗d5+ ♕f7 33.♕xg6+.

Esipenko-Salomon
Moscow 2018 (6)

26.♕e7+! 1-0

Fedoseev-Matlakov
Moscow 2017 (8)

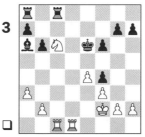

27.g3! Creating a second front. **27...fxg3+ 28.hxg3 g6** 28...♔f7 29.♖d7+ ♔f8 30.a4 b5 31.a5 b4 32.♖c5+–. **29.f4 ♗b7?** 29...h5 30.♔e3 ♖e8 31.f5+ gxf5 32.♘d4+ ♔e5 33.♘xf5 ♖ad8 34.♘g7+–. **30.f5+! 1-0**

page 180   NI 27.2

Svane-Socko
Germany Bundesliga 2015/16 (14)

The best move is **15.g3!**, preserving a good structure. After **15...♕d7** White has the strong exchange sac **16.♖b1!**. Svane played 15.♖b1 immediately, allowing 15...♗d6!.

Costachi-Lupulescu
Romania tt 2016 (7)

The best move is **14.c4!** and compared to Schoppen-D. Horvath, Black's position is weakened with the pawn on f5. In the game White swapped on g5 instead, giving Black a good game.

Gähwiler-Georgiadis
Leukerbad ch-SUI 2019 (6)

Black should just castle, with an excellent game. He played **14...♕f6** instead, and after **15.♗g2 ♘e7** White could have gotten an edge by 16.c4 or 16.e4 with the idea 16...dxe4 17.♘d2.

Jankovic-Pavlidis (analysis)
Kavala 2012 (6)

25...♘xd5! 26.exd5 26.♘xd5
♕g5∓. **26...♖xg2+! 27.♔xg2**
♕g5+ **28.♔h2** 28.♔f3 ♕h5+−+.
28...♖g8!−+

Tsygankov-Lanz Calavia (analysis)
cr 2015

27...♖f4! 28.♗g3 ♖h8!

Kozul-Freitag
Austria Bundesliga B 2010/11 (3)

25...♕h4! 25...♗xb5? was played
in the game. **26.♘h3 ♗xg4**
27.♘df2 ♘f6−+

Ding Liren-Carlsen (analysis)
Chessable Masters rapid 2020 (2.14)

16...♖d8!⇄

J.Hansen-Tunega
cr 2016

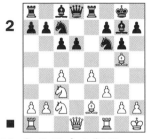

12...♘e6! 13.♗e3 ♘h5!⇄

Gustafsson-Kramnik
Dortmund 2012 (2)

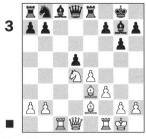

13...a5!

Parkhov-Asadli
Poprad jr 2016 (6)

11...b5! 12.dxc6 12.cxb5 cxb5
13.0-0 b4 14.♘a4 ♗a6 15.♖fc1
♗b5∓. **12...♘e5 13.♕e2 bxc4**
14.0-0 ♗a6↑ and Black looks
nicely placed.

Tahbaz-Nyazi
Dubai 2018 (4)

12...b5! A strong tactical blow!
Black sacrifices a pawn for quick
development with ...♗b7. **13.cxb5**
13.♘xb5? ♘xe4−+, but now
13...♗b7! 14.♘f3 14.♗f3 ♘b6↑.
14...♘xe4 15.♘xe4 ♗xe4∓ and
White can't solve the problem of
his king.

V.Stefansson-V.Ivic (analysis)
Konya jr 2018 (1)

15...♖xf3! A great exchange
sacrifice to crush White's
kingside! **16.gxf3 ♘xe5 17.♕e2**
♗b7 And Black is winning.

Grandelius-Kukk
PRO League Stage 2020 (9)

Black could have played **19...♗c3**, as after **20.♕xd6 ♕xd6 21.♖xd6 a4** the bishop pair gives Black full positional compensation for the pawn.

Baburin-Gullaksen
Port Erin 1998 (1)

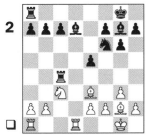

14.♗xb7?! ♖b8∞ was played in the game. **14.♖ac1!** with the idea to trap the black rook with 15.b3 ♖b4 15.♗c5: **14...e4 15.b3 ♖c6 16.♘xe4! ♖xc1 17.♗xc1!**

Baburin-Gullaksen (analysis)
Port Erin 1998 (1)

White can protect everything with **16.♗b5!** and after the forced sequence **16...♖xc3** (16...♖d6 17.♗xa7+−) **17.bxc3 ♖xb5 18.♖d8+ ♗f8 19.♖h6 ♘d7 20.♖d1**, with the unstoppable threat of 21.♖1xd7, White wins.

Goganov-Indjic
Yerevan 2014 (3)

32...♖xf2! 33.h6+ ♔f6 34.♘xb4 cxb4 35.♔c1 ♖g2 36.♗xg4! White decided to enter a pawn-down endgame rather than face a hopeless position after 36.♖h1? ♖xg3. **36...♖xd2 37.♗xd7 ♖xd5∓**

Blagojevic-Ivanisevic
Podgorica 2011 (5)

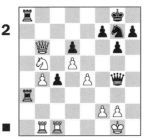

26...♘h5!→ Suddenly Black's dormant knight springs to life with devastating effect. **27.♘xa3 ♘f4! 28.g3 ♖xa3−+**

Krasenkow-Kurmann
Germany Bundesliga B 2012/13 (3)

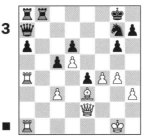

27...♕b7!, attacking the pawn on d5, thus forcing White to play c3-c4, which helps Black because the 3rd rank is opened after Black's rook lands on b3, e.g. **28.c4 h5⇄ 29.♗f2 ♕e7 30.♖xa6 ♖xa6 31.♖xa6 ♖b3∞**.

Van Egmond-Van de Griendt
(analysis)
Netherlands tt 2019/20 (3)

25...♘c7! 26.♘xc7 ♖xb2+ 27.♔g1 and now the surprising zwischenzug **27...♗b7!−+**.

Rudd-Webb (analysis)
Cardiff 2016 (8)

17.♗h8!! f6 17...♔xh8 18.♕h6 ♖g8 19.♘g5! ♖g7 20.♘xh7 ♔g8 21.♘f6++−. **18.♕h6 ♖f7 19.♗xf6! ♖a6 20.♗e5 ♖xd5** 20...♕xd5?! 21.♗e4! ♕xe4 22.♖xe4 ♗xe4 23.♘g5 ♖c6 24.♗c3±. **21.♘g5 ♕b4** And after the rook moves along the first rank, 22...♖af6 23.♘xf7 ♗xf7+=.

Polugaevsky-Kholmov
Tbilisi ch-URS 1967 (16)

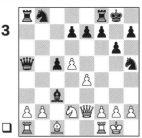

13.♘c4! 13.bxc3?! ♘f4!= and next Black will take on c3 due to the fork on e2. **13...♕b5 14.a4 ♖xa4 15.♖xa4 ♕xa4 16.bxc3 d6 17.e5±**

Cruz-Moiseenko

Riga blitz 2019 (12)

No, that was not his best option, because after **10...exd3?** White could have played **11.♘xc6!+–** instead of the game continuation 11.♕xd3 0-0!=.

Shtembuliak-Zierk

St Louis 2019 (5)

He should have played **24.♘xg7! ♕xd2+ 25.♔f1 ♘f4 26.♖e1+–**.

Liang-Sadhwani

Sitges 2018 (4)

15...♗f5 as 16.e4 meets with 16...♗xh3 and if 17.♕e2 ♖fe8∓.